Public Administration

The Profession and the Practice

A Case Study Approach

GERALD GARVEY

Princeton University

ST. MARTIN'S PRESS   NEW YORK

This book is dedicated to Scott Geraldson Garvey

SPONSORING EDITOR: Beth A. Gillett
MANAGER, PUBLISHING SERVICES: Emily Berleth
SENIOR EDITOR, PUBLISHING SERVICES: Douglas Bell
PROJECT MANAGEMENT AND GRAPHICS: Omega Publishing Services, Inc.
PRODUCTION SUPERVISOR: Kurt Nelson
COVER DESIGN: Evelyn Horovicz
COVER ART: Rebecca Rüegger

Library of Congress Catalog Card Number: 95-73319

Manufactured in the United States of America.

1 0 9 8 7
f e d c b a

For information, write:
St. Martin's Press, Inc.
175 Fifth Avenue
New York, NY 10010

ISBN: 0-312-10580-0

Acknowledgments

Pages 11–12: Albert R. Jonson and Stephen Toulmin, "Casuistry: The Analysis of Complex Cases in Light of 'A Thousand Difficulties'" from *The Abuse of Casuistry: A History of Moral Reasoning.* Copyright © 1988 by The Regents of the University of California. Reprinted with the permission of University of California Press.

Page 26: Mircea Eliade, Rabbi of Cracow story, from *Myths, Dreams, and Mysteries: The Encounter between Contemporary Faiths and Archaic Realities,* translated by Philip Mairet. Copyright © 1957 by Libraire Gallimard. English translation copyright © 1960 Harvill Press. Reprinted with the permission of HarperCollins Publishers, Inc.

Pages 33–35: Charles Goodsell, "Defense of Bureaucrats as Ordinary People" from *The Case for Bureaucracy: A Public Administration Polemic, Second Edition.* Copyright © 1983, 1985 by Chatham House Publishers, Inc. Reprinted with the permission of the publishers.

Pages 36–38: David Osborne and Ted Gaebler, "Personnel System for the Twenty-First Century" from *Reinventing Government: How the Entrepreneurial Spirit is Transforming the Public Sector.* Copyright © 1992 by David Osborne and Ted Gaebler. Reprinted with the permission of Addison-Wesley Publishing Company, Inc.

Pages 43–47: Frank J. Thompson, "Five Competing Values in Civil Service Systems" from "Managing within Civil Service Systems" in James L. Perry, editor, *Handbook of Public Administration.* Copyright © 1989 by Jossey-Bass, Inc., Publishers. Reprinted with the permission of the publishers.

Acknowledgments and copyrights are continued at the back of the book on pages 517–518, which constitute an extension of the copyright page.

CONTENTS

▼◆●■▼◆●■▼◆●■▼◆●■▼◆●

PREFACE

▼ ◆ ● ■ ▼ ◆ ● ■ ▼ ◆ ● ■ ▼ ◆ ● ■ ▼ ◆ ● ■ ▼ ◆ ●

We study public administration because some of us will actually become government officials. But public administration is as important for the general citizen as it is for the student bound on a career in public service. In a democracy, we all need to know what we may sensibly ask government to do. Because power flows from the people and accountability returns to them we also should know what level of performance we have a right to expect from government. For these reasons, Woodrow Wilson, more than a century ago, wrote that the primary aim of administrative study should be to discern "what government can properly and successfully do."

This book is intended to meet both of the purposes that are implicit in the forgoing paragraph: to provide an introduction to public administration for the student who's headed toward a career in public service, or at least who might be considering a trial period in government work; and to foster in others an appreciation of the nature of public administration—its extreme difficulties as well as its enormous satisfactions.

There's an impression abroad that administration is synonymous with "bureaucracy" and that public administrators are sentenced to lives of dull routine without the possibility of parole. It is certainly true that most public administrators work in bureaucratic organizations. And, admittedly, elements of routine usually figure into their jobs. But at the core of their professional lives, most public administrators are neither "mere bureaucrats" in the pejorative sense nor prisoners of routine and red tape. They are, before everything else, problem solvers. That's what this book is about: *problem solving*. More precisely, it's about the very special challenges to problem solving that administrative officials at every level of government encounter in the *public sector*.

Highlights

The text incorporates three kinds of study materials: original essays, texts drawn from the scholarly literature, and case studies. By interweaving these strands, students can gain a true appreciation of the profession of public administration while, at the same time, exercising the real-life skills of practitioners in the field.

Problem-Solving Approach

From the problem-solving approach of the volume follow certain decisions about its analytical framework and mode of presentation—about how materials are offered as well as about the concepts used to organize them. The concepts at the center of the analysis capture what's arguably the most basic characteristic of problems in public administration: their formidable difficulty. The situations that public administrators confront on a daily basis resist easy-fit, deterministic solutions. Practitioners often find

xiii

that they must search for "proximate solutions to impossible problems." Students who come to appreciate that a proximate solution may represent the best achievable combination of desirability and doability will be better prepared for the real-world problems that many of them will someday face.

Multilayered Cases

There are sound reasons to believe that the dissection and discussion of complex cases is the best way to develop the motivation and analytical skills needed for work or serious study in the field. The complex case is the form in which most public administrators confront the tangles of interdependent issues that have come to characterize problem solving in the public sector. The case method embodies the belief that vicarious experience—best gained by "entering into a story"—is a useful way to heighten interest and cultivate appreciation.

The situations in our scenarios are intended to reflect the actual experiences and to represent the typical problems of public administrators. The stories have been located in recognizable kinds of settings—a rural area in the upper Midwest, and a Sunbelt metropolitan center with a pronounced ethnic heritage. There are occasional references to statutes and court decisions; in context, it should be clear when such references are to actual laws and decisions rather than merely to hypothetical ones. Otherwise, the figures in the stories, their situations, and for the most part the organizations and even locales depicted in the scenarios are fictional. Resemblances to actual persons, places, events, enterprises, or organizations are coincidental. Some of the numerical materials and calculations have also been adjusted in ways that seemed appropriate.

Lively Narrative Reinforced by Pedagogy

The materials are presented in a direct, jargon-free style. Key concepts are defined in the text and in the end-of-book glossary. Boxed inserts contain matter that may require further explanation. Discussion questions at the end of each case should help students structure their analyses of the issues in the scenarios.

Instructor's Resource Manual

A comprehensive guide, written by the author, has been designed to meet the needs of veteran and novice professors alike. The *Instructor's Resource Manual* provides guidance on effective classroom use of the case study approach. It contains a detailed discussion of teaching options, sample syllabi, instructional suggestions, complete lecture outlines, test banks, and drafts of student exercises. For instructors who want to customize their courses, the manual also offers thematic summaries of all chapters and worksheets that can be copied and handed out in class. Special features are detailed budget exercise packages and scenarios for use by instructors who like the role-playing format. Together with the cases, original essays, and outside reading selections in the text, the *Instructor's Resource Manual* rounds out a complete course in public administration.

Acknowledgments

In the course of developing the original essays, gleaning for the most apt selection of outside readings, and preparing case materials, I have profited greatly from the help of many others. Let me extend thanks to just a few of them: Sharon Barrios, Daniel Carpenter, Erhan Cinlar, John DiIulio, Michael Dark, my wife LouAnn Garvey, Scott Garvey, Robert George, Gigi Georges, John Glascock, Jim Green, Fred Greenstein, Constance Horner, Patrick Horvath, Saul Kripke, Rosemary Little, John Londregan, Steven Maynard-Moody, St. Martin's marketing manager Rob Mejia, Tali Mendelberg, Milena Novy, Anna Maria Ortiz, Thomas Romer, James Trussell, David Wilkinson, and dozens of Princeton University undergraduates and graduate students in several versions of Politics 326 (Public Administration), Politics 420 (American Bureaucracy), and Public Affairs 501 (Public Management) who suffered much of the prose, worked through many of the cases, and generally tested the materials from the most demanding standpoint of all—that of the students themselves.

Several referees provided comments that were helpful at multiple points; to these reviewers—and to my editors at St. Martin's, who arranged for their assistance—I owe a special debt of thanks: Carolyn Ban, SUNY Albany; R. Steven Daniels, University of Alabama at Birmingham; Dennis Dresang, University of Wisconsin–Madison; Michael Harris, Eastern Michigan University; Ralph Hummel, University of Oklahoma; Kenneth Hunter, University of Tennessee at Chattanooga; Steven Maynard-Moody, University of Kansas; Christopher Mobley, De Paul University; Marjorie Sarbaugh-Thompson, Wayne State University; Michael J. Scicchitano, University of Florida; James R. Simmons, University of Wisconsin–Oshkosh; Jeffrey Straussman, Syracuse University; and Homer Williamson, St. Cloud State University.

In the same vein, I am pleased to add my name to those of the many other authors on the St. Martin's list who have had Don Reisman—one of the truly influential academic editors of his generation—to thank for his professionalism and support through much of the period of preparation of this book. To Beth Gillett, who inherited me and my project when she took over as St. Martin's political science editor, I express my equally sincere thanks for the uncanny way she has managed to balance the forces of push with those of lift during the final stages of drafting and production. Thanks also to Rich Wright of Omega Publishing Services, who has forgotten more about the book business than most writers ever learn, for teaching me a great deal during our collaboration on this book. Finally, I can't find just the right word to describe the extraordinary level of art that Bob Weber brings to the craft of copyediting—but I know that he could.

Gerald Garvey
Princeton, New Jersey

[N]o practical science is ever studied where there is no need to know it. The very fact, therefore, that the eminently practical science of administration is finding its way into college courses in this country would prove that this country needs to know more about administration. . . . It is the object of administrative study to discover, first, what government can properly and successfully do, and secondly, how it can do these proper things with the utmost possible efficiency and the least possible cost either of money or of energy. On both these points there is obviously much need of light among us; and only careful study can supply that light. . . . The task is great and important enough to attract the best minds.

From Woodrow Wilson, "The Study of Administration,"
2 *Political Science Quarterly* (June 1987): 197.

▽◆●■▽◆●■▽◆●■▽◆●■▽◆

CHAPTER 1

Introduction:
Ten Cues for Case Analysis

The practice of public administration reaches back to the beginnings of organized society—indeed, back to the creation of a special sector of human life consisting of projects that are defined and managed by collective action. The Greeks of classical Athens recognized the public realm as a unique kind of "space," the space in which citizens interacted with one another to settle issues of general concern. The Romans named this special sector *res publica,* "the public thing."

Given the importance that men and women have attached to our subject from the very beginning, it isn't surprising that the study of public administration has drawn from the works of thinkers who have shaped the course of Western history. In his description of the ideal state, *The Republic,* Plato spent whole sections on administrative issues. Over the centuries, Christian and Jewish thinkers—the former dealing with the problems of empire, the latter with the challenge of the Diaspora—strove for better ways to structure authority relations, lines of communication, and mechanisms for the making and enforcement of rules within and among their communities. The coming of the modern nation-state in the 1500s and 1600s saw a redoubling of interest in the theory and practice of public administration.

The framers of the U.S. Constitution took administrative issues with utmost seriousness, just as their predecessors in Western statecraft had. Alexander Hamilton in *Federalist* No. 68 went so far as to assert that "the true test of a good government is its aptitude and tendency to produce a good administration." Public administration attained status as a formal field of professional study in the United States, however, little more than a hundred years ago. For practical purposes, the story began with the **Progressives,** who dominated much of American political life during the latter decades of the nineteenth century and early years of the twentieth. The Progressives numbered among their leaders some of the most colorful and innovative figures in American history: Theodore Roosevelt and Woodrow Wilson; Frederick Winslow Taylor, the father of "scientific management"; the eminent lawyer and later Supreme Court Justice Louis Brandeis; Gifford Pinchot of the Forest Service; Senator "Fightin' Bob" LaFollette of Wisconsin; the civil service reformer George W. Curtis.

A Special Way of Thinking, a Special Kind of Preparation

The Progressives believed that the problems of industrial America could be solved only by highly trained experts. Adopting a theme popularized by the scientific managers, the Progressives reasoned that expert administrators would use their specialized knowledge to find the **One Best Way** for any job of work. One-Best-Way thinking suggested that administrators would be dealing, in the main, with relatively clear-cut problems. *Clear-cut* didn't necessarily mean easy. It did, however, imply that expert administrators would be facing problems with unambiguous solutions, provided only that the specialists were in place to find them. The Progressives' problem-solving imagery suggested the analogy of a mathematical formula. A properly trained analyst could plug in the right numbers and compute a value for the unknown term. That value would correspond to the One Best Way of dealing with the problem at hand. A problem of this description is said to be *determinate;* it contains just enough structure, just enough information, for the knowledgeable problem solver to determine a single correct answer.

The determinate nature of the problems that face public administrators—if it ever existed—has largely vanished over the years. Today there are too many bureaucratic actors on the scene, too many questions of policy to consider, too much confounding of "politics" with "objective analysis" and "administrative technicalities," too many variables to control. Often, authority is divided among multiple actors. Again, an analogy occurs: the analogy with an equation that contains many unknowns, each of which can be assigned a value by a different decision maker acting more or less independently. Unlike the determinate problems envisioned by the Progressives of a century ago, problems of the sort regularly encountered by today's public administrators are said to be *underdetermined.* An **underdetermined problem** signifies the existence of a system with too many variables, variables that move under the influence of too many forces, or variables that are too poorly understood for easy control.

Incomplete Control:
Problems of Underdetermination in Public Administration

There are many sources of underdetermination in our administrative system. Among the more important are organizational contingency; goal diversity; defective information (or, in modern parlance, "bounded rationality"); and fragmentation of authority.

> **Organizational contingency** refers to the situation, faced in many organizations, in which external conditions change over time. These contingencies require adaptive action. By definition, a contingency originates in conditions or developments beyond the immediate control of actors within the system or organization; it originates in *external* failures of control. Contingency theorists see organizations as organisms struggling to stay in equilibrium with their environments.
>
> **Goal diversity** refers to divergences in the preferences or values of different individuals in an organization. No leader has total control over every subordinate. Hence a subordinate might pursue goals in conflict with the those of the organization. Shirking on the job or subversive actions by disloyal employees represent *internal* failures of control.

Defective information causes an administrator to lack control simply because he or she doesn't know about important external or internal factors (organizational contingencies, goal diversities within the group). Or a decision maker may lack an adequate model of the problem. Without a valid *causal theory*, he or she won't know which variables to change in order to bring about desired results.

Fragmentation of authority is perhaps the most pronounced characteristic of the American political system. Power is parceled out among multiple office holders and many wielders of informal influence, such as lobbyists or members of a leader's "kitchen cabinet." Dispersal of control may prevent any one decision maker from determining outcomes, even within areas for which he or she is formally responsible.

Extending our simple mathematical analogy, we can liken an underdetermined problem in administration to an equation such as

$$x + y = 100$$

in which there aren't enough data given to solve for both x and y, or in which two different decision makers may independently decide what values to substitute for certain of the unknown terms. Neither decision maker is under the other's control, yet each may have an opinion regarding the policy (say, the values of x and y) that should be pursued. An infinite number of x-y combinations might be selected that will add up to 100. There's no way within the structure of the problem as given to determine a uniquely satisfactory outcome.

Let the decision makers in our example be X, who controls variable x (but not y), and Y, who is in the reverse situation. The choice made by each decision maker is likely to appear arbitrary when viewed from the standpoint of the other. X will have to find some way to limit Y's freedom of action. Given whatever value X hopes to assign to x, he or she must somehow motivate Y to choose an appropriate value for y.

Contemporary public administration is filled with problems of the "X and Y" type. The challenge for the problem solver is to create conditions in which X and Y will end up coordinating their actions. Perhaps one decision maker can persuade the other to go along. Or maybe both can be "restructured" into a new relationship in which a single superior commands the actions of both. For a third possibility: What if X and Y can be hauled in front of a judge empowered to settle whatever dispute has kept them from agreeing? Or . . . well, you get the idea. Much of our study throughout the following pages will center on the potential of rhetorical argumentation (*persuasion*), organizational change (*restructuring*), courtroom litigation (*adjudication*), and other means of dealing with problems of underdetermination in administrative settings.

Inconsistent Criteria: Problems of Overdetermination in Public Administration

Let's carry our analogy a step further. Suppose X not only has to worry about coordinating with Y but isn't even sure what value should be assigned to x. Further suppose that this uncertain state of affairs is the result of X's awareness that multiple, inconsistent criteria can be applied, both when deciding what the variable x should refer to and how many xs there should be.

To flesh out the notion of "multiple, inconsistent criteria"—it's a recurrent phrase in the literature of contemporary public administration—imagine that X is an official in a government agency. The agency is undergoing a cutback in its workforce. (A cutback management scenario, in more concrete form, underlies our first case study, in Chapter 2.) Let x plus y signify the number of workers to be retained after the layoff. Our equation might then be interpreted in the following way: X and Y are directors of independent divisions. Each must cut his or her workforce back to values of x and y, which, together, lie within an overall personnel ceiling of 100 workers. In general, each decision maker might be expected to fight for the highest number in his or her own unit, even though every added worker in one division will come at the expense of the other. However, the minimum number of xs that X needs will depend in some degree on their quality—in other words, on what the abstract term x refers to.

Higher-ups in the organization tell X and Y to rank the individuals in their units, mindful that various workers' chances of keeping their jobs will depend on their standings in the supervisors' lists. X might reasonably consider any of the following criteria (along with many others) when ranking the individuals:

Criterion 1: Minimize the payroll.

Rank individuals in decreasing order of salary; once the number of xs is known, choose workers from the bottom of the list up, thereby minimizing the total wage bill for a given number of employees retained.

Criterion 2: Reward workers' seniority.

Rank individuals in decreasing order of seniority; choose from the top down, in order to keep the most-experienced workers ("Last hired, first fired").

Criterion 3: Keep the most-competent workers.

Rank individuals in decreasing order of performance; choose from the top down, so that, whatever the final number of x, the best workers will be kept irrespective of their present salary level or years in the organization.

At the end of the day, each of these criteria will produce a different force of retained workers. If X relied solely on criterion 1, 2, or 3, the rank-ordering of individuals might be relatively easy to decide. But the presence of three inconsistent conditions makes for a problem with no unique solution. It is possible for x to take on any numerical value from 0 to 100, but practically speaking, it's not possible for x simultaneously to consist of the 50 least-skilled workers, the 50 most-senior workers, and the 50 most-competent workers. Inconsistency of criteria makes for a problem that's technically known as *overdetermined,* the mirror image of an underdetermined one.

In an **overdetermined problem,** too many—rather than too few—conditions or criteria have to be realized. The problem isn't too much *in*dependence, as occurs when neither decision maker has control over the other; but too much *de*pendence, since each variable simultaneously depends on multiple contradictory conditions. Some criteria won't be achievable in full, and it may not be possible to satisfy other criteria at all. Among the more important sources of overdetermination are multiple goals, resource constraints, and role-based obligations.

Primary goals. Ultimately, a public administrator traces his or her authority to a provision of law, usually a statute that sets up a government agency and authorizes programs for its employees to administer. The "intent of the lawmaker" is usually the first criterion for a public administrator to consider when acting in an official capacity.

Contextual goals. In addition to the primary goals are a host of so-called contextual goals. For example, a welfare caseworker must deal with the specific needs of clients while satisfying procedural requirements ("due process of law"), protecting the privacy of individuals on the welfare rolls, and collecting statistical information for public record-keeping agencies. Such ancillary criteria set the context for the pursuit of primary goals. Contextual goals complicate the jobs of almost all public officials.

Resource constraints. Officials must pursue primary and contextual goals within the limits of the agency's budget, its personnel allocation, and so forth. In an era of cutback management, public administrators often complain that they're asked to do more and more with less and less.

General role obligations. A person who accepts a public role incurs certain *outcome-centered* obligations (such as the duty to achieve beneficial outcomes for the constituency served—for example, farmers or low-income citizens) as well as certain *action-centered* obligations (such as the duty to give impartial treatment to all citizens who are entitled to service). As we'll see in Chapter 8, conflicts between outcome-centered and action-centered obligations are common.

Specific role obligations. Particular government positions may carry additional, special obligations. For example, some roles (a police officer serving on a SWAT team; a safety inspector in the Federal Aviation Agency) call for strict adherence to procedures. Other roles may require an official to put the interests of clients or patients *above* the obligation to obey orders from a superior officer. Most vexing are situations—we'll consider specific examples in our case for Chapter 10—in which an official simultaneously fills several roles that make conflicting claims.

Why Case Analysis?

If most problems in contemporary public administration were determinate—well structured, subject to One-Best-Way thinking, governed by completely consistent criteria—they would, for the most part, be solvable through the straightforward application of technical expertise. That's apparently what the Progressives had in mind when they called for "a science of administration" and moved to create "a corps of civil servants prepared by special schooling." (The quotes are from a famous 1887 article by Woodrow Wilson.[1]) Today, however, problems in public administration—or at least the most interesting, most representative problems—not only are not determinate but also combine elements of both underdetermination (lack of control, inadequate information) and overdetermination (inconsistent criteria, usually requiring the compromise of some goals

---

[1]"The Study of Administration," 2 *Political Science Quarterly* (June 1887): 197–222. All quotes from Woodrow Wilson come from this article.

and the outright sacrifice of others). To deal with such problems requires a special way of thinking. In turn, this special way of thinking calls for a special kind of preparation.

The Geometrical Intelligence and the Discerning Intelligence

Philosophers through the ages have tried to distinguish between the different kinds of thinking that are appropriate in different kinds of problem-solving situations. Aristotle drew a contrast between theoretical knowledge (*episteme*) and practical wisdom (*phronesis*). From the time of the Roman republic until early in the modern era, the practitioners of a method of ethical inquiry known as **casuistry** distinguished between "questions," which they defined as moral problems for which general solutions could be found, and "causes," for which special responses might be appropriate depending on the details of each situation. The seventeenth-century thinker Blaise Pascal elaborated these lines of thought by distinguishing between the **geometrical intelligence** and the **discerning intelligence**.

Pascal, who was both a great mathematician and a great theologian, considered theoretical science—the kind of science we associate with chemistry or physics—to be the essential field of the geometrical intelligence. The geometrical intelligence works through the process of abstraction. The problem solver strips away details to lay bare deeper general principles. For example, "force of gravity" and "conservation of energy and mass" are among the general principles that we learn in the first course in physics. Even at the introductory level, natural science involves the study of regularities so dominant and certain that all other factors can be "abstracted away." Hence a physicist, when demonstrating the physical law that governs a body in free fall, may feel perfectly justified in ignoring the object's color and composition; the rate of descent depends, to a very close approximation, only on the force of gravity (and perhaps wind resistance).

Repeatedly in the chapters that follow, we will experiment with the uses of formal, geometrical reasoning in public administration. Arguably, the most powerful analytical tendencies within the field since World War II—usually collected under an umbrella term such as *formal policy analysis*—display the impulses to quantify and simplify. Both impulses are characteristics of the geometrical intelligence. None of our simple algebraic analogies, none of our analytical methods (such as cost-benefit analysis, the main subject of Chapter 9) should suggest that public administrators need to be mathematicians or computer jocks. But administrators *do* need to appreciate the role of formal methods. It's essential for our public servants to feel comfortable and intellectually confident when deciphering a table of figures or interpreting a simple algebraic description of a problem.

The geometrical style is often especially useful when an analyst tries to isolate the inner kernel of an administrative problem. (Indeed, we've already used this style to illustrate the concepts of underdetermined and overdetermined systems.) But getting to the kernel is usually only a start. If the process is left there, it's as likely to distort the problem as solve it. We've noted that the situations confronting public officials often involve many variables in complex, sometimes contradictory relationships with one another. Furthermore, the relationships among the variables in a typical administrative problem are often rather weak. *Weak* here doesn't mean that any one variable is unimportant; it only means that no single factor dominates the situation—in the way, for example, that force of gravity may dominate a problem in physics. The analyst can't ignore one set of variables in favor of some limited set of other variables that control the entire problem. On the contrary, it is essential to consider details in all their richness and variety, weighing their offsetting impacts.

The besetting error of the geometrical thinker is to suppose that abstract analysis—however necessary in some situations—can be sufficient for practical problem solving. Pascal concluded that, when dealing with human problems, one must consider factors "so delicate and so numerous that you must have a very delicate and clear sensitivity to feel them; and you must judge aright and with precision according to that feeling, usually without being able to prove them in an orderly fashion as in geometry. . . . It is not that the mind does not reason, but it does so tacitly, naturally, and without art."[2] The problem solver must *feel* the situation, must cultivate an "appreciative sense" for the nuances of the case.

Both the geometrical and the discerning intellects have their places in public administration, but the more important of the two is the discerning intelligence. Moreover, it is the discerning intellect that the case study mode of analysis is intended to cultivate. Aristotle's *phronetic* knowledge and Pascal's discerning intellect are both species of practical—as opposed to abstract or theoretical—wisdom, and practical wisdom generally comes out of experience among the masters of a calling. In the field of ethics, for example, abstract treatises on Truth or Goodness teach less about moral behavior than does the experience of living with good people and learning from their example. It is experience, albeit vicarious experience, that case analysis is intended to provide.

Case studies have long been preferred as the vehicles by which the masters in crafts such as law, medicine, and public administration pass practical knowledge on to the apprentices in their fields. Our aim is to work through the kinds of vicarious experiences that will help cultivate not only the skills but also the sensitivities that administrators need: circumspection and discernment, moral acuity, practical wisdom.

SECTION ● ■ ▼ ◆ 2   Cultivating the Discerning Intelligence: Ten Cues for Case Analysis

Few public administrators expect ever to find a "one size fits all" problem-solving approach for the vast range of situations that they are likely to encounter—partly (one suspects) because they acknowledge that the problems of public administrators have become harder over the years and partly (one hopes) because public administrators themselves may have grown wiser since the scientific managers taught that One Best Way can always be found to solve any problem. Still, with wisdom has come not only humility but also the notion of a *discipline* of case analysis.

The most disciplined bodies of knowledge contain materials encapsulated in rigorous problem-solving methods called **algorithms**—routines to be followed in exact order. Unfortunately, no script has ever been written for an administrator to follow exactly and literally when dealing with case materials. Because case analysis in public administration can't be undertaken through formulas, the notion of an algorithm should

---

[2]Blaise Pascal, *Pensées* (Thoughts), No. 38.

be taken suggestively, not literally. Nevertheless, the following ordered steps provide a useful checklist.

Gather the Facts; Find the Issues; State the Case. (Cues 1 through 3)

What's the *story*? What lessons can we draw from an understanding of the way the situation developed? What are the *choices*? Who must make what decisions, resolve what conflicts, take what actions?

Is the Problem Underdetermined? Overdetermined? (Cues 4 through 6)

Is *control* over critical variables unified or diffuse? If the situation is underdetermined, might persuasion, restructuring, negotiation, adjudication, or other techniques be used to establish control?

What are the main figures' *goals*? What changes in the situation would lead to those goals? What conditions or *criteria* (including resource constraints and role-based obligations) limit the options? Multiple criteria may make for an overdetermined problem, either because the criteria are inconsistent among themselves or because they severely limit the policies that can be adopted. In an overdetermined case, might priority setting, parameter changing, or policy adjusting be used to mitigate the inconsistencies?

Is the Pattern Familiar? How So—and How *Not?* (Cue 7)

Does the problem evoke one of the established *paradigms* of public administration? Does the paradigm suggest a way to proceed? *What if?* How might the "progression of circumstances" change the decision regarding what to do?

Discuss and Defend: Why *This* Action Instead of Another? (Cue 8)

Good decisions most often emerge from dialogue, and they need to be sustained in rhetorical argument. In a democracy, decisions must be defended. Can you *justify* your recommended action?

As is indicated, the steps in our algorithm (loosely interpreted) correspond to a series of cues that experience has shown to be helpful in case analysis. You might want to keep these cues in mind, both when working through your classroom case assignments and in real-world problem solving.

Cue 1.   **Cases are stories; they teach what stories teach—which just happens to be what administrators most need to learn.**

The editors of a popular introduction to literature, Carol Bain and associates, have stressed that stories "tell us not so much what life means as what it's like."[3] In the same vein, our cases are intended to take you inside the world of public administrators—to communicate what the lived experience is really like. The stories of which case studies are composed should help you appreciate what it is that public administrators do and how they do it—which, after all, is what public administration is.

There's a maxim of case analysis known as *Goldberg's Rule.* Avram Goldberg, the former president of the Stop & Shop food chain, used to ask his employees "What's the

---

[3]Carol E. Bain et al., *The Norton Introduction to Literature* (New York: Norton, 1982), p. 5.

story?" instead of the more general, abstract question "What's the problem?" By focusing on the story behind the problem, the case analyst can often best discern *who* must make *what* choices, and *how* the issues in the case emerged to begin with. The "stories administrators tell" suggest that effective performance depends as much on the intangibles of relations among bosses and subordinates—on the subtle manifestations of institutional leadership or organizational sabotage, on the ability to identify the critical decision maker or opportune moment—as it does on the problem solver's ability to apply deductive logic. The cultivation of an "appreciative sense" is a feature of story-based knowledge. The first move on the path to effectiveness as an administrator isn't to learn a list of handy-dandy administrative principles but to develop a sense of the human milieu in which administrative issues arise and must be resolved.

Cue 2.   Public administration is politics—not the "obvious politics" of high-stakes electioneering and policy making, but the "other politics" of small-scale, behind-the-scenes problem solving; the nature of administrative casework follows accordingly.

For most purposes, public administration can be thought of as the calling of all those men and women who hold appointive (instead of elective) jobs in government, and who conduct the "other politics"—the less visible, less dramatic politics of everyday governance. The term *other politics* suggests what public administrators do, in a way that most of us who read the papers or watch TV can easily understand. The featured players in most political stories are prominent leaders of coalitions (Jesse Jackson, Ralph Nader, Gloria Steinham), cabinet officers, legislative deal makers, and, of course, the president. But everyone knows that another kind of politics starts up where high-level statecraft and power brokering leave off. This awareness takes us to the realm of ordinary citizens in daily interaction with their government. Public administration is also about the tired citizen waiting in line for a driver's license, the accident victim applying for a federal disability allowance, the farmer hoping for a drought-year crop subsidy, and, of course, the student anxiously awaiting action on a government college loan request.

The "other politics" includes most of the problems of governance that the professors don't cover in their lectures on election hoopla; that the pundits ignore when they analyze the inner workings of the White House; that the network anchors skip in their reports on foreign policy crises. From none of these sources, however, do we learn why Jane Roe had to wait three hours on line to renew her driver's license and why John Doe never seems to get his Social Security check on time. What the practitioners of the obvious politics do affects all of us. That's the point of most courses in political science. But it's also true that elected officials, who wheel and deal with the millions in mind, must eventually rely on appointive administrators to apply the laws to individual citizens—to all the Jane Roes and John Does whom the entire system was supposedly designed to serve in the first place. That's a main point of our course in public administration. Our cases are designed to underscore the importance as well as the difficulty of the quotidian in modern governance.

The scenarios that we'll be considering don't deal with great issues of war or peace. They involve more modest matters: How to make cutbacks in the local public workforce. How to ensure order in the neighborhood. How to arrange for efficient waste disposal. Cases about budget officers, beat cops, and managers of recycling centers may lack drama. But they more than make up for this in realism and relevance. The novelist James Michener once defined a civilized society as a "body of people who can supply their community with potable drinking water, proper sewage disposal, and someone skilled enough in radio transmission to bring huge airplanes to safe landings."[4] All the items on Michener's list, and thousands like them, presuppose the existence of successful, supporting public administrative structures.

What are stories of problem solving in the public sector really about? Nothing less than what's necessary to keep life for all of us civil, decent, and sustainable.

Cue 3.   Stories don't come readymade but must be formed through selection and shaping from the flow of events: "Case synthesis precedes case analysis."

In the real world, administrative problems come with information that is incomplete, enshrouded in "noise." So do the scenarios in the following pages. All our cases have a degree of richness, of texture—in other words, of complexity and confusion. Our scenarios are meant to model the complexity of real-world administrative situations rather than the structure of academic exercises. Therefore, the case write-ups don't flag approved problem-solving methodologies. Nor do they contain the kinds of neat textbook exercises that you know you've solved when a nice round number pops out at the end. The analyst must piece together a coherent story from materials that may seem (and probably are) disjointed, even contradictory. If you don't start from a position of some bewilderment after perusing each case for the first time, the case itself will not have done *its* job of modeling a complex real-world administrative situation.

On the other hand, after a reading or two of a case, if you don't move to draw from the stream of events a coherent story, then you'll not have done *your* job as a case analyst. The principle underlying this admonition—"Case synthesis precedes case analysis"—is familiar in all fields of study that are case-based or casuistic in spirit. (You might want to acquaint yourself with some of the history and methodology of the problem-solving approach known as casuistry; see Box 1.1. Our work throughout this book will draw from the casuistic tradition, which is currently enjoying an intellectual renaissance.)

For law and medical students, problem solving routinely begins with case synthesis. Class discussion in a law school typically takes off from a statement by a designated student who presents a summary of the facts of the case, organized to show how and why particular legal issues came to be joined. Medical residents make their morning rounds in teaching hospitals using a similar approach. For each patient, a student describes the case history, recounting the development of symptoms and reporting on the success of treatments tried to date.

In public administration as in law or medicine, step 1 is to "state the case" by presenting for open discussion a brief précis of the story, leading to a definition of the conflict or conflicts that need to be resolved and the choice or choices confronting the principal actors in the scenario.

Optimally, the relevant choices should be stated in both abstract and concrete forms. At the abstract level, for example, a case might involve a choice between certain

---

[4]*The Key Reporter* (newsletter of the Phi Beta Kappa Society, Spring 1994), p. 5.

BOX 1.1 ▬▬▬▬▬▬▬▬▬▬▬▬▬▬▬▬▬▬▬▬▬▬▬▬▬▬▬ ■-■-■

Casuistry: "The Analysis of Complex Cases in the Light of 'A Thousand Difficulties'"

The problem-solving approach known as casuistry was practiced in one form or another by some of the finest minds in Western history—by Socrates, Cicero, St. Augustine, and Maimonides, among others. Unfortunately, the term *casuistry* has fallen into some disfavor. Today it connotes hairsplitting and strained interpretations to rationalize morally lax behavior. Yet the basics of casuistry survive in the methodology of law (to this day, Anglo-American common law is casuistic in form), in the curricula of our business schools and public policy programs, in the practice of medicine, and in the study of public administration.

The Roman politician and philosopher Cicero was the classical period's greatest exponent of the casuistic method. Cicero also authored one of the first treatises to use the case method in an explicit way. Today we recognize Book III of Cicero's *De Officiis* ("Of Public Office: On the Conflict between the Right and the Expedient") as the forerunner of the modern casebook. The moral philosophers of the Middle Ages preserved the Ciceronic tradition. They passed the casuistic method on to the Christian ethicists of the high period, in the early seventeenth century. Much of Jewish moral thought, expressed in the *responsa* of the medieval and modern talmudists, is also basically casuistic in nature. We needn't, however, reach to the greats of civic and moral discourse for our examples. In a recent study, the philosophers Albert Jonsen and Stephen Toulmin pointed out that Ann Landers, the advice-to-the-lovelorn columnist, is a capable contemporary practitioner of the craft of casuistry.

In the following passage, Jonsen and Toulmin give the flavor of the casuistic method, explicitly relating it to three features of the case method: the practical (or, in Aristotle's term, *phronetic*) style of thought; the technique of paradigmatic analysis; and the concept of the progression of circumstances.

> Casuists of the high era organized their cases . . . in a way that showed the connection between a specific kind of case and a given principle. In treating killing under the fifth commandment, for example, or false witness under the eighth, the casuist first offered a definition of key terms, such as "killing" or "lying," usually drawn from some renowned author such as Cicero, St. Augustine, or St. Thomas. He then proposed sample cases in which the question can be raised whether an action described in a certain way might fall under the moral offense so defined. . . .
>
> These extreme examples served as "paradigm cases" illustrating the most manifest breaches of the general principles, taken in its most obvious meaning. . . . Then, in succession, cases were proposed that moved away from the paradigm by introducing various combinations of circumstances and motives that made the offense in question less apparent. . . . This gradual movement from clear and simple cases to the more complex and obscure ones was standard procedure for the casuist; indeed, it might be said to be the essence of the

casuistic mode of thinking. . . . [C]ases of progressive difficulty were constructed by the addition of complicating circumstances to the paradigm cases. The casuists drew on the traditional list of circumstances—"who, what, where, when, why, how and by what means." . . . These were the qualifications that Aristotle, Cicero, and the classical rhetoricians had taught. . . . The casuists incessantly called these circumstances to attention; they insisted that "circumstances *make* the case" and inevitably modified moral judgment about it. . . . [T]he further one moved away from the paradigm, the more arguable—in terms of pro and con—the case became. . . .

The work of the casuists was precisely the analysis of complex cases in the light of "a thousand difficulties." . . . [I]n morals, as in medicine, difficult cases can never be resolved by logical deductions leading to certain conclusions. . . . [W]hat matters most is an ability to recognize, in full subtlety and detail, the relevant features of any particular case—both "circumstances of the action" and "conditions of the agent." . . .

Beyond all necessary inferences and deductions from general rules, there thus lie other, more basic issues of moral and judicial *judgment* about just how close the facts of any particular case lie to the facts of the relevant paradigm. . . . The kind of wisdom involved in answering questions of this kind is just the personal talent Aristotle described as practical wisdom, or **phronesis**. This does not demand only the capacity to learn general rules and to make valid deductions; it rests, rather, on having a feeling for or a grasp of what is . . . equitable, fair, fitting, or reasonable—given all the detailed circumstances of some particular practical situation.

From A. Jonsen and S. Toulmin, *The Abuse of Casuistry* (Berkeley CA: U. of California, 1988), pp. 251–258.

---

general principles, such as the competing principles of "efficiency" and "fairness," both of which are relevant to typical administrative problems such as the awarding of licenses, the allocation of beds in homeless shelters, or the acceptance of applicants for welfare payments. The corresponding concrete issue would involve the way these principles apply to the particular factual situation: Should *this* child care provider (who may have a spotty safety record) get her or his license renewed? Should *this* homeless individual get space for the night (even though the space limit set by the fire department has already been reached)? Should *this* claimant's General Assistance allotment be increased? Should a public health specialist divulge *this* person's positive HIV status in an effort to protect other individuals?

Cue 4.   **Keep your eye on the entire set of interacting decision makers and interlocking policies; it's there you're most likely to find any lurking problems of underdetermination.**

Problems of underdetermination, we have seen, most typically occur when a decision by one actor can arbitrarily change the conditions under which another must act. For example, the way an urban leader decides to encourage inner-city development will influence the number of homeless persons in the population. Should the city planner promote low-cost housing or encourage upscale businesses? Affordable housing should ease homelessness, while commercial development might preempt space that low-income citizens need for residential development. In turn, homeless people are the responsibility of officials in a different agency of city government. Homeless persons also have a higher-than-average chance of becoming public health statistics, involving administrators from yet a third city bureaucracy. Public health problems may call for budgetary increases in the medical area, thereby creating pressures on the resources available for housing, commercial development, homeless support programs, and so forth. (In several of our cases, we'll be dealing with just this tangle of intersecting concerns in the fields of urban development, housing, and public health.)

Let's return to our example of decision makers X and Y, each empowered to assign a value to "his" or "her" variable. Each decision maker might regard the other's ability to make this kind of assignment as arbitrary (just as the homeless assistance administrator might think it arbitrary if a community developer presses for the demolition of marginal housing to make room for new businesses, thereby pushing some individuals out onto the street). These kinds of underdetermined situations naturally make for conflict. How do such scenarios of conflict play out in actual experience? In the pages that follow, we'll be considering five primary ways to deal with underdetermined situations:

Persuasion. X and Y might each try to persuade the other to assign a value that the first feels able to live with. Even if the rhetorical process doesn't change anyone's mind, the offering of explanations and justifications may soften disagreements and help future working relationships.

Restructuring. X and Y might be brought (whether they like it or not) into a new hierarchical structure under Z. As an organizational superior, Z could either issue commands tailored to specific situations or impose general rules that X and Y must follow.

Negotiation. X and Y might retain their independence while bargaining directly with each other. Negotiation ("haggling over the price") is characteristic of free-market transactions. It's also increasingly important in bureaucracies, where, because of goal diversity, problems of underdetermination may surface even though there's a superior, Z, formally in charge. Z may find it impossible to exert the desired degree of control. Instead, Z may try to lead by bargaining with both subordinates and peers (leading to the concept of an organization as a dynamic "negotiated order"). Chapter 5 includes a section about bargaining theory as a subfield of public administration. Then, in Chapter 6, we'll see how informal groups play a vital role in administrative systems by facilitating ongoing processes of negotiation.

Adjudication. What if negotiators find they can't hammer out mutually satisfactory voluntary agreements? X and Y might find themselves arguing before a judge—or before a special kind of public administrator who is filling what's known as an adjudicative role—empowered to settle matters in accordance with a preexisting code of rules.

Strategic interaction. Suppose X and Y want to retain as much independence of action as they can (they resist restructuring); suppose they also refuse to negotiate (which implies a willingness to compromise); finally, suppose they reject the risky process of adjudication (in which a judge or administrative official will settle their case by picking a winner and a loser). *X* and *Y* may each independently try to calculate which strategy will best advance his or her own interests, given an estimate of the strategies that the adversary might pursue. **Game theory** is the formal study of strategic action; we'll see vignettes of "gaming" throughout our cases.

Most of our case scenarios involve one or more elements of underdetermination. Keep in view the entire chain of interlinked decision makers and interlocking policies that so frequently gives rise to issues of underdetermination. Persuasion, restructuring, and the other methods can then be used as a kind of rough-and-ready checklist of possible responses.

A final point, but an extremely important one: The admonition to keep interlocking issues in view doesn't mean that you should try to reconcile them all. We have long had the advice of the sage Rabbi Tarfon: "You are not required to finish the work, but neither are you at liberty to desist from your portion of it." A public administrator's work involves not only problems too complex for determinate solutions but also problems that tend to be too large for complete responses. *You are not required to finish the work!* You're not expected to propose even proximate resolutions for all the issues raised in a case scenario. But neither, on the other hand, should you "desist from your portion of it." Use the scenario in its entirety as context; against that backdrop, select one or two concerns to focus on.

Our cases, like administrative situations in the real world, are exercises in selectivity as well as in circumspection and discernment. The difficulties most of us have with unsolvable problems of this kind are emotional as much as they're intellectual. It's not easy to end a day's labors knowing that three problems remain unsolved for every one that's been dealt with. But an important part of "learning public administration" is learning to live with the sensation of discomfiture when a job can't be done as well as you'd have liked. Don't be surprised to feel that way, not only as you end your own reading of a case but also as you conclude your class discussion of the issues. ("But we didn't get to debate this!" "Why didn't we find time to talk about that?") Uneasiness over work undone isn't the feeling of failure. Rather, it's the feeling—again in Professor Bain's words—of what administrative life is really like.

Cue 5.   **It's usually helpful to break out the goals being pursued, the variables that must be modified to move toward the goals, and the criteria to be borne in mind when pursuing the goals; it's in those criteria that problems of overdetermination are likely to originate.**

In our discussion of overdetermination, we saw that multiple criteria may limit the decision maker's freedom to act. For example, the criterion of economy may limit the dollars available for solutions. Or a hiring restriction of some kind may prevent a manager from staffing up with the kinds of experts needed to do an important job. For the kinds of overdetermined problems that we commonly encounter in public administration, it's usually helpful to ask if different weights should be assigned to the different criteria or conditions—a process known as **priority setting**.

Which criteria should an administrator scrupulously try to satisfy? Which ones might be safely deemphasized? An extreme form of priority setting occurs when an official decides for some reason that it's necessary to achieve a heroic simplification of the problem by "zeroing out" certain criteria altogether. Instead of trying to balance primary and contextual goals, resource constraints, and a long list of role-based obligations against one another, a decision maker might declare that certain contextual goals should be ignored lest they interfere with the pursuit of some all-important primary goal. Such a judgment would have to depend on the circumstances of the case.

An administrator can sometimes eliminate an inconsistency among competing criteria by changing one or more of the criteria themselves. For example, in our first chapter case, involving a management scenario of cutbacks, the manager of a layoff in the ·U.S. Department of Agriculture is supposed to compile lists of workers whose jobs are interchangeable. The more-senior employees on each list will "bump" junior ones, since (according to the interchangeability requirement) they should be able to take over the duties of the displaced individuals. But maybe the manager thinks that the more-senior workers are deadwood, that the organization would be better off if they—instead of the more-vulnerable junior employees—were let go. The manager could consider redefining jobs in a way that prevents bumping. The criterion of interchangeability would be changed; this kind of modification is known technically as **parameter changing.** The list of interchangeable jobs could be revised to bring the criterion that applies to bumping an employee into line with another obvious criterion, namely, the criterion of excellence in the workforce. Note, however, that this kind of parameter changing might violate yet a third criterion, the criterion of good-faith interpretation of the civil service rules. Seniority protections are intended to prevent just this kind of game playing, which may have the effect of rigging the outcome of a cutback in personnel.

The worst instances of overdetermination occur when criteria are literally inconsistent with one another, meaning that they must be weighted (priority setting) or modified (parameter changing). A less severe but still problematic kind of overdetermination can occur when so many different criteria exist that they can all be satisfied only by a specially tailored policy. This kind of problem can lead to a process of **policy adjusting.**

Public administrationists used to teach that a gap existed between policy makers, who formulated goals, and the administrators who were merely to execute orders from above. This notion of a **policy-administration gap** applied to a context in which the policy makers were free to order whatever actions they thought were in the public interest. Theoretically, administrators were also free to do whatever they had to in order to get the job done. To exemplify this approach, Woodrow Wilson wrote that administrators should enjoy "unhampered discretion" to choose whatever legal means were necessary for the efficient execution of commands.

But the situation is very different today. Neither policy makers nor administrators act in unconstrained contexts. If politics is "the art of the possible," so is administration! Policy makers who care about results can't set goals without thinking through the potential problems of implementation. Reciprocally, when dealing with overdetermined situations, administrators can't simply stand passively by, ready to execute any comand that comes their way. They must tell their superiors what's feasible. The resulting tension between policy and feasibility is a defining element in most administrative actions.

Box 1.2 contains a more formal discussion of the techniques of priority setting, parameter changing, and policy adjusting.

Cue 6.   Remember Miles's Law: "Where you stand depends on where you sit."

Different actors in an administrative situation are likely to have different priorities. We've already encountered this phenomenon under the technical term *goal diversity*, which underlies a maxim of administrative problem solving known as **Miles's Law:** "Where you stand depends on where you sit." This is attributed to a distinguished public administrator, Rufus Miles. Miles, who served from the 1940s through the mid-1960s in a series of high federal posts. While working in the Executive Office of the President, Miles observed the change in attitude that overtook a subordinate who left the budget office for a job in a cabinet department. The individual had been a vigorous cutter of fiscal fat, but he quickly became an advocate of increased spending to support his new department's mission. "Where you stand" (the interests you're most likely to try to promote) invariably reflects the expectations and obligations of "where you sit" (the job you hold, the organizational position you occupy).

Miles's Law underscores the importance of an actor's social role. A role in a play comes with a set of prescribed lines to speak. In the same way, an administrative role, which encodes the ought-tos and should-dos of an organizational position, comes with explicit or implicit rules of behavior. Role analysis will therefore be one of our main concerns in case analysis. "What's the story?" (Cue 1) usually leads to a statement of the choices facing the main figures in a case scenario. The roles filled by those figures are usually among the predictors of the actions that are appropriate for them to take.

The roles that are relevant in public administration aren't confined to formal titles such as secretary of agriculture, chief of police, or director of planning (to cite some of the formal offices filled by actors in our first three cases). Roles of a more general kind are also powerful indicators of appropriate action. For example, an administrator responsible for implementing a specific program, such as a license examiner at a motor vehicle bureau, may prefer not to obey a disagreeable order from above ("Make sure you *see* proof of auto insurance before you renew a driver's permit, no matter what kind of hard-luck story the applicant tells"). But the license clerk is under a strong obligation to follow the agency's established procedures, whether they're pleasant or not. By contrast, an official in the role of a service professional—say a doctor serving as a public health officer—may have an ethical obligation to question a higher order if it might harm a patient. A hard-luck story could be highly relevant, depending on the official's specific role and the facts of the particular case.

Cue 7.   Search for the paradigm of the case, but expect departures from the underlying pattern; explore the progression of circumstances.

Case analysis typically involves a search for a *paradigm* (from the Greek word meaning "pattern"). For most purposes, *archetype, model,* or *pure case* can be used synonymously with the word *paradigm*. There's nothing fancy about the paradigmatic concept except perhaps the term itself. The **paradigm of the case** simply refers to whatever

BOX 1.2 ■■■■

Dealing with Overdetermination: Priority Setting, Parameter Changing, and Policy Adjusting

We've looked informally at some typical instances of priority setting, parameter changing, and policy adjusting—for example, at the decision of the administrator who changes a parameter in the personnel system (the definition of interchangeable jobs) to gain flexibility when managing a personnel cutback. If you've taken a course in college-level algebra—or even if you recall simple simultaneous equations from your high school math—you might find it useful to have a more formal treatment of the key concepts of underdetermination and overdetermination. *The following discussion is strictly optional.* And keep in mind that although an algebraic illustration can be used to clarify nonalgebraic ideas, it can't convey the sense for details that an administrator needs in concrete cases.

Consider an agency with two subunits that are to be staffed by our now-familiar x- and y-type workers. As before, the total number of workers must equal the authorized personnel strength of 100. Now add two additional criteria: Suppose that x-type workers are paid at rate r_1 and y-type workers are paid at rate r_2, and that the total agency payroll has to equal dollar total R. Further suppose that x-type workers require s_1 square feet of office space per worker while y-type workers require s_2 square feet, and that the total footage allotted to both units should equal S. The agency head must decide how many xs and ys to recruit. Algebraically, we have:

$$\text{Criterion 1:} \quad x + y = 100$$
$$\text{Criterion 2:} \quad r_1\,x + r_2\,y = R$$
$$\text{Criterion 3:} \quad s_1\,x + s_2\,y = S$$

In its present form, this system is underdetermined. It consists of three equations with only a single fixed term: the workforce total, 100. (Implicitly, in criterion 1 both x and y have coefficients of 1; technically, those 1s are also fixed, but they don't affect the problem in any way.) There are eight "free" terms: x, y, r_1, r_2, R, s_1, s_2, and S. One way to proceed would be to assign values to six of the eight free terms in order to ensure that the remaining two—presumably the dependent variables of interest, x and y—can be solved for. A mathematician would call this procedure "arbitrarily fixing terms."

Unfortunately, in the world of political and administrative decision making, it might prove very difficult indeed to fix the appropriate free terms in a consistent way. In our fragmented decision-making system, different actors control different terms. Let's list the main categories of free terms and the decision makers who might have jurisdiction over them:

100 A *central personnel agency* (corresponding to the Office of Personnel Management in the federal government) sets the workforce ceiling.

R A *legislative appropriations committee* allots total dollar amount R for salaries.

S   A *central facilities management agency* (in the federal government, it would be the General Services Administration) allocates total office space S.

r_i An independent *civil service pay board* fixes the salary rates r_1 and r_2 of workers with particular skills.

s_i Under a special law to ensure standardized working conditions, a *workplace equity officer* within the agency—but authorized to act independently of the agency head—sets the space requirements s_1 and s_2.

Inconsistent decisions about the personnel ceiling (fixed here as 100), the personnel budget (R), the overall space allotment (S), salary rates (r_1 and r_2), and per-worker space entitlements (s_1 and s_2) seem inevitable. *Thus does an underdetermined situation easily give way to a problem of overdetermination as well.*

Suppose the decision makers, acting independently, assign values as shown below to the terms they control:[7]

$$
\begin{aligned}
x + y &= 100 \text{ total employees} \\
40x + 60y &= \$4,800 \text{ total payroll} \\
50x + 100y &= 7,500 \text{ total square feet}
\end{aligned}
$$

The agency head can satisfy any two of these criteria simultaneously by choosing a unique set of values for x and y. For example, criteria 1 and 2 are satisfied when $x = 60$ and $y = 40$. These values, however, violate criterion 3, since

$$(50)\,60 + (100)\,40 = 7,000 \text{ square feet}$$

instead of 7,500. On the other hand, if decision makers recruit 50 workers apiece for x- and y-type jobs, criteria 1 and 3 can both be satisfied—albeit at the cost of violating criterion 2. Finally, criteria 2 and 3 can be met by setting $x = 30$ and $y = 60$, but then criterion 1 is violated, since the total staffing falls 10 short of the required 100. What's the agency head to do?

Priority Setting

In an extreme case, the decision maker might simply declare criteria 1 and 2 to be of overriding importance and ignore criterion 3. By treating one or more uncomfortable criteria as though they didn't even exist, the decision maker can eliminate inconsistencies and render the problem determinate. But this kind of solution may be costly. The General Services administrator may set off some fireworks when he or she learns that the agency head has ignored the required space assignment.

In a less extreme case, instead of literally zeroing-out one or more criteria, the administrator who must decide on values for x and y might emphasize certain crite-

---

[5]Note that, to save space, dollar figures have been abbreviated to thousands. Hence the parameter values should be read in the following way:

Salaries: R = \$4,800 thousand total payroll
                  \$40 thousand per year per x-type worker
                  \$60 thousand per year per y-type worker

Space: S = 7,500 total square feet
                50 square feet per x-type worker
                100 square feet per y-type worker

ria and give short shrift to others. This kind of weighting procedure would come closer to what we usually mean by priority setting. However, assigning weights to criteria doesn't eliminate inconsistencies. It only mitigates them. So priority setting in this sense isn't so much a way to solve an overdetermined problem as it is to find a *proximate solution*. The decision maker tries to come close to his or her objectives based on the selective weighting of criteria.

Parameter Changing

Instead of dropping or deemphasizing criteria, the agency head might modify one or more of the factors that make them up. These factors—in our example, r_1, r_2, s_1, and s_2—are (somewhat loosely) called *parameters*. For example, if the criteria in our problem are changed to

$$x + y = 100 \text{ total employees}$$
$$40x + 56y = \$4,800 \text{ total payroll}$$
$$50x + 100y = 7,500 \text{ total square feet}$$

by substituting the parameter 56 for 60 in criterion 2, we can meet all three conditions simultaneously. This occurs at $x = 50$ and $y = 50$. There are usually an infinite number of ways in which the parameters that define criteria can be changed to nudge an overdetermined system toward consistency. But note: Any change of this kind produces a solution to a different problem from the one initially given! Again, from the standpoint of the original problem, the solution is only proximate.

Policy Adjusting

The numbers—100; \$4,800; 7,500—make up an expression known as a *column vector*, usually written as

$$\mathbf{p} = (\ 100\ \$4,800\ 7,500\ )^t$$

This expression is labeled **p** because it can be thought of as a *policy vector*. Taken together, the three numbers specify a policy to be achieved—targets for the agency head to shoot for when recruiting *x*s and *y*s: how many workers to hire, how much to pay them in aggregate, how roomy their work stations should be. The problem, we have seen, is that the uncoordinated assignment of values by different decision makers is likely to produce a policy vector that contributes to the inconsistency of the system. In our illustration, the policy vector **p** combines with the parameters $r_1 = 40$, $r_2 = 60$, and so forth, to define three criteria that can't simultaneously be satisfied by any combination of the two dependent variables *x* and *y*.

The agency head might persuade one of the policy makers to make a small adjustment in the term that he or she controls. Suppose the appropriations chairperson agrees to change **p** to

$$\mathbf{p}' = (\ 100\ \$5,000\ 7,500\ )^t$$

by adding some money to the personnel budget, *R*. Then it will be possible to satisfy all three criteria at $x = 50$ and $y = 50$ without deemphasizing any criteria or changing any parameters. But, again, instead of giving an exact solution to the original problem, policy adjusting solves a different problem. Alternatively, it yields a "proximate solution to an insoluble problem."

In linear algebra, there's a technique known as singular value decomposition for finding the best proximate solution to an overdetermined problem. And as we'll see in Chapter 9, the practitioners of systems analysis—an important subfield of contemporary public administration—have developed an alternative mathematical method known as linear programming for approximating solutions to problems such as the one in our example.

But after all that has been said, the fact is that most administrative situations don't have the definable structures of math exercises. In the real world, criteria rarely occur in the form of simple equations. It isn't always easy to isolate every criterion or identify all the parameters. Sometimes it's even hard to spell out the policy vector in the problem. Nor should terms borrowed from algebra, such as *parameter* and *vector*, be taken literally. Nevertheless, it's helpful to reflect that at the kernel of many a real-world administrative situation is an underdetermined problem which multiple decision makers have transformed into an overdetermined one, meaning that some combination of priority setting, parameter changing, and policy adjusting will usually be necessary if an administrator is to achieve even a proximate solution.

——————————————————————————————————— ■-■-■———

cluster of central ideas the analyst uses as a point of reference when ordering data, developing a model of the problem, and proposing a line of response. (A **model** is simply a representation of the main variables in a problem and their relationships with one another.)

Even in our everyday lives, we routinely size up situations, trying to discern the categories into which they fall and the rules governing appropriate behavior. Consider this example: You see a person suddenly lurching in pain on a city street, the apparent victim of a heart attack. The ethical paradigm "Comfort the afflicted" applies; immediately, instinctively, you feel obliged to call for medical help. But suppose instead you notice an individual experiencing a mild, merely embarrassing physical problem (say a bad case of hiccups in public). The applicable paradigm becomes "Mind your own business," with the behavioral rule: "Don't stare!" Infinite shadings of degree separate the life-threatening seizure from the trivial social incident. No computer has ever been programmed to distinguish in a mechanical way between the two kinds of situations, their paradigms, or the applicable actions. The difference between theoretical inquiry and paradigmatic analysis lies precisely in the greater degree of subjective, intuitive, experience-based practical judgment that goes into the choice of the paradigm and its translation into a course of behavior. But the idea of paradigmatic analysis is the same, whether in the events of everyday life or in the issues of public administration.

There is no agreed-upon paradigmatic framework in public administration, any more than there are any all-purpose solutions to the problems of everyday life. Nevertheless, certain patterns recur in the situations that administrators regularly encounter. We'll be dealing in the pages to come with some of the more important paradigms of organization and coordination (Chapters 3 and 6), paradigms of assignment (Chapters 6 and 7), and paradigms of obligation (Chapters 8 and 10).

The most frequently encountered **paradigms of organization** are the hierarchical or bureaucratic and the free-market paradigms. These paradigms involve different ways of dividing functions, arranging communications, and structuring relations of authority in an organization.

Different formal organizational structures imply different **paradigms of coordination.** For example, bureaucratic structures involve centralized planning and the coordination of workers' actions by commands from organizational higher-ups: *coordination by direct supervision,* usually supplemented by routinization (also called *coordination by standardization*). This approach was the norm in classical public administration. By contrast, many organizations today are being "reinvented" to encourage dialogue, consensus building, and bargaining—in other words, to facilitate *coordination through mutual adjustment.* For many purposes, the informal organization model that we'll take up in Chapter 6 can also be considered as a paradigm of organization, again with mutual adjustment as the associated paradigm of coordination.

Paradigms of assignment identify the conditions under which certain functions (such as policing) normally get assigned to public officials, while others are left as the responsibilities of families, private business corporations, markets, or charitable organizations. Within the public sector, there are also certain general principles for assigning jobs to federal, state, or local officials and, at each level, to legislative, executive (generally meaning administrative), or judicial actors.

Paradigms of obligation refer both to *general* duties of public officials (who, for example, are expected to treat all citizens impartially) and to certain *specific* duties that are associated with particular offices or roles. For many purposes, a paradigm can be thought of as a cluster of rules which oblige an administrator in a given role to follow a particular routine under specified conditions. Finding the appropriate classification of the role is often equivalent to identifying the applicable paradigm of obligation.

Paradigms refer to pure cases. But pure cases are rare. Although virtually every administrative situation contains analogies with other cases, every situation is also in some ways unique. So in the very act of identifying the appropriate paradigm, the administrator must try to discern those respects in which the immediate situation departs from the type. The casuists referred to departures from the paradigmatically pure case as the **progression of circumstances.**

The challenge of case analysis is most interesting when the "circumstances of the action" or the "conditions of the agent" diverge from the pure example along multiple dimensions. Thus case analysis normally concludes with the *What-if?* question: Under what progression of circumstances would the analyst change priorities, follow a different rule, pursue a different goal, adopt a different paradigm?

Cue 8.   Cases involve choices; in a democracy, choice demands justification, which further implies a process of dialogue and an effort at persuasion.

Case synthesis involves the framing of a beginning and a middle of a story: How did the situation arise? How did the conflict emerge? In the old expression, it then becomes "an exercise for the student" to come up with an ending—a suitable resolution, given the facts of the case.

Yet mere *resolution* of the issues in a case isn't enough. In a democracy, politicians and administrators must do more than satisfy themselves that they have quietly settled an issue or efficiently implemented a program. An administrator's superiors or professional colleagues may ask why a particular decision was made. Questions can often be expected from journalists and scholars, and, above all, from plain citizens who want to know why they got the treatment they did from government bureaucrats who are supposed to be working for them. Democracy involves accountability. It requires *justification* as well as resolution.

The nature of justification in public administration reflects the nature of administrative problem solving itself. Reasoning is probable and persuasive rather than certain and logical. Arguments are rhetorical rather than deductive. In the words of the ethicist David Smith:

> A rhetorical argument . . . is concerned with guiding action in a practical world of uncertainty. It deals with . . . best guesses, probabilities, assessments of circumstances, rough-and-ready rules of thumb, and the accumulation of reasons. . . . Practical knowledge turns not on general principles and deductive logic, but on recognizing pattern in the details of the case. . . . The arguments are rather like strands to a rope or roots to a tree than like the links in a chain. In the latter each link controls the strength of the chain; in the former a single strand or root may fail, but the whole may still remain intact or standing.[5]

Rhetorical argumentation is (in the terms preferred by some modern social philosophers) a **dialogic process** rather than a contemplative one. There is no substitute for careful reading of materials and reflective consideration of the factors in the case. But something in the very nature of administrative action also invites dialogue, discussion, debate. Disputants criticize one another's analyses while adjusting their own. The more robust the dialogue with others who bring different points of view to the case, the closer one is likely to get to an acceptable answer. (Several, if not all, of our cases are, by design, complex beyond the level at which a student working alone should expect to piece together the full pattern. Again, dialogue is the best approach. Discussion of the givens of a scenario in a group may turn up insights that no single case analyst is likely to achieve. The group approach models the way complex problems must often be tackled in the real world—as team efforts of synthesis and analysis.)

Incidentally, the requirement of justification doesn't mean that administrators must literally defend their every action. It does, however, require a public administrator to cultivate habits of demonstrable fairness, probity, reasonableness, and regularity in the conduct of everyday duties. The official who has developed such habits is best able to vindicate the correctness of a particular action which later comes under scrutiny.

---

[6]"Stories, Values and Health Care Decision," in Charles Conrad, ed., *The Ethical Nexus* (Norwood, NJ: Ablex, 1993), pp. 130–131, 137–147.

Cue 9.   **An effective administrative analyst must be ready to "speak in tongues"; expect to work in a variety of idioms and vocabularies.**

Historians of philosophy sometimes use a term from Aristotle—*architectonic discipline*—to describe a field of knowledge whose practitioners draw concepts from a variety of supporting fields, the way an architect synthesizes the knowledge of the designer, the economist, the structural engineer, the builder. Public administration is an architectonic discipline in this Aristotelian sense. As a field of study, it has central concepts and themes of its own. But in its practice, administrators also have to draw on insights from accounting, economics, law, political science, and—most important—moral philosophy and ethics (see Box 1.3). The openness of public administration to influence by other academic disciplines makes it one of the most expansive, progressive fields in contemporary academic endeavor.

As new topics have found their ways into the syllabus, the practicing administrator has had to extend his or her mastery of methods and vocabularies. To apply the insights, principles, and techniques of traditional political and legal study, contemporary social science, and quantitative analysis, public administrators must be able to converse with professionals from all these fields.

Four ways of packaging and presenting information have attained special prominence: first, the language of the law; second, the language of formal analysis, typically involving graphs or sketches of models that show how key variables in a problem relate to one another; third, the language of the organizational chart; and fourth, the language of statistical display—often expressed in simple tables containing budget information (numbers of dollars), personnel data (numbers of workers who possess different skills), and program information (numbers of actions planned or actually taken, broken out over a span of time). Few cases in public administration absolutely require the application of all four of the following rules. But the majority—including the cases in this book—call for combinations of two or three of them.

1. **Know the law.** What are the applicable statutes, court interpretations, administrative regulations? What actions do they require the administrator to take? What do they prohibit? What actions are permitted but left to the good judgment—the discretion—of the administrator?

2. **Sketch a model.** What's the underlying structure of the problem? What causal theory applies? What are the key variables, and how do they interrelate?

3. **Review the organization.** Who may do what to whom? How are authority and responsibility formally divided, and what do these jurisdictional considerations suggest regarding the "turf" of different actors? Organizational arrangements are often critical to the important issue of control: Who's in charge? Or—as the pervasiveness of underdetermination suggests may be more to the point—why does it seem *no one's* in charge?

4. **Check the numbers.** What information can be gleaned from a display of figures summarizing important factors—dollars, numbers of workers, estimated costs and benefits of different programs?

BOX 1.3 ■■■

Public Administration: A Vast and Expanding Field of Study

Partly as a result of elaborations in its own core concepts and partly as a result of intellectual grafts from other disciplines, public administration has undergone a continuous process of expansion and enrichment. Practitioners have always emphasized a central core of topics. These include *PPA,* or *public personnel administration* (including the civil service system and, more recently, the trend toward unionization among government employees); classical organizational theory; federalism (more recently brought under the heading of *intergovernmental relations,* or *IGR*); rule of law and the control of administrative discretion; and the relationship between politics and administration. These subjects remain as vital today as they were in the early days of administrative study.

Since World War II, whole new areas have been annexed to the field. In their range and diversity, the added subjects overshadow the original list of must-cover topics. The new subjects include privatization (that is, shifting functions from government back to private businesses); contemporary organizational theory (including the theory of informal organizations); motivation theory; formal policy analysis; decision making and bargaining theory; and implementation research.

Certain other topics that have always had a place in public administration have recently gained in interest and importance. Red ink in the ledgers of government has led to some bold experimentation in one of the oldest concerns within public administration, budgeting. Scandals in high places—wrongdoing in Pentagon contracting, in General Services Administration procurement practices, in the federal housing program—have prompted a series of new ethics laws and renewed the attention of professional ethicists to the field of public administration.

The literature of public administration reflects the vastness, diversity, and difficulty of the subject. Our readings come from thinkers representing a variety of disciplines. Their writings aren't always easy or entertaining, nor will you always find their solutions satisfying. But persevere as you read our selections, from authors as diverse as the psychologist Stanley Milgram, the organizational theorist Henry Mintzberg, the philosopher Thomas Nagel, the bargaining theorist Thomas Schelling, and the constitutional scholar Kathleen Sullivan. And bear in mind that difficult writing is a characteristic of scholarship in a dynamic field, where there's a need for new concepts and categories to provide a framework for the analysis of difficult issues.

■■■

Keep in mind, though, that "Know the law," "Sketch a model," "Review the organization," and "Check the numbers" are not so much special techniques as they are prods to use a whole repertoire of research skills and techniques of analysis.

Cue 10.   Most important of all: Trust your own experience and instincts!

We are about to begin a long journey. On the way, we'll encounter some exotic intellectual animals—critters bearing technical names like "discounted cash flow," "integrative bargaining," and "synoptic analysis." We have already met beasts called "overdetermined systems" and "paradigmatic analysis". But the issues and techniques signified by these terms aren't the core stuff of our subject. Nor is the kind of knowledge they imply the core knowledge. The habit of circumspection, the capacity for discernment, and the appreciative sense of administrative relationships count for more than formal analytical techniques do. *Never underestimate your own experiences and instincts as a source of relevant knowledge.*

We all bring to the practice of case analysis a store of knowledge compounded of organizational understanding, political lore, and moral insight. Your sense of organizational life may be informal and even unconscious, but it's there. It's based on experiences that may have started years ago, in, say, the small-group activities of Brownies or Boy Scouts (and may more recently have been amplified in the regimentations of life on today's bureaucratized college campus). The typical American collegian also knows the essentials of our civic culture. We've all grown up taking for granted such principles as "government by consent," "rule of law," and the accountability of public officials for their actions. Additionally, all sensitive human beings—regardless of their prior formal training (or lack of it)—recognize and value the qualities of compassion, empathy in human relations, and respect for the dignity of others. These sensitivities may be the most important data of all, since so many public officials deal primarily with strangers; bureaucratized "stranger relationships" hardly make for settings in which it's easy to sustain caring human connections. Finally, every student comes to a course in public administration having learned something of the dynamics—if not the formal vocabulary—of authority, hierarchy, contracting, free-market transacting, and bargaining. These are among the basic phenomena of modern life. Learning about them is a by-product of everyday experience with parents, teachers, employers, and merchants.

In other words, the vast majority of college-age Americans have already spent most of their lives experiencing certain core realities of our society. Many of the same organizational, human, and political realities are also the basic stuff of our subject. So trust your own insights and instincts; they're based on the life experiences that are the best-possible preparation for formal administrative study.

All this leads us to a curious conclusion: In a sense, you probably already have most of the *answers* (although it may take some effort to dig them out of your own store of basic instincts and ethical intuitions). The hard part in case analysis is usually to come up with the right *questions*. This paradox underlies the main difference between the cases in the following chapters and the kinds of exercises (including case studies) you're likely to find in most other texts.

A typical chapter in a typical textbook contains an expository section in which the author introduces a new principle or problem-solving method. Exercises follow. These exercises evoke obvious questions—"obvious" because they explicitly challenge the student to apply the principle or method that's just been presented. The trick isn't to discern what's important. That's given. The task is rather to demonstrate mastery of the main theory or problem-solving methodology in the chapter. In the cases we'll be working with, by contrast, multiple issues crowd one another. The challenge is to identify the questions and then select the most critical ones. ("One must consider factors so delicate and so numerous . . . ," Pascal wrote of the problems that call for exercises of the discerning intellect.) Once a key question has been clearly phrased, the answer is more likely to call for common sense and intuitive judgment than it is to depend on an abstract principle or technical method.

An oft-told story points up the relevance of life experience to our subject. The parable of the Rabbi of Cracow, presented here in the version by the sociologist of religions Mircea Eliade, epitomizes a thought that you should keep in mind when traveling the pathways of public administration:

> This pious rabbi, Eisik of Cracow, had a dream which told him to travel to Prague; there, under the great bridge leading to the royal castle, he was to find a hidden treasure. The dream was repeated three times, and the rabbi decided to go. Upon arrival at Prague he found the bridge; but, as it was guarded day and night by sentinels, Eisik dared not dig. But as he continued to loiter in the vicinity he attracted the attention of the captain of the guard, who asked him, kindly, if he had lost something. The rabbi then innocently narrated his dream; and the officer burst into laughter. "Really, poor man," he said, "have you worn out your shoes coming all this way simply because of a dream?" This officer, too, had heard a voice in a dream: "It spoke to me about Cracow, ordered me to go over there and look for a great treasure in the house of a rabbi whose name was Eisik, Eisik son of Jekel. The treasure was to be found in a dusty old corner where it had been buried behind the stove." But the officer put no trust whatever in voices heard in dreams; the officer was a reasonable person. The rabbi, with a deep bow, thanked him and made haste to return to Cracow; there, he dug in the neglected corner of his house and discovered the treasure; which put an end to his poverty.[7]

Like Eisik of Cracow, you are likely to find the necessary treasure of knowledge and sensitivities right at home. But the process of discovery begins with the departure that must precede the return—and the unearthing of what's been there all along. The rabbi found his journey, in the end, to be more than worthwhile. You've every right to expect the same of the trip on which you now set forth.

Each of the following chapters will contain an original essay, one or more selections from major contributors to public administration as a field of contemporary study, and a case. Each case should be rich enough in narrative texture to suggest what administrative life is really like, complex enough to challenge your skills in case synthesis and case analysis, relevant enough to satisfy the good citizen's interest in the public policy issues of the day, and detailed enough to invite exploration of the progression of circumstances. Our materials should amply justify Woodrow Wilson's conviction that public administration sets tasks "great and important enough to attract the best minds."

---

[7]*Myths, Dreams, and Mysteries* (New York: Harper Torchbook [1957], 1960), pp. 244–245.

Administrative analysis also involves problems difficult enough to engage and sustain them.

 ## FOR FURTHER READING   ◆ ◆ ◆

The three classic primary sources on Progressive Era public administration doctrine are Woodrow Wilson's seminal essay ("The Study of Administration," cited in note 1) and

> Goodnow, Frank, *Politics and Administration: A Study in Government* (New York: Russell & Russell, 1900).
>
> White, Leonard, *Introduction to the Study of Public Administration* (New York: Macmillan, 1926).

The following volumes contain highly readable introductory treatments of the Progressive Era:

> Goldmann, Eric, *Rendezvous with Destiny* (New York: Random House, 1952).
>
> Haber, Samuel, *Efficiency and Uplift* (Chicago: U. of Chicago Press, Midway Edition, 1964); see especially chaps. 1–3.
>
> Hays, Samuel, *The Response to Industrialism, 1885–1914* (Chicago: U. of Chicago Press, 1957).

The portions of the writings of Aristotle that are relevant to the concepts of "practical wisdom" *(phronesis)* and architectonic branches of knowledge are

> *Nicomachean Ethics,* books I, parts A–B; IV, parts A–C; V, part H (especially chaps. 9, 10); and *Politics,* book IV, part E. These works are, of course, widely available in many different translations and editions.

Additional useful works in the Aristotelian vein are

> Green, Richard, and Robert Zinke, "The Rhetorical Way of Knowing and Public Administration," 25 *Administration and Society* (November 1993), 317.
>
> Morgan, Douglas, "Administrative Phronesis: Discretion and the Problem of Administrative Legitimacy in Our Constitutional System," in Kass and Catron, eds., *Images and Identities in Public Administration* (Newbury Park CA: Sage Publications, 1990), p. 67.

On the history, uses, and value of stories and case studies in public administration, see

> Dandridge, Thomas, "Organizational Stories and Rituals," in R. Tannenbaum et al., eds, *Human Systems Management* (San Francisco: Jossey-Bass, 1985).
>
> Hummel, Ralph, "Stories Managers Tell: Why They Are Valid as Science," 51 *Public Administration Review* (January–February 1991), 31.
>
> Maynard-Moody, Steven, and Marisa Kelly, "Stories Public Managers Tell about Elected Officials: Making Sense of the Defunct Dichotomy," in Barry Boseman, ed., *Public Management: The State of the Art* (San Francisco: Jossey-Bass, 1993), chap. 8.

For contingency theory as an approach to organizational study (also known as the organic approach), see

Lawrence, Paul, and Jay Lorsch, *Organization and Environment* (Boston: Graduate School of Business Administration, Harvard U., 1967); see especially chaps. 6, 8.

Thompson, James, *Organizations in Action* (New York: McGraw-Hill, 1967).

Most contemporary scholarship on defective or incomplete information as a source of underdetermination in administrative problem solving traces to the writings of Herbert Simon; we'll deal with Simon's contributions in Chapter 11, but for those interested it certainly wouldn't hurt at this point to check out his pioneering work on "bounded rationality." See

Simon, Herbert, *Administrative Behavior* (New York: Free Press, 1947); see especially Simon's "Introduction to the Second Edition."

The best (if somewhat difficult) recent discussion of role-based obligations—that is, roles as predictors of "appropriate behavior"—is

March, James, and Johan Olson, *Rediscovering Institutions* (New York: Free Press, 1989).

The attention of public administrationists to the problem of "multiple, inconsistent, vague" criteria—the main source of overdetermination in administrative problem solving—probably owes mainly to the influence of James Q. Wilson. See

Wilson, James Q., "The Bureaucracy Problem," 6 *The Public Interest* (Winter 1967), 3.

Wilson, James Q., *Bureaucracy: What Government Agencies Do and Why They Do It* (New York: Basic Books, 1989); see especially chap. 7.

The clearest, most accessible formal treatment of the technique of singular value decomposition (that's mathematical language for the "solution" of an overdetermined algebraic system) is

Strang, Gilbert, *Linear Algebra and Its Applications* (San Diego: Harcourt, Brace, Jovanovich, 1988).

Goldberg's Rule is discussed—along with many other issues relevant to our concerns in this book—in the highly readable (and anecdote-filled) volume co-authored by a political scientist and a historian:

Neustadt, Richard, and Ernest May, *Thinking in Time* (New York: Free Press, 1986).

▼◆ ● ■ ▼ ◆ ● ■ ▼ ◆ ● ■ ▼ ◆ ● ■ ▼ ◆

CHAPTER 2

Public Personnel Administration

In the paper of 1887 in which he presented what many still regard as the clearest statement of the Progressives' administrative concepts, Woodrow Wilson called for reform of the governance process in three key areas: *personnel, organization,* and *methods.* It's significant that Wilson listed the need for high-quality people at the top of his agenda. To Wilson, improvements in public personnel administration—the specialists usually shorten it to PPA—had to be the basis on which all the other Progressive reforms would have to rest:

> [C]ivil service reform must . . . expand into efforts to improve, not the *personnel* only, but also the organization and methods of our government offices. . . . Civil service reform is thus but a moral preparation for what is to follow. It is clearing the moral atmosphere of official life by establishing the sanctity of public office as a public trust, and, by making the service unpartisan, it is opening the way for making it businesslike.

The reforms to which Woodrow Wilson referred originated in the determination of the Progressive reformers to root out the corrupt and crassly political influences of the nineteenth-century **spoils system.** Under this system, politicians doled out government jobs (patronage) to their supporters, often without reference to their qualifications. Although the reformers aimed especially at the abuses of this practice in the machine-dominated big cities, they worked to eliminate the spoils system in federal and state governments as well. Despite variations in the details of their various programs, the Progressives generally agreed on certain broad policy aims. The civil service structures that gradually emerged therefore broadly resembled one another across the federal, state, and local levels. With a few notable exceptions, they continue to do so even today.

Origin and Evolution of the Civil Service

The supporters of Andrew Jackson who installed the spoils system didn't view their practices in the jaundiced way that the reformers of a few generations later would. As

President Jackson himself put it in 1829, "The duties of all public officers are, or at least admit of being made, so plain and simple that men of intelligence may readily qualify themselves for their performance. . . ."[1] The Jacksonians saw the appointment of "plain and simple" citizens—based on their support of electoral victors rather than on proved technical qualifications—not as an invitation to corruption and mediocrity but as a way to guarantee democratic governance.

In theory, patronage-based job filling ensured an unbroken line of responsiveness running from the majority of the people through their elected representatives to the appointive officials who would actually carry out the duties of day-to-day administration. (As we'll see later, twentieth-century scholars of public administration would call essentially the same concept by a fancier name, "the principal-agent chain.") The rotation of incumbents into and out of office with changes in administration would automatically produce civil servants whose opinions reflected the views of elected leaders. By extension, civil servants would reflect the views of the electorate itself. Defenders of the spoils system saw it as a contributor to the important value of political responsiveness. So, at least, went the theory.

As the system worked in practice, however, the victors after every election often simply hired their cousins and cronies. The scandal of public job filling on the basis of political connections became a defining moral issue in the late nineteenth century, much as slavery had been before the Civil War. Worse, patronage-based appointments prevented the buildup of the kind of expertise needed for the problems of a complex urban society. Perhaps the most perceptive observer of all, the German sociologist Max Weber, wrote that only an extravagantly wealthy country could afford the "corruption and wastefulness" of politicized, amateur public administration. "Dilettante management," Weber called it. Not even the United States was rich enough to support so irrational a public personnel system indefinitely. By the late nineteenth century, Weber wrote, "irrefrageable needs of the administration" had forced reforms. Weber saw the old system of personnel staffing based on partisan favoritism and political patronage "inevitably and gradually giving way formally to the bureaucratic structure."[2] (We will return to Weber and his theory of the bureaucratic structure in Chapter 3.)

Three Foundational Civil Service Principles

The spoils system had made it relatively easy for an individual to enter federal service—or to leave it, since patronage-based appointees could be dismissed for causes having nothing to do with their technical competence. The **Pendleton Act of 1883**, the culmination of decades of of civil service reform agitation, changed all that. The 1883 act enshrined the principle of **appointment by merit**, the first foundational principle of the civil service. Under the merit principle, a candidate for civil service appointment had to pass a standardized written civil service test or possess formal academic credentials for the job. Though the written-test requirement initially applied primarily to clerk-level positions, the idea of merit-based appointment gradually spread through the higher

---

[1]Andrew Jackson, message to Congress, Dec. 8, 1829.

[2]In H. Gerth and C. W. Mills, eds., *From Max Weber* (New York: Oxford U. Press, 1946), p. 88; see also pp. 201, 211.

administrative, professional, and technical jobs (**APT** is the term personnel specialists use in reference to workers in such slots). More realistic evaluation procedures gradually spread throughout the civil service. Today the merit requirement of the typical APT job is satisfied not by a written test but by a careful assessment of the candidate's educational qualifications and prior experience in jobs like the one being considered.

The civil servant, after a probationary period, enjoys **civil service tenure**—the promise of steady government work with the right not to be let go except for cause. The Progressives expected that job security would encourage a civil servant faithfully to execute his or her office without fear of reprisals: A tenured official can't be fired for taking the politically incorrect position. Closely related to the principle of tenure was the criterion of seniority, eventually given a firm statutory basis in another major piece of Progressive Era legislation, the Lloyd-LaFollette Act of 1913. To this day, seniority significantly affects a civil servant's pay level and also offers significant protections against being laid-off in a **reduction in force (RIF)** necessitated by a budgetary shortfall or a change in the mission of a public agency.

Federal statutes from as far back as the 1850s had anticipated in rudimentary form the third foundational principle, **position classification.** The original federal classification laws required department heads to grade their clerk-employees and pay them at a level prescribed by law for each step in the scale. Municipal and state governments eventually began experiments with more elaborate classification formulas. In 1912 the City of Chicago, and shortly thereafter the State of Illinois, installed classification systems of their own. Other cities and states followed suit. A line from a 1920 textbook—one of the first to treat personnel administration as a special body of expert knowledge—captured the spirit of the position classification movement: "The job is the molecule of industry; and what molecular study has done for physics and chemistry job study with the aid of every possible instrument of precision can begin to do for industry."[3]

The Classification Act of 1923 completed the basic structure of the federal civil service. Position classification was in essence an enactment into law of the much-maligned modern concept of **comparable worth,** which requires that salaries be fixed by administrative decision rather than by market forces. The pay that goes with a job is supposed to reflect the economic value of the skills that a worker brings to the position. Personnel experts in a central office—the Civil Service Commission—were to decide what skills were needed and what level of pay they should command. The "equal pay for equal work" standard became official, as did the "rank in the job" principle, under which civil service status broadly depends on the position that an employee fills. An incumbent who, through extra education or in some other way, becomes overqualified can't readily convert his or her higher level of competence into an increase in authority or a raise in pay unless a vacant position exists into which the individual may be promoted.

The Public Personnel Structure Today

The Civil Service Reform Act of 1978 renamed the Civil Service Commission the federal Office of Personal Management (OPM) and, at least in theory, underscored that

---

[3]Ordway Tead and Henry C. Metcalf, *Personnel Administration: Its Principles and Practice* (New York: McGraw-Hill, 1920), p. 255.

the OPM was on a par with the powerful Office of Management and Budget within the Executive Office of the President. The 1978 act also provided for increased flexibility in federal personnel appointment and promotion processes and created the **Senior Executive Service (SES),** intended as an elite cadre of public management generalists capable of filling the critical job slots between the president's political appointees at the pinnacle of the federal bureaucracy and lower-level career civil servants. Finally, the act confirmed today's unified system of civil service grades, each with its internal promotional steps carrying increased pay with increased seniority in the grade.

At the top of the personnel structure of the federal executive branch are the president and from two thousand to three thousand political appointees—in effect, presidential patronage employees. (Typically, in state and local governments the governor or mayor makes reduced numbers of political appointments. Numbers aside, the basic pattern's the same at all levels. Chief executives everywhere try to fill the top posts with loyalists who, because they share the boss's views, can be trusted to convey his or her intentions to the career appointees in the lower ranks.) In the federal government, the political layer includes cabinet officers and officials such as the president's Special Trade Representative and the White House "Drug Policy Czar," who hold cabinet rank even though they don't head major departments of government. The political layer also includes deputy secretaries, undersecretaries, assistant secretaries, *principal* deputy assistant secretaries (no fooling!), deputy assistant secretaries, and other relatively high-level executive-branch officials.

Beneath the political layer, nonpolitical civil service appointees fill slots known as *general schedule (GS) grades.* Most occupants of the top three grades, GS-18 down through GS-16, belong to the SES. Career officials in grades GS-15 down through GS-9 are the workhorses of the federal service. These—the APTs who constitute almost 50 percent of the total civilian classified service—are the degree-holding accountants, civil engineers, economists, lawyers, soil conservationists, and so on, through all the separate occupational series in today's federal bureaucracy. Clerical and custodial personnel (grades GS-8 down to GS-1) complete the structure.

In the early 1990s the federal classification system contained some seven hundred separate occupations, eighteen GS grades, and ten "steps" within each grade. The number of separate job slots in state civil service systems varies from over five hundred in South Dakota to more than seven thousand (yes, you read it right!) in New York. The jobs themselves are customarily divided to form hierarchies of organizational units: Agencies split into bureaus, bureaus into divisions or offices, offices into branches, branches into sections, and so forth on down to individual frontline administrators. In this way the civil service personnel structure has evolved as the perfect complement to the bureaucratic organizational structure of most government agencies.

In recent years some leaders in the personnel subfield have touted a **human resources approach,** sometimes called "the new PPA." Proponents of this approach seek to shift the focus of "the old PPA" from its alleged fussiness, its traditional preoccupation with the intricacies of the classification system, and its "triumph of technique over purpose," in the oft-quoted words of one authority.[4] Champions of the new per-

---

[4]This characterization of the public personnel process was the title of an article by Wallace Sayre, 8 *Public Administration Review* (Spring 1948): 134–139.

sonnel approach want to be less bureaucratic and more concerned with the development of professional capacity by recruiting individuals with the needed abilities ("external extraction" of talent, in the language of PPA) and developing intra-agency methods for the adaptation and upgrading of workers' skills ("internal extraction"). Doubters say that the human resources approach is merely the old personnel routines without some of the petty regulations and procedures. Even advocates of the approach admit that it can work only if public managers are free to increase workplace flexibility and develop rewards for individual performance.

The proponents of the human resources approach are converging toward the kinds of arguments for a loosening-up of the civil service that have been popularized by another group of analysts: the *New Theorists,* who start from very different assumptions about the motives and creativity of public-sector employees. The New Theorists are among the most influential thinkers in contemporary public administration. We'll come back to them after we sample a range of opinions about PPA by some commentators who are less given than the New Theorists are to the use of technical terms and a highly formal style of analysis.

Our first selection comes from a leading scholar of public administration, Charles Goodsell of the Virginia Polytechnic Institute and State University. Goodsell's voice is perhaps the most eloquent yet to be raised on our civil servants' behalf. His spirited defense of bureaucrats as intelligent, energetic, and innovative servants of the people counters the stereotype. Is Goodsell too soft on our public servants? Is his panegyric for bureaucracy overstated? Many critics think so. But some overstatement on the pro-bureaucracy side of the PPA debate may be in order at this point—if only to counterbalance some of the bureaucrat bashing that we'll be witnessing in the pages to come!

Charles Goodsell on the Defense of Bureaucrats as Ordinary People

Let us begin by elaborating common depictions of public bureaucracy so that we can appreciate what making the case for it confronts. As for portrayals in mass media, we encounter a relatively simple picture, confidently expressed. The employee of bureaucracy, that "lowly bureaucrat," is seen as lazy or snarling, or both. The office occupied by this pariah is viewed as bungling or inhumane, or both. The overall edifice of bureaucracy is pictured as overstaffed, inflexible, unresponsive, and power-hungry, all at once. These images are agreed upon by writers and groups of every shade of opinion. One is hard pressed to think of a concept more deeply ingrained and widely expressed in American cultural life....

One way to strip the bureaucrat of his or her supposed distinctiveness is simply to note how many bureaucrats there are. The club of bureaucrats is not exclusive enough to be very ominous. A sizable proportion of Americans belong, in fact more than one out of six employed persons. The overall figures, rounded off, are that the federal government employs 5 million (3 civilian, 2 military), state governments 4 million, and local governments 9 million. This adds up to 18 million people.

Besides their vast numbers, another feature of bureaucrats that places them on a fairly ordinary and unawesome plane is what they do. They do not simply shuffle papers, attend meetings, and telephone laconically with no hands. Nor do they just give orders; managers in government are a distinct minority of the whole. What bureaucrats do is nothing less than the myriad of highly specialized tasks performed in a modern technological society—the matter is both that complex and that simple.... Bureaucrats operate bridges, investigate crimes, manage forests, program computers, arbitrate labor disputes, counsel teenagers, calculate cost-benefit ratios, operate sea-rescue cutters, run libraries, examine patent applications, inspect meat, negotiate contracts, and so on and so forth. . . . Occupational directories and job classification handbooks put out by government personnel agencies run to the hundreds of pages. The point is simply that bureaucrats don't "bur"— there is no common occupational activity they all perform. These men and women do almost everything, which means that even at face value generalizations about their nature or behavior are strongly suspect. . . .

Who, then, are the bureaucrats? They are a great bunch of us, in the first place. In the second place they are not generalizable in terms of occupational activity. Third, bureaucrats are representative of the public at large in terms of education, social status, religion, income, and party affiliation. Minority bureaucrats are disproportionately present in overall numbers but do not hold their fair share of high-level jobs. Women are underrepresented on both counts, although this is changing. Finally, bureaucrats and the rest of us have similar political and policy views. . . .

One may reply . . . by saying that certainly these ordinary Americans do not leave their homes at night to join conspiracies, but on arriving at the office the next morning, something even worse happens. They become transformed into petty tyrants. This argument has been taken very seriously in academic circles for some forty years and should be examined closely. The contention is formidable: The structure of bureaucracy itself produces a distinctive mentality or personality on the part of its full-time, appointed staff. Whether by self-selection in entering bureaucratic employment or by socialization once in it, the bureaucrat is deemed to possess a particular turn of mind and pattern of behavior. These attributes and behaviors are said to be quite nasty, at the least.

This school of analysis began with a famous article by Robert Merton, "Bureaucratic Structure and Personality," published in 1940.[5] Merton argued that . . . the specialized nature of bureaucratic work causes

"an inadequate flexibility in the application of skills." This is said to occur because an extreme narrowness in scope of work does not allow the functionary to be capable of adapting to ever-changing conditions. Second, the need for reliability and discipline in bureaucratic output causes officials to overemphasize the importance of rules. They then forget the initial reason for the rules, and in a "displacement of goals" phenomenon, enforcement of the rules surpasses in importance in the bureaucrat's mind what the organization is trying ultimately to achieve. . . .

Endless additional pieces of published writing could be cited on this bureaucratic mentality, inasmuch as it is a favorite theme not merely among professional critics of bureaucracy but among journalists, novelists, and writers of letters to the editor. Like the stereotype of bureaucracy, the image conveniently captures the many frustrations of those who work in or with large governmental organizations, a group that includes just about everyone that is of school age or over. Moreover, within the social sciences the notion has acquired its own momentum as an idea in vogue, and this momentum has scarcely slowed over four decades. To that extent, then, is the model verified empirically?

Perhaps the best-known empirical study, and partly for that reason one of the most controversial, is a project undertaken by Melvin Kohn. In it he attempted to measure the effects of employment in a bureaucracy, whether private or public. Kohn's interest extended to the employees' values, social orientation, and intellectual functioning. A national sample of 3,101 men employed in civilian occupations was surveyed by structured interview. . . . Kohn's main finding was simple: Correlations of bureaucratization with these factors [the list included conformity to external authority; a personality orientation of an authoritarian, legalistic, and noninnovative nature; and low problem-solving intelligence scores] were notably small. Even more interesting, the directions of correlation *consistently contradicted* what the bureaucratic personality is supposed to be like!

Men who work in bureaucratic firms or organizations tend to value, not conformity, but self-direction. They are more open-minded,

[5]We will consider Merton's seminal essay with some care in Chapter 4.

have more personally responsible standards of morality, and are more receptive to change than are men who work in nonbureaucratic organizations. They show great flexibility in dealing both with perceptual and ideational problems. They spend their leisure time in more intellectually demanding activities.[6]

. . . We discover, then, that the empirical evidence reviewed concerning the "bureaucratic personality" is generally disconfirming rather than supportive. Bureaucrats are no less flexible, tolerant, and creative than other people—perhaps they are a little more so. Compared to business executives, bureaucrats may

be less risk-prone but do not seem less motivated, assured, or decisive. Welfare bureaucrats, with their terrible reputation for being disrespectful to clients and overzealous in rule enforcement, entertain positive images of clients more often than negative ones, and exhibit flexible attitudes toward compliance with regulations. . . .

"Well, maybe it's time to challenge the stereotype, to say something nice about the faceless millions who labor for government all over the country," admits one columnist.[7]

From Charles T. Goodsell, *The Case for Bureaucracy,* 2d ed. (Chatham NJ: Chatham House, 1985), pp. 2, 82–83, 91, 95, 103, 109.

[6]Melvin L. Kohn, "Bureaucratic Man: A Portrait and an Interpretation," 36 *American Sociological Review* (June 1971): 461–474.

[7]Bob Willis, *Roanoke Times & World News,* Sept. 16, 1980.

Notwithstanding the appreciation of our public servants offered by scholars such as Charles Goodsell, from an early point in the history of the civil service onward, critics have argued that centralized hiring and firing, detailed position classification by personnel specialists, and lockstep advancement through a rigid personnel structure couldn't help but promote inflexibility and inefficiency in the public service. Arguably the central issue in PPA today is whether the apparatus of personnel principles and procedures that the Progressives erected to facilitate efficient governance have somehow evolved into a system of barriers to sound administration.

The following excerpt, which represents an offsetting opinion to that of Professor Goodsell, comes from David Osborne and Ted Gaebler's *Reinventing Government,* published in 1992—reputedly the greatest popular best-seller in the history of public administration. President Bill Clinton ordered the senior members of his administration to use the Osborne-Gaebler volume as a kind of do-it-yourself kit for overhauling the federal bureaucracy.

Osborne and Gaebler didn't pretend to give a balanced picture of the current personnel system. They also didn't purport to be bureaucrat bashers, yet that's the way many readers interpreted their critique of the civil service. How, then, are we to account for the influence of their rather-biased analysis? The answer—as our reading from Goodsell will already have suggested—is probably that Osborne and Gaebler express a mood of dissatisfaction common both among opinion shapers and among ordinary citizens. Note, however, that the Osborne-Gaebler critique has to do with alleged inefficiencies in the public bureau*cracy,* whereas Goodsell's defense was of the bureau*crats* themselves, rather than of the institution in which they work.

As you read the Osborne-Gaebler selection—which includes the authors' account of traditional public-sector budgeting practices along with their critique of civil service inefficiencies—take special note of the distinction they draw between a **mission-driven organization** and a **rule-driven organization.** It's a distinction you'll want to keep in mind as you deal with our chapter case.

David Osborne and Ted Gaebler on a Personnel System for the Twenty-First Century

Most public organizations are driven not by their missions, but by their rules and their budgets. They have a rule for everything that could conceivably go wrong and a line-item for every subcategory of spending in every unit of every department. The glue that holds public bureaucracies together, in other words, is like epoxy: it comes in two separate tubes. One holds rules, the other line items. Mix them together and you get cement.

Entrepreneurial governments dispense with both tubes. They get rid of the old rule books and dissolve the line items. They define their fundamental missions, then develop budget systems and rules that free their employees to pursue those missions.

Some rules are necessary to run any organization. But as James Q. Wilson writes, "The United States relies on rules to control the exercise of official judgment to a greater extent than any other industrialized democracy." Wilson ascribes this tendency to our system of checks and balances, which makes each power center so weak that everyone falls back on rules to control what everyone else can do. But the tendency escalated dramatically during the Progressive Era, when reformers were struggling to control Boss Tweed and his cronies. To control the 5 percent who were dishonest, the Progressives created the red tape that so frustrates the other 95 percent.

To this day, whenever things go wrong, politicians respond with a blizzard of new rules. A business would fire the individual responsible, but governments keep the offenders on and punish everyone else by wrapping them up in red tape. They close the barn door after the horse has escaped—locking in all the cowhands.

We embrace our rules and red tape to prevent bad things from happening, of course. But those same rules prevent good things from happening. They slow government to a snail's pace. They make it impossible to respond to rapidly changing environments. They build wasted time and effort into the very fabric of the organization. . . .

Creating a Mission-Driven Budget System

Government's rules are aggregated into systems— budget systems, personnel systems, purchasing systems, accounting system. The real payoff comes when governments deregulate these systems, because they create the basic incentives that drive employees. If leaders tell their employees to focus on their mission, but the budget and personnel systems tell them to follow the rules and spend within the line items, the employees will listen to the systems. The leaders' mission will vanish like a mirage.

Few people outside government pay any attention to budget systems. But budgets control everything an agency does. They are onerous and omnipresent, useless and demeaning. They suck enormous quantities of time away from real work. They trap managers in yesterday's priorities, which quickly become tomorrow's waste.

At the root of these problems lies a villain. Most public budgets fence agency money into dozens of separate accounts, called line items. This was originally done to control the bureaucrats—to hem them in on all sides, so they could not spend one penny more than the council or legislature mandated on each item of government. But once again, our attempt to prevent bad management made good management impossible.

If you started a business, you would ask your bookkeeper to track how much you spent on travel, supplies, personnel, and so on. But you surely wouldn't let the bookkeeper control how much you spent under each account. The same is true of family budgets: you may set aside so much for groceries, so much for the mortgage, and so much for car payments every month. But if the washing machine breaks, you find the money to fix it, and if manufacturers offer rebates on new cars, you seize the opportunity.

Public managers cannot do this. Their funds are fenced within line items that are often absurdly narrow. In one branch of the military, base managers have 26 different accounts for housing repairs alone! A typical manager of a city department has 30–40 line items for every program or division. In most cities and many states, legislatures not only dictate line items, they tell each unit how many full-time employees it can have. . . .

Transforming a Rule-Driven Personnel System

The only thing more destructive than a line item budget system is a personnel system built around civil service. Most personnel systems in American government are derivatives of the federal Civil Service Act of 1883 [the Pendleton Act], passed after a disappointed office seeker assassinated President Garfield. A typical Progressive reform, civil service was a well-intentioned effort to control specific abuses: patronage hiring and political manipulation of public employees. In most places, it accomplished its goals. But like a howitzer brought out to shoot ants, it left us with other problems. Designed for a government of clerks, civil service became a strait-jacket in an era of knowledge workers.

Fifty years ago, governments were not unionized. Nor had the courts outlawed most patronage hiring and firing and protected most employees from wrongful discharge. In other words, most of what civil service procedures were established to prevent has been ruled illegal or made impossible by collective bargaining agreements. Yet the control mentality lives on, creating a gridlock that turns public management into the art of the impossible. . . .

In business, personnel is a *support* function, to help managers manage more effectively. In government, it is a *control* function—and managers bitterly resent it. Civil service rules are so complex that most managers find them impenetrable. The federal personnel manual, to cite but one example, is 6,000 pages long. Consider just a few of the major problems.

Hiring. Managers in civil service systems cannot hire like normal managers: advertise a position, take résumés, interview people, and talk to references.

They have to hire most employees from lists of those who have taken written civil service exams. Often they have to take the top scorer, or one of the top three scorers—regardless of whether that person is motivated or otherwise qualified. (In San Francisco, if two applicants tie for the top score, the one with the highest social security number gets the job.) . . .

Classification. Civil service jobs are classified on a graded scale, and pay within each classification is determined by longevity, not performance. Personnel departments spend thousands upon thousands of useless hours deciding whether such-and-such a job is a GS-12 or a GS-13, telling managers they cannot pay the salary they want to because the classification doesn't allow it, and blocking their efforts to reclassify people. Even when classification changes are approved, the process takes forever. In Massachusetts, where local governments have to get approval from the state, it can take two years.

Promotion. When people hit the top of their pay range, they cannot earn a raise without earning a promotion into a new type of work. But promotions are controlled by the personnel department, not the manager. They seldom have anything to do with performance. In a typical line job—in a police department, or data processing office—managers have to promote from among those already in the proper career track who have scored highest on the promotional exam.

Firing. There's an old saying: "Government workers are like headless nails: you can get them in, but you can't get them out." Federal employees cannot be fired until a manager has spent months (if not years) carefully documenting poor performance and the employee has then exhausted three appeals processes—the first two of which alone take an average of 224 days. State and local governments have their own versions of this scenario. The process is so time consuming and difficult that few managers ever fire anyone. (James Q. Wilson estimates that in one recent year, fewer than two-tenths of 1 percent of federal civil service employees were fired.) Instead managers tolerate incompetents, transfer them, or bump them upstairs.

Layoffs. When governments reduce their numbers through layoffs, civil service employees with seniority can bump those with lesser seniority. Middle managers can bump secretaries who can bump mail room clerks. In the Reagan cutbacks of 1981, a secretary at the Department of Energy who had worked her way up to running a program—and was proud of it—was bumped back to secretary. When New Jersey laid off 1,000 employees in 1991, 20,000 people received notices that they might be bumped. . . .

At the federal level, things may be even worse. Federal employees we know describe colleagues who spend their days reading magazines, planning sailing trips, or buying and selling stocks. Scott Shuger, who interviewed several dozen federal employees for the *Washington Monthly,* found that most estimated the number of "useless personnel" in their offices at 25 to 50 percent.

The waste in this system is mind-boggling. With 17.5 million civilian government employees (roughly 15 million of them full-time), our public payrolls approaches $500 billion a year. Benefits add another $100 billion or so. . . . No one can say how much lower our personnel costs could be with a rational system, but 20 percent is not an outlandish guess. . . .

The task is less to reform civil service than to define the appropriate personnel system for a modern government and create it. When we ask entrepreneurial public managers what they would do with civil service, most simply say, "Scrap it and start over." . . .

We obviously need some protection against patronage hiring and firing. But it is time to listen to our public entrepreneurs and replace a civil service system designed for the nineteenth century with a personnel system designed for the twenty-first.

From David Osborne and Ted Gaebler, *Reinventing Government* (Reading, MA: Addison-Wesley, 1992), pp. 110–111, 117–118, 124–130.

SECTION 2   The New Theorists on Public Personnel Administration

Among critics of bureaucrats and bureaucracies, some commentators—Osborne and Gaebler are probably the best examples—focus quite specifically on practices in our *public* service as sources of major inefficiencies. Other analysts argue that public-sector inefficiency isn't peculiar to the civil service but rather represents in extreme form certain deficiencies that are inherent in all large organizations. The most influential of these critics is a group of scholars who are variously called public-choice theorists, rational-choice theorists, or—as we've simply referred to them—**New Theorists.** These scholars draw most of their premises from economic theory. Whereas traditional public administrationists stressed government officials' dedication to some notion of the public interest, the New Theorists emphasize instead the power of self-interest in human affairs and the consequent need to get incentives right when structuring organizations.

The New Theorists and the Varieties of Incentive Impairment

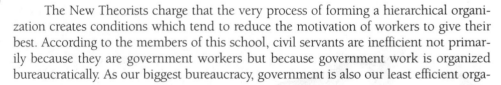

The New Theorists charge that the very process of forming a hierarchical organization creates conditions which tend to reduce the motivation of workers to give their best. According to the members of this school, civil servants are inefficient not primarily because they are government workers but because government work is organized bureaucratically. As our biggest bureaucracy, government is also our least efficient organization. Bureaucratic organization, the New Theorists point out, severs the link between rewards and performance. Civil servants know that tenure and seniority make it difficult to fire them. They also know that position classification procedures make it difficult to promote outstanding performers much in advance of the normal career progression. To ease the resulting motivational deterrents—called **incentive impairments**—the New Theorists support a shift in the organizational paradigm so that administrative practice would be patterned less on the bureaucratic model and more on the image of the free market. In the market, the New Theorists contend, everyone competes, no one has job security, and remuneration is tied to performance. Unlike bureaucracies, free markets reward energetic and innovative performers with higher profits, and they punish sluggards and incompetents with the threat of bankruptcy.

Adverse Selection, Moral Hazard, and Asymmetric Information

The New Theorists have argued that the civil service is acutely susceptible to two forms of incentive impairment, adverse selection and moral hazard. **Adverse selection** refers to conditions that reduce the incentives of outstanding individuals to become civil servants or, if they do enter government work, to remain in the public service. The New Theorists claim that the kinds of workers who seek career cushions rather than career challenges will feel more comfortable in organizations with lockstep promotion patterns and predictable salary graduations. **Moral hazard** refers to conditions that impair the incentives of workers to perform with care and diligence. The New Theorists also contend that the dangers of moral hazard increase in precisely the kinds of working conditions that are characteristic of the civil service.

Adverse selection may operate at several points in the career of a civil servant: at the initial point of career selection (when a candidate decides whether to apply for government work or to remain in the private sector); at points of possible departure from the civil service (for example, when an offer of higher pay beckons a civil servant to private industry); and in the course of a layoff affecting the individual's agency. At the point of career selection, the idea is that jobs which carry civil service protections inherently invite the lazy or unambitious to apply in the first place. An applicant might be motivated by the desire to serve. But the motivation might also lie in the attractiveness of a job with regular salary increases and virtual immunity from firing unless underperformance becomes flagrant.

You probably recall those high school algebra problems in which water pours from a faucet into a cask at a certain rate of inflow while, from the bottom of the cask, water is being drained by a hole that allows a larger rate of outflow. The objective of the exercise is to compute the time it will take for the cask to become empty, taking into account the differential rates of simultaneous inflow and outflow. The theory of adverse selection implies the possibility of a similar phenomenon in the civil service. At the same time that adverse selection is allegedly producing a less-capable public workforce through an inflow of poorer-quality applicants, outflows from the ranks of our civil servants may be occurring, with outstanding people leaving at a higher rate than are the less-able workers.

Private employers are constantly trying to entice knowledgeable civil servants by offering higher salaries, better working conditions, and greater opportunities for promotion. And periodically, reductions in force occur in the public service. A senior official who receives notice that his or her job is to be eliminated in a RIF may have the right to bump a more-junior person. Unfortunately, however, it may be the more-senior official who has the poorer record of job performance. For this reason, bumping rights can make it difficult to reduce the size of the public-sector workforce except at the cost of eliminating younger workers whom managers want to keep. A kind of adverse selection will then have occurred in which the less qualified, less energetic workers can use their seniority to displace those with the greatest promise of future contributions. The critics argue that adverse selection on both the inflow and outflow sides can gradually convert a civil service intended to ensure competence into a workforce of tired hangers-on who are more concerned with security than with performance.

The New Theorists argue that once applicants have been hired, the assurance of job security even at substandard levels of performance may induce them to display *moral hazard,* a term coined in the insurance industry for an individual's tendency to exercise less care if an insurer will indemnify negligent behavior. In the civil service system, the "insurer" is the government, who will pay the tenured worker even when the work itself isn't up to snuff. Less work for the same pay, some would suggest, is an all-but-inevitable consequence.

Furthermore, the New Theorists argue that the conditions of work typically encountered in the civil service exacerbate the problem of moral hazard by creating patterns of **asymmetric information.** Government agencies tend to be relatively large bureaucracies whose employees process highly technical data. But highly technical data can be mastered only by the individuals who are actually processing specific cases. Those caseworkers' superiors can never possess more than a generalized sense of the work done by individuals beneath them in the organization. Because the frontline workers know more about their respective jobs than their supervisors do, workers who are inclined to shirk (that is, indulge in morally hazardous behavior) may be able to do so with impunity, trusting that their superiors won't ever even know.

Given their acceptance of the theories of adverse selection, moral hazard, and asymmetric information, the New Theorists quite naturally would prefer a public personnel system based more on individual than on collective evaluations and rewards. They therefore argue that a move in agency organization toward the free-market paradigm would give public managers greater freedom to hire and fire workers based on job qualifications or actual performance. Free-market personnel practices would also confer greater freedom on workers to demand salaries commensurate with their contributions rather than at levels fixed by a pay scale keyed to the "rank in the job" principle. At minimum, most New Theorists favor proposals to "deregulate the public service" as a way of freeing up the public sector so that market forces can work. Conversely, the New Theorists tend to oppose moves to strengthen collective forces in PPA—for example, moves to increase the influence of public-sector unions in personnel policy making (see Box 2.1).

Are the New Theorists Right?

Are the New Theorists right? The question merits serious thought and open discussion, if only because the widespread influence of the New Theorists has encouraged

BOX 2.1 ■ ■ ■

Two Subthemes in PPA:
Deregulation and Public-Sector Collective Bargaining

The critics of traditional PPA contend that even the most dedicated and imaginative government employees may fail under the frustrations of an overregulated public workplace. In 1987 Constance Horner, former director of the federal Office of Personnel Management, put the case for civil service deregulation:

> The size of the government workforce could be substantially reduced if public managers had more flexibility in making basic personnel and purchasing decisions, and if lower paperwork requirements freed them to focus more on the services they are supposed to provide. [There are] tens of thousands of pages of regulations restricting their every move. Federal managers have little discretion to use pay to reward and retain good employees. As a rule, superior performance goes unrewarded with better pay. Nor does promotion come more swiftly to workers who show superior commitment and talent. Status on the basis of seniority is the dominant ethos of civil service administration. . . . It would be much better if senior managers could get their appropriated budgets and decide how many people to hire, at what pay level, to get the job done.[8]

Pressures have long been felt to relax appointment procedures, permit public managers a freer hand to fire mediocre performers, and increase flexibility in job assignment, promotion practices, and pay scales. Dozens of experiments along these lines have been tried, with mixed success. Early in the Clinton presidency, Vice-President Al Gore, in his capacity as director of a major initiative to "reinvent government," announced yet another effort to adopt results-oriented personnel policies.

The issue of workplace flexibility runs directly into the issue of public-sector unionism, since the matter of on-the-job working conditions plays a relatively larger role in government collective bargaining than it does in private industry. Overall today, some 35 percent of the state and local public workforce is unionized. The pattern of union membership, however, is highly uneven both across the nation and among different occupational classifications. Some state and local public-service sectors (fire, police, education, sanitation) are more heavily unionized than others. By contrast, doctors, lawyers, and other service professionals have often resisted union commitments that they feared would brand them as "blue collar" or, indeed, as less than fully "professional." This partly explains why the increase in public-sector union membership at the federal level over the past few decades has occurred primarily in the lower grades. (It should be emphasized, however, that the main federal collective bargaining organization, the American Federation of Government Employees—AFGE—includes white-collar as well as blue-collar employees.) The percentage of dues-paying federal

[8]"Beyond Mr. Gradgrind," *Policy Review* (Spring 1988): 34–35.

workers also varies widely from agency to agency, averaging by some estimates around 10 percent, although as many as 60 percent of federal civil servants may be in work units covered by collective bargaining agreements.

Most personnel experts foresee both bad and good news for public-sector unions in the near future. The bad news applies mainly at the state and local levels, where some nasty bills have begun to come due for bargains that union leaders successfully negotiated decades ago. In the 1960s and 1970s, some governors, county executives, and big-city mayors granted hefty pay raises and generous benefits to their unionized employees. ("Fringes" are traditionally high in the public sector, partly as compensation for salaries that tend to be low relative to those of comparable private-sector workers.) But these negotiated wage levels couldn't always be sustained. In time, some union leaders had to concede "givebacks." Then workers covered by the earlier agreements began retiring, often needing increased levels of medical attention as they aged. Their employers—cities which were often themselves financially troubled because of shrinking tax bases—had difficulty funding promised fringe benefits. The situation bodes to get worse before it gets better.

At the federal level, the main problem in management-labor relations has taken a somewhat different form. Congress determines federal civil servants' pay scales, and so union leaders have bargained mainly for favorable agency working conditions and better protections from the classification system itself. In early 1993, President Clinton pledged to create a federal bureaucracy that "works better and costs less." But the Clinton reinvention initiative couldn't succeed without support from federal employees. The President ordered all federal agencies to set up "partnership councils" with representatives of organized labor. Subjects that were traditionally excluded from collective bargaining become mandatory topics of negotiation, including issues relating to the numbers, types, grade levels, organizational divisions, and work methodologies of employees in federal units. Some observers suspected that President Clinton had privately cut a deal with AFGE leaders. Under it, the government would in time permit public employees' unions to bargain over salaries. In exchange, the AFGE leaders would tacitly support the Clinton plan to cut the federal workforce and move toward the human resource approach by simplifying civil service rules.

---

some of the bureaucrat bashing that's become common in recent years. Answers can come at three levels of analysis.

First, there are the findings of scholars other than New Theorists who have tried to assess both the quality of civil servants as workers and the average efficiency levels of government programs. We've already considered Charles Goodsell's claim that the imagery of civil servants as drones or malingerers is rooted in myth, not fact. Others have supported Goodsell's side of the argument. Arthur Speigel, a Harvard Business School consultant called in during the 1970s to overhaul one of the nation's most hidebound and complex bureaucracies, the New York City Department of Human Services, has emphasized the willingness and ability of professional civil servants to respond to higher directives—*on condition* that the directives lie within a zone of reasonableness: "I experienced several pleasant surprises in dealing with the civil service. First, their support was available. It hinged on four factors—proof of our competence, the mayor's backing of our effort, our respect for their standard bureaucratic procedures, and insight into the mutuality of our objectives." Speigel added that he and his shaker-uppers "found a richness of management talent buried under the civil service promotion system. By working around the regulations, we were able to put these people into the strategic positions that called for professionals."[9] (Note, however, that as Spiegel tells the story, the regulations didn't help the political leaders activate the latent capabilities of the professional administrators; the regulations had to be circumvented if the capacities of the permanent personnel were to be fully realized.)

Second, there is the test of experience and instinct. The New Theory assumes a cynical view of human nature—that workers in large numbers seek out jobs where they can be lazy (adverse selection) and that employees will routinely take advantage of informational asymmetries to goof off on the job (moral hazard). These arguments don't ultimately rest on hard data but instead appeal to some people's beliefs about human behavior. Does the picture of organizational life as presented by the New Theorists correspond to your own observations and experiences? In what respects does it ring true, and in what ways does it oversimplify or even falsify the pattern of human motivations? (We'll return to some of these questions in Chapter 10.)

Third, *if* our public-sector bureaucracies suffer from inefficiency, the reasons might not be that inferior employees take advantage of incentive-impairing conditions but that well-qualified, conscientious civil servants must divert their energies to deal with a surfeit of procedures, bureaucratic rules, and demands imposed by decision makers from without the organization.

[9]Arthur H. Spiegel III, "How Outsiders Overhauled a Public Agency," *Harvard Business Review* 53 (January–February 1975): 116, 120.

CHAPTER READING ▼ ▼ ▼

The following selection, by Frank J. Thompson of the State University of New York at Albany, explicitly raises the issue of competing criteria in the field of PPA and, implicitly, the problem of overdetermination. Thompson suggests that the discontent which is so commonly voiced by critics of the civil service ultimately reflects value judgments— that is, people's different weightings assigned to different values. As we'll see in our chapter case, the difficulties that public administrators encounter when they engage in priority setting are perhaps nowhere more acute than in civil service decision making.

Five Competing Values in Civil Service Systems
Frank J. Thompson

Certain core values compete for expression in civil service systems: instrumental goals, merit, political responsiveness, social equity, employee rights and well-being. In essence, discontent springs from the inability to forge a consensus on the appropriate weight to be assigned to particular values—to define the optimal mix of achievement on the various dimensions.

In managing human resources, public administrators tend to operate within civil service systems. These systems refer to the formal structures of authoritative rules that govern personnel practices in government programs and activities. Some public managers in very small jurisdictions do not, in any meaningful sense, manage human resources in the context of these systems, but in most local governments of any size, and certainly at the state and federal levels, civil service systems markedly influence the day-to-day management of personnel.

Reformers of various stripes have not underestimated the importance of civil service systems. The struggle against the spoils politics of the late nineteenth century evoked intense feelings and impassioned rhetoric. The Pendleton Act of 1883 forged the basic template for the spread of merit systems throughout the country. . . .

The new merit systems spawned their own discontents. . . . A study sponsored by Ralph Nader referred to federal personnel practices as *The Spoiled System.* Two top administrators in New York City government suggested that the city's personnel practices were "meritless." They claimed that the city's civil service system produced "mindless bureaucracies that appear to function for the convenience of their staffs rather than the public." They concluded that the city's personnel system had developed "rigor mortis"; it had "been warped and distorted to the point where it can do hardly anything at all." Discontent with civil service systems also found expression in the common view that public organizations lack the efficiency and effectiveness of their counterparts in the private sector. This belief fueled the privatization initiatives of the 1980s, which, among other things, urged that government's work be arranged through contracts with the private sector.

Most people who have spent any time working in the public sector sense that the criticisms of civil service systems are often excessive. Effective human resource management does occur in public agencies. Nevertheless, expressions of discontent with civil service systems occur with enough regularity to demand attention. . . .

Competing Values

Certain core values compete for expression in civil service systems. . . . [O]ne can make a strong case for focusing on five basic values: instrumental goals, merit, political responsiveness, social equity, and employee rights and well-being. At times, the perceived performance of civil service systems with respect of any one of these values has prompted discontent to simmer and, less frequently, to boil over into a reform initiative.

Civil service systems can facilitate or impede the efforts of public managers to accomplish *instrumental goals*—economy (cost containment), efficiency (as expressed in the ratio of output to cost), and effectiveness (achievement of program goals). In cities with political machines, the absence of merit systems has often forced public managers to put up with many marginally skilled or incompetent employees. This situation has heightened the risk that city agencies would be inefficient and ineffective.

More recent criticism holds that civil service systems impeded instrumental achievement by undermining managerial discretion. Some analysts see the restrictive character of government's personnel systems as the critical difference between managing in public and private organizations. The rules embedded in civil service systems presumably hamstring managers, who would otherwise use discretion over personnel decisions to enhance the efficiency and effectiveness of agencies' operations. Nowhere can one find a more piercing expression of this view than in a report released by the National Academy of Public Administration. In reviewing federal personnel practices, the report noted that the *Federal Personnel Manual* had 8,814 pages, and that the personnel system "does not seem to work very well for anybody." According to the report, "executives and managers feel almost totally divorced from what should be one of their most important systems." The report called for substantial deregulation of government managers and stressed that the U.S. Office of Personnel Management should delegate more authority to line departments.

Among other effects, restrictions on managerial discretion allegedly make it more difficult to motivate employees. Observing practices in New York City, Savas and Ginsburg charged that promotion tests robbed managers of opportunities to motivate subordinates; they further asserted that "the knowledge that it is almost impossible to penalize or discharge the barely competent or even incompetent permanent employee" is "demoralizing for supervisors." At the state level, a survey of top executives found 30 percent who indicated that they faced serious or very serious problems in disciplining or dismissing inept employees. These observations, from all levels of government, echo a common theme: that the rules of civil service dampen motivation because they weaken relationships between performance, on the one hand, and pay, promotion, disciplinary actions, and firing, on the other. In a related vein, Golembiewski focused on job design and description in arguing that civil service systems "fail to respond to the need to facilitate the management of work by increasing supervisory power." Excessively constraining rules march hand in hand with the charge that much of public personel administration represents the triumph of technique over purpose.

Merit is a second core value. Meritocratic norms have deep roots in the classic, liberal tradition of the United States. In the case of personnel, they emphasize that rewards ought to go to the most competent individuals—those with the best records of or potential for achievement. A sense of society as a market, where individuals compete and prizes go to the most adroit, undergirds this view. Therefore, strong sentiment and legal requirements often insist that public managers hire the most competent people from pools of eligible applicants. More recently, various policies have called for managers to allocate pay increases to the most meritorious performers.

While civil service systems often promote merit ideas, the 1960s and the 1970s witnessed countless accusations that the systems left much to be desired in this regard. Recruitment policies, in particular, came under fire. Hiring practices in the past had clearly excluded many well-qualified applicants on the grounds of race and sex. Moreover, very few civil service tests had been strictly validated (proved predictive) via scientific research. Thus, in reviewing the situation in New York City, Savas and Ginsburg noted that out of four hundred civil service examinations, "not a single case could be found where the validity of a written test . . . was ever proved." Moreover, merit hiring practices sometimes had unanticipated consequences. In New York City, delays between the scoring of tests and the actual hiring of individuals produce a situation in which candidates with low passing grades were more likely to be hired than those with higher marks.

The value of *political responsiveness* asserts that the preferences of elected officials and their appointees ought to weigh heavily in personnel management. The civil service reform movement of the late nineteenth century grew up in an effort to reduce the weight assigned to one form of political responsiveness, that associated with spoils systems. Spoils aimed primarily at maintaining the electoral coalition that had allowed politicians to stay in office by providing patronage in the routine, lower-level jobs of government. The institutions spawned by civil service reform made the practice of such patronage more difficult. Written tests for employment, quite aside from their capacity to predict the best person for a job, made it harder (although by no means impossible) for elected officials to practice patronage. "Independent" civil service commissions served a similar function. While some manifestations of low-level patronage politics persist, the spoils system is not a major rallying point for reform in the current era. For instance, one survey of over eight hundred state executives found that only 5 percent viewed patronage in filling positions as a serious problem.

In another sense, however, issues of political responsiveness remain on the front burner. The rise of the administrative state presents perplexing issues of accountability and control in a democracy. How can the elected representatives of the people ensure that government administrators remain sensitive to their concerns and not become autonomous power holders? More specifically, what role should personnel administration play in the quest for such responsiveness? In this regard, top policy jobs in the bureaucracy tend to be a central target of concern, as elected officials strive to place loyal people in strategically sensitive positions. . . .

Civil service systems can, however, tip the balance too far in the direction of this form of political responsiveness. Democracy requires not only responsiveness but also nonpartisan technical competence and respect for law among public managers. In this regard, some observers criticize civil service systems for facilitating too much political responsiveness. They see many top political appointeees as transient birds of passage, who all too frequently possess minimal qualifications for the jobs they hold and whose zealotry can lead to an administration that departs from both the spirit and the letter of the law. These observers note how heavy emphasis on political responsiveness can yield declining appreciation of career civil servants' professional expertise. In turn, morale among these civil servants may plummet, and turnover may increase. Administrative capacity thereby diminishes. These observers hold that civil servants, within the bounds set by law, will usually attempt to be responsive to their political masters. Civil servants understand that a political executive who goes too far in seeking to control personnel processes may paradoxically wind up with administrators who are unresponsive—not because they lack loyalty, but because they lack the skill to carry out the executive's wishes.

Social equity concerns the uses of government employment practices to help groups who are deemed disadvantaged or potentially disadvantaged. One variation on this concern involves the declaration that certain characteristics of groups are off limits in personnel decisions, an action that helps protect these groups from adverse discrimination. Job applicants, for instance, generally enjoy the right not to be discriminated against on the basis of being Catholic or fifty years old. Another version of this commitment to social equity goes beyond protection to representation. In this regard, various affirmative action plans have urged government officials to seek out and hire women and minorities. Other groups, such as veterans and the handicapped, have also received preferential treatment in the name of social equity.

Social equity concerns are sometimes at the heart of the criticisms and legal actions directed against civil service systems. Protected groups, such as women and minorities, frequently complain that the practices embedded in these systems continue to perpetuate injustice. Others complain because civil service systems do not officially recognize their characteristics as deserving of protection or proactive treatment. Hence, gay rights leaders charge that civil service systems permit discrimination against gay and lesbian applicants and employees. From another perspective, white male job applicants sporadically complain of not having obtained employment or promotion because of so-called reverse discrimination.

Employee rights and well-being also constitute a salient value in civil service systems. A pervasive norm, buttressed in many instances by law and regulation, asserts that an individual enjoys certain substantive and procedural rights as an employee of an organization. These rights increase to the degree that four conditions, among others, hold. First, they expand to the extent that rules limit the reasons for which executives can take actions (firing, demotion) perceived as adverse to employee interests. For instance, laws often constrain public executives from punishing subordinates for engaging in certain activities off the job, such as contributing money to political campaigns. Second, employee rights grow as the procedures (for example, appeals systems) for taking adverse action become more elaborate and place a greater burden of proof on executives. Third, employee rights loom larger when employees with more seniority in an agency enjoy greater protection from adverse action than employees with less seniority. Fourth, employee rights grow as formal procedures require executives to consult or bargain with official representatives of subordinates (say, union leaders) over a broader scope of issues. Beyond these formal safeguards, the notion of employee well-being implies a concern with the quality of work life. Work that provides employees with psychological gratification and promotes their physical well-being goes to the heart of this concern.

Some criticize civil service systems for being excessively deferential with respect of employee rights. Among other things, employees are allegedly too hard to fire or lay off. Seniority, critics claim, receives excessive weight in decisions. Skirmishes over these and related issues erupt sporadically. Other critics, however, charge that civil service systems fail to demonstrate sufficient respect for employee rights and well-being. For instance, concern over drug use and AIDS in the 1980s had fueled debate over employee rights to control who can monitor their physical condition. Guidelines issued by President Reagan required federal agencies to test designated employees for marijuana and cocaine use. The guidelines permitted employees to provide urine samples without observation, unless agency officials believed that subordinates would alter or substitute samples. To guard against such "cheating," the guidelines recommended such steps as the use of bluing agents in the toilet water at testing sites, to prevent employees from diluting their samples. Union leaders denounced the plan as "tidy-bowl justice" and a violation of the constitutional rights of employees. . . .

The Optimal Mix. These five core values of the personnel arena have several implications for those who seek to assess civil service systems and the practices of human resource managers. In some in-

stances, a given personnel practice does not serve any of the core values well. In other cases, a practice may promote all of them. . . . The presence of trade-offs means that civil service systems run the risk of being "damned if they do and damned if they don't." In essence, discontent springs from the inability to forge a consensus on the appropriate weight to be assigned to particular values—to define the optimal mix of achievement on the various dimensions. This inability to reach consensus means that reform movements often contain the seeds of new discontent and assume a cyclical pattern. When some reformers succeed in causing civil service systems to increase their emphasis on certain values (for example, more political responsiveness), they prompt others to seek change on behalf of other core concerns (merit, for example, or instrumental goals). . . .

From Frank J. Thompson, "Managing within Civil Service Systems," in James L. Perry, ed., *Handbook of Public Administration* (San Francisco: Jossey-Bass, 1989), pp. 359–366, 368–372.

CHAPTER CASE

Today federal, state, and most local government agencies of any size rely on career public-sector employees to conduct the day-to-day business of government. In the civil service, we find the vast majority of our fellow citizens who qualify for the title of public administrator. In the civil service, we probably also find the most rule-bound sector of the entire American workforce. The resulting tension has been a major theme in our discussion of public personnel administration. Arguably, the central challenge in PPA today is to develop administrative capacity suitable for modern circumstances (that personnel system designed for the twenty-first century which Osborne and Gaebler sought), while recognizing that long-established rules and traditions make change difficult in the civil service. Many civil servants oppose any weakening of these rules and traditions, since they protect the employee rights and well-being that Frank Thompson emphasized in his discussion of public-sector personnel planning.

The pervasive tension between the striving for results and the inhibiting effect of rules frames any survey of modern public administration. We find this tension in the following scenario, which introduces Mary Martengrove and tells us something about the geographic area and formal organization—the St. Croix Development Commission—in which Mary works. Closely interlocked with the work of the commission are the activities of the dominant federal agency in the St. Croix region, the U.S. Department of Agriculture ("the USDA" to most locals). This interdependency leads to Mary Martengrove's involvement in an action that the major figure in the scenario, USDA county coordinator Roman Drnda, has under way; Drnda has the unpleasant job of preparing for a RIF in the local workforce.

As you read through the case materials, look with some care at the excerpts from the official federal RIFfing regulations. Their language may seem awkward—bureaucratic gobbledygook. But deciphering bureaucratese (both what's explicit and what's between the lines) often proves to be an important part of the lived experience of administration. Similarly, you're likely to find the densely arrayed numbers in the retention registers to be cryptic and off-putting. But remember, case analysis requires close attention to the details. The details that really count often come in precisely the forms illustrated by these excerpts from federal personnel rules and sample retention tables. (By the way, you might be surprised at how much you can infer about the lives, talents, and vulnerabilities of "the sisters" in the story—Lief Pink, Bobbie Boo, and Lisa Hepburn—from a careful study of the numerical data in the retention registers. There's a lesson in that fact, too.)

A final caveat: At one point Guy Strumi, a figure in the scenario, muses on the "twisty-turny" thought processes of his boss, a public-sector union leader named Walt March. March's convoluted reasoning results from his decision to approach the impending RIF *strategically,* based on calculations of the following sort: "If I do this and my opponent does that, the results will be such-and-such; on the other hand, if I do something else and my opponents counters with . . ." and so forth, and so forth. Calculations of this kind are usually hard to follow unless the various combinations of strategies are carefully sorted out and represented in some simple way. One objective of the scenario is to set up the quest for that simple way of seeing the strategic situation in which Walt March finds himself.

CASE 1
. . . .

Cutback Management in the St. Croix: A RIF in the USDA

The Upper St. Croix River rises in two branches out of the boglands of Apostle County in northwest Wisconsin. The Upper St. Croix watershed embraces an area of relatively low-impact development—mostly seasonal-use cabins, fishing camps, and small resorts, plus a small manufacturing operation, Polaris Corporation's old wood-pulp processing plant at Half Day Rill. From its headwaters, the St. Croix angles in a southwesterly direction through some of the best freshwater fishing lakes in North America. It reaches a point on the Wisconsin-Minnesota boundary about 60 miles above Minneapolis–St. Paul, the Twin Cities. There the river itself becomes the border between the two states. There, too, it becomes one of the most spectacularly scenic waterways on the continent, a rushing flow enclosed by more than 25 miles of deep gorge, interrupted at bend after bend by rapids, and enclosed by overlooks of dense hardwood foliage.

A few miles south of Minneapolis–St. Paul, the St. Croix pays its own tribute to the Mississippi River, which has cut through the Twin Cities from the northwest. Thereafter, the St. Croix is no more, having joined the great river which marks the

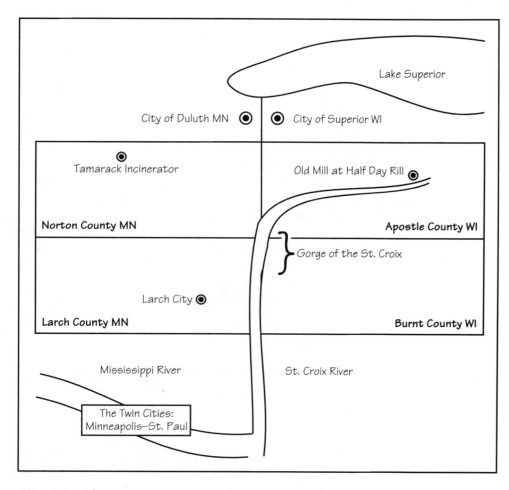

Sketch 2.1 The Four-County Region Known as "The St. Croix"

boundary between Wisconsin and Minnesota from its point of confluence with the St. Croix southward (see Sketch 2.1).

The St. Croix has given its name to the four-county area that it drains (Norton and Larch counties on the Minnesota side of the border, Apostle and Burnt counties in Wisconsin). The "mini–twin cities" of Duluth and Superior, on Lake Superior, lie just beyond the northern border of the four-county area. From the southern edge of the four-county region, it's a 30-mile drive on Interstate 35 to Minneapolis–St. Paul. Within the area are dozens of mink ranches and tree farms, a well-developed community college system, a medium-security federal prison at Vikingsholm, Minnesota (there's also a second federal correctional institution in Duluth), and perhaps three dozen market-center towns of varying sizes. Only three bridges cross the Upper St. Croix within the four-county region, so there's not as much travel as you might suppose back and forth between the two states. Yet common problems and shared economic interests cause both the Minnesotans and the Wisconsinites, in general, to think of themselves for most purposes as residents of an identifiable area. They customarily refer to the region simply as "the St. Croix."

• • • • •

Not too many decades ago, the economic base of the St. Croix was agricultural. There was some logging, especially on the Wisconsin side (where substantial numbers of folks continue to count on paychecks earned in silviculture, lumbering, and wood pulping). Mink ranches dot the region, and, of course, many natives of the St. Croix trap seasonally for fox, lynxcat, and muskrat. But the traditional foundation of the four-county region's prosperity had rested, in the main, on its dairy farms.

Folks joked that troubles had begun "when Carter killed the cows." Under President Jimmy Carter, officials of the USDA decided to deplete the nation's dairy herds as a way of reducing overproduction of milk, butter, and cheese. Many eligible dairyfarmers in the St. Croix area took up the USDA's offer to buy their cows and dispose of them. Within a few years, however, residents of the four-county region recognized that they had lost an important part of the local culture. The farmers never found a way to convert their one-time infusion of federal funds into a continuing cash flow. Mink ranching and expanded tree farming couldn't offset the deficit left by the sell-off of the herds.

For some years after "Carter killed the cows," local business and professional people had been promoting a "coordinated approach" (whatever that meant) to economic recovery. The message went from town to town that the area's Kiwanians and Lions and Rotarians were ready for a concerted effort on the region's behalf—if only someone would take the initiative. In 1984 Andy Byce, a consulting engineer and surveyor with offices in Larch City, proposed that all members of area service organizations chip in to set up a clearinghouse for information.

"I know, from our surveying work," Byce asserted, "that there's federal money from the Environmental Protection Agency we can get for some anti-pollution or water treatment projects, and I think the Corps of Engineers might have some money to put up too. Ellen Moe [the Minnesota congresswoman from the area] . . . she'll help, as always, to bring money from Washington into the district." What about the Small Business Administration: Doesn't it make grants? And of course the USDA itself had tons of programs and subsidies. All you had to do was know what was available, put together a credible plan, and collect the money. Byce convinced area bankers, lawyers, and realtors to kick in the necessary seed money. Byce himself agreed to chair the St. Croix Growth Council.

In the late 1980s, the county commissioners and county managers¹ in the St. Croix region collectively decided that the Growth Council should be expanded and

¹Outside of New England—and certainly in the midwestern states—counties are extremely important units of local governance. In most areas of the United States, the senior elected county officials are called "commissioners," although other titles are also used, such as *freeholder* and (as in most Wisconsin counties) *supervisor.* Many counties around the country also have an appointed professional county manager or county executive, whose main duties are executive in nature. These managers run day-to-day county operations subject to the oversight of the commissioners. When speaking of matters relating to the four-county development commission, residents of the St. Croix region have fallen into the habit of using the more common generic terms for officials whose formal titles vary somewhat from state to state and even county to county. Thus, citizens speak of "commissioners" when referring to their county-level legislators, although those officials in Wisconsin would properly be called "supervisors," and they speak of "managers" in all four counties, even though Norton County's senior executive official has the formal title of county executive.

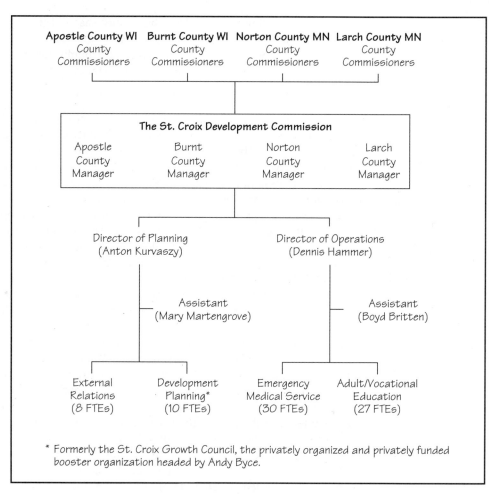

Sketch 2.2 Organization of the St. Croix Development Commission

professionalized by making it an official arm of a new four-county development commission. Henceforth, each county manager would wear two hats. Each would continue to supervise his or her own county's court services, oversee the sheriff's department, collect local taxes, and so forth (hat 1). Additionally, each county manager would serve by formal appointment as a commissioner on the newly created St. Croix Development Commission, or SCDC (hat 2).

The four-member SCDC met every other week with a director of planning and a director of operations. Together, these six framed coordinated policies in four areas of governmental activity: grant applications prepared by the SCDC's Division of External Relations, general economic development planning, regional emergency medical service, and adult/vocational education. The SCDC staff had grown to a total of seventy-nine full-time equivalent (FTE) employees, organized as shown in Sketch 2.2.

The SCDC's planning director, Anton Kurvaszy, had come to the St. Croix from somewhere in the southeast. His two units occupied a suite of offices in the Jackson

Professional Building in Larch City, the county seat of Larch County. Kurvaszy often thanked himself for having had the sense to hire as his staff aide a native of the St. Croix region, Mary Martengrove, fresh out of the public administration program at the University of Wisconsin-Eau Claire, to be his staff assistant.

• • • • •

Mary Martengrove knew that just about every county seat in the states of Minnesota and Wisconsin had its own version of the Jackson Building, a central place with office space for both businesses and government officials. Not many years earlier, four Larch City lawyers with some extra cash to invest had financed the construction of this new "professional building." The lawyers took the best locations for themselves and offered the remaining space for rent. Congresswoman Moe kept an office for constituent services on the first floor; the congresswoman's local representative, Dagmar Blaine, maintained a full-time presence there. The planning division of the SCDC also had its suite on the ground floor, along with some local engineers and surveyors (including Andy Byce and his partner, Boyce Winkwiak) who worked out of the Jackson building. "White-Collar Walt" March was a main shaker in the local chapter of the American Federation of Government Employees (AFGE), the bargaining agent for many of the federal workers across northern Minnesota and Wisconsin. March also rented space in the Jackson Building. His travels kept him from spending much time there, but most days you could find his assistant, Guy Strumi, in the AFGE office.

The other renters were all government officials. Next door to the SCDC offices on one side was the USDA's Soil Conservation Service office. Down the corridor was where the Agriculture Extension field-workers hung out when they weren't criss-crossing the region "jawing" with mink or poultry ranchers. From the SCDC offices going the other way, you reached the door of the USDA program coordinator, Roman Drnda.

Upstairs in the Jackson Building was a five-room layout where "the welfare" administered the Social Security disability program, Medicaid, and so forth. "The welfare" was a collective term used by most St. Croix residents when they referred to employees of the federal Department of Health and Human Services. "The welfare" folks from HHS also worked in close coordination with state and county officers administering shared programs such as the old federal-state Aid to Families with Dependent Children program. Next to "the welfare" were offices for food stamps and the local Commodity Credit Corporation, both USDA programs. Traffic to and from the CCC was especially heavy at planting and harvest times, when farmers signed up for federal crop subsidy programs, and again toward the end of the growing year, when they returned to claim benefits under the CCC's nonrecourse loan programs.[2]

Nearly everyone in the Jackson Building knew everyone else's first name. And of course they all knew about the looming problem that would end up touching everyone in the St. Croix—the impending RIF in the USDA.

---

[2]*Nonrecourse loan program:* Traditionally, many of the subsidies administered by the Department of Agriculture have taken the form of loans made to farmers on the understanding that all or part of the debt incurred would be forgiven if the farmer's crop didn't fetch a specified price at harvest time. In that event, the U.S. government would "have no recourse" to the money that the farmer could keep as a form of price support. In 1996, Congress passed a law changing the structure of the price-support program. The new legislation provides for a slow phaseout of many forms of nonrecourse loans.

Roman Drnda, who was going to have to "run the RIF," had spent twenty-five years in agriculture. Early in his career, he'd moved from extension work in Iowa, Minnesota, and Wisconsin to a stint with the American Farm Bureau Federation (the nation's leading agribusiness trade association and lobbying organization). From the AFBF Drnda had gone on to a job at one of the University of Minnesota's agricultural research stations. Drnda had then worked in the USDA's Washington headquarters office before moving into his present position. As county coordinator of all farm programs in a troubled area of the country, Drnda in effect functioned as the local spokesperson, chief negotiator, and occasional "hatchet man" for Secretary of Agriculture Nyby himself.

Because any problem affecting agriculture also affected prospects for economic growth in the region, the rumored RIF order also became the official concern of Anton Kurvaszy in his capacity as planning director of the St. Croix Development Commission. Drnda had asked Kurvaszy, representing the SCDC; Dagmar Blaine of Congresswoman Moe's staff; and Chris Clairy from the office of Wisconsin state senator Ben Loffel to meet informally at the Golden Gopher Grill for a discussion of the expected cutback order. As a courtesy to Walt March, Drnda also included Guy Strumi. And at Anton Kurvaszy's request, Mary Martengrove would also attend, bringing the number at the Golden Gopher meeting to six.

• • • • •

In farming circles around the country, there's a familiar joke:

A civil servant of the U.S. Department of Agriculture is seen standing on Independence Avenue in Washington, next to the USDA building, weeping uncontrollably. A compassionate passerby asks the official what happened. The bureaucrat replies: "My farmer died."

No one around the table with Roman Drnda retold the old joke. No one had to.

Over the years since the sell-off of the herds, the overall population in the St. Croix—about 120,000 souls—held almost steady. But the number of active farmers steadily declined. All the while, the number of USDA technical specialists remained as it had been when many times the current number of farmers were being serviced. Meanwhile, the number of USDA employees who performed social service functions was increasing apace with the increased need to administer federally supported relief programs (food stamps and the rest). People in the know realized that the personnel trend had long alarmed the bureaucracy watchers in Washington, especially among the would-be budget cutters in Congress.

Drnda said to the group assembled at the Golden Gopher: "Study commission after commission has recommended that we downsize Agriculture. For years, congressmen and congresswomen horsetraded with one another to protect USDA offices and jobs in their districts. No longer, I'm afraid."

Dagmar Blaine confirmed Drnda's opinion: "I got it from Ellen [Congresswoman Moe] herself this morning on the phone. Nyby's signing the RIF order today. That means Ellen will get her courtesy advance soon, maybe tomorrow. . . ."

Courtesy advance? Mary Martengrove didn't know the term.

"As a courtesy to M.C.s [Members of Congress]," Blaine explained, "a departmental secretary 'consults' with them before closing facilities in their districts. What that means is, the secretary sends a copy of the orders before they go to the field."

"So the M.C. can make the announcement?"

Blaine laughed. "The M.C. makes the announcement when there's a *new* facility to be *built.* When it's an *old* one to be *closed,* she lets the secretary—in this case, Secretary of Agriculture Nyby—put out the nasty news. Then the M.C. blasts the action as 'heartless, ill-advised, penny-wise-and-pound-foolish. . . .' Pick any other adjectives."

"What exactly's in the RIF order?" state senator Loffel's man, Chris Clairy, asked Drnda.

"Word is, we'll have to let go 1 in 3." No one around the table envied Drnda's job—to decide who would be fired.

Drnda continued: "Here's some background: The USDA has seventy-four employees, in all, in the St. Croix. Scheduled retirements, combined with clear lines of bumping rights, should make the RIF pretty straightforward for the very-senior people, the very-junior people, and for the clericals and custodials. Everyone already knows who'll have to go (the newest workers) or who's already planning to go (pending retirees, whose attrition should pretty much give us our quota of layoffs, at least in those categories). The tough problem is with thirty-nine APTs we have in grades GS-9 through GS-14. On the 1-in-3 basis, thirteen of those thirty-nine will be let go. Of those thirty-nine, however, seven are service veterans. For practical purposes, their jobs are protected—unless, of course, some of them are put in special competitive levels of their own.

"So, say we set aside the seven vets," Drnda continued, "leaving thirty-two problematic cases. Those thirty-two will have to take the entire 1-out-of-3 hit as we downsize from our thirty-nine APTs to a staff of twenty-six. The question is: Who should be let go? Or—what's almost the same question—what kinds of jobs should the remaining APT staff be tailored to perform in the St. Croix after all the ripple effects of the RIF have washed away?"

Drnda distributed a paper. "Here's a worksheet showing my guesses about the thirteen individuals among the thirty-two nonveterans who, after bumping, are likely to lose their jobs" (see Table 2.1).

In multiple columns, Drnda had noted each individual's civil service grade, gender, veteran's status (or lack of it), and job category: an *F* for workers who spend time mostly in the field giving hands-on advice to farmers, fur ranchers, and silviculturalists; an *A* for administrative employees who specialize in office-based paperwork—processing price-support and acreage-reduction forms for subsidies, and the like; an *S* for employees in social work, such as the second-floor workers in the food stamp group or the WIC counselors. (Women, Infants, and Children, a program for nutritional supplements). Drnda's worksheet also showed each worker's job location by state, years of service, and average of the last three performance ratings on the standard federal civil service 1–5 scale. And although he worried about creating a written record of factors that might be inappropriate to consider in the impending RIF, Drnda had also added marks showing which workers are Native Americans or members of other minority groups.

Table 2.1 Roman Drnda's Worksheet: Tentative Retention Register for 39 St. Croix Region APT-Level Employees

	General Schedule (GS) Grade	M/F Vet*	Specialization†	Job Location	Seniority	Average Job Rating	Performance Credit	Register Rank
7 APT-Level USDA Employees Protected by Veterans' Status								
Abernaz	14	M, V	F	MN	26	5	+ 20	46
Morton	9	M, V	F	WI	24	3	+ 12	36
Angiulio	13	M, V	S	WI	11	4	+ 16	29
Ntaba‡	13	M V	F	MN	25	2		25
Quirk	9	M, V	A	MN	12	3	+ 12	24
Hackney	14	M, V	S	MN	15	2		15
Murchisan	7	M, V	F	WI	7	2		7
19 APT-Level USDA Employees Likely to Survive the RIF								
Two Bear‡	13	M	F	WI	21	4	+ 16	37
Zerbe	11	M	F	MN	18	4	+ 16	34
Madison	9	M	F	WI	11	3	+ 12	33
Haberler	9	F	S	MN	21	3	+ 12	33
Phaltz	11	M	A	MN	20	3	+ 12	32
Houlihan	11	M	F	MN	19	3	+ 12	31
Eagle‡	12	F	S	WI	10	5	+ 20	30
Pink	9	F	F	MN	14	4	+ 16	30
Safter	11	M	A	WI	8	5	+ 20	28
Sorenson	11	M	A	MN	14	3	+ 12	26
Jones, F	12	M	A	MN	13	3	+ 12	25
Farnsworth	12	M	F	WI	9	4	+ 16	25
Loblick	10	F	A	WI	7	4	+ 16	23
Jones, B	10	M	F	MN	21	2		21
West	13	M	A	WI	21	2		21
Beckel	9	M	F	MN	9	3	+ 12	21
Boo	9	F	A	MN	8	3	+ 12	20
Dernbach	14	F	F	WI	18	2		18
Praski	9	F	S	MN	6	3	+ 12	18
13 Vulnerable to Layoff Because of Low Retention-Register Rank								
Hepburn‡	9	F	S	WI	1	4	+ 16	17
Johnson	9	F	S	WI	3	3	+ 12	15
Laurie‡	11	F	A	MN	3	3	+ 12	15
Charles‡	11	M	A	WI	3	3	+ 12	15
Kinsallas	9	F	S	MN	3	3	+ 12	15
Edelweiss	10	F	S	WI	2	3	+ 12	14
Cloudie‡	12	M	F	WI	11	2		11
Doggett‡	11	F	S	WI	10	2		10
Sturdiven	9	F	A	WI	8	2		8
Smathers‡	11	M	S	MN	7	2		7
Schmeirer	9	F	A	WI	6	2		6
Manley‡	10	M	S	WI	3	2		3
Martens	9	F	F	MN	2	2		2

*V = veterans' preference.

†F = field-worker; S = social worker; A = administrative staffer.

‡Native American or other minority affiliation.

"I've listed our seven protected vets at the top," Drnda said. "The remaining thirty-two are listed in descending order on the retention register, assuming that we lump everyone into a single competitive level."

Retention register? Competitive level? To Mary's ears this was more civil service jargon.

Anton Kurvaszy called for a pause to give his new assistant a brief explanation (see Box 2.2). "A retention register," he told Mary, "is the listing of people subject to a RIF, graduated according to their level of protection, from the highest-ranked individuals in a 'competitive level' to the lowest. The competitive level is the listing of all those workers who have roughly substitutable skills. By definition, anyone in a competitive level should be able to make a transition into anyone else's job within that level. Anyone can bump a worker in the same competitive level if that worker has a lower retention rank." Kurvaszy pointed to the bottom of Drnda's worksheet: "The last thirteen names, the underlined ones, have no one beneath them to bump. They're the thirteen who will have to go."

"How do you establish the retention ranks?"

Drnda answered Mary. "Civil service rules award a tenured worker—that is, anyone who has successfully completed an initial probationary period in career government employment—1 point for each year of service. Then you add a credit based on the worker's average job performance over recent rating periods. The retention rank is the seniority score plus the performance credit."

After a silent minute or two, while everyone tried to take in the codes and numbers on Drnda's worksheet, Dagmar Blaine addressed Drnda: "Okay, Roman. Is this meeting for real, or just a charade? Have you already made your decision about who's going to get RIFfed, and this coffee-klatsch is really just a sociable way to tell us which of our constituents are going to lose their jobs?" Blaine pointed at the underlined names on Drnda's worksheet: "Poor Hepburn, and Johnson, and the others on your list of the luckless."

"No, Dagmar. No decisions have been made. I want input from all of you. If any of you can come up with a better way to run this RIF, I'd like to know it. All I ask is, you don't divulge this tentative information, which is just a straw man for planning purposes, to anyone but your own principals." In other words, Dagmar Blaine could talk the entire problem over with Congresswoman Moe; Chris Clairy could talk with Senator Loffel; and Guy Strumi could confer with Walt March. But none of the attendees at the Golden Gopher coffee-klatsch was to leak names of probable layoff candidates to the press, or even to tell the vulnerable employees about their place on Drnda's list.

Chris Clairy spoke up. "I can give you one bit of input right now." He stabbed a finger toward the bottom category on Drnda's list: "The way you have it set up, Roman, eight or nine of the people to be RIFfed would be from the Wisconsin side, just because they're junior. Look at the list. Most of those are women or Native Americans, or they have excellent performance records—a lot better than the records of some of the more-senior people, who'll use pure longevity to bump better workers."

"I *don't* have it 'set up,' Chris," Drnda countered, his voice betraying some testiness. "There's nothing definite yet—nothing, of course, except (if our advance word is right) that thirteen people will have to go. If you want to change my list, which is only a draft, tell me how."

BOX 2.2 ▬▬▬▬▬▬▬▬▬▬▬▬▬▬▬▬▬▬▬▬▬▬▬▬▬▬▬▬▬▬▬▬▬▬▬▬   ■ ■ ■

A Primer on Federal RIFfing Procedures

At all levels of government, RIFfing procedures, as they are called, are elaborately limited by personnel laws. They are also controlled by civil service regulations, which have the force of law, and often by the terms of contracts negotiated with government employees' unions. These too are legally binding.

Title V, Chapter I, *Code of Federal Regulations* requires that "competitive areas"—areas within which federal employees will compete for the jobs that remain after a RIF—be designated within all federal agencies and departments. Each competitive area (1) must embrace a definable geographic region and (2) must have a reasonable organizational rationale. Two units from different departments of government—say from the Agriculture Department and from Health and Human Services—can't share a competitive area even if they have offices in the same region or, for that matter, in the same building. A competitive area also must encompass a single "local commuting area." According to the Office of Personnel Management (OPM) RIFfing handbook:

> A Local Commuting Area is a geographic area that usually includes any population center and the surrounding communities in which people live and reasonably travel back and forth to work.

A RIF administrator is required to study the position descriptions of every employee within each competitive area and, *strictly on the basis of these descriptions,* must group interchangeable positions into competitive levels. Another pertinent provision from the OPM handbook reads:

> The competitive level is based on each employee's position description, not on the employee's personal qualifications.
>
> Two positions that are similar (e.g., same grade, series, work schedule, etc.), but are not identical, may be placed in the same competitive level if the position descriptions show that each employee would need less than 90 days to perform the key tasks of the other position.

(You should note that Drnda, when developing his draft retention register, treated every worker on the list—whether an *F,* an *A,* or an *S*—as interchangeable with every other one. Was that a defensible judgment? Or might the difficulty of an *F* worker's transition to an *A* or an *S* worker's duties subject a RIF that Drnda runs under that arrangement to challenge in court, based on the charge that it violated the rule of interchangeable positions?)

Once competitive levels have been defined, the administrator prepares formal retention registers by rank-ordering individuals within each level using a format minutely prescribed in 5 *CFR* I, subpart E, sections 351.501–351.506. The handbook is explicit: "Tenure is the most important factor [when determining an individual's rank order for a layoff] while performance is the least important factor." Think that one over a while!

All workers in the same *tenure* bracket are grouped together; in this phase of the RIFfing process, career workers compete against career workers, political appointees compete against other political appointees, probationary workers (who haven't yet gained civil service tenure) compete against their counterparts, and so forth. Next, within each tenure group, *veterans* are subgrouped for preferential treatment. Under most conditions, a veteran can bump a nonveteran, even if the latter has more experience and higher performance ratings. Third, individuals in each subgroup are listed in order of *seniority*. Finally, excellence in *performance* is reflected by adding a seniority-equivalent number to certain individuals' rankings—an additional twenty years' credit for workers who averaged the highest performance rankings in recent job evaluations (performance rating of 5), sixteen years for a 4, and twelve years for a 3.

Broadly, bumping provisions permit a worker who is subject to layoff to displace a lower-ranking employee on the retention register, provided that the displacement occurs (1) within the same competitive level; (2) within a specified number of civil service grade levels, normally three—meaning, for example, that a GS-13 usually may not bump a GS-5; (3) into a job for which the bumping employee can be fully qualified after no more than ninety days of training (the aforementioned interchangeability requirement); and (4) into a position that is not covered by a special exception. Section 351.607 of the federal RIFfing regulations specifies the most important exception:

> An agency may make exception to the order of release . . . when needed to retain an employee on duties that cannot be taken over within 90 days and without undue interruption to the activity by an employee with higher retention standing.

(Again, Drnda has bent the rules—in this case, by stretching the competitive level to cover all employees between GS-9 and GS-14, inclusive, instead of confining the level to workers within three civil service grades of one another. Here too, as with Drnda's parameter change concerning interchangeable positions, it's the *reasonableness* of Drnda's judgment that could become a crucial issue if a challenger were to contest his RIFfing procedure. What do you think?)

-- ■ ■ ■

"Why not make two competitive levels?" Clairy asked. "Use one level for everyone on the Wisconsin side, and the other for everyone in Minnesota. That way senior Minnesotans could bump junior ones in Minnesota, but they couldn't bust out junior people on the Wisconsin side. We'd end up with roughly equal sharing of the layoffs by people from both states. That's fair."

Drnda was about to answer Clairy, but he was interrupted by Anton Kurvaszy: "Roman, look at the way your list ends up RIFfing not only disproportionate numbers on the Wisconsin side but also people on the welfare and service ends of the work—the very ones we need most as long as the St. Croix continues on the economic downside."

It was true. In general, the technical advisers and administrators of traditional agriculture programs—the officials, for example, who evaluate local farmers' applications for crop subsidies—had seniority over administrators and caseworkers in the welfare areas. On average, workers with *F*s on Drnda's list had been in the USDA harness longer than those hired to deal with the recent problems of social and economic distress in the area. The way Drnda had approached the ranking, the variations in the patterns of longevity on the job couldn't help but cause disproportionate hurt to social workers—those coded S on Drnda's list.

"I don't think," Kurvaszy added, "you intended 'Last hired, first fired' to be your rule of selection, Roman."

Drnda thought for a second and then acknowledged the validity of Kurvaszy's observation. "You're right. Even though the regulations favor seniority, they don't require us to put our brains entirely in cold storage! We can't do this RIF thing in a vacuum." The nature of USDA work in the St. Croix was changing. Arguably, the department didn't need all those agricultural technicians any more. Drnda's retention register would guarantee continued employment for people with the traditional USDA skills, even though they weren't needed as much in the region as they had been in the old days. Drnda's listing would also result in the RIFfing of workers with expertise and (presumably) interest in socially oriented jobs.

"The number of social service jobs goes up every year," Drnda admitted. He wondered out loud if it would really be so easy for senior technicians—agronomists, crop specialists, soil experts, and so forth—to take over the work of the more-junior social service professionals whom, under Drnda's scheme, the technicians might bump.

Mary Martengrove asked: "Since the point seems to be, how to prevent the service professionals who do more and more of the work of the department from being bumped by workers with more seniority but less critical skills, why not put the Fs, As, and Ss in separate competitive levels?"

Dagmar Blaine didn't seem to get Mary's drift. Drnda, sensing her puzzlement, explained: "The more competitive levels we create, the fewer individuals who can bump others, since each one is competing within a smaller group. That gives us better control over the outcome. At the extreme, if you could put every worker in his or her own competitive level, you could pretty much choose whom to lay off by declaring certain competitive levels superfluous. By definition, a released individual couldn't bump a worker lower down in the register because there wouldn't be anyone else in that specific individual's category to bump!"

Blaine, catching the point, nodded. Nevertheless, something in Drnda's voice conveyed that he would be leery of a retention register that contained too many competitive levels.

The six talked a bit longer, and then Drnda adjourned the meeting. "Look it over," he said in closing. "I'll be fooling with this retention register all day tomorrow. Give me a call if you have further reactions, or if you can think of a better way to approach all this."

• • • • •

The next day, Mary asked Kurvaszy: "What kind of manager wants to eliminate all judgment and just go by the numbers—which seems to mean mostly seniority?" Mary confessed that she didn't understand why Drnda seemed willing to let abstract rules, abstractly applied, decide which workers would remain to staff the USDA organization in the St. Croix region.

"Why," Mary asked, "wouldn't the guy running the RIF identify the best performers on a staff? Then the worst ones? And then design the retention register so that, when the required number of people are laid off and all bumping rights have been exercised, the best have been protected, and the duds are the ones eliminated? Why not use a little discrimination when defining interchangeable positions and competitive levels?"

Kurvaszy could think of several reasons why Mary's approach might be problematical, and his almost-perceptible wincing at the word *discrimination* suggested what one of them might be.

"Some managers *do* let the dice fall just that way, going strictly by the numbers," Kurvaszy acknowledged. "Any other way, any attempt to 'game' the process, and a manager's open to appeals through the higher echelons in the department, through the civil service system appeals process—that's run by OPM itself—and, of course, through the courts."

Kurvaszy thought a moment before continuing. "The whole point of all those RIFfing rules is to prevent the person who runs the operation from exercising personal control—and to prevent the abuse that can go with so much control." The RIFfing procedure, Kurvaszy added—and especially the requirement to collect slots into competitive levels based strictly on job descriptions, not on the performance records of the people filling existing positions—had been designed to keep an administrator from rigging a RIF to favor particular individuals.

"Besides," Kurvaszy added, "the public employees' unions watch the RIFfing process closely. So, of course, do the affected workers—and so do their lawyers, if it comes to that. Any listing of retention entitlements has to comply with the rules. Managers aren't supposed to gimmick-up a RIF for the purpose of beating the tenure protections of the more-senior workers. There have to be reasonable justifications for any departures from the RIFfing rules, read in the most straightforward way. If a RIF manager bends the rules too far, he or she will just land the department in court.

Anton shrugged philosophically. "Just going by the numbers may not be the best way to protect the best workers, but it still may be best from the bureaucratic standpoint. Like it or not, it's not necessarily *un*reasonable for a RIF manager to take the line of least resistance. I agree with you," Kurvaszy admitted, "that's what Roman seems to be doing here. Just line 'em up using the simplest imaginable ranking procedure—that's what Roman's done; then shoot as many hostages as the boss orders, making no judgments about whom should be spared. So—as Dagmar Blaine pointed out—poor Hepburn and Johnson and the others among the unprotected thirteen lose out." He added that, if Mary could devise a better way, Drnda—whose life had been devoted to the cause of American agriculture and those who worked in it—would surely be happy to hear about it.

Later, at her desk, Mary picked up from Drnda's question about a three-way breakout of competitive levels. Table 2.2 shows the alternative retention register that Mary, after some playing with the names and numbers, came up with.

"What do you think?" she asked Kurvaszy.

Anton looked at the names Mary had underlined on her suggested alternative listing. "You want to RIF deeply into the *F* category...."

Table 2.2 Mary Martengrove's Alternative Retention Register Based on Three Competitive Levels (F/S/A)

	General Schedule (GS) Grade	M/F Vet*	Specialization†	Job Location	Seniority	Average Job Rating	Performance Credit	Register Rank
APT Competitive Level 1: Interchangeable F Skills								
Abernaz	14	M, V	F	MN	26	5	+ 20	46
Morton	9	M, V	F	WI	24	3	+ 12	36
Ntaba‡	13	M V	F	MN	25	2		25
Murchisan	7	M, V	F	WI	7	2		7
Two Bear‡	13	M	F	WI	21	4	+ 16	37
Zerbe	11	M	F	MN	18	4	+ 16	34
Madison	9	M	F	WI	11	3	+ 12	33
Houlihan	11	M	F	MN	19	3	+ 12	31
Pink	9	F	F	MN	14	4	+ 16	30
Farnsworth	12	M	F	WI	9	4	+ 16	25
Jones, B	10	M	F	MN	21	2		21
Beckel	9	M	F	MN	9	3	+ 12	21
Dernbach	14	F	F	WI	18	2		18
Cloudie‡	12	M	F	WI	11	2		11
Martens	9	F	F	MN	2	2		2
APT Competitive Level 2: Interchangeable S Skills								
Angiulio	13	M, V	S	WI	11	4	+ 16	29
Hackney	14	M, V	S	MN	15	2		15
Haberler	9	F	S	MN	21	3	+ 12	33
Eagle‡	12	F	S	WI	10	5	+ 20	30
Praski	9	F	S	MN	6	3	+ 12	18
Hepburn‡	9	F	S	WI	1	4	+ 16	17
Johnson	9	F	S	WI	3	3	+ 12	15
Kinsallas	9	F	S	MN	3	3	+ 12	15
Edelweiss	10	F	S	WI	2	3	+ 12	14
Doggett‡	11	F	S	WI	10	2		10
Smathers‡	11	M	S	MN	7	2		7
Manley‡	10	M	S	WI	3	2		3
APT Competitive Level 3: Interchangeable A Skills								
Quirk	9	M, V	A	MN	12	3	+ 12	24
Phaltz	11	M	A	MN	20	3	+ 12	32
Safter	11	M	A	WI	8	5	+ 20	28
Sorenson	11	M	A	MN	14	3	+ 12	26
Jones, F	12	M	A	MN	13	3	+ 12	25
Loblick	10	F	A	WI	7	4	+ 16	23
West	13	M	A	WI	21	2		21
Boo	9	F	A	MN	8	3	+ 12	20
Laurie‡	11	F	A	MN	3	3	+ 12	15
Charles‡	11	M	A	WI	3	3	+ 12	15
Sturdiven	9	F	A	WI	8	2		8
Schmeirer	9	F	A	WI	6	2		6

*V = veterans' preference.

†F = field-worker; S = social worker; A = administrative staffer.

‡Native American or other minority affiliation.

"Maybe my exact number's off," Mary said, "but it seems reasonable to concentrate the layoffs where the demand for skilled workers is thinnest, among the field technicians, the Fs."

Kurvaszy nodded. "Under your RIF plan, poor Pink here gets the ax, even though she's been a good, loyal DA type for more than a dozen years and has a fine work record, . . . and has a retention register total of 30. While"—Anton scanned Mary's worksheet, looking for a comparison case to make his point—"while Lisa Hepburn, a brand-new worker at the same grade as Pink, but with a register total barely more than half of Pink's, keeps her job just because it carries a 'social work' code!"

• • • • •

As bargaining agent for most of the organized federal workers in the four-county area, "White-Collar Walt" March was a figure of importance across upper Minnesota and Wisconsin. He listened as Guy Strumi described Drnda's tentative retention register. Guy went on to fill March in on the alternative approach that Anton Kurvaszy and Kurvaszy's new assistant, Mary Martengrove, had suggested. Strumi referred to the plans, respectively, as the "inclusive" retention register (Table 2.1) and the "discriminating" three-level register (Table 2.2).

"Under Drnda's inclusive plan," Strumi summarized, "all APTs in the area would be thrown into a single competitive level. Veterans would be protected. Bumping would proceed until only thirteen workers remain who have no one below them to displace. Under Mary Martengrove's alternative, the retention registers would be drawn up in a way that discriminates among the three kinds of workers: field-workers, social workers, and straight administrators. In other words, the Fs, Ss, and As would have separate registers, preventing cross-bumping. The justification suggested by Kurvaszy and Martengrove at the Golden Gopher meeting had been that a higher percentage of Fs could be let go under the discriminating approach than under the inclusive plan. Anton and Mary had reasoned that fieldwork—that is, providing extension services to working farmers—seemed almost superfluous under current conditions. As Kurvaszy had put it, the shrinkage in the farm population had made what many of the Fs used to do almost irrelevant, while hard times were making the work of the Ss—food stamps, WIC outreach—more vital than ever before.

March frowned. Strumi thought he knew what was on March's mind. Among the area's USDA workers, as among federal employees generally, actual card-carrying, dues-paying membership in unions had long been patchy and irregular. It happened that the more-senior USDA workers in the St. Croix area—Drnda's Fs—constituted the core organized group, while most Ss had decided not to join the union. The As were evenly split; 50 percent were AFGE members, 50 percent were not. Walt March understood the mechanisms (and all the tricks) of a RIF, and he could see what might be in store for his members, depending on the RIFfing approach that Drnda finally used. Under the inclusive approach, March's members' jobs would mostly be protected—although that wouldn't have been any part of Drnda's reason for going with Table 2.1. By contrast, the discriminating approach would end up RIFfing Fs and effectively favoring the nonunionized Ss.

March pondered the options. He suspected that Drnda would prefer the discriminating approach after he had thought through all the twists, since—as Kurvaszy and Martengrove had argued—it would leave the department with a workforce better suited to the current USDA mission in the region. March knew Roman Drnda well. He told Strumi that Drnda wouldn't be prejudiced against a better way of running the RIF just because someone else had suggested it. Drnda wasn't afflicted by the "not invented here" syndrome.

"In other words," Guy responded, "you think Roman will scrap his own inclusive retention register and adopt the more discriminating approach?"

March considered another moment. "That's what I'd kind of expect," he said tentatively.

What strategy should March play in response? Both he and Strumi knew that the bottom line for a union negotiator in the private sector is the threat of a strike. But things are different in federal government collective bargaining.[3] The ultimate sanction against management—in this case, against Roman Drnda and Drnda's boss, Secretary Nyby—is the threat of litigation. A willingness to litigate shows gumption on the union leader's part, demonstrates the solidarity of the membership, and warns management not lightly to mess with workers' rights.

And how did all that apply to the coming RIF of the St. Croix USDA workers?

March said: "My thinking now, off the top of my head, is this: On the merits, the inclusive approach would obviously be better from our standpoint than the discriminating plan would be. Furthermore, we'd probably lose if we sued to keep Drnda from RIFfing on the basis of the discriminating, three-level plan."

March thought for a second, then said: "But win or lose, I think it might be time to litigate on this RIF—tie 'em up in court, let everyone know we don't mean to go quietly while they cut back all over the federal government. Sue the bastards!—whether Drnda uses the inclusive *or* the discriminating plan."

Strumi liked to hear March talk union tactics. The union had to pick a fight every now and then. Cutbacks were never to be conceded—even when a leader, such as March, knew in his heart of hearts that some personnel trimming has become unavoidable. It was the threat of legal hassles that kept cabinet officers such as Nyby, and their henchmen (such as Drnda), honest.

"I don't mind telling you," March added, "considered strictly as a legal strategy and for political effect, I'd rather sue if Drnda goes with the inclusive plan than with the discriminating one." After all, the aim of a suit would be to make a gesture. All other things being equal, March obviously would prefer to litigate in a case that the union actually had a chance to win. Legally, a stronger case could surely be made against the inclusive plan than against the discriminating, three-level approach. A RIFfing plan, if litigated, would have to pass what lawyers call "the test of reasonableness," and a judge might well find the discriminating approach to be the more reasonable one because it would permit patterns of layoff (of *F*s) and retentions (of

[3]In contrast with the practice in some municipal and state public-sector unions, where "job actions" and strikes have become relatively common, federal unions rarely call strikes or even quietly approve "wildcat" walkouts. Federal civil servants' salaries are set by Congress rather than in collective bargaining. (See the discussion in Box 2.1.) Part of the reason why strikes are rarely used in federal labor disputes is that they are unlikely to be effective means of bringing pressure to bear in Congress. Indeed, striking may boomerang by offending public opinion. Legislative lobbying and providing campaign support to congressional candidates have proved over the years to be more successful union tactics.

Ss) in better alignment with projected USDA workloads. In other words, the union faced a greater risk of losing a case brought to block implementation of the discriminating retention register even though implementation of the inclusive register would be less harmful to the immediate interests of March's union members.

Strumi had to agree. There might be just enough rule bending in the inclusive approach for a federal judge to void a RIF run on the basis of Drnda's original retention register. (See, for example, the doubts about Drnda's methods mentioned in Box 2.2.) One problem from March's viewpoint was that the blanket threat of a legal challenge might give Drnda the nudge to scrap Table 2.1 and draw up retention registers in closer conformity with the spirit of civil service rules and current USDA personnel needs in the four-county region. On the other hand, for any number of reasons, Drnda could decide to proceed with his original, inclusive retention register, especially if he didn't think that a RIF based on Table 2.1 would face a challenge in court. Table 2.1 would certainly be simpler to administer than Table 2.2. That might be grounds enough for Drnda to favor it *if* he thought he wouldn't have to worry about defending the inclusive approach before a federal judge.

Strumi said: "You think Drnda will assume he has an open ticket to bend the RIFfing rules unless he suspects the union will take him to court."

March nodded, adding: "That's one reason why we probably *will* take him to court, no matter which approach he takes. The worst strategy—at least from the union's standpoint—would be if Drnda goes with the discriminating plan and we just sit by without acting. That would give Drnda a free ride. He'd go ahead and RIF people who are counting on the union to protect them. Next worse would be for us to go for an injunction against the discriminating plan, since we'd be more likely to lose. Still in all, if we sue—even if we lose—we'll salvage credibility, both with the USDA muckety-mucks and with our own members. That's probably better than doing nothing."

It was more than a bit confusing. Strumi wanted to be sure he understood March's rather twisty-turny reasoning: "I hear you saying that you'd prefer 'going quietly'—not litigating—under the inclusive plan rather than litigating under the discriminating plan."

"That's right," March replied, "but we'd probably prefer suing even under the inclusive plan rather than accepting the RIF quietly, even on the inclusive plan. And we'd prefer going quietly under the discriminating plan least of all."

•   •   •   •   •

Late in the afternoon of the day after the Golden Gopher meeting, Roman Drnda received the call that he had half expected to get, given the evident dissatisfaction of Chris Clairy over Drnda's initial plan for the RIF. After some time Drnda recradled the phone, his head shaking and ears burning. Mary Martengrove was visiting in Drnda's office at the time. Kurvaszy—though somewhat skeptical of Mary's plan—had told her to show the three-way breakout to Drdna as a possible alternative.

The call had been from Clairy's boss, Senator Ben Loffel. "Chris Clairy really got the senator's dander up over the 'unfairness' of my RIF plan," Drnda explained to Mary.

Mary's alma mater, "U-Wis at Eau Claire," was on the edge of Ben Loffel's state senatorial district. Mary knew of Loffel's long history of support for affirmative action programs. His efforts had helped dozens of kids like herself get through college and into good jobs. Mary had grown up in Minnesota, but had she been a Wisconsin native, she might well have gone to Eau Claire under one of the in-state scholarship programs that Senator Loffel had fought through Wisconsin's state legislature. Furthermore, Loffel's aides—including Chris Clairy—had always tried to help the beneficiaries of the senator's educational programs when it came time to move on into entry-level government jobs. A high percentage of these Loffel protégés were (like Mary) women, Native Americans, or both. Under Drnda's tentative RIFfing plan, a disproportionate number of Loffel's protégés—Wisconsin-based jobholders—would be bumped out of work.

Drnda told Mary: "What Ben wants is exactly what Clairy suggested at the Golden Gopher meeting: Protect workers in each state separately. Since the seniority's mostly in the *F*s, and it just happens that the *F*s are mostly in Minnesota, the best way to protect junior Wisconsin people is by giving them their own competitive level so Minnesotans can't bump 'em."

"Here," Drnda said, wheeling his swivel chair over to the fax machine and drawing a sheet from its output tray. "Here's Loffel's idea of a 'fair' retention register" (see Table 2.3).

● ● ● ● ●

By coincidence "the sisters," as they called themselves, met in the same booth at the Golden Gopher Grill where Drnda, Kurvaszy, and the others had discussed the impending RIF a few days earlier. Lief Pink had been in the Larch City Big Sister program when she was in high school, with Bobbie Boo as her charge. Bobbie became Lisa Hepburn's big sister a few years later. The three remained close despite the differences in their ages. When Lisa came back home for visits from her Ag Department position across the bridge in Wisconsin, the sisters often got together for coffee and gossip. All three held USDA jobs; all three knew of the impending RIF; and all three knew that their names were on a retention register somewhere.

Lief Pink was not only the oldest but also the most knowledgeable about the ways of the civil service. She didn't like one bit what she surmised must be going on over at Roman Drnda's office. Lief—a federally funded extension agent specializing in dairy, sheep, and goat herd management—didn't care for the thought that Drnda had probably reduced her fourteen years of exemplary service to a single statistic, her standing on an impersonal retention register.

"We're three," Lief said to Bobbie and Lisa, "and on the probabilities alone, that means one of us will go." Which one? Lief knew that it would depend pretty much on the way Roman Drnda drew the retention registers. To her, that came close to saying that the decision about their jobs would be arbitrary.

"I need the job," Lisa Hepburn had repeated several times during their conversation. By dint of extraordinary grit and sacrifice, Lisa had scraped her way to a two-year's associate degree in management science at a local community college, after which she won a permanent job in the USDA. Lisa's family, trappers in the winter and

Table 2.3 Ben Loffel's/Chris Clairy's Suggested Retention Register Based on Separate State Competitive Levels

	General Schedule (GS) Grade	M/F Vet*	Specialization†	Job Location	Seniority	Average Job Rating	Performance Credit	Register Rank
Competitive Level M, confined to APTs working in Minnesota								
Abernaz	14	M, V	F	MN	26	5	+20	46
Ntaba‡	13	M V	F	MN	25	2		25
Quirk	9	M, V	A	MN	12	3	+12	24
Hackney	14	M, V	S	MN	15	2		15
Zerbe	11	M	F	MN	18	4	+16	34
Haberler	9	F	S	MN	21	3	+12	33
Phaltz	11	M	A	MN	20	3	+12	32
Houlihan	11	M	F	MN	19	3	+12	31
Pink	9	F	F	MN	14	4	+16	30
Sorenson	11	M	A	MN	14	3	+12	26
Jones, F	12	M	A	MN	13	3	+12	25
Jones, B	10	M	F	MN	21	2		21
Beckel	9	M	F	MN	9	3	+12	21
Boo	9	F	A	MN	8	3	+12	20
Praski	9	F	S	MN	6	3	+12	18
Laurie‡	11	F	A	MN	3	3	+12	15
Kinsallas	9	F	S	MN	3	3	+12	15
Smathers‡	11	M	S	MN	7	2		7
Martens	9	F	F	MN	2	2		2
Competitive Level W, confined to APTs working in Wisconsin								
Morton	9	M, V	F	WI	24	3	+12	36
Angiulio	13	M, V	S	WI	11	4	+16	29
Murchisan	7	M, V	F	WI	7	2		7
Two Bear‡	13	M	F	WI	21	4	+16	37
Madison	9	M	F	WI	11	3	+12	33
Eagle‡	12	F	S	WI	10	5	+20	30
Safter	11	M	A	WI	8	5	+20	28
Farnsworth	12	M	F	WI	9	4	+16	25
Loblick	10	F	A	WI	7	4	+16	23
West	13	M	A	WI	21	2		21
Dernbach	14	F	F	WI	18	2		18
Hepburn‡	9	F	S	WI	1	4	+16	17
Johnson	9	F	S	WI	3	3	+12	15
Charles‡	11	M	A	WI	3	3	+12	15
Edelweiss	10	F	S	WI	2	3	+12	14
Cloudie‡	12	M	F	WI	11	2		11
Doggett‡	11	F	S	WI	10	2		10
Sturdiven	9	F	A	WI	8	2		8
Schmeirer‡	9	F	A	WI	6	2		6
Manley‡	10	M	S	WI	3	2		3

*V = veterans' preference.

†F = field-worker; S = social worker; A = administrative staffer.

‡Native American or other minority affiliation.

on welfare the rest of the year, depended on her for financial support. She was the first woman from the band[4] to complete a degree; she was a role model for all the younger girls.

"You're pretty junior in rank, Lis'," Bobbie said, "and that makes you pretty bumpable, depending on how they draw the retention register." None of the three sisters uttered the thoughts they all had about "Lisa the 'twofer.'" As both a woman and a Native American, Lisa Hepburn counted for two credits in the affirmative action ledger that everyone thought existed in the locked drawer of a shadowy personnel manager somewhere in the civil service. Of course, any filling of affirmative action "quotas" was illegal, and USDA officials denied that personnel decisions were ever made on any bases other than seniority and merit. Nevertheless, most lower-level workers suspected that considerations of "political correctness" figured subtly in procedures for appointment, advancement, and separation.

Over their second cups, Lief—a single mother who thought she needed the work every bit as much as Bobbie and Lisa did—explained the ins and outs of a RIF to the other two: what "competitive areas," "commuting areas," "competitive levels," and the rest meant and how the system worked in practice.

Bobbie Boo worked out of the Jackson Building. Her job was to assess local crop-farmers' acreage-limitation applications. With eight years of tenured service, Bobbie thought herself too far into a government career to consider a switch, and yet she recognized her vulnerability to bumping from above. Furthermore, Bobbie recognized that her job skills would have relatively little carryover to nongovernment work if she were among the 1 in 3 who would bear the burden of the RIF and so would have to look for jobs outside the civil service.

"You know Roman Drnda," Bobbie said to Lief. "Is he the kind who tries to think about us as persons, instead of just names on lists?"

• • • • •

Across the alley from the Golden Gopher in his Jackson Building office, Roman Drnda sat, feeling the pressure. His friend and boss Secretary Nyby himself had called from Washington to tell Drnda that he'd better get on with it. The RIF order was official. Nyby had prodded Drnda: "If 'tis done, 'twere well it were done quickly."

Drnda looked again at the three drafts of retention registers. Indeed, he very much appreciated that the underlined names stood for real people, not for impersonal slots in a table of organization. Drnda's eyes flicked to the corner of his desk, where the RIFfing rules lay waiting for a final check over, lest his decision go too far afoul of any official requirement. Drnda knew that the boss was right: It was time to do what he had to do.

---

[4]*Band:* Members of the Ojibway Tribe—also called Chippewas—are organized into subunits known as bands. Each band has a geographic base. Lisa Hepburn (like Mary Martengrove) belongs to the Thunder Bay Band.

Questions for Discussion
· · · · · · · · · · · · · · · · ·

The following queries might help you frame your thoughts and organize a discussion of the case.

1. What's the story? Who must make what decisions, resolve what conflicts, take what actions? Bearing in mind that situational factors are all-important in case analysis, what circumstances of the action and conditions of the agents should be kept in mind when pondering the steps that the figures in the case should take?

2. How does the conflict discussed by Osborne and Gaebler—the conflict between organizational *mission* and organizational *rules*—present itself in this case? How should the changing pattern of demand for USDA services—a decreasing need for extension work, although technical assistance has traditionally been the focus of USDA employee skills—condition the way that Drnda manages the RIF? In what forms (if any) do the concerns we've identified in relation to underdetermination and overdetermination enter into the case?

3. Which ways of dealing with conditions of underdetermination—restructuring, litigation, strategic interaction, and so forth—seem most likely to be helpful to the figures in the case? Which of these terms best describes the situation in which Roman Drnda and Walt March find themselves? How should Drnda react when he gets wind of the strategy that March seems bent on using (namely, "go to court no matter which RIFfing strategy Drnda uses")? What do you think of the arguments March gives Guy Strumi for adopting this highly combative strategy? Since "circumstances make the case," what changes in the givens of the scenario might modify your views regarding the courses of action that Drnda and March should take?

4. Our reading from Frank Thompson underscores the multiple criteria that characteristically apply to civil service personnel actions. Which of the following criteria should a supervisor like Roman Drnda seek primarily to satisfy in an era of cutback management: performance of the agency (the mission), scrupulous adherence to civil service rules, compassion for workers who suddenly become vulnerable to layoffs, or deference to persons (such as sponsors in Congress) whose support may be needed to sustain the agency over the long haul? Taking Drnda's situation as an instance of an overdetermined administrative problem, what uses might he make of such techniques as priority setting, parameter changing, and policy adjusting?

5. In your opinion, whose retention register—Roman Drnda's (Table 2.1), Mary Martengrove's (Table 2.2), or Senator Loffel's (Table 2.3)—can be supported with the most persuasive arguments? "Discuss and defend"; justify your selection.

6. What's the appropriate way for Roman Drnda to think about the personal concerns of employees like "the sisters"? If you were running a RIF, would you try to keep the process impersonal and manage it by the numbers, or would you "put faces on the procedure" by trying to gain knowledge of individuals' specific situations? What do you see as the main pros and cons of each approach?

● ● ●

FOR FURTHER READING ━━━━━━━━━━━━━━━━━━━━━ ◆ ◆ ◆

PPA is probably the subfield of public administration that has been studied most intensively and over the longest stretch of years—going back at least to the period of the civil service reformers. Thus it isn't surprising that a well-developed literature exists. Some of the best overviews of the subject are

> Dresang, Dennis L., *Public Personnel Management and Public Policy* (New York: Longman, 1991).
> Nigro, F. A., and L. G. Nigro, *The New Public Personnel Administration* (Itasca IL: Peacock, 1991).
> Shafritz, Jay, et al., *Personnel Management in Government,* (New York: Marcel Dekker, 1992).
> Sylvia, Ronald D., *Public Personnel Administration* (Belmont CA: Wadsworth, 1994).

Arguably the most influential interpretetive essay on the subject of PPA in recent years is

> Mosher, Frederick C., *Democracy and the Public Service* (New York: Oxford, 1968); this is still probably the best, most readable introductory essay on PPA.

The standard history of our federal civil service (which, unfortunately, breaks off in the late 1950s) is

> Van Riper, Paul, *A History of the United States Civil Service* (Evanston IL: Row, Peterson, 1958).

Van Riper's book might be consulted in conjunction with the following study, which is particularly helpful on the ideological and moral motivations of the civil service reformers:

> Nelson, William, *The Roots of American Bureaucracy* (Cambridge MA: Harvard U. Press, 1982).

The best recent books on the higher civil service and political-appointee ranks are

> Heclo, Hugh, *A Government of Strangers: Executive Politics in Washington* (Washington: Brookings Institution, 1977).
> Light, Paul, *Thickening Government: Federal Hierarchy and the Diffusion of Accountability* (Washington: Brookings Institution, 1995).

The two standard works on the representativeness of civil service systems in the United States are

> Kingsley, J. Donald, *Representative Bureaucracy* (Yellow Springs OH: Antioch U. Press, 1944).
> Krislov, Sam, and David Rosenbloom, *Representative Bureaucracy* (New York: Praeger, 1981).

Finally, excellent brief overview treatments of the civil service systems and their contemporary problems by two of most knowledgeable scholars writing in this subfield these days are

Ingraham, Patricia, and David Rosenbloom, "The New Public Personnel and the New Public Service," 46 *Public Administration Review* (March–April 1989), 116.

Ingraham, Patricia, and David Rosenbloom, "Political Foundations of the American Federal Service: Rebuilding a Crumbling Base," 50 *Public Administration Review* (March–April 1990), 210.

▼◆●■▼◆●■▼◆●■▼◆●■▼◆

CHAPTER 3

Introduction to Organizational Theory

The second item on Woodrow Wilson's three-point agenda for the upgrading of public administration, you might recall, looked to improvements in the *organization* of the public service. Wilson and most of his colleagues in the Progressive movement regarded rationality as generally applicable as well as highly desirable in human activity. They therefore assumed that it should be possible to develop a **generic theory of organizations,** a theory that would rest on universal truths of human motivation and behavior. "Organization as a technical question," some exponents of classical thought called it.

To the Progressives, bureaucracy was the paradigm of rational and efficient organizational structure. Today we might consider the Progressives' faith in bureaucracy as quaint, even naive. Yet the bureaucratic form endures, and "restructuring the organization" in accordance with bureaucratic principles remains a common way to deal with problems of inefficiency and underdetermination. The persistence of bureaucracy in private organizations such as corporations, as well as at all levels of our government, suggests that powerful historical or theoretical causes may be at work. Organizational theorists try to identify and understand the causes that explain the attractions of this distinctive structure.

We turn now to the contributions of some of most influential of all organizational theorists, members of the so-called classical school: preeminently Frederick Winslow Taylor and the other enthusiasts of scientific management; Max Weber, the seminal theorist of modern bureaucracy; and Luther Gulick, the intellectual leader of the administrative management school. During the heyday of classical thought—roughly, from the 1880s to the late 1930s or early 1940s—theorists such as Taylor, Weber, and Gulick pretty much assumed that structural solutions could be found for most if not all problems of organizational communication and control. By "restructuring," the classicists usually meant changing the way that jobs within an organization were clustered, the aim being to group complementary functions together under the jurisdiction of a single director. The director was to coordinate the activities of subordinates using the technique that the organizational theorist Henry Mintzberg has called **direct supervision.** Mintzberg developed his concept of direct supervision in a now-standard work in the field in which he presented a useful three-way classification of the paradigms of coordination.

71

Henry Mintzberg on Three Paradigms of Coordination

Every organized human activity—from the making of pots to the placing of a man on the moon—gives rise to two fundamental and opposing requirements: the *division of labor* into various tasks to be performed and the *coordination* of these tasks to accomplish the activity. The structure of an organization can be defined simply as the sum total of the ways in which it divides its labor into distinct tasks and then achieves coordination among them. . . .

Mutual Adjustment

Mutual adjustment achieves the coordination of work by the simple process of informal communication. Under mutual adjustment, control of the work rests in the hands of the doers. . . . Because it is such a simple coordinating mechanism, mutual adjustment is naturally used in the very simplest of organizations: for example, by two people in a canoe or a few in a pottery studio. Paradoxically, it is also used in the most complicated, but because . . . it is the only one that works under extremely difficult circumstances. Consider the organization charged with putting a man on the moon for the first time. Such an activity requires an incredibly elaborate division of labor, with thousands of specialists doing all kinds of specific jobs. But at the outset, no one can be sure exactly what needs to be done. That knowledge develops as the work unfolds. So in the final analysis, despite the use of other coordinating mechanisms, the success of the undertaking depends primarily on the ability of the specialists to adapt to each other along their uncharted route, not altogether unlike the two people in the canoe.

Direct Supervision

As an organization outgrows its simplest state—more than five or six people at work in a pottery studio, fifteen people paddling a war canoe—it tends to turn to a second coordinating mechanism. Direct supervision achieves coordination by having one individual take responsibility for the work of others, issuing instructions to them and monitoring their actions. . . . In effect, one brain coordinates several hands, as in the case of the supervisor of the pottery studio or the caller of the stroke in the war canoe.

Consider the structure of an American football team. Here the division of labor is quite sharp: eleven players are distinguished by the work they do, its location on the field, and even its physical requirements. The slim halfback stands behind the line of scrimmage and carries the ball; the squat tackle stands on the line and blocks. Mutual adjustments do not suffice to coordinate their work, so a field leader is named, called the quarterback, and he coordinates the work by calling the plays.

Standardization

Work can also be coordinated without mutual adjustment or direct supervision. It can be *standardized*. . . . Coordination is achieved on the drawing board, so to speak, before the work is undertaken. The workers on the automobile assembly line and the surgeons in the hospital operating room need not worry about coordinating with their colleagues under ordinary circumstances—they know exactly what to expect of them and proceed accordingly. . . .

The . . . school of thought . . . popularized in the English-speaking world by Luther Gulick and Lyndahl Urwick (1937) was concerned primarily with formal authority, in effect with the role of direct supervision in the organization. These writers popularized such terms as *unity of command* (the notion that a "subordinate" should have only a single "superior"), and *span of control* (the number of subordinates reporting to a single superior).

[A] second school of thought really includes two groups that, from our point of view, promoted the same issue—the standardization of work throughout the organization. Both groups were established at the turn of the century by outstanding researchers, one on either side of the Atlantic Ocean. In America,

Frederick Taylor led the "Scientific Management" movement, whose main preoccupation was the programming of the contents of operating work—that of pig iron handlers, coal shovelers, and the like. In Germany, Max Weber wrote of machine-like, or "bureaucratic" structures where activities were formalized by rules, job descriptions, and training.

And so for about half of this century, organization structure meant a set of official, standardized work relationships built around a tight system of formal authority.

From Henry Mintzberg, *The Structuring of Organizations* (Englewood Cliffs NJ: Prentice-Hall, 1979), pp. 2–10.

Under the paradigm of direct supervision, lower-level workers know what to do because they get marching orders from an organizational higher-up. Though direct supervision is the paradigm of coordination that is most closely associated with the bureaucratic paradigm of structure, as Mintzberg points out, the administrators of the classical period also emphasized the coordinative technique of **standardization.** Functions that could be reduced to common routines were more easily grouped together and taught to workers in specialized units.

As we will see, many public administrationists today believe that the governance process has come to involve too many functions with too many shifting interactions for a clear-cut, once-and-for-all grouping of tasks. These theorists reject the approach of the classicists and argue instead for flexible, *non*bureaucratic organizational models. In general, proponents of this view also contend that the job of coordinating subordinates' actions from above has become too difficult for assignment to a supreme director, even when the director has the help of a battery of analyst-advisers and planners called "staff officers." Therefore, contemporary organizational theorists usually emphasize the third paradigm of coordination, **mutual adjustment,** over direct supervision and standardization. Mutual adjustment, these theorists say, is the best way to coordinate the activities of individuals who must constantly learn new skills, deal with decision makers not under their own control, and rearrange relationships with one another.

SECTION 1 Classical Organizational Theory: The Bureaucratic Paradigm

Frederick Taylor (1856–1915), the eloquent proponent of the movement that his disciples simply called Taylorism but was known more generally as **scientific management,** first attained prominence in the 1890s as a leading figure in the newly formed American Society of Mechanical Engineers. The engineer's habits of orderly, quantitative, scientific thought, Taylor thought, displayed exactly the qualities that were needed to develop sound management for industrial America.

Perhaps better than any other writer of his time, Taylor expressed the characteristic Progressive desire to move in all departments of human endeavor beyond *craft knowledge*—knowledge that's empirical, intuitive, and artful rather than scientific in nature. Taylor hoped to create a "science of work"—in effect, a universalized version of Woodrow Wilson's "science of administration"—based on quantitative study of production processes. Taylor perfected his ideas by actually observing workers in machine shops and steel mills, where he sought numerical measures of the time required to perform each step in an orderly sequence of operations. Shoveling coal, a favorite example of Taylor's, required a laborer to engage in a specific sequence of bendings, liftings, and turnings. Once the discrete steps in this sequence had been identified, precise procedures for the easiest, speediest execution of the function could be formulated and taught to workers.

"[F]ixed principle," Taylor wrote, must replace "rule-of-thumb methods."[1] Action based on fixed principle assumed a scientific base, an understanding of causal theory so complete and reliable that a problem solver could say with certainty: To achieve result y in the most efficient way, do x. Taylor's idea of the One Best Way—the scientifically established optimal procedure, to be followed by the worker in a highly standardized manner with as little conscious thought as possible—was an expression of the engineering approach as he understood it. As we've noted, the One Best Way was an idea for which the scientific managers are remembered (and often ridiculed) even today.

Organizational Implications of Taylor's "Science of Work"

When the One Best Way of completing an individual job had been established, the larger task of combining functions and dividing assignments into an efficient overall organization could be undertaken. Common elements in an operation could be grouped together in whatever way would maximize the contribution of each subunit to the whole. Cooperative human activity could be organized and work processes could be structured for maximum efficiency. Ideally, the specialized functions assigned to each unit in the organization would consist of standardized activities that all members of the work team could perform in identical fashion.

Interestingly, Taylor's preferred organizational model differed in significant ways from the pyramidal structure of most formal bureaucracies. In effect, Taylor reversed the familiar "one boss over several workers" imagery and proposed a "several bosses to each worker" doctrine instead. Taylor referred to the pyramidal form of organization as "military." In the military organization, a single top commander (or factory manager, or agency head) barks orders to a few lieutenants, who then pass them on to a larger number of sergeants, and so forth down the line to the privates in the trenches. Taylor, however, thought that pyramid builders missed the central problem of modern industrial organization, which was to match skills (expertise, information, and aptness to do the job—whatever its level of intellectual or physical demands) with positions on the production line.

Skills had to be fitted exactly to jobs. Taylor recognized the critical need in modern organizations to acquire and employ expert information. To Taylor, information included messages of command based on authority as well as messages containing craft and professional knowledge. No one should know less—but neither should anyone know more—than his own job absolutely required. Because higher levels of skill implied higher personnel costs, Taylor argued that an organizational designer should fill a given slot with a worker who possessed the minimum skills for the task. The pyramidal form, Taylor thought, demanded too much in the way of skills at the top. The pyra-

[1]*Scientific Management* (New York: HarperCollins [1911], 1947); see for example p. 63.

midal chain of command also prevented the experts at the pinnacle of the organization ("brain workers," Taylor called them) from giving needed guidance to workers lower down in the hierarchy. **Functional management** was Taylor's way to ensure that the right information would get to the workers who needed it at the right time (see Box 3.1).

Taylor was especially interested in the "how to" knowledge of the machine-shop worker, but he saw no reason why the notion of the One Best Way couldn't be applied as aptly to the work of clerks as it did to the labor of employees on a production line. Scientific management could revolutionize work in the office, as Taylor thought it would in the factory. The apparent transferability of scientific principles from the blue-collar world of the steel mill to the white-collar world of public administration suggested the emergence of a social form so basic that it transcended the distinctions between private corporation and public agency, between manual labor and administrative action. That emerging social form was, of course, bureaucracy.

Bureaucracy as a Paradigm of Organizational Structure

Bureaucracy. The very term calls to mind the writings of Max Weber (1864–1920), who set forth the ideal type of this organizational form. *Ideal type* was Weber's own term, coined to emphasize that his aim was not to draw a literal picture of a typical modern organization but to give a logical description of a phenomenon in its purest form—its paradigm. A social scientist can analyze a system by assessing how closely it resembles its paradigm or ideal type.

In one ideal type of authority system studied by Weber, the members of an organization acknowledge that a leader is supreme only if he or she possesses an almost-magical ability to inspire followers; Weber called the special grace possessed by such a leader *charisma*. In a **charismatic organization**, the relationships of control are intensely dependent on the personality of the leader. In a second type of authority system, known as a **traditional organization**, a leader's orders are acknowledged as legitimate only if they are in accordance with custom. In Weber's third system, the **rational-legal organization**, citizens accept authority because it is rationally justified—not necessarily charismatic or traditional, but "reasonable"—and organized in an orderly way. According to Weber, precisely the qualities of discipline, rationality, and orderliness that one finds in the third system explained the inexorable pressures that organizational designers feel to adopt the bureaucratic model.

A Weberian bureaucracy is a permanent organization. Individual workers may move in and out; the mission of the organization may change over time; but the basic structure remains. The personnel system, organizational structure, and pattern of authority in a bureaucracy have the following distinctive characteristics:

1. *Merit.* Recruitment and promotion of workers in a bureaucracy is based on merit rather than on "connections" or any quality other than a worker's objective ability to perform the assigned functions of the specialized unit.

2. *Tenure.* A bureaucracy offers secure employment, supporting the further expectation that steady advancement up a career ladder will be the reward of good performance in the job. Tenure in Weber's analysis, as in the minds of the American civil service reformers, would ensure political neutrality and encourage faithful

BOX 3.1 ■■■

Frederick Taylor on Functional Management in a Machine Shop

The foreman usually endeavors to lighten his burdens by delegating his duties to the various assistant foremen or gang bosses in charge of lathes, planers, milling machines, vise work, etc. Each of these men is then called upon to perform duties of almost as great variety as those of the foreman himself. The difficulty in obtaining in one man the variety of special information and the different mental and moral qualities necessary to perform all of the duties demanded of those men has been clearly summarized in the following list of the nine qualities which go to make up a well rounded man:

Brains. Education. Special or technical knowledge; manual dexterity or strength. Tact. Energy. Energy. Grit. Honesty. Judgment or common sense. . . . Good health.

Plenty of men who possess only three of the above qualities can be hired at any time for laborers' wages. Add four of these qualities together and you get a higher priced man. The man combining five of these qualities begins to be hard to find, and those with six, seven, and eight are almost impossible to get. . . .

[In functional management] each workman, instead of coming in direct contact with the management at one point only, namely, through his gang boss, receives his detailed orders and help directly from eight different bosses, each of whom performs his own particular function. Four of these bosses [route clerk, instruction-card clerk, time-and-cost clerk, shop disciplinarian] are in the planning room. . . . Four others [gang bosses, speed bosses, inspectors, repair bosses] are in the shop and personally help the men in their work, each boss helping in his own particular line or function only. . . . Thus the grouping of the men in the shop is entirely changed, each workman belonging to eight different groups according to the particular functional boss whom he happens to be working under at the moment. . . .

A glance at the nine qualities . . . will show that each of these men requires but a limited number of the nine qualities in order to successfully fill his position; and that the special knowledge which he must acquire forms only a small part of that needed by the old style gang boss.

From "Shop Management," in Frederick Winslow Taylor, *Scientific Management* (New York: Harper and Row [1911], 1947), pp. 95–100.

■■■

job performance since workers wouldn't have to fear reprisals simply because they carried out duties that were unpopular with party politicians in power.

3. *Specialization.* A bureaucracy has division of labor based on separate units (traditionally called *bureaus*) whose members perform specialized—and preferably standardized—tasks.

4. *Hierarchy.* A bureaucracy's structure is pyramidal, with a single head at the top and tiers of subordinate managers who direct and coordinate the work of employees in the specialized units beneath them.

5. *Rationalization.* Bureaucratic authority is rooted in the expertise of those who occupy supervisory positions in the hierarchy and is exercised in such as way as to achieve results efficiently.

6. *Rule-boundedness.* A bureaucracy organizes work under explicit rules, preferably in written form, to ensure the regularity of procedures for those who are inside the structure and standard treatment for the outsiders with whom they do business. Rule-boundedness is intended both to ensure that authority remains rationalized and to prevent arbitrary action or abuses of administrative discretion. We'll consider the phenomenon of rule-boundedness in some detail in Chapter 4.

Weber extolled bureaucratic coordination as "superior to any other form in precision, in stability, in the stringency of its discipline, and in its reliability." A bureaucracy can harmonize the work of many individuals, each of whom possesses specialized skills. Weber commented, in oft-quoted words:

> The decisive reason for the advance of bureaucratic organization has always been its purely technical superiority over any other form of organization. The fully developed bureaucratic mechanism compares with other organizations exactly as does the machine with the non-mechanical modes of production. . . . Its specific nature, which is welcomed by capitalism, develops the more perfectly the more the bureaucracy is "dehumanized," the more completely it succeeds in eliminating from official business love, hatred, and all purely personal, irrational, and emotional elements which escape calculation.[2]

Weber versus Taylor, Control versus Efficiency

Weber argued that, as an instrument which responds mechanically to orders issued by a leader, a bureaucratic organization is a powerful tool of social control. Weber's emphasis on control suggests why, in his ideal type, he rejected functional management, under which each worker would have several specialized bosses. Taylor had justified functional management as a means of economizing on scarce talents. Because it would be difficult to find commanders with the full range of skills needed to run complex organizations, Taylor emphasized the need to divide labor among supervisors as well as among their subordinates. However, the multiplication of supervisory roles, as in functional organization, also multiplied the difficulties of control. What if a worker's different bosses gave inconsistent orders? One obvious way to minimize this danger—Weber's way—was to require that all orders emanate from a single head. The concept that underlay this approach would later come to be called the **unitary principle.**

On the other hand, Weberian unity of command quickly ran into the problem foreseen by Taylor. In Weber's executive pyramid, each worker has a single boss, and the

[2]"Bureaucracy," in Gerth and Mills, eds., *From Max Weber* (New York: Oxford U. Press [c. 1910], 1946), pp. 215–216.

entire structure of authority builds to a single peak. But few individuals can master all the knowledge needed to plan and supervise the efforts of large numbers of workers, even when they have intervening ranks of staff officers to help them. Under the unitary approach, different supervisors wouldn't have to coordinate decisions with one another. But—just as difficult—a single commander at the top would have to be able to coordinate solutions to many different problems within his or her own head. To do so, the leader would need information from every recess of the organization, information packaged and presented in a digestible form. The burden of high command under the Weberian model creates a need for sophisticated information systems, which is one reason why the acquisition, processing, and utilization of information by managers is a central topic in contemporary administrative study.

The Administrative Management School

In the United States, the move to apply scientific principles and bureaucratic theory to public administration culminated in the work of President Franklin D. Roosevelt's "Committee on Administrative Management," chaired by a prominent public administrationist, Louis Brownlow.

"The president needs help," went a famous line from the 1937 Brownlow report. The executive branch of the federal government had grown rapidly since the late nineteenth century, and without apparent design or discipline. No chief executive, the Brownlow committee members felt—not even one with the leadership skills of FDR— could make efficient use of the vast but rather ramshackle administrative apparatus at his disposal. Fortunately (Brownlow and his cohorts believed), help was available in the form of certain universal principles of efficient organization. According to the administrative managers, President Roosevelt could best help himself by reorganizing the executive branch in accordance with these **canons of efficiency.** The administrative managers influenced the reshaping of the American presidency in the late 1930s—the modern Executive Office of the President was created along lines recommended in the Brownlow report—as well as the structuring of Allied military command relations during World War II.

The Brownlow committee members drew heavily on the work of British, French, and American administrative theorists who, working by and large independently of one another in the late 1920s and throughout the 1930s, pursued the quest for universally valid organizational principles. Luther Gulick (1892–1993), a Brownlow committee member, co-edited a volume of essays by these theorists. This volume, completed in collaboration with the organizational theorist Lyndahl Urwick and entitled *Papers on the Science of Administration,* appeared in 1937. *Papers* is still widely regarded as the authoritative statement of the classical canons. As you consider the canons of efficiency, take particular note of the emphasis that the administrative managers gave to the principle of specialization (what Gulick called "work division") and to the challenge of coordination, which becomes more difficult as the number of specialized subunits proliferates.

The Structure of the Executive Pyramid

What, ideally, should the executive pyramid look like? What should be its basic structure, its dimensions, and overall shape?

1.   *Centralization.* The administrative managers wrote of the need in any organization for a "supreme coordinating authority" at the apex of the executive pyramid. Commands from the chief executive are just what the word implies: *commands,* not proposals for discussion and debate. Ideally, the centralization of administrative authority ensures a single statement of organizational goals, providing coherent direction to all who are lower down in the organization.

2.   *Hierarchy.* Authority is graduated from the supreme power wielder at the top through successively lower tiers of subordinate management. Gulick elaborated three subcanons:

a. Subordinates' responsibilities are precisely defined, resulting in increasingly detailed descriptions of duties, such that discretion diminishes as one moves lower and lower in the hierarchy.

b. Supervisors at each level have total responsibility for every aspect of their respective subordinates' work; there's no division of supervisory duties, as in Taylor's functional organization. In Gulick's words, "A workman subject to orders from several superiors will be confused, inefficient, and irresponsible."[3]

c. Clear, unbroken authority runs from the top of the hierarchy to every corner of the undertaking.

3.   *Span of Control.* If a supervisor is to have complete responsibility over subordinates, in accordance with canon 2b, it is necessary that she or he closely monitor, evaluate, and ultimately control the subordinate's activities. For supervision to be effective, the right number of workers must be assigned to a boss—as many as the boss can fully control, but no more, lest his or her supervisory capacities be swamped. (See Sketch 3.1.)

Specialization and Distribution of Functions

In a famous passage of his 1776 book *Wealth of Nations,* Adam Smith estimated that pin making could be made vastly more efficient if functions were divided among each of ten workers, assembly-line style, instead of having employees individually complete all the tasks necessary to produce a single pin. With division of labor, one worker straightens the wire, another sharpens it, a third puts heads on semifinished pins, and so forth. The same division-of-labor principle applies in administrative organization, giving rise to the classical theorists' second set of canons. In Gulick's words, "Work division is the foundation of organization; indeed, the reason for organization."

4.   *Specialization.* All members of the organization beneath the peak of the pyramid are grouped into subunits with their own specialized functions. Specialized assignments permit workers to become expert in their duties—in other words, to build up knowledge. Thus specialization represents an important organizational means to solve the informational problem that is central to modern enterprise. (We'll shortly see this principle expressed in the "specialized-line" version of the organizational pyramid.)

---

[3]"Notes on the Theory of Organization," in Gulick and Urwick, eds., *Papers on the Science of Administration* (Clifton NJ: Kelly [1937], 1973), p. 9. All Gulick quotes come from this essay.

As an organization increases in size, there is the danger that the number of subordinates assigned to a given supervisor will grow beyond the supervisor's managerial ability. The chief executive may have to add staff assistants and middle managers to transmit orders, monitor workers lower in the hierarchy, and communicate information about goings-on within the organization. One name for this process—which we'll discuss more fully in Section 3 of this chapter—is **radial expansion.**

The addition of personnel at intermediate tiers reduces each manager's span of control, but does so at the cost of **organizational layering** (also called *organizational thickening*), with a resultant increase in the height of the structure, the steepness of its authority gradient, and often in the difficulty of getting ungarbled messages from top to bottom or vice versa.

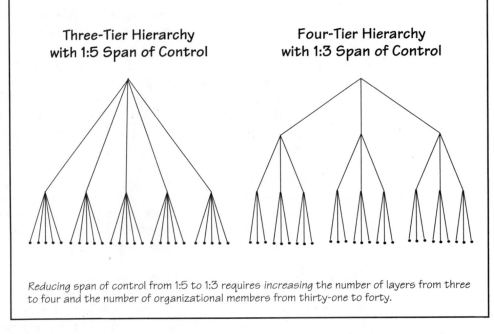

Three-Tier Hierarchy
with 1:5 Span of Control

Four-Tier Hierarchy
with 1:3 Span of Control

Reducing span of control from 1:5 to 1:3 requires increasing the number of layers from three to four and the number of organizational members from thirty-one to forty.

Sketch 3.1 Shape of the Executive Pyramid as a Function of Span of Control and Number of Layers

5.   Standardization. The functions of a given unit should, wherever possible, be standardized—in part because, as noted already, functions that can be standardized can also more easily be grouped together in specialized subdivisions of the organization.

6.   Homogeneity. "[T]he efficiency of a group working together," Gulick wrote, "is directly related to the homogeneity of the work they are performing, of the processes they are utilizing, and of the purposes which actuate them." Gulick's guidance for the grouping of homogeneous functions applied primarily to the portion of an organization that theorists refer to as "the line" as contrasted with "the staff." The **line-staff distinction** is itself, of course, an extension of the division-of-labor principle. The line consists of those units which perform the primary mission of the agency. In a police department, the line workers are the beat cops and the detectives, not the booking sergeants and the jail keepers. In an army, the line comprises the actual fighting force, not intelligence-gathering or supply units. In a state college, it is the classroom teachers who are "on the line," not the campus maintenance workers or the administrators in the registrar's office.

Gulick wrote that the subunits in the line portions of an organization, such as a police force, could be assembled on the basis of any one of four primary aggregative principles:

Purpose (for example, solving crimes after the fact, deterring future crimes, providing social services)

Process (nonuniformed detective work, foot patrol, patrol using police cars, crowd control duty)

Persons or things dealt with or served (victims of violent crime, traffic violators, abused children or battered spouses)

Place (1st precinct, 2d precinct, and so forth; within each precinct, beat 1, beat 2, and so forth)

7. Aggregation. Homogeneity with respect, say, to the kind of work performed might require diversity with respect to technology or purpose. The organizer must identify the **primary basis of aggregation** and then try to minimize the inefficiencies that secondary instances of nonhomogeneity will inevitably cause by carefully selecting a **secondary basis of aggregation** and—if need be—tertiary and even quarternary bases.

The traditional organization of an urban police department illustrates the processes of primary and secondary aggregation of subunits. The patrol function (officers walking beats or cruising in squad cars) has always been at the center of American police practice. In patrol, the dominant basis of aggregation is geographic. Within each precinct, officers individually or in teams work distinct beats. Within each precinct, however, there may also be further breakouts of a nongeographic nature. Some officers will work the lockup unit, others will join teams of gang-suppression experts, and so forth. The organizational principles of these supplementary units represent secondary bases of aggregation.

8. Scale. The volume of work produced in an administrative organization limits functional specialization, just as the extent of the market limits the division of labor in economic life. It would have made sense, in Adam Smith's example, for a factory owner to reorganize production with division of labor to increase the output to 4,800 pins per day (instead of the 200 that Smith estimated could be made without division of labor) *only if* a large enough market for pins existed to justify the increase in output. The larger the scale of an organization's operations, the greater the opportunity for specialization within it.

The Theory of the Line-Staff Distinction

We have seen that Taylor translated the functional distinction between the thinkers who analyze a job and the laborers who actually perform it into a structural distinction. Taylor stressed the need for brain workers to conduct studies and develop optimal procedures. Hands-on operators would then do the actual work, following the routines (the One Best Way) that the brain workers had devised. In the vocabulary of classical organizational theory, the workers in the former group belong to the staff. The members of the staff departments have the right to demand information from individuals in the line units. Based on data from sources both internal and external to the organization, staff officials give advice to the commander—*not* directly to the line operators who eventually will have to carry out the main work of the organization. In theory, the leader considers the staffers' advice and decides what action to take. The leader issues appropriate orders to the senior-most line officers, who transmit more detailed versions of the leader's commands down the line for implementation.

Even the classical theorists recognized that the process rarely works in real life the way it does in theory. Staff officials in most large organizations constantly interact with the line officers even though they have they have no formal command authority over the latter. There are good reasons for this departure from strict theory. Staffers normally work near the pinnacle of the pyramid and therefore should "know the commander's mind" better than line officers in the field do. In practice, therefore, line officials regularly try to tap into the knowledge that their counterparts on the staff possess. In the real world of modern organizational life, staff officials spend much of their time in the process of **informal coordination**—explaining, negotiating, and sometimes cajoling line officials to behave as they think the chief executive wishes and, occasionally, threatening them from the privileged positions that they occupy near the seat of ultimate power.

Intervention by staff officials in the command chain is natural and often necessary, notwithstanding that the practice of informal coordination breaks the direct line of communication from the commander to lower-level line officials (canon 2c). Informal coordination may effectively create a system resembling either Taylor's scheme of functional management or Mintzberg's coordination by mutual adjustment. In any event, organizational control in most complex structures becomes more than an exercise in direct supervision. Through the process of informal coordination, it becomes a continuing exercise of information exchange, persuasion, and negotiation. Members of the staff and members of the line stay in regular and direct touch, although in theory they're to communicate only indirectly, by way of staff recommendations which the leader converts into orders for the line to execute.

The Organizational Trade-Off

Gathering the varieties of classical theory up and sorting them out yields three broad approaches to organization: the *unitary* approach, the *staff* approach, and the *specialized-line* approach.

In the **unitary approach,** an all-knowing commander develops plans and issues the orders that orchestrate everyone else's activities into a coherent whole. The accuracy of reports from below is assumed, so there's little need for staff officers to glean through the ranks for evidence of errant behavior. Obedience to authority is also assumed, so the commander can trust that an order will be followed once it has been issued. The challenge in this model is to find the extraordinary leader who can process all the needed information in his or her own head. Absent such an individual, staffers will have to support a less-than-all-knowing commander by gathering intelligence, analyzing it, and preparing plans for the leader's review and approval—thereby bringing us to the second organizational approach.

The **staff approach** emphasizes those whom Taylor called the "brain workers." It entails the creation of a cadre of intelligence gatherers, analysts, and planners who do most of the organization's thinking. The challenge is for these staff officers to communicate what they have learned in a persuasive, digestible form both to the commander at the pinnacle and, through the process of informal coordination, to the hands-on line workers in the ranks.

In yet a third scheme, the **specialized-line approach,** an organizer can deemphasize the staff and can form teams of specialized frontline workers. The narrowness of the workers' tasks within each specialized-line unit should permit them to learn their jobs so well that they needn't depend on "brain workers" for advice. In a sense, specialized-line workers are expected to become their own staff officers. On the other hand, the leaders of the specialized teams must coordinate their activities with one another, since, by hypothesis, they function in an organization with a relatively weak supporting staff apparatus. Unfortunately, the difficulties of constant coordination may distract unit leaders from their line responsibilities and, in the extreme case, may lead to a sense of fragmentation and incoherence throughout the organization. With the specialized-line approach, problems of underdetermination may originate more in the structure of the organization than in the complexity of the issues.

A central issue in classical organizational theory—arguably, *the* central issue—involves the location of authority and expert knowledge. Should authority be centralized at the pinnacle, or should it be decentralized throughout the structure? Should all knowledge be imputed to a single supreme coordinating authority? Should it be the province of a staff of "brain workers," or should an effort be made to encourage the development of expertise in specialized frontline units? As Sketch 3.2 suggests, all three approaches are broadly consistent with the pyramidal outline of the bureaucratic paradigm. In general, however, effective organization requires trade-offs among the three approaches. Pure cases can rarely be achieved in the real world, and so an organizer must try to find an optimal point within a field bounded by the unitary, staff, and specialized-line approaches.

SECTION 2
Dealing with Goal Diversity: Supervision in the Modern Organization

The classical theorists—and especially the administrative managers—lavished so much thought on the principle of span of control primarily because of the importance of *supervision* in an organization that was to be both hierarchical in structure and efficient in operation. The aim of the administrative managers, of course, was to identify the ratio of supervisors to subordinates, as needed for adequate surveillance and given the nature of the work, without overdoing the numbers of intermediate managers and thus wasting personnel. The classical thinkers' emphasis on direct supervision reflected—in addition to their acceptance of the bureaucratic paradigm as a matter of general intellectual conviction—their expectation that employees would understand and diligently obey commands. Weber, Gulick, and most of the other classicists didn't much worry that subordinates might pursue personal goals different from those of their organizational leaders. (Among classical theorists, Frederick Winslow Taylor was the exception; in fact,

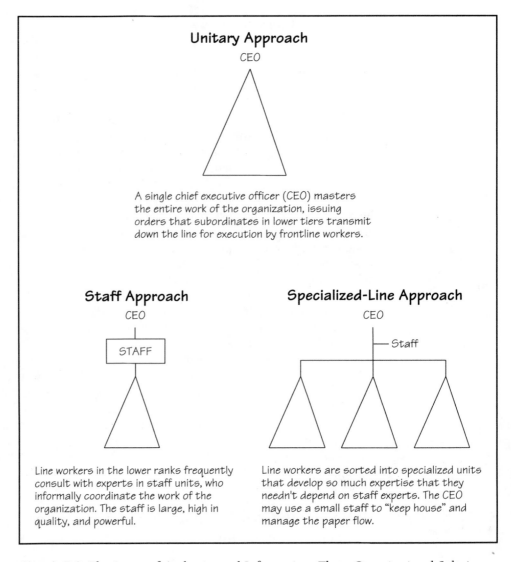

Sketch 3.2 The Locus of Authority and Information: Three Organizational Solutions

Taylor's study of organizational dynamics originated in his concern over the problem known in his time as "soldiering," or slacking on the job—what today is simply called "shirking" or, more pretentiously, *moral hazard*.)

Viewed in retrospect, the assumption that workers would be highly tractable seems almost as naive as was the classical thinkers' belief in the superiority and "rationality" of the bureaucratic paradigm of structure. This assumption is at odds with the phenomenon we identified in Chapter 1 as a common cause of the problem of underdetermination: **goal diversity.** Goal diversity originates in the organizational process itself. More precisely, it originates in the variety of interests and values that individuals bring to this process. The individual is a flesh-and-blood human being with personal preferences as well as obligations to the group. Gather a number of individuals within a single structure, ask that they coordinate their actions over time, and disagreements are all but inevitable. Divergencies are also likely between the goals of individuals and groups, on the one hand, and the objectives of the organization, on the other. For these reasons, most theorists today recognize that every organization is a **mixed-mode entity** which combines opportunities for *cooperation* with the potential for *conflict* (see Box 3.2).

An organization is in trouble if its official decision makers announce a policy, only to see it ignored or even subverted because those who are supposed to carry it out are battling with one another or pursuing goals of their own. Such instances of incomplete control are among the more common examples of the problem of underdetermination in modern organizations. Of course, some kinds of organizations are more apt than others either to provide conditions that encourage shirking or subversive behavior or to make it possible for members to engage in such conduct without getting caught. It is an important focus of organizational thought to identify the kinds of structures that permit—or even encourage—shirking or subversion by workers. (*Shirking* refers to laziness or malingering on the job; *subverting* is behavior that actively undercuts the policies set by organizational higher-ups.)

One of the most problem-prone organizational situations, we noted in Chapter 2, occurs under conditions of asymmetric information. Workers who, for whatever reason, have the disposition to pursue interests of their own will find it easier to act in ways that are harmful to the organization if they know their behavior is shielded from surveillance or if, even under surveillance, supervisors find it difficult to assess workers' performances with any accuracy. We've seen that a condition of asymmetric information exists whenever the superior in a relationship knows less than the subordinate does about any aspect of the situation—about the technical requirements of a particular job, for example, or about the employee's diligence in performance. Asymmetric information seems especially apt to cause problems when the implementers are **street-level bureaucrats.** Building and health inspectors, police officers, probation officials, and social outreach workers, among others, carry out their duties for the most part alone, in decentralized locations, and without close supervision. For another example, consider the goings-on in a typical state college system. *You* might see what the professors do (or don't do) in class, but you can be sure that their deans don't know with any certainty; and the state legislators who appropriate faculty salaries haven't got even a clue!

As we noted in Chapter 2, all these problems of asymmetric information may be worsened in a bureaucratic structure. There's a nice irony here: Hierarchical organization, although usually justified as a way to ensure the close surveillance of subordinates by supervisors in the next tier above them, may actually contribute to a pattern of asymmetric information. Hierarchy may provide the means for frontline workers to free themselves from effective surveillance by supervisors who are more than a layer or two above them. As the number of layers increases, so do the opportunities to lose information going both up and down the chain of command. Instructions get garbled as they're passed from the tip of the pyramid down to the frontline workers. And information about what's really happening gets distorted (or, maybe, purposely suppressed) as it travels from bottom to top. Together, these phenomena are known as **information absorption.** The expertise of lower-level employees can ensure competence; but it can

BOX 3.2

Organizations as Mixed-Mode Entities: A Preview of Modern Bargaining Theory

The conception of organizations as mixed-mode entities goes beyond classical ideas, for it emphasizes potentially conflicting factors that many of the classical organizational theorists all but ignored. These factors include goal diversity (employees who have varied objectives of their own, which are not necessarily identical with the goals of the organization) and directly opposed interests (such as competitors for organizational resources—perhaps shares of an agency's budget—who know they'll confront each other again and again in the future; they have an interest in preserving cordial relations, but in every encounter they must try to win approval from the boss at each other's expense).

The relative importance of the cooperative and the conflicting elements in a particular setting largely determines how to balance two of the main ways we identified in Chapter 1 to deal with underdetermination: formal organizational structuring ("Put someone in charge!") and negotiation ("Let's see if we can work this disagreement out"). We'll come back repeatedly to bargaining theory as a theme—indeed, as a major subfield—in contemporary public administration. For the moment, it's probably enough merely to point out how the mixed-mode concept creates an opening for the study of negotiation as a necessary complement to organization—and vice versa.

When people share a critical level of agreement on goals, and hence can expect to succeed in cooperative action, it makes the most sense for them to create a formal organization. But initial agreement won't ensure permanent accord. Individuals have multiple and divergent objectives (again, the phenomenon of goal diversity). Some conflicts will surface only with time. Different values may lead members of an organization to act at cross-purposes regarding particular issues even while they remain connected in a general way by bonds of common purpose or loyalty. When the members of a going concern feel that the issues dividing them have become too deep or too difficult for business as usual, they must bargain out their differences or risk an organizational breakup.

Most organizations are the products of negotiations. (In Chapter 6 we'll explore not only why but also how men and women create organizations.) Once an organization has been set up, however, conflict may break out over an interpretation of the "fine print" or over issues that never even occurred to the parties during the original negotiation. Further bargaining will be necessary to produce new agreements about disputed interpretations or unexpected issues. If the negotiators succeed, they will have preserved the original organizational pattern. They will also have refined the structure of expectations within which all parties work, lifting relationships up to a higher plane of cooperation and trust. Each success in one of these follow-up bargaining rounds should make it easier to deal with subsequent misunderstandings.

It is this procedure, repeated over and again, that bargaining theorists have in mind when they speak of an organization as a **negotiated order**—a dynamic structure whose elements are constantly being tinkered with, bargained over, and finely tuned in the thousands of negotiating processes that are occurring all the time at all organizational levels. The concept of a negotiated order can apply to a highly structured formal organization such as a classical bureaucracy. But it can also encompass a relationship as loose as the one in which two satisfied traders tacitly agree to continue doing business with each other. Because *all* organizations are, in some sense, negotiated orders, the bureaucracy of classical organizational theory turns out not to be as rigid as the Weberian model would imply; even superiors and subordinates are always negotiating around the edges of their hierarchical relationships. On the other hand, the free market turns out not to be as atomistic as economic theorists sometimes imply, because individuals are constantly negotiating deals that bind them, at least temporarily, in contractual relationships.

But negotiation may be a symptom of organizational decline as well as a means of organizational development. An association initially founded on expectations of cooperation may gradually dissolve as the number or intensity of conflicts grows. In classical theory, an organization is a structure of authority. It is precisely this element of authority that becomes problematic in a dissolving organization. Relationships become less and less "organizational" as subordinates resist orders or subvert the rules; responsibilities come more and more to be defined by separate issue-by-issue agreements. The element of negotiation increases in prominence; the sense of formal organizational integration diminishes.

So goes the rhythm of organization and negotiation:

> *Organization is the structure produced by a negotiation; negotiation is the process that creates or maintains organization; because organization is constantly affected by internal and external sources of conflict, negotiation must be ongoing; because negotiation is ongoing, organizational structure is constantly changing.*

The term *negotiated order* taps into a way of thinking about organizations that emphasizes the need to keep negotiation always in mind. And the modern negotiated-order model, which assumes a continuous process of mutual adjustment, suggests a more flexible (and probably more realistic) picture of organizational life than does the traditional bureaucratic paradigm centered on coordination by direct supervision.

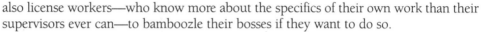

also license workers—who know more about the specifics of their own work than their supervisors ever can—to bamboozle their bosses if they want to do so.

Our next selection comes from one of the most influential writers in the field, James Q. Wilson, who classifies the products of government work as either outputs or outcomes. *Outputs* refers to the day-to-day work activities and work products of an organization. *Outcomes* refers to the actual social consequences that result from the outputs. How are outputs and outcomes to be measured? The challenge of **performance measurement** has attracted much interest over the years, for reasons that are perfectly natural and rooted in the classical tradition of public administration. The classical theorists emphasized efficiency as the test of effective administration. The classical concept of efficiency involves a ratio of costs to gains: How much must go in (inputs) to achieve what comes out (outputs or outcomes)? Traditionally what goes in is measured in dollars, and proponents of the classical, efficiency-based approach to management have always sought for better ways to measure what comes out.

Examples of output measures readily occur: the number of application forms that clerks in a government agency process within a period of time (for example, applications for federal grants so that transportation experts can study highway safety techniques); the number of students assigned to a classroom (used to compute the traditional teacher-pupil ratio); and the number of felony arrests made by the members of a sheriff's force. Outcome measures corresponding to these output measures would include the actual improvements in traffic safety, the learning that actually goes on in the classroom, and the actual improvement in neighborhood order that is achieved as a result of higher arrest rates. Alas, such outcome measures are often far more difficult to establish than are the corresponding output measures. As an observer of the Washington bureaucratic scene has commented, "There's a world of difference ... between counting how many grants the Department of Transportation processes, for example, and figuring out whether the roads have fewer potholes"[4]—let alone measuring the ultimate contribution of the transportation study to the achievement of a safer, faster traffic pattern.

Wilson underscores that many areas exist in public administration in which neither outputs nor ultimate outcomes can even be effectively monitored, let alone measured in any precise, numerical way. Wilson contends that these variations in observability are critical factors in agency management. Asymmetric information is a problem in three of the four types of agencies that Wilson identifies. In the type of organization with the most severe problem of asymmetric information, one that Wilson calls a **coping organization,** neither outputs nor outcomes can be effectively observed. The Wilson selection ends with a discussion of the kinds of expedients that are most frequently found in police forces, which Wilson cites as typical coping organizations. You'll find this discussion of the supervisory function in police forces, by one of the country's leading criminologists, useful when you get to our chapter case about the move to community policing.

[4]John Meacham, "What Al Gore Might Learn the Hard Way," *Washington Monthly* (September 1993): 18.

James Q. Wilson on the Observability of Outputs and Outcomes

From a managerial point of view, agencies differ in two main respects: Can the activities of their operators be observed? Can the results of those activities be observed? The first factor involves *outputs....* Outputs consist of the work the agency does. The second factor involves *outcomes*—how, if at all, the world changes because of the outputs....

Outputs—work—may be hard to observe because what the operator does is esoteric (for exam-

ple, a doctor performing a diagnosis or a physicist developing a theory) or because the operator acts out of view of the manager (for example, a police officer handling a family quarrel or a ranger supervising a forest). If operator actions are esoteric or unobserved, the problem of moral hazard arises: the operator may shirk or subvert. Outcomes—results—may be hard to observe because the organization lacks a method for gathering information about the consequences of its actions (for example, a suicide-prevention agency may actually prevent suicides but it has no way of counting the number of potential suicides that did not occur); because the operator lacks a proven means to reduce an outcome (for example, prison psychologists do not know how to rehabilitate criminals); because the outcome results from an unknown combination of operator behavior and other factors (for example, a child's score on a test reflects some mix of pupil intelligence, parental influence, and teacher skill); or because the outcome appears after a long delay (for example, the penalty imposed on a criminal may lead to a reduction—or even an increase—in the offender's behavior five years later). . . .

Observing outputs and outcomes may be either difficult or easy. Taking the extreme case produces four kinds of agencies: Agencies in which both outputs and outcomes can be observed [*production* organizations]; agencies in which outputs but not outcomes can be observed [*procedural* organizations]; agencies in which outcomes but not outputs can be observed [*craft* organizations]; and agencies in which neither outputs nor outcomes can be observed [*coping* organizations]. . . .

Production Organizations

Where both outputs (or work) and outcomes are observable, managers have an opportunity to design (within the limits established by external constraints) a compliance system to produce an efficient outcome. . . .

A problem that confronts the managers of all production agencies is that by plan or inadvertence they may give most of their attention to the more easily measured outcomes at the expense of those less easily observed or counted. There is a kind of Gresham's Law at work in many government bureaus: Work that produces measurable outcomes tends to drive out work that produces unmeasurable outcomes. Consider the IRS. It wishes to get the maximum amount of tax revenues from the work of its auditors. It is therefore tempted to judge auditors solely on the basis of how much money they produce from each audit and how many audits they conduct. This can lead the auditors to become so zealous in auditing that they annoy taxpayers who feel they are being treated unfairly or hounded about minor errors.

Similarly with intake workers in a welfare office. Certain aspects of its work—the number and accuracy of claims processes—are readily observable. Being observable, welfare-office managers may press their operators to maximize the number of claims or minimize the number of errors. (Doing both simultaneously is no easy trick; more claims requires speedy clerks, fewer errors requires careful clerks. Careful, speedy clerks are in short supply.) But another, less easily observed outcome thereby will be neglected—being helpful to clients. If careful, speedy clerks are in short supply, careful, speedy, friendly clerks are even harder to find. And when they are found, numbers-oriented managers can lead the clerks to emphasize speed or accuracy at the expense of kindness and civility.

In his study of a state employment agency, Peter Blau observed that when managers counted the number of applicants referred to employers by each interviewer, both good and bad things happened. Because interviewers were judged by how many unemployed persons were informed of job openings, any tendency the (predominantly white) interviewers had to discriminate against black applicants was suppressed: A black referral counted for just as much as a white one. At the same time, however, clerks would refer even unqualified applications to employers, where their chances of getting or keeping a job were poor, because a marginal referral counted for as much as a qualified one. There was no incentive to spend a lot of time on hard cases. In addition, clerks competed with each other for placements, sometimes concealing from each other the existence of a job opening. . . .

Procedural Organizations

When managers can observe what their subordinates are doing but not the outcome (if any) that results from those efforts, they are managing a procedural organization. The administrators of a mental hospital can learn what the medical staff is doing but cannot easily (if at all) observe the results of many kinds of treatment, either because there is no result or because it will occur in the distant future. . . .

The conditions that define a procedural bureaucracy seem to make it ripe for management in ways that encourage the development of professionalism. What better way, one might ask, to manage organizational activities, the outcomes of which cannot be observed from any administrative perch, than by recruiting professionals to do the work in accordance with the highest professional standards? These standards would constrain the practitioners to put the client's interests ahead of their own and to engage in behavior that is most likely to produce the desired outcome. This sometimes happens (as in the case of better-run mental hospitals), but more often it does not. The reason, I believe, is that a government agency cannot afford to allow its operators to exercise discretion when the outcome of that exercise is in doubt or likely to be controversial. . . . If the manager cannot justify on the grounds of results leaving operators alone to run things as they see fit, the manager will have to convince political superiors that the rules governing government work are being faithfully followed. Putting the fig leaf of professionalism over the nakedness of unknown outcomes will not fool anybody.

In short, because it is constraint driven, management becomes means-oriented in procedural organizations. *How* the operators go about their jobs is more important than whether doing those jobs produces the desired outcomes. . . .

Craft Organizations

. . . A craft organization consists of operators whose activities are hard to observe but whose outcomes are relatively easy to evaluate.

. . . Peter Blau described a "federal enforcement agency" (almost surely the Wage and Hour Division of the U.S. Department of Labor) in which the key operators, called "compliance officers," spent much of their time working away from their offices, unobserved, investigating complaints that employers have violated federal laws governing the pay and hours of work of their employees. These officers interviewed

employers and employees (often in their homes), inspected records, and negotiated compliance agreements with the employers that included a promise of future good behavior and, sometimes, a bill for back wages that had to be paid. Defiant employers were referred to federal attorneys for legal action.

The day-to-day activities of the Wage and Hour employees were much less minutely regulated than those of the workers in the state employment agency that Blau also studied. The reason was clear: The former could be judged on the basis of the results they achieved in a way that the latter could not. The compliance agreements and legal complaints brought in by the Wage and Hour officers could be reviewed for legal accuracy and substantive completeness. The law and agency rules clearly described what constituted a correct outcome, and that outcome could be observed. The compliance officers either produced that outcome or they did not. No law or rule prescribed with equal clarity for the employment service interviewer what constituted the right outcome (A referral? A job obtained? A job held for a year? A career begun?) and in any case there was no way for the agency to observe any outcome other than a referral. Because of these differences management in the Wage and Hour Division was goal-oriented; management in the employment service was means-oriented. . . .

Coping Organizations

Some agencies can observe neither the outputs nor the outcomes of their key operators. . . .

The managers of these agencies must cope with a difficult situation. They can try to recruit the best people (without having much knowledge about what the "best person" looks like), they can try to create an atmosphere that is conducive to good work (without being certain what "good work" is), and they can step in when complaints are heard or crises erupt (without knowing whether a complaint is justified or a crisis symptomatic or atypical). . . .

Where both outputs and outcomes are unobservable there is likely to be a high degree of conflict between managers and operators in public agencies, especially those that must cope with a clientele not of their own choosing. The operators will be driven by the situational imperatives they face—... the officers' desire to create order on the street or restore order in the quarreling family. The managers will be driven by the constraints they face, especially the need to cope with complaints from politically influential constituencies.... [C]oping agencies are precisely those that do not know with confidence what behavior occurred and cannot show with persuasiveness what outcomes resulted. And so managers, depending on their personal style, cope with the complaints as best they can. In doing so, they must strike a delicate balance:... Police officers do not like captains who fail to back them up in conflicts with citizens and lawyers.

For many years the dominant doctrine of police professionalism was based on the view that the police administrator had to get control of his department to prevent corruption or abuse of authority and to bring to bear on the crime problem the methods of rapid response, scientific investigation, and complete record keeping. This led police managers to treat their departments as if they were production agencies: Officers were asked to follow standardized procedures, keep careful records of what they did, stay close to the police radio always to be on call, and generate statistical evidence of their productivity. This in turn led the officers to emphasize those aspects of their job that were most easily standardized and recorded, that could be directed by radio transmissions, and that generated statistics. These included written reports of crimes (mostly thefts and burglaries that occurred in the past) and making easy arrests (for example, handing out tickets for traffic violations and making arrests for such "on view" offenses as public drunkenness and disorderly

conduct). It led them to de-emphasize managing family or barroom quarrels and handling rowdy street youths. In short, one part of the police job, order maintenance, was sacrificed to another part, law enforcement. The difficulty was that for many citizens order maintenance was more important than law enforcement and for many officers the bureaucratic supervision was an impediment rather than an aid to solving crimes.

Because of increased citizen dissatisfaction with the disorderliness of the urban environment some police departments began moving to redress the balance by involving their officers more deeply in order-maintenance activities. Officers were instructed to walk beats rather than ride in cars, report broken street lights or abandoned cars as well as crime, and handle the homeless and disorderly as well as the truly criminal. But many police managers resisted for quite understandable reasons. Order-maintenance work (such as coping with rowdy youngsters or handling quarrelsome families) produces few if any statistics, puts the officer in conflict-ridden situations, and increases the risk of complaints about officer misconduct from people who disagree with the officer as to what constitutes an acceptable level of order or how best to achieve it. The order-maintenance role of the police is threatening to many police managers, and so many departments are split between managers (and many officers) who believe that the dominant mission ought to be law enforcement and those who believe it ought to be order maintenance (or community service or problem solving).

From James Q. Wilson, *Bureaucracy* (New York: Basic Books, 1989), pp. 158–170.

The tendency of managers to substitute output measures—which are often easier to establish—for outcome measures calls to mind the joke about the drunken person who looks for a set of lost car keys under the nearest streetlight—not because that's where the keys were dropped but because that's where the light is. Output measures, although difficult enough in themselves to come by, can be downright misleading if they poorly reflect the outcomes that ultimately are desired.

Contemporary Organizational Theory: From the Bureaucratic to the Market Paradigm

Although the bureaucratic model retains a powerful hold on the modern administrative imagination, one of the most insistent impulses in contemporary organizational practice is the urge to reduce reliance on direct supervision even in large, complex organizations, including the bureaucracies in which most public administrators work. The aim is to encourage workers' initiative, problem solving (instead of robotlike order taking or rule following), and coordination by mutual adjustment. In the corporate world as in government, there's a move on to flatten hierarchy, to organize for flexibility rather than for routine, to liberate procedures in cases where yesterday's manager would have tried to standardize them—in short, to "end bureaucracy as we know it," in the words of one leading contemporary theorist.[5] Organizers are relying less and less on direct supervision and standardization as techniques of coordination and are emphasizing mutual adjustment—in other words, bargaining and negotiation.

Beyond the Pyramid: M-Form, Matrix, and Network Organizations

Ironically, irresistible pressures to modify the bureaucratic structure appeared in the United States at just about the same time that Max Weber was describing the finished form of the executive pyramid. Private corporations continued to grow in size and complexity, and so, for that matter, did the American public bureaucracy. In the 1920s it was the pressure of growth that led to the first major organizational innovation: the **M-form (multidivisional) organization.**

The M-Form Corporation

The term *M-form* was coined by the economist Oliver Williamson, one of the leading New Theorists. Williamson ascribed the rise of the multidivisional corporation to problems that organizations with the classical form—which he called the **U-form (unitary) organization**—encountered in the normal course of corporate growth.

Williamson imagined a medium-sized business firm organized in the classical manner, along pyramidal lines. With success in the market, the firm grows by adding workers. More frontline workers permit it to produce more finished items and thereby to satisfy the increasing demand. But expansion increases the average span of control at the lower tiers of the organization. Supervisors find that they can't keep track of subordinates' activities. The effectiveness of surveillance wanes; moral hazard sets in, and quality falls.

In Williamson's scenario, the company's top managers respond by following the classical theorists' advice: They add layers of middle managers and thereby restore the firm's control structure. In this scenario, therefore, growth in demand eventually leads to a roughly proportional growth in the size of the organization along all dimensions—horizontally (with the addition of production workers) and vertically (with the addition of supervisory layers). Williamson called this kind of expansion, which preserves uni-

[5]Warren Bennis, "Organizations of the Future," 30 *Personnel Administration* (September–October 1967): 6.

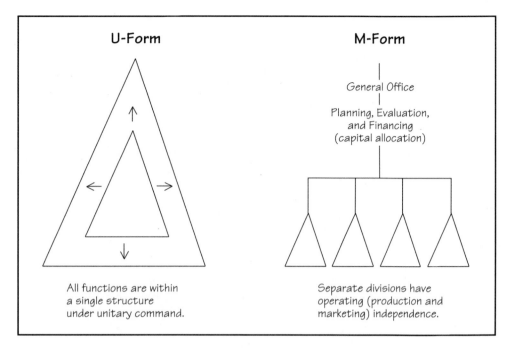

Sketch 3.3 From the U-Form to the M-Form Organization

tary command and the classical pyramidal (or U-form) shape, **radial expansion.** The larger triangle superimposed over the smaller one in Sketch 3.3 suggests the results of a growth process in which managers simply "scale up" the organization as demand increases for its products.

Radial expansion as a response to the challenge of organizational growth puts an extraordinary burden on the chief executive. Even a leader who is surrounded with a capable top-management team—the staff officers and handful of senior executives near the pinnacle of the pyramid—will eventually be swamped by the information-processing and decision-making requirements of an organization whose every line of action runs to the chief executive for approval.

In the early 1920s, American corporate managers began searching for ways to transcend the limits of the U-form organization. At General Motors, Alfred P. Sloan came up with the idea of breaking the company into semi-independent divisions. Each division became, for operating purposes, a separate company (again see Sketch 3.3). The delegation of operating responsibilities to the divisions left the central managers in the so-called general office free to devote all their time to long-range planning and investment decision making for the corporation as a whole. At GM, the prototype M-form corporation, the top executives in Detroit set overall policy and made the basic corporate financial decisions. But they left it to management teams in the divisions—Chevrolet, Pontiac, Oldsmobile, and so forth—to run their own production lines and sales operations. Chevrolet had to compete against Pontiac, although both remained divisions of General Motors, just as today they also compete with Ford and Mercury (both of which, of course, are operating divisions of Ford Motor Company).

The M-form structure expressed a new distinction in American business, between the operating functions of the separate divisions and the planning, evaluation, and financing functions of the general office. It was in the latter functions that the "market-mimicking" advantage of the M-form organization most clearly appeared. If each division were actually an independent company (instead of merely functioning *as though* it were one), its finance officers would periodically have to arrange with bankers or equity investors for infusions of funds with which to expand plant, retool equipment, and open new territories.[6] Reciprocally, financiers would have to evaluate the profit-and-loss ledgers of all the independently competing companies to see where they should put their money: Will Chevy or Pontiac, Ford or Mercury yield the best return on invested capital?

In a free economy populated by independent firms, the functions of evaluating and financing business operations are normally performed by the capital market (what most people mean by "Wall Street"). However, in an M-form corporation, it is the managers in the general office who evaluate their divisions' performances and allocate capital. Some of the capital will come from overall corporate profits (called *retained earnings*); some will have to come from outside investors. In an economy populated by M-form corporations, bankers and investors need merely decide which company—in our example, GM or Ford—has the better general office and the most-promising overall prospects. The financiers invest their money in the overall corporation, leaving it to the general managers—who should know more about any real problems in the divisions than external investors do—to allocate capital among the different operating units.

What advantages does the M-form offer over the U-form? First, of course, is the injection of marketlike competition into the regular workings of a large organization. When Chevrolet has to compete against Pontiac, the level of effort in each division is likely to be higher than if all models just roll out as different models in a single product line. Then, too, in the multidivisional structure, the general managers can focus their attention on the big picture, since they needn't worry (as the overloaded leader does under the unitary form) about day-to-day operations. Conversely, the managers of the operating divisions can make everyday decisions within an overall corporate plan drawn by knowledgeable decision makers in the general office. The rewards for a profitable division's year-end balance sheet will come in the form of a larger allocation of capital in the next go-round of central corporate decision making. The divisional managers who compile the best operating records know that they'll be in line for promotion to the general office.

Matrix Organization

The next major innovation in organizational form appeared after World War II. A new competitive environment—based on research and development, characterized by constant and rapid change—called for highly adaptable structures. The executive pyramid's, fixed structure of authority, standardized jobs, and formal channels of communication seemed too rigid. Executives in the U.S. aerospace industry found that they had to assemble large project teams to complete defense contracts and then had to disas-

---

[6]Bankers (and holders of bonds) *lend* money to businesses; equity investors *buy* stocks in companies and thereby become part-owners. Thus, debt and equity are alternative ways by which private corporations raise capital needed to expand.

semble the teams and construct new task forces for the next set of contracts. Furthermore, the dynamic scientific and technical base of modern industry required work units made up of specialists from multiple disciplines and capable of absorbing information from a multitude of sources. To meet these challenges, aerospace managers devised the form known as **matrix organization.**

The proponents of matrix organization argued that modern governmental and industrial operations routinely require members of organizations to consult multiple information sources, satisfy multiple criteria, and simultaneously respond to multiple line commanders and staff advisers. Therefore, they argued, we might just as well recognize the inevitability of multiple chains of command. The implication: Scrap the pyramidal form. As a corollary, the matrix theorists urged, we should also supplant direct supervision with mutual adjustment as the predominant paradigm of coordination.

Matrix organization permits—indeed, facilitates—ongoing coordination between the staff officials, who are today's embodiment of Taylor's "brain workers," and the line employees who must take the staff officials' new ideas and actually turn them into "better mousetraps." The nature of such coordination requires give-and-take—in other words, mutual adjustment. In Mintzberg's account of work in contemporary industrial organizations and public agencies, mutual adjustment occurs through various liaison devices such as special problem-solving task forces (which Mintzberg calls "adhocracies") and conference committees. The members of interacting subdivisions within an organization use these committees as forums to exchange information, discuss disagreements, and generally decide how to adapt their activities to one another. The point of it all is to provide a vehicle for the expression of multiple, often-competing interests and sources of information.

Whereas the manager in the classical organization believed that, in Gulick's words, "A workman subject to orders from several superiors will be confused, inefficient, and irresponsible," the proponent of the matrix form argues that the worker who gets marching orders from a single superior will almost certainly slight the requirements of the multiple interests that tend to be involved in modern corporate and government projects. And whereas the classical organizational designer assumed that—again in Gulick's words—"[T]he efficiency of a group working together is directly related to the homogeneity of the work they are performing," the matrix manager recognizes that the dynamism of modern organizations derives precisely from the confluence of heterogeneous kinds of information: the economist contributing to an effort in which the engineer, marketing manager, legal adviser, and others are all vital participants.

Sketch 3.4 shows a typical example of matrix organization. Each individual works on a team to which she or he is temporarily assigned. The employee answers to at least two superiors: (1) the head of a staff office organized around some special skill (such as accountancy or engineering); and (2) the director of the team made up to complete a specified task. In matrix organization, a worker over the course of a career may serve on dozens of teams, usually in sequence. Sometimes, however, an employee may have part-time assignments on two or more project teams simultaneously. The job of the chief operating officer is itself divided and distributed to form a series of supervisory offices (thereby violating the administrative managers' canon 1). The fixed hierarchy of tiers has been abolished in favor of the boxiform structure (violating canon 2), subjecting the members of the task forces to multiple authorities (violating canon 2b), and giving staff

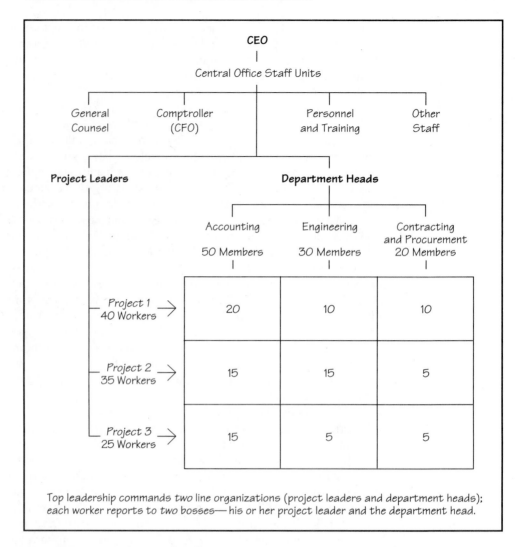

	Accounting	Engineering	Contracting and Procurement
	50 Members	30 Members	20 Members
Project 1 40 Workers →	20	10	10
Project 2 35 Workers →	15	15	5
Project 3 25 Workers →	15	5	5

CEO
|
Central Office Staff Units

General Counsel　　Comptroller (CFO)　　Personnel and Training　　Other Staff

Project Leaders　　Department Heads

Top leadership commands two line organizations (project leaders and department heads); each worker reports to two bosses— his or her project leader and the department head.

Sketch 3.4 Typical Example of Matrix Organization

officials—listed as department heads in Sketch 3.4—a share of formal command authority over their employees. As new projects come into view, the teams are reorganized pretty much without regard to classical axioms of unity of command, homogeneity of subunit organization, or strict line-staff distinctions.

Incidentally, a glance at Sketch 3.4 suggests that the matrix idea resembles Frederick Taylor's scheme of functional management, at least in the sense that each worker (within a given cell of the matrix) must respond to at least two bosses. But despite their superficial resemblance, the purpose of functional management differs dramatically from that of matrix organization. Taylor wanted to subject the individual worker to strict control by a series of supervisors, each the master of a narrowly defined skill. Matrix managers, by contrast, focus on the expertise and ingenuity of the workers themselves, rather than on the staff directors and team leaders. Matrix managers want to bring workers into daily contact with one another, trusting that the chemistry of interaction will generate team spirit and joint problem-solving skills.

Network Organization

The loose-jointed matrix organization, designed to facilitate rapid internal re-arrangement and adaptation, gets carried to the extreme in the structure known as **network organization** (see Sketch 3.5, page 98).

Instead of building on teams temporarily assembled from workers who possess the specific skills needed for a particular project, network organizations consist of free-floating and essentially self-seeking nodes of expertise. Each node consists of a few individuals or teams of individuals who are expected to act to the greatest possible extent on their own initiative, opportunistically bonding to others who can help in a given undertaking. The spokesperson for a given team may come up with a new idea and then negotiate with the leaders of other teams to set up a temporary organization able to execute the plan. If the spokesperson can't sell the idea to others within the organization, he or she is equally free to contract with suppliers of needed skills or resources from outside. Individuals freely communicate with one another, often across long distances by electronic means and even across the lines that separate them from their counterparts in competing organizations. In the network world, everyone is free to pursue new, more profitable arrangements unless he or she is bound by an existing contract. Everyone competes with everyone else, both within and without the organization. And every project expresses an agreement achieved through mutual adjustment rather than a plan hatched at the top and ordered to be carried out by workers below.

Operators within a network organization are encouraged to act almost as independent decision makers, modifying plans to accommodate local circumstances. In Chapter 11, we will see this organizational concept reemerging as an implementation approach called *backward mapping*. It is not coincidental that network organization and backward mapping are both phenomena of an era marked by rapid communication, a willingness by workers to take the initiative, and widespread recognition that adaptability is a requisite of organizational effectiveness (not to say survival).

A special instance of network organization is the **internal service unit (ISU).** The standard example is a motor-pool operation set up to service the members of different units within a single large organization (see Box 3.3, page 99). An ISU produces billable goods or services, such as cars to be "rented" by members of the organization. The ISU's managers deal with other units in the organization on a fee-for-service basis: Customers must pay for the goods they take or services they use. Fee levels, however, aren't determined by supply and demand, as they would be in a true market; they must be set administratively. It is a frequent subject of controversy in organizations with ISUs whether fees are too high (the usual complaint of users) or too low. Low fees imply that the central office is subsidizing the use of the service, since it must make up any deficit after all fees have been collected. The "sale" of a service at too-low rates—even if it occurs within the context of an organization rather than in a free market—may invite abuse, since potential users tend to overpurchase cheap services.

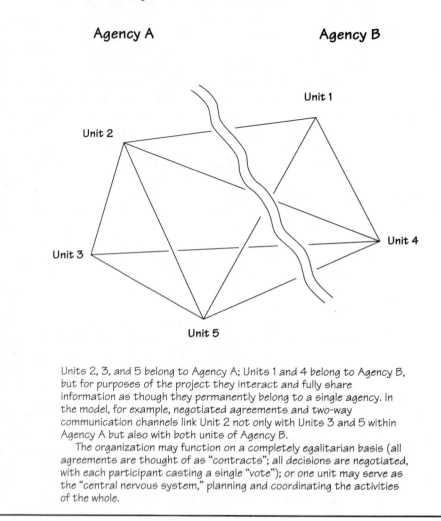

Self-contained product-development or production units rearrange agreements and connections with one another across organizational lines and often over great distances, using modern communications technology and information systems. Absence of a traditional hierarchical chain of command means that each unit pursues its own incentives; information flows generally and freely throughout a network, instead of through hierarchical channels.

Agency A   **Agency B**

Unit 1

Unit 2

Unit 4

Unit 3

Unit 5

Units 2, 3, and 5 belong to Agency A; Units 1 and 4 belong to Agency B, but for purposes of the project they interact and fully share information as though they permanently belong to a single agency. In the model, for example, negotiated agreements and two-way communication channels link Unit 2 not only with Units 3 and 5 within Agency A but also with both units of Agency B.

The organization may function on a completely egalitarian basis (all agreements are thought of as "contracts"; all decisions are negotiated, with each participant casting a single "vote"); or one unit may serve as the "central nervous system," planning and coordinating the activities of the whole.

Sketch 3.5 Model of Network Organization

Network Organization and the Information Revolution

Why have efforts to "hollow" the modern organization (as some have described the trend toward the network form) become so pronounced in recent years? The

BOX 3.3 ▪▪▪

An Internal Service Unit: The Motor Pool

Sketch 3.6 illustrates a typical problem in a large organization. Top managers realize that members of the company or agency occasionally need to have access to automobiles. To provide a "company car" for everyone, however, would be prohibitively expensive. What about assigning a certain number of vehicles to each unit in the company—giving each department its own dedicated minifleet of automobiles? Unfortunately, the only-*occasional* need of workers for such cars would imply a surplus of cars. "Dead time" in each minifleet would, again, make for a prohibitively expensive arrangement. So the top managers set up a companywide motor pool—an internal service unit—in a staff-type location within the overall organizational structure.

On some kind of priority schedule (probably "first come, first served"), any worker from any unit can use a car from the common pool as long as he or she has the unit director's permission. The unit director must approve car use because the unit's budget limits the amount for the rental of cars from the central motor pool. Through experimentation, an effort will be made to find just the right level of inventory in the motor pool—a number that presumably will be less than the sum of the cars in the minifleet system. The top managers of the company, in conference with the unit directors and the manager of the motor-pool operation itself, will have tried to set the charge for the use of a company car at just the level that will give everyone the right incentive to use the common facility in a way which efficiently advances company or agency goals. In other words, the ISU will be set up as a market-mimicking device. Thus, through the use of the ISU arrangement, the attempt is made both to reduce the total number of resources (number of cars) and to apply market disciplines (the charge per trip or per mile) to their use.

▪▪▪

impulse to free-up relationships and break through the rigidities of the bureaucratic structure accounts for part of the answer. Belief in the efficiency-fostering potential of market-mimicking forms of organization, inspired especially by the writings of the New Theorists, also helps explain why many managers want to flatten hierarchies and ease the patterns of internal authority. But there is more to the story: Moves toward network-type linkages reflect the extent to which modern technology has undermined the classical case for a pyramid of tiers.

As we saw in Section 1 of this chapter, basic to the theory of the executive pyramid, especially as the administrative managers developed it, was the span-of-control problem. A manager at any level must acquire and process information about the doings of his or her subordinates; a narrow span of control, the classical theorists taught, helps in the accomplishment of this goal because fewer subordinates can be monitored more

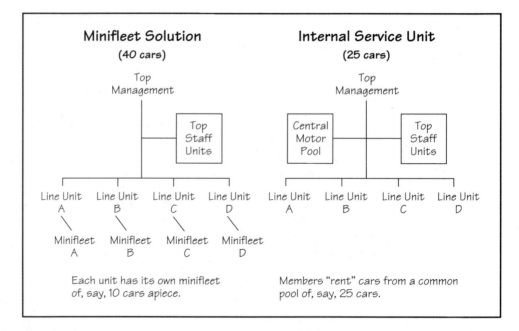

Sketch 3.6

closely. But narrowing the span of control implies an increase in the number of layers. What the supervisor gains in the way of a heightened surveillance capability may be more than lost in other ways. Organizational thickening adds middle managers, swelling payroll costs. Some of those intermediate supervisors may have goals of their own to pursue, contrary to the goals of the organization. Furthermore, as organizational distance increases with layering from top to bottom in a bureaucratic hierarchy, so does the potential for serial information losses and other forms of information absorption. Orders from the top get muddled on the way down; reports from the bottom get lost or distorted on their way up. Hierarchy, intended to promote obedient behavior, may end up frustrating it.

Accurate, complete information is a precious asset in private and public organizations that depend on economic statistics, accurate internal performance reports, word of scientific innovations, and reliable processing of complex messages. Fortunately, modern information-processing technology makes the kind of layering illustrated in Sketch 3.1—the traditional way to reduce the average span of control in an organization—less necessary than it was when the classical axioms were developed. Across the U.S. economy, senior managers are discovering that they can use well-designed management information systems instead of pyramids of fact finders to get the data they need. They can use telephones or E-mail instead of the old chain of command to send orders anywhere in the structure. Thus computers, electronic mail, and the like have permitted corporations to downsize by eliminating middle-management slots while at the same time providing the flexible connective tissue that facilitates networking.

CHAPTER READING ▼ ▼ ▼

In the following selection, the British administrative analyst Christopher Hood discusses the phenomenon of information absorption in hierarchies. Hood goes on to consider some practical ways—other than close surveillance, which so often can't work—of dealing with asymmetric information and a related problem: opportunism. **Opportunism** usually refers to the tendency of workers whose personal objectives conflict with the goals of the organization to take advantage of loopholes in the rules or weaknesses in organizational procedures. Hood argues, however, that if a worker's personal objectives can be aligned with the organizational goals, his or her pursuit of self-interest may be helpful rather than harmful.

Hood's relatively formal approach to his subject, plus the emphasis he gives to self-interest as a motivator of behavior, qualifies him as a New Theorist. Hood offers three bracketing strategies for dealing with opportunism. You might want to invoke some mixture of Hood's strategies when you get to certain problems in the relationship of superiors to subordinates (the "master-servant relationship," in British usage) that loom in our chapter case. In that scenario, the leading figures contemplate a move to community policing. Such a move requires decision makers to decentralize organizational authority and release frontline police officers from the kind of intensive direct supervision that's been traditional in American law enforcement agencies.

To Control Opportunism—Or Capitalize on It?
Christopher Hood

One way of tackling opportunism is by making servants act as fiduciaries, solely for the benefit of the master. An opposite approach is to accept opportunism but limit discretion. The third approach is to devise a rule structure such that opportunism and discretion produce positive results.

There are at least three ways in which information may be distorted in a subordinate-superordinate relationship. Each type of distortion is likely rise with the number of hierarchical levels in an enterprise:

(a) Self-interested distortion of information by a servant to his master. . . . Suppose that the proportion of the "total picture" (whatever that is) which is distorted for this reason at any level of the hierarchy is given as: a_1.

(b) "Natural" (i.e. unintended) distortion of information due to error. It is a commonplace of storytelling games or "whispering" experiments that unintended error steadily creeps into a message as it passes from one person to an-

other, especially if transmitted by word of mouth alone. This kind of distortion is likely to be most serious when employees are physically scattered, when they possess a diversity of specialized skills such that information must be repeatedly translated from technical into lay language and back, or when action may have to take place very fast, for instance on the basis of telephone messages rather than written reports. Suppose that the proportion of the "total picture" distorted for this reason at any level of the hierarchy is given as: b_1.

(c) Distortion arising from deliberate simplification of messages as they travel upwards in a hierarchy, or bulking out messages as they travel downward. . . . [E]ven if there is no self-interested distortion whatever on the part of servants, some distortion is bound to arise simply because of the functional need to cut down on the detail known to a servant in order to convey the "bottom line" of a situation to a busy master with other things on his mind and a finite capacity to absorb and process information. Similarly, when a message goes down from the top, "implied terms" must be progressively introduced in order to convey its practical meaning in terms of work routines and the like. Call the proportion of the total picture distorted for this reason at any level of the hierarchy: c_1.

The proportion of any message distorted (L) as it crosses any level in an enterprise's hierarchy is then:

$$(1 - [a_1 + b_1 + c_1]).$$

L will grow larger the more levels there are in the hierarchy. If there are n levels, the total distortion of any message as it passes from the bottom of the enterprise to the top will be:

$$(1 - [a_1 + b_1 + c_1])^{n-1}$$

. . . Even if one makes conservative assumptions about what values to attach to each of these three distortion factors, the cumulative effects are potentially dramatic in long hierarchies. For instance, if the proportion of the total picture distorted by each of these three factors is 0.1 at each stage (little enough, it may be agreed), it only takes a three-level hierarchy for the distortion factor to climb above half of the total message conveyed, so that the picture which gets to the top is more wrong than right. If accurate decision-making at the top requires the combination of several separate messages, the likelihood that the enterprise directorate will *ever* make any correct decisions becomes very low. . . .

[T]here are broadly three strategies which can be used to counter the discretionary behavior/information distortion problem in larger scale master-servant organizations;

(1) Seek to reduce opportunism.

(2) Seek to limit discretion.

(3) Fix the rules of the game such that opportunism and discretion produce positive rather than negative results; in other words, changing the *consequences* of opportunism and discretion.

(1) Limiting Opportunism

We have already seen that discretionary behavior and information impactedness[7] within a master-servant relationship is a "problem" only if the servants are opportunistic. So one way of tackling the problem at the root is by trying to limit opportunism, making servants act as fiduciaries (acting solely for the benefit of their master) rather than looking after Number One. Such an approach can hardly be avoided where servants are sent out to far-flung districts where the exercise of discretion, local monopoly, and information-impactedness is unavoidable, as in the case of missionaries, spies, colonial administrators. Traditional public administration theory emphasizes this approach, seeking to put the running of public services in the hands of people not subject to worldly corruption—sometimes with explicit comparison to a priesthood. . . .

Conventional means used to limit opportunism by employees include the following, none of which is foolproof and many of which overlap:

Accepting as employees only people who show signs of vocation or permanent calling to the work in question, as tested by rigorous scrutiny, screening and probation procedures, not casual job-hoppers momentarily attracted to the pay or the job;

[7]*Information impactedness:* A term coined by Oliver Williamson for a situation in which one party in an arrangement, such as a contract to perform a highly technical task, learns so much about the peculiarities of the job that he or she has a huge advantage when the time comes for the other party to think about selecting a new contractor for an extension of the work. The bidding will inescapably be impacted by the privileged information that the first party has gained. See Williamson's *Markets and Hierarchies* (New York: Free Press, 1975), pp. 14, 31–32.

Lifetime career service (another facet of "vocation"). This may encourage people to take a "long view" which may limit opportunism, especially if allied to more or less automatic progression by seniority and "cradle to grave" benefits from the employer. Just as those who regularly deal with one another in trade have more reason to act honestly than those who interact only in discrete or on-off transactions, employees who must work with one another in a group for decades before they get pensions or promotions cannot easily indulge in fly-by-night tactics of getting rich quick and then moving on to something else.

Long induction and training procedures, to cultivate a sense of enterprise solidarity and to limit the grosser aspects of self-serving behavior. This is, for instance, the intended purpose of the rule that English lawyers eat a stipulated number of dinners at an Inn of Court before they become barristers, so they absorb the atmosphere and ethics of the legal profession and become socially involved with their peers, rather than merely studying the law in the books.

(2) Limiting Discretion

Whereas the "priesthood" approach aims to tackle the servant problem by limiting opportunism, a logically opposite approach is to accept opportunism but limit discretion. This is, of course, a rule design problem. . . . Organization theorists conventionally use the term formalization to denote the degree to which enterprises govern their affairs by explicit formal rules for the conduct of business, reporting requirements, authorization and appeal procedures to check and limit the discretion of agents, closely specified performance targets. As with "laws not men" rules more generally, it has often been noted that the more formalized the operations of an enterprise are, the more decentralized it can be. This is because the formal rules are intended to limit discretion and stop servants from turning their office to private advantage. The logical development of this approach (as with minimal discretion rules in gen-

eral) is the automated factory or office, in which the rules are physically programmed into the structure.

(3) Harnessing Discretion and Opportunism

Tackling the servant problem at its source—either by limiting discretion or damping down opportunism—is not without its drawbacks. In principle, discretion has many advantages. . . . Too many rules can be stultifying. Notoriously, strictly defined output targets such as distance driven by police cars or number of traffic tickets issued will distort performance, causing statistics to be created for the record without regard for the real value of such activities. Damping down opportunistic tendencies by servants may have negative side-effects too. It may exchange competence for loyalty, effectiveness for honesty, independent thought for groupthink, analytic capacity for piety, capability for seniority. It may mean being too kind to employees with burnout, declining competence, skill obsolescence (or who are just plain failures)—in short, to do without all the potential benefits of opportunism, in terms of dynamism, quick-wittedness, adaptivity. Such approaches tend to kill (or at least weaken) the patient as well as curing the disease.

An alternative approach is to take both opportunism and discretion by servants for granted, but to devise a rule structure such that these forces produce positive rather than negative results. Among the many devices which build on this general approach are the limitation of tenure, the creation of cross-cutting structures, the creation of league tables, and the engineering of payment on performance.

(1) Limited Tenure. One of the traditional ways of harnessing opportunism and discretion is to give servants only limited or conditional tenure. The servant's continuance or advancement in office is made to depend on the fortunes or approval of the master. If this can be done, the servant's interest is unavoidably linked to that of the master, so discretion and opportunism on the part of the former automatically works for the latter. This is, of course, completely different from limiting opportunism by lifetime career struc-

tures. Many rulers, from earliest times to the present day, have tried to obtain loyalty by drawing their servants from people without independent resources or authority (outsiders, aliens, people of low esteem), so that the careers of these agents cannot continue to prosper if their principal's fortunes sink.

(2) *Cross-Cutting Structures.* Downs' "Law of Control Duplication"[8] says that if you want to control one large bureaucracy, you must create another. Flippant as this may seem, it has sound intellectual underpinnings. "Control" is conventionally defined in control theory as the capacity to keep the state of a system within some sub-set of all its possible states, such that the state of the system can be changed at any time. (This may seem rather abstract; think what it means, say, for driving a car.) Ashby's "Law of Requisite Variety"[9] says that control in this sense can exist only to the extent that the number of states that the controller can take up at least matches the number of states that the object of control can take up (the driver must have a response to every state that the car may get into). This is the logic of developing large audit offices, "second guessing" institutions, adversary bureaucracies, duplication and rivalry within employment enterprises.... [C]ontradictions may come into rules and criteria in order to give power to adjudicators. Rival opportunists with stakes in different rules will conflict, such that "outside" resolution will be needed.

Thus, both economics-based and cybernetics-based ideas about large enterprises stress the need for "redundancy" (duplication, overlap, competition) and built-in conflict to keep such enterprises under control. This applies especially to enterprises which do not compete in a market and thus run little risk of being driven out of business—meaning that there is no inherent congruence of interest between master and servant. This "cross-cutting structures" approach conflicts sharply with a style of thinking

about administrative organization which seeks to minimize duplication, conflict, and overlap....

(3) *League Tables and Competing Teams.* A particular application of the cross-cutting structure approach is what Williamson calls "capitalism's creative response" to the problems of self-regarding discretionary behavior and information distortion within large corporations. This approach began to be applied within General Motors and DuPont in the 1920s. It involves:

(a) "double-sourcing" (avoiding dependency on any one single plant for important products or services, usually by running duplicate plants in different countries); and

(b) changing from what Williamson terms a unitary-form enterprise (that is, one with an unbroken hierarachical chain of command from top to bottom) to a multidivisional form of enterprise (M-form). M-form enterprises consist of competing plants constituted as quasi-enterprises—that is, trading with one another on a charging basis, competing in a league and operating with independent profit-and-loss accounts. This means that the plants are in continuous rivalry.... The top directorate ceases to exercise close supervision in an unbroken chain of hierarchical command reaching into every nook of the enterprise (with all the distortion of information problems that such a structure invites in a large enterprise). Instead, it acts as a holding company or merchant bank, allocating capital to individual sub-companies in the light of rival bids for capital or profit performance, promoting or firing managers on the same basis....

(4) *Payment on Performance.* Discretion and opportunism may be harnessed by linking employee rewards to performance, as with commission fees, piece rates, stock options. A specific performance contract is laid on top of an employment contract.[10] If an employee's reward comes from a fixed salary

---

[8]Hood here refers to a standard analysis of bureaucratic organization, Anthony Downs's *Inside Bureaucracy* (New York: Wiley, 1967).

[9]Hood's reference here is to one of the classic early works of **cybernetic theory**; see Ross Ashby, *Introduction to Cybernetics* (London: Chapman and Hall, 1956).

[10]We'll go into the theory of this kind of contract, also known as an **employment macrocontract,** in Chapter 6.

alone, he or she cannot benefit from saving costs or raising output, nor suffer from failure to do so. . . . Thus if fixed-salary employees are opportunistic, they have little incentive to raise output or cut costs. Adam Smith drew the moral that "Public services are never better performed than when their [public officials'] reward comes only in consequence of their being performed, and is proportionate to the diligence employed in performing them.". . .

Performance-related reward systems raise exactly the same problem as setting measurable output targets . . . —namely that opportunists produce the right statistics for the record, whether or not that reflects high-quality work. If academics are rewarded by number of words written, pitiless verbosity is the inevitable result. If architects or other professionals are rewarded by "scale fees" (a share of the final cost of projects), the incentives are to push project costs up as far as possible rather than to aim for savings. Output-linked rewards can easily be perverse. . . .

These four approaches do not exhaust the possibilities. They merely show some possible ways of designing institutional structures so that employees' opportunism and discretion can be led to produce positive effects. They all reflect the view that (to modify another dictum of Adam Smith) it is not from the benevolence or altruism of employees that we must normally expect public services to be provided, but from their pursuit of self-interest. . . . [T]he problem is to find a way to anchor the servant's pursuit of self-interest with the interest of the master without destroying either opportunism or discretion.

From Christopher Hood, *Administrative Analysis: An Introduction to Rules, Enforcement and Organizations* (New York: St. Martin's, 1985), pp. 105–116.

▲ ▲ ▲

CHAPTER CASE ●●●

From the viewpoint of ordinary citizens, the authority of the state is probably at its most awesome when it's personified in officials who wield public power backed with the symbol of the badge and the threat of the baton. For this reason, great emphasis in American police organization has always been placed on the imperative of control. It's not surprising that police administrators have traditionally accepted the bureaucratic model, favoring hierarchical organizations with clearly differentiated subunits (narcotics, traffic control, and so forth); strong lines of direct supervision; and, whenever possible, coordination by standardization in the form of strictly prescribed procedures to be followed by officers on the street. Some within our criminal justice community, however, think it's time to rethink the applicability of classical thought to police administration. As police missions change, so must police organizations.

The hot topic these days is the move to community policing. Almost all experts agree that community policing requires at least a partial retreat from the traditional pyramidal model, toward a more decentralized structure of flexibly operating line units. Much beyond that point, however, there is disagreement. Should community-based units be staffed with generalists, or should they consist of experts in community relations, gang suppression, and so forth? Should frontline police officers think of themselves primarily as law enforcers or as administrators of "street justice" (conflict resolvers, dispute adjudicators)? The community-based approach delegates discretion to beat cops. But everyone has heard the stories about bribe taking, the allegations of police brutality, the reports of cops who look the other way when they know they're not being looked at themselves. Proponents of decentralized authority must somehow ensure against the kinds of abuses that community-based tactics make it easier for street cops to commit.

One final point: The French organizational theorist Henri Fayol—whom the administrative managers in particular viewed as an authority—was the first theorist to emphasize the organizational chart as an essential "administrative tool":

> Organization charts, with branches like genealogical tables, permit us to seize at a glance, better than we could with a long description, the organization as a whole; the various activities and their boundaries; the ranks of the hierarchy; the position occupied by each employee, the superior to whom he reports and the subordinates under his control. The organization chart draws attention to overlappings and encroachments, to dualities of command and to offices without incumbents. It is a kind of model which shows the imperfections of the staff as a whole and which can be used each time the whole or any part of the organism is reorganized or modified.[1]

Fayol probably overstated the value of the organizational chart. Nevertheless, a well-crafted schematic can point up the trade-offs that an organizer must make, and in a way that clarifies the strengths and weaknesses of competing organizational proposals. As you work your way through the following scenario, try to translate the organizational issues you uncover into schematics that highlight alternative ways of locating authority and expertise, dividing functions, and providing for lines of coordination.

CASE 2
. . . .

Controlling Urban Crime: The Move to Community Policing

It was plain to everyone at the conference table that the mayor liked Police Commissioner Tarn's vision of the new policing approach. But "Hizzoner" (as the mayor's staffers always referred to him) also foresaw organizational and political problems with a move to community policing. Such a move would rankle some within the mayor's own inner circle. And everyone in attendance took it for granted that most of the city's old-line cops would resent the organizational changes that the commissioner was proposing.

Police Commissioner Grace Tarn herself had started the argument when, at a meeting of the mayor's cabinet, she muscled into a discussion of economic-development issues. Tarn pointed out that tax breaks and zoning variances couldn't attract job-creating new businesses into the inner city if prospective employees felt unsafe and hence refused to accept steady jobs in the area. Tarn passed out copies of a summary statement and a map of the city's central ward area, roughly coincident with the 4th, 5th, and 6th police precincts. The statement read, in part:

[1]"The Administrative Theory in the State," [1923], trans. Sarah Greer, in Gulick and Urwick, eds., *Papers on the Science of Administration*, p. 106.

Although community policing has no single definition, all advocates of this approach emphasize certain themes: an emphasis on "order maintenance," perhaps even at some sacrifice of the traditional police function, "law enforcement"; extending police operations through the supportive activities of ordinary citizens (as in crime watches); street cops acting preventively, as problem solvers rather than mere after-the-fact cleaner-uppers of messy situations. These aims require less hierarchy, less control of beat cops through direct supervision, more reliance on police officers' acting independently, and more emphasis on teams of social program specialists.

Under Tarn's plan, an inner city area of some 20 square miles—more than 1,000 square blocks—embracing the three designated precincts would be reorganized for an experimental community policing program. ("Experimental"? That's how Commissioner Tarn billed her plan. But some of those in attendance at the mayor's meeting doubted that such a massive effort could easily be undone even if it proved unsuccessful.)

"Why the three precincts in question?" asked Sis Pfundapfel of the mayor's personal staff.

"Look at the central ward's crime stats," Tarn replied. Over the past few years, felonies had increased alarmingly within the 4th, 5th, and 6th precincts. Tarn said that four categories of major crime were of special concern:

Narcotics trafficking and dealing, with a rising number of "incidents gone bad" (police jargon for drug deals that ended in serious violence)

Gang activity, which was known to be the basis of much of the drug trade, handgun distribution, and local crimes against property—many of which were planned by and executed under the direction of gang leaders

Daytime burglary (which, for reasons only partly accounted for by the drug and gang statistics, had risen sharply); and

Domestic violence, especially violent abuse of spouses and partners.

"And what's it going to cost to bring all this crime under control?" The mayor's question was inevitable.

"I'm not asking for any new people," Tarn answered. "We'll move to community policing by reorganizing the force we already have in the area. There'll be the same number of people as now—750 from the P.D. plus some health people and the human services caseworkers who normally have duties in the central ward area. Police, Public Health, and city BHS [the city's Bureau of Human Services] now act separately, and there's a continuing problem of coordination. In fact, there's almost *no* effective coordination at all at the street level." Commissioner Tarn emphasized that under her plan the three city agencies—and probably representatives from some of the relevant county departments as well—not only would "coordinate" their efforts but also would actually "integrate" assigned employees on multifunction street-level teams.

The mayor repeated the commissioner's number: "We've got 750 cops there? In three precincts? That seems high—*Too* high."

Tarn nodded. "Those precincts are our most intensively patrolled in the city. When you count in sick time, vacation days, court appearances, and all the rest . . . well, it takes five cops on the force to put one out on the street." Besides, Tarn added, not all 750 were actually cops. Currently in the three precincts there were 600 sworn officers[2] (including uniformed "blues" and detectives) plus about 150 civilians, serving mostly in administrative and support (including janitorial) positions.

Some 150,000 souls lived in the three precincts. Currently, Tarn explained, each precinct was separately organized along traditional lines, each with its own command structure. Traffic and patrol sections were broken out geographically, into beats. Although most detectives on the city's police force worked out of central, each precinct also had a small investigative unit.[3]

Commissioner Tarn wanted to operate the three precincts as a single unit. One-third of the patrol officers, give or take, would form a *rapid response force* consisting of teams cruising the streets, both on foot and in squad cars. These teams would deploy to trouble spots as directed from a dispatching point in the central ward. Most of the remaining officers—two-thirds of the available central-ward force—would work as members of small *community service teams* oriented toward neighborhood relations, order maintenance, and crime prevention. Each community team would consist of police officers, one or more public health workers, and a complement of community action specialists, "family builders," and social caseworkers from the city BHS. Caseworkers from the county DWS (Department of Welfare Services) would probably also get into the act. Each team would have its own storefront miniprecinct house. Its members would concentrate on face-to-face work in "the hood"; on working health watches (immunization drives, AIDS and venereal-disease outreach); on engaging in social service casework; offering DARE counseling (*Drug Abuse Resistance Education*) and PAL (*Police Athletic League*) leadership; and so forth.

Tarn continued: "The point of the community teams is to have police, health, and welfare in common units, working the streets together."

Arpad Gasper, Number 2 in the city's Public Health Department, interrupted: "In other words, each of your community teams will have one or more cops, public health workers, and welfare types all handling 'drunk and disorderlies,' seeing to rat control, doing AFDC casework, plus all the old cop-on-the-beat duties."

Tarn nodded: "A matrix setup seems workable to me."

Gasper continued: "If each team is to function as a unit, it'll need a leader."

The commissioner's expression suggested that she hadn't figured out how to select the leaders of community service teams—or even who would do the selecting.

Gasper went on: "So each cop, each health aide, and each social worker on each team will have two bosses—the one back in the P.D., or in Public Health, or in the Bureau of Human Services who details that worker to the team; and the leader who's the day-to-day boss in the field."

The mayor interjected: "Will that work? Two bosses?" He wheeled in his chair and put it to one of his assistants, Peter York: "Do these kinds of two-boss organizations work?"

The mayor liked what he had seen since Peter York joined his staff just a few months earlier. York had a low-key manner and unassuming demeanor—not exactly

---

[2]*Sworn officers*: Professional policemen and policewomen who are legally authorized to carry deadly weapons and make arrests.

[3]Most major felonies (homicides, sex crimes, and so forth) are dealt with entirely by senior detectives based at headquarters. But each precinct has a unit of burglary detectives and may have one or more additional units specialized for any problems in the particular area, such as vice or bunco.

universal personality traits among individuals who gravitate toward jobs near the seat of power in city hall. His duties within the mayor's entourage were also unusual. He served as an adviser to the mayor pretty much without portfolio, taking on odd jobs of administrative analysis. "What about [County Executive] Eller's new proposal or [Police Commissioner] Tarn's latest idea?" the mayor might ask. Or: "Pete, so-and-so wants us to do such and such—Is that idea feasible? Can we afford it? Do some research; see if it makes sense, and report back."

Commissioner Tarn had nothing against Peter York, and she certainly had no authority to interfere with the mayor's request for one of Peter's fast studies. But Tarn wanted Hizzoner to know that she had already committed some high-level talent to the effort. She said: "I think we should move on this community-based approach just as soon as the chief signs off on the reorganization that Reuben Mann's been working on." Tarn was referring to Chief of Police T. G. Singh and his chief of staff, Captain Mann.

Commissioner Tarn nodded confirmation when Hizzoner asked if he was to understand that Reuben Mann was already at work on a formal organizational plan for the new policing concept. "The main outlines—breaking the force out, organizationally, into a rapid response force and community service teams—are settled," the commissioner added; "but, yes, Captain Mann's working out the details. Of course, I've instructed Mann to stay in close touch with planners from the other departments that would be involved." Tarn tossed what she apparently took to be a reassuring glance toward Arpad Gasper. But Peter York knew that, no matter how highly the mayor regarded Captain Mann, he'd never accept Commissioner Tarn's proposal on the basis of staff work completed entirely within the police department.

"However good community policing sounds in the abstract," the mayor said, closing the subject for the moment, "there's no sense in rushing it if it won't work organizationally—or politically. Let's mull it over before taking the next step."

• • • • •

Peter York walked from the mayor's cabinet room to his own office. He slipped behind his desk and reached for the phone. After a few tries, he got through to Captain Reuben Mann. He gave Mann the gist of the discussion that had just broken up. "Hizzoner wants me to give him a background paper on the community policing concept," Peter told Captain Mann. Then he asked if it would be possible to stay in touch with Mann through the remainder of the planning process.

Naturally, Mann treated a request from the mayor's office as a command. A captain on the force for almost eight years now, Reuben Mann had demonstrated a knack for problem solving. When Commissioner Tarn had decided to push for community policing, it was natural that she'd ask Mann (reputedly, "the best mind in the department") to help her develop an organizational plan. Mann told York that he had begun to meet with representatives of other city and county bureaus—Public Health, BHS, and so forth—to consider problems of interagency coordination in a community policing context. Mann said that he'd let York know about any meetings of that group. Of course, Peter should feel free to sit in as the mayor's personal representative.

Captain Mann wished that the commissioner had conferred with him before she unveiled her reorganizational scheme. Years of experience in the police bureaucracy told Mann what Hizzoner seemed to have sensed intuitively: Commissioner Tarn's New Age ideas might not be so easy to implement. Organizational problems—that "two-bosses" issue, and integration of the police with the public health and social service workers—still needed to be worked out. Reuben knew, too, that Chief Singh, who favored an approach known as crackdown policing, had been thinking along lines very different from the ones that the police commissioner was now proposing.

Officers trained in the traditional ways referred to community policing as "the touchy-feelies." Reuben Mann himself remained open to evidence either way. It wasn't clear whether the rising crime rates called for "harder" policing (more arrests, stern suppression of neighborhood disorder, strict *law enforcement*, deployments of special police units to crime-ridden areas) or the "softer" social touch (emphasis on community interactions, neighborhood crime watches, storefront precincts—all in a program of *order maintenance*). Of only one conclusion did Mann feel reasonably sure: At some point, the kinds of attitudes and organizational structures needed to support hard-line law enforcement began to undermine a force's ability to operate on an order-maintenance philosophy, and vice versa. And Mann instinctively suspected that the resource requirements of community policing would preempt any chance to launch the crackdown effort that Chief Singh wanted.

Yes, Mann wished that Commissioner Tarn had given him more time to ponder this reorganization before she started selling community policing to Hizzoner. And while he was thinking about it, did he really need this bright young man from city hall looking over his shoulder?

• • • • •

Commissioner Tarn, knowing Reuben Mann's capacity for work, simply took it for granted that her top planner would throw himself fully into the new reorganizational assignment. At the same time, he'd find ways to continue carrying out all his regular duties as chief of staff—Number 2 in the department, after Chief Singh himself. "Maybe the Commissioner wouldn't be so sure I could keep all my plates in the air," Reuben thought to himself, "if she knew what it meant to have Gwen Wong on the staff!"

Wong headed the Division of Criminalistics and Forensics. Mann considered Wong his most promising, most innovative staff member: "Gwen the Go-Getter." So loaded with ideas was Gwen Wong, however, and so relentlessly energetic was she in their pursuit, that managing her sometimes seemed a full-time job in itself, one that left little time for other chores—such as the minor matter of reorganizing policing in the central ward. In Chief Mann's in-box was another in an endless stream of memos from Wong:

MEMORANDUM

FOR: Capt. Reuben Mann, C/S
FROM: Lt. Gwen A. Wong, Chief, C&F
SUBJECT: Electronic Print Scanning System

Attached are the latest brochures regarding the availability and pricing of the automated/electronic fingerprint-scanning systems that I have talked to you about.

Attached too are reports of conversations I have had with C&F people in some other departments around the country where they already have electronic systems. We are behind the times in this respect.

I envision, with your support, an expedited procurement action, permitting us to acquire and install central databank hardware and software in my office immediately. All components of automated fingerprint-scanning systems are now available almost literally off the shelf at standard prices. Hence the limiting time factor will be our own ability to cut a purchasing contract. A rough cost breakout follows:

Central computerized print-scanner system and supporting data base management software	$3,250,000
Installation, debugging, shakedown of 400 mobile scanners @ $1,000 each	400,000
Instructional programs to prepare our personnel for system use	
Central staff personnel	20,000
Field personnel	60,000
O&M expenses (first 5 years) for on-line links to other automated systems (including FBI database in Washington)	200,000
Total	$3,930,000

I've checked with the Controller's Office and with Marcia Walkington in our Division of Accounts; there's more than enough slack in the P.D.'s capital and operating budgets to absorb these costs if you, Chief Singh, Commissioner Tarn, and the mayor give the word. (I assume the mayor will say go if the commissioner recommends it.) In fact, Deputy City Controller Basker said that there's a window of opportunity: enough slush has actually accumulated in the accounts for an immediate reprogramming of loose money, assuming he gets the go-ahead from the mayor.

With rapid action, we should have the new print-scanning system debugged and operational citywide, served from central staff (C&F), within a year. The system should pay for itself in increased efficiencies within a very short time.

As I mentioned when we spoke last time, automated fingerprint scanning and computerized print matching, when combined with an automated system for blood typing and DNA typing, will put us on the forefront of criminal forensics. For this reason, unless I receive a contrary indication from you, I will proceed to take the following two steps:

1. Prepare the procurement-request paperwork, notify Deputy City Controller Basker to stand by for reprogramming of funds per our earlier discussions, and contact our own procurement people about ways to shortcut (or if possible eliminate) competitive bidding.

2. Begin planning for the integration of the fingerprinting system with our current manual blood-typing and DNA-typing systems (both of which, of course, we'll eventually have to upgrade through computerization, whether we go to automated fingerprinting or not).

Mann smiled: "Gwen the Go-Getter." He tilted back, his smile erupting into an audible laugh as he reflected on Wong's suggestion that the new system be purchased "off the shelf," thus bypassing the time-consuming process of competitive bidding for purchases of new equipment. Gwen always seemed sure she could find a way around, over, or (if need be) *under* the established bureaucratic obstacles. "Yea, right!" Mann muttered.

Still, the move to automate the department's antiquated, manual fingerprint-matching operation deserved study. No, it deserved *sympathetic* study. That was the least he could do, Mann thought, to repay the gumption of a real go-getter like Gwen Wong.

●   ●   ●   ●   ●

From the clipping file of Peter York. Subject: Computerized fingerprinting systems. Source: Jacques Steinberg, "Coming Soon: Fingerprints at Many Fingertips," New York Times, Jan. 10, 1994.

A fingerprint, thanks to recent technological advances, can now be captured in a flash by an optical scanner and entered into a personal computer. No ink involved. And that new ease in taking prints—which some say removes the air of being arrested—means that the demand for fingerprints may rise the same way that demand for Social Security numbers has risen over the last 50 years. This cheers some police departments and worries some civil libertarians. . . .

The new fingerprint technology has been slowly developed over the last 20 years for its obvious first customer, law enforcement agencies.

Already, more than half the states and several major cities have set up their own data bases that, sometimes within hours, can electronically identify fingerprints lifted at a crime scene. Once, a detective's only options were to send in a list of suspects with the prints, or request a print-by-print search that might take weeks or months by hand.

The Federal Bureau of Investigation has converted the prints of about 24 million criminals into mathematical formulas. It has the prints of another 4 million criminals, plus the prints of 38 million other Americans, most of them military veterans or Federal employees, on file cards. Right now, despite what television has led people to think, the police rarely dust for fingerprints except in murders and other serious crimes. It is expensive and time-consuming. . . .

In two years, the F.B.I. says, fingerprint scanners tied to a national computer network will be in some police cruisers, letting officers know, for example, whether a speeder is a wanted fugitive.

The new technology is already being used by other agencies to prevent things like welfare fraud.

Social service officials in California's Los Angeles County and in two upstate New York State counties are fingerprinting welfare applicants to prevent them from collecting duplicate benefits by registering at several offices under different names. In the California program's first 16 months, officials said, it saved $7.8 million because 314 applicants were caught filing duplicate applications and another 3,010 were dropped from the rolls after refusing to be fingerprinted.

The new technology converts the unique pattern of a fingerprint's ridges, bifurcations and endings, called minutiae, into a mathematical formula. . . .

But it's expensive. A minimal system, like that used by one county, costs over $2 million. A large one like that used by California's Department of Justice costs over $30 million. . . .

Civil libertarians fear that the confidentiality of fingerprint data gathered to fight crime will quickly be breached. What, some ask, would keep immigration authorities from retrieving the fingerprints of welfare recipients, or even of credit-card holders, to ferret out illegal aliens? . . .[4]

● ● ● ● ●

Every other day or so, Captain Mann liked to start the morning with a brief sit-down in Chief Singh's office. If no current business required them to coordinate plans and reactions, fine. If, on the other hand, ends had begun to fray anywhere in the department, regular meetings between the chief and the force's second in command gave Singh and Mann a better chance of nipping any incipient problems before they become too serious.

Tarlock Gura Singh, the most decorated police officer on the force, left no doubt who was running the department—or what kind of department he wanted it to be. Chief Singh believed that good cops go first by the book and, where procedures leave room for interpretation (which is often), by their instincts. You get instincts only from experience—lots of it, on the street in the thousands of different situations that a cop will already have had to deal with while still a rookie. Singh, a disciple of Commissioner George O'Connor of Troy, New York (see Box 3.4), didn't much believe in the value of line specialization. Of course, there were the obvious requirements for experts in specific areas, such as narcotics and gang suppression, and for functional specialists to pull traffic duty and the like. But in the main, police officers should be jacks-of-all-trades not only in their assignments (especially the most basic assignments, those of beat patrol and motorized patrol) but also in the knowledge and instincts they took out onto the streets.

Nor, Reuben Mann knew, would Chief Singh's views on police administration make it easy for him to accept the kind of community-based approach that Commissioner Tarn was now pushing. Singh believed that the deteriorating quality of life in the central ward could be reversed only by crackdowns on the drug trade and on the gangs whose leaders—many of them career criminals—organized much if not most of the lawbreaking in the city.

● ● ● ● ●

[4]Jaques Steinberg, "Coming Soon: Fingerprints at Many Fingertips," *New York Times*, Jan. 10, 1994, p. 6.

BOX 3.4 ■ ■ ■

The Perils of Line Specialization: A Vignette from the Career of George O'Connor, Former Police Commissioner of Troy, New York

Police officers admonish, chase away, and counsel youths on the street much more frequently than they take them into custody. Almost always an officer's decision not to arrest is unknown beyond the circle of participants. There is no firm evidence to show under what circumstances each course of police action is effective in deterring disruptive behavior among either the youths caught or their friends who run away. The assumption underlying police contact with youths is that, if a police officer intervenes in some fashion with youths who are commiting a nuisance or crime, they and their friends are less likely to commit subsequent offenses than if the officer ignores the situation. . . .

Before 1977 the rate of arrest and referral for youths in Troy was low, and the number of unrecorded interventions on the street was probably likewise low. Youth arrests remained below two hundred a year from the late 1960s through 1976. Then, from 1976 to 1977 the number of youths brought to the station doubled and in 1978 rose further. . . . The commissioner's step in April 1977 that brought about this increase was to abolish the separate youth services division and to place the youth services positions within the criminal investigation division. His action came as a shock, because the police field had developed these specialist units in the 1950s to cope with increases in youthful crime and had come to regard them as standard. . . .

The logic behind O'Connor's move is that whenever a specialist unit is responsible for a function that is also among the responsibilities of the patrol division, patrol officers tend to neglect situations in which they might otherwise take action: "This is *their* problem." Thus, even in the hey-day of community relations units, when O'Connor was commissioner in Cleveland, he had refused to create one lest patrol officers regard community relations as the concern only of the specialists. Because youths were the cause of numerous problems, O'Connor sought to increase all patrol officers' attention to those problems by eliminating the label on a specialist unit to which the buck could be passed. . . .

From Dorothy Guyot, *Policing as if People Matter* (Philadelphia: Temple U. Press, 1991), pp. 124–126.

■ ■ ■

Reuben Mann scanned the note from Henry Brekken, the P.D.'s director of public affairs. It was Henry Brekken who had to explain police policies to the press and to rationalize them to citizens' groups. "Where you stand depends on where you sit," and where Henry sat went far to explain his reaction to the word that Gwen Wong was pushing again for a big new computer system.

MEMORANDUM

FOR: Capt. Reuben Mann, C/S
FROM: Capt. H. Brekken, Director, PA
SUBJECT: Electronic Print-Scanning System

Reuben—

I hear that Gwen W. is back on that electronic fingerprinting kick of hers. Please *talk to me* before you go forward on this idea.

Gwen might be right: Print scanning may help with the fancy criminalistics and forensics. But it'll do zip—absolutely *ZIP*—for the cops out there on the streets. How many DARE programs could we fund with that computer money? How many PAL teams and tournaments? How many storefront precinct offices? (I'm not able to give figures because G. just gives me vague answers when I ask how much her grand computer plan will cost.)

This is the *wrong time* to divert resources for computers. Anyway, don't let Gwen rush you. I think the commissioner (I don't know about the chief) will nix the proposal if she has a chance to think it through, since moving toward high tech instead of toward the people orientation conveys the wrong emphasis in the department at this time.

•   •   •   •   •

Gene Petitsaint, a recent graduate of the University of Washington, had loved his four years in Seattle, but he was also glad for the opportunity his new job gave him to live in a different part of the country. Gene had been surprised about the range of tasks assigned him during his stint so far in the Office of Policy Planning of the city's Public Health Department. Even so, he was more than satisfied with his working conditions, with his varied duties, and certainly with his boss, Nora Smith. There was no doubting Smith's technical credentials; she held an advanced degree in health economics from the University of Michigan. Gene was also coming to appreciate Nora's savvy as a bureaucratic operative and her skills as an office manager.

During the six months or so that he'd been in Public Health, Gene had learned to distinguish between Nora's "thinking-out-loud" conversations and her "let's-get-moving" tone. Thinking out loud called for no action. Often it never led much beyond toying with ideas. But once Nora Smith had decided on a course of action, everyone on her staff had better snap into motion.

Gene could see that Nora was in her thinking-out-loud mode.

"You know," Nora said, "there's talk of the cops springing for a fancy new system to take fingerprints electronically—no ink, no muss. The new system has a gizmo that searches through a database of prints to make instantaneous matches."

Gene couldn't quite see where this sudden interest of the city's director of public health policy might be heading.

"Bert Herbert told me about this new fingerprinting system that the cops want," Nora continued. Albert Herbert was, roughly, Nora Smith's counterpart in the county Department of Welfare Services. Herbert headed DWS's policy-planning shop. His status as a senior county official would usually have exempted him from certain kinds of pesky chores, such as service on interagency planning groups. But all the talk currently about a major police reorganization in the central ward was of special interest to Bert Herbert. Not only might DWS personnel have to be involved in the community service teams that Commissioner Tarn was talking up, but the core idea of neighborhood involvement was in line with Herbert's sense of the right way to promote urban redevelopment. Herbert had therefore taken the unusual step of assigning himself, rather than one of his underlings, as the DWS liaison to a panel that Captain Reuben Mann had assembled to study a possible move to community policing.

Smith briefly described Mann's interagency group to Petitsaint. She then said that she wanted him to serve as one of the Public Health Department's representatives on the interagency group and also to give some thought to a proposal that Herbert had mentioned to her.

"At Mann's next meeting," Nora told Gene, "Bert Herbert's going to float an idea. The idea doesn't relate to the community policing project directly, as far as I can see, but Mann's reorganization planning group has members from all the important offices, both city and county. It seems a good place to sound out people informally."

Smith continued: "Herbert thinks an electronic print database can help them over in Welfare Services in dealing with the old WFA [waste, fraud, and abuse] problem. In some states, they already cross-check the prints of welfare recipients to identify cheaters. You can't do that manually—searching and comparing takes too long, and it's too error-prone. Bert thinks a system to handle both crime and welfare investigations will need to be twice the size of the setup the police are thinking of. The trick is, because of economies of scale, twice the size shouldn't be anything like twice the cost. Herbert wants to go in with Mann and get a joint P.D.–DWS computer identification system, splitting the cost."

Petitsaint, although relatively new on Smith's staff, knew Nora's instincts well enough to sense now where she was heading. Why not add Public Health to a P.D.–DWS automated database system?

"Gene," Nora said, "with all the matching and tracing we have to do in Public Health—contact tracing on sexually transmitted diseases, hepatitis histories, tuberculosis exposures, whatnot—we should hook into the same system that the cops, and maybe the county welfare people, are thinking about setting up. If what Herbert says is true, they're already planning to put a blood-typing and a DNA-typing database into the police system."

Gene listened as Nora verbally sketched out her image of a new office, a kind of city-county joint venture of the Police Department, Public Health, the Bureau of Welfare Services, and interested county agencies (such as the DWS and the Sheriff's Department) as well. Smith envisioned a fully computerized "integrated regional database"—a central memory bank of fingerprints, blood types, genetic data, and other items of personal identification useful to government officials in the fields of public safety, public health, and social welfare. "Of course," Nora added, seemingly as an afterthought, "the kind of shared database I have in mind would have to be moved out of the P.D. It would have to be organized as a central facility serving everyone in city or county government who can add to the information and contribute to the funding."

"*One big central information system,*" Nora emphasized to Gene. "Turn the idea over a few times, and let me know if you think it's something we should push for."

• • • • •

Toward the end of each working day, Hizzoner the mayor liked to stroll briefly through the suite of offices near to his own city-hall inner sanctum. It was a way to chat with staffers who hadn't, for one reason or another, seen him in a formal meeting for a while. Hizzoner found Peter York working on his study of Commissioner Tarn's community policing plan. The mayor dropped into a nearby chair and asked how the work was going.

Peter had scribbled some numbers on a rough diagram. He pointed to his sketch. "Right now, sir," he told the mayor, "I'm trying to decide whether Commissioner Tarn and Chief Singh can both have the kinds of policing programs they want in the central ward. If it turns out they can't, someone's going to have to make a hard choice—either community policing or crackdown policing, but not both." Hizzoner knew that York knew that the "someone" who generally had to make such hard choices was the mayor himself.

Hizzoner wanted to hear more, and he wanted Peter to explain the numbers and lines on the chart. What did he mean by his remark about Chief Singh and crackdown policing? Was the chief fighting the police commissioner over the move to community policing?

"No," Peter answered. "Not 'fighting.' But yes, apparently there *is* a problem between Chief Singh and Commissioner Tarn. It goes back to something the commissioner mentioned at the cabinet meeting when she brought up her community policing plan. You remember what she said about needing five cops on the roster to put one out on the street? Well, when you work through the numbers, that turns out to set a pretty significant limit on the kind of policing we can provide in the three central ward precincts."

Peter emphasized that the commissioner's 5:1 figure was no more than a rule of thumb. The actual numbers of police officers on watch varied around the clock. Day work required more officers in every category (patrol, traffic, detectives, and so forth) than night duty did. But given those caveats, the 5:1 rule roughly meant that a complement of 600 sworn officers assigned to the three central ward precincts translated into only about 120 policemen and policewomen actually available for frontline duty on an average watch. The others were out sick, on vacation, tending to administrative duties in the precinct house, or home getting ready to report for duty on one of the other two shifts. Furthermore, at least half of those actually available for street work were effectively preempted from assignment to special duties—such as community problem solving or intensive crime suppression—by essential work of a nondiscretionary nature.

York explained: "The precinct captain needs some minimum number of cops to direct traffic, at least on the day watch. There are essential chores at the precinct house that civilians can't handle, such as managing the lockup. There's also a minimum number of supervisors needed for every so many officers actually working the streets."

The mayor interjected: "That figure of 750 in the central ward impressed me when Gracie Tarn mentioned it. But you're telling me it boils down pretty quickly to a much smaller number of men and women doing the real work of the force."

Peter nodded, gesturing toward the pad on which he had been figuring. "First," he said, "deduct the 150 civilians who never get active policing assignments, since they're clerks and custodians and whatnot. Right away, the 750 shrinks to 600. Of the 600, no more than 120 are actually on the line at any one point—more by day, fewer at night, but 120's a good number, give or take. Next, deduct the 60 nondiscretionary assignments. In sum, both the commissioner and the chief have known all along that they'll have to squeeze any changes they hope to make on the ground out of the officers who remain after all those discounts are applied to the initial 750 figure."

"The bottom line?" Hizzoner asked.

"The commissioner has, at most, 180 sworn officers—that's 60 discretionaries times 3 watches—for community policing, not the 750 officially assigned to the central ward. Break it out the way Commissioner Tarn expects, and that's 60 cops for rapid response, with 120 divided among the community service teams."

York slid his roughly drawn chart across the desk and positioned it next to a map of the central ward. He said that the mayor could probably best get the essence of the community policing plan by noting the number of storefront miniprecinct stations the commissioner hoped to establish. On the map, Peter had drawn a star at every planned miniprecinct location in the central ward. He had labeled the map "Optimistic Case." The map showed 20 stars, based on the assumption that the commissioner would be able to establish the maximum number of storefronts within the foreseen limits of personnel—120 cops, all dedicated to the new community policing mission. Peter explained: "Commissioner Tarn wants 6 officers at each storefront, 4 on days and 1 each on the other two shifts. She's still optimistic that arrangements can be worked out with Public Health and the BHS so the officers will work on integrated social action teams."

The mayor nodded. "So there'll be 120 divided by 6 equals 20 storefront miniprecincts scattered through the central ward."

"Yes, sir."

"And do I understand Singh doesn't like that idea?" the mayor asked. "Is he opposed to the storefronts as a concept, or is it the number—20 miniprecincts—that bothers him?"

"It's not so much that he doesn't like the storefront idea," Peter answered. "But the chief doubts we can afford the people needed for more than a fraction of those assignments unless enough cops are assigned to clean up major crime in the central ward *before* the shift to community policing. Chief Singh's been just as worried about crime in the central ward as Commissioner Tarn, only his solution's different. He thinks there's no way 'social action' will fix what's wrong unless we first clean up the drugs and the gangs. That'll take a different *kind* of operation—crackdown policing instead of community policing."

Peter told the mayor about experiences in other cities with serious drug and gang problems: "According to Captain Mann—and what I've found in the police and criminology literature seems to confirm it[5]—the best way to beat the drug trade or

[5]See, for example, Alok Beveja et al., "Modeling the Response of Illicit Drug Markets to Local Enforcement," 27 *Socioeconomic Planning Sciences* (June 1993): 73; and Jonathan Caulkins et al., "Geography's Impact on the Success of Focused Local Drug Enforcement Operations," 27 *Socioeconomic Planning Sciences* (June 1993): 73.

interrupt the gangs, at least at the street level, is through a two-phase 'crackdown strategy.' You pick a high-crime area and send in a 'crime suppression unit'—a CSU. Each unit has 8, 10, up to 12 officers—some working undercover, some in uniform. The more, the better. Beginning with the worst open-air drug markets or gang turfs, these CSUs blanket a defined area for 4, 6, maybe 8 weeks. The CSUers make life so miserable for the dealers or gang bangers—often they're the same—that they either move or actually go out of business. If enough crackdowns are under way in the same general area, such as in the central ward, the crooks can't move, and so they fold. Then the suppression unit moves on to another market. After the shock troops leave, you 'maintain' the neighborhood that's just been cleaned up. A small patrol force—3 cops taking shifts—works the area. Social workers and community development people also move in to make sure the neighborhood doesn't backslide."

York waited for his description to sink in. The mayor seemed to find the crackdown theory plausible. Then Peter continued: "I got the impression that the chief was thinking about launching crackdowns in the central ward when the commissioner came up with her community policing plan. It's worked in cities like Hartford and Houston, but only when the actual crackdown tactics met certain criteria. CSUers need close contact with one another to share information and carefully plan the next day's moves against dealers and gang leaders. The frontline officers get explicit instructions from their team leaders for the next day's work—whom to bust, where to get permission for phone taps, and so forth. Direction has to be close and constant. The structure is strict and clear, like in a commando unit—which, of course, is what the CSUers think they are. The organization needs tight controls, and the organization of the units has to facilitate complete, 'real-time' sharing of information. Also, drugs mean money, and money means potential corruption. It's to everyone's interest that every cop work under close surveillance by higher-ups who can ensure—and if need be, can testify—that everyone has stayed clean."

Peter noted that, historically, the FBI had been late getting into the business of narcotics suppression because Director J. Edgar Hoover had feared the corrupting potential of drug money. Nor could the kinds of undercover operations that narcotics suppression required be reconciled easily with the bureaucratic organizational approach. Hoover had always emphasized exhaustive log keeping within the bureau, intensive internal reporting, and close supervisory control of frontline agents. The same problems that had worried Hoover were just as relevant today. Peter wasn't sure how Chief Singh meant to solve the problem of police control if he launched a crackdown program. But as tough as a problem of control would be under a crackdown approach, Peter knew that it would surely be even harder if the department moved to the kind of loose, decentralized organization that community policing implied.

Peter York summarized for the mayor: "A crackdown doesn't work if every officer has to make it up as it goes along. And the professionals say that decentralized decision making is out, too. A crackdown doesn't work if every officer is told, 'Use your judgment and initiative; fix whatever you find wrong on your beat when you find it.' It's not an exercise in social action or incident-by-incident problem solving. What's more, a crackdown calls for undivided attention to the mission. You can't take time out from drug surveillance or gang suppression to chase purse snatchers or roust hustlers. That may mean you can't crack down for long enough periods in enough markets if you're assigning potential CSU cops to do storefront social work."

"So it really *is* either-or: community policing or crackdown?" asked Hizzoner.

Peter said that until he had "worked the numbers" he couldn't be sure, but conceptually his analysis seemed to point that way. "Chief Singh's been careful in what he's said. I think he doesn't want to undercut Commissioner Tarn. Community policing, Tarn-style, calls for a high level of police presence spread across the entire central ward—that's why she wants as many storefronts as can be managed. But Chief Singh thinks there's no way you can divide 120 cops among 20 miniprecinct stations *and at the same time* divide them into a workable number of crackdown units—each with, say, 12 members plus follow-up maintenance teams of 3 members."

"Might it be possible," Hizzoner asked, "to split the difference, or at least to program a smooth transition from community policing to crackdown, or vice versa?"

"By 'split the difference,' you mean launch both a crackdown strategy and move to community policing, with each staffed at a reduced level? That's what I was trying to figure out just now," Peter answered. "Chief Singh thought you needed the number of crackdown points to exceed some threshold. Otherwise, it's too easy for dealers just to move their locations. Of course, the commissioner also sees a need for some minimum number of miniprecincts. Maybe the critical threshold doesn't have to be set at 20, but it has to be high enough to show that the commitment to community policing is real, not merely symbolic." Peter ended by saying, "I'm trying to work out a simple model of the problem."

Hizzoner wondered if the model would help him make the choice that the dispute between his police commissioner and his police chief seemed to be forcing on him.

"No, sir, but it might tell you *whether* you have to choose at all."

That kind of information, Hizzoner knew, could be even more useful than a firm recommendation favoring a decision for either community policing or crackdown policing.

• • • • •

Commissioner Tarn asked Reuben Mann to come to her office; there was something she didn't want to discuss over the phone.

Tarn told Mann about her conversation earlier that day with Claire Nagamura, a reporter for the major daily newspaper in the metropolitan region, the *Tribune-Examiner.* Nagamura had nosed out word of Bert Herbert's proposal to establish a new central database. The recommended computer system, Nagamura had told Tarn, would allow officials to collect "personal information ranging from credit records to hair-loss information on every man, woman, and child in the city and surrounding county." Nagamura intended to break the story in the next day's edition, followed by a series of articles about the battle over "electronic snooping" that seemed certain to ensue. Nagamura's editor wanted her first follow-up story to feature a lawyer named Ann Brown from the local chapter of the American Civil Liberties Union who threatened court action to block "plans for Orwellian dossiers—fingerprints, DNA, drug histories, HIV status, sexual contacts, *everything!*—available to any city or county bureaucrat who dials in and asks."

"Central database?" Reuben's eyes widened. "Is that the proposal Gwen Wong's been working on—for a new C&F computer system?"

Tarn nodded. "Nagamura knows that the idea started here in the P.D. and that Wong's been pushing for a computerized fingerprinting system. Pushing hard. Somehow, Nagamura got the idea that I've recommended a go-ahead to Hizzoner."

Mann wouldn't have put it past Gwen the Go-Getter to butter up the area's best political reporter if she thought a discrete leak would add some steam to her campaign for the new computer system. But Reuben couldn't envision Wong telling a reporter about communications between the police commissioner and the mayor, let alone about communications that hadn't even occurred.

The commissioner continued: "Nagamura's also talked to the crowd over in county DWS, and to some folks in city Public Health as well. Nagamura says they want an even bigger system than the one Wong's been pushing."

Mann told Commissioner Tarn that a senior DWS administrator named Bert Herbert had been coming to the interagency meetings on community policing. Mann described the trial balloon that Herbert had floated at the last meeting: Herbert wanted the mayor to get together with his counterpart in the county government, County Executive Julio Eller, and appoint a group to study the feasibility of a much bigger computer system. The system Herbert envisioned wouldn't be bought and operated by the police department. It would belong instead to a consortium of city and county agencies—the P.D., county DWS, city BHS, Public Health, and perhaps some others.

Mann told the commissioner: "I agreed, at Herbert's request, to save some time for a further discussion of his idea at the next meeting of the interagency group."

Commissioner Tarn expressed her supposition that it had been Herbert himself who, in a bid to build a broader base of support for the integrated computer system, had leaked word of "interagency negotiations" to the *Trib'-Examiner* reporter. Mann relaxed a bit, pleased that the commissioner didn't think that Gwen Wong had been the source. Besides, Gwen was pushing for a configuration very different from the one that Herbert was advocating.

Chief Mann said: "Gwen Wong and her forensics people have been hounding me for six months to get them an electronic scanner. But her idea was to keep it a dedicated police system in our own central staff, to service our cops, and probably [County Sheriff] Rilleau's force too. *If* we went for Wong's idea at all—some of the storefront police-types don't want to spend any money in that direction—it'd be a police-only system, not an interagency outfit. As far as the multi-agency notion goes, I only heard of the idea when Herbert brought it up out of a clear blue sky at our last meeting on community policing. I haven't had time to consider it, and I don't really know what I think about it."

Tarn raised her hand, as if testing the wind. "I get the feeling that some issues we're working on are going to come to a head. I better be ready with answers."

"For what questions?"

"Do I favor a computerized identification system at all? If not, why? If so, what kind of system should it be? The possibilities range from Gwen Wong's police-only setup to Herbert's integrated database."

Commissioner Tarn asked Reuben Mann to give her any thoughts he came up with in time to help her with the questions she was sure to get after Claire Nagamura's article appeared. "While you're at it," Tarn added, "why don't you gather up what you have about the central ward project. I'll be meeting soon with Hizzoner, and I'd like to talk to him in concrete terms about the police department's official position on an organizational structure for the move to community policing."

Questions for Discussion

The following queries might help you frame your thoughts and organize a discussion of the case.

1. What's the story? Who must make what choices, and how must they interact with one another in order to accomplish anything? What "circumstances of the action" and "conditions of the agents" should be kept especially in mind when thinking through the actions that the figures in this case should take?

2. Which ways of dealing with conditions of underdetermination—persuasion, restructuring, litigation, negotiation, strategic interaction—seem most likely to be helpful to each of the following actors (each of whom has an agenda to push despite opposition from others who are beyond his or her control): Commissioner Tarn, Chief Singh, Gwen Wong, and Bert Herbert?

3. Does the move to community policing sound, at first hearing, like a good idea? What about the contrary preference of Chief Singh for the crackdown approach? (No, you're not an expert in police administration. But you are a citizen, and one way or another, you've been dealing with law enforcement officials all your life. What do your own experiences, instincts, and common sense tell you about the best way to tackle urban crime?) Remember the "progression of circumstances." Under what conditions would you favor community policing over the crackdown strategy or vice versa?

4. Any move to decentralize police operations or to focus on order maintenance will tend to make both supervision and performance measurement more difficult. Based on the selections from James Q. Wilson and Christopher Hood, how—if at all— might you try to deal with these issues? Are the potential problems of asymmetric information, opportunism, and control of police discretion so grave that decision makers should avoid making the kinds of changes that might interfere with traditional hierarchical supervision or might erode performance measurement?

5. Limited resources will obviously be a factor in the decision about the central ward's police organization and tactics. Peter York knows that he can help Hizzoner "see the problem" by drawing a picture of the situation. Can you use Commissioner Tarn's assumption of 120 sworn officers for duty in the new mode—community policing, crackdown policing, or some combination of the two—and sketch a model that displays the key factors affecting whether to adopt community policing, crackdown policing, or a combination approach (such as "splitting the difference," as Hizzoner asked about)?

6. To what extent do the classical (bureaucratic) and contemporary (marketlike) paradigms help us envision structural patterns that can be used as templates for police organization in the central ward? Which paradigm best applies to Gwen Wong's and to Bert Herbert's different visions of a computerized personal identification system?

7. Moving to a finer level of detail in your organizational thinking: How do those central issues of classical organizational theory (how to structure authority; where to locate expert knowledge) present themselves in the case? Specifically, how would you mix features of the unitary, staff, and specialized-line approaches if you were called on to design the central ward's police force? What should be the primary and secondary bases of aggregation? Try to display the main features of the setup you propose in an organizational chart.

8. An organizer should consider whether it's desirable to set up a specialized unit. In what guises does the specialist-generalist controversy appear in this case?

9. Suppose Hizzoner asked Peter York to begin his study of the community policing proposal with a list of criteria that should be met by a decision maker in the mayor's position. What might such a list look like? Which techniques (priority setting, parameter changing, policy adjusting) would *you* use to deal with any multiple, inconsistent criteria that you identify in Hizzoner's situation? In the other main actors' situations?

FOR FURTHER READING

One probably can't find more comprehensive or more lucid expositions of organizational theory in all its aspects than

> Harmon, Michael, and Richard Mayer, *Organization Theory for Public Administration* (Boston: Little, Brown, 1986); this is the best introduction, all around, available.
> Rainey, Hal, *Understanding and Managing Public Organizations* (San Francisco: Jossey-Bass, 1991). Pitched at a somewhat more scholarly level than the Harmon-Mayer book, this is probably the better choice if you're interested in organizational theory as it has developed in the academic literature.

The following four volumes must be on any list of the modern classics of organizational theory:

> March, James, and Herbert Simon, *Organizations* (New York: Wiley, 1957).
> Mintzberg, Henry, *The Structuring of Organizations* (Englewood Cliffs NJ: Prentice-Hall, 1979).

Perroux, Charles, *Complex Organizations* (New York: Random House [1972], 1986).

Thompson, James, *Organizations in Action* (New York: McGraw-Hill, 1967).

The subject of bureaucracy in particular has generated a scholarly literature of remarkable breadth and quality; three of the best recent sources are

Meier, Kenneth J., *Politics and the Bureaucracy* (Pacific Grove CA: Brooks-Cole, 1993).

Stillman, Richard, *The American Bureaucracy* (Chicago: Nelson-Hall, 1995).

Wilson, James Q., *Bureaucracy: What Government Agencies Do and Why They Do It* (New York: Basic Books, 1989).

And see, for a fine collection of representative standard sources,

Shafritz, Jay, et al., *Classics of Organizational Theory* (Chicago: Dorsey Press, 1987).

On bureaucracy, pro and con, also see the following articles and books, all somewhat polemical in tone but thoughtful and stimulating:

Cleveland, Harlan, "The Twilight of Hierarchy: Speculations on the Global Information Society," 45 *Public Administration Review* (January–February 1985), 185.

Goodsell, Charles, *The Case For Bureaucracy* (Chatham NJ: Chatham House, 1994); recall that you got a taste of Goodsell's approach in one of the readings in Chapter 2.

Hummel, Ralph, *The Bureaucratic Experience* (New York: St. Martin's Press, 1994).

Thayer, Frederick, *An End to Hierarchy! An End to Competition!* (New York: Franklin Watts, 1973).

The continuing influence of the teachings of the administrative managers is demonstrated and discussed in

Conant, James K., "In the Shadow of Wilson and Brownlow: Executive Branch Reorganization in the States, 1965 to 1987," 48 *Public Administration Review* (September–October 1988), 892.

The best introductory treatment of performance measurement is in

Swiss, James E., *Public Management Systems* (Englewood Cliffs NJ: Prentice-Hall, 1991), chap. 5.

On the concept of organizations as negotiated orders, see

Nathan, Maria, "The Use of Negotiated Order Theory as a Tool for the Analysis and Development of an Interorganizational Field" 27 *Journal of Applied Behavioral Science* (June 1991), 163.

Schulman, Paul, "The Negotiated Order of Organizational Reliability," 25 *Administration and Society* (November 1993), 353.

Strauss, Anselm, *Negotiation* (San Francisco: Jossey-Bass, 1978), especially chap. 1.

Strauss, Anselm, et al., *The Social Organization of Medical Work* (Chicago: U. of Chicago Press, 1985).

A full account of the theory of the M-form organization is in

> Williamson, Oliver, *The Economic Institutions of Capitalism* (New York: 1985), chap. 2.

The standard source on the matrix approach is still

> Davis, S. M. and P. R. Lawrence, *Matrix* (Reading MA: Addison-Wesley 1976). The date correctly suggests that the matrix-management vogue may have passed; but, if so, it has probably passed in favor of the shift to more marketlike structures (such as networks) rather than back to classical bureaucracies.

And see, for an interesting case study,

> Sunon, May Ellen, "Matrix Management at the U.S. Consumer Product Safety Commission," 43 *Public Administration Review* (July–August 1983), 357.

On network organizations in business and government, see these two featured articles in *Business Week:* "The Virtual Corporation" and "The Hollow Corporation" (Feb. 8 and Mar. 3, 1993); and

> Landau, Martin, "On Multiorganizational Systems in Public Administration," 1 *Journal of Public Administration Research and Theory* (January 1991), 5.
> Milward, H. Brinton, et al., "What Does the Hollow State Look Like?" in Barry Bozeman, ed., *Public Management Theory: The State of the Art* (San Francisco: Jossey-Bass, 1993), chap. 20.
> Tully, Shawn, "The Modular Corporation," *Fortune* (Feb. 6, 1993), 106.

H. Brinton Milward, the leading scholar on this subject, has assembled an excellent symposium on the "hollow organization" in the public sector; see especially the articles by Eugene Bardach and Cara Lesser, William Gormley, Laurence Lynn, and Laurence O'Toole in

> "Symposium on the Hollow State: Capacity, Control, and Performance in Interorganizational Settings," 6 *Journal of Public Administration Research and Theory* (April 1996).

▼◆●■▼◆●■▼◆●■▼◆●■▼◆

CHAPTER 4

Democratic Accountability versus Administrative Discretion

The sixth—and in some ways the most important—feature in our listing of the characteristics of a Weberian bureaucracy was **rule-boundedness,** to use the somewhat-awkward term that's common in the literature. So central is the bureaucratic paradigm to public administration (notwithstanding moves toward the market paradigm as an alternative), and so important are rules in bureaucratic practice, that it's worth turning at this point to the main problem which rule-boundedness was supposed to solve: the problem of administrative discretion. In a democracy we want appointed officials, who don't owe their jobs directly to the people, to be answerable to the elective policy makers, who do. It's no surprise, then, that so many of the rules which control administrative actions exist mainly to ensure that appointed officials will execute the intentions of the people's chosen representatives. These rules come from legislators, judges, and, of course, from top decision makers within the administrative agencies themselves.

There are also rules—for the most part, written by appointed officials rather than by legislators—to control certain actions either of citizens in general or of members of special groups, such as factory owners and beneficiaries of government grants (food stamps, welfare payments, and so forth). Examples of such rules include most environmental regulations, product-safety standards, and the procedural requirements that are exacted of applicants for public benefits. As Americans, we live under "a government of laws not of men." But every day, more and more of the laws under which we conduct our affairs consist of rules issued by public administrators rather than enacted by elected legislators.

In this chapter we take up both kinds of rules—those imposed *on* officials by legislators, judges, and senior public administrators themselves as well as those framed or interpreted *by* officials and imposed on citizens who come under the jurisdictions of administrative agencies. We'll also give special attention to two specific kinds of roles that many public administrators fill in our system—the quasi-judicial role of administrative adjudicator and the quasi-legislative role of administrative rule maker. Judges, lawmakers, and scholars have expended much brainpower trying to define (1) how much discretion adjudicators and rule makers should enjoy and (2) how formal regulations might be used to discipline administrative discretion once its proper limits have been marked out in some way.

The Public Bureaucracy as a Rule-Bound Environment

In general, the Progressives trusted that government officials would use any discretion they possessed responsibly, because, the Progressives assumed, administrators would bring appropriate values to their new jobs in public service. In his 1887 paper on administrative reform, Woodrow Wilson argued that America's civil servants could be expected to react in most situations pretty much as ordinary folk would. After all, except for their superior levels of technical preparation, they'd be ordinary Americans themselves. Wilson argued that administrators would be answerable not only to elected legislators and organizational higher-ups but also to public opinion. The desire of bureaucrats to retain the respect and support of the citizenry would, almost by itself, prevent the emergence of "a domineering, illiberal officialism." Wilson expected a civil service "so intimately connected with the popular thought, by means of elections and constant public counsel, as to find arbitrariness or class spirit quite out of the question."

Public administrators not only would have internalized the values of the citizenry in general but also would have committed themselves to the highest moral and practical standards of their professions. The final decades of the nineteenth century saw the establishment of many of America's leading professional associations. Professionalism implied a heightened level of attention to academic credentials as well as a stiffening of intellectual and professional standards. The ethic of professionalism became a powerful force in the higher civil service. As professionals educated at the best schools and imbued with the high standards of their callings, they were expected to use their specialized knowledge selflessly and responsibly.

We've seen that the staffers whom the Progressives hoped to recruit into the burgeoning agencies of government would bring knowledge of the One Best Way to their jobs. The proof that administrators were experts—which, after all, was the basic assumption of the civil service, especially in the upper ranks—would lie in their knowledge of superior methods. The proof that they were professionals would lie in their adherence to the high standards of their callings when applying the best methods. Appointive officials would feel intellectually and even morally obliged to use "standard accounting procedures," "best engineering practice," or whatever other best way of tackling problems represented the state of the art in their fields of expertise.

The theory of expertise supported the early reformers' willingness to legislate in broad, even vague terms. Believing as they did in an internalized ethic of service that reduced the need for extensive external regulation, the Progressives were willing to delegate discretionary authority to appointive officials whose specialized knowledge they then trusted to produce proper decisions in specific cases.

Unfortunately, however, the Progressives overestimated the disciplining potential of expertise. Lobbyists began pressing officials to adopt their own biased interpretations of the vaguely worded statutes. As we'll see in Chapter 6 when we take up the theories of "iron triangles" and "issue networks," it's easy to overstate the *capture* of administrative agencies by agents of the very industries those administrators are supposed to be regulating. Nevertheless, there's some validity in the charge that administrators have occasionally (and perhaps more than just occasionally) gotten too close, too cozy with their counterparts in the private sector. As concerns increased about the potential for abuses of discretion, so did efforts to control administrative action. There gradually developed a web of rules imposed on our appointive officials by legislators, judges, and often by senior administrators themselves. Much of the bureaucratic red tape to which today's public administrators are subject exists to hamper just the kind of "unhampered discretion" that Progressives such as Woodrow Wilson wanted to confer on them.

Rules Imposed by Legislators and Judges

Legislators are far more likely today than they were in times past to write laws that prescribe in meticulous detail what administrators must do to whom—and, often, exactly how they may do it. The result has been an externally imposed regime of detailed rules that crimp appointive officials' freedom of action. This process is sometimes referred to as **legislative micromanagement.**

At the federal level, Congress since the early 1960s or so has taken to passing laws remarkable for their length and specificity. The 1970 Occupational Safety and Health Act, the 1974 Employees Retirement Income Security Act, the 1976 Federal Land Policy and Management Act, the 1978 Natural Gas Policy Act, the amendments to the Clean Air Act (1970, 1977, 1990), and literally dozens of other major federal statutes all contain minutely detailed provisions. Executive-branch officials must follow these legislative requirements when administering programs of great technical complexity. James Q. Wilson has observed that state legislatures seem these days to be just as apt as Congress is to micromanage. For example, Wilson writes, the elementary and secondary schools in his state of California "are governed by the better part of five volumes of the state's education code, 2,846 pages in all (including commentary). And all this is just the legislature's contribution to defining a good education. . . ."[1] Similar descriptions can be multiplied for most other states, and even for the actions of county and city councils in many areas of the country.

Procedurally, the most important general statutory limit on federal administrators' discretion is the 1946 **Administrative Procedures Act (APA).** The federal APA became the pattern for most state and even municipal statutes passed to define the procedures that administrators at those levels must follow. The years since passage of the APA have seen a vast and complex body of administrative law develop, aimed at limiting exercises of administrative power that are "arbitrary, capricious, an abuse of discretion, or otherwise not in accordance with the law." The procedures mandated by the APA and kindred statutes have exposed administrative actions to close review by the courts, which brings us to our second main category of action-oriented restrictions: those imposed by judges rather than by legislators.

When a public administrator interprets a law passed by the legislature, adjudicates a dispute between citizens, passes on a claim for some public benefit, or implements a regulation issued by the administrative agency in which he or she works, a person affected by the action may contest the administrator's decision. Over the decades, administrative actions have been subjected to literally hundreds of thousands of court challenges, many of which have resulted in judicial decisions that have crystallized into additional, judge-made rules for administrators to follow in subsequent cases. These

[1]"Can the Bureaucracy be Deregulated?: Lessons from Government Agencies," in John J. DiIulio, ed., *Deregulating the Public Service* (Washington: Brookings, 1994), p. 44.

judge-made rules are important elements in the branch of law known as **administrative law.** Administrative law also includes the statutes that legislators have passed to define the powers, duties, and procedures of administrative officials (such as the federal APA). It further includes the caselaw generated by regulatory commissioners, senior administrators, and administrative law judges[2] in their capacities as adjudicators of disputes. And it includes many of the procedural rules that administrative officials themselves issue to structure their own agency activities.

In turn, the statutes that frame the general rules of administrative law (again, the APA is the standard example) are controlled by a still-higher body of law, known as **constitutional law,** which consists of the provisions of the U.S. Constitution itself and—more important—of judicial interpretations of the constitutional document. A special kind of judicial scrutiny is triggered when a citizen can make a reasonable case that an administrative official has violated one of his or her constitutional rights, especially procedural or substantive due process rights. We'll come back to the subject of these special rights in Chapter 8.

Rules Imposed on Public Administrators by Other Public Administrators

To this point, we have emphasized the rules that decision makers other than administrators—legislators and judges—impose on agency officials. In addition, vast and important portions of the regime of rules have been put in place by senior administrative officials themselves. Organizational and procedural requirements in some bureaucracies seem to propagate organically. The literature of public administration contains story after story of regulations germinated and nurtured within the administrative system, as if by a process of "bureaucratic genesis."

Many of the *standard operating procedures (SOPs)* that structure activities in a typical bureaucracy are in the nature of simple housekeeping measures or "traffic rules" to maintain the flow of work. These internally generated administrative regulations rarely attract much notice—except, of course, by the officials who must follow them. Rules of this nature rarely turn out to be worthy subjects for congressional investigation or litigation in courts. Yet, cumulatively, SOPs may represent a heavy weight on the governmental process, especially when they are considered in conjunction with externally imposed regulations. Individual rules, whether internally generated or imposed from

---

[2]**Administrative Law Judge (ALJ):** An appointive official in an administrative agency—usually a lawyer in a relatively senior civil service grade—who conducts formal courtlike hearings in important cases. A hearing before an ALJ is highly structured and often is focused on technical issues. Usually the hearing is used to gain a careful preliminary examination of the facts and applicable law (ALJs used to be called "hearing examiners") and of an opinion by a seasoned adjudicator about the proper disposition of the main issues in the case. The ALJ's decision then goes to the commissioners or top administrators in the agency for review. This review process means, in effect, that the losers at the level of the ALJ's hearing normally may appeal to the commissioners or top administrator for a reversal of the ALJ's decision. In the same way, the losers at the commissioners' or administrator's level can go beyond the agency by appealing an adverse administrative decision to the courts. In a major federal regulatory case, issues may be formally litigated through no fewer than five stages: at the hearing before the ALJ, in further argument within the agency in front of the commissioners or top administrator, on appeal to a district court, on further appeal to a higher circuit court, and (in the most important cases) on final appeal to the U.S. Supreme Court.

the outside, add up. The overall ambiance of rule-boundedness can engender resentment, discouragement, indifference, or timidity among civil servants who find that following the rules may hinder, not help, them do their work. Critics charge that the weight of rules has slowly transformed many of the Progressives' administrative structures into unresponsive "old-line agencies."

It's almost always possible to find a reason somewhere along the line for a given bit of red tape. As an eminent public administrationist, Herbert Kaufman, has argued, this or that rule may have originated in the best of intentions—to plug some loophole or prevent an administrative abuse.[3] But rule writing can become habit forming; and so, some critics charge, can mindless rule following.

The classic description of the rule-bound environment of modern bureaucracy appeared in a 1940 article by the sociologist Robert Merton. Virtually all subsequent critics of bureaucracy owe something to Merton. It was Merton who first suggested that rule-boundedness—although a source of inefficiency and even of perverse behavior when viewed by an external observer—can create within the workers themselves a sense of comfort and security. As the process of governance becomes increasingly complex and the cross-play of interests more dynamic, harried officials may yearn for refuge from hostile litigators, importunate special-interest representatives, and investigators from Congress or the home department's inspector general. Often an administrator finds it prudent to retreat behind some rule: "I was only following regulations!"

According to Merton, life in a hierarchical organization may produce not the efficiencies that the founders of our public bureaucracies expected but fussiness and **trained incapacity,** defined as the condition in which the carefully cultivated ability of a worker to perform in exactly the way required precludes adaptation even when the needs of the organization call for imagination and initiative. Related to trained incapacity is the pathology of **goal displacement,** whereby the worker displaces his or her primary concern from the achievement of the objectives that the organization has been set up to advance; instead, such a bureaucrat makes zealous adherence to the rules a goal in itself, whether such dutiful behavior contributes to the real mission or not. The ironic result, Merton writes, is that "the very elements which conduce toward efficiency in general produce inefficiency in specific instances."

[3]*Red Tape* (Washington: Brookings Institution, 1977).

Robert Merton on the Bureaucratic Personality

As Weber indicates, bureaucracy involves a clear-cut division of integrated activities which are regarded as duties inherent in the office. A system of differentiated controls and sanctions are stated in the regulations. The assignment of roles occurs on the basis of technical qualifications which are ascertained through formalized, impersonal procedures (e.g., examinations). Within the structure of hierarchically arranged authority, the activities of "trained and salaried experts" are governed by general, abstract, clearly defined rules which preclude the necessity for the issuance of specific instructions for each specific case. The generality of the rules requires the constant use of *categorization,* whereby individual problems and cases are classified on the basis of designated criteria and are treated accordingly. . . .

The chief merit of bureaucracy is its technical efficiency, with a premium placed on precision, speed, expert control, continuity, discretion, and optimal returns of input [in other words, "efficiency"]. The structure is one which approaches the complete elimination of personalized relationships and of non-rational considerations (hostility, anxiety, affectual involvements, etc.). . . .

In these bold outlines, the positive attainments and functions of bureaucratic organization are emphasized and the internal stresses and strains of such structures are almost wholly neglected. The community at large, however, evidently emphasizes the imperfections of bureaucracy. . . .

If the bureaucracy is to operate successfully, it must attain a high degree of reliability of behavior, an unusual degree of conformity with prescribed patterns of action. Hence, the fundamental importance of discipline which may be as highly developed in a religious or economic bureaucracy as in the army. Discipline can be effective only if the ideal patterns are buttressed by strong sentiments which entail devotion to one's duties, a keen sense of the limitation of one's authority and competence, and methodical performance of routine activities. The efficacy of social structure depends ultimately upon infusing group participants with appropriate attitudes and sentiments. As we shall see, there are definite arrangements in the bureaucracy for inculcating and reinforcing these sentiments.

At the moment it suffices to observe that, in order to ensure discipline (the necessary reliability of response), these sentiments are often more intense than is technically necessary. There is a margin of safety, so to speak, in the pressure exerted by these sentiments upon the bureaucrat to conform to his patterned obligations, in much the same sense that added allowances (precautionary overestimations) are made by the engineer in designing the supports for a bridge. But this very emphasis leads to a transference of the sentiments from the *aims* of the organization onto the particular details of behavior required by the rules. Adherence to the rules, originally conceived as a means, becomes transformed into an end-in-itself; there occurs the familiar process of *displacement* of goals. . . .

Discipline, readily interpreted as conformance with regulations, whatever the situation, is seen not as a measure designed for specific purposes but becomes an immediate value in the life-organization of the bureaucrat. This emphasis, resulting from the displacement of the original goals, develops into rigidities and an inability to adjust readily. Formalism, even ritualism, ensues with an unchallenged insistence upon punctilious adherence to formalized procedures. This may be exaggerated to the point where primary concern with conformity to the rules interferes with the achievement of the purposes of the organization, in which case we have the familiar phenomenon of the technicism or red tape of the official. An extreme product of this process of displacement of goals is the bureaucratic virtuoso, who never forgets a single rule binding his action and hence is unable to assist many of his clients. A case in point, where strict recognition of the limits of authority and literal adherence to rules produced this result, is the pathetic plight of Bernt Balchen, Admiral Byrd's pilot in the flight over the South Pole.

> According to a ruling of the department of labor Bernt Balchen . . . cannot receive his citizenship papers. Balchen, a native of Norway, declared his intention in 1927. It is held that he has failed to meet the condition of five years' continuous residence in the United States. The Byrd Antarctic voyage took him out of the country, although he was on a ship flying the American flag, was an invaluable member of an American expedition, and in a region to which there is an American claim because of the exploration and occupation of it by Americans, this region being Little America.
>
> The bureau of naturalization explains that it cannot proceed on the assumption that Little America is American soil. So far as the bureau is concerned, Balchen was out of the country and *technically* has not complied with the law of naturalization.[4]

[4]Actually, Merton's account was overstated, and even unfair. In the end, the bureaucrats relented. Balchen got his exception and received his citizenship papers. Nevertheless, the vignette seems to have rung so true with so many readers as a description of bureaucracy that it has become a kind of parable—an oft-quoted fable in the literature of public administration regarding the effects of rule-boundedness.

Such inadequacies in orientation which involve trained incapacities clearly derive from structural sources. The process may be briefly recapitulated. (1) An effective bureaucracy demands reliability of response and strict devotion to regulation. (2) Such devotion to the rules leads to their transformation into absolutes; they are no longer conceived as relative to a given set of purposes. (3) This interferes with real adaptation under special conditions not clearly envisaged by those who drew up the general rules. (4) Thus, the very elements which conduce toward efficiency in general produce inefficiency in specific instances. Full realization of the inadequacy is seldom attained by members of the group who have not divorced themselves from the "meanings" the rules have for them.

From Robert K. Merton, "Bureaucratic Structure and Personality," 18 *Social Forces* (May 1940): 560–564.

SECTION ● ■ ▼ ◆ **2**

Administrative Adjudication and Administrative Rule Making

Generally speaking, we have seen, the trend in public administration since World War II has been toward increasingly detailed statutory and judicial restrictions on public officials—legislators minutely prescribing what public officials should do and how they should do it (legislative micromanagement); and detailed judicial pronouncements that have added to the density and difficulty of the action-oriented restrictions on public administrators. Nevertheless, vast areas remain in which administrators enjoy broad discretionary opportunities. Administrative discretion is a source of concern—if by no means always of active worry—almost wherever it's found, but there are two areas in which the deployment of discretion raises issues of special interest: in *adjudication* and in *rule making*.

Administrative Adjudication

Across the United States there are literally thousands of officials whose basic job it is to resolve conflicts or allocate benefits and penalties after weighing competing claims. Conflict resolution and equitable decision making are the classic functions of judges. Hence these functions, when performed by regulators or other officials in administrative agencies (rather than in courts), are called by a term that combines both the administrative and the judicial elements: **administrative adjudication.**

The process of administrative adjudication has traditionally found its purest expression in the workings of an important group of agencies known as the **independent regulatory commissions (IRCs).** These commissions were among the important institutional innovations of the Progressive Era. In 1877, the U.S. Supreme Court upheld the constitutionality of state laws regulating private businesses that were "affected with a public interest."[5] Subsequently, the Court approved special administrative bodies—today called *public utility commissions (PUCs)*—that state legislators empowered to regulate industries ranging from local livery companies (the forebears of today's urban taxi fleets) to urban electric, telephone, and water utilities. Then, in 1887, Congress established the first federal regulatory commission, the Interstate Commerce Commission to

[5]*Munn v. Illinois*, 94 U.S. 113, 126.

regulate the railroads. The ICC set a pattern for other independent federal administrative agencies, such as the Radio Commission (later renamed the Federal Communications Commission), Federal Trade Commission, Federal Power Commission (later renamed the Federal Energy Regulatory Commission), and Securities and Exchange Commission.

These administrative agencies were called "independent" because they were to function as quasi-judicial, or *adjudicative,* bodies, outside both the legislative and the executive branches. The appointive officials who headed the IRCs at both the federal and the state levels were to apply laws that the legislature passed to regulate specific industries. But, at least in theory, these officials—called *commissioners*—were answerable only to the courts for their interpretations of the applicable standards. Unlike the cabinet officers who head executive departments such as State, Treasury, and so forth, the independent status of commissioners meant that their chains of command didn't run up to the president or governor. (We'll come back to this unusual and important notion of administrators answerable not to elected or appointed officials who are above them on the organizational ladder but to a "legal code" or "higher standard" that's to be applied in the manner of a judge.)

The first chairman of the ICC was an eminent legal scholar and judge named Thomas Cooley; he faced a daunting challenge—and an unprecedented opportunity. The lawmakers of the Progressive Era rarely provided detailed instructions when they legislated new agencies into existence. They thought that the individuals to be appointed to the new commissions would be experts in their subject and hence would best be able to sort out how to handle their jobs based on objective, technical considerations. Since the ICC came into existence with the typical Progressive open-ended legislative charter, Cooley was able almost singlehandedly to decide how he and his fellow commissioners should conduct the agency's business. Cooley adopted the practices of court trials in commission proceedings. Ever since, regulatory agencies at all levels of our government have tended to function as quasi-judicial institutions. Lawyers for private companies formally appear seeking regulatory approval for some action, such as raising their rates or making a new capital investment. In response, agency staff members argue "the public's side" of the case ("The proposed price hike isn't justified"; "The proposed new investment would be unnecessary and wasteful"). After hearing both sides, the commissioners decide.

Agencies with adjudicative responsibilities today exist at all levels of government. Their jurisdictions range from traditional public utility regulation to modern entitlements administration (disability policy, welfare policy, and the like).

Adjudicative roles may be distinguished not only on the basis of agencies' jurisdictional subject areas but also according to the levels of formality that are expected of an official when he or she is functioning in an adjudicative capacity. At one extreme is the regulatory commissioner taking evidence in a formal proceeding. Depending on the jurisdiction of the administrative agency in question, the commissioner may be deciding whether a regulated electric company deserves to raise its rates, whether an indigent mother qualifies for a welfare check, or whether an injured worker deserves disability benefits under the Social Security Act. At the opposite end—the informal end—of the adjudicative continuum is the street cop. Should the officer make an arrest, let a troublemaker off with a warning, or simply ignore the offense if it seems minor enough? The underlying requirement for an individual functioning at any point along this continuum is to exercise judgment. Hence, the governing paradigm of the adjudicative process is the **judgmental paradigm,** the central value of which is *fairness in the resolution of disputes or disposition of benefits.*

A scholar who has thought deeply about the adjudicative role in public administration, Jerry Mashaw of Yale Law School, has summed it up this way: "The goal in individual adjudications is to decide who deserves what." In this formulation of the adjudicative function, fairness is closely tied to the intuitive concept that most of us have of justice: A fair resolution is one that gives every party what he or she deserves after all relevant factors (the circumstances of the action, the conditions of the agents) have been taken into account. In a difficult but rewarding book based on a study of the adjudicative process in the federal Social Security Administration (see Box 4.1), Mashaw described adjudicative decision making as a "search for moral deservingness." Professor Mashaw's description applies up and down the administrative structure, from the work of the commissioner making a billion-dollar judgment in a rate case to the action of a patrol officer dispensing street justice.

Whether in formal legal proceedings or in the day-to-day resolution of minor disputes, the adjudicative function presupposes that some overarching moral or political standards can be invoked for the case at hand. Such a set of overarching standards typically involves questions like these: What's fair? What should a "reasonable, prudent person" have done in the circumstances? What's in the public interest? As a check against an erroneous interpretation of the standards that they identify as relevant, regulatory officials and most other administrative adjudicators must be ready to justify their decisions in court. Since argumentation in most adjudicative situations has to do with the application of standards ("Who deserves what?") rather than with automatic rules, adjudicators aren't expected to present geometric proofs but to justify the "reasonableness" of the particular principles they choose to emphasize. As a result, those staple considerations of the casuistic method—the circumstances of the action and the conditions of the agents—loom large in adjudicative judgments.

The regulatory field provides some of our best examples of adjudicative reasoning based on overarching standards rather than on hard-and-fast general rules or explicit commands from higher-ups in the organizational structure. We've noted that the legislators of the Progressive Era liked to pass broadly worded, open-ended regulatory laws. These Progressive Era statutes would typically authorize commissioners on adjudicative agencies such as the state public utility commissions to issue licenses to public utility companies. A licensed company—say a local electric, telephone, or water company—could then legally operate as a natural monopoly as long as its actions served "the public convenience and necessity." The commissioners were to audit the books of these companies to ensure that their rates were "just and reasonable." Needless to say, however, what "the public convenience and necessity" required varied from case to case and from industry to industry. And what the commissioners found to be "just and reasonable" in one set of circumstances might have been unfair or irrational in another. Administrators in adjudicative roles couldn't be asked to obey a rigid code of rules, good for all cases.

It's a subject of continuing debate how closely a formal adjudicative proceeding—such as a regulatory rate setting proceeding or a disability determination hearing—must

BOX 4.1 ▬▬▬▬▬▬▬▬▬▬▬▬▬▬▬▬▬▬▬▬▬▬▬▬▬▬▬▬ ■ ■ ■

Jerry Mashaw on Competing Models of Justice in the Social Security Administration

Under the federal Social Security Act, citizens who become disabled and can't continue working may qualify for special compensation from the government. Officials in the Social Security Administration (SSA) of the U.S. Department of Health and Human Services, working in collaboration with state-level medical and vocational officials, must determine whether claimants are entitled to receive benefits under the terms of the law. It's not nearly as straightforward an administrative problem as you might suppose, in part because the applicable statute is itself somewhat vague. In the language of the act:

> an individual shall be determined to be under a disability only if his physical or mental impairment or impairments are of such severity that he is not only unable to do his previous work but cannot, considering his age, education and work experience, engage in any other kind of substantial gainful work which exists in the national economy . . . (42 U.S.C. 423 (d)(2)(1976)).

Many of complications in the implementation of the Social Security law derive from the simultaneous applicability of three competing *models of justice*. The term is Jerry Mashaw's, from his detailed study of the disability program. Mashaw describes three models—**bureaucratic rationality**, **moral judgment**, and **professional treatment**. Of these, the moral judgment model corresponds most closely to our judgmental paradigm.

Bureaucratic Rationality: Obedience with Efficiency

The touchstone of Mashaw's bureaucratic rationality model is *correctness*, by which Mashaw means action by an administrator on a given case which accurately reflects the intention of the lawmakers (in other words, "obedience to authority") and which disposes of cases in the most cost-effective way (in other words, the criterion of "efficiency"). Mashaw writes:

> . . . [T]he administrative goal in the ideal conception of bureaucratic rationality is to develop, at the least possible cost, a system for distinguishing between true and false claims. Adjudicating should be both accurate (the legislatively specified goal) and cost-effective. . . .

Moral Judgment: Who Deserves What?

The lawyers in the Social Security Administration, as Mashaw observed them, envision disability determination as an adjudicative process rather than as a bureaucratic one. The lawyers prefer a moral judgment paradigm in which (as noted in the text) *deservingness* emerges as the key value:

The traditional goal of the adjudicatory process is to resolve disputes about rights, about the allocation of benefits and burdens. The paradigm adjudicatory situations are those of civil and criminal trials. In the former, the contest generally concerns competing claims to property or the mutual responsibilities of the litigants. Property claims of "It has been in my family for generations" confront counterclaims of "I bought it from a dealer" or "I have made productive use of it"; "The smell of your turkey farm is driving me mad" confronts "I was here first." In the latter, accused murderers claim self-defense or diminished responsibility. The goal in individual adjudications is to decide who deserves what. . . .

The moral judgment model views decisionmaking as value defining. The turkey farmer's neighbor makes a valid appeal not to be burdened by "noisome" smells, *provided* his conduct in locating nearby is "reasonable" and he is not being "overly sensitive." The turkey farmer also has a valid claim to carry on a legitimate business, *provided* he does so in ways that will not unreasonably burden his neighbors. The question is not just who did what, but who is to be preferred, all things considered, when interests and the values to which they can be relevantly connected conflict.

Acting in the name of due process of law, the members of the agency's legal staff see it as their duty to ensure that all applicants are treated fairly—"fairness" being achieved when every party gets what he or she deserves. The key concern is neither efficiency in claims processing nor customized personal treatment of disabled citizens; it is the obligation to see that every applicant receives the entitlements which the law provides for anyone in the same situation.

Professional Treatment: Service to Patients

By contrast with the professional administrators and the lawyers, doctors—whom we would also expect to play a major role in a disability-determination program—tend to favor a professional treatment model in which the highest value is *service*. Whereas the rational bureaucrat tries to act impersonally, simply processing papers on the basis of objective information about the applicant's level of disability, and the judge aspires to make proper judgments of deservingness, the proponent of professional treatment tries to consider each case individually but nonjudgmentally. As one would expect in any doctor-patient relationship, the decision maker tries to see the patient as a person, not merely as an additional bit of "casework." What's more, the service provider might be willing to bend the rules (or incur additional expenses) if the applicant's special needs seem to require it. In Mashaw's words:

> The goal of the professional is to serve the client. The service delivery goal or ideal is most obvious, perhaps, in the queen of the professions, medicine; but it is also a defining characteristic of law and the ministry and of newer professions such as social work. . . . The objective [of medical treatment] is to wield the science [that the doctor possesses] so that it produces good as defined by the patient. This entails interpersonal and diagnostic intuition—clinical intelligence—as well as scientific knowledge.

An administrative system for disability decisonmaking based on professional treatment would, therefore, be client-oriented. It would seek to provide those services—income support, medical care, vocational rehabilitation, and counseling—that the client needed to improve his well-being. . . . Disability decisions would be viewed not as attempts to establish the truth or falsity of some state of the world, but rather as prognoses of the likely effects of disease or trauma . . . and as efforts to support the client while pursuing therapeutic and vocational prospects. . . .

When action comes to be justified, sound professional judgment is an adequate explanation. And the adequacy of bureaucratic organization will be evaluated in terms of its tendency to permit fulfillment of the professional's role in relation to client or patient needs. . . .[6]

Mashaw concluded that the first paradigm—bureaucratic rationality—is the dominant one in the Social Security Administration. Bureaucratic rationality alone among the three approaches promised implementation of the disability program as members of Congress envisioned it, "rather than the pursuit of some other set of values." Nevertheless, the important roles of both lawyers and doctors in the disability program result in constant pressures for the use of criteria drawn from the competing moral judgment and professional treatment models. In each individual case, decision makers must "triangulate" to a compromise among the three approaches. This kind of indeterminacy, we have seen, is common in public administration.

[6]Jerry Mashaw, *Bureaucratic Justice: Managing Social Security Disability Claims* (New Haven CT: Yale U. Press, 1983); see especially pp. 23–34.

follow the paradigmatic example of adjudication, a formal court trial. Carelessness in accepting evidence, failure to compile a written record of sufficient thoroughness, or other procedural lapses might constitute a denial of due process. Yet even in formal adjudicative hearings, the applicable precedents generally end up leaving ample room for the adjudicators to exercise substantial discretion when making their judgments in specific cases.

Of course, an even-higher level of discretion usually applies in less formal episodes of adjudication, as in the examples of the street cop or of an administrative supervisor who must decide how to deal with a misbehaving subordinate. In informal adjudicative situations, it may be quite proper for an administrator to make a decision based on common sense, organizational custom, or ordinary morality: What does simple decency require, given the circumstances of the action? Who is the more deserving party to the dispute, given the conditions of the agents? How do principles of fair dealing, honesty, and respect for the other person affect the parties' entitlements?

Administrative Rule Making

Discretionary action enters the administrative process not only by the quasi-judicial route of administrative adjudication but also by the quasi-legislative path of administrative rule making. The opportunity for administrators to function, in effect, as lawmakers often arises because the legislators themselves may lack the interest, the information, or the political courage to settle every last provision of a new public program. Besides, even the most meticulous turn of phrase in a statute may miss some complication in the way the world actually works. Recognizing these realities, lawmakers often explicitly instruct administrators to spell out the statutory interpretation that they (the administrators) mean to adopt and the procedures that they intend to use when implementing a new law. In effect, the lawmakers tell the administrators to write a regulation that will limit their own discretion. The process by which such an administrative regulation is conceived, drafted, discussed with the parties who are likely to be affected by it, and finally issued as a formal order with the force of law is called **administrative rule making.** It is probably the primary formal method by which administrators, in effect, "legislate" in the sense of issuing rules to be followed by specified groups of ordinary citizens.

The rule maker's role—one of the most important in public administration—requires administrators to function as lawmakers, or at least in a quasi-legislative mode. That mode casts appointive officials in a role which strict democratic theory once reserved for elected representatives sitting in formal legislative bodies.[7] As would be expected, delegations of lawmaking power to administrative officials are still hedged about with restrictions. These restrictions take the form of both specific procedures that have to be followed and more general principles that guide administrators during the rule-writing process. Toward the end of this section we'll list some of these basic principles. We'll also see that they often cut against one another, thereby becoming yet another source of overdetermination in public administration.

The procedures that administrators follow when developing rules are set forth in the federal Administrative Procedures Act, in various state-level versions of the APA, and in many specific statutes that prescribe special procedures to be followed in particular agencies or circumstances. Most of the key provisions in these statutes have been challenged in the courts, so judicial interpretations must also be considered when an administrative rule maker sets out to frame a new regulation.

The rule-making process has many variations, ranging from the almost casual to the highly formal, from the quick and simple to the exceedingly costly and cumbersome. When the solution to a problem is obvious and uncontested, or when the problem itself is relatively simple, the rule-making process may proceed relatively swiftly. But when high financial stakes are implicated, when a new law calls for administrative action that members of some constituency oppose on ethical or ideological grounds, or when difficult technical judgments must be made, the rule-making process can become a cockpit of contending interests and conflicting positions. "Intervenors" may enter the

---

[7]In the strongest form of this reservation, the political philospher with the greatest influence on the framers of the U.S. Constitution, John Locke, wrote: "The legislative cannot transfer the power of making laws to any other hands: for it being but a delegated power from the people, they who have it cannot pass it over to others"; see sec. 141, *Second Treatise of Civil Government.* For some time, it has been recognized that the nondelegation principle, if literally applied, would prevent the administrative process from functioning. For this reason, the courts permit lawmakers to "pass the power over to others," those others being appointive administrators. Yet suspicion of delegated power persists. Because discretionary administrative power seems inherently less responsive to the popular will and hence more liable to abuse, it remains an object of close scrutiny by judges and by members of an **oversight committee** (the legislative committee or subcommittee responsible for "riding herd" on the administrative agency assigned to its jurisdiction). Just as inevitably, delegated powers are subject to elaborate disciplining rules.

fray and challenge the rule makers at almost any stage. The multiple points at which spokespersons for affected interests can intervene make the formal rule-making process cumbersome and prone to delay. In the following discussion, we'll concentrate on the complexities of large, formal rule makings; then in our chapter case, we'll try to apply some of the relevant principles to a relatively informal municipal rule-setting process.

Rule making most commonly begins in one of two ways. As mentioned, legislators may require the intended administrators to set forth in explicit terms how they read a new statute and what procedures they intend to follow under it. Alternatively, the officials of an administrative agency themselves may sense a need for action to correct some problem, modify some agency procedure, or clarify some provision of existing law; a formal rule is the usual device for announcing the action, changing the way business has been conducted, or explicating the statutory interpretation which officials henceforth intend to use when enforcing or executing a law that's already on the books.

Usually a special team of experts within an agency will be assigned to see a rule-making exercise through from start to finish. The members of this team will make as careful a study of the problem as time and money allow. They will review pertinent judicial rulings and any relevant decisions by administrators in earlier cases that might bear on the problem at hand. The rule makers may then conduct formal studies to determine the costs and benefits of different ways to achieve the intended goals of the new rule. It's often necessary to hold open hearings, at which virtually anyone who wishes to participate may offer testimony about the pros and cons of the options that the rule writers are considering. Seemingly endless hours may be spent in consultation and negotiation with representatives of groups whose members will be affected by whatever rule finally emerges. At last, the team may publish a final statement of the rule, which will thereafter have the force of law.

Even in the simplest kind of proceeding (known as *informal rule making* or *notice-and-comment rule making*) the rule writers must provide public notices to inform attentive citizens of their intentions, must arrange to receive written comments by anyone who wishes to submit materials, and must publish a final written summary of the rationale for the rule in the form in which it ultimately appears. In major federal rule making, at appropriate points officials also have to publish a series of statements, along with supporting data, called the *Advanced Notice of Proposed Rule (ANOPR); the Notice of Proposed Rule, (NOPR);* the penultimate draft of the proposed rule itself (the *PR*); and, at last, the final rule in whatever form emerges after all the pushing, massaging, revising, and editing are done. At every stage, the administrators must report and attempt in writing to meet all serious objections that commenters on the proposed rule have made at earlier stages in the process. Furthermore, once the administrators adopt a rule, they will be expected to follow it closely unless they can adduce very solid reasons for departing from it. Only if administrators, like ordinary citizens, play by the rules can all affected parties know the terms of the game. Again, it comes back to the idea of fairness, which underlies the legal concept of due process.

Using some variant of this process, officials at all levels of our government issue many hundreds of administrative regulations every year on subjects ranging from the procedures that Treasury Department officials will use to fix the interest rates of certain government bonds to the definitions that public health officials will use when administering laws affecting persons with "AIDS-related diseases," that welfare agency officials will use to decide when a family is living "in poverty," and that Environmental Protection Agency administrators will use when applying the protections of the Endangered Species Act. At the federal level, final administrative rules fill almost two hundred small-print volumes in the *CFR (Code of Federal Regulations)*.

If a proposed rule finally does make it to publication in the *CFR* or in a comparable state or municipal code, the implementers may turn up unexpected bugs when they try to put the regulation into practice. They'll then have to start a mini rule-making process to enact amendments needed to rectify the problems that have been discovered in the original rule. At the same time, citizens who are finding compliance with the original rule to be costly or inconvenient may be lobbying the administrators for informal adjustments in the way the rules are interpreted and applied. Meanwhile, legislators who feel the heat from the same lobbyists may amend the original statute to mandate adjustments in the implementing rules. Needless to say, while all this is in the works, the original problem may be changing. Through it all, claims that the rule violates due process or some other requirement of law are likely to be in active litigation. In the end, the courts remain involved right along with legislatures and the rule-making agencies themselves as full partners in the making of administrative law.

Years—not months, but *years*—may intervene between the legislative floor debate on a proposed new law and final court review of the implementing regulations. The process may culminate in the general acceptance of a rule with multibillion-dollar impacts on the economy or profound implications for individuals. But it may also end up producing little more than a paper trail of controversy, litigation, and paychecks for all the administrators, consultants, and lawyers who were involved in the process.

 CHAPTER READING ▼▼▼

Illustrative of what can go wrong in the rule-making process is the following story by journalist Robert Reinhold of an abortive effort in the Food and Drug Administration (FDA). Although the disappointing result (or, rather, the *non*result) in this episode was unusual, Reinhold's account emphasizes other aspects of the rule-making process that are typical of current administrative practice. These include the political environment in which the technical experts work, the openness of the administrative process to pressure from outsiders, and the importance of tactics and timing to success or failure (illustrated, for example, by the impact of a "late" cost-benefit study).

How One Rule-Making Process Worked (or Didn't Work) in the U.S. Food and Drug Administration
Robert Reinhold

The FDA may have been its own worst enemy, given the anti-regulatory mood of the country. With its soft underbelly exposed, the FDA ventured bravely into battle. Daggers were drawn at every turn.

As any consumer who has ever purchased a prescription drug knows, the container in which it comes has almost no information on the label other than instructions on how many times a day to take it and perhaps a little sticker warning against combining it with alcohol consumption. Consumer activists have long argued that because many drugs are extremely hazardous the patient has a right to know more about what he or she is taking. . . . [T]he FDA began in 1974 to investigate the issue, with a view toward new rules requiring [patient package inserts, or *PPIs*] with prescription drugs. . . .

The project was headed by an affable young psychologist from Brooklyn, Louis Morris, who had come to the agency after taking a Ph.D. at Tulane, where he studied the placebo effects of drugs on patients. He was soon to learn that the hardball world of Washington politics bore little resemblance to the polite academic world of science and objective facts.

On November 7, 1975, the FDA published one of those turgid gray notices in the *Federal Register* saying that it was considering requiring PPIs generally, and inviting comments. It received more than 1,000—from consumers, doctors, druggists, and professional organizations. It also commissioned studies of the issue and sponsored conferences and symposia in conjunction with the American Medical Association (AMA) and the Pharmaceutical Manufacturers Associations (PMA). It reviewed all the scientific literature on the value of PPIs. All of this was necessary to meet any later challenge claiming that the agency had not given full consideration to the implications of its actions. But even before the agency made up its mind on a full-blown program, trouble began brewing when it issued an estrogen PPI rule in 1978. Morris explained in an interview:

> That started to bring out a lot of the professionals against PPIs. The estrogen insert was frightening to people—it stressed the risks, and it was very difficult to read. It was a fear-inducing document, written by doctors at the FDA. Estrogen sales were cut in half. That's not what we wanted. But unfortunately the message in the insert was one of fear. We could have written it a lot clearer.

Despite this harbinger of trouble, the FDA plunged ahead. . . .

Thus on Friday, July 6, 1979, a dry notice appeared in the *Federal Register* announcing a "proposed rule." The rule would have required inserts for 375 of the most widely prescribed of the 5,000 prescription drugs on the market. It proposed to phase in the plan over several years, starting with about 50 to 75 drugs and drug classes the first year. . . . The rule would have required drug makers to prepare and distribute through pharmacies a leaflet written in nontechnical and nonpromotional language. It would list, among other things, the proper uses of the drug, circumstances under which it should not be used, and possible side effects. It would have to be given to all drug buyers, except those deemed legally incompetent, whose primary language was not English, or who were blind, whose doctors directed the insert withheld, patients in emergency treatment, and institutionalized persons.

The response was not entirely what the FDA might have hoped for. . . . Druggist groups, doctors, drug makers, and others began to write letters to members of Congress. The proposal elicited about 1,300 written comments, not all of them unfavorable, and other reactions were expressed at hearings held in three cities.

In all these preliminaries, required before a regulation takes effect, the FDA may have been its own worst enemy. Given the anti-regulatory mood of the country at the time, it did something its officials now admit was naive. The proposed rule was advanced before the agency had done an economic analysis of whether the benefits of implementing the rule were worth the costs, or had examined if there were any cheaper alternatives that would achieve the same end. "We failed to protect where we were most vulnerable—on the economic side," said Morris. "We put out the regulation and then did the cost-benefit analysis. It did not have the documentation it should have had. We found out what concerned people most was the economics. How naive of us."

Naive indeed. With its soft underbelly thus exposed, the FDA ventured bravely into battle. Daggers were drawn at almost every turn. . . .

The druggists said they would have to redesign their stores to build huge pigeonhole racks to hold the little flyers, hire extra help to fumble with them, and otherwise alter their operations to cope with the new rules. The American Pharmaceutical Association (APhA), representing 55,000 pharmacists, calculated that the cost would amount to $235 million for the first year and possibly as much as $1.8 billion over five years. The National Association of Retail Druggists, representing 33,000 independent pharmacy owners who fill 70 percent of all prescriptions, came up with a figure of $250 million for the first year and $100 million to $150 million for each subsequent year. The National Association of Chain Drug Stores, to which 194 chains belong, put the price at $312 million to $532 million a year. And Eli Lilly, a leading drug maker, estimated that the cost to manufacturers alone would run to about $140 million annually. . . .

The consumer or "public interest" proponents of PPIs were not inactive in all this, but they were outgunned. While such groups are frequently effective at stirring up issues and provoking general alarm, they do not always have the sticking power of industry. While industry can marshall all of its resources in support or defense of a few major issues, public interest groups by their very nature must concentrate on several fronts at once. Marsha Greenberger is a lawyer for the Center for Law and Social Policy in Washington. . . . "The opponents have enormous resources available to them," she said in an interview. "They have gone to congressmen, the White House, they have filed lawsuits. They do have access. We have access too. But we've got limited staff. No one in the consumer movement can devote sustained and regular attention to this issue." . . .

In the words of a former FDA lawyer who now represents the drug makers, the druggists "lobbed a shell into the White House compound" with an analysis of the economic consequences of the proposed regulation. The complaints struck a responsive chord with the President's Domestic Policy Staff, his science advisers, and the Small Business Administration. The only high-level ally to come to the aid of the drug agency was the President's consumer adviser, Esther Peterson.

Then on top of all this, the proposal got "rarged" early in 1980—a Carterism meaning that the regulation was subjected to close scrutiny by a special interagency panel called the Regulatory Analysis Review Group (RARG), an arm of the Council on Wage and Price Stability. President Carter had set up the panel to review regulations with substantial economic consequences to make agencies more sensitive to the economic effects of what they did. The panel had no direct authority to alter regulations, but agencies had to respond to its inquiries and pronouncements. The panel, made up mostly of economists, tended to be sympathetic to business. . . .

The final RARG report took the drug agency to task, saying it had failed to consider many potential costs of the rule. Moreover, it observed, "We are troubled the FDA had not stated how the knowledge gained in its initial implementation steps will be reflected in subsequent ones." It suggested that the agency consider a limited phased-in test of the inserts rather than starting out with a full-blown program. . . .

At first the agency was distressed over the "rarging." But Louis Morris, the psychologist who headed the insert project, said that the ultimate RARG report was a "reasonable" one. "The decision of how many drugs how fast is basically a political decision," he said. "The FDA welcomes advice on that."

By the fall of 1980, the leadership of the drug agency had changed hands. . . . Dr. Jere Goyan . . . had been dean of the pharmacy school at the University of California at San Francisco. He came to the FDA job with a reputation as a champion of consumer rights. He once described himself as a "therapeutic nihilist," and had often said that Americans were "overmedicated." He seemed to many, after some months on the job, to be somewhat out of his element in the highly charged political atmosphere surrounding the FDA.

With his reputation as a foe of overmedication, it was widely assumed that Dr. Goyan would push full-speed ahead on the PPI rule. But shortly after taking office, he surprised everybody by letting it be known that he planned to scale back the regulation to include just 10 drugs on an experimental basis. . . .

The industry lobbyists had been at work on Capitol Hill and had elicited a positive response from the

House Appropriations Subcommittee on Agriculture, which handles the FDA budget. Dr. Goyan found himself under hostile questioning at a hearing of the subcommittee in March of 1980, particularly from Representative Bill Alexander, an Arkansas Democrat who had received a $250 contribution from the National Association of Chain Drug Stores Political Action Committee the year before. Minutes after Dr. Goyan testified that "I would not want to swallow a pill about which I knew nothing," Alexander extracted a promise from him that the PPI program would begin with no more than 10 drugs. . . .

Dr. Goyan indicated in the interview on the PPI issue that he feared that the Appropriations Committee would pass a bill forbidding the insert program altogether and the scaled-back scheme seemed like a politic way of getting half a loaf, or at least a few slices. "Politics is not necessarily a bad word," he said. . . .

And so the FDA proceeded to hammer out its final, much less ambitious, rule. . . . It was to be a three year pilot program involving new prescriptions for 10 drugs or drug classes. Refills were exempted from the insert requirement. . . . Two days later, on September 12, the full rules were spelled out in 63 pages of small type in the *Federal Register.* . . .

In November 1980, two months after the drug agency issued its "final" rule, Ronald Reagan was elected president on a platform that included the promise to roll back what he called costly, overly burdensome, and ineffective government regulations. The opponents of PPIs, having reached a reasonably satisfactory accommodation with the Carter admin-

istration, saw the opportunity to reopen the issue and force the FDA to back off even further. . . .

By this time, Dr. Goyan had been swept out of his job as FDA commissioner along with the rest of the top Carter appointees. The new FDA commissioner was Arthur Hull Hayes, Jr., a cardiologist who had been head of the Hypertension Clinic at the Hershey Medical Center, affiliated with Pennsylvania State University. . . .

Meanwhile, while the Reagan administration was reconsidering, a long-awaited study of the efficacy of PPIs by the RAND Corporation was released. The study, done under a $525,000 contract from the FDA, seemed to suggest that PPIs were neither as good as their proponents suggested nor as bad as their detractors feared. It found that 70 percent of patients would read the inserts. But the study also found that they did not substantially influence the way the medicine was used, nor encourage patients to return prescriptions for refunds.

Finally, under court order to announce a decision by December 24, 1981, Dr. Hayes and Secretary Schweiker [the new head of the Department of Health and Human Services, FDA's parent department] issued a joint statement in late December saying that they would scrap the entire proposal. . . . And so, after years of painful labor, the regulatory system gave birth to nothing.

From Robert Reinhold, "An Aborted Regulation," in Allan Sindler, ed., *American Politics and Public Policy: Seven Case Studies* (Washington: CQ Press, 1982), pp. 84, 87–89, 91, 94–99, 100, 103–105.

SECTION **3**
● ■ ▼ ◆

How Much Discretion? The Rules-versus-Standards Debate

What happens if a new rule makes it to formal publication? The discretion of administrators will have been reduced, to be sure—reduced but *not* eliminated. As we've noted, the rule will itself be subject to a process of continual rethinking and reinterpretation, particularly if it deals with a changeable area of public policy; if it covers subjects that can't be described with mathematical precision; or if it has been framed in the form of a general standard rather than as the kind of precise command that (in the words of the legal scholar Kathleen Sullivan) "binds a decisionmaker to respond in a determinate way to the presence of delimited triggering facts."

The so-called **rules-versus-standards debate** has long been one of the most important in public administration. The conflict in this debate is felt in both administrative adjudication and administrative rule making. Professor Sullivan of the Stanford Law faculty has put the matter succinctly:

> Here is the rules and standards debate in a nutshell. Law translates background social policies or political principles such as truth, fairness, efficiency, autonomy, and democracy into a grid of legal directives that decisionmakers in turn apply to particular cases and facts. . . . These mediating legal directives take different forms that vary in the relative discretion they afford the decisionmaker. These forms can be classified as either "rules" or "standards" to signify where they fall on the continuum of discretion. Rules, once formulated, afford decisionmakers less discretion than do standards. . . .
>
> (a) *Rules.* A legal directive is "rule"-like when it binds a decisionmaker to respond in a determinate way to the presence of delimited triggering facts. . . . A rule necessarily captures the background principles or policy incompletely as so produces errors of over- or underinclusiveness. But the rule's force as a rule is that decisionmakers follow it, even when direct application of the background principle of policy to the facts would produce a different result.
>
> (b) *Standards.* A legal directive is "standard"-like when it tends to collapse decisionmaking back into the direct application of the background principle or policy a fact situation. Standards allow for the decrease of errors of under- and overinclusiveness by giving the decisionmaker more discretion than do rules. . . .
>
> Why would anyone choose a rule over a standard or a standard over a rule? . . . [R]ules require a decisionmaker to act consistently, treating like cases alike. On this view, rules reduce the danger of official arbitrariness or bias. . . . [R]ules afford certainty and predictability [and minimize] the elaborate, time-consuming, and repetitive application of background principles to facts. . . . Standards are . . . less arbitrary than rules. They spare individuals from being sacrificed on the altar of rules, . . . are flexible and permit decisionmakers to adapt them to changing circumstances over time.[8]

More than a century of experience with administrative rule making and implementation has convinced most students of the subject that the question isn't so much *how* to eliminate discretion, which is impossible, as it is *who* in the overall system shall be entrusted with what kinds of discretion and how much of it. Should legislators confer substantial discretion on the administrators who will have to execute the legislative intent? Should administrators who find themselves implementing a vague statute try to confine their own room for maneuvering by issuing a rule-like clarifying regulation? Or should they try, on the contrary, to preserve as much discretion for themselves as they possibly can in the expectation that they, as the experts responsible for day-to-day administration of the law, will best be able to exploit any discretion in the system for the

---

[8]"Forward: The Justices of Rules and Standards," 106 *Harvard Law Review* (November 1992): 57–66.

benefit of citizens? Of course, both the statute and any rule that's issued may be reviewed in the courts. How tightly should a court try to confine the discretion of administrators by insisting, when they review a challenged rule, that a regulation provide for explicit requirements and elaborate procedures?

In our underdetermined system of governance—a system of fragmented jurisdictions and shared powers—it's rarely possible to predict in advance exactly how the pattern of discretion will end up distributed among lawmakers, judges, and administrators. Nevertheless, the rule-making process must be recognized as fundamental to the mechanisms in our system for making this distribution. The choice between a more rule-like and a more standard-like approach in the implementing of regulations is one of the most basic ways to "tune" the amount of discretion that the administrators of a statute enjoy. Among the principles for both the writers and the reviewers of an administrative rule are the following:

Respect for legislative intent. Elected representatives write the laws which, when duly enacted, should be executed in a responsive manner. Rule writers should normally try to express the intent of the lawmakers, albeit in more precise or more concrete terms than are contained in the pertinent statute.

Respect for administrative expertise. Administrators receive delegations of authority from legislators because they are more expert than the lawmakers are. Excessive limits on administrative discretion deprive government of precisely the expertise that the administrative apparatus was designed to give it.

Fairness and the principle of *promulgation*. A rule can't be fair unless those to whom it applies know what it requires. Any meaningful sense of promulgation requires reasonable clarity and specificity—the quality that Colin Diver, in our next reading, calls *transparency.*

Appropriate inclusiveness. An administrative rule must not err either on the side of over- or underinclusiveness—a criterion that brings up two other qualities discussed by Diver: *congruency* and *simplicity.*

Flexibility. Excessive rigidity either in the wording of a rule or in its mode of application may end up frustrating the intent of the lawmakers by preventing the administrators from tailoring their exercises of governing power to the needs of particular cases.

Significantly, these same principles apply, in a general way, to administrators when functioning in adjudicatory capacities. Adjudicative decision makers should consider both the legislative intent behind the statute that applies to the case and any recommendations that are based on the special technical knowledge of administrative staff members.

The principle of flexibility (which in some ways encompasses all the others) is perhaps the most difficult to apply in a general way. The following reading selection, from an article by Dean Colin Diver of the University of Pennsylvania Law School, explains why it's often so difficult to decide where a regulation should be located on the spectrum between a precisely worded rule and a more loosely phrased standard. Picking up on the point made by Kathleen Sullivan about the twin dangers of underinclusiveness and overinclusiveness, Diver identifies the three values—**transparency, congruence,** and **simplicity**—which, he argues, should ideally be embodied in an administrative rule. Diver claims that the basic problem in rule making derives from the inherent inconsistencies among these values. In other words, Diver directs our attention yet again to the pervasive and recurrent problem of overdetermination in administrative analysis.

Colin Diver on the Requisites of a Rule

If, as Oliver Wendell Holmes once said, "a word is . . . the skin of a living thought," then a "rule" is the skin of a living "policy." A rule is the verbal manifestation of a policy that is typically—but not necessarily—encased within a written text and issued with the formality suited to a solemn occasion. . . .

Rules may, like skin, be the visible manifestation of an unseen reality, but unlike skin, they are the product of conscious choice. The framing of a rule is, indeed, the climactic act of the policymaking process. Any system of advice calculated to improving that process must, then, include criteria for making the choice. In the following pages I develop an efficiency criterion for selecting the optimal "precision" of a regulation. . . .

Criticisms of legal rules tend to cluster in three discernible camps: the vagueness critique, the over-inclusiveness critique, and the complexity critique. The evil on which the vagueness critique focuses is indeterminacy. Vague rules leave persons whom they affect (or whom they may affect) to guess at their meaning in particular circumstances. They confer large areas of largely uncontrollable discretion on those entrusted with their enforcement. Vagueness is a common affliction of regulatory standards, especially those that rely on such open-ended terms as "in the public interest," "feasible," or "reasonable."

Recent criticism of specification standards in health and safety regulation illustrates the overinclusiveness critique. The problem with overinclusive rules is not that they are vague—their meaning is usually commendably clear—but that they command (or forbid) many actions that are not beneficial (or are harmful) to society. The fit between the outcomes demanded by literal adherence to the rule and those desired by the policymaker is poor. The complexity critique focuses on the sheer length and intricacy of a rule's verbal formula. Complex rules, like the tax code or many environmental regulations, make the determination of legal consequences turn on a maze of considerations, conditions, and exceptions. The consequence is to drive the cost of applying the rule to excessive levels.

These three critiques suggest three corresponding qualities that should characterize well-drafted rules: transparency, congruence, and simplicity. A transparent rule, like a transparent window, allows each observer to see the same image—to reach the same conclusion about legal consequences when confronted with the same evidence. Transparency thus increases the likelihood that the rule maker's intention will be communicated without distortion to the rule's audience. A congruent rule identifies as proscribed (or mandatory or permitted) only those actions that ought—under the policy maker's governing normative system—to be proscribed (or mandated or permitted). Congruence, in this sense, essentially determines the efficacy of a rule's verbal formulation in achieving its intended outcome. Simplicity, finally, is a function of the number of steps required by the regulation's decision rule and the quantity and accessibility of the evidentiary inputs that it demands. The simpler the rule, the more likely that its audience will remember it and the less costly its application to concrete situations.

Determination of the appropriate verbal form in which to cast regulatory policy decisions, then, could be understood as a problem of simultaneously maximizing a rule's transparency, congruency, and simplicity. Unfortunately, these values frequently conflict. Consider, for example, a rule setting a highway speed limit. A uniform speed limit like "maximum speed 55 m.p.h." has the virtues of transparency and simplicity. Virtually everyone understands the meaning of "55 m.p.h." (it is interpreted as "any speed at which the needle on my speedometer lies to the right of '55'"). The differences of interpretation that arise (resulting mostly from variations in the calibration of speed-measuring equipment) will be modest in all but the rarest of cases. The rule is also simple: the legal test relies on a single variable (speed), and the evidentiary input (speedometer reading) is easily accessible and relatively objective.

The problem with the rule is its incongruity. Under any plausible assumption about the purpose of highway speed regulation, a uniform speed limit will overinclude or underinclude. If the objective were absolute safety (zero accidents), a uniform speed limit (of zero) might be defensible. But more realistically, one must assume a policy objective that combines concerns about safety with other values such as the facilitation of movement and efficient consumption of motor fuel. However one might combine these values into a single objective function, it is inconceivable that a uniform speed would maximize that function. An "efficient speed" criterion (minimize the sum of the costs of accidents, delays, fuel consumption, and so forth), for example, would surely require a speed limit that varied with weather conditions, time of day, type of vehicle, purpose of travel, and the like. A variable speed limit of this sort might significantly enhance the rule's congruence but with an unavoidable loss of simplicity (since the decision rule would contain multiple criteria and perhaps require less objective and accessible evidentiary inputs, such as "time value of vehicle's occupants"). Transparency might also suffer if the new variables (such as "icy conditions") are less susceptible to uniform interpretation than a simple speed limit.

One could restore at least the appearance of simplicity with a rule such as "do not exceed a reasonable speed." But transparency suffers badly in such a formulation. And one has little basis for confidence that such a congruent-sounding rule will in fact produce congruent outcomes, since it effectively confers a broad, unlimited discretion upon drivers and enforcers. . . .

One possible way to make choices among such competing verbal formulations is to invoke some a priori moral value such as fairness or equity. Unfortunately these principles frequently conflict. The principle of "fair notice" may require the interpretive clarity of a highly transparent rule, while the principles of "participation" and "individualized treatment" may require the flexibility of a more opaque formulation. Even taken singly, moreover, few plausible moral principles point in an unambiguous direction. "Equity," for example, may be interpreted to require all three qualities: transparency, to assure equivalent interpretation by those subject to the rule; congruence, to assure equivalent treatment of those similarly situated in relation to the ultimate policy objective; and simplicity, to minimize differences in treatment resulting from cognitive or litigative advantages.

Constructing a metric for evaluating the work product of regulatory drafters, then, requires us, however crudely, to measure and compare the competing interests at work, in an effort to locate the appropriate mix of transparency, congruence, and simplicity. Adoption of this approach may convert the argument from the elevated rhetoric of moral principle to the crasser language of costs and benefits. But it provides a more promising basis for making the unavoidable tradeoffs entailed in decisions about the form of rules.

From Colin Diver, "Regulatory Precision," in Keith Hawkins and John Thomas, *Making Regulatory Policy* (Pittsburgh: U. of Pittsburgh Press, 1989), pp. 199–202.

CHAPTER CASE ●●●

The following scenario involves a set of rules to be promulgated by city administrators from two different agencies, acting under the authority of a new local law intended to promote inner-city residential development. The rule makings will govern the annual disbursement of several million dollars of tax money, to be collected in a special Housing Trust Fund. Several million dollars isn't exactly chump change; but neither is it of the magnitude—often mounting to the billions—that major federal rule makings often involve. The point is, rule-making actions like the ones described in our case are replicated thousands of times every year at all levels of government and at every scale of financial effect. The proceedings in the following scenario raise, in microcosm, virtually all the issues encountered when a public administrator ponders the pervasive problem of controlling administrators' actions by setting limits to the discretion they enjoy.

As you sort through the issues in the case, keep in mind that the problem isn't so much how to eliminate discretion, which usually proves to be impossible, as it is to decide who shall be entrusted with what kinds of discretion and how much of it.

1. Which individuals or organizations in the scenario are involved in the allocation and exercise of discretionary power? Can you suggest any general principles for the division of discretion? Should legislators try to tie down administrative rule writers? What values should administrative rule writers, in their turns, try to serve? How narrowly, in general, should they try to confine the actions of the frontline officials who will have to implement the rules?

2. How closely, and by means of what coordinating mechanisms, should the members of the two groups of rule writers in the scenario try to harmonize their work? Should both (or either) of the rule-writing groups described in the scenario emphasize rules over standards, or vice versa?

3. Which of the qualities that are desirable in a rule—transparency, congruence, and simplicity—should be stressed in the rules to be turned out by each of the rule-writing groups in the case? Should any one of these qualities be specifically emphasized—or consciously ignored—in any of the particular provisions of either rule?

CASE 3

· · · · · · · · · · · · · · · ·

Renewal in the Inner City:
A Housing Trust Fund for the Central Ward

For almost a decade, city watchers had been aware that something curious was happening in the rundown neighborhoods around the old central business district. Urban decay seemed to be in stiff competition with spontaneous renewal. No one could predict which of the contrary tendencies would finally win out.

Word had filtered out that Police Commissioner Grace Tarn was working on a new plan for the inner-city neighborhoods of greatest concern, the central ward area encompassing the 4th, 5th, and 6th police precincts. Those who knew about the project hoped the commissioner would hurry. Even as she worked, the statistics on crime, illegitimacy, unemployment—you name it—got worse. Almost 20 percent of the once-residential structures in the area were already gutted or on the edge of abandonment. Druggies occupied most of the abandoned buildings that hadn't been consumed by arsonists' fires. Yet in the midst of the blight, there were signs of life. Developers were starting to appeal to the city's Board of Zoning Commissioners for the "downgrading" of whole blocks in the most dilapidated residential neighborhoods. Downgrading from a residential rating to zoned-for-business was the first step before buying old multi-unit apartment buildings and razing them to make room for new hotel or office construction.

Few owners of close-in multi-unit residential structures could resist the offers of the developers. But although it was true that every contract to clear a large old apartment building for a new hotel or office building added to the sense of economic recovery, this kind of "progress" further reduced the city's stock of affordable close-in housing. Among the prime targets for demolition were multi-unit buildings used as *single-room-occupancy apartments (SROs)*. There were literally hundreds of these seedy hotels in the central ward. Poverty-line families (more often than not, fatherless) and troubled single men (some of them with drug habits, mental illnesses, and criminal records) were the main occupants of the city's SRO space. These residents were also the ones least able to adjust when the eviction notices came from the developers who had just purchased the buildings in which they were living. The low-income population of the central ward represented the city's main reserve army of the homeless.

At the same time that commercial developers were eyeing potential comeback areas of the central ward, relatively young and affluent business and professional couples were "gentrifying"—buying up old two- and three-story brownstones or loft buildings for refurbishment, often with an eye to eventual resale at premium prices. Inevitably, gentrification—city Housing Department staffers called it "the assault of the yuppies"—added to the tendency of commercial development to take low-rent units out of the available residential inventory. Rising rents combined with the sheer physical withdrawal of low-rent space as a result of gentrification and commercial development had brought affordable residential housing to the crisis point in the near-downtown precincts.

Evelyn Alvarado, who headed the Housing Department, a major division within the city's Bureau of Human Services (BHS), wanted to encourage business growth and even some gentrification in the central ward. But she also wanted to balance these forces with an inner-city low-income housing program. To this end, Alvarado had developed her idea of a *housing trust fund (HTF)*. Alvarado missed few opportunities to preach for a mixture of residential and commercial development, renovation and new construction, new enterprises and (if necessary) life-support systems for inner-city commerce in the form of public subsidies to languishing business establishments. Evelyn Alvarado had sold the HTF idea first to her boss, Aaron Haber; then to Haber's boss, Hizzoner, the mayor himself; and finally, with the mayor's support, to a narrow majority of City Council members. When the council finally passed the HTF ordinance, an editorial in the *Trib'-Examiner* recognized it as both a personal and a professional triumph for the city's Housing Department director. The editorial writer called the money that would be paid into the HTF "Evelyn's fund"—which, to be truthful, was how Evelyn Alvarado herself thought about it.

The HTF program had two components.

First, the City Council defined the existing tax level on real property and improvements within the HTF area as a "predevelopment baseline." (The actual boundaries of the HTF area weren't specified in council legislation, but were to be drawn later in an administrative rule-making procedure.) Note: The taxes on inner-city properties were *not actually frozen* at the baseline level. On the contrary, the HTF idea depended on the expectation that with development, actual tax rates in the area—and hence the absolute level of tax receipts—would rise. For a twenty-year period, the *dif-ference* in any year between actual property tax receipts and the baseline figure would be diverted into the special housing trust fund. No one could predict the course of development for the full two decades of the HTF's expected existence. But Alvarado was convinced that a rising economic tide should pay about $2 million each year into the fund for the first four or five years of the baseline arrangement.

Second, a special tax would be collected on all transfers of title to land or buildings within the inner-city area. The exact amount of the transfer tax would be set as a flat rate in a special biennial resolution of the City Council. It would consist, for each two-year period, of a set number of dollars per square foot of property purchased, with one rate for vacant land and a different rate for "improved" real estate. For the first two years of the fund's operation, the transfer tax had been set at a level projected to pay a million dollars annually. Like the difference between the property tax collection and its baseline, the transfer tax dollars would go directly into the HTF.

In brief, "Evelyn's fund" should take in—and pay out—roughly $3 million each year for the first couple of years. All parties understood that rules would have to be written specifying precise HTF procedures. And, of course, some person or persons (presumably in the Housing Department) would have to do the actual administering. Alvarado had proposed that Aaron Haber, the head of the BHS, expand the mission of the Real Estate Planning Board, a small staff unit in the Housing Department. She assumed that the planning board would be the issuing agency for all rules required by the HTF program. Also, although it had no history as an operating body, the board would assume responsibility for implementing HTF rules when they were issued, in a manner consistent with the intent of the council.

· · · · ·

Most of Claire Nagamura's readers probably assumed that she was always busy—ferreting out information, writing copy, checking those "reliable sources" of hers. In truth, though, she spent much of her time just hanging out, walking the corridors of city hall and the county building. As Yogi Berra put it, "You can see a lot by watching."

Nagamura just watched as Esty Lee and the other inner-city community leaders swept by, obviously on their way to the mayor's office. Normally, there'd have been some chitchat. Local politicos like Esty Lee rarely missed an opportunity to massage influential journalists. This time, however, Lee—apparently the organizer and spokesperson of the passing group—merely nodded. The group later came to be called the Central Ward Delegation. From the looks on some of their faces, serious business was at hand, but Nagamura had no way of knowing that the issues for discussion related to the new HTF. Whatever concern had moved the members of the delegation to ask Hizzoner for an audience, however, from the looks on their faces Nagamura surmised that it probably had the makings of a story.

· · · · ·

As the city's housing director, Evelyn Alvarado had a full plate of duties and concerns. There was no way she could personally oversee the unfolding of her pet project, and so she turned to one of her aides, a staff assistant named Kendra Quinn.

Evelyn told Kendra that she would start immediately to sit in as her representative on the Real Estate Planning Board. Kendra would participate in the rule-making processes that would be required to implement the HTF ordinance. She would also take on any additional chores (within reason) assigned by Wayne Elsie, who chaired the planning board. Needless to say, it would also be Quinn's duty to keep Alvarado aware of any problems that Elsie and others on the board encountered trying to get the HTF program off the ground.

Back at her desk, Kendra began to work through the materials in the file that Evelyn had handed her. The first item was a copy of the HTF ordinance itself, which read in part:

AN ORDINANCE

WHEREAS it is the sense of this Council that dilapidation and abandonment of residential structures represents a threat to the quality of life of citizens, and inasmuch as dilapidation and abandonment have been found to be factors contributing to crime and drug abuse, to the reduction of affordable housing, and general community deterioration, especially in that portion of the inner city known as the central ward.

THEREFORE, be it enacted that . . .
    [At this point, the ordinance contains technical language describing the baseline comparison tax and the transfer tax.]

PURPOSES. All funds derived from the forgoing sources are to be maintained in trust and administered, managed, and disbursed for the purposes of promoting and stabilizing affordable housing within a context of balanced development in areas of the city to be designated by administrative rule making as eligible for financial support under this ordinance; WITH THE FURTHER PROVISO that no funds are to be used in support of analytical studies, such studies of those expenditures which will best promote balanced development being proper purposes of regular annual appropriations.

FULL EFFECT. The effective date of operation of the Housing Trust Fund will coincide with the publication of rules specifying criteria and methods of fund allocation.

As Kendra Quinn worked through the pile of backup memoranda and studies, something in Evelyn Alvarado's account of the theory behind the HTF kept gnawing at her mind. Quinn took a sheet of paper and sketched a set of axes. She drew a downward-sloping line, thinking to herself as she did so: "Obviously, the higher the total tax imposed on anyone who wants to buy property in the center city, either for 'rehabbing'—in other words, gentrification—or for commercial development, the less will be the demand for the taxed property." Hence the line of negative slope: With everything else held equal, the higher the dollar amount represented at any time by the HTF, the less commercial development will be occurring.

At the same time, if the expenditures go as Alvarado wants them to—into some sort of support for low-income housing—outlays from the HTF would be increasing the quantity and quality of the central ward's stock of residential space. Quinn sketched a second graph. This time, the line sloped upward: "The higher the HTF, the more residential space should come into existence."

Quinn doodled and tugged at her chin, thinking. What was the relationship between commercial and affordable residential space? Better housing because of HTF outlays, Quinn supposed, should further stimulate commercial growth. Customers were more likely to book rooms in a hotel that wasn't surrounded by seedy housing. Better close-in housing might also imply the proximity of a better workforce to staff jobs in the new hotels and office buildings. But Quinn recognized that forces would also be working in the opposite direction: A trend toward better housing—especially when supported by public subsidies from the HTF—might exacerbate the run-up of real estate costs. Gentrifiers and commercial developers not only would have to pay higher taxes but also would have to pay more in market prices for land and buildings within the HTF area. A price run-up would tend to depress demand, just as a higher tax rate would.

"Somewhere here," Kendra Quinn thought, "there's at least the potential for equilibrium—the mix at which residential and commercial development in the area *both* increase because the HTF tax isn't too high to deter the hotel builders and office developers but is just high enough to produce the margin of subsidy needed to save and rebuild decent housing." Sooner or later, she thought, the forces better balance out. The trick in implementing the new HTF program will be to "tune" the tax. The wrong decisions, Quinn noted to herself, won't merely slow the pace of improvement but could actually worsen matters by making commercial development unattractive and drying up the very source of funding for residential expansion that the HTF was supposed to ensure. The HTF could have an outcome exactly opposite to what Evelyn Alvarado was trying to promote.

•　•　•　•　•

Aaron Haber knew that Evelyn Alvarado wanted to keep in her own hands a high level of control over the rules governing the management of the HTF. Unfortunately, however, her expectations were not to be realized, and it was Haber's unpleasant duty to tell her why.

As director of the BHS and a full member of the mayor's cabinet, Aaron Haber met regularly with Hizzoner, both in general meetings and head to head. Haber owed it to Evelyn Alvarado to brief her as quickly as possible about his most recent private get-together with the mayor. At that meeting, Hizzoner had told Haber about a recent encounter the mayor had had with the Central Ward Delegation. Hizzoner had described the concessions that he'd felt forced to make under pressure from Esty Lee and other community leaders from the central ward area. *They* lived in the inner city; *they*—not the mayor's bureaucrats—delivered the votes Hizzoner depended on; and they felt that *they*, not Evelyn Alvarado, should control any spigot of funds into the central ward. The upshot of the delegation's meeting with the mayor would have to change everyone's (especially Alvarado's) initial ideas about the purposes and administration of the central ward HTF.

The Central Ward Delegation's leaders had pressed the mayor to commit the HTF money for pet projects of their own. In the end, Hizzoner had promised that HTF proceeds would be divided "in some reasonable way" among the items in the following four-point program:

1. Small housing-supplement grants to senior citizens with homes in the central ward area, many of whom wanted desperately to remain in their own homes but

were having trouble doing so on the small, fixed annuities that they collected in Social Security and pension benefits.

2. Substance-abuse clinics, to be located in abandoned storefronts that the city would buy or lease with HTF money, renovate, and turn over to community-based nonprofit organizations; the nonprofits would then operate the programs with funds from private foundations and grants from two federal departments: Health and Human Services and Housing and Urban Development.

3. Financial assistance to day care providers, many of whom were glorified baby-sitters helping out friends and family members who had to leave their children somewhere if they were to hold down steady jobs. Most of these care providers' homes were ill equipped, and some were probably downright unsafe. The Central Ward Delegation wanted HTF funds to be used to subsidize upgradings for the neediest providers.

4. Subsidies to the owners of selected dilapidated multi-unit inner-city residential buildings; with rehabilitation subsidies from the HTF, these buildings could be refurbished to augment the dwindling stock of affordable rental units within easy reach of the city's central business district.

This four-point agenda came to be known as the *diversion program* because—if adopted as the mayor promised—it would divert resources from low-income housing to a broader set of social goals. Only points 1 and 4 seemed consistent with the original intent of the HTF program as Evelyn Alvarado had conceived it.

Esty Lee and the others had never known Hizzoner to renege on a promise. But by itself that fact wasn't any assurance that a mayoral initiative couldn't be sabotaged by underlings in the agencies of city government, where promises by the boss had to be carried out. The members of the Central Ward Delegation were experienced and savvy. Each of them could tell stories of deals cut with top-level politicians which lower-level administrators (like Alvarado) had subsequently found ways to subvert.

When pressed about how he might ensure that the diversion program would be implemented fully, Hizzoner had replied: "Why, that's simple. We'll write right into the rules that these four points will be the purposes of the spending. All money that goes into the HTF will have to be divided among our four points because the rules will explicitly require it. Deal?"

The mayor had made sure that there were nods all around. "I'll tell Aaron Haber and [City Engineer] Kent Buchanan, who together will be in charge of the rule makings. They should put enough detail into the rules so there'll be no wiggle room when it comes time to spend the dough. All HTF monies will have to be apportioned among the four uses—senior housing, storefront substance-abuse clinics, day care, and subsidies to rehabilitate dilapidated residential structures."

•   •   •   •   •

Housing policy! Housing policy was an area about as far as it could get from the kinds of issues Gene Petitsaint had thought he'd be working on when he joined Nora Smith's policy staff in the Public Health Department. But there it was—a note from Nora assigning him to a new interagency task group, one responsible for drafting an administrative rule on the use of funds to save dilapidated residential buildings from demolition and assist in their rehabilitation.

Petitsaint read through the supporting papers clipped to Smith's note, trying to reconstruct the background of his new assignment. Apparently, the City Council had established some kind of new funding mechanism called an HTF. The city engineer, Kent Buchanan, had been made responsible for drafting a rule to govern the disbursement of certain HTF monies. In turn, Buchanan had assigned one of his assistants, Dave Cook of the Department of Inspections and Licenses (I&L), to write the rule, which would deal with inner-city demolition policy. ("*Demolition policy?* Give me a break!" thought Petitsaint.) Cook was assembling a special task group, with representatives from all concerned city agencies. Nora Smith, tasked to designate the delegate from Public Health, had—not surprisingly—decided that Gene Petitsaint could be spared to represent the policy planning staff on Cook's interagency committee.

As the junior person in Nora Smith's office, Gene Petitsaint knew that he had dues to pay before he'd be able to start picking his own assignments. Until then, Smith would continue to finger him for . . . well, it seemed, for any odd job that came along. Here was the current list of Gene's assignments: the County Council on Handicapped Services, the Public Facilities Coordinating Committee, the Special Community Policing Task Force, the Regional Automated Identification System Planning Group, and now the newly formed interagency rule-drafting group named the Inner-City Residential Rehabilitation Panel.

Gene accepted the assignment with grace. But when he next met with Nora, he asked how it was that *anyone* from the Public Health Department should be involved in residential housing policy. Gene hadn't known that the writ of city health officers gave them any jurisdiction over dilapidated apartment buildings.

"It doesn't," Nora answered. "But Public Health has lots to do with policy on drugs in the inner city. Those dilapidated houses are prime locations for the pushers and junkies, who turn them into shooting galleries." Gene and Nora talked a bit about inner-city decay: Turn an abandoned SRO or apartment building into a crack house, and everything else starts to go as well. Undesirables of all sorts come onto the scene. There's more trouble in the neighborhood, more fear, and more "broken windows"—the classic symbols of neighborhood decay and harbingers of more serious crime to come. Gangs move in. Arsonists set fires. All this leads to more abandonments. The process feeds on itself.

Nora told Gene she had an additional stack of materials relevant to his new assignment. Handing him a filled manila folder, Nora said that Gene's years in Seattle might prove helpful. "It's all there in the file," she added. "They've done similar rehab programs in other cities. One of the model programs was in Seattle. Since you went to school there, you might be able to make better sense of the data. I assume that'll make you more helpful to the panel."

Gene wondered to himself: Where had Nora gotten the idea that he knew anything about demolition or rehabilitation, whether in Seattle or anywhere else? "I did a public administration degree in Seattle, not civil engineering or urban renewal," Gene reminded her. But he knew as he said it that the way his job seemed to be developing, those might be distinctions without differences.

• • • • •

Aaron Haber had seen that his account of the mayor's deal with the Central Ward Delegation wasn't going down very well with Evelyn Alvarado. After all her efforts to find a way to subsidize a low-income residential housing program, she was now being asked to absorb the news that Hizzoner had caved in the first moment local politicians pressured him to divert money into favored projects of their own.

"Hizzoner had no real choice," Haber said. "Politically, he's got to deal with them." And besides, as the mayor had wryly put it to him, "There *is* something to be said for listening to the people who live in the central ward when deciding what should be done in their own neighborhood. If they want seniors' subsidies and day care, maybe they should have them, instead of just spending all the money to shore up the low-cost housing stock."

"But that's not the issue," Alvarado protested. "It's not a question of who speaks for whose interests, or even of what's the 'best' in a policy sense. On the best policy, reasonable persons can agree to disagree. But as for spending priorities with HTF money, it's a question of legality. What did the council say it intended when it passed the ordinance? Surely, Aaron, you're not saying the mayor can override that, no matter how Esty Lee and the other ward heelers try to bully him politically."

"We'll just have to live with it," Haber responded weakly. "With that . . . and even more."

In some ways, the worst news Aaron had for Evelyn was the mayor's decision to involve City Engineer Buchanan in the HTF rule-making process. Although the Real Estate Planning Board would (as Evelyn had recommended) have overall rule-making responsibility for the HTF, by Hizzoner's own decree a separate rule would have to be written covering the disbursement of HTF monies for residential building rehabilitation—point 4 in the Central Ward Delegation's diversion program.

Aaron tried to explain why the mayor had felt it necessary to splinter authority by delegating a portion of the rule-drafting responsibility to an agency outside the BHS. The central ward's underground utilities (especially water and sewer lines) were ancient. Inner-city residents suffered frequent main breakages and power outages. Some of the mayor's advisers had underscored the need for extreme care when making decisions about physical infrastructure in the inner city. The locations of demolitions predicted where future commercial development was most likely to occur. The pattern of development obviously had to affect the city engineer's long-term plan for infrastructure maintenance and upgrading. The mayor himself had decided that the rule governing antidemolition expenditures should therefore be the responsibility of engineers, not of the city's housing officials.

"So," Alvarado said, "we're to have *two* rules governing outlays of HTF money. My people—Wayne Elsie's group on the planning board—will write a rule governing points 1 through 3 of the diversion program. A completely separate group over in I&L will do a separate rule governing subsidies to rehabilitate demolition-prone buildings. . . ."

"No," Haber corrected her. "Obviously *not* 'completely separate.' Since both rules—the one Wayne Elsie's group will write and the one from Dave Cook in I&L—deal with funds flowing from the same source, the HTF; they'll have to be written in coordination. Remember, too, the group in I&L will only *write* the subsidy rule, to make sure there's engineering expertise in any plans for the demolition or salvaging of buildings in an area with a decrepit infrastructure. Once the rehab rule is written, the actual administration of that part of the HTF will switch back to the Housing Department, meaning to the Planning Board, which will have had complete responsibility all along for the first three points."

•   •   •   •   •

From the journal of Gene Petitsaint. Subject: Predictors of demolition for buildings in the residential building stock.[1]

One of the best studies of efforts to save demolition-prone residential structures was conducted in inner-city Seattle. Researchers there concluded that five variables can be used as key indicators of the likelihood that an abandoned residential structure would be demolished to make room for new development. The Seattle researchers used codes to identify each key indicator and conducted computer-based analyses to determine whether the direction of association was positive or negative (that is, whether a relatively high or low score tends to suggest that a building, once abandoned, is likely to be demolished). The Seattle findings:

Variables correlated with a high chance of demolition

CVCT   (Number of vacant buildings on land adjacent to the building under study). The higher the CVCT score, the more likely the chance of demolition of the building.

PKG   (Number of parking lots in immediate vicinity of the building). The higher the PKG score, the greater the chance of demolition.

UNT   (Number of separate dwelling units in the building; a dwelling unit may be a single room or a suite of rooms). The higher the UNT score, the greater the chance of demolition.

Variables correlated with a relatively lower chance of demolition

RST   (Number of residential buildings in area). The greater the number of residences in the area, the greater the supportability of shops and services, making abandonment less likely for any one building; hence demolition is less likely.

FAR   (Ratio of floor space on all stories of the building to the area of land occupied by the building). The higher the FAR score, the more costly demolition is likely to be; hence—holding all other factors equal—the less likely the building owner is to decide to demolish.

•   •   •   •   •

Evelyn Alvarado told Wayne Elsie that Kendra Quinn from her immediate staff would join the Real Estate Planning Board to help Wayne's regular people write a rule covering the points 1 through 3 in the diversion program. Kendra would also be responsible for coordinating the work of Wayne's staff with that of the interagency task group responsible for the rule governing point 4, the antidemolition program.

It would be a problem for Elsie, Cook, and their respective workers to decide how HTF monies should be divided among the four uses. Given the assurances that Hizzoner had made to Esty Lee and the others, how much discretion should the rules

[1]Based on E. J. Bell and D. Kelso, "The Demolition of Downtown Low-Income Residential Buildings: A Discriminant Analysis," 20 *Socioeconomic Planning Sciences* 1 (1986): 17–24.

confer on the administrators who would actually have to disburse HTF revenues for the next twenty years? Assuming the legality of the diversion program—an issue about which Evelyn Alvarado still had doubts—competition for shares of the $3 million each year among proponents of the four goals couldn't help but influence the eventual administration of the HTF fund.

Prominent in the Central Ward Delegation had been Esty Lee's ally, Council-woman Laura "Larry" Coe. Coe had delivered the crucial vote to swing the council majority behind the HTF plan. What repayment could Councilwoman Coe claim morally or politically as her reward for helping to make Evelyn Alvarado's dream a reality? Everyone knew of Larry Coe's interest in promoting substance-abuse clinics. Wayne Elsie, who was responsible for the rule covering point 2 of the diversion program, expected Larry Coe to use all her considerable influence as a City Council member to siphon as much money as she could out of the HTF for her favorite inner-city social program. To this end, Larry Coe could be counted on to press for the most-liberal-possible reading of the HTF legislation. As far as she'd be concerned, any outlay of HTF monies even remotely associated with "affordable housing within a context of balanced development" (such as outlays for storefront clinics) would fall within the council's intent. But Wayne Elsie had to take more than a program's merits or political prefer-ences into account. Any rule governing the disbursement of HTF monies might be challenged in court. As the official in charge of a rule making, Elsie had to worry, lest the courts find any rule that his group issued to be outside the legislative mandate.

•   •   •   •   •

Most first meetings of most task forces get off to slow starts. The members sip coffee, break donuts, and chat with one another to get acquainted. After the usual ini-tial milling about, Dave Cook called the group to order. Cook briefly summarized the background of the HTF program, passed out summary reports about the antidemoli-tion programs in Seattle and several other cities, and explained the work of the Inner City Residential Rehabilitation Task Force:

"First, we need to write a rule outlining how money from the HTF is to be allo-cated among demolition-prone buildings. How should the HTF administrators choose which buildings to try to save for residential use by offering rehab funds to their own-ers? Which ones should be written off—letting their owners either abandon them or (for the lucky few who get offers) sell them for demolition, followed by commercial development?

"Second, we have to ask how our rule should affect the *amount* of HTF money each year that goes into the antidemolition program. We've been given as a planning figure $3 million per year to be divided among all four items in the so-called diversion program. But there's no procedure set up to decide how the Real Estate Planning Board, which will eventually administer the whole pile, should allocate the amount.

"No matter who administers the HTF," Cook cautioned, "they'll only be able to spend what the special tax arrangements bring in. That isn't fixed; it will depend on other factors. The rules we write and how they're implemented may decide the long-term success or failure of inner-city renewal as a whole."

The gentleman sitting immediately to Cook's left asked for recognition—he didn't give his name but identified himself as a member of the I&L staff—and asked whether the group could simplify its task by getting a copy of a successful rule from one of the test cities, such as Seattle, and adopting it outright.

Cook replied that some members of the task force might want to propose anti-demolition criteria that weren't contained in any of the model programs. "For example," he added (nodding in the direction of a woman named Barbara Crofter, who was sitting in on the task force as a private-sector representative of the Chamber of Commerce), "the Chamber people have let me know that they want all the help they can get to shape up neighborhoods likely to be seen by visitors to the city."

"I don't see anything wrong with that," a task force member without a name tag interjected.

"I don't either," said Cook. "But just as the Chamber of Commerce has its special concerns and priorities, so do other constituencies. Take the historic sites people: The preservationists think that some kind—any kind—of historic connection, such as with the history of the city or one of its famous Mexican families, should land an old house at the top of the list for a renovation subsidy. And I gather the professional planners from the mayor's office have some more-objective, 'scientific' criteria they think should be used to decide rehab priorities."

Gene Petitsaint took it from what Cook said that the professional city planners regarded the "scientific" findings of the Seattle studies as the most-objective, least-political basis for action. The planners apparently thought that funds should be disbursed strictly on the basis of the five criteria that predicted whether an abandoned building was likely to undergo demolition: To the most vulnerable should go the most money.

Cook, Crofter, and the two planning board representatives on the task force went back and forth for a while over the relative merits of tourism and "the Seattle findings" as criteria for determining which buildings should get HTF support.

Joyce Ruhe, a senior attorney from the City Solicitor's office, had been silent up to this point. She asked for the floor, and Gene discerned an attitude of deference even in Dave Cook's manner.

"If I follow," Ruhe said, "we could write a rule with three parts.

"Part 1, 'Extent,' would define a specific area on the map. No building of any kind outside that boundary would qualify. But a building inside could qualify if it's residential in structure, if it's abandoned or seems on the verge of abandonment, if it meets certain other criteria—especially if it's vulnerable to demolition, and if there's money left in the fund.

"Part 2, 'Criteria,' would list the five factors that the planners want"—Ruhe read from her notes—"namely, . . ." and she repeated the five Seattle variables. "But the Chamber people might want to use a different eligibility area in Part 1, and also might want to change or add to the five criteria I've listed for Part 2. For example, 'proximity of candidate building to areas of likely development, use, or visitation based on known patterns of tourism,' or some such phrasing, could be added as a sixth criterion; or it might be substituted for one or more of the planners' five 'Seattle criteria.'

"Part 3, 'Allocation,' would contain at least two subrules: how the planning board administrators would decide how much to give for each rehabilitation project and—interdependent with the first—how the selection and award procedures will work. Do owners of dilapidated buildings have to apply for funds, or will inspectors go out and propose candidate buildings for rehab? Will grants go out whenever a good case comes up—first-come, first-serve—or should some kind of panel collect all the candidates proposed during a period, set priorities, and divide the money accordingly?"

Gene Petitsaint, taking his own notes as Joyce Ruhe spoke, noted that the three-part rule that she had so remarkably drafted almost extemporaneously could easily contain a dozen or more subrules, not just the ones Ruhe mentioned. At the other extreme, it would be possible to leave certain provisions—such as the boundary area—out altogether and simply trust Wayne Elsie's planning board members, as the designated administrators of the program, to use good judgment when deciding if a candidate building has a location appropriate for HTF support.

• • • • •

At the next meeting of Cook's group, Ashley Kopper—one of those to whom Cook had referred as "the professional planners from the mayor's office"—proposed a discretionless rule, as she described it. Kopper's rule would be based on a building's five-variable scores, on weightings of those scores that everyone could understand (since they would be applied in a simple worksheet), and on a "rule of proportional funding" in the distribution of rehabilitation funds during each six-month period.

The procedure would work in the following way: Using standardized rating forms, building inspectors from Dave Cook's shop would survey the central ward (defined as the area of the present 4th, 5th, and 6th police precincts) twice yearly. They would assign numerical scores, from 1 to 5, to buildings that they "eyeballed" as potential candidates for HTF support, based strictly on the Seattle variables. The assigned scores would be multiplied by weightings and then added up. Fund allocation would follow automatically, based on the resulting weighted sums. The entries in Table 4.1 illustrate the Kopper algorithm.

In the Kopper scheme, for example, if $100,000 were available in a given six-month period for rehab, and the three hypothetical buildings shown in Table 4.1 were the only candidates, funds would be apportioned to the building owners in the ratio 6:5:3—that is, the ratios of the weighted numerical scores shown on the "total" line

Table 4.1 An Illustration of Applying Kopper's Algorithm to Rate a Building for Rehabilitation Funding

Survey to be completed every six months for all vacant multi-story buildings sited within the 4th, 5th, and 6th police precincts.

	Weight	Building 1		Building 2		Building 3	
		Score	× Weight	Score	× Weight	Score	× Weight
CVCT	2	5	10	3	6	4	8
PKG	1	5	5	5	5	1	1
UNT	3	2	6	4	12	3	9
(−) RST	1	1	−1	4	−4	5	−5
(−) FAR	2	1	−2	2	−4	2	−4
Total	1		18		15		9
Ratio			6		5		3
Funding			$42,900		$35,700		$21,400

of Table 4.1. Thus, $42,900 would be awarded as a renovation subsidy from the $100,000 to building 1, the candidate for HTF funding with the highest weighted score on the Seattle variables during that six-month period.

"But what happens," Myra Biller from the Fire Department asked, "if building 1 just happens to be on a site where the mayor for some reason *wants* demolition? Or where creeping urban blight makes it desirable to clean out the old eyesores and heartbreak hotels and run-down brownstones? Your mechanical, numerical method for choosing, Ashley—well, your procedure just won't leave us any room for judgment. Your procedure will just churn out money by formula even to buildings that *should* be demolished."

"Should the *mayor* have the right to make that kind of decision," Ashley Kopper asked, "or should it be done objectively, nonpolitically? You talk about judgment, Myra. The judgment's in the procedure, which applies to everyone without special pleading. How else can a process be fair? Isn't that why we're in this exercise to begin with, instead of just saying to Hizzoner or Larry Coe or the head of housing in the BHS: 'Here, here's $3 million. Spend it how you want?'"

Johnson Brickell from the Education Department chimed in. "Ashley, what if building 1 in your example is a crack house right in the midst of other vacant buildings all around it? That means that if building 1 gets a high score, some of the nearby ones will too, because they're automatically in the CVCT category; and that means that they automatically get a weighting of 2 on your scale. So you might have half a dozen buildings—all the property of different owners—that qualify for funds at about the same high level. Instead of concentrating a high allocation on one building—the most deserving one—the money gets splintered. It's easy to imagine cases where, because we're tied to the formula, no one owner gets enough to make much of a difference. That's what I don't like about automatic weightings or automatic proportional distributions. It's better to concentrate funds where they'll do the most good. No proportional formula—no formula of any kind—can guarantee that."

Ashley Kopper came right back: "'Do the most good' from whose standpoint? At least doing everything possible to set forth clear rules will let everyone know how decisions will be made. We can live with an occasional mistake. We can't live with arbitrary decisions."

"From this very discussion, you can see where part of the problem lies," Petra Messersmith from City Sanitation said. "What's the real point, anyway, of this rule we're supposed to be drafting? I thought it was to put money where it'll save old buildings and help retain affordable housing in the inner city. But now from where Johnson's coming from, I'm getting vibrations that the point may be different, say to drive out crack houses. Or maybe it's to preserve quaintness for tourism."

Cook rapped his knuckle on the table. "Ladies . . . gentlemen: Let's pull ourselves together. Let's start over. What do we want to accomplish with this rule, and how should we go about doing it? The floor is open for anyone who can give us a fresh idea."

• • • • •

Claire Nagamura had built a reputation as a reporter who broke news based on information pieced together from bits and slips passed to her from sources in city hall or the county building. The area's political junkies followed her *Trib'-Examiner* stories closely. They were surprised to find under her byline—instead of hard news—a rather leisurely overview of the entire HTF controversy.

Delivering Defeat from a Program Everyone Thought a Sure Winner: Future Uncertain for the HTF

by Claire Nagamura

Inner-city neighborhoods in all of America's great cities have undergone immense changes. As more jobs, especially in manufacturing, have moved from inner-city factory locations to new sites around the suburban peripheries, populations have thinned in the once densely inhabited central areas. Those who remain experience higher-than-average unemployment rates and often find themselves caught in the cycle of neighborhood decay. In every big city, a primary symptom of decay is the abandonment of residential buildings—this at a time of increasing national concern over the problems of homelessness, "affordable housing," and lagging rates of new housing starts.

In several of the big cities, programs have been initiated to subsidize the rehabilitation of dilapidated residential structures, especially old hotels or apartment buildings located close to the traditional central business districts. Unless empty structures are reoccupied within a reasonable period, they become arson statistics, crack houses, or fall to the wrecking ball, usually to make space for nonresidential development. In any event, abandonment almost always attracts scavengers, so that literally within days a house not occupied by tenants will be looted of all removable electrical and plumbing fixtures, making it that much harder and more costly to restore for habitation.

The Housing Trust Fund set up less than six weeks ago by the City Council was intended to provide a steady flow of funds to subsidize building owners who are considering abandonment or demolition of their prop-

erties. Another, complementary purpose was to subsidize affordable housing for the neediest inner-city residents. The HTF plan was that rarity in our city's politics: a policy with seemingly universal support. The evaporation of that support is one of this year's great local political mysteries.

Apparently, the erosion of confidence in the ability of HTF administrators to rescue residential properties in the central ward began when inner-city community leaders convinced the mayor to divert money from the rescue of demolition-prone buildings into projects of their own. As goals remote from the original conception of the plan were added, one by one, the problems of allocating funds among claimants became more complicated. The critical defection from the pro-HTF coalition came when local business leaders decided that prospects were poor for the fund to realize its objective. As these business leaders saw it, that objective was to support commercial redevelopment of the central ward by ensuring a stable residential base.

Feeling is widespread that the mayor, by mishandling the HTF issue, has converted a promising and broadly popular urban renewal policy into a cause of bitterness and unexpected controversy. His most ardent and loyal supporters are watching closely for evidence that he will be able to reverse the negative momentum and block calls, which are now being voiced, for a new vote in the City Council. If such a vote were held today, the Housing Trust Fund ordinance would probably be repealed.

• • • • •

Hizzoner looked glumly at the letter from John Spadely, the area's leading banker. Spadely had written only after discussing the current imbroglio over the HTF with other members of the local Business Council. Spadely confessed puzzlement over the events that had transpired in connection with the HTF. Spadely's letter continued:

> The sentiment throughout the business community is widespread that the diversion of HTF moneys to storefront clinics and so forth not only would reduce the dollars available for residential rehabilitation but also could have deleterious effects on economic activity within the central ward neighborhoods. Needed are major job-creating projects to reverse the pattern of decay and impoverishment. Those major projects won't materialize in a context characterized by financial life support for marginal activities.

> Though I don't myself like to use fighting words, and though some of what's being said is an overreaction, you should know that one man from the front ranks of local business said of this diversion program: "It's bad public policy, and what's worse about it, is it creates a climate that's bad for private business, too."

> As you know, the institutions with potential financial stakes in inner-city redevelopment informally pledged, both to you and to particular members of the City Council, that venture capital and home mortgage money would be directed into central ward projects, consistent with an overall plan for the general area. The careful targeting of HTF money seemed in line with such an overall plan, but that sharpness of focus has now been lost, and so has the confidence of some leaders within the business community. To save a program that could still accomplish much by returning to its original housing-related purposes, I and those for whom I speak think it necessary for you to assert leadership by restoring a carefully limited conception of the Housing Trust Fund.

> If you would like to discuss this important issue at greater length, I will be happy to set up a luncheon at University Club with some of the civic leaders whom I know to be deeply concerned.

> As ever,
> /s/ J.
> John Spadely
> Chairman and President
> First National Bank

Hizzoner was now in the middle of a fight that he'd just as soon have avoided. He wasn't looking forward to a political bloodletting over the HTF issue in the City Council.

The mayor asked a few significant figures from his administration to send brief position papers on aspects of the inner-city development program to one of his staff assistants, Peter York. It would be York's job to take the inputs, digest them, and prepare a comprehensive statement for the mayor to issue when the HTF battle broke out in the council.

One of those tasked by the mayor was Aaron Haber at the BHS, who bucked the job down to Evelyn Alvarado. Evelyn in her turn asked Kendra Quinn to jot down some notes about what she, as the Housing Department's "official staffer on the case," thought should be done about the HTF issue. Quinn had the best feel of anyone for the current state of the relevant rule makings.

Another person contacted by the mayor was Arpad Gasper at the Public Health Department. Gasper phoned Nora Smith of the department's policy-planning shop to ask her for input. (Incidentally, Nora was a family friend of the mayor's from way back; for personal as well as professional reasons, she wanted to respond in a creditable way to his request for input from Public Health.) Nora caught Gene Petitsaint and asked him to shove other business off his desk for a couple of hours and write a page of suggestions: What should she recommend be done about the HTF?

Questions for Discussion
········

The following queries might help you order your thoughts and organize a discussion of the case.

1. What's the story? What competing values and contending interests complicate the position of Evelyn Alvarado? The position of her boss, Aaron Haber? ("Where you stand depends on where you sit.") And then there's Haber's boss: What lessons can we draw from an understanding of the way Hizzoner got himself into his current political fix? Could the mayor have avoided the problem he now faces, or does it seem to have arisen from decisions by him and others that were, at the time made, justifiable based on the information available? (By the way, who does the scenario suggest is Hizzoner's "boss"?)

2. In this chapter, we've considered a central conflict in public administration: the requirement for democratic accountability versus administrative officials' need for reasonable discretionary authority. In what ways does this conflict present itself in the scenario? "Democratic accountability" reminds us that officials are ultimately answerable to the voters, but rejection at the polls doesn't apply to appointive officials, and anyway, there are ways other than elections for citizens to put pressure even on elected officeholders. In what ways do individuals in the case try to elicit responsive action from public officials? How would you rate the appropriateness of the various means used, given that our system is supposed to be democratic at its core?

3. "Know the law." Are the kinds of expenditures that the mayor promised to the Central Ward Delegation consistent with the intent of the City Council members who voted to set up the HTF? If you don't think so, how should Wayne Elsie deal with that fact in the rule that his group has been instructed to write?

4. How do you react to the HTF method as an administrative technique, given Evelyn Alvarado's objectives as a city official? What do you see as the principal advantages and disadvantages of trust-fund financing of public projects as opposed to funding out of general tax revenues—which implies, among other things, that the level of support each year will be whatever legislators decide to appropriate in the annual budget process? Again: Can you describe the dynamics of trust-fund financing versus general-revenue financing using a simple model? How do you suppose the choice between these two financing modes influences the allocation of discretion in the governance process?

5. "Sketch a model." Can you express the basic ideas of Kendra Quinn's equilibrium analysis using graphs?

6. As simply as you can, state the main issue or issues that Wayne Elsie and Dave Cook have to resolve in their rule-writing efforts. How would you decide whether the regulations to be drafted by Elsie's and Cook's groups should be "rule-like" or "standard-like"? With respect to the rule that will govern the antidemolition program, what would be the advantages and disadvantages of moving toward the kind of procedure advocated by Ashley Kopper?

7. To what extent can the issues facing Elsie's and Cook's groups be dealt with independently, and to what extent do they interlock in a way that makes for an underdetermined situation? Insofar as the situation is underdetermined, what techniques—persuasion, restructuring, and so forth—should Elsie and Cook employ as they work through their respective rule-writing assignments?

8. In his essay on the requisites of a rule, Colin Diver emphasizes that inconsistencies are likely to crop up among his three criteria, making the classic problem of overdetermination common in the administrative rule-making process. How should Wayne Elsie and Dave Cook try, in their respective rule-writing groups, to balance the claims of congruency, transparency, and simplicity? Would parameter changing or policy adjusting have a role to play along with priority setting?

 # FOR FURTHER READING

A representative sampling of the classic titles on American administrative law and process would include:

Goodnow, Frank, *The Principles of Administrative Law in the United States* (New York: Putnam, 1905).
Landis, James, *The Administrative Process* (New Haven CT: Yale U. Press, 1938).
Waldo, Dwight, *The Administrative State* (New York: Ronald Press, 1948).
Davis, Kenneth Culp, *Discretionary Justice* (Baton Rouge LA: Louisiana State Press, 1969).

Several excellent textbooks of administrative law, with sections on both administrative adjudication and administrative rule making, are available; among the more accessible of these are

Barry, Donald, *The Legal Foundations of Public Administration* (St. Paul MN: West, 1987).
Carter, Lief, and Christine Harrington, *Administrative Law and Politics* (New York: HarperCollins, 1991).
Mashaw, Jerry, et al., *Administrative Law: The American Public Law System* (St. Paul MN: West, 1992).

Strauss, Peter, et al., *Administrative Law* (Westbury NY: Foundation Press, 1995).

Among the better contemporary overview treatments of administrative law and the formal administrative process are

Byner, Gary, *Bureaucratic Discretion* (Elmsford NY: Pergamum, 1987).

Kolko, Gabriel, *Railroads and Regulation* (Princeton NJ: Princeton U. Press, 1965); the standard, if somewhat overstated, development of the "agency capture" thesis.

McConnell, Grant, *Private Power and American Democracy* (New York: Knopf, 1966).

Shapiro, Martin, *Who Guards the Guardians?* (Athens GA: U. of Georgia Press, 1988).

Williams, Jere, "Cornerstones of American Administrative Law," in D. Barry and H. Witcomb, eds., *The Legal Foundations of Public Administration* (St. Paul MN: West, 1987).

The best short treatment of "administrative policy making" (that is, administrators' serving as quasi-lawmakers) is

Maynard-Moody, Steven, "Beyond Implementation: Developing an Institutional Theory of Administrative Policy," 49 *Public Administration Review* (March–April 1989), 137.

On an important modern variation in the rule-making process—negotiated rule making, see

Perritt, Henry H., "Negotiated Rulemaking in Practice" 5 *Journal of Policy Analysis and Management* (Spring 1986), 482.

The following (along with the Reinhold and Diver selections excerpted in the text) are a sample of illuminating case studies in the workings of the administrative process:

Bishop, Peter, and Augustus Jones, "Implementing the Americans with Disabilities Act of 1990: Assessing the Variables of Success," 53 *Public Administration Review* (March–April 1993), 121.

Cofer, Donna Price, *Judges, Bureaucrats, and the Question of Independence: A Study of the Social Security Administrative Hearing Process* (Westport CT: Greenwood Press, 1985).

Mashaw, Jerry, *Bureaucratic Justice* (New Haven CT: Yale U. Press, 1983); a study of the Social Security disability-payments program.

Mashaw, Jerry, and John Harfst, *The Struggle for Auto Safety* (Cambridge MA: Harvard U. Press, 1990).

Melnick, R. Shep, *Between the Lines: Interpreting Welfare Rights* (Washington: Brookings Institution, 1994).

Schmandt, Jurgan, "Managing Comprehensive Rule Making: EPA's Plan for Integrated Environmental Management," 45 *Public Administration Review* (March–April 1985), 309.

West, William, "The Politics of Administrative Rule Making," 42 *Public Administration Review* (September–October, 1982), 420; an excellent brief coverage of rule-making procedures at the Federal Trade Commission.

▼◆●■▼◆●■▼◆●■▼◆●■▼◆

CHAPTER 5

The Politics of Administrative Choice: Creating Winners, Compensating Losers

The first two items on Woodrow Wilson's agenda for administrative reform centered on *personnel* (primarily the civil service system) and *organization* (which, for the Progressives, meant structuring government agencies in accordance with the bureaucratic paradigm). The third item—"to rescue executive *methods* from . . . confusion and costliness"— referred to certain technical procedures that the Progressives thought would increase efficiency in the governance process. Wilson and his cohorts had in mind a series of reforms to be implemented by public administrators laboring in a field of action distinct from that of the elective politicians. Wilson's call for "better methods of executive organization and action" implied a shift away from political deal making based on local interests and piecemeal analysis.

The Progressives believed that politics could be distinguished from administration because they also believed in a fairly clear-cut distinction between ends and means. In a democracy, the people's elected representatives should choose the ends of policy. But they couldn't be trusted to select the means. Too often, the Progressives feared, vote-conscious politicians failed to make decisions based on rational methods of systemwide planning. Local incentives constantly tugged elected officials toward implementation strategies that favored their own constituents. Instead of looking at the big picture, politicians naturally emphasized the concerns of the folks who elected them: "Put the new jobs program in *my* ward"; "Build the highway through *my* town"; "Put the new army base in *my* congressional district." The precinct, the county, the district, the home state have always been the base areas of American politics. From the systemwide perspective, however, such areas are mere parts of larger wholes. What's optimal from the standpoint of the part may be suboptimal for the system considered in the large. (We'll come back to those terms *optimal* and *suboptimal* in just a bit.)

The Progressives became convinced that only the separation of politics and policy making from administration could keep the politicians from messing with administrative activities that they were likely to botch. Reciprocally, only the separation of admin-

167

istration from politics could prevent appointive officials from making decisions that properly belonged to elected representatives. The Progressives thought that any involvement by administrators in the seamy processes of politics would distort their ability to choose the One Best Way based on the technical judgments that their expertise qualified them to make.

To the Progressives, systemwide planning seemed the best way to approach the problems of a nation of interlocking systems. In the America that the Progressives saw taking shape, urban populations increasingly depended on vast agricultural hinterlands and far-flung utility systems. The continental resource base was best viewed as a system of interconnected waterways, regional mineral deposits, national forests and grazing lands, and recreational areas. As rationalists, the Progressives hated the wasteful and haphazard. Efficiency and order could best be attained by methods that optimized the use of resources over entire systems. Contemporary public administrationists sometimes refer to the kind of all-seeing study of public policies that the Progressives espoused as *synoptic analysis* (from the Greek words which mean, roughly, "to see everything at the same time"). **Synoptic analysis** of the country's major engineering and social problems was a priority item on the Progressive agenda right along with the establishment of a merit-based public service, rational structuring of the public bureaucracy, and the reciprocal separation of politics and administration.

SECTION 1
● ■ ▼ ◆

The Progressives and Synoptic Analysis: Conservationism, a Case Study in Systemwide Planning

The Progressives' conviction that problem solvers had to take entire systems into account went far to explain their hostility not only to the impulses of localism and decentralization but also to the politicians who represented these persistent forces in American public life. A gifted twentieth-century politician, the late Speaker of the U.S. House of Representatives Tip O'Neil, once said that all politics is local. It has always been thus, and never more surely than in the waning years of the nineteenth century. Ward-level politicians bent on advancing ward-level interests ran the big cities, trading patronage jobs and public works contracts for votes and campaign donations (and occasional bribes). The Progressives wanted cities run by professional managers who would make the streetcars run on time, plan for urban growth, and see to efficient systems of trash pickup. Synoptic analysis and systemwide planning were implicit in the Progressive vision of the well-run city. Transit managers, development planners, and sanitation engineers needed the authority to override the local ward heeler or neighborhood patronage dispenser when the welfare of the body politic as a whole required it.

Similarly, at the national level, it was the Progressives who pushed for executive budgeting as a way to bring rationality and systems thinking into government financial planning (see Box 5.1).

It was the Progressives too who perceived a logical connection between natural resource policy making and the quest for efficiency through systemwide planning. Indeed, of all the major governmental initiatives undertaken by the Progressives, the conservation movement illustrated Wilson's third agenda item—the improvement of administrative methods—in the most coherent and sustained way. Conservationism originated not in the desire of nature lovers to preserve the land but in the determina-

BOX 5.1

The Progressives on Public Finance: From Line-Item Budgeting to Executive Budgeting

We saw in Chapter 2 that some contemporary critics rank **line-item budgeting** second only to civil service classification as a force for inefficiency. The objections of contemporary commentators such as Osborne and Gaebler to the line-item budget echo complaints made more than a century ago by the Progressives.

Throughout most of the nineteenth century, the main technique of legislative spending control was the listing of specific appropriations under budgetary headings known as line items: personnel, equipment, operations and maintenance, and suchlike. Line itemization facilitated legislative control. Auditors could check the record of disbursements for compliance with the itemized purposes of the appropriation. A million-dollar appropriation for personnel generated a paper trail of paychecks to a fixed number of staff members.

Precisely because it implied clear audit trails and controls on administrative action, however, the line-item technique denied agency officials the discretion they thought they needed to choose the best means to do their jobs. The reformers believed that administrators should be free to "reprogram" money when priorities changed by shifting funds among the different lines in their budgets. They also thought that a unified view of public needs—a view only the chief executive could provide—would permit the kind of synoptic budgetary planning that decision making by separate legislative committees prevented.

The **executive budget**, formally recommended in 1912 by the members of President Taft's Commission on Economy and Efficiency, was installed piecemeal over the years as the federal government's standard budgeting method. In 1922, Congress created the Bureau of the Budget (BOB) to bring a coherent perspective to public financial planning. Based on BOB advice, the president would propose a single budget incorporating balanced estimates of the individual departments' needs. Congress later reemphasized that executive department heads must deal directly with their appropriate legislative committees on agency financial matters—an effort to reclaim control from the president. Nevertheless, the BOB provided a vehicle for presidential administrators to inject a central viewpoint into the budgetary process. By and large, the Bureau of the Budget—renamed the Office of Management and Budget in 1972—has compiled a record of growing influence, based on administrative control of the critical process of comprehensive executive budget preparation.

---

tion of scientific managers to extract the "maximum sustainable yield" from America's forests, grasslands, mineral deposits, and waterways by exploiting them systematically and scientifically. The doctrine of the maximum sustainable yield was a perfect example of One-Best-Way thinking. It implied that there existed a single, optimal level of resource use that experts could discover if only they were free to apply the right analytical methods.

We'll see in our chapter reading, however, that the Progressives were self-deluders when they described themselves as experts or technicians who were above engaging in political wheeling and dealing. The Progressives may have preached the reciprocal separation of politics from administration, but their actions belied the theory. Progressive conservationists used every trick they could think up to cajole, intimidate, or stampede elected representatives into adopting policies favored by the natural resource experts. The most notable feature of the scientific resource managers' position, then, wasn't its nonpolitical nature. On the contrary, conservationism was inescapably enmeshed in politics from the start. What fundamentally distinguished the conservationists' position was the disposition to use whatever administrative *and* political means were necessary to achieve the best results for systems taken in their totality.

CHAPTER READING ▼ ▼ ▼

The following selection from Samuel Hays, a historian of Progressive Era conservation policy, documents one of the bitterest chapters in the historic struggle between localism and centralism—and the parallel struggle between the politicians and administrators who embodied these motifs in our national life. The representatives of local interests thought the technical experts were too ready to sacrifice the welfare of a mere part in order to promote an optimal solution for the overall system. Alas, the experts' willingness to sacrifice the part bespoke a willingness to treat as expendable the very interests that mattered most to the politicians. Thus the struggles that Hays describes became inevitable from the moment that technical expertise and scientific analysis emerged as significant elements in the governance process.

You should take note of some additional points in the Hays reading, for they illustrate important aspects of the workings of our administrative system even today. Among these are the role of professional associations as lobbying groups, the practice—perfected by President Theodore Roosevelt—of constituting high-level study panels (today they're called "blue-ribbon commissions") as advice-giving and consensus-building bodies, and the importance of informal connections in the policy-making process. It all adds up to a revealing case study in the workings of the administrative process at the highest level of government. Hays tells the tale with a historian's careful attention to the details of time, place, and person.

The Progressive Struggle for Systemwide Planning: Conservationists versus Congress

Samuel Hays

The crux of the gospel of efficiency lay in a rational and scientific method of making basic technological decisions through a single, central authority. Administrators thought that competing claims should be resolved by a scientific calculation of benefits rather than through political struggle. Westerners did not agree. To them the "scientific expert" became simply a "bureaucrat."

[L]et us examine more precisely the framework of political structure within which conservation in the Progressive Era had meaning.

The dynamics of conservation, with its tension between the centralizing tendencies of system and expertise on the one hand and the decentralization and localism on the other, is typical of a whole series of similar tensions between centralization and decentralization within modern American society. . . . To many people the external characteristics of this process—efficiency, expertise, order—constituted the spirit of "progressivism." . . .

The new forms of organization tended to shift the location of decision-making away from the grass roots, the smaller contexts of life, to the larger networks of human interaction. This upward shift can be seen in many specific types of development: the growth of city-wide systems of executive action and representation in both school and general government superseding the previous focus on ward representation and action; the similar upward shift in the management of schools and roads from the township to the county and the state department of public instruction and the state highway commission; the upward shift in regulation of economic life from the state to the federal regulatory agency. . . .

Natural resource policies played an integral role in these processes at the national level. From the point of view of the larger context of historical, social and political change, they involved both the extension of the new techniques of modernization—system, expertise, centralized direction and manipulation—and the activation of tensions between centralizing and decentralizing forces. Conservationists were led by people who promoted the "rational" use of resources, with a focus on efficiency, planning for future use, and the application of expertise to broad national problems. But they also promoted a system of decison-making consistent with that spirit, a process by which the expert would decide in terms of the most efficient dovetailing of all competing resource users according to criteria which were considered objective, rational, and above the give-and-take of political conflict. . . .

By 1906 [Chief Forester Gifford] Pinchot, [Frederick] Newell [Director, U.S. Reclamation Service], and other officials had formulated comprehensive land management concepts which during the remainder of [Theodore] Roosevelt's presidency they tried to apply to the public domain.

This program required, first of all, a thorough revision of the public land laws, which Congress had passed originally to promote rapid disposal to private individuals rather than to aid in systematic development. To some resources no specific laws applied; for others, existing law hampered rather than promoted efficient growth. In 1873, for example, Congress passed a coal land act which provided for such a limited maximum acreage per entry that it prevented larger and more efficient coal development. Laws restricting land entry to 160 or 320 acres hardly sufficed for grazing, which required as much for each head of cattle. . . . This lack of system appalled those who were enthusiastic about more efficient growth; new management plans required major legislative reforms. "The possibilities of a wiser system of land laws," declared Pinchot, "grow to almost boundless dimensions."

In the fall of 1903 President Roosevelt appointed a Public Lands Commission, "to report at the earliest practicable moment upon the condition, operation and effect of the present land laws, and on the use, condition, disposal, and settlement of the public lands." . . .

The work of the Public Lands Commission reflected the concern of the Roosevelt administration for a more orderly and planned approach to the public lands. The Commission never officially completed its work, but continued as an informal group of administration leaders who backed a new set of land management principles. The most obvious of these principles was public ownership. The old practice of disposing of nonagricultural lands to private owners, Pinchot and the others argued, must give way to public ownership and the controversy over public or private resource management was the crucial conservation issue. But, to the officials of the Roosevelt administration, public ownership was merely a means to an end; it alone would permit rational development. The significance of the new public lands program, therefore, lay, not in the method of public ownership, but in the objective of efficient, maximum development. . . .

Efficient development required carefully regulated conditions of use as well as a scale of priorities. Grazing, for example, should not exceed the carrying capacity of the land. By issuing permits to use the public lands, the federal government could control the conditions of use. These permits, Pinchot argued, should run for only a limited period of time, so that if an area later could be developed for a more valuable use, it could be reclassified. Permits should prevent speculation by requiring prompt development. Moreover, the administration believed, public land users should pay for their privilege a fee approximately equal to that paid to owners of private lands. The administration applied these basic conditions—a limited permit, prompt use, and a user fee—to all resources on the public lands.

Finally, the new land management entailed administrative innovations. Experts rather than politically appointed officials, for example, should take charge of the program. Pinchot had long emphasized both scientific training for foresters and the use of civil service examinations to select them for government work. He hoped to establish schools to train irrigation and land management experts, as he had for forestry, but these plans fell through. Nevertheless, the Roosevelt administration constantly increased the number of trained foresters, range specialists, and geologists in its public lands program. . . .

Earlier experience with reclamation and forest affairs seemed to point toward a multiple-purpose river basin program. The Geological Survey had brought forward the concept of water as a single resource with many uses. The Reclamation Service was constructing reservoirs to control water for irrigation, and had become aware of the possibilities of combining irrigation storage with hydroelectric power production. The Reclamation Service developed power at its first reservoir project, and Congress in 1906

authorized that agency to undertake its general development and sale. Practical experience with these problems prompted officials of the Roosevelt administration almost inevitably to think in larger terms.

The enormous possibilities of basin-wide river development suddenly captured the imagination of Newell, Pinchot, [Secretary of Interior James] Garfield, and other conservation leaders. Flood waters, now wasted, could, if harnessed, aid navigation, produce electric energy, and provide water for irrigation and industrial use. It also became clear to these men that maximum development required multiple-purpose development. Engineering works which tapped a river for one use alone might rule out other uses which could yield even greater benefits. A low dam for navigation, for example, might prevent construction of a higher dam at the same site that would produce hydroelectric power as well. . . .

The multiple-purpose concept required attention to the entire river basin as well as to the size and design of reservoirs. Failure to control erosion and silt might impair the long-range value of engineering works. The multiple-purpose approach, therefore, brought together federal officials in both land and water agencies in a common venture. . . .

Agitation for inland waterways provided the opportunity for federal leaders to carry out their multiple-purpose views. Waterway associations supported only their particular navigation projects; they displayed little interest in larger ideas. But administration leaders hoped that they could marshal this interest in limited plans to support their broader objectives, and for a time it appeared that they might succeed. W. J. McGee linked these two groups. Geologist, anthropologist, philosopher, former member of the Geological Survey, and assistant to John Wesley Powell, the head of the Bureau of Ethnology, McGee became the chief theorist of the conservation movement. He also became one of its most crucial promoters within the Roosevelt administration and in the country at large. Almost daily he presented new ideas to Roosevelt, Pinchot, and Garfield; he drew up presidential letters and messages, formulated policies, and organized conferences. . . .

In February 1907 he outlined his broader views in an article in *The World's Work*. Each stream, he wrote, is "an interrelated system in which the several parts are so closely interdependent that no section can be brought under control without at least partial control of all other portions.... It is in this concept of the river as a power to be controlled by engineering projects, and at the same time as an agency of interdependent parts, that the view of the engineer and the geologist must meet and merge...." McGee had described with great accuracy the very process whereby the views of resource leaders in the Roosevelt administration had met and merged.

McGee worked quickly and energetically to implement his views.... On February 21 he left St. Louis ... with petitions and asked the President to create an Inland Waterway Commission. On March 12 he formally presented these to Roosevelt, and two days later the President announced the appointment of the Commission.

The Inland Waterways Commission

... McGee had selected a commission of four experts, one from each of the federal departments involved in water problems: Gifford Pinchot from the Forest Service, Frederick H. Newell from the Reclamation Service, Brigadier-General Alexander Mackenzie, Chief of the Corps of Engineers, and Lawrence O. Murray, Assistant Secretary of the Department of Commerce and Labor. The President, more aware of the Commission's political ramifications, added to this group two members of the House, Theodore E. Burton of Ohio and John H. Bankhead of Alabama, and two from the Senate, Francis G. Newlands from Nevada and William Warner from Kansas.... [A]fter appointing McGee to a post in the Bureau of Soils so that he would be eligible, [the President] selected him as the Commission's Secretary....

Roosevelt made clear in his letter of appointment that he intended the Commission to take a multiple-purpose viewpoint. He wrote:

> Works designed to control our waterways have thus far usually been undertaken for a single purpose, such as the improvement of navigation, the development of power, the irrigation

of arid lands, the protection of lowlands from floods, or to supply water for domestic and manufacturing purposes.... The time has come for merging local projects and uses of the inland waters in a comprehensive plan designed for the benefit of the entire country. Such a plan should consider and include all the uses to which streams may be put, and should bring together and coordinate the points of view of all users of water....

The Inland Waterways Commission ... emphatically supported the multiple-purpose idea. "Hereafter," it recommended, "plans for the improvement of navigation in inland waterways ... should take account of the purification of the waters, the development of power, the control of floods, the reclamation of lands by irrigation and drainage, and all other uses of the waters of benefits to be derived from their control." This proposal, the Commission continued, required a single executive agency to coordinate all water resource administration....

Senator Newlands Presents a New Bill

In December 1907 Senator Francis G. Newlands presented to Congress a bill to carry out the recommendation of the Inland Waterways Commission. A permanent body appointed by the President would continue to investigate water problems, authorize projects, supervise construction, and coordinate the activities of all federal water resource agencies. To finance the work, Congress would establish an Inland Waterway Fund.... The Commission could draw upon this Fund at its own discretion, without annual authorization from Congress....

To his reluctant colleagues in the Senate [Newlands] argued:

> Large powers and a comparative free hand should be given to an administrative body of experts in the full development of projects, lest the complexity of the transaction, the time necessary to secure Congressional approval, the difference in view as to purpose or method, may result in indecision and delay, the worst enemies of effective development.... I hope to

see a commission of experts that will have the power to initiate both investigation and construction and with ample funds to complete its projects, not a commission that will have to wait on the tardy initiative of Congress as to projects the details of which it is incapable of dealing with. . . .

The Roosevelt administration readily agreed with these views. Congress, far more responsive to the demands of local constituents than to the requirement of scientific planning, could not select projects rationally. It preferred to carry forward many projects at once, though with meager funds for each, rather than take them up in the priority of their greatest economic value. Unless a multiple-purpose program could circumvent these practices, the water conservationists argued, it would fail.

The Newlands bill met with a cool reception in the Senate. . . . The lawmakers as a whole opposed an independent body that would take from Congress the power to decide each project. . . .

By the spring of 1913 the water power struggle in Congress had deadlocked. Congress had checked the Roosevelt policy, but conservationists had also blocked perpetual, free grants to private corporations. This stalemate halted all water power development on the navigable streams at a time when it proceeded rapidly on the public lands. After a decade of legislative struggle the compromise water power Act of 1920 once more permitted development. This Act dealt solely with water power. It failed to realize the hopes of conservationists that power development would go forward as an integral part of a multiple-purpose river program. . . .

[T]he thread of resource policy had become interwoven in a single coherent approach: the use of "foresight and restraint in the exploitation of the physical sources of wealth as necessary for the perpetuity of civilization, and the welfare of present and future generations." This, in 1908, was conservation, a concept which formerly had referred to reservoir storage of flood waters and controlled grazing on the Western range, but had now come to connote efficiency in the development and use of all resources. . . . Indeed, for many the term implied the need for

efficiency in social and moral affairs as well as in economic life. Like Theodore Roosevelt, they looked upon conservation as a major step in the progress of civilization; it would bring conscious foresight and intelligence into the direction of all human affairs.

The conservation movement was closely connected with other organizations which attempted to promote efficiency. Leaders of the Roosevelt administration, for example, maintained close contact with the four major engineering societies, the American Society of Civil Engineers, the American Society of Mechanical Engineers, the American Institute of Electrical Engineers, and the American Institute of Mining Engineers. The societies spearheaded the drive for efficiency. They argued that the potential electric energy in the nation's streams should be harnessed to lessen the drain on exhaustible coal supplies. They promoted more efficient mining methods and the utilization of by-products in the iron and steel industry, and pressed upon manufacturers the need for scientific management in the plant. Professional engineers felt a close kinship with the scientific and technological spirit of the Roosevelt administration. They took a keen interest in resource problems, publicized conservation affairs in their journals, and defended the administration from attack. They applauded when the President sought to bring order, efficiency, and business methods into government. . . .

This expanded philosophy of efficient planning found tangible expression in the Governors' Conference in 1908 and in the subsequent inventory of natural resources undertaken by the National Conservation Commission. . . .

The proposal for a national resources inventory came initially from the engineering societies. These organizations had maintained contact with the Roosevelt administration for a number of years through a National Advisory Board on Fuels and Structural Materials, established to supervise the testing of the quality of fuels and construction material used by the federal government. . . . In March 1908 Charles Whiting Baker, editor of *Engineering News,* suggested the national inventory project to Pinchot as a proposal to be sponsored by the four engineering societies. . . .

To many conservationists this inventory merely applied sound business principles to the entire nation. In his first report on the Commission's work, Roosevelt echoed this viewpoint:

> All we are asking . . . is that the National Government shall proceed as a private business man would, as a matter of course, proceed. He will regularly take account of stock, so that he may know just where he stands. . . . The same measures of prudence demanded from him as an individual, are demanded from us as a nation. . . .

The National Conservation Commission, however, soon faced opposition from Congress which led to its demise. . . . This controversy went to the heart of the conservation idea itself, the view that experts alone should make resource decisions. Congress, so the argument ran, could not deal with complex questions; it was better able to fulfill the immediate desires of its local constituents than to carry out a rational resource program in the light of scientific facts. Moreover, the great number of differing opinions among congressmen rendered them incapable of acting with the dispatch essential to operate large and intricate programs efficiently. . . .

Dissatisfaction with the inability of Congress to act efficiently cropped up continually during Roosevelt's term of office. In 1905, speaking of the need for a more efficient federal administration, the President declared: "to make it so is a task of complex detail and essentially executive in its nature; probably no legislative body, no matter how wise and able, could undertake it with reasonable prospect of success." Senator Newlands criticized the inefficient logrolling methods used by Congress to undertake rivers and harbors improvements. He threw up his hands in disgust when congressmen refused to adopt a system of priorities in public works projects. . . .

In the spring of 1908 Congress refused to appropriate funds to continue the work of the Inland Waterways Commission. Immediately after Congress adjourned, Roosevelt reappointed the Commission as a section of the more extensive National Conservation Commission which he established also without legislative sanction. Those were the last straws. In February 1909, when Roosevelt sought funds for the work of the National Conservation Commission, Congress not only denied his request but also approved the Tawney amendment to the Sundry Civil Bill, prohibiting any federal administrative official from aiding the work of any executive commission not authorized by Congress. This was the final answer of Congress to an administration which the lawmakers thought had gone too far in assuming legislative powers. . . .

How should conflicts among Western resource users be settled? This problem illustrated concisely the ambivalent Western attitude toward the federal conservation program. To Roosevelt administrators its solution lay at the heart of the conservation idea. Competing claims to resources should be resolved, they argued, by a scientific calculation of material benefits rather than through political struggle. How else could one guarantee maximum efficiency? Westerners did not agree. To them the "scientific expert" became simply a "bureaucrat" whose decision a local group could rarely affect. Open economic competition, court action, or political pressure provided far more effective opportunities for resource users to fight their own battles. The cry of "dictator" rarely arose until a federal bureau decided an important case in favor of one group and against another. But an accumulation of discontent in specific cases grew into a widespread regional attack against the "undemocratic methods" of the federal experts. . . .

The deepest significance of the conservation movement, however, lay in its political implications: how should resource decisions be made and by whom? Each resource problem involved conflicts. Should they be resolved through partisan politics, through compromise among competing groups, or through judicial decision? To conservationists such methods would defeat the inner spirit of the gospel of efficiency. Instead, experts, using technical and scientific methods, should decide all matters of development and utilization of resources, all problems of allocation of funds. Federal land management agencies should resolve land-use differences among livestock, wildlife, irrigation, recreation, and settler groups. National commissions should adjust power, irrigation, navigation, and flood control interests to promote the highest multiple-purpose development of river basis. The crux of the gospel of efficiency lay in a rational and scientific method of making basic technological decisions through a single, central authority.

. . . [T]he conservation movement raised a fundamental question in American life: How can large-scale economic development be effective and at the same time fulfill the desire for significant grass-roots participation? How can the technical requirements of an increasingly complex society be adjusted to the need for the expression of particular and limited aims? This was the basic political problem which a technological age, the spirit of which the conservation movement fully embodied, bequeathed to American society.

From Samuel Hays, *Conservation and the Gospel of Efficiency* (New York: Atheneum [1959], 1969), introduction and pp. 66–72, 100–115, 121–138, 145–146, 248–249, 271–272, 275–276.

SECTION 2

Efficiency for What—and Whom? Distributing the Benefits

We might say, using the jargon of modern decision-making theory, that the Progressive reformers hoped to replace "suboptimal" decision making by politicians with "optimal" decision making by experts. What exactly does it mean to optimize? Literally, it means to do one's best or, in economics, to get the maximum benefit out of a situation after all costs have been taken into account. For most purposes, therefore, the terms *optimizing* and *maximizing* are interchangeable. **Optimizing,** the term preferred by operations researchers and systems analysts, gives more explicit emphasis to the search for the best balance of gains and costs. (We'll take up operations research and systems analysis as a formal subfield of public administration in Chapter 9.) **Maximizing,** the term more frequently used in economic theory, leaves implicit the accounting of costs; in other words, the term *maximizing* puts a bit more emphasis on the decision maker's search for the highest level of net benefit—always remembering, however, that "benefit" is a meaningful concept only if the price paid to gain it has been taken into consideration.

The Progressives' aspiration to optimize—the ultimate purpose of synoptic analysis and systemwide planning—reflected certain themes and theories that were revolutionizing the discipline of economics, especially in European intellectual circles, at about the same time that the Progressives were developing the outlines of public administration in the United States. Alfred Marshall in England and Vilfredo Pareto, an Italian who divided his time between universities in France and Italy, were building on the foundations laid by Adam Smith ("classical economics") to raise the pillars of modern economic theory ("neoclassical economics"). We will consider several of Marshall's innovations—graphical analysis of supply-and-demand curves, the concepts of "willingness to pay" and consumer surplus—in Chapter 9; the latter concepts are building blocks of modern cost-benefit analysis, the central optimizing methodology in contemporary public administration. Right now, we want to consider the contribution of the other great neoclassical innovator, Marshall's contemporary, Pareto.

Economic Theories of Optimizing: Pareto Optimality and Kaldor-Hicks

Pareto studied the conditions under which a rational individual making purchases in a free market will draw the maximum benefit from his or her expenditures. Pareto's analysis gave rise to the modern theory of consumer demand. Although Pareto focused on the problem of rational behavior for an individual, he went on to consider how economic welfare might be optimized for a society as well.

Pareto imagined a decision maker who acts on behalf of an entire community. The decision maker considers a whole series of policies, trying to find the best course of action while taking into account the welfare of all the individuals who are under his or her care. Different policies will change one or more citizens' levels of welfare. Many policies, Pareto observed, will make some citizens better off, but they'll do so by hurting others. For example, redistributive programs may put money into some citizens' pockets that has been taxed away from others. Pareto's analysis implied that policy makers should search for ways to improve the lot of some without harming anyone else in society. A position is said to be **Pareto optimal** when there's no way to make even a single individual better off without making at least one other person worse off. By definition, any policy that improves efficiency moves society in the Pareto-optimal direction because it permits more goods to be produced with the same input of resources. The extra increment produced will obviously redound to some person's or group's benefit, making that individual or set of individuals better off while not hurting any one else.

The intimate link between the Pareto-optimal concept and the value of efficiency suggests why the basics of neoclassical economic thought should have had special appeal to America's scientific managers. Yet as a practical matter, the concept of Pareto optimality had little direct impact on public administration either in the United States or in Europe—partly because "better off" and "worse off" are rather abstract notions, often hard to flesh out in practice, and partly because few policies can be imagined for which no one pays any net cost (that is, for which no on ends up worse off, however that is defined). What, however, if those who stand to benefit will gain more than those likely to be hurt will lose? It remained for some of Pareto's successors in the economic profession to point out that such a policy could be defended even though it would violate the strict form of the Pareto condition. Such a policy would achieve a *net* improvement after all effects were taken into account—not necessarily improvements for every individual considered one by one, but an overall gain for society taken as a whole. The same notion suggests a further possibility—namely, that the winners might somehow compensate the losers.

The **Kaldor-Hicks principle**, named after the two mid-twentieth-century economists who formulated it, expresses these ideas. Unlike the concept of Pareto optimality, the Kaldor-Hicks principle permits a policy to be adopted that may make some individuals worse off if it will make other individuals more than proportionately better off. The essential point is in the qualification "more than proportionately." The Kaldor-Hicks principle says that decision makers should look for policies under which those who win have their situations sufficiently improved so that some of their gains could be drained off and used to offset the losses of anyone who, absent compensation, would be left worse off. Theoretically, the optimal position for society as a whole would be reached when no possibilities remain to level out gains and costs by compensating losers from the excess benefits reaped by the winners.

The Kaldor-Hicks principle suggests that it's usually desirable to funnel some of the gains of improved systemwide efficiency back to those who will continue to fight change if it threatens to help others—even a majority of citizens—by making themselves worse off. The problem is, it's often very hard to come up with an administratively feasible way to achieve this redistributive objective. In practice, a whole lot of political tugging and pulling may take place in the struggle to decide *what* a fair compensation pattern would look like, *who* should be included, and *how* it can best be administered.

An Example: Efficiency and Compensation in a Local Solid-Waste Disposal System

Let's use a simple example to see how the Kaldor-Hicks principle relates to the quest for efficiency through systemwide planning. Suppose that three individuals form a society. Tom, Dick, and Mary each must pay $240 annually (either to government or to private trash haulers) for garbage service. Then someone finds a way to improve life for at least some of the participants in the system, say by offering a better method of waste disposal. Assume, however, that the more efficient arrangement benefits only certain citizens and actually hurts others. Suppose that henceforth two customers (Dick and Mary) will have to pay only $160 per year, but because of some peculiarity in the improved garbage disposal system—maybe an excessive distance from Tom's home to a new, low-cost dump—it will actually cost more for haulers to truck his garbage away. In effect, Dick and Mary together will gain a total of $160 per year if the new policy is instituted. But because of the peculiarity, the overall improvement in the system will mean a net loss to Tom, whose charge under the new scheme will have to increase from $240 to $280 per year to cover the extra cost of long-distance haulage.

The new policy can't be adopted under the strict form of the Pareto-optimal criterion, for although two persons will be better off, the third—Tom—will be hurt. Under the Kaldor-Hicks principle, however, there's a different calculation. The net gain to two individuals

$$\$80 + \$80 = \$160$$

should easily support a $40 transfer from the winners to offset Tom's disadvantage. Table 5.1 shows one formula ($20 apiece from Dick and Mary) for the transfer money to make Tom "whole."

Who should be included in the compensation scheme for our three-member society may seem clear enough, and also *what* a fair compensation pattern might look like: namely, Dick and Mary should each compensate Tom by paying him $20 per year. But

Table 5.1 Kaldor-Hicks Compensation following the Adoption of an Improved Waste Disposal System in a Three-Person Society

	(1)	(2)	(3)
		Charges for Waste Disposal	
	Under the Old System	Under the Improved System	
		Before Compensation	With Compensation
Tom	$240	$280	$240
Dick	240	160	180
Mary	240	160	180
Systemwide cost	$720	$600	$600

as we'll see in a moment, *how* to engineer the compensation scheme in practice may pose a problem.

There are other difficulties besides administrative feasibility. Unfortunately the notion of compensation in most Kaldor-Hicks arrangements—and perhaps in this one—implies that all individuals put the same intrinsic value on a dollar. It's a doubtful assumption at best. In fact, there exists no precise way to make what economists call "interpersonal comparisons." Hence it's technically impossible to show that any compensation scheme actually wipes out a loser's deficit in a completely fair way. Suppose, further, that the hauler manages to forget Tom's trash pickup every once in a while simply because it's inconvenient to make the long trip between Tom's place and the new dump. A requirement that Dick and Mary spend $20 apiece will compensate Tom only for his ostensible pecuniary loss. But Tom's higher dollar costs now aren't the only factor; under the new scheme, he must also periodically put up with substandard service. Does that square with our intuitive idea of a fair social arrangement?

It may also be hard to devise satisfactory practical mechanisms for achieving even a rough level of fair compensation. The difficulty of Kaldor-Hicks implementation is just one of the measures of the contemporary challenge to public administration. Let's consider some varieties of administrative procedures that might be used to achieve compensation in the case of Tom, Dick, and Mary. As we do so, you might find it helpful to sketch out simple models of our three-person society, showing the channels through which money flows—both the channels that run from Tom, Dick, and Mary to the service provider (the hauler) and the channels through which compensation payments flow from Dick and Mary to Tom.

Administrative Applications of the Kaldor-Hicks Principle

Superficially—and setting aside the problem of interpersonal comparisons—the allocation of waste-disposal costs in Column 3 of Table 5.1 ("With Compensation") seems to satisfy the Kaldor-Hicks requirement: Tom ends up no worse off because he has been compensated; Dick and Mary end up better off than they were under the original arrangement. But how are the transfers accomplished? Who collects the money needed to defray the costs of trash disposal, and what happens to those extra dollars that Dick and Mary gain as a result of an improvement in systemwide efficiency?

Case 1. Efficiencies Achieved Solely by Private Action

Suppose that Tom, Dick, and Mary are all private citizens who pay private waste haulers. Public officials never get into the act. As profit seekers, the haulers all search for better ways to provide their service. A hauler who can lower his or her costs will beat out the competition. Assume that the savings to Dick and Mary result from a more efficient logistical pattern developed by one of the system's private haulers. The hauler opens a new dump that's much closer to Dick's and Mary's homes (although somewhat farther from Tom's), making it possible to reduce average transportation costs throughout the entire waste disposal system, thereby lowering the total cost of service, from $720 to $600 per year.

In this case, the private service provider is the sole intermediary; he or she collects all the money paid by Tom, Dick, and Mary. What's more, as a private entrepreneur, the hauler is under no obligation to mitigate the loss—a $40 hike in the yearly charge for garbage service—that Tom incurs under the new system.[1] Nor, for that matter, could we expect Dick and Mary to be very concerned about Tom's predicament. Unless something fundamental changes, Dick's and Mary's savings will remain in their pockets.

The extra $40 per week that Tom must pay will go directly to the hauler, who will have to use this sum to cover the higher costs of trucking trash the longer distance from Tom's home to the new dump. How might Tom be made whole? Only by going "outside the market." A special tax may be assessed against Dick and Mary. After all, both Dick and Mary come out of the deal relatively wealthier than Tom does (each is $80 richer every week, and Tom is $40 poorer), making themselves liable to a higher tax rate under the principle of progressivity.[2] The government could collect an extra $20 apiece from the two winners in the form of higher taxes and then award $40 to Tom as a grant justified in the name of equity. Alternatively, the $40 could be transferred to the hauler as a subsidy. Under this subsidy, the hauler would be prohibited from charging Tom extra for long-distance haulage, since the $40 to cover the higher-cost service would now be covered by the subsidy out of tax funds. Furthermore, the provision of a public subsidy would, in effect, make garbage service a public utility, subject to public regulation. The hauler would have to promise not to scrimp on service to Tom just because he lives at an inconvenient location.

Case 2. Efficiency Indirectly Stimulated by Public Action

In our second case, the improvement in area waste disposal capabilities results not from private innovation but from public action. An example would be a publicly funded road improvement program. Any road system favors certain locations over others. In case 2, Tom, Dick, and Mary remain private citizens who continue to pay a private waste hauler. Following the road improvement, the hauler can selectively lower costs because more efficient routings are possible from two customers' homes. Because the savings reaped by the winners result from the publicly funded new transportation configuration, the relatively richer citizens (Dick and Mary) become richer because of the indirect help they get from the government. Of course, the government is also to blame for the $40 potential loss to Tom, who actually contributed with his taxes to the construction of public facilities that now bode to hurt him. Because government has "harmed" one of its own citizens, some might think that government has a more compelling obligation than in case 1 to compensate him.

[1]Why wouldn't Tom switch to a competing hauler? The likely reason would go roughly as follows: When one hauler somehow achieves a competitively superior system, as in this case, he or she can underbid all other comers for Dick's and Mary's business. Furthermore, potential competitors won't even be able to match the efficient hauler's increased ($40 per year) charge to Tom because, having been wiped out of the competition for Dick's and Mary's business, they must defray the total costs of any service they continue to provide out of whatever fees they would hope to collect from the single remaining customer. That necessity would probably drive the cost of service to that customer up to a prohibitively high level. By contrast, the innovative hauler will be able to spread costs over the service offered to all three customers—even though one of them, Tom, will have to pay a somewhat jacked-up price. Obviously, innovation can (as in this case) put a successful competitor on the road to monopoly.

[2]*Principle of progressivity:* The idea that those who are better able to pay should bear a higher portion of the collective burden. This principle underlies the progressive income tax, under which richer citizens pay higher percentages of their extra increments of income (the "marginal tax rate") than poorer citizens do.

Again, the savings to Dick and Mary and the loss to Tom will remain in private channels of money flow *unless* public officials take steps to achieve compensation. A tax-and-transfer approach might be taken, as in case 1. Or perhaps tolls could be collected on the new roads, with a portion of the take used to subsidize trash haulers (again, subject to regulated rate setting and public monitoring of the service level to all customers, even distant ones like Tom). The aim, as in case 1, would be to compensate the loser while retaining overall efficiency gains in the form of lower charges to Dick and Mary.

Case 3. A Public Agency as a Financial Intermediary

In our third case, the government not only is an active force in the promotion of systemwide efficiencies but also is involved from the very start in the waste disposal business. Suppose that Tom, Dick, and Mary each pay an annual fee to a public waste disposal agency or, what's almost the same, pay a private waste hauler who has always operated subject to public regulation. Say that systemwide savings become possible because of an administrative innovation—for example, the adoption of a computerized dispatching and routing system. All trucks can be directed from pickup points to their lowest-cost ultimate disposal sites. Suppose, however, that some old dumps were filled to their capacity and were closed, again leaving Tom so far from active landfills that, even with the new system, the cost of hauling his waste increases. Thus the pattern of gains and losses is the same as in cases 1 and 2.

The easiest way to achieve compensation will be through selective changes in charges to customers, combined with a series of internal accounting and fiscal adjustments. The hauler can cut Dick's and Mary's charges from $240 to $180 and use the resulting surplus—which will amount to a $40 fund in excess of the firm's true expenses—to cover the higher cost of serving Tom. Another solution might be to take the total cost of systemwide service after gains from the improvement have been deducted from the original $720; divide that by 3

$$\frac{\$280 + \$160 + \$160}{3} = \$200$$

and charge every customer the same amount irrespective of the actual cost of service to a particular address. Charging a uniform $200 annual rate would yield an across-the-board reduction of $40 in everyone's original ($240) rate. No one would be advantaged or penalized by the luck of his or her location within the disposal network.

In case 3, Kaldor-Hicks compensation occurs with a minimum of fuss. The key is the replacement of separate, privately controlled cash streams with a single administrative entity—whether a private firm operating under public regulatory authority (a public utility) or a public waste authority that actually hauls the trash—to manage the flow of funds as an internal bookkeeping procedure.

Case 4. Funding from Taxes rather than from Fees

In our final example, Tom, Dick, and Mary rely for garbage service on a sanitation force supported by taxes. Customers don't pay separate fees to have their waste removed. Instead, the sanitation workers' wages and all equipment costs are publicly funded. No direct market transactions enter the picture, putting this case at the opposite end of the spectrum from case 1.

In case 4, dollars spent on trash service never get broken out into separate expenditure streams. In fact, no longer are there even any "customers" for trash collectors in the normal meaning of that word. Tom, Dick, and Mary fill only the roles of "citizens" who pay general taxes. Public officials must divide the total tax return into separate money streams that will support public education, a police department, trash service, and so forth. No market transactions occur; all transfers of funds result from political or administrative decisions. This result may make it somewhat easier to redistribute any gains achieved by adopting more efficient trash disposal procedures, but it also severs the direct link that individuals in cases 1 through 3 felt between the money they paid for haulage and the level of service they got in return.

As intelligent citizens, Tom, Dick, and Mary recognize that any systemwide efficiencies will cut the true costs of trash disposal. If they see a roadway improvement under way or hear of a new computer-based dispatching system, they will probably anticipate a reduction in the true cost of waste service and expect to see some benefit themselves. The citizens may expect a prorated tax cut, some kind of administered Kaldor-Hicks compensation arrangement, a diversion of money from waste disposal into the school system or other worthwhile public undertakings, or some combination of all the above.

You might want to ask yourself if funding a public service by general taxation, by separate assessments tied directly to the service, or by market arrangements with private providers (whether publicly regulated or not) should make it easier or harder to spread any systemwide benefits fairly over the entire society. You'll want to keep your answer in mind when, in our chapter case, you encounter a testy small-town official named Finn Ebertsen who has certain opinions of his own about a proposal to achieve systemwide efficiencies in trash disposal throughout the St. Croix region—but with little promise of immediate gain for Ebertsen's own constituents.

Blind Spots in the Progressive Outlook

So far in this chapter, we've considered three themes: the doctrine of the politics-administration gap; the Progressives' campaign for "better methods of executive action," which boiled down to the application of synoptic analysis and systemwide planning; and the issues of fair compensation that naturally emerge whenever citizens find themselves divided into potential winners and losers.

The Progressives never saw the inconsistency between the politics-administration gap and the systemwide planning orientation—an orientation which would have to be realized in a political system that's designed as much to express local interests as it is to attain overall efficiencies. That was blind spot number 1. Systemwide planning inevitably involved the technicians in politics because the attempt to optimize over total systems (executive budgeting, improved public services for entire cities, "comprehensive development" of multistate river basins, and so forth) often required sacrifices by some to benefit the many. That goal made sense to reformers acting on behalf of the "public interest," but it had the potential to create local losers. Understandably, the potential losers used all available political means to block plans that threatened them. Politicians can be expected to interfere in the "separate" province of administration whenever appointed officials come up with plans that are likely to harm their constituencies. (Our chapter reading was about precisely that dynamic—about local actors mobilizing against conservation experts who sought overall gains while ignoring the selective losses that systemwide planning would cause.)

The Progressives looked first and last for efficiency in their "better methods of executive action," but they failed to see the implications of efficiency gains all the way through; that was blind spot number 2. Specifically, the Progressives rarely considered how extra increments of welfare might be redistributed to provide fair compensation for those threatened by their schemes. Of course, fair compensation is a value-charged concept. It has to do with the division of benefits and allocation of harms. It necessarily evokes a process of political choice, albeit one that may succeed or fail as a function of the kinds of administrative arrangements that can be made to implement a compensation agreement. Recognizing this fact, we can appreciate that the intermixing of politics with administration, the quest for efficiency through systemwide planning, and the need to think through winner-loser issues are necessary and interrelated aspects of administrative analysis. Our chapter case will give us a chance to explore some of the implications—and the difficulties—of this insight.

SECTION 3
● ■ ▼ ◆

Beyond Kaldor-Hicks:
An Introduction to Modern Bargaining Theory

The central issue in a Kaldor-Hicks scheme is the distribution of the benefits that may be achieved, systemwide, if a more efficient approach to some function—such as waste disposal—is adopted. It sometimes happens that a unitary decision maker (the "supreme command authority" of classical organizational theory) has been empowered in advance to decide on a fair distributional arrangement. It also sometimes happens that the situation itself, so to speak, gives clues of its own about the kind of distribution that might satisfy fair-minded participants. Bargaining theorists call such a "natural" or intuitively "fair" distribution a **resting place.**

We can return to our hypothetical three-person society to illustrate the usefulness of this concept of a distributional resting place. It is at least arguable that no fairer result is likely to be found in our waste disposal example than the one in which each winner contributes $20 to make Tom whole. On the other hand, why should Tom have to pay $240 just because he happens to live farther from a new dump than Dick and Mary do? Tom might decide to make an issue of it, arguing that since Dick and Mary both improve their situations, they should contribute enough to level out the distribution of benefits across society as a whole, as in the "$200 solution" of case 3. On second thought, then, maybe there's no intuitively "fair" resting place after all. Or, rather, perhaps there are *two* resting places, one that merely leaves Tom as well off as before but greatly benefits Dick and Mary, and one that evenly divides the benefits among all three without regard to variations in the true cost of serving any one of them.

Unfortunately, in many real-world problems, there may be neither a unique distributional resting place (and so the problem remains indeterminate) nor an authoritative unitary decision maker to choose a course of action, even arbitrarily, within the range of indeterminacy. The actors who have interests in the outcome but can't control one another's decision will have to sit down and negotiate. Each actor may try some fairly standard bargaining tactics in an effort to gain an outcome favorable to his or her own interests. Yet it's in the nature of most bargaining situations that a large number of outcomes—some favorable to a given participant, many less so—may be equally feasible; that, in fact, is what the bargaining theorists' term *range of indeterminacy* means. Between a would-be buyer's best offer and a would-be seller's minimum demand, for example, there may be an infinite number of possibilities and no natural resting place. Which bargainer will the final price end up favoring? The outcome may depend more on the skills of the negotiators than on the structure of the situation.

In our three-person society, the Kaldor-Hicks principle points to a possible—but not unique or even compelling—solution, namely, the "Make Tom Whole" distribution shown in Column 3 of Table 5.1. That distribution can be thought of as a resting place. But as we have seen, the "Equal Benefits" distribution, at which each citizen pays $200, can also be considered as a possible resting place. The mixed-mode nature of the situation is evident. Although all three citizens have an incentive to cooperate in getting the better waste disposal system implemented, there's also a basis for conflict in the situation. Even if Dick and Mary can be persuaded that fairness requires compensation up to the "Make Tom Whole" point, they have an obvious interest in preventing any more-generous level of compensation. Tom's interest, on the other hand, is to keep the settlement as close as he can to the three-way $200-per-year split. Between these two resting places lies the range of indeterminacy. As with all indeterminate problems, there's no clear-cut solution.

Modern bargaining theory extends the study of distributive arrangements for situations such as the one in which Tom, Dick, and Mary find themselves. What tactics might the three of them use to decide how benefits will be divided within that "pure bargaining" range between the two resting places? In part because of its relevance to problems for which Kaldor-Hicks may suggest an opening position but not a unique solution; in part because negotiation is so commonly used in situations that call for coordination by mutual adjustment; and in part because we want to prepare for certain issues in our chapter case, we turn now to some basics of this important subfield of our subject.

Distributive Bargaining

Distributive bargaining occurs in situations of relatively simple opposed interests, as when a buyer wants to bargain for the lowest-possible price while the seller is trying to get as much as he or she can—or, again, when an actor like Tom in our illustration is trying to hold an agreement close to one resting place while opponents like Dick and Mary want to drive the outcome in exactly the opposite direction. Let's consider the simpler buyer-seller model first, and then we'll extend it to the situation with Tom, Dick, and Mary.

A shopper wants a product for less than the seller is demanding, so the two haggle over a price. A diplomat wants to get a more favorable trade concession than the other negotiator wants to give, so they go back and forth until the tariff gets cut or the bargainers—despairing of an agreement—break off talks. Negotiations of this sort, whether in the bazaar or in the arena of high statecraft, go back to the beginnings of institutionalized human interaction. Although these examples presuppose conflict, each

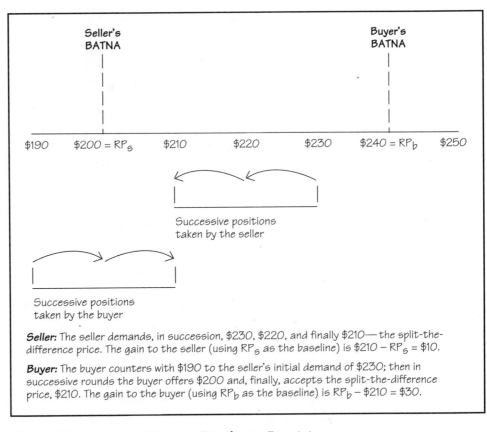

Seller's BATNA   Buyer's BATNA

| $190 | $200 = RP_S | $210 | $220 | $230 | $240 = RP_b | $250 |

Successive positions taken by the seller

Successive positions taken by the buyer

Seller: The seller demands, in succession, $230, $220, and finally $210—the split-the-difference price. The gain to the seller (using RP_S as the baseline) is $210 − RP_S = $10.

Buyer: The buyer counters with $190 to the seller's initial demand of $230; then in successive rounds the buyer offers $200 and, finally, accepts the split-the-difference price, $210. The gain to the buyer (using RP_b as the baseline) is RP_b − $210 = $30.

Sketch 5.1 Reservation Pricing in Distributive Bargaining

also involves the shared goal of finding a peaceful way to distribute or redistribute goods. The aim is to leave each party better off than he or she would be if the negotiation hadn't occurred and, therefore, the trade hadn't been made.

A distributive negotiation implies a process known as **positional bargaining** along a single axis. Two bargainers engage in a ritual of offer and counteroffer, the buyer trying to hold down the amount that he or she will have to pay and the seller trying to extract the highest price. Thus there's a direct opposition of interests; what the buyer wins, the seller loses, and vice versa.

Sketch 5.1 depicts two adversaries, a buyer and a seller, haggling over the sale of some good or service. The first requirement is to establish a feasible bargaining range— a range within which the parties can engage in the so-called "dance of negotiation." If (under any circumstances) the seller will demand a higher price than the would-be buyer can (under any circumstances) pay, no bargaining range exists. Both parties might as well fold up immediately, since there is no basis for ultimate agreement, which implies that there's also no range for good-faith bargaining.

Fortunately, in the situation of Sketch 5.1, it turns out that there *does* exist a potential for agreement. The question is, will the adversaries have the sense and the skills to capitalize on that opportunity? The least that the seller will accept is $200, and the most that the buyer will pay under any circumstances is $240. As we will see, however, not only is it *not* assumed that the bargainers truthfully communicate their minimum and maximum requirements to each other but also, in distributive bargaining, it is often desirable—at least as a tactic—that each bargainer conceal information from adversaries. In Sketch 5.1, $200 and $240 define the range within which bargaining will have to proceed if a deal is to be made. But since each bargainer may conceal vital information from the other, much of the point of negotiation is to discover (1) what that range really is and (2) whether any resting places exist within it.

As we have just seen, if the would-be purchaser refuses to offer at least the minimum price that the seller is willing to consider, the negotiation will end before any real bargaining has even begun. The seller's walking-away price in such a case is known as the seller's **BATNA** (*best alternative to a negotiated agreement*). On the other side, if the seller holds out for too high a price—a price higher than the buyer's BATNA (in our example, $240)—then the latter should take his or her business to some other seller or, perhaps, try to get along without the item altogether. "Know thine BATNA" is the first law of distributive bargaining. Traders shouldn't get caught up in the emotions of the market and be tempted, as a result, to "breach their BATNAs." Bargainers who succumb to the excitement of the bidding may end up selling their wares for too little or buying items for too much.

A BATNA, also known as a *reservation price, (RP),* refers to a true minimum or maximum requirement. In contrast, a *position*—the key concept in negotiation conceptualized as positional bargaining—refers to an announced requirement, which may be either true or false. A would-be buyer is likely to understate the price that he or she would, in actuality, be willing to pay; conversely, the would-be seller may overstate the minimum price that he or she demands. *Positioning*, then, refers to the information that each bargainer communicates to the other, whether it is truthful or not. A bargainer chooses a position in order to elicit a desired response from the adversary. When a seller announces an untruthfully high opening position, the purpose is to warn the buyer that the latter's initial offer will have to be jacked up if there's to be any chance of a trade.

In Sketch 5.1, the seller opens with a position (that is, a demanded price) of $230, even though he or she will actually accept as little as $200—the reservation price, RP_s. The buyer feigns a lack of interest and offers $190, even though he will actually be willing to pay up to $240 if the seller holds out for no less than that amount. In other words, the price above which the buyer will walk away, RP_b, is $240. The bargainers are really haggling over the distribution of the difference between their reservation prices, in this example, $40. Each will be sufficiently satisfied at any price between the two RPs to close the deal, but within those limits any gain to one bargainer will come at the cost of the other.

One can easily imagine the negotiation playing out as follows:

Seller: "I need $230."
Buyer: "I'll give you $190."
Seller: "$190 won't even cover my costs. Make it $220."
Buyer: "$200."

So they split the difference at a final exchange price of $210, halfway between the two bargainers' last bids. The $210 sale price is also halfway between their initial positions—

their $230 and $190 offers. Split-the-difference is a reasonable-sounding decision rule and one that fair-minded individuals often adopt in distributive negotiations. But split-the-difference—or, for that matter, any hard-and-fast decision rule, if mechanically applied in a negotiation—may create an incentive for bargainers to engage in **strategic misrepresentation.**

Strategic Misrepresentation: Insincere Reporting

The scenario as presented in Sketch 5.1 illustrates the element of compromise that is implicit in most distributive negotiations, but so far it ignores the deeper ethical challenges that positional bargaining, reservation pricing, and strategic misrepresentation imply in negotiation analysis.

In the scenario each bargainer concealed important information. Within limits, untruthful position taking (also called *insincere reporting*) is usually regarded as an acceptable practice, at least in distributive negotiations. Consider the price that a bargainer might end up paying for negotiating sincerely against an insincere adversary. Suppose each actor opened the bidding by truthfully announcing his or her reservation price:

> *Seller:* "The true value of my service is $200."
> *Buyer:* "I'm willing to pay as much as $240."

Again the negotiators split the difference. At a final exchange price of $220, each of these sincere bargainers would have gained $20 relative to his or her reservation price:

$$RP_b - \$220 = \$20$$
$$\$220 - RP_s = \$20$$

In the example of Sketch 5.1, however, both parties engage in strategic misrepresentation. Neither opens the bidding with a truthful report of his or her RP. Interestingly (and rather perversely), the bargainer who indulges in the more-extreme falsification—the buyer—is the one who gains at the other's expense. Recall that at the $210 split-the-difference price, the seller gains $10 over her RP, while the buyer gains $30. The buyer saves more, and the seller earns less, because of the former's misrepresentation—positioning at $230 instead of $240 to start the bidding.

The accuracy with which a bidder can estimate the adversary's reservation price determines how "hard" a position the bidder can take. It is this peculiarity of distributive bargaining that inherently invites strategic misrepresentation and can ultimately serve as a continuing temptation to employ unethical practices. Because the outcomes of many bargaining episodes depend on the truth-telling propensities of the bargainers, negotiation theorists have invested very considerable amounts of brainpower trying to find ways to promote sincere reporting.

Back to Tom, Dick, and Mary: Arbitration, Irreversible Commitments, and Coalition Formation

Under some conditions, distributive bargaining concepts can be used to analyze problems like the one facing Tom, Dick, and Mary. The situation of these three citizens calls for bargaining if all three share in the decision-making process but no one fully controls the others' actions—our familiar situation of underdetermination. No dictator exists with the power to impose whatever waste-haulage rates he or she wishes to, even to the point of discriminating arbitrarily among different customers. Furthermore, each citizen may walk away from any proposed deal. By refusing to agree to a new arrangement because one finds its terms objectionable, the walker can force this three-person society to retain its old waste disposal system. In actual administrative practice, this kind of blackmailing power is often expressed in obstructionistic tactics; an opponent may not have formal veto power but may be able to tie up a project in, say, environmental litigation. The result might be tantamount to killing the proposal outright. This kind of power roughly corresponds to the power of the walking-away threat that's implicit in the BATNA concept. Obviously, the power to hold everyone else in an unsatisfactory existing arrangement can be used coercively. The dog-in-the-manger policy isn't pretty, but it's often effective: "Meet my minimum demands, or no one else will get theirs!"

Dick and Mary could proceed in several ways. They might try to avoid all hassle by persuading Tom to join in hiring an impartial outsider to arbitrate. In effect, the three citizens would appoint a dictator to settle the distributional issue, having bound themselves in advance to accept the arbiter's decision. Alternatively, Dick and Mary could hire an agent to bargain with Tom on their behalf. Their agreement might restrict the agent's freedom of action in certain ways. As we'll see in our reading, restrictions of this sort often reflect carefully considered tactical choices. As such, they are not mere "administrative preliminaries" but key elements in the bargaining process itself. Dick and Mary, for example, might specify that any settlement negotiated by the agent must involve equal waste disposal payments for them; or they may demand that any deal must leave them at least as well off as they would have been if the new waste disposal system hadn't ever become a possibility.

The requirement to be "at least as well off" functions as a kind of BATNA: The agent must break off negotiations rather than agree to any scheme that will require Dick and Mary to pay more than $240. This means that in the very best of all worlds (from his standpoint), Tom can't possibly negotiate an annual rate lower than

$$\$600 - 2(\$240) = \$120$$

At the other extreme, Tom too would be better off under the old system than under any deal that would require him to pay more than $240. Tom would walk away and force a continuance of the old disposal system before agreeing to the distribution that would lower Dick's and Mary's rates to the $160 level of Column 2 in Table 5.1.

Within the resulting range, strategic concealment doesn't seem to promise much benefit either to Dick and Mary's agent or to Tom. Both bargainers know the true costs of disposal under the old and new systems; the two possible resting places also become evident on a quick inspection of the problem. All parties also see that, except for the resting places, the bargaining range appears to be essentially indeterminate. If Tom convinces Dick and Mary's agent to consider a better rate than $240—say $220 on the scale in Sketch 5.1—why shouldn't the agent come back and demand that Tom give equally serious consideration to a $230 rate—which is still a $10 saving over his current service charge (and the charge that Tom would continue to pay under a simple Kaldor-Hicks compensation scheme). The reading that ends this chapter covers such a situation, in which *irreversible commitments* (instead of strategic misrepresentation) are often the best ways to deal with a range of indeterminacy.

Two other variations in the givens of this bargaining problem should be noted.

First, situations sometimes occur in which there are more than two parties but no obvious basis for particular individuals to form the kind of unified negotiating blocs that Dick and Mary represent. What if Dick and Mary were complete strangers and could find no reason to join together as a single bargaining unit? Suppose that the three citizens had previously agreed to majority rule with no prohibition against **coalition formation.** With Tom, Dick, and Mary each acting independently in pursuit of his or her own self-interest, the way might be open for *any* two of them to form a voting bloc adverse to the interests of the third. Suppose that Tom saw an agreement evolving in which he would have to pay $220, with the remainder

$$\$600 - \$220 = \$380$$

split equally between Dick and Mary. Dick might be open to a bribe from Tom. Under one coalition that Tom might propose, Tom's charge would be cut to $180, and Dick's would stay at $190. However, a $20 bribe from Tom would effectively reduce Dick's annual outlay to $170[3] (and would effectively increase Tom's to $200—which is still better than the $220 figure from which he started). This deal would leave Mary to pick up the remainder, $230—still beneath her walking-away limit. If you were Mary, how would you counter such a threat from Tom and Dick?

A second kind of complexity occurs when individuals can look beyond a single dimension (such as the splitting of disposal costs) and bargain for the best mixture of benefits measured along several dimensions (different splits of disposal costs, water service costs, public recreation costs, and so forth). This possibility brings us to the next major subject in modern bargaining theory: integrative bargaining.

Integrative Bargaining

Integrative bargaining applies to more complex situations, such as those in which several bargainers deal with many issues. The manipulation of information also tends to become more problematical, both ethically and pragmatically, in integrative than in distributive bargaining.

An integrative negotiation always involves multiple dimensions. This characteristic often produces opportunities for trades that would be impossible to make in distributive bargaining. Asymmetries in the bargainers' patterns of preferences can often be used to advance a negotiation by creating "package deals." The parties to the negotiation may see in such packages more gains than can be realized by simple "What you win, I lose" trading along a single dimension. For this reason, professional negotiators who find themselves in a distributive negotiation will typically try to find a way to transform the situation into an integrative bargaining session.

Suppose that Ms. Jones and Mr. Smith are bargaining over two different services, each of which can be represented using a conventional distributive bargaining model. Service 1, which Jones provides, can be purchased by Smith—if, of course, Smith pays a price that Jones finds satisfactory. How high a price should Jones hold out for? How hard should she bargain? There's a very real danger here that the dynamics of positional posturing by the two adversaries may result in a total breakdown of negotiations. Even

---

[3]Tom would save $40 by paring his annual charge from $220 down to $180; he would use half of that saving as the $20 bribe—called a **side payment**—needed to convince Dick to go along.

if the participants' true BATNAs create the potential for a trade, "hard bargaining" (possibly compounded by strategic misrepresentation) may leave Smith at the end of the day without service 1 and Jones without the payment she would have received if the two had found a way to make a trade.

Suppose further that Smith controls the supply of service 2, which Jones wants—and wants very much. Service 2 represents a second dimension, a second distributive bargaining problem. Jones must be concerned lest she lose a sale of service 1 through inept negotiation with Smith. Jones must also take care lest she "lose" in the parallel distributive bargaining process by which the two actors will try to decide on a price at which Smith will sell Jones service 2, which she very much wants to purchase on favorable terms.

The key to integrative bargaining lies in treating the two dimensions as potential bases for a single package in which trades of both services will be linked rather than negotiated separately. Suppose that Jones, in her heart of hearts, isn't really desirous of extracting the highest possible price for the service she's selling (service 1) but is for some reason exceedingly anxious to get the best possible deal on the service offered by Smith (service 2). Reciprocally, for reasons of his own, Smith values service 1 very highly indeed, but he is willing to "be reasonable" in setting the price at which he'll supply service 2 to Jones. Stated differently, asymmetries in the bargainers' values—**asymmetric preferences,** in the terminology of modern bargaining theory—imply that Jones may be willing to "lose" when negotiating the price of service 1, since she doesn't much care about winning or losing along this dimension. Jones is willing to "lose" along one dimension in exchange not only for the payment she gets for service 1 but—more important—also for a "win" along the other dimension, which from Jones's standpoint is the really significant one. Reciprocally, the "bad deal" that Jones may be willing to accept along the first dimension will represent a valuable gain from Smith's standpoint—a gain for which he should be willing to compensate Jones in the form of a concession on the price at which he will furnish service 2 to her. The chance to make out where it really counts—on the issues of principal concern to each participant—should cause reasonable bargainers to be willing to lose, within limits, along the dimensions that are of lesser concern to them.

In our example, Jones and Smith strike two little bargains as a way of making one big one. The smaller bargains are the trade of service 1 at a price favorable to Smith and the trade of service 2 at a price favorable to Jones. The large bargain—and the crucial one for achieving the two smaller ones—is in the fact that each negotiator takes something of value away from the session (although failure to bridge the two dimensions might have left Jones and Smith both walking empty-handed away from a potential win-win situation if they had approached each other envisioning two completely independent distributive bargaining problems). The idea, then, is to integrate two or more distributive bargaining situations and thus create a single multidimensional negotiation in which advantage can be taken of the participants' asymmetric preferences, with each bargainer "winning" along his or her dimensions of primary interest.

It is important when organizing a negotiation to promote integrative rather than distributional bargaining. When different participants have different value scales along different dimensions, chances improve for finding creative trade-off combinations. Everyone will give up something. But with imaginative exploitation of the possibilities of asymmetric preferences, the something that everyone gives up should represent relatively lower-valued losses, while everyone also gains more than a series of separate distributive bargains could ever produce.

Uncertainty and Contingent Claims Contracting. Integrative negotiation often requires an elaborate process of compromising across many dimensions—the more dimensions, the better, since the opportunities for creative combinations increases with the number of issues. BATNAs must be established for all dimensions, adding to the complexity of the process. The end point of such a process is likely to be an agreement specifically framed to take into consideration not only the bargainers' different values (including their time values or discount rates) but also any differences that exist in their estimates of future probabilities. In other words, integrative bargaining usually takes the element of uncertainty into consideration.

An agreement that reflects different assessments of the likelihood of future events is called a **contingent claims contract.** It specifies a series of actions to be taken if specified conditions occur. Negotiation theorists sometimes refer to this kind of contingent agreement as a *vector*—a series of numbers with meanings that are defined in advance by the parties to the contract. The six-component vector

$$\{10, 20, 15, 0, 5, 5\}$$

might refer to a series of three payments that the buyer would have to make to the seller, depending on the appearance of specified future circumstances, and three rebates or refunds that the seller might have to make to the buyer—also contingent on the occurrence of specific future developments. Thus, the buyer might have to pay the seller $10 immediately in order to take possession of a shipment of some good, followed by another payment of $20 in a month's time, followed in two months by still a third installment of $15 *contingent on an increase over the sixty-day period in the market price of the product.*

In this hypothetical contingent contract, *0* in the fourth position might indicate that the buyer would owe the seller no third payment if the market price of the good fell or held steady for some agreed-upon period of time. The fifth and sixth components in the vector would refer to contingent refunds owed by the seller to the buyer. Thus, the two 5s might indicate that the seller must rebate $5 at the end of the first month if she or he has not made full delivery of the purchased item by that time and that the seller must rebate another $5 if the price of the good falls by more than a specified amount over a two-month period.

Asymmetric Preferences and Principled Bargaining. Bargaining theorists point out that contingent claims contracting is a technique of integrative negotiation. It is, in effect, a way to create new dimensions of choice and, hence, situations of asymmetric preferences. If one bargainer sets a high value on certainty while the other is a born risk taker, they may adjust the terms in the vector in a way that (1) ensures the first bargainer a certain minimum guaranteed return while (2) enabling the other bargainer to gamble for a high future reward if specified—but uncertain—future contingencies occur.

The process of integrative negotiation imposes some stiff demands on those who participate. The bargainers need to cultivate high levels of tolerance for complexity, since the more complex they are willing to make their negotiations, the better is the chance that they'll find trade-offs across dimensions. If they are to make integrative negotiation work, bargainers also have to trust one another—which often requires them to break the habits of strategic misrepresentation that they are likely to have learned in simpler positional bargaining situations. Trust alone—the basis of **principled bargaining**[4]—can induce negotiators to reveal both their true preferences and their true assessments of future probabilities. In turn, only mutual knowledge of true preferences and assessments can make it possible for two bargainers to recognize a situation of asymmetric preferences and thereby see ways to trade across sets of lesser and greater values.

Informational Bargaining

Informational bargaining emphasizes the knowledge-sharing functions of the negotiation process. As such, it involves a pronounced shift in emphasis by comparison with the other two kinds of bargaining modes that we've considered. We usually think of integrative negotiation, like distributive bargaining, primarily as a mode of conflict resolution. But the same process that can yield complex package deals—the aim in integrative bargaining—can also produce a valuable by-product: shared information. When shared information is important for its own sake—especially information about potential adversaries' values and goals, irrespective of any immediate conflict—a well-organized process of negotiation may be an effective way of managing complexity and reducing uncertainty by giving decision makers the data they need to deal intelligently with their environments. Increasingly in modern administrative contexts, the process of negotiation serves this primarily informational purpose.

Expressed differently, one reason why administrators rely increasingly on mutual adjustment rather than direct supervision lies in the greater capacity of coordination, when achieved through negotiation, to facilitate flows of information. Direct supervision works best when orders are as crisp, concise, and clear as they can possibly be, in order to minimize the chance that the subordinate will misunderstand what the superior wants done. In this sense, direct supervision works through a kind of communication that transmits as little information as possible—just enough to let the implementer of the order know what's expected. By contrast, mutual adjustment, whether through open discussion (as in "brainstorming sessions") or bargaining, usually involves much chit-chat, conversation on the margins of the main issues, and exchanges of information with the purpose of setting a context, communicating attitudes (determination or flexibility), and exploring possibilities ("What if I give in on x; will that bring forth the concession on y that I've been seeking?").

The generation and sharing of information is the purpose of the third kind of negotiation, informational bargaining. Gilbert Winham, a Canadian expert on negotiation, has undertaken the most systematic analysis of bargaining as a process of information exchange.[5] Winham accepts the thesis—consistent with the concept of negotiated order in Chapter 3—that organization and negotiation are complementary ways of achieving the same objective. That objective is to increase control over a complex, uncertain environment. One way to promote this end is by enlarging the sphere of bureau-

[4]*Principled bargaining:* A term developed by Roger Fisher and William Ury of the Harvard Negotiating Project. Unlike positional bargaining, in which each negotiator stakes out positions to defend in an adversarial confrontation with opponents, principled negotiation proceeds subject to commonly agreed guidelines. All parties try to understand one another's interests and to accommodate them where reasonably possible.

[5]"Negotiation as a Management Process," 30 *World Poltics* 1 (October 1977): 93–97.

cracy, since clear-cut structures of authority and standardized procedures can exert a powerful stabilizing force. Winham argues that the function of bargaining is often essentially the same—to reduce uncertainty, but through information exchange rather than through rule making.

From this conception of the negotiating process, important conclusions follow. When bargaining is viewed as a technique to reduce uncertainty, conflict resolution and dispute settlement become relatively less important as motives to negotiate. Negotiators also have much less reason to engage in strategic maneuvering—concealment, dissembling, efforts to "psyche out" the adversary. In informational bargaining, instead of trying to "win," all parties try to sustain a *process of continuing interchange.* The negotiators don't think in terms of minimum acceptable outcomes; if the concept of a reservation price applies at all, the factors entering into its computation will probably have changed long before an informational negotiation approaches any kind of decision point.

The informational bargainer tries to sustain the process of exchange because all relationships, whether formalized as legal agreements or informally worked out as tacit understandings, have temporal limits. In organizations considered as negotiated orders, all relationships are subject to review, reassessment, and revision. By promoting continuing relationships of trust, informational bargainers can better sustain the conditions in which productive reviews, reassessments, and revisions can occur. Because a negotiated order needs to be worked at, a forum for continuing interchanges of information may also provide an institutional setting for problem solving over time, even among—indeed, *especially* among—negotiators who don't share exactly the same goals. This insight, incidentally, anticipates a central lesson that we'll draw, in Chapter 6, from the modern theory of informal organizations.

Paradox in Bargaining

The following excerpt, from the Harvard economist Thomas Schelling's *Strategy of Conflict,* hints at the variety of problems and techniques that are encompassed within the field of modern bargaining theory. Schelling focuses explicitly on the most interesting—and most difficult—kind of conflict situation, one with an underdetermined structure. Note how Schelling develops the paradoxical idea that apparent weakness in positional bargaining can sometimes actually be cultivated and converted into strength through the making of irreversible commitments. (It just might have occurred to you that a situation involving a "range of indeterminacy" and a paucity of resting places may emerge in our chapter case.)

Thomas Schelling on the Paradox of Bargaining Power

When the business is finally sold to the one interested buyer, what price does it go for? When two dynamite trucks meet on a road wide enough for one, who backs up?

These are situations that ultimately involve an element of **pure bargaining**—bargaining in which each party is guided mainly by his expectations of what the other will accept. But with each guided by expectations and knowing that the other is too, expectations become compounded. A bargain is struck when somebody makes a final, sufficient concession. Why does he concede? Because he thinks the other will not. "I must concede because he won't. He won't because he thinks I will. He thinks I will because he thinks I think he thinks so. . . ." There is some range of alternative outcomes in which any point is better for both sides than no agreement at all. To insist on any such point is pure bargaining, since one always *would* take less rather than reach no agreement at all, and since one always *can* recede if restraint proves necessary to agreement. Yet if both parties are aware of the limits to this range, *any* outcome is a point from which at least one party would have been willing to retreat and the other knows it! There is no resting place.

There is, however, an outcome; and if we cannot find it in the logic of the situation we may find it in the tactics employed. . . . The essence of these tactics is some voluntary but irreversible sacrifice of freedom of choice. They rest on the paradox that the power to constrain an adversary may depend on the power to bind oneself; that, in bargaining, weakness is often strength, freedom may be freedom to capitulate, and to burn bridges behind one may suffice to undo an opponent.

Bargaining Power: The Power to Bind Oneself

"Bargaining power," "bargaining strength," "bargaining skill" suggest that the advantage goes to the powerful, the strong, or the skillful. It does, of course, if those qualities are defined to mean only that negotiations are won by those who win. But, if the terms imply that it is an advantage to be more intelligent or more skilled in debate, or to have more financial resources, more physical strength, more military potency, or more ability to withstand losses, then the term does a disservice. These qualities are by no means universal advantages in bargaining situations; they often have a contrary value. . . .

Bargaining power has also been described as the power to fool and bluff, "the ability to set the best price for yourself and fool the other man into thinking this was your maximum offer."[6] Fooling and bluffing are certainly involved; but there are two kinds of fooling. One is deceiving about the facts; a

[6]Citing J. N. Morgan, "Bilateral Monopoly and the Competitive Output," 63 *Quarterly Journal of Economics* (August 1949): 376, n. 6.

buyer may lie about his income or misrepresent the size of his family. The other is purely tactical. Suppose each knows everything about the other, and each knows what the other knows. What is there to fool about: The buyer may say that, though he'd really pay up to twenty and the seller knows it, he is firmly resolved as a tactical matter not to budge at sixteen. If the seller capitulates, was he fooled? Or was he convinced of the truth? Or did the buyer really not know what he would do next if the tactic failed? If the buyer really "feels" himself firmly resolved, and bases his resolve on the conviction that the seller will capitulate, and the seller does, the buyer may say afterwards that he was "not fooling." Whatever has occurred, it is not adequately conveyed by the notions of bluffing and fooling.

How does one person make another believe something? The answer depends importantly on the factual question, "Is it true?" It is easier to prove the truth of something that is true than of something false. To prove the truth about our health we can call on a reputable doctor; to prove the truth about our costs or income we may let the person look at books that have been audited by a reputable firm or the Bureau of Internal Revenue. But to persuade him of something false we may have no such convincing evidence.

When one wishes to persuade someone that he would not pay more than $16,000 for a house that is really worth $20,000 to him, what can he do to take advantage of the usually superior credibility of the truth over a false assertion? Answer: make it true. How can a buyer make it true? If he likes the house because it is near his business, he might move his business, persuading the seller that the house is really now worth only $16,000 to him. This would be unprofitable; he is no better off than if he had paid the higher price. . . .

If both men live in a culture where "cross my heart" is universally accepted as potent, all the buyer has to do is allege that he will pay no more than $16,000, using this invocation of penalty, and he wins—or at least he wins if the seller does not beat him to it by shouting "$19,000, cross my heart." If the buyer is an agent authorized by a board of directors to buy at $16,000 but not a cent more, and the directors cannot constitutionally meet again for several months and the buyer cannot exceed his authority, and if all this can be made known to the seller, then the buyer "wins"—if, again, the seller has not tied himself up with a commitment to $19,000. Or, if the buyer can assert that he will pay no more than $16,000 so firmly that he would suffer intolerable loss of personal prestige or bargaining reputation by paying more, and if the fact of his paying more would necessarily be known, and if the seller appreciates all this, then a loud declaration by itself may provide the commitment. The device, of course, is a needless surrender of flexibility unless it can be made fully evident and understandable to the seller.

. . . Consider a culture in which "cross my heart" is universally recognized as absolutely binding. Any offer accompanied by this invocation is a final offer, and is recognized as such. If each party knows the other's true reservation price, the object is to be first with a firm offer. Complete responsibility for the outcome then rests with the other, who can take it or leave it as he chooses (and who chooses to take it). Bargaining is all over; the commitment (that is, the first offer) wins.

. . . Suppose only part of the population belongs to the cult in which "cross my heart" is (or is believed to be) absolutely binding. If everyone knows (and is known to know) everyone else's affiliation, those belonging to this particular cult have the advantage. They can commit themselves, the others cannot. If the buyer says "$16,000, cross my heart," his offer is final; if the seller says "$19,000" he is (and is known to be) only "bargaining."

If each does not know the other's true reservation price there is an initial stage in which each tries to discover the other's and misrepresent his own, as in ordinary bargaining. But the process of discovery and revelation becomes quickly merged with the process of creating and discovering commitments; the commitments permanently change, for all practical purposes, the "true" reservation prices. If one party has, and the other has not, the belief in a binding ceremony, the latter pursues the "ordinary" bargaining technique of *asserting* his reservation prices, while the former proceeds to *make* his.

The foregoing discussion has tried to suggest both the plausibility and the logic of self-commitment.

Some examples may suggest the relevance of the tactic, although an observer can seldom distinguish with confidence the consciously logical, the intuitive, or the inadvertent use of a visible tactic. First, it has not been uncommon for union officials to stir up excitement and determination on the part of the membership during or prior to a wage negotiation. If the union is going to insist on $2 and expects the management to counter with $1.60, an effort is made to persuade the membership not only that the management could pay $2 but even perhaps that the negotiators themselves are incompetent if they fail to obtain close to $2. The purpose—or, rather, a plausible purpose suggested by our analysis—is to make clear to the management that the negotiators could not control the members or because they would lose their own positions if they tried. In other words, the negotiators reduce the scope of their own authority and confront the management with the threat of a strike that the union itself cannot avert, even though it was the union's own action that eliminated its power to prevent the strike.

Something similar occurs when the United States Government negotiates with other governments on, say, the uses to which foreign assistance will be put, or tariff reduction. . . .

When national representatives go to international negotiations, knowing that there is a wide range of potential agreement within which the outcome will depend on bargaining, they seem often to create a bargaining position by public statements, statements calculated to arouse a public opinion that permits no concessions to be made. If a binding public opinion can be cultivated and made evident to the other side, the initial position can thereby be made visibly "final."

. . . These examples have certain characteristics in common. First, they clearly depend not only on incurring a commitment but on communicating it persuasively to the other party. Second, it is by no means easy to establish the commitment, nor is it entirely clear to either of the parties concerned just how strong the commitment is. Third, similar activity may be available to the parties on both sides. Fourth, . . . they all run the risk of establishing an immovable position that goes beyond the ability of the other to concede, and thereby provoke the likelihood of stalemate or breakdown.

Institutional and Structural Characteristics of the Negotiation

Some institutional and structural characteristics of bargaining situations may make the commitment tactic easy or difficult to use, or make it more available to one party than the other, or affect the likelihood of simultaneous commitment or stalemate.

Use of a Bargaining Agent. The ... agent may be given instructions that are difficult or impossible to change, such instructions (and their inflexibility) being visible to the opposite party....

Secrecy vs. Publicity. A potent means of commitment, and sometimes the only means, is the pledge of one's reputation. If national representatives can arrange to be charged with appeasement for every small concession, they place concession visibly beyond their own reach....

Intersecting Negotiations. ... The advantage goes to the party that can persuasively point to an array of other negotiations in which its own position would be prejudiced if it made a concession in this one....

Continuous Negotiations. [T]o persuade the other that one cannot afford to recede, one says in effect, "If I conceded to you here, you would revise your estimate of me in our other negotiations; to protect my reputation with you I must stand firm."...

The Possibility of Compensation. ... When agreement must be reached on something that is inherently a one-man act, any division of the cost depends on compensation.... If a drainage ditch in the back of one house will protect both houses; and if it costs $1,000 and is worth $800 to each homeowner; neither would undertake it separately, but we nevertheless usually assume that they will get together and see that this project worth $1,600 to the two of them gets carried out. But if it costs 10 hours a week to be scoutmaster, and each considers it worth 8 hours of his time to have a scout troop but one man must do the whole job, it is far from certain that the neighbors will reach a deal according to which one puts 10 hours on the job and the other pays him cash or does 5 hours' gardening for him. ... Measures that require unanimous agreement can often be initiated only if several are bundled together....

Principles and Precedents. To be convincing, commitments usually have to be qualitative rather than quantitative, and to rest on some rationale. It may be difficult to conceive of a really firm commitment to $2.07½; why not $2.02¼? The numerical scale is too continuous to provide good resting places, except at nice round numbers like $2.00. But a commitment to the *principle* of "profit sharing," "cost-of-living increases," or any other basis for a numerical calculation that comes out at $2.07½, may provide a foothold for commitment....

From Thomas C. Schelling, *The Strategy of Conflict* (New York: Oxford U. Press, 1963), pp. 21–25, 27–35.

CHAPTER CASE ● ● ●

Environmental policies remain today, as they were during the glory years of Teddy Roosevelt and Gifford Pinchot, among the most difficult and contentious issues in American politics. In our own time, as when the conservation movement was in its infancy, these issues involve questions of value, technical knowledge, outcomes that are hard to measure, and all the tensions that must be expected when local actors fear that systemwide efficiencies may come at their own expense. The framing, selection, and implementation of environmental policies vex politicians and administrators not only at the national level but also at the regional and local levels—as in the following scenario of "The Great Four-County Garbage War."

After you've read through the scenario a time or two, ask yourself if the systemwide project hatched by Anton Kurvaszy, an administrative official of a regional development commission, represents an appropriate policy initiative on his part or an improper trespass into the realm of local politics. (Finn Ebertsen, the feisty mayor of the town of Brownlea, Wisconsin, leaves little doubt about *his* opinion on this issue.) Is the old policy-administration gap thoroughly discredited, or can you frame any general principles to support a broad differentiation of the functions of elected officials and appointive administrators?

You might also take special note of Kurvaszy's hope that brainstorming by some leading citizens of the St. Croix will produce the breakthrough idea needed to convince decision makers that the Area Waste Authority proposal makes sense all around. Any politically acceptable agreement will require inventive administrators and suitable administrative arrangements to make it work. If you found yourself sitting in at the meeting at Antoine's Ante, could you help find the needed administrative mechanism? And once you identified an approach that seemed acceptable, given your position somewhere in the St. Croix area governmental structure, could you draw on any principles of modern bargaining theory to help you get it accepted by other participants—who have other interests to advance—around the table?

The Antoine's Ante meeting is not only a brainstorming session. It's also a negotiating session—or at least it may develop into one if Kurvaszy can convince the assembled officials to search for a joint solution to a common problem. Students of negotiation quickly learn to ask questions of the following kind: What stakes are the various principals in the scenario playing for? In what ways does the situation call for distributive, integrative, or informational bargaining? How (even if in very rough and impressionistic terms) should each player think about his or her BATNA? Does an analysis of the problem suggest any resting places? What incentives do the principals in the scenario have to misrepresent their aims or values, and how might the organizer of a negotiation arrange proceedings in order to deter insincere reporting? Might any of the actors consider using contingent claims contracting to deal with uncertainties?

CASE 4
....

An Area Waste Authority (AWA) for the St. Croix: "The Great Four-County Garbage War"

About four times every year Anton Kurvaszy, Director of Planning at the St. Croix Development Commission, was the featured presenter at a special meeting of the SCDC. At these so-called development-plan sessions, Kurvaszy reported to the county executives on the results of his latest studies. Ideas for projects came from thoughtful residents of the region, from entrepreneurs seeking SCDC support for potentially profitable ventures, and, of course, from members of Kurvaszy's development-planning staff.

Kurvaszy's first act as planning director had been to hang a yellowed parchment over his desk in the Jackson Building. The scroll, a commendation of some sort, testified to Kurvaszy's years of experience in systemwide planning with the Tennessee Valley Authority. Kurvaszy liked to emphasize that the TVA model—"a system that works!"—underlay his proposal for an areawide waste authority serving the St. Croix. Kurvaszy's staff members recognized in his notion of an integrated disposal system an engineer's concern for technical soundness and economic efficiency. Kurvaszy hoped to gain commission approval for his Area Waste Authority proposal at the next development-plan meeting. Following formal SCDC endorsement, his idea for an integrated regional waste disposal system should have an easy time gaining final approval from all four counties' boards of county commissioners.

"In TVA," Kurvaszy had explained, "computers decide which electric generators to turn on and which to turn off, depending on minute-to-minute monitoring of electric demand in seven states. Computers ensure just the right mix, taking high-polluting plants off line when the wind shifts and firing up expensive old generators only when demand suddenly surges. Balanced operations save millions every year by optimizing flows of electricity across the whole TVA region. Why can't the same concept work in waste disposal?"

Kurvaszy's disposal plan was to be the subject of a serious conversation with his assistant, Mary Martengrove. Anton finished marking a chart spread before him as Mary entered his office. Mary saw two ordinary gas-station road maps, taped together to form a single picture of the SCDC area. Kurvaszy had inked color-coded spots throughout the region to show the locations of the four-county area's current working disposal sites: a huge incinerator in Norton County, a handful or so of landfills, and several dozen recycling facilities. "Every town in the St. Croix," Anton told Mary, "has at least one recycling center for paper and usually another one for multiple duty: plastic bottles, glass, metals, and all."

Kurvaszy summarized waste disposal procedures under the existing system (or, as he put it, "under the existing *non*system") in the four-county area: "The town governments run trash disposal as a public service in their areas—actually, as monopolies. The counties manage the system in unincorporated areas. Towns and counties coordinate their operations, working through private contractors. Every week or so, private companies operating under franchise to a town or a county pick the stuff up from the recycling centers. They truck it off somewhere to market it. These haulers take reusable glass, paper, and so forth to sell wherever it will fetch the most."

Mary asked, "Is that what I've heard referred to as 'flow control'?"

"No, 'flow control' is almost the exact opposite. Instead of letting the haulers sell recyclable waste where it'll bring the highest price, and dump the rest where it can be gotten rid of cheaply—in other words, instead of using the free market—under flow control, administrators *order* the waste to specific locations."

"Lately," Anton continued, "politicians and administrators in some areas have been trying to keep all their trash as close to home as they can for final disposal."

Mary's expression betrayed puzzlement. "They want to *keep* their trash?"

Laughing, Anton jabbed a finger at a spot on his map, up in what Mary knew to be a sparsely populated area of Norton County. "Let me tell you about the infamous Tamarack incinerator."

• • • • •

Incineration has a long history in the upper Midwest, where strong prevailing upper winds quickly scavenge and spread airborne waste across vast areas. In fact, on a per capita basis, Minnesotans burn a higher fraction of their solid wastes than do the citizens of any other state. Wisconsin isn't far behind. Furthermore, the importance of the water table to tourism and the general quality of life in the two states had sensitized Minnesotans and Wisconsinites to the dangers of toxic seepage from landfills. Every ton of garbage burned takes one more ton's worth of pressure off the underground waste disposal network.

In the early 1980s, the Norton County commissioners had floated a $20 million bond to finance a huge new waste combustor—the Tamarack incinerator. Kurvaszy emphasized that the Tamarack facility was "state of the art, technologically speaking," and had been sold as a stimulus to Norton County growth. The $20-million figure covered not only a big new combustor itself but also a new roadway intended to improve the local arterial system.

Salespeople from a national firm had convinced Erwin Snyder, a Norton County commissioner, that Tamarack would handle virtually all the solid waste from all the towns in the county, with enough spare combustion capacity to dispose of additional garbage trucked in from Apostle, Burnt, and Larch counties as well as from Duluth, Superior, and maybe even the Twin Cities (Minneapolis–St. Paul). Charges at Tamarack might be as low as $20 per ton of waste burned, making incineration the best disposal deal in the upper Midwest. Big-city administrators, the salespeople were sure, would pay Norton County to take their trash, with the result that the Tamarack incinerator might actually run at a profit. Erwin Snyder persuaded the other four commissioners that an annual net cash inflow of almost $3 million per year seemed a reasonable expectation. If it all went according to Snyder's initial projections, the Norton County commissioners would be able to cut their constituents' taxes, since the combustor would return enough revenue to retire the $20-million debt, pay for most county services, and maintain Norton's share of financial support for the four-county SCDC programs (the emergency medical service, the vocational/technical programs, and so forth).

Alas, however, within just a few years after the new combustor went into service, it became clear that the commissioners had overestimated the project's revenue stream. A canvas of conditions in the waste disposal industry nationally established that the Norton County politicians weren't alone. Through the 1980s and 1990s, both nationally and in the St. Croix, the actual rate of increase in solid-waste volumes lagged behind the projections that planners had used when making disposal-facility decisions. Excessive disposal capacity had gradually accumulated. Minneapolis, Duluth, and the other potential sources of Tamarack's waste stream had ample disposal facilities of their own. Why would city planners from outside the St. Croix region want to pay Norton County for incineration services? Instead of attracting upward of

150,000 tons from all over the area for burning at Tamarack, the new combustor was working on a waste stream of only 21,000 tons per year—all of it from points within Norton County, since other potential waste suppliers found that they didn't have as much garbage to get rid of as initially projected and, anyway, that there were cheaper places to dump their waste. Unless control measures were imposed to ensure a minimum level of waste for incineration, the total volume of trash expected at Tamarack wouldn't generate the revenue needed to pay off the plant's huge debt.

Mary Martengrove was listening carefully. Garbage management wasn't exactly what had attracted her to public administration. It took a substantial effort to concentrate her attention on the subject.

Anton Kurvaszy told Mary that recycling withdrew about 20 percent of the waste stream from the volume that had to be finally disposed of by burning or dumping. Currently, haulers took the remaining 80 percent of the trash generated in the St. Croix area to whoever would accept it at the lowest cost per ton. That obviously wasn't the Tamarack incinerator, since the combustor operators had to charge high rates in order to service that huge debt. With all the excess capacity in the region—much of it accounted for by the ill-advised facility at Tamarack—dump operators had started lowering their tipping fees. Haulers naturally responded by taking more and more of their tonnage to landfills. Residents of the St. Croix referred to the cutthroat competition for disposal business as "The Great Four-County Garbage War."

The dump operators were processing more waste, true, but their falling fees meant that area landfills were showing less and less profit on average for every ton disposed of. Some observers feared that the narrowing margins created incentives for dump operators to begin cheating on environmental requirements. Landfill operators were required to test for toxins, to lay bottom barriers against leakage, and so forth—all relatively expensive operations. Kurvaszy believed that the dynamics of the four-county garbage war were destructive all around, which, of course, was why he thought that the area needed a rational integrated waste disposal system.

●　　●　　●　　●　　●

On May 16, 1994, the U.S. Supreme Court announced its decision in the most recent of a series of flow control cases, *Carbone* v. *Clarkstown*. Justice Anthony Kennedy, writing for the majority, summarized the facts of the case in his opinion:

> We consider a so-called flow control ordinance, which requires all solid waste to be processed at a designated transfer station before leaving the municipality. The avowed purpose of the ordinance is to retain the processing fees charged at the transfer station to amortize the cost of the facility. Because it attains this goal by depriving competitors, including out-of-state firms, of access to a local market, we hold that the flow control ordinance violates the Commerce Clause.
>
> The town of Clarkstown, New York, lies in the lower Hudson River valley.... In August 1989, Clarkstown... agreed to close its landfill located on Route 303 in West Nyack and build a new solid waste transfer station on the same site. The station would receive bulk solid waste and separate recyclable from nonrecyclable items. Recyclable waste would be

baled for shipment to a recycling facility; nonrecyclable waste, to a suit-able landfill or incinerator.

The cost of building the transfer station was estimated at $1.4 mil-lion. A local private contractor agreed to construct the facility and operate it for five years, after which the town would buy it for one dollar. During those five years, the town guaranteed a minimum waste flow of 120,000 tons per year, for which the contractor could charge the hauler a so-called tipping fee of $81 per ton. If the station received less than 120,000 tons in a year, the town promised to make up the tipping fee deficit. . . .

The problem, of course, was how to meet the yearly guarantee. This difficulty was compounded by the fact that the tipping fee of $81 per ton exceeded the disposal cost of unsorted solid waste on the private market. The solution the town adopted was the flow control ordinance here in question. . . . The ordinance requires all nonhazardous solid waste within the town to be deposited at the Route 303 transfer station. [Justice Kennedy here notes that the requirement applies both to "waste generated within the town" and to "waste generated outside and brought in."] . . .

Carbone operates a recycling center in Clarkstown, where it receives bulk solid waste, sorts and bales it, and then ships it to other processing facilities—much as occurs at the town's new transfer station. While the flow control ordinance permits recyclers like Carbone to continue receiv-ing solid waste, . . . it requires them to bring the nonrecyclable residue from that waste to the Route 303 station. It thus forbids Carbone to ship the nonrecyclable waste itself, and it requires Carbone to pay a tipping fee on trash that Carbone has already sorted. . . .

While the immediate effect of the ordinance is to direct local trans-port of solid waste to a designated site within the local jurisdiction, its eco-nomic effects are interstate in reach. The Carbone facility in Clarkstown receives and processes waste from places other than Carkstown, including from out of state. By requiring Carbone to send the nonrecyclable portion of this waste to the Route 303 transfer station at an additional cost, the flow control ordinance drives up the cost for out-of-state interests to dispose of their solid waste. . . . These economic effects are more than enough to bring the Clarkstown ordinance within the purview of the Commerce Clause. It is well settled that actions are within the domain of the Commerce Clause if they burden interstate commerce or impede its free flow. . . . [W]e find that the ordinance discriminates against interstate commerce. . . .

Discrimination against interstate commerce in favor of local busi-ness or investment is *per se* invalid, save in a narrow class of cases in which the municipality can demonstrate, under rigorous scrutiny, that it has no other means to advance a legitimate local interest. . . .

The Commerce Clause presumes a national market free from local legislation that discriminates in favor of local interests. Here Clarkstown has any number of nondiscriminatory alternatives for addressing the health and environmental problems alleged to justify the ordinance in question. The most obvious would be uniform safety regulations enacted without the object to discriminate. These regulations would ensure that competitors like Carbone do not underprice the market by cutting corners on environmental safety. . . .

The flow control ordinance does serve a central purpose that a non-protectionist regulation would not: It ensures that the town-sponsored facility will be profitable, so that the local contractor can build it and Clarkstown can buy it back at nominal cost in five years. In other words, . . . the flow control ordinance is a financing measure. By itself, of course, revenue generation is not a local interest that can justify discrimination against interstate commerce.

•   •   •   •   •

"Take down some figures," Anton instructed Mary. She scribbled quickly as he began to rattle off estimates of recycling rates, incineration costs at different points in the four-county region, and so forth.

"Let's say that overall, 20 percent of everyone's waste—that's from households and businesses, including factories and farms—gets recycled. Whoever has title to that recyclable 20 percent at the point of final resale then reaps a small net return. Say that return is $10 per ton for usable old paper, plastic, metal, whatever.

"When you shift from recycling to combustion, the figures of course are very different. In Norton County, the Tamarack debt bind has already forced the commissioners to use flow control. Up there they send 70 percent of all waste generated in the county to the new combustor. Tamarack charges $90 per ton to burn trash, a price set artificially high for debt-service purposes. The remaining 10 percent of Norton garbage and junk—after the 20 percent to recycling and the 70 percent to Tamarack for burning—goes to landfills. Tipping fees in the area today average $30 per ton."

Mary scribbled numbers as Anton spoke. "How much waste comes each year out of Norton County?"

"Say, 30 thousand, give or take. That's 30 thousand *tons.*"

Mary blinked. Anton told her that his number was rough but in line with the national average—a ton of trash per year per person, and Norton County had about 30,000 permanent residents.

Mary figured quickly. At a weighted average disposal cost of about $64 per ton, based on a simple computation . . . giving full credit for the *negative* $10 that someone—in this case, the haulers—got for recycling . . .

For Norton County:
$$(.2) \times (-\$10) + (.7) \times (\$90) + (.1) \times (\$30) = \$64$$

Thus, Mary estimated, a 30-thousand-ton waste stream implied . . .

$$\$64/\text{ton} \times 30,000 @ 1 \text{ ton/person} = \$1,920,000$$

Mary wrote the number and told Anton: "That makes the total Norton County waste disposal cost under the existing system about $1,920,000."

"Okay," Kurvaszy affirmed, "*assuming* that they keep rolling those exorbitant Tamarack incineration fees into the figure." He continued: "Of course, people in the other three counties have no reason to send their nonrecyclable waste to Tamarack.

They don't have to worry about the Tamarack debt, and they certainly don't want to pay those high $90-per-ton incineration fees when, on average, they can get away paying $30 to dump operators with whom they have contracts. So Apostle, Burnt, and Larch county haulers truck the 80 percent that doesn't get recycled to landfills."

Since each of the other three counties had about 30,000 people, like Norton, Mary's calculation for the average annual cost went as follows:

For Apostle, Burnt, or Larch County:
$$(.2) \times (-\$10) + (.8) \times (\$30) = \$22$$
$$\$22/\text{ton} \times 30,000 @ 1 \text{ ton/person} = \$660,000$$

Mary, her head full of numbers, would have happily ended the conversation, but Anton wasn't yet ready. "Of course," he said, "those numbers you just computed don't give *total* trash management costs, since they don't cover the pickup portions of the service—workers' salaries, a depreciation reserve for trucks and other equipment, and like that." Kurvaszy said that the pickup portions in each of the four counties came to about three-quarters of a million dollars per year.

"In other words," Mary summarized, "the total service cost is the sum of a disposal cost—almost $2 million annually for Norton County these days, but much lower for Apostle, Burnt, and Larch—and a pickup portion."

"Right. It's a pretty close estimate that the resulting figure then gets divided among all the paying customers in the county."

"Divide by 30,000?" Mary asked.

"Mary, think a second," Anton ordered mildly. "30,000 is the population, yes, but it's households and businesses, not individuals, who pay for trash service." He paused, then said: "The rough rule sets the number of paying subscribers at 1 in 3. So the county-total disposal charge based on your formula

County total = Disposal cost + Pickup portion

gets divided by 10,000 to give you an idea of the annual layout of a household or business for trash service in each of the four counties." It came to about $267 per year per paying customer in Norton County, compared with $141 annually in Apostle, Burnt, and Larch counties.

•   •   •   •   •

All over the United States, local officials are experiencing versions of the Norton County commissioners' problem. All over, troubled politicians and administrators are trying to find legal methods of imposing flow control on their local waste streams, as the Norton commissioners had already done with the order directing haulers to take a percentage of all county trash to Tamarack.

Of course, political choices have political consequences. The Norton taxpayers blamed their elected legislators, the county commissioners, for higher trash fees when the county's flow control requirement began routing 70 percent of all the county's trash to Tamarack. It came as no surprise when residents of Norton County objected to paying almost twice what everyone in Apostle, Burnt, and Larch counties paid ($267 versus $141). Rumor had it that the Norton County commissioners had already agreed informally among themselves to repeal the flow control ordinance. If a much smaller percentage of the waste stream were directed to the high-priced Tamarack disposal facility, trash fees could be cut. The commissioners would no doubt claim credit for sound management.

"But if they cut the waste stream to Tamarack, and hence the revenues," Mary asked, "how will the county pay for an overpriced, underused plant? And if the commissioners buckle under and close Tamarack entirely, don't they still have to pay off the debt the county incurred as a legal obligation?"

"Flow control," Kurvaszy emphasized, "is more a political than an administrative problem. The hard choice for politicians in the position of the Norton commissioners is whether to raise fees—which you have to do when you use flow control to direct waste to a high-cost local incinerator or dump—or blow the town's credit. Raise fees, and your constituents raise hell. But default on your debt, and you can't borrow money for future improvements—in other words, you're selling out your successors' constituents."

Anton told Mary of another rumor. Apparently, the commissioners were actually considering the "unthinkable option": defaulting. Under this option, instead of continuing to mix recycling, incineration, and landfill utilization in the {.2, .7, .1} proportions, a new Norton County flow control ordinance would be passed calling for a {.2, .2, .6} mix: 20 percent to recycling; only 20 percent to incineration (but still at $90 per ton); and 60 percent to area landfills. The $10 credit for recycling and $30 landfill tipping fee would remain unchanged. Changing from a {.2 .7 .1} mix to {.2 .2 .6} would yield a net reduction in the average disposal-cost portion of the trash fee, from $64 to $34 per ton, based on the revised weighted-average calculation:

For Norton County under the new plan:
$$(.2) \times (-\$10) + (.2) \times (\$90) + (.6) \times (\$30) = \$34$$

The reduced cost to the county would permit the commissioners to cut trash fees substantially. Instead of the current $267 per year, Norton residents would see their bills cut to about $177—still embarrassingly high when compared with the $141 being paid by residents in the other three counties, yet enough of a reduction to require serious consideration by the Norton commissioners. Of course, there would be a terrible downside: Forgoing the cash stream needed to support the Tamarack debt service would probably also force a default on Norton County's debt, ruining the county's Dun and Bradstreet rating for years into the future.

Kurvaszy said there was an outside chance that the commissioners would try to make up the shortfall in Tamarack's revenue stream through a subsidy out of county tax receipts. But paying that much money out in an annual subsidy—a bit more than three-quarters of a million dollars annually—would force Norton County onto a starvation diet for many other services. The county might have to withdraw its contributions to the four-county emergency medical service and the adult/vocational education programs. Needless to say, the commissioners in the other three counties regarded the possibility of withdrawal as a serious areawide threat.

•   •   •   •   •

Kurvaszy hoped to create a new operating division of the SCDC to manage a flow control system covering the entire St. Croix region, instead of just in Norton

County. Kurvaszy slapped a copy of the SCDC organization chart on the table and penciled in a new box labeled *AWA* under Dennis Hammer.

"Over here on the planning side," Anton told Mary, "we'll lay out the whole system—design the computer programs, figure out what new equipment may be needed to manage all four counties' wastes as though they were a single, integrated unit. Then the operation will be turned over to Dennis Hammer, who'll run it, same as EMS and adult/vocational education."

Kurvaszy expected major gains from administering "the whole shootin' match" as a single waste system. His idea was to balance all the waste flows to the Tamarack combustor, all the landfills, and all the recycling points within reasonable distance in order to achieve the lowest average cost, spreading it over everyone in the four-county area. The idea was simplicity itself: Truck all waste from all points to the most efficient disposal site, taking into consideration transportation costs, the estimated fair market costs of handling the waste at the selected facility, any recycling credits, *and* a commitment to complete payment on the troubled Tamarack incinerator. Of course, some areas might see their fees rise slightly because their rate payers would have to help subsidize the high-cost operations, especially the action up at Tamarack. But improved systemwide efficiency should make for lower total costs across the area.

"These numbers come from a computer model of an areawide waste disposal system," Anton told Mary, giving her three tables of figures (see Tables 5.2, 5.3, and 5.4). The modelers estimated that the combustion fee at Tamarack could be cut from its $90 per ton to $50 per ton if the facility were operated at a higher capacity: The more trash, the lower the fee per ton. "We get more trash up to Tamarack by flow control—directing a percentage of the waste from Apostle, Burnt, and Larch as well as from Norton. At $50 per ton, if we can get 63,000 tons per year up to Tamarack through four-county flow control, it should be possible to restore the situation to where the Norton County commissioners expected it to be when they issued the Tamarack bonds. Yet rolling the $50 fee into a single average cost over the entire system—defined as the four-county area—should make it absorbable."

Kurvaszy explained that, with a unified bargaining agent acting on everyone's behalf across the entire region, it should be possible to push landfill operators to cut their fees still further, say to $20 per ton. With systemwide planning and operation, Kurvaszy also thought, a higher recycling proportion than at present could also be achieved; and better bargaining should fetch fees closer to $20 than the present $10 per ton. "The extra cost to citizens of Apostle, Burnt, and Larch would be relatively small," Kurvaszy commented, "but total systemwide savings relative to the present arrangement should be in the range of $530,000 every year."

Mary wanted to get her boss's claim clear in her own mind: "That's a total saving to customers, spread over the entire St. Croix, based on the difference between the current $6,900 thousand (counting both waste disposal and the pickup portion) and the projected customer costs in your Table 5.3 of about $6,370 thousand per year."

Anton checked Mary's figures against his own computations. "Yes, that's one way of sorting the numbers out." Then, to make sure that he and Mary saw the situation in the same way, Kurvaszy insisted that they take a few extra minutes to work up a summary "before and after" table (Table 5.4), explicitly breaking out the extra overhead charge for the layer of activity represented by the AWA.

Table 5.2 Waste Disposal Options in the St. Croix Development Council Area

| | Percent of Waste to Recycling Incineration, Landfill | Disposal Cost/Ton | | | Weighted Cost/Ton |
		Recycling	Incineration	Landfill	
Current:					
Norton	(.2, .7, .1)	−$10	$90	$30	$64
Apostle Burnt Larch }	(.2, .0, .8)	−$10	$90	$30	$22
Options:					
Under the default options being studied by Norton County commissioners:	(.2, .2, .6)	−$10	$90	$30	$34
Under Kurvaszy's plan for an Area Waste Authority to spread costs over all four counties:					
Norton	(.3, .6, .1)	−$20	$50	$20	$26
Apostle Burnt Larch }	(.3, .5, .2)	−$20	$50	$20	$23

Disposition of wastes under Kurvaszy's plan:
63,000 tons to Tamarack, $50/ton = $3,150,000/year incineration
21,000 tons to landfills, $20/ton = $420,000/year tipping fees
36,000 tons to recycling, $20/ton = $720,000/year credit to AWA

Note: As we'll see in our case for Chapter 9, Anton Kurvaszy already has in mind a further arrangement whereby one-half of the 36,000 recyclable tonnage would be sold under long-term contract to Polaris Paper Corporation for use at the old mill out at Half Mile Rill in Apostle County.

• • • • •

Dagmar Blaine was on the phone with the news from Washington that Anton Kurvaszy had been waiting to hear. Blaine's boss, Congresswoman Ellen Moe, always seemed to come through when the task involved pork for her district. Moe's clout in the appropriations process had enabled her, Blaine told Kurvaszy, to reserve an **earmark** in a forthcoming money bill. Based on the word from Congresswoman Moe, Blaine assured Kurvaszy that every member of the relevant congressional appropriations subcommittee approved of the earmarking. Such informal approvals had the practical effect of guaranteeing passage when the bill went to the floor of the House for a final vote. By congressional pork-barrel standards, the amount of the earmarking—a paltry $50,000—was trivial. But the number was merely a "hook" on which to hang the real purpose of the earmarking. It was a vehicle by which Congress could convey official approval for the project that was to be undertaken with the allotted funds.

"You'll be happy to know, Anton," Dagmar said, "that the $50K[1] is to be paid out in equal installments over four years to the SCDC. In other words, it'll mean a few

[1]K: In Washington lingo, K (for the Greek *kilo*, "thousand") is often used to abbreviate dollar amounts.

Table 5.3 Cost Comparison, Independent versus Integrated Four-County Waste Management

	Yearly Solid-Waste Volume in SCDC Area (Tons × 10³) Total	Costs			
		Under Current Disposal System		With Integrated Waste Management	
		$/Ton	Total	$/Ton	Total*
Wisconsin:					
Apostle	30	$22	$ 660,000	$23	$ 690,000
Burnt	30	$22	660,000	$23	690,000
Minnesota:					
Norton	30	$64	1,920,000	$26	780,000
Larch	30	$22	660,000	$23	690,000
	120		$3,900,000		$2,850,000*

Note: The $2,850,000 can also be broken out based on Table 5.2:

$3,570,000 (incineration + landfill)
−   720,000 (recycling)
$2,850,000

*Refers to fees charged by ultimate disposers, that is, by incinerator operators and landfill operators. The collection fees actually charged to customers of the proposed AWA will include these sums plus a general operating charge for the AWA service (10 percent of the cost attributable to incineration, dumping, and recycling, plus sums invested every other year on replacement equipment) less a deduction for credits paid to AWA by recyclers. The resulting total *disposal cost* of AWA operations to customers would equal $28.1/ton. Thus total annual net receipts to AWA are given by:

$28.1/ton × 120,000 tons/year = $3,372,000/year

To this figure it is necessary to add a $3,000,000 annual *pickup portion*, covering all four counties. Dividing the sum $6,372,000 by 40,000—the total number of paying customers in the St. Croix—gives an average customer cost of $159 (plus change) per year.

thousand a year in extra funds for your planning division. The final wording of the earmarking language hasn't been worked out, but the gist will be to express congressional encouragement of 'cooperative multistate, multicounty experiments in governance.' Specifically, the earmarking language will require you to study and experiment with innovative approaches to environmental quality, including 'cooperative, multicounty experiments' in solid-waste disposal practices."

Anton was, of course, pleased at the news—the more so, he told Dagmar, because he had that same day received a call from Wisconsin State Senator Ben Loffel. Unlike Congresswoman Moe, Loffel hadn't come up with any money for Kurvaszy and his planning staffers to spend, but he gave Kurvaszy something almost as good. Senator Loffel, working with Minnesota State Senator Axel Loncaric, had gained support in their respective state legislatures for resolutions that would officially endorse "cooperative, bi-state, multicounty experiments in governance." The resolutions would explicitly commend a proposal that people were talking about for a new four-county flow control and waste disposal system in the area of the St. Croix River.

• • • • •

Mary Martengrove was surprised (but later decided that she really shouldn't have been) when the mayor of Brownlea, Wisconsin, appeared in the Jackson Build-

Table 5.4 Summary Table, Costs Independent versus Integrated Waste Management

	Under Current Disposal System		With Integrated Waste Management	
Wisconsin				
Apostle				
Disposal	$ 660,000		$ 690,000	
Pickup	750,000		750,000	
Prorated overhead (AWA)	—		130,000	
	$1,410,000	$1,410,000	$1,570,000	$1,570,000
Burnt				
Disposal	$ 660,000		$ 690,000	
Pickup	750,000		750,000	
Prorated overhead (AWA)	—		130,000	
	$1,410,000	$2,820,000	$1,570,000	$3,140,000
Minnesota				
Norton				
Disposal	$1,920,000		$ 780,000	
Pickup	750,000		750,000	
Prorated overhead (AWA)	—		130,000	
	$2,670,000	$5,490,000	$1,660,000	$4,800,000
Larch				
Disposal	$ 660,000		$ 690,000	
Pickup	750,000		750,000	
Prorated overhead (AWA)	—		130,000	
	$1,410,000	$6,900,000	$1,570,000	$6,370,000

Note: Total saving across the four-county area projected as a result of AWA operations:

$6,900,000 − $6,370,000 = $530,000/year

With AWA, the $6,370,000 four-county cost is divided equally among 40,000 paying customers, resulting in $159.25/year service cost.

ing offices of the SCDC. Finn Ebertsen had heard about the "harebrained scheme," as he phrased it, and wanted to make known "to whoever is responsible" his own views and those of the citizens of Brownlea for whom he spoke. Brownlea, Mary knew, was one of the towns in Burnt County whose residents' trash fees would have to be increased somewhat—if the estimates were right, from $141 to almost $160 per year—if Anton Kurvaszy's four-county plan went into effect.

Currently, the waste haulers for Brownlea, Wisconsin, a town of about 7,000 in the southern part of the SCDC area, trucked nonrecyclable waste to the relatively new North Harbour landfill, where they benefitted from the lowest tipping fees in the area. (The $30 landfill fee that Kurvaszy used in his planning estimates was itself a systemwide weighted average; actually, North Harbour charged a rock-bottom $25 per ton.) Mayor Ebertsen was unimpressed when Mary Martengrove pointed out that, according to the computer model, the rate increase to towns such as Brownlea would be much less than the average savings realized in the towns that would be the main beneficiaries.

"Show me," Ebertson demanded. He wanted Mary not only to track him through Kurvaszy's figures but also to explain how *his* town and *his* constituents—the voters of Browlea—stood to be beneficiaries of the proposed Area Waste Authority.

Mary dug through some scratch papers on which she had been trying to smooth out the details of Kurvaszy's rough-and-ready cost estimates. "Take Sbabler, for example," she said, flipping one of her pages from the stack. Sbabler, Minnesota, in Norton County, one of the part-owners of the Tamarack incinerator, was about the equal of Ebertsen's town in population, but its waste fees were currently almost twice Brownlea's.

"Why," Ebertsen demanded of Mary, "should Brownlea have to start paying more to truck some of its garbage over to Tamarack when we've already got a good deal with North Harbour? Why should Sbabler be able to cut its fees because Brownlea's paying the freight?"

Mary made a mental note to check on the financial condition of the area's landfill operators, including North Harbour. Naturally, she didn't mention it to Ebertsen, but she thought it worth asking if systemwide planning didn't require attention to the people who'd be hurt as flow control cost them business as well as the service providers, such as those at Tamarack, who might be saved from bankruptcy.

Ebertsen protested that, "unlike the Norton crowd," Brownlea and Burnt county officials had been careful when they made decisions for their citizens, including decisions on waste disposal. Why should they be penalized now because their counterparts in Norton had been greedy, or at least imprudent? "Norton wouldn't be offering to share profits with us if the Tamarack project had succeeded, I'm sure," Ebertsen said. "Why should they ask us to bail them out, now that their plant's become a white elephant?"

Ebertsen added, "You know we haven't had it so easy lately in our area."

Mary knew that Burnt County over in Wisconsin, heavily invested in logging, had begun to suffer the same kind of decline—now that demand for wood pulp was ebbing—that Norton and Larch counties in Minnesota experienced after "Carter killed the cows." Ebertsen stressed that unemployment was high in Brownlea. The local banks were talking higher rates of foreclosure; two small businesses on Brownlea's main street—a cafe and a hardware store—had recently closed for good. "Me and Winston Hemp [president of the Brownlea Dry Goods, and a Burnt County commissioner] supported the SCDC because we thought it would help to set up an organization for the whole St. Croix across the state line, and because we thought you SCDC people would find ways to bring money into the region. Now it turns out you want to build empires at our expense."

Martengrove respectfully disagreed with the characterization. With a centrally administered system, she told Mayor Ebertsen, there would be a big enough scale of operations to support a sophisticated information and planning system. Ebertsen's eyes glazed, but Mary persisted: "Right now, your waste haulers have to spend time searching out the lowest-cost disposal sites, transportation costs considered. They have no way to tell just when and how and where to adjust routes or change the mix between burning and dumping, and truckers operating singly have no market clout to force down the prices of the people they have to deal with. It's a volatile field," Mary continued. "Today landfills are cheaper; but ten years ago everyone thought we were running out of dump space. We have too much burning capacity today, but what if the early predictions of high waste volumes finally materialize, or we suddenly discover *real* environmental problems with dumps, so that landfill costs suddenly skyrocket? The idea is to hedge our bets over space and time. There's value to spreading costs and gains over everyone in the system."

Yes, Ebertsen admitted. But whose system? "*My* system, it's Brownlea. That's not the same system as the SCDC's, is it? And their interests aren't necessarily in line either."

At the end of their interview, Mayor Ebertsen seemed mollified by Mary's courtesy and forthrightness. But he was by no means ready to let her boss make decisions about costs and municipal services that were important to the voters of Brownlea. "I've been nosin' around," he told Mary. "I found out, I'm not the only one whose nose is out of joint."

Ebertsen explained that, as near as he could estimate, half the towns and unincorporated areas in the St. Croix could absorb a small increase with little inconvenience. Maybe their voters wouldn't even notice. One-fourth of the population—practically speaking, everyone in Norton County—would "make out." But that left another quarter of the citizenry of the area, consisting mostly of small-towners spread across the other three counties, whose combination of favorable local disposal costs and worsening economic conditions would make even small losses painful. There'd be plenty of local politicos, Mary knew, who would exploit the controversy and tell a "bad guys–good guys story" around the four counties—a story in which feckless Norton County commissioners and SCDC administrators would be cast as villains—as a way of hyping opposition to a plan that Anton Kurvaszy had thought was a straightforward technical solution for a systemwide problem.

Mary was ruefully thankful after Finn Ebertsen left. If nothing else, the mayor had convinced her that the problem wasn't simple and that it certainly wasn't only technical.

• • • • •

If you drive across Antoine's Bridge from Minnesota into Wisconsin and go on another quarter mile or so, you'll see Antoine's Ante Club. Actually, it's a major resort, with hotel and cottage facilities, two restaurants, and halls to rent for receptions, square dances, and even small conventions. Antoine's Ante was the natural place for Anton Kurvaszy to hold the meeting of selected area "influentials." After Mary told Anton about Finn Ebertsen's concerns—and based on reports of doubts throughout the four-county region about the "sellability" of his integrated waste management plan—Kurvaszy decided to take the initiative. He had assembled a list of individuals who, he thought, would be willing to discuss the sticking points about the proposed AWA. Perhaps a candid exploration of ways to meet dissenters' objections represented the best way to create a favorable climate of opinion for the plan.

Almost every one contacted by Kurvaszy agreed to attend the meeting at Antoine's Ante. Those present found the standard setup for a conference: four long tables topped with green felt, arranged in a square. A blackboard on casters stood ready for service as a visual aid. On a second blackboard, the inevitable gas-station road maps of the St. Croix area had been neatly taped. Erwin Snyder, the Norton County commissioner generally "credited" as the promotional genius behind the

Tamarack venture, winced as he entered the room and noticed how prominently the location of the huge incinerator facility had been highlighted on the map.

On a side bar near the conference table, the Antoine's Ante Club staff had laid on carafes of beverages and plates of finger food. Each place at the conference table had a name card (not that every attendee didn't already know every other one), a pad of paper, a sharpened pencil or two in case anyone had come without such equipment, and a sheet of St. Croix Development Commission stationery on which had been typed:

PROSPECTUS

Meeting of the Ad Hoc Consultative Group
on Integrated Regional Solid-Waste Planning
Antoine's Ante Club
Antlers, Wisconsin

In attendance:

Guy Ambrose, County Manager, Apostle County WI

Tabitha Brock, Mayor, Sbabler (Norton County) MN

Erin Crum, Commissioner, Apostle County WI

Finn Ebertsen, Mayor, Brownlea (Burnt County) WI

Adam Fencl, County Manager, Larch County MN, and current Chairman, St. Croix
    Development Council

Dennis Hammer, Director of Operations, SCDC

Martin Johanssen, President, Antlers WI Rotary Club

Anton Kurvaszy, Director of Planning, SCDC

Erin McCloskey, Mayor, Deerslip (Larch County) MN

Mary Martengrove, Staff, SCDC

Douglas Naismith, Commissioner, Apostle County WI

Erwin Snyder, Commissioner, Norton County MN

Arne Temple, County Manager, Burnt County WI

Ferdy Washburn, City Manager, Wells (Norton County) MN

Kurvaszy gave everyone the usual ten minutes of grace time to greet one another, pour second cups of coffee, and stack Danish pastries or creamed cheese and bagels on plates to take to their places around the green-topped tables. When everyone was situated, Anton thanked them for coming on relatively short notice, adding that he appreciated the way several opponents of his AWA proposal had come forward with their objections.

No, Kurvaszy assured everyone, no, he wasn't being sarcastic in using the word *appreciated.* He pointed out that the whole idea behind the AWA proposal was "to create a win-win situation, an arrangement that will make *everyone*—not just the Norton County folk—better off, at least *in the long run.*" Eyeing Finn Ebertsen in particular, Anton pointed out that full approval by majorities on all four county boards would be needed before a single regional system could be set up. In turn, the county commissioners, meeting separately and voting, surely wouldn't act favorably on Kurvaszy's recommendation unless they received strong endorsements of the AWA plan from their respective county managers. The latter—as everyone at the Antoine's Ante conference knew—were slated to take the matter up in their capacities as members of the SCDC at the next special development-plan meeting of the commission.

"The thrust of it all," Kurvaszy said, "is that there are several points where the AWA idea can be vetoed. In fact, the sequence of decisions needed to move forward are, if anything, rigged *against* approval. . . . If the county managers bring only a tepid endorsement out of the SCDC meeting . . . if *any three* members out of five on *any one* of the county commissions vote no—even if majorities on the other three boards approve the plan . . . well, at any one of these switch points, the train can be derailed." Kurvaszy emphasized that *that* was why he appreciated the chance to air everyone's concerns—to try for a way to satisfy even the current naysayers, lest they use whatever political leverage they could muster to block approval.

Anton took a sip from his cup and then walked to the blackboard. "What I want to do is set forth the situation as I see it. Maybe by brainstorming we can find a way to get both the politics and the administration right."

Kurvaszy said that the pickup portion of St. Croix area trash service charges, being about equal for all counties and unlikely to change, could be factored out of the discussion. He'd confine himself, for the moment, to summarizing waste disposal costs only. Kurvaszy turned back to the board and wrote numbers as he spoke.

"As things now stand, we have a two-tiered waste disposal system in the St. Croix, with Norton on the top tier—in the sense that those Tamarack costs jack disposal costs to Norton way up—and the other three counties all coming in at a very much lower level. At 30 thousand tons per county per year"—Kurvaszy was working with round numbers, but he emphasized that they were in the ballpark for all four counties—"and taking into consideration the different costs to Norton and the others, we're spending about $3.9 million every year with the present uncoordinated and unplanned operation." Anton scratched out numbers showing his derivation:

$$\text{Norton:} \quad 30{,}000 \text{ tons} \times \$64/\text{ton} = \$1.92 \text{ million}$$

$$\left.\begin{array}{l}\text{Apostle} \\ \text{Burnt} \\ \text{Larch:}\end{array}\right\} \quad 90{,}000 \text{ tons} \times \$22/\text{ton} = \underline{1.98} \text{ million}$$

$$\$3.90 \text{ million}$$

Kurvaszy quickly surveyed his audience. No rebuttals. "Okay," he said, "we'll take $3.9 as our base. Now, as you know, with the AWA we'd be set up to run waste disposal a whole lot more efficiently, in part because we could take advantage of any targets of opportunity as they appear in the recycling and landfill markets. The SCDC Operations Division would run garbage disposal for the whole area, and that would add a layer of administrative costs. We estimate the added overhead charge at about $529,000 per year." He explained that in his cost workups he had rounded this sum to a prorated overhead charge of $130,000 per year for each of the four counties.

Kurvaszy continued: "Central direction of our system should more than pay for itself. By operating the four-county disposal setup as a single system, we could centrally direct wastes to their most efficient points of disposition. We'd also get bargaining power: The commission—the SCDC—acting as agent for the entire region could negotiate with recyclers, dump owners, and even combustors both in the St.

Croix and outside. With that kind of bargaining power, I assume that right from scratch we could get better deals than the towns and counties have been able to do acting on their own."

"What are your key assumptions here, Anton?" Kurvaszy knew that he'd have to answer that question in detail when he made the presentation at the development-plan meeting of the SCDC. He thought it was fair for the commission's chairman, Adam Fencl, to ask it now.

Kurvaszy said he expected a unified bargaining agent to be able to push area landfill operators to cut their tipping fees, say to $20 per ton. "And don't forget," he added, "with systemwide planning, it should also be possible to achieve a higher recycling proportion than at present. Better bargaining should enable us to recover fees closer to $20 than the present $10 per ton." Anton then noted that quite a few states had set objectives on the order of 40, 50, or even 60 percent of their solid waste to be recycled before the year 2000. With the kind of efficient, integrated operation he was proposing—he assured everyone—it wasn't unreasonable to look for a much higher recycling rate within the St. Croix than the 30 percent his SCDC staffers were currently using as a planning assumption.

Facing the blackboard again, Kurvaszy showed the first-year gains that he was confident the new AWA could achieve. Efficient areawide waste management should yield a constant stream of annual savings to the citizens of the St. Croix. Anton estimated that the region's total waste load of 120 thousand tons could be disposed of for a weighted cost of $28.1 per ton. That included tonnage trucked to Tamarack and burned at the rate of $50 per ton, and it multiplied out to the total annual cost figure that the meeting's attendees had doubtless heard about: $6,370 thousand (including waste disposal and the pickup portion). That $6,370,000 would be spread over the entire four-county area.

"Right," Finn Ebertsen interjected. "But what the fuss is all about isn't your $6.37 million figure standing alone. It's about the *spread* of the charges among the counties. Why should we in Burnt pay extra to bail out Norton?" Ebertsen didn't hesitate to look Erwin Snyder in the eyes as he said it. "Why should we give up arrangements we've made that work for us, when we see no benefit in this 'systemwide' deal you keep talking about?"

"Fair questions," Kurvaszy conceded. "But maybe the answer isn't to think in terms of a bailout for Norton."

"What other way is there to think about it?"

Kurvaszy asked everyone to join in a mental experiment. "Assume we were already organized on a regional basis, so we could think about waste disposal from the integrated perspective instead of as separate towns and counties."

"Sounds awfully like 'Assume we have a can opener,'" Ferdy Washburne quipped. Washburne was an economist by training.[2]

Most of those around the table laughed mildly. So did Anton Kurvaszy, who then proceeded:

[2]Washburne's allusion is to an old joke among policy analysts about a physicist, an engineer, and an economist stranded with nothing but a supply of canned beans: How to get at the food? The physicist says she can figure out how hot a fire it would take to raise the pressure in a can to the explosion point. The engineer says he'll compute the force with which a can would need to be hurled against a rock. Then it's time for a contribution from the economist, who suggests: "Assume we have a can opener."

"Assume we were already operating at a generally higher level of governmental integration, with a single four-county office carrying out most of the governance functions for the entire St. Croix. But suppose that as a kind of holdover from earlier days of town-by-town, county-by-county governance, we were continuing to dispose of our waste in an uncoordinated way, for our agreed baseline cost of $3,900,000 (waste disposal only) or $6,900,000 (when you include the pickup portion in the baseline as well). Finally, suppose some promoter comes and offers us a deal along the following lines:

> "'It's possible to buy a magic machine that does the same physical job of four-county waste disposal, but for $6.37 million, waste disposal and pickup portion. Logically, we . . . I mean, all of us together in the St. Croix . . . should be willing to pay up to the amount of the difference between $6.37 and the baseline figure of $6.90 million, since *collectively*, the difference—$530 thousand—is what we'd save by going to the new system.'"

Kurvaszy gave his listeners some time to fix the terms of the mental experiment in their minds. Then he continued: "Here's what I want us to try to brainstorm: Assuming we all think it worthwhile to buy the new system for some amount up to the full amount of money that we'd collectively save:

"*One*, what would be a fair way to divide the contributions of the four counties to the $6,370 thousand needed to fund the AWA? Is the idea of a uniform $159 charge, give or take, to every customer in the four-county region the best way to spread the costs of service? Or should existing disparities caused by the Tamarack debt overhang be taken into account when spreading the fees, and if so, how?

"*Two*, is there any way to think about using that $530-thousand annual saving to make everyone really feel like a winner after the charges have been spread over the area? In other words, is there a way to salvage what's now a win-lose situation—with the folk over in Norton County the main losers, but in a way that could hurt us all if Norton has to pull back on its SCDC support—into a win-win situation for everyone in the St. Croix?"

Questions for Discussion
. . . .

The following queries might help you frame your thoughts and organize a discussion of the case.

1. What's the story? What lessons can we draw from an understanding of the way "The Great Four-County Garbage War" developed? Are "Tamarack-type problems" essentially inevitable? If so, should that have any bearing on the way conflicts brought on by these kinds of problems are handled?

2. "Why should [the Norton commissioners] ask us to bail them out, now that their plant's become a white elephant?" Finn Ebertsen asked Mary Martengrove. In any negotiations over future waste disposal arrangements in the St. Croix, how should Norton County officials handle the "threat" they could make to cover their Tamarack financing deficit by withdrawing support for various four-county programs

of value to citizens in Apostle, Burnt, and Larch counties? How should officials from the latter counties respond, mindful that "abandoning" their Norton colleagues to pay for their own mistakes could boomerang by causing Norton to abandon the SCDC and a series of shared services (the regional emergency medical service, adult/vocational education, and so forth) along with it?

3. How is this scenario shaped by two of the central issues of this chapter: (a) the tension between synoptic analysis and local interests and (b) the conflict between rational planning and decision making through negotiation? To what extent do you see planning and bargaining as opposing approaches? To what extent do you see them as complementary?

4. In what forms (if any) do the elements of underdetermination and overdetermination occur in this case? Review the problem-solving techniques in Chapter 1 (persuasion, restructuring, and so forth; priority setting, parameter changing, and policy adjusting). Which of these would you use to deal with issues of incomplete control and multiple, inconsistent criteria?

5. Suppose that Anton Kurvaszy and Finn Ebertsen had to make their cases—Kurvaszy, for adoption of the proposed Area Waste Authority; Ebertsen, for the status quo—before a wise and objective visitor from outside the St. Croix. What do you think would be the strongest points that each could make? Who, in your opinion, would finally convince an impartial judge?

6. "Know the law." What do you think of the arguments offered by Supreme Court Justice Kennedy in the *Carbone* case against the Clarkstown, New York, flow control program? (You might want to think a bit about the larger constitutional scheme within which regional, state, and local administrative entities—such as the St. Croix Development Commission—function. The Commerce Clause of the Constitution itself rests on a "systemwide conception" of the American economy.) Can you see any connection between Congresswoman Moe's earmarked appropriation, the impending resolutions of the Minnesota and Wisconsin state legislatures, and the legality of the four-county waste disposal plan that Anton Kurvaszy wants adopted?

7. How would you respond to Kurvaszy's request for suggestions about ways to use the dollar savings that he's convinced can be realized through the AWA? How might estimates of these savings affect any bargaining that might ensue over the distribution of gains? Can you think of a workable administrative scheme to capture the savings and redistribute them in a way that leaves everyone represented at the meeting better off?

8. What kinds of bargaining—distributive, integrative, informational—are likely to take place at Antoine's Ante Club?

9. Do any of the negotiating techniques described by Thomas Schelling seem applicable to the principal figures at the meeting? What about the technique of coalition formation? Does this technique have any relevance to the tasks confronting Kurvaszy, Ebertsen, or the others?

FOR FURTHER READING

Two classic works of the Progressive period which elucidate the belief in planning are

> Croly, Herbert, *The Promise of American Life* (New York: Macmillan, 1909).
> Veblen, Thorstein, *Engineers and the Price System* (New Brunswick NJ: Transaction Books [1921], 1983), especially chap. 6.

Interesting—and somewhat iconoclastic—treatments of the theory of reciprocal separation (the politics-administration gap) are in

> Roberts, Alasdair, "Demonstrating Neutrality: The Rockefeller Philanthropies and the Evolution of Public Administration, 1927–1936," 54 *Public Administration Review* (May–June 1994), 221.
> Martin, Daniel W., "The Fading Legacy of Woodrow Wilson," 48 *Public Administration Review* (March–April 1988), 631.

See also, for interesting applications of the doctrine of the policy-administration gap,

> Koven, Steven G., "Base Closings and the Politics-Administration Dichotomy Revisited," 52 *Public Administration Review* (September–October 1992), 526.
> Thomas, Christine, "The Policy/Administration Continuum: Wisconsin Natural Resources Board Decisions," 50 *Public Administration Review* (July–August 1990), 435.

The standard work of contemporary scholarship on the search for efficiency in government is

> Downs, George, and Patrick Larkey, *The Search for Government Efficiency* (Philadelphia: Temple U. Press, 1990).

A superb treatment of the economic theories behind the optimizing approach—together with complete coverage of Pareto optimality, the Kaldor-Hicks principle, and related materials—is in

> Baumol, William, *Economic Theory and Operations Analysis,* (Englewood Cliffs NJ: Prentice-Hall, 1977), chap. 21.

The standard works in contemporary scholarship on bargaining tactics and negotiation theory—all representative of the "Harvard approach"—are

> Fisher, Roger, and William Ury, *Getting to Yes* (New York: Penguin, 1981); lucid, readable, and probably the best exposition in the literature of "principles negotiation."
> Lax, David, and James Sebenius, *The Manager as Negotiator* (New York: Free Press, 1986); we'll see an extended excerpt from this popular treatment of the subject in Chapter 11.
> Raiffa, Howard, *The Art and Science of Negotiation* (Cambridge MA: Harvard U. Press, 1982).

A readable introduction to negotiation theory, taking a less formal approach than the one associated with the Harvard Negotiating Project, is

> Freund, James C., *Smart Negotiating: How to Make Good Deals in the Real World* (New York: Simon and Schuster, 1993).

For useful treatments of selected special topics in bargaining theory and case studies of negotiation, see

> Carpenter, Susan, and W. J. D. Kennedy, *Managing Public Disputes* (San Francisco: Jossey-Bass, 1988); a well-written all-around handbook for the public official in the role of dispute mediator.
>
> Lewicki, Ray J., et al., *Negotiation: Readings, Exercises and Cases* (Burr Ridge IL: Irwin, 1993); arguably the best single introduction for those who seek a combination of bargaining theory, concrete examples, and interesting negotiating exercises.
>
> Quandt, William B., *Camp David* (Washington: Brookings Institution, 1986); probably the best insider account available of an actual major negotiating exercise.

▼◆●■▼◆●■▼◆●■▼◆●■▼◆

CHAPTER 6

What's Private? What's Public? What's the Relationship between the Two?

The Progressives thought that a modern industrial society required a high level of public action. In their time, unregulated private conduct had produced monopolistic corporations, cutthroat competition, and dirty, overcrowded cities—all problems that the Progressives proposed to fix through a more enlightened, more vigorous process of governance. How much bigger and more active did the public sector have to become in order for the **New American State**[1] to undertake the tasks that the Progressives had in mind? This was the question implicit in an assertion by Woodrow Wilson, in his 1887 article, that administrative study should center on "what government can properly and successfully do."

The balance between activities that remain in the private sector and those which the people delegate to government defines the **institutional division of labor.** Over the long haul, most Americans have taken it pretty much for granted that "private is best." In general, Americans prefer to rely on markets, families, churches, and other private-sector associations whenever these can do the job. We call on government mainly when our private-sector institutions prove to be severely inefficient; when they fail to satisfy certain minimum standards of social equity; when they seem inappropriate to perform functions traditionally regarded as "inherently political," including functions that express "the moral writ of the community"; or when procedures (*how* functions are performed) seem to be as important as *what* functions are actually undertaken. Our main aim in Section 1 of the chapter will be to demystify these four reasons for moving functions out of private hands and defining them as public responsibilities.

We shouldn't, however, consider the paradigms of private and public assignment—that is, the criteria by which certain functions are reserved to private institutions

---

[1] *New American State:* The term coined by Steven Skowronek, a historian of the Progressive Era, to describe the administrative institutions (new regulatory agencies, comprehensive planning approaches, and so forth) the Progressives set up to meet the challenges of industrial America. See Skowronek's *Building a New American State* (Cambridge, England: Cambridge U. Press, 1982).

and others are assigned to government—as expressions of hard-and-fast dogmas. *In theory,* we may make rather clear distinctions between the functions of private and public institutions. *In practice,* the administrative process requires continuing interactions across the private-public boundary. A strict separation of the private from the public, like a strict separation of policy making from administration, would make the governance process unworkable. Many public administrators routinely operate across the public-private boundary, in constant contact with their counterparts in private companies, lobbying firms, and think tanks. In doing so, they conduct much of the day-to-day work of modern governance in the context of informal organizations.

In Section 2 of this chapter, then, we'll consider how actors in the private and public sectors cooperate to create a single private-public system even though traditional American administrative theory might have suggested the need for separate spheres of private and public action. Why this merging of private with public has occurred is a major concern in contemporary political science and public administration. Of even greater importance, perhaps, are certain problems that result from the permeation of the boundary between private actors and public officials, problems such as "influence peddling" and preferential treatment of some citizens based on their connections with public officials. We'll give special attention to the explanations that the New Theorists offer for the importance—indeed, the inevitability—of informal organizations as institutions of governance.

SECTION 1 ● ■ ▼ ◆
The Paradigms of Assignment: Why Public Action?

The philosophy of individual freedom that undergirds our political system traces back to the writings of the seventeenth-century English political theorists Thomas Hobbes and John Locke. Hobbes and Locke envisioned a state of nature that existed before governments were created. The individuals who inhabited the state of nature formed organized societies by negotiating social contracts.

Locke, the social contract theorist with the greatest influence on the framers of the U.S. Constitution, envisioned the natural human state as one in which markets functioned with reasonable reliability and security. Even in the state of nature, Locke thought, men and women were guided by moral sentiments and rational calculations of self-interest. These habits of mind permitted human beings to carry on trading relationships. In general, they could depend on one another to follow through on their contracts. Yet even among the basically benevolent inhabitants of Locke's state of nature, squabbles would occasionally occur and disputes arise over the terms of agreements that rational individuals had struck. It therefore made sense to set up a government empowered to enforce rules of social and commercial intercourse. Locke, however, believed that rational individuals would give up no more freedom than they had to in order to achieve social order. Hence their social contract set up a liberal state. (*Liberal* in this usage connotes no particular social ideology but only that the state's powers over citizens are strictly limited.)

The same postulate of rational individualism that led political philosophers to the theory of the liberal state has traditionally led economists to champion the market as the most important institution of a free society. "In the beginning was the market. . . .": One comes across this striking sentence here and there in the writings of the scholars known as the New Theorists.

In the same way that Hobbes and Locke thought it helpful to envision society as originating in a pregovernmental state of nature, the New Theorists find it useful to think of institutions as originating in some primeval (if hypothetical) market. The ideal market is said to be atomistic, inhabited by individuals (the "atoms" of society) who pursue their interests by trading with one another. The competitive market plays the important role that it does in our system because it efficiently organizes the production and distribution of so many of the goods and services that all individuals seek. Agreements freely made to trade goods or services are contracts, and so freely negotiated contracts are the basic instruments of market transactions.

Under certain conditions, however, individuals will forgo negotiation and accept a different kind of transaction—an administered decision, in which a command or a general rule instead of a negotiated agreement guides behavior. Whereas market transactions involve buyers and sellers negotiating and freely contracting with one another, administered decision making involves order giving by superiors and order taking by subordinates. The transition from **negotiated decision making** to **administered decision making** marks the transition from the free market to the hierarchical organization (and, ultimately, to bureaucracy, which many still regard as the central structure of public administration). Under what conditions will this transition occur?

Why Organize? The Theory of Market Failures

Obviously, when transactions are administered (that is, commanded by superiors) instead of negotiated, much of the individual freedom that the institution of the market preserves vanishes. There are many who believe that efficiency erodes right along with freedom. Why then would rational human beings ever forgo the benefits of negotiated dealing and submit to administered decision making? Why organize by creating hierarchical structures? These questions bring us to a body of thought that is crucial to an understanding of the institutions of contemporary public administration: the **theory of market failures.**

Transaction Costs: The First Category of Market Failure

The New Theorists argue that certain inconveniences in the free-market negotiating process can become so severe that individuals will choose to become employees of firms (thereby binding themselves to obey bosses) or form governments (thereby subjecting themselves to the regulatory authority of public officials). According to the New Theorists, **transaction costs** cause the most serious free-market inconveniences. Transaction costs include the costs in time, energy, and emotional wear and tear of the bargaining process itself, and also the costs of finding out who's selling what and for how much. Bargaining costs and information costs effectively add to the dollar price that a buyer must pay, making the real cost of a traded item its listed price *plus* any external costs, such as the costs of any pollution that the makers of the good generate in the course of producing it, *plus* the transaction costs of the exchange.

Many kinds of goods involve relatively low transaction costs, so little incentive exists to economize on the transaction costs of exchanging them. These goods will normally be traded item by item in free markets. However, for many items, transaction costs are large. High transaction costs represent a special kind of market failure, since they signify that buyers and sellers are losing time, energy, and resources to the frictional activities of acquiring information (Where are the goods? What are they really worth? Are there hidden defects? Are there catches in the fine print of the sales contracts?) and then haggling over the prices at which those goods will be traded.

A pioneer among the New Theorists, the economist Ronald Coase, illustrated the transaction-cost concept in a famous analysis of the value of human labor.[2] A worker's skill normally improves with experience on the job. Should the worker therefore renegotiate his or her contract every week to reflect the improving skill levels? No, because the transaction costs of constant bargaining would offset any possible gain in productivity. Lest the transaction costs of renegotiation become excessive—as would occur with periodic reviews of every individual's pay rate—all workers instead collectively agree once and for all to a special kind of contract, an employment macrocontract.

An **employment macrocontract** is a special kind of contract by which the parties agree to set up a hierarchical structure in which administered decision making will supplant free-market bargaining and item-by-item contracting. The process of order giving by superiors and order taking by subordinates will eliminate the need for negotiations over a wide range of issues covered by the terms of the macrocontract. The superiors promise that the employees will receive automatic raises with seniority so long as they do as they are told when on the job. For their part, all employees of the organization accept a standard set of work rules. The personnel structure in which most public administrators spend their working lives—the civil service system—illustrates the schedule of salary guarantees and the encompassing code of rules that are typical elements of an employment macrocontract.

Transaction-cost analysis explains when decision making should be administered rather than negotiated—that is, when the disadvantages of transaction costs in the free market exceed the disadvantages of the restrictions on individual freedom that accession to an employment macrocontract implies. But the New Theory doesn't tell us whether the new organization should be private (a business firm) or public (a government agency). Having suggested when negotiated decision making should give way to administered decision making, can we take the next step and say when administered decision making should be taken out of the private sector and assigned to a public organization?

Economists and those political scientists who subscribe to the New Theory (which ultimately derives from economic premises) explain the move to the public sector mainly in terms of the drive for rationality. Economists equate rationality with efficiency, so the rule becomes: *Assign functions either to the private sector or to the public sector, depending on where they can be performed more efficiently.* To many Americans, brought up on suspicion of bureaucracy, it's a bizarre thought that efficiency might ever actually be a reason for assigning functions to government. Nevertheless, for centuries, considerations of efficiency have helped explain the proper role of public agencies.

We have just seen that markets become inefficient whenever transaction costs—including information costs and bargaining costs—become excessive, for then the

[2]"The Nature of the Firm," 4 *Economica* (New Series, 1937): 386.

processes of information seeking and negotiation absorb so much of buyers' and sellers' energy that it becomes impossible to complete the number of item-by-item trades that are needed to produce a free-flowing stream of commerce. Markets are also said to fail when monopolies appear. Monopolies destroy the disciplining force of competition that should guarantee efficiency by driving prices down and the quality of products up. Finally, markets fail when the transactions among individuals or organizations affect persons other than the buyers and sellers who are directly involved. Such effects are said to be "external" to the market transaction in question. Let's see how these concepts—particularly those of monopoly power and external effects—can be used to frame a theory centered on the criterion of efficiency which justifies transferring certain functions out of private hands and assigning them to public agencies.

Monopoly Power: The Second Category of Market Failure

Monopoly power can't exist in the kind of atomistic market that economic theorists like to write about. In an atomistic market, so many individuals pursue their interests in so fragmented a social environment that no one person, or even any conspiratorial group of persons, can amass enough power to control the supply of any good or service. Markets in industrial societies are rarely atomistic, but they may remain reasonably competitive as long as no firm in a given line of commerce grows large enough to dictate terms to others.

Traditionally, the threat of monopoly comes from predatory individuals who manage somehow to acquire enough market power to drive their competitors out of business. The concept of monopoly also applies to a markets in which only a few firms control the entire supply of a product, since it's not hard for a small number to meet in a closed room and plot against the public interest. A conspiracy to limit output or to fix prices is a form of monopoly known as a *cartel*. There is also a third possibility, one that is of special relevance in the history of American public administration: The technology in an industry may make monopoly "natural," as, for example, in modern water supply. A central water system requires large investments of capital in costly piping and pumping plants; these can be planned and operated most efficiently over an entire region by a single company. As we saw in Chapter 4, much of the regulatory apparatus of the modern American administrative state originated in the attempt to control natural monopolies.

However achieved, the existence of a monopoly indicates a market failure, since a monopolist can limit the supply of a good and thereby unfairly drive prices up. Because competition and the efficiencies that it should bring about are deemed to be in the public interest, the appearance of monopoly power gives one of the classic reasons for government to move in—either through the creation of a public agency to provide the goods or services in question or through the empowerment of a regulatory commission to oversee the workings of an industry in which monopoly power has begun to appear (whether through predatory action, cartelization, or the emergence of conditions that justify a natural monopoly).

External Effects: The Third Category of Market Failure

Like the threat of monopoly, the problem of external effects was recognized long before the New Theorists appeared on the scholarly scene with the modern theory of transaction costs. Using a concept that's all but identical to the contemporary notion of an external effect, John Dewey (1859–1952), the leading American philosopher of the Progressive Era, developed a "public philosophy" that contained many of the essentials of modern doctrine. Dewey's focus on transactions, his interest in the reasons why individuals form themselves into organized groups, and his account of the distinction between private and public activity foreshadowed the ideas of the New Theorists:

> We take . . . our point of departure from the objective fact that human acts have consequences upon others, that some of these consequences are perceived, and that their perception leads to subsequent effort to control action so as to secure some consequences and avoid others. Following this clew [sic] we are led to remark that the consequences are of two kinds, those which affect the persons directly engaged in a transaction, and those which affect others beyond those immediately concerned. In this distinction we find the germ of the distinction between the private and the public. . . . When A and B carry on a conversation together the action is a transaction: both are concerned in it; its results pass, as it were, across from one to the other. One or other or both may be helped or harmed thereby. But, presumably, the consequences of advantage and injury do not extend beyond A and B; the activity lies between them; it is private. Yet if it is found that the consequences of conversation extend beyond the two directly concerned, that they affect the welfare of many others, the act acquires a public capacity. . . .
>
> Those indirectly and seriously affected for good or evil form a group distinctive enough to require recognition and a name. The name selected is The Public.[3]

Dewey anticipated the so-called pluralist explanation of public agency creation (see Box 6.1). His analysis suggested that "the public" isn't a fixed population of citizens but instead consists at any instant of a series of overlapping **subpublics.** A new subpublic comes into existence whenever supposedly private actions have "indirect consequences" and begin to affect persons other than those who perform them. Willy-nilly, individuals and groups are constantly finding new ways to affect their neighbors. Therefore, new subpublics are constantly being created. By definition, a new subpublic comes into being whenever a new external effect appears.

Public Goods, Public Bads, and the Criterion of Efficiency

Social scientists today call a positive external effect an **external economy** or a **public good.** A private factory owner who beautifies a plant site or develops a smoothly working labor market produces an external economy; everyone in the neighborhood will gain from the improved appearance, and other employers—even competitors—may benefit from the availability of workers attracted into the area. Other standard examples of public goods are national defense, roadways, fire protection, and basic medical research. A negative external effect is called an **external *diseconomy*** or a **public**

[3]*The Public and Its Problems* (Chicago: Swallow Press [1927], n.d.), pp. 12–13, 35.

BOX 6.1 ■■■

The Pluralists' Theory of Agency Creation

According to most **pluralists** (sometimes called *group theorists*), the members of sub-publics eventually form themselves into pressure groups and demand remedies for the market failures that affect them. Consumers organize in opposition to monopolists who they think are ripping them off; environmentalists lobby against those they identify as despoilers of the land.

The group-forming and interest-articulating process accounts for the creation of new government agencies and expansion of old ones. That's how we got such Progressive Era agencies as the Food and Drug Administration (FDA) to test foods for purity—an information-gathering task that would be performed inefficiently or not at all if consumers had to make an item-by-item inspection of every purchase in a grocery store. That's also how we got the Interstate Commerce Commission (ICC) to regulate the railroads, and a beefed-up Forestry Service to plan for the development of the nation's timber resources—an important public good from which we all benefit. That too is how, more recently, we got the federal Consumer Product Safety Commission and the Environmental Protection Agency (EPA).

If for some reason lawmakers prefer not to set up a new public agency, pressure from the members of a mobilized subpublic may move them to add to the responsibilities of an existing organization. That's how rate-setting authority over the interstate trucking industry came to be added to the responsibilities of the original ICC; that's also how regulatory authority over the natural gas industry was added in 1938 to the existing hydroelectric jurisdiction of the Federal Power Commission.

Throughout, we discern a pattern of agency-by-agency, problem-by-problem response as groups mobilize to lobby for public regulation of private actions that affect them. From the early years of progressivism onward, Americans have displayed a quickness to pass a law, create a bureau, issue a new rule. Government has become a kind of residual problem-solving instrument—an institutional solution to be tried whenever a problem appeared that traditional private-sector institutions seemed incapable of handling. In this evolutionary history lies much of the explanation for the patchwork structure of our government. That patchwork structure, in turn, helps to account for the fragmentation of authority in the American public bureaucracy. Because different officials have jurisdictions over different aspects of interlocking problem areas, underdetermination emerges as a recurrent problem, and coordination is a primary challenge in American public administration.

■■■

bad. Note that these positive and negative terms are to an extent interchangeable: The suppression of a public bad (for example, pollution abatement) is itself a public good. Conversely, the failure by government to produce a public good (for example, failure to fund some kinds of public health research that no private drug manufacturer finds it profitable to finance) can be branded a public bad.

An external economy possesses the quality known as *nonexcludability;* it produces a **nonexcludable good.** For example, no one in the neighborhood can be prevented from gaining the beneficial effects of a factory owner's beautification program, any more than anyone can be excluded from the harmful effects of a local polluter's emissions. Public goods and bads are "public," then, because they have spillover effects. which make it impossible to confine the impacts of nonexcludable actions to the immediate transactors. For this reason, a producer can't sell a public good to a given customer without giving every one of the customer's neighbors the opportunity to share in it as well. Some individuals, called **free riders,** will take advantage of their ability to benefit from a public good without paying for it.

Public Goods and the Collective-Action Problem

Consider what effect the possibility of free riding will have on the behavior of individuals who would otherwise be inclined to purchase the good: They will soon realize how foolish it is to pay for an item that others in the neighborhood are getting free. The logic of the situation will cause the number of paying customers to shrink as more and more individuals try to become free riders. Eventually, shrinkage in the number of paying customers will reach the point at which demand can't support the production of the good. After all, few producers will set up in business to provide a good or service for which customers won't appear in adequate numbers. Free riders create what's known as a **collective-action problem,** for they force the members of a community to ask how public services—which typically possess the quality of nonexcludability—can be provided collectively, with everyone paying his or her fair share.

The implication of the collective-action problem is of fundamental importance in the analysis of the division of labor between private and public institutions: The point is, a nonexcludable good tends to be underproduced, if produced at all, by private entrepreneurs. Public agencies must be set up to provide such a good. Representatives of the people impose taxes and use some portion of the revenues they collect to pay public administrators, who either produce the public good themselves or contract with some private supplier to produce it in an amount that the decision makers deem to be in the public interest. Because of the nonexcludable nature of the good, every citizen gets the benefit. No one has to haggle with a private producer, as would have to occur if free-market transactions were relied on to ensure that the good in question will be produced and distributed. Administered decision making replaces negotiation.

Public Bads and Transaction Costs

A slightly different line of reasoning applies when setting up public agencies to control negative externalities. Consider a person harmed by smoke from a nearby factory, the standard example of a public bad. In a free-market situation, such an individual might find it worthwhile to pay the offending industrialist to abate the nuisance. In theory, the affected individual could bribe the polluter to stop spewing dirt into the air. A process of negotiation would take place over the amount to be paid. The payment— in effect, a bribe—would have to be just high enough to induce a reduction to exactly the level at which the price paid offsets the harm done by the smoke to that individual.

But in practice it would be impossible for each of a thousand neighbors, say, to figure out the level of harm that he or she has suffered and then to arrange a separate bribe with the factory owner such that just the right amount is paid in aggregate to bring about the satisfaction of all individuals' preferences for clean air.

In the smoke-pollution case, high transaction costs rule out reliance on negotiated decision making. There must emerge some single agent to act on behalf of all citizens, who will have to pay for clean air through taxes rather than through individual transactions (bribes). In this case, two kinds of market failure—external effects and high transaction costs—combine to justify the setting up of a public authority empowered to make collective decisions on behalf of individuals who aren't able to look after their interests singly. Laws will be passed and regulations will be issued to specify some maximum level of pollution that factories in a given industry may emit. In this way, the government, acting on behalf of the public—or, more precisely, on behalf of members of the affected subpublic—forces the producer to "internalize costs" by paying to install anti-pollution equipment or suffer criminal penalties. Again, administered decision making replaces negotiated decision making.

The Criterion of Social Equity

High transaction costs, the appearance of monopoly power, and the presence of external effects all involve breakdowns in the classical free market. An additional issue in contemporary public policy can also be discussed under the heading of a market failure, although it does not, technically speaking, involve a breakdown in any of the classical market mechanisms. That issue arises because of the severe inequities which can result from an overreliance on the free market. If the urge to rationality (again, in the sense of encouraging efficiency) in the division of functions offers one important explanation of the decision to assign certain tasks to government, the urge to social equity offers a second one. Under the second approach, the criterion of public assignment becomes: *Assign functions to government whenever public action seems likelier than private decision making to provide all members of the community—especially the most vulnerable—with minimal opportunities to lead lives of dignity and sufficiency.*

Free markets give the edge to the productive and the efficient. They favor those who have knowledge, skills, or strength to sell to employers. The employers are then supposed to compensate their workers roughly in proportion to the latters' economic contributions (their "marginal productivity"). But the men and women who fare most successfully in this kind of system aren't necessarily those who have "earned it" in a moral sense. A high IQ doesn't by any means give evidence of virtue. Neither does diligence in the pursuit of ignoble goals (although that may be profitable) or the ability to hit a soft jump shot or whack a baseball 450 feet (although those capabilities may command millions in professional athletics). And what about those who, through no fault of their own, have been left behind by the market: elderly workers whose occupational skills have become obsolete; those whose educational attainments suddenly leave them ill equipped to compete in a high-tech economy? Critics of the market urge that a decent society must somehow realize certain minimum standards of sustenance and dignity for all. If the market fails in *human* terms—even though its working mechanisms are in sound repair—the community must act in its collective capacity to fill the gap.

Can both efficiency and equity be achieved at the same time? Probably not, at least not completely, since these values are prime examples of inconsistent criteria—in other words, of the problem of overdetermination. Nor is it easy even to strike a balance between the contending values of efficiency and social equity. Much heated controversy has occurred over the point at which income redistribution in the name of social equity begins to destroy the market incentives that traditionally prod the most aggressive and most talented individuals to higher levels of achievement. Many analysts of the American economy contend that policies such as income redistribution and affirmative action end up shrinking the size of the economic pie for all. These proponents of the free market believe that the undermining of efficiency in the name of social equity threatens to create a poorer society in which both justice and efficiency must finally be losers.

Within the limits of validity, the logic of the argument from social equity extends to institutions other than the market. If families can't meet the most basic needs of some citizens (What about the battered spouse? The abused child?), the community may assert the importance of the unsatisfied human values by acting where the private institution has failed. Americans continue to debate the extent to which government officials should be cast in "helping" roles, whether acting to compensate for malfunctioning markets or dysfunctional families, but there seems to be general agreement about the rightness of the social equity argument in its basic outline.

The Appurtenances of Sovereignty as a Criterion of Private-Public Assignment

A third set of arguments for the assignment of functions to government hinges on the belief that some tasks express the "majesty" of the community or the collective sense of common need. According to these arguments, which are rooted in the classical theory of the state, traditional public functions such as the conduct of foreign affairs and the steady dispensation of justice are inherent appurtenances of sovereignty. They symbolize the collectivity of concerns within a community. As such they shouldn't be performed within the private sector. Certainly they can't be entrusted to profit-seeking entrepreneurs. Under this approach, the criterion becomes: *Assign those functions to government which seem, in terms of the traditions of the community, inherently "political"—for the most part, functions that express the majesty the public sector.*

Public administrationists who espouse this argument tend to stress the symbolic content and moral implications of public action. The symbolic includes those aspects of public life that are emotion laden, evocative, capable of charging citizens' loyalties and firing their enthusiasm rather than merely being efficient or instrumental. As critics of the **instrumental theory of institutions,**[4] some commentators charge that an overemphasis on efficiency, combined with an undervaluation of symbolic and moral factors, causes those who accept this theory—**instrumentalists**—to assign the wrong functions

---

[4]*Instrumental theory of institutions:* The view that institutions—including the institutions of government—are artificial rather than natural and are no more than means to be used in pursuing given ends. In this view, there's nothing sacred or symbolic about institutions. Since they are merely instruments or tools designed for specific purposes, institutions should be employed as needed in the pursuit of particular objectives but modified or even discarded when they have outlived their usefulness.

to the wrong kinds of organizations, usually by arguing for private takeovers of functions whose symbolic or moral content make them inherently public.

Is government, as the instrumentalists contend, just another tool, to be enlarged or overhauled in good times and trimmed or mothballed when more efficient tools appear to be available? You should consider, in this connection, the following passage by the political scientist and criminologist John DiIulio, an influential contributor to the debate over the desirability of privatizing prisons. Suppose the statistics showed that private companies such as CCA—the Corrections Corporation of America, Inc. (a real firm)—can operate prisons more efficiently than our federal and state correctional departments can. DiIulio, who heads the Brookings Institution Center for Public Management, argues that "the moral writ of the community" would still require that incarceration must remain a public function, an obligation of the sovereign. According to DiIulio, if we were to privatize prisons, we would forgo the symbolic benefit of using public authority to dramatize our collective revulsion against lawbreaking.

John DiIulio on "The Moral Writ of the Community"

[L]et us grant for the sake of argument that private prisons and jails are eminently feasible. Must it then follow that they are desirable? Is the private operation of prisons and jails, however instrumental it may prove to be in reducing costs and bettering services, justifiable morally? . . .

In my judgement, to remain legitimate and morally significant, the authority to govern behind bars, to deprive citizens of their liberty, to coerce (and even kill) them, must remain in the hands of government authorities. Regardless of which penological theory is in vogue, the message that those who abuse liberty shall live without it is the philosophical brick and mortar of every correctional facility—a message that ought to be conveyed by the offended community of law-abiding citizens, through its public agents, to the incarcerated individual. The administration of prisons and jails involves the legally sanctioned exercise of coercion by some citizens over others. This coercion is exercised in the name of the offended public. The badge of the arresting police officer, the robes of the judge, and the state patch of the corrections officer are symbols of the inherently public nature of crime and punishment.

The moral implications of privatizing the administration of this central communal function—administering justice for acts against the public welfare—can be felt by entertaining morally analogous situations. . . .

[S]uppose that CCA has made it really big. They have proved that they can do everything the privatizers have promised and more. The corporation decides to branch out. The company changes its name to CJCA: the Criminal Justice Corporation of America. It provides a full range of criminal justice services: cops, courts, and corrections. In an unguarded moment, a CJCA official boasts that "our firm can arrest 'em, try 'em, lock 'em up, and, if need be fry 'em for less." Is there anything wrong with CJCA? . . .

Where the governing of prisons is concerned, is management by private hands morally distinguishable from management by public hands? At a minimum, it can be said (both in theory and in practice) that the formulation and administration of criminal laws by recognized public authorities is one of the liberal state's most central and historic functions; indeed, in some formulations it is the liberal state's *raison d'etre.* In the opening chapter of his *Second Treatise of Government,* Locke defines political power itself as "a right of making laws with penalties of death, and consequently all less penalties, for the regulating and preserving of property, and of employing the force of the community, in the execution of such laws . . . , and all this only for the public good." Criminal law is the one area in which Americans have conceded to the state an almost unqualified right to act in the name of the polity, and hence one of the few placed in which one can discern an American conception of political community that is not a mere collage of individual preferences. It is not unreasonable to suggest that "employing the force of the community" via private penal management undermines the moral writ of the community. . . .

The central moral issues surrounding private prison and jail management have little to do with the profit motive of the privatizers and much to do with propriety, in a liberal constitutional regime, of delegating the authority to administer criminal justice to nonpublic individuals and groups. For much of American history, government has allowed too many of the community's prisons and jails to be ill managed, undermanaged, or not managed at all. Especially in light of the progress that has been made over the last two decades, no self-respecting constitutional government should again abdicate its responsibility to protect and guide criminals in state custody. . . .

In conclusion, while corrections firms like CCA have run admirable juvenile centers and other facilities, we are most likely to improve our country's prisons and jails if we approach them not as a private enterprise to be administered in the pursuit of profit but as a public trust to be administered on behalf of the community and in the name of civility and justice. The choice is between the uncertain promises of privatization and the unfulfilled duty to govern.

From John J. DiIulio, *No Escape* (New York: Basic Books, 1991), pp. 196–203.

The case discussed by DiIulio exemplifies the problem of overdetermination in public administration: the presence of multiple criteria that point to contradictory courses of action. In corrections as elsewhere, justifications for private or public action based on the arguments from efficiency, social equity, and symbolic value may all be relevant; but each argument may imply a different conclusion in a particular situation. For example, the value of efficiency, if assigned premier weight, might require privatization of the correctional function, even though—as Dr. DiIulio argues—symbolic and moral factors could suggest that incarceration must remain a public responsibility.

When "*How* It's Done" Is as Important as "*What* Is Done"

Whereas an essential feature of private life is exactly that—*privacy*—public action usually implies a high degree of openness to general scrutiny, suggesting a higher level of answerability by public officials than almost any private citizen ever has to meet. Private actors can often flee from inquiry by hiding behind "the corporate veil"[5] or invoking the privileges of "proprietary interests."[6] When all that matters is the delivery of the promised good or service on time and at some minimum level of quality, it may be perfectly acceptable to contract with a private supplier. But the exposure of public action to the public eye makes government the agent of choice when citizens want to ensure that their decision makers are behaving with fairness and procedural correctness. In

[5]*The corporate veil:* A corporation is a "legal person" distinct from the shareholders who own it. Thus any legal liability—for selling a defective product, for example—attaches to the corporation, not to its owners or managers. For most purposes, the latters' actions are treated as separate from those of the company, as if shielded from view (and from legal action) by a veil.

[6]*Proprietary interest:* An ownership interest in a business carries with it the right to make a profit by exploiting knowledge (such as the know-how needed to work a patented industrial process) that has been developed by the proprietors. The proprietary interest would be defeated if the owners of the intellectual property in question had to make it public or divulge it to competitors.

Chapter 8, we'll return to this issue of procedural correctness, which is at the core of one of the most important paradigms of obligation in the field of public administration.

It's rarely enough that citizens trust those who wield power to use it fairly. They must be able to *see* that justice is done. If for any reason they come to doubt the correctness of the procedures that are in use, the citizens in a democracy may insist that those procedures be changed. The best way to ensure both visibility and amendability is often to place the power to act within the public realm. Under this approach, the criterion of public assignment becomes: *Assign functions to government when a special requirement exists to expose and, if necessary, modify the manner in which agents carry the function out—in other words, when* how *it's done is as important as* what *is done.* The author of our chapter reading gives special attention to this fourth justification for public action.

CHAPTER READING

John Donohue, a public administrationist at Harvard's Kennedy School of Government, sets his analysis of the case for public action in a framework based on three "organizing principles for production and exchange." Two of these principles (voluntarism, markets) typically imply private action. The third principle (government) implies public action. Nevertheless, many examples of administered decision making occur in the private sphere, just as innumerable instances of volunteer activity and marketlike decision making are to be found in the public arena. Try to identify the basic tests that Donahue explicitly or implicitly contends we should use when deciding how labor should be divided among volunteers, government bureaucrats, and private profit seekers. Our chapter case will raise questions about the desirability not only of private versus public action but also of voluntary versus profit-seeking behavior.

Three Ways of Organizing Production and Exchange in a Modern Society
John Donohue

There is an inherent tension between paying for activity and paying for results. The typical governmental organization is oriented to process rather than product. The rationale is control over means, either because means are more observable than ends or because means are important ends in themselves.

Every culture, guided by the values it cherishes, builds its own institutional structures for creating and distributing wealth.... [O]ne can distinguish three organizing principles for production and exchange.

The first is *voluntarism*. People act in the interest of others uncompensated and uncompelled, animated by tradition, or by a sense of religious, social, or familial duty, or out of empathy, joy in the work

itself, or the thrill of power implicit in magnanimity. While participants in a culture of voluntarism may anticipate benefiting in their turn, they do not keep accounts, expect reciprocity on each transaction, or have any recourse should they end up, over the course of their lives, as net benefactor rather than net beneficiary. The volunteer fireman, for example, is doubtless motivated in part by the prospect of assistance should his own house catch fire, but he does not insist upon a pledge of reciprocal aid from each fire victim before he connects the hose.

The most obvious instances of voluntarism may seem economically marginal. The gardener next door shares his tomato harvest with the neighborhood; you give a panhandler a quarter, or pledge some small fraction of your income to the United Way. But in fact transactions based particularly or predominantly on voluntarism are pervasive. Except in the most peculiar of families, they include the bulk of the production and exchange that occurs within the household. They include philanthropy in cash and in kind.

There are also mixed transactions in which voluntarism figures prominently but not exclusively. When a soldier steps forward for a dangerous assignment, the extra degree of commitment is voluntary, even if he is compelled to military service by the draft and is paid a salary for his time in uniform. There is an element of voluntarism when people chose work—as ministers, schoolteachers, or general practitioners, for example—because they feel that it is meaningful or novel, and in spite of the greater ease or compensation other occupations offer. . . .

The second broad principle for organizing production and distribution is the price system, the manifestation, in Adam Smith's words, of our species' "propensity to truck, barter, and exchange one thing for another." . . . The organizing principle is reciprocal, self-interested exchange. The result is often a marvel of coordination. "Give me this which I want, and you shall have this which you want," Smith wrote. "It is in this manner that we obtain from one another the far greater part of those good offices which we stand in need of." When the circumstances are right, market forces orchestrate a community's material interactions with astonishing speed and precision. . . .

The third broad organizing principle is *government*. Political decisions backed by authority, rather than benevolence or price signals, determine what is produced and how it is distributed. . . . The archetypal bargain of government spending, complementing the individual promise of "give me this which I

want, and you shall have this which you want," is the collective "we mutually pledge to pay for this which we all want." How are we to know when this is the right arrangement? How shall we strike such a bargain?

. . .

The more precisely a task can be specified in advance and its performance evaluated after the fact; the more certainly contractors can be made to compete; the more readily disappointing contractors can be replaced (or otherwise penalized); and the more narrowly government cares about ENDS to the exclusion of MEANS, the stronger becomes the case for employing profit-seekers rather than civil servants. . . . Only if performance will be properly evaluated and contactual terms enforced does competitive bidding have much meaning. If profit-seekers fear no penalties for incompetence, negligence, or other failures to deliver as promised, then the bid process becomes a contest in fabricating extravagant claims. And the less the government knows or cares about the means by which the public's business is accomplished, the looser the rein that can be granted to profit-seekers to devise efficient and innovative ways of delivering specified results. . . . [W]hat the public *loses* by choosing a bureaucratic over a profit-seeking agent is the cost discipline of competition and the benefits of accelerated innovation. What the public *gains* are control over methods, and the right to change mandates as circumstances require. . . .

Consider one particular public task—applying a fresh coat of white paint to the White House. Suppose that the building manager can specify the scope and durability of the painting project and can verify by personal inspection the quality of the job. Suppose that several contractors submit sealed, final bids, and that the contract leaves the building manager the right to replace incompetent contractors in midproject. Finally, imagine that the manager has no special insights into the best way to paint the White House, and does not care whether the contractor uses brushes, rollers or spray guns, ladders, scaffolds, or hydraulic lifts, big crews or small crews, union or nonunion labor, so long as the job is done well and on time. In these circumstances, it makes sense to write up specifications to solicit bids from profit-seekers, and to select the lowest-bidding contractor and let her figure out the best way to paint the White House, pocketing the profit if she does it efficiently.

Consider another public task, protecting the president from aspiring assassins. Suppose that the presidential schedule is contingent on events and thus frequently revised, so that neither the amount of protection required nor the conditions of the task can be specified in advance. Suppose that it is impossible (because of the variability of the task) or unwise (for security reasons) to distribute bid specifications for a month's worth of bodyguarding; or that only a few firms are equipped for a job of that scale and sensitivity; or that it would be difficult to switch security firms after an incumbent contractor masters routines and develops relationships with the president and his staff. Suppose too that it is hard to gauge different degrees of risk short of an actual attack, or to count the number of assassination plots deterred, but relatively easy to tell if an alert bodyguard is on the scene. Suppose further that experience has demonstrated the effectiveness of certain procedures, the departure from which is far more likely to degrade security than to enhance it. Finally, suppose that it matters *how* the president is protected. Many conceivable tactics—keeping all crowds one-half mile away, transporting the president in an armoured car or in disguise, opening fire on all shady looking characters—are unacceptable. Under such circumstances, the potential gains from competitive contracting are swamped by the potential losses. It makes sense to set up a governmental security organization, to establish rules and standard operating procedures for it, and to evaluate agents largely by their fidelity to routine.

So long as our painting and presidential protection examples remain hypothetical, we may as well proceed to imagine the results of alternative choices. Suppose that the building manager at the White House insists upon civil servants to do the paint job. With a typical governmental organization, oriented to process rather than product, the cost would very likely be somewhat higher than with a contractor selected through competitive bidding. If the building manager hoped to retain civil service arrangements *without* sacrificing cost control—and if he were au-

thorized to use *any* form of contracting—he might set up a new bureaucracy along these lines: The painting staff is unconstrained by routine. Workers are urged to experiment with new methods for painting the White House. Each worker can propose an approach and each submits a budget. The building manager selects the most attractive proposal and appoints its author as the leader of the painting team. If expertise and innovations enable it to do the job for less than the budgeted sum, the team gets to keep any excess, with the leader to decide how it well be shared among the members.

Analogously, if the presidential security director strongly prefers private sector protection services he could, in principle, write a contract enumerating the job requirements in full. Since the output (protection from a range of imperfectly observable risks) cannot be completely defined or measured, payment would have to be based in large part on activity rather than on results. The security firm would provide bodyguards to accompany the president as needed—using an agreed upon set of acceptable security tactics—and would be paid for the time and materials spent on the job.

But in the case of the White House paint job, the result is a bureaucracy that mimics private contracting, and in the case of the presidential protection arrangements, a private contractor comes to resemble a public bureaucracy. The civil service painting contract (as incentives are arranged to achieve low costs and innovation) surrenders control over means. The private sector security arrangements (as the contract dictates protocol and specifies activity rather than results) will lose the virtues of cost-based competition and innovation. . . .

There is an inherent tension, that is, between paying for activity and paying for results. To the extent that civil servants hew to output-based contracts, they will tend to shed both the virtues and the defects of bureaucracy and to take on the virtues and defects of profit-seekers. To the extent that profit-seekers contract to accept instruction, rather than to deliver a specified result, that will tend to assume certain fundamental characteristics of civil servants.

If the White House building manager insists on the option to change in midstream the specifications on the paint job, or reserves the right to suspend work during unanticipated state functions, or requires that the paint be American made, or that the workers be unionized, or Republican, or that they be subjected to security checks, or that specified numbers be minorities or women, then each of these process specifications will tend to erode the efficiency advantages of outside contracting. The rationale for privatization is that competition among contractors will inspire more efficient procedures; as their discretion to innovate is restricted, the benefits of competition are lost. Similarly, if the security director seeks to cut the costs of protecting the president by cutting back on monitoring, eliminating standard procedures, and offering bonuses to agents who experiment with ways to foil assassins more cheaply, breakdowns are as likely as breakthroughs. The issue, in both cases, is how much cost minimization *matters* and how well quality can be *measured*. The rationale for bureaucracy is control over means, either when means are more definable or observable than ends, or when means are important ends in themselves.

The point here is to caution against undiscriminating enthusiasm for hybrid organizations that promise all the virtues of both public and private forms and none of the defects of either. . . . My argument, rather, is that if a task allows for clear evalua-

tion by results, then the bias should be toward turning the task over to profit-seekers, instead of structuring elaborate performance incentives for civil servants. And if a task is so delicate and so difficult to evaluate that the contracts that govern it must be layered with constraints and specified procedures, it may be better to abandon outside contracts and to set up a bureaucracy. . . .

This is not to say that bureaucracies cannot be made more efficient, or that profit-seeking firms cannot be made more broadly accountable, through carefully balanced contracts that tailor the mix of incentives to the task at hand. But it does suggest caution in efforts to make public agencies more businesslike, or to make private suppliers more responsive to considerations that are not covered in the contract. Isadora Duncan once suggested to George Bernard Shaw that the two of them owed it to humanity to have a child who would combine her beauty with his brains. Shaw declined, horrified at the prospect that their joint effort could instead produce the opposite combination—her intellect and his looks. A comparable wariness should inform efforts to blend public and private styles of organization.

From John D. Donohue, *The Privatization Decision* (New York: Basic Books, 1989), pp. 14–17, 79–80, 83–84.

SECTION 2 Breaching the Private-Public Boundary: Informal Organizations in the Administrative Process

"What government may properly and successfully do"—to use Woodrow Wilson's words again—has been a subject of continuing debate among Americans because each generation, it seems, confronts new challenges to the institutional division of labor. Market failures occur in different ways at different times. Members of different generations have also held different views both of social equity and of the symbolic role of government. Not surprisingly, perceptions of the best way to divide responsibilities among private and public actors have changed over time along with changes in citizens' perceptions of political and social priorities. During the Progressive Era, the problem of monopoly power was foremost in reformers' minds. The 1960s, by contrast, were a decade dominated by the drive for social equity, most notably expressed in the civil rights movement and the beginnings of the modern campaign for gender equality.

Today, some commentators urge the wholesale transfer of public functions to private operators through *contracting out, deregulation,* and *privatization.* These terms refer to different ways of dividing three kinds of activities between the private and the public spheres:

> *Decision making:* Someone has to choose whether or not to take on a job, produce a good, or provide a service, and at what level of output to do it.
> *Financing* (including budgeting and—stretching the point a bit—logistics): Someone must arrange to provide the resources needed to do the job.
> *Implementation:* Once the necessary resources have been made available, someone needs to oversee the actual production and manage delivery of the service to clients or customers.

Table 6.1 suggests that there exist many different ways to mix and match these responsibilities. Let's quickly touch on the main idea of each category in this table.

To begin with, all three critical activities may be assigned to public officials—to the entry listed as **public provision** (the top category in Table 6.1). Not only do public officials make the decision to provide a given service, but the work is then financed out of tax receipts and actually carried out by government workers.

With **contracting out,** the production decision and all or portions of the financing process remain within the public sector, but officials move implementation into the private sector. The implementers may be employees of private firms working under contracts with government agencies or (as we'll see in our chapter case) volunteers—that is, implementers working without compensation or at pay levels below those their services would command if they were priced in markets.

Under **regulation**—the table's third category—legislators pass laws and administrators issue rules that set certain requirements: "Install airbags in all new cars"; "Put your household trash out bagged in plastic every Friday." It's then up to the private actors to find the money (financing) and actually to do whatever is necessary for compliance (implementation). **Deregulation** refers to the easing of publicly imposed rules.

Table 6.1 Ways of Distributing the Operating Activities of Decision Making, Financing, and Implementation

	Decision Making	Financing	Implementation
Public Provision			
Public	X	X	X
Private			
Contracting Out			
Public	X	X	
Private			●
Regulation			
Public	X		
Private		●	●
Privatization and Commercialization			
Public			
Private	●	●	●

Deregulation has been under way for some time in certain traditionally regulated industries, such as broadcasting, commercial aviation, and long-distance telephone service.

Privatization and **commercialization** move all three functions into the private sector. The advocates of privatization and commercialization tend to rely heavily on the criterion of efficiency. The case is strongest for privatizing a public function if the government isn't providing it efficiently, and yet there's reason to think that a profit-seeking entrepreneur may be willing to provide the service in question. Commercialization differs from privatization in that it applies to a service that could be performed efficiently either by a government agency or by a private firm; but for some reason—usually a preference for free enterprise—public officials decide to let commercial firms take over the entire action. The rationales for privatization and commercialization may seem confusing at first, but the distinction is an essential one in an era marked by pressures to displace functions from the public sector to the private. Technically, the distinction turns on two kinds of analysis: *cash-flow analysis* (CFA), which applies to financial planning in the private sector, and *cost-benefit analysis* (CBA), which applies to public-policy decision making. We'll take up these two evaluative techniques in Chapter 9.

Public provision, contracting out, and regulation all bring private actors into continuing relationships with government decision makers. Typically these relationships involve repeated contacts across the private-public boundary, as when a government agency regularly renews contracts with a particular supplier on whom it relies for a certain product. Relationships across the private-public boundary often imply reciprocal dependencies. Many private companies count on government contracts for most of their business, and government officials may come to depend on the expertise possessed by members of firms with which they have long standing purchasing agreements.

Even privatization and commercialization—which imply the withdrawal of functions from government for reassignment to private businesses or volunteer organizations—presuppose substantial interactions across the private-public interface. The lobbyists and influence peddlers of whom we hear so much these days earn hefty fees trying to affect the decisions of politicians and public administrators. Which public functions should be privatized? When should commercial firms be licensed to use new technologies that have been developed with public funds? Such decisions aren't made in a vacuum; they involve inputs from interested representatives of private interests.

We thus come to a basic point about the actual workings of the American governance system: *There exists a definite private-public distinction in theory, but private-public interaction—a sharing of work rather than a clear-cut division of labor between private actors and government officials—is more often the reality.*

From Adversarial System to Information Exchange and Negotiation

The relationship that should exist between private actors and public officials can appear in two contrasting images—one adversarial, the other cooperative.

The **adversarial imagery** presents the private and public spheres as separate arenas of action that are inhabited by essentially hostile players. This viewpoint suggests that the private-public relationship can best be managed through processes of arms-length bargaining[7] and adjudicative dispute resolution, although command relationships and strategic actions also have important roles. (Perhaps some of these terms jog your memory. It might be worthwhile to review our list in Chapter 1 of the main techniques for dealing with underdetermination.)

In contrast, the **cooperative imagery** presents the two spheres as interpenetrant, as being populated by private citizens and public administrators working in close, generally amicable contact with one another. The proponents of the cooperative image suggest that everyone will lose if public officials behave toward their private-sector counterparts with suspicion, let alone outright antagonism. Although the adversarial image is the older one, and though it remains vital in some fields of administrative activity (for example, in much of regulatory practice), the cooperative imagery probably gives the more accurate picture of the mechanisms of private-public coordination in our system.

The cooperative imagery underlies the modern theory of **informal organizations.** The proponents of this imagery suggest that the private-public relationship can best be managed through ongoing processes of information exchange in support of persuasion and principled negotiation as techniques for dealing with the problem of underdetermination. Informal organizations exist to provide forums for the exchange of information and the conduct of negotiations. Often, we will see, these informal organizations function as "committees" with recognizable memberships, agreed agendas, and established rules of procedure.

Administrative Adjudication and the Adversarial Model

Within the American administrative process, the adversarial system has traditionally found its purest expression in the workings of the *independent regulatory commissions*—the *IRCs* whose origins we considered in Chapter 4. Thanks very largely to the efforts of Judge Cooley, the first chairman of the Interstate Commerce Commission, regulatory agencies at all levels of our government have tended to function as quasi-judicial institutions—through adversarial proceedings in which lawyers for contending parties offer arguments, often in elaborate trial-like proceedings, in front of adjudicatory officials (administrative law judges, commissioners) who function more or less as judges. It is in these highly legalistic proceedings of the federal regulatory commissions and state public utility commissions that the administrative rituals are most formal, most elaborate, and often most costly.

In the most rigid versions of these adjudicative proceedings, any information used in making a formal decision must be spread openly "on the record" for anyone to see. All representations from either side in an adjudicative proceeding are subject to challenge and cross-examination. Strict rules prohibit even commissioners from talking over certain aspects of pending cases among themselves unless they notify all parties who might want to participate in the discussions. Must the process really be this convoluted and cumbersome?

Gathering and processing information, negotiating, and presenting and debating evidence are among the characteristic activities of modern public administration. They

[7]*Arms-length bargaining:* A term used to describe a negotiation in which the adversaries bargain from positions of financial and emotional distance from each other. No implicit agreements, cozy understandings, or interdependent relationships moderate the bargainers' opposed interests.

are also inherently costly transactions—costly in time, in money, and often in emotional wear and tear on the participating parties. What worked for Judge Cooley isn't necessarily suitable today. The modern administrative process would choke on its own information costs if ways weren't available to cut through some of the formalities. It is this realization that has gradually led many students of the administrative process to move from the adversarial model to an imagery that emphasizes cooperative exchanges of information and amicable negotiation rather than adversarial litigation. Informal organizations are the vehicles used to facilitate these processes. In the context of the present chapter, the relevance of the move toward the cooperative model derives from the fact that the exchanges of information and negotiating processes that this model implies routinely cross the private-public boundary.

The Emergence of Informal Organizations

Just as rational individuals will try to reorganize their relationships when transaction costs in the free market become excessive (recall the New Theorists' answer to the question "Why organize?" from Section 1), so will public officials and their counterparts in the private sector think of forming a new kind of organization—albeit an informal one—when the transactions in which they regularly engage come to involve cumbersome, costly procedures. The adversarial postures of individuals in formal adjudicative proceedings involve precisely the kinds of inconveniences and inefficiencies that give rational individuals incentives to reorganize their relationships.

Once a *formal* organization (usually a hierarchy) has been brought into existence, a network of new communication channels usually evolves. As expressions like "office politics" and "water-cooler conversation" imply, a going organization typically creates a context in which a richer, more permanent set of *informal* relationships can emerge. The network of informal relationships that evolves within a formal organizational structure becomes a system for the gathering, interpretation, and dissemination of knowledge. Information readily flows through the informal communications channels of mature organizations. The "grapevine," scuttlebutt, plain old-fashioned gossip, and channels of "informal consultation" eliminate the need for each individual to hunt out scraps of data as best he or she can. It is this fact which establishes the link between the New Theorists' transaction-cost framework and the theory of informal organizations.

Informal organizations emerge not only within and around formal structures but also as vehicles to facilitate contacts across the boundaries that divide different formal organizations from one another. In the modern administrative system, informal organizations embrace both private actors and public officials. The flows of data run both ways—from private citizens to public officials and also back from government administrators to the citizens who are their clients or customers or the targets of their policies. Thus, it's common today for an official in an executive department or an independent regulatory commission to stay in continuous contact with a host of "networkers" who hold jobs outside that official's formal organization—with staff members of legislative committees, researchers from nearby think tanks, and representatives of lobbying firms and public interest advocacy groups. Additional informal linkages will keep the same official in regular touch with administrators from other agencies, academic specialists, and—as was well illustrated in our reading from Samual Hays in Chapter 5—spokespersons for the professional associations (accountants, engineers, lawyers, and so forth).

Obviously, there are dangers as well as benefits in the institutions of informal organization. Informal contacts can grease the gears of government. But—as proponents of the adversarial imagery emphasize—the lines of communication across the private-public boundary may also be used to facilitate forbidden deal making. The contacts that count may be informal almost to the point of invisibility. In the bit of gossip over lunch with a colleague from a neighboring agency or the innocent phone call from a professional acquaintance may lurk potential ethical problems—made all the more difficult because the efficiency of the administrative process may depend on public officials' continuing participation in the very informal relationships which create the danger. Because participation in informal organizations may create the appearance of impropriety—and sometimes may lead to the reality—there are laws and rules to regulate behavior at the boundary between the private and the public sectors. Illustrative are regulations limiting the freedom of retired public servants to accept jobs from industry figures with whom they have dealt while on the government payroll, laws limiting the right of officials to hold stock in companies whose profitability might be affected by their decisions, and elaborate rules detailing the procedures public officials must use when negotiating contracts with private companies. The list goes on and on.

The rules laid down to govern behavior at the porous private-public interface are among the most important sources of overdetermination in public administration. In Chapter 1 we referred to such criteria as *contextual goals*—requirements that are secondary, in a sense, to the primary goals of the organization, yet which may complicate the pursuit of those objectives. The multitude of requirements that an official must observe when dealing with a representative from a regulated company or contracting for products from a private vendor can't help but slow the decision-making process. Most citizens would probably judge it worthwhile to sacrifice some efficiency for a gain in ethical administration. But acceptance of that trade-off in principle doesn't help us set the balance in particular cases. Again, we find that the essence of administrative excellence isn't in any general formula but in the acumen and judgment of the official who must "feel" the situation, note the circumstances, and carefully weigh the criteria of action.

The Structures of Informal Organizations

Over the years, terms such as *iron triangle, community power structure,* and *issue network* have been coined by scholars to point up specific aspects of the informal organizations that bridge the private-public boundary.

The Iron Triangle

According to the literature, an **iron triangle** is a continuing, informal organization consisting of one or more administrative bureaus, legislative committees or subcommittees, and associations of individuals or companies from the industries that are under the regulatory authority of the bureaus. As the word *iron* suggests, the emphasis is on the allegedly rigid and unbreakable nature of these connections.

The iron triangle model enjoyed its widest acceptance for about twenty-five years after World War II, from 1945 to 1970 or so. There is some dispute today among students of public administration about whether iron triangles even exist, let alone function as essentially conspiratorial arrangements in which public officials (administrators, legislators, legislative staffers) and private representatives (industry lobbyists, trade association staffers) advance their own interests at the expense of the public's. Nevertheless, it is useful to consider the iron triangle model as an example of the abuses to which contacts across the public-private boundary may lead. Moreover, the iron triangle model suggests how the formal structure of an organization can influence certain informal relationships that grow up inside and around it. To develop this point, it would be helpful to go back for a moment in history and note that the formal structure of many of the agencies of the modern administrative state to this day reflect a practice of the Progressives called **counterpart organization.**

In the 1870s and 1880s, as the U.S. economy was rapidly industrializing, the Progressives turned their attention from one new problem to another. When the railroads threatened to choke the flow of commerce with monopolistic rates, the Progressives set up the aforementioned state-level and federal commissions to regulate them. When the electric companies began to build hydroelectric dams helter-skelter across the country, Progressive conservationists called for—and got—legislation setting up a Federal Power Commission to make sure that projects were developed in accordance with systemwide plans for the nation's waterways. Over the years, the agency builders extended this reactive approach in such fields as maritime regulation, securities regulation, natural-gas regulation, and so forth. The growth of agencies with conservation and promotional missions—the Forest Service, the Extension Service of the Agriculture Department, the Bureau of Reclamation, among dozens of others—followed much the same pattern. Whenever an industry seemed a candidate for regulation or promotion (or both), legislators would simply set up a counterpart agency. Often, for good measure, the lawmakers would also create a new legislative subcommittee to oversee the work of the new bureau and periodically consider whether additional legislation might be needed to keep the industry on track. Thus did the outline of the iron triangle appear: a new bureau (angle 1) linked to a new legislative subcommittee (angle 2) as well as to the firms in the particular counterpart industry that would henceforth be under the bureau's administrative jurisdiction (angle 3).

Because members of the iron triangle are in constant contact with one another—discussing problems in the industry; preparing, presenting, or reviewing lobbying documents—relationships of friendship and mutual understanding gradually develop. An agency-industry consensus emerges to guide the decision making of both public officials and company executives. In the iron triangle model, behavior becomes collusive, not adversarial. Industry representatives make campaign contributions to the legislators on the counterpart committee; the legislators in turn recommend subsidies, tariff protections, or tax breaks that favor the client industry. Meanwhile, the expectation of lucrative jobs in private industry ensures sympathetic attitudes on the part of the administrators who implement the laws. According to the proponents of the iron triangle model, the industry eventually "captures" the agency that is supposed to be regulating it.

The Community Power Structure

Whereas the iron triangle theorists focused on the informal organizations that they saw shaping flows of information and patterns of influence within government agencies—especially the independent regulatory agencies—scholars of the **community**

power structure (members of a school known more broadly as the *power elite theorists*) focused on the informal groups that they saw dominating state and local governance.

In 1957, a political scientist named Floyd Hunter published an influential book that depicted decision making in modern societies as a product of informal discussion and behind-the-scenes consensus building. Hunter had intensively interviewed a sample of residents in "Regional City, U.S.A."—a metropolitan area later identified as Atlanta, Georgia. When Hunter asked his interviewees to rank well-known Atlantans, he found a strikingly high level of agreement about the existence of a relatively small, close-knit elite. The support of the members of this elite was required for action on any major project, such as the construction of a new public building complex or a revision of the municipal tax code. Hunter located a few senior business leaders—*not* Atlanta politicians—at the apex of the power pyramid. These leaders operated as an informal committee. In effect, they decided how Atlanta should be run. Then they recruited less-powerful members of area institutions (corporations, agencies of city government, and so forth) and area associations (the bar association, the churches, and so forth) for assistance as needed, depending on the nature and importance of the project. Midlevel public administrators were called in to ensure smoothness in project execution after most of the critical decisions had been made.

(In the years since Hunter published his book, Atlanta has unquestionably become a "national city." Indeed, as the headquarters city of major multinational corporations and host of the 1996 Olympic Games, it has become an international one. With growth and increased relative influence has come a degree of socioeconomic differentiation and dynamism that belies the somewhat parochial, static picture of the Atlanta governance process drawn by Hunter.)

Floyd Hunter on the "Fluid Committee Structure" of Community Policy Making

The committee is a phenomenon which is inescapable in organized community life in American hamlets, villages, small cities, and great metropolitan centers. Almost every activity of any importance in our culture must be preceded by committee work, carried on by committee work, and finally posthumously evaluated by a committee. Regional City is no exception. . . .

The outstanding characteristic of the ordinary committee meeting is its fluidity and its adaptability in adjusting to changing conditions, which are so essentially a part of our modern urban culture. . . .

While it is important to stress the fluidity of committee structure, it must also be pointed out that there is a stable base of personnel who are seen time and again in a variety of committee meetings. There are men in any community who devote large por-

tions of their waking hours to attendance at one meeting or another. Public-relations men in industry and associational secretaries are paid to devote considerable of their time to meeting attendance. It becomes commonplace among this latter personnel group to see one another at committee meetings, and such personnel become familiar with community leaders who operate on a similar level with them. There is a tendency to judge the importance of these meetings by who is in attendance.

Most of the top personnel of the power group are rarely seen at meetings attended by the associational understructure personnel in Regional City. The exception . . . may be found in those instances in which a project is broad enough so that the "whole community needs to be brought in on the matter." Such meetings as bring in the understructure personnel are usually relatively large affairs, rather than the smaller, more personal meetings which characterize policy-determination sessions. . . .

In matters of power decision the committee structure assumes keystone importance. The committee as a structure is a vital part of community power relationships in Regional City.

From Floyd Hunter, *Community Power Structures* (Chapel Hill NC: U. of N. Carolina Press, 1957), pp. 88–90.

Do iron triangles and community power structures really exist? Probably. Most communities require the occasional convening of movers and shakers to set goals and recruit lieutenants who can help "put projects over." Hunter's informal organization of top decision makers represented such a committee of movers and shakers. (And wasn't Anton Kurvaszy, in the last chapter's case, trying to duplicate the informal organizational tactic at the meeting at Antoine's Ante Club?)

But do iron triangles and community power structures function monolithically, almost conspiratorially? Probably not. The iron triangle and community power models both imply that the members of the informal organization enjoy a high level of consensus. In theory, all participants agree on what's good for a particular industry or community. Therefore, they can concentrate their influence and advance their agendas, unbothered by internal dissension. This view, however, discounts the possibility that the members of the group will have honest disagreements over values and goals. Such disagreements are inevitable in human affairs. Most actual decision making occurs in the zone somewhere between the constant conflict envisioned in the adversarial model and the virtually complete consensus represented by the iron triangle or a power elite.

The Issue Network

In 1978 the political scientist Hugh Heclo—recognizing the need for a more accurate description of informal organizations than was implied by the concepts of iron triangle, community power structure, or power elite—introduced the concept of an **issue network:**

[T]he iron triangle concept is not so much wrong as it is disastrously incomplete. . . . Looking for the few who are powerful, we tend to overlook the many whose webs of influence provoke and guide the exercise of power. . . .

The notion of iron triangles and subgovernments presumes small circles of participants who have succeeded in becoming largely autonomous. . . . Iron triangles and subgovernments suggest a stable set of participants coalesced to control fairly narrow public programs which are in the direct economic interest of each party to the alliance. Issue networks are almost the reverse image in each respect. Participants move in and out of the networks constantly. Rather than groups united in dominance over a program, no one, as far as one can tell, is in control of the policies and issues. Any direct material interest is often secondary to intellectual or emotional commitment.[8]

[8]Hugh Heclo, "Issue Networks and the Executive Establishment," in Anthony King, ed., *The New American Political System* (Washington: American Enterprise Institute, 1978), 87–123, pp. 88, 102–103, 118–121.

Heclo wanted to capture the mixture of conflict and consensus that exists in the middle zone where most actual decision making occurs. The concept of an issue network also shifts the emphasis somewhat from participants' self-serving *interests* to the *information* that they must bring as the price of admission to the policy-making process. An issue network, then, is an informal organization created to facilitate flows of information among all the interested parties in a given arena of policy.

Membership in a network (as in one of Hunter's community decision-making "committees") is not formal, and it isn't fixed. Players select in and out, easily forming and defecting from coalitions within the network. Even ostensible adversaries within a broader community of common concerns may belong. In fact, a major purpose of an issue network is to provide a forum in which adversaries can interact, bargain, and reach accommodations. To this end, the participants in the network develop certain rules of acceptable behavior and expectations of give and take. Network members learn that reasonableness and moderation can serve everyone's interests. Even when two participants find themselves in adversarial positions over a specific question, they will recognize their long-term interest in compromise and in obeying the rules of the game. Once understandings are in place, it is unnecessary to renegotiate every point from scratch. Thus a major benefit of the existence of an informal group is a reduction in the players' transaction costs.

None of this is to imply that the members of issue networks periodically assemble in official meetings. Meetings are indeed necessary, but in practice they usually consist of a circuit of conferences stretched out in time and space, rather like the "oldest permanent established floating crap game in New York" celebrated by the gambler Nathan Detroit in Damon Runyon's *Guys and Dolls.* Just about every identifiable area of public policy—from accounting standards in government, through education and environment, to welfare—has its own permanent established floating seminar, its own conference circuit. An administrator in a typical government agency can expect an occasional trip to a trade convention, a formal study-group meeting at a think tank or university, a legislative hearing, an advisory panel session. Some participants in the conference circuit spend much of their lives on the road, trading information with one another in elaborate rituals of exchange across the private-public boundary.

Job switching is another way to transfer information and an important mechanism in the workings of issue networks. An official may work a few years in government to learn firsthand the folkways of public administration. The individual then takes the know-how he or she has picked up to a private law firm, trade association, or industry job. Such job switching is known as "moving through the **revolving door.**" In the new position, the individual may earn a comfortable living telling clients how to deal with the government regulators in the agency he or she has recently left. Of course, the revolving door turns both ways: Government recruiters want private-sector expertise as much as industry recruiters want what experienced public administrators can bring to the business world. The in-and-out employment pattern is especially pronounced in the independent regulatory commissions. It's generally estimated that about half of all sitting commissioners typically come either from the industry that they end up regulating or from law firms with practices (and therefore clients) in the field.

To sum up: *Much of the administrative process today works through information sharing and negotiation in a context of informal organizations.* This, indeed, is the central lesson of the literature on iron triangles, community power structures, and issue networks. Should we be surprised at this conclusion? Not really. When viewed in light of the New Theory, informal organizations are natural responses to the complexities of the modern governance process (we might also say they're rational and even inevitable). Legalistic, adversarial procedures inhibit information sharing and encumber decision making. In contrast, informal organizations make it possible to communicate information, especially across the private-public boundary, more cheaply than would otherwise be possible, thereby reducing transaction costs. Additionally, by creating forums for bargaining, informal groups facilitate decision making in contexts of fragmented authority and competing interests.

Networks may also make it easier for decision makers to narrow the range of criteria they're considering and, hence, may permit them to mitigate the problem of overdetermination. In the network context, it's easier to confine attention to a limited set of values—the values that are shared by participants who have a long-standing interest in the issue. Of course, there's also a downside to these forms of priority setting and policy adjusting; they can imply close-mindedness and parochialism. In Chapter 7 we'll consider the uses of issue networks to mitigate problems of underdetermination and overdetermination in the intergovernmental context, where informal groups have become regular institutions in patterns called picket-fence federalism and executive federalism.

 CHAPTER CASE ● ● ●

Although the author of our chapter reading, John Donohue, cautions against excessive enthusiasm for hybrid arrangements, private-public combinations are increasingly the norm in American public administration, as are mixed structures in which public subsidies supplement revenues from private fees (such as the user fees charged to visitors in our national parks) or in which volunteers work side by side with civil servants and profit-seeking private contractors. The following case deals with the mixing of private and public in one of the most demanding fields of contemporary public administration, the correctional system. How in your opinion does John Donohue's analysis of the trade-offs among voluntary, market-based (profit-seeking), and governmental action play out?

The scenario finds Julio Eller, the county executive in a major metropolitan area with a large city at its center—you will find the setting familiar—readying a proposal for a new "intermediate criminal sanctions" policy. Eller's proposal would almost surely extend the range of support services (substance-abuse counseling, job-placement assistance, and the like) that county correctional officials must contract *out* to private-sector companies. At the same time, Eller is working through the implications of a plan devised by two of his subordinates for yet-another innovative program within the county's correctional system. Under the proposal, idle inmates could volunteer to prepare take-out meals for the area's elderly. Officials of the jail would, in effect, contract *in* from the administrators of the area's meal-support program for senior citizens.

Of course, County Executive Eller isn't functioning in a vacuum. Hizzoner the mayor has learned of some of Eller's plans. The mayor knows that Eller's initiatives, if carried out, will affect citizens of the city. The interests of Hizzoner's inner-city constituents may be rather different from those of residents of the outer suburbs, who provide the county executive's main electoral support. The county executive and mayor have to get together about plans that seem likely to affect the entire area. In the course of their thinking about the condition of the local correctional system, they both find themselves on the receiving end of advice from participants in the local issue networks and community power structures. What's your opinion of the contacts that certain actors in the scenario—Deb Springer of Gus De Gustibus caterers, for example, and John Spadely of the Business Council—make across the private-public boundary?

You should, as always, read the case with pencil in hand and scratch pad at the ready. Some of the materials in the following scenario are rather technical, which is by no means unusual in administrative problem solving. You're likely to find one of our maxims, "Sketch a model," especially pertinent as you try to make sense of the workings of the correctional system. And remember: "Check the numbers." Again, it's helpful to underscore that the details often come in tables of figures that may be hard to look at but are important to read with care nevertheless.

CASE 5
....

Contracting Out and Contracting In: A County Correctional System

It's no secret that politicians around the county have been feeling the heat over the way crime's gotten out of hand. County Executive Julio Eller supposed that just about everyone approved of the "get tough" policies that his criminal justice officials were talking up. But getting tough meant that more convicted lawbreakers were being sentenced, which also meant that decision makers such as Eller had to find ways of adding capacity within the local correctional system. Building new jail cells was one way to do so. The draft resolution that Eller would shortly send to the county commissioners represented a less obvious way to absorb some of the increased flow of convicted offenders.

Eller wanted to send some nonviolent criminals to intensively supervised probation instead of packing them off to prison. Some experts tout the *intermediate criminal sanction (ICS)* as a sentencing option cheaper than traditional incarceration but much rougher on offenders than standard probation. Under Eller's plan, judges would assign certain probationers to special supervisory centers within local communities. These probationers could hold down jobs and have regular contact with their families but would remain under the close scrutiny of officers in the correctional system. Extensive social services, such as substance-abuse treatment and job counseling, would come in the ICS package.

In a *Tribune-Examiner* article, Claire Nagamura, the area's most knowledgeable political reporter, had learned of the ICS proposal and labeled it "Eller's leniency plan." The tag stuck. Some local pundits thought that the stigmatic term *leniency,* whether deserved or not, would undermine County Executive Eller's ability to assemble the political support he'd need to gain approval for his resolution, which follows.

/DRAFT/

A RESOLUTION
Sentencing Guidelines for Nonviolent Offenders

It is the finding and sense of these County Commissioners that rising crime rates, leading to higher levels of incarceration of convicted felons and misdemeanants, has caused corrections-related costs to rise out of proportion to the benefits of imprisonment, and in a way that endangers the fiscal integrity of the county.

To bring corrections-related costs under control, BE IT RESOLVED that sentencing guidelines, pursuant to Sec. 86-324, State Penal Code, and County A-326 (Stat. CC December 1, 1994), be revised to encourage the use of alternative intermediate criminal sanctions wherever feasible, *viz.*—The county sentencing guidelines shall be adjusted to include recommendations of alternative intermediate sentences for all offenders who are otherwise eligible (see below) and whom the sentencing judge deems likely to profit from participation in an intermediate criminal sanctions program, insofar as capacity remains for additional probationers within the program;

PROVIDED THAT offenders convicted of aggravated violent crimes, or crimes committed with lethal weapons, or felony drug-trafficking shall not be normally eligible for alternative intermediate sanctions as a substitute for physical incarceration. THAT IS, present sentencing guidelines will continue to apply to offenders convicted of aggravated violent crimes, or crimes committed with lethal weapons, or felony drug trafficking.

In support of a program of alternative intermediate sanctions, there is herewith obligated a sum of $3,200,000 from general county revenues, to be administered over the present fiscal year and following three years for purposes as outlined in the forgoing sections of this Resolution; provided that an initial expenditure of $35,000 is herewith made for purposes of a planning study prior to initial implementation of the aforementioned alternative intermediate sanctions program.

•   •   •   •   •

When you looked at a map of the area, you could hardly fail to think of a donut, consisting of the city in the center (the hole) and, entirely surrounding it, the county. The configuration of the two jurisdictions required constant negotiations to ensure a reasonably equitable division of their many overlapping responsibilities. As a result, a complicated pattern of interaction—in part competitive, but largely cooperative—had evolved. The pattern presupposed a broad division of labor. The county and city each had its own police force, but the county handled the bulk of welfare services, court services, and correctional facilities ("county jail") for both jurisdictions. Reciprocally, the city owned and managed most public housing facilities (including emergency shelters for the homeless). The city also provided fire protection throughout the county as well as within its own legal borders. Further, city officials ran the public elementary and secondary schools, serving children with addresses in the county as well as those who lived within the limits of the city proper.

But general cooperation didn't necessarily mean that political leaders in the two jurisdictions agreed on every particular program. Hizzoner the mayor wasn't so sure that Julio Eller's new approach to criminal sentencing jibed with his own views about the needs of the justice system in the area. Nor, for that matter, was Hizzoner inclined to think that the county executive's plan supported his own political interests. Actually, Eller hadn't yet formally advised the mayor of his proposal, which probably meant that the "leniency plan" was still in its relatively early stages of development within the county executive's staff.

Eller's plan would require scattered siting of monitoring facilities called *Daily Reporting Centers (DRCs)* and live-in *Community Corrections Centers (CCCs)*. Because the idea was to let convicted offenders continue working, the offenders would have to be placed close to where the jobs were. The mayor feared that a more-than-fair share of these facilities would have to be sprinkled throughout city neighborhoods.

Hizzoner didn't think that the idea of halfway houses for convicted felons would go down very well with his constituents. The typical citizen responds to a proposal for, say, a probationers' or parolees' halfway house with the typical *NIMBY* reaction: "Not in *my* backyard!" Urban planners refer to such a facility as a *LULU*, a "*locally unwanted land use.*" Common reactions among citizens ticketed to receive a LULU in their locale are fear of traffic at unpopular hours, increased crime in the neighborhood, "undesirables" in residence and as regular visitors, and general deterioration of property values—classical negative externalities. Governments are supposed to prevent public bads, not create them. Yet neighborhood negative externalities seemed to be exactly what County Executive Eller's ICS program would unavoidably create. Worse, as far as Hizzoner could see, the burden of a plan hatched mainly to benefit the county would fall disproportionately on citizens of the city.

Hizzoner knew that Julio Eller must have thought through the arguments for and against his proposal from the standpoint of the county's needs. Now the matter needed some serious thought from the standpoint of the city's interests. The mayor buzzed for Peter York. Hizzoner needed more information and a fresh look at the problem. He couldn't rely on rumors and press reports while waiting for Julio Eller to fill him in authoritatively. Hizzoner said that he wanted Peter to find out what he could about the Eller plan, to think it through—"not just the economics, but the political aspects, and any potential administrative hang-ups"—and to report back.

•   •   •   •   •

York strode down the hall from the mayor's office. He turned the knob to the unmarked door of a custodial closet. An inch or so down in the stack of discarded newspapers, left there for recycling, Peter found the edition of the *Trib'-Examiner* that had contained Claire Nagamura's article breaking the news of Eller's pending proposal.

High-Tech Corrections May Be Coming

by Clara Nagamura

Many criminologists and penologists around the country have been urging alternatives to outright incarceration (too costly) and traditional probation (too lenient) for certain convicted offenders. ICSs—intermediate criminal sanctions—typically involve the release of convicted offenders to the community, where they must maintain strict work schedules and submit to intensive supervision.

The prison industry is among the fastest-growing in the state. At about $20 thousand per year to incarcerate a convicted offender, the cost of putting more criminals behind bars mounts up. Overcrowding has already necessitated costly new construction programs for needed cell space.

Although the professionals call them "correctional institutions," critics label prisons training schools for crime. Some criminologists want nonviolent criminals sentenced to controlled living centers in their communities, where they can hold meaningful jobs. In most ICS programs, special social services, such as drug treatment and employment counseling, are intended to prepare convicted offenders for useful positions in society. ICS advocates claim that this outcome is more difficult to achieve with incarcerated individuals, who are constantly exposed to the criminogenic influences of life behind bars.

ICSs currently operate in more than forty states, using a variety of techniques: intensive probation, house arrest, incarceration of young offenders in military-type boot camps, assignment of participants to community-based homes. Electronic monitoring programs are at work in more than thirty states; a probationer wears an ankle bracelet that gives a constant signal indicating her or his whereabouts, or a periodic beep which registers how close the person is to a designated telephone box. In the main, civil service correctional officers run intensive probation programs and boot camps. But nationally, almost all group domicile arrangements and most electronic monitoring services are run by nonprofit private firms working under contract to government agencies and, of course, subject to regulation by public correctional officials.

By no means are ICS programs universally supported, either by professionals in the correctional industry or by ordinary citizens.

Opponents of ICS ask how it can be fair for serious white-collar criminals and drunk drivers who kill pedestrians to be given "country-club sentences." MADD chapters around the country have banded together against "leniency programs" such as the one County Executive Julio Eller will reportedly soon propose to the Board of County Commissioners. Public employee unions and some academic experts also oppose ICSs, claiming that they don't end up cheaper than outright incarceration, either because the wrong detainees are diverted into the programs or because a high percentage of probationers get caught in additional criminal activity or for "technical violations." These offenders get recycled back into prison anyway.

• • • • •

"What about this claim, in the *Tribune-Examiner* story, that ICSs don't necessarily end up saving any money?" Peter York put the question to Henry Hallam, chief of the County Probation Service. It would be Hallam who'd have to run the ICS program if Eller's plan went into effect.

According to Hallam, everything depended on the way ICS would be implemented. Hallam said that ICS *might* work, but *only* if it were confined to the diversion of prison-bound offenders into intensive probation. Lots of offenders, Hallam emphasized, are never ticketed for prison to begin with. The danger, Hallam said, was that judges would divert offenders slated for regular probation or parole into an ICS program. "We won't save the money that goes into incarceration if the convicts who are diverted to ICS wouldn't have been the ones incarcerated, would we?"

Peter asked if, in Hallam's opinion, the special ICS social service programs—drug treatment and the like—would "prepare convicted offenders for useful positions in society" (in the words of Claire Nagamura's article) and so reduce recidivism?

"Some people make the case for ICS on grounds of rehabilitation," Hallam replied, "just as you say. With *intensive* supervision while they're out in the community, 'clients' may develop good habits. And just as the proponents say, because these clients are not in prison, they're not constantly exposed to those bad influences behind the walls. But even if the extra social services *can* successfully rehabilitate offenders, we shouldn't oversell ICS as a preventive of recidivism. Not all prison-bound convicts are eligible for ICS. The rules in all ICS programs I know of exclude murderers, rapists, and anyone who commits a crime with a weapon. They also usually exclude felony drug offenders, who are upward of 50 percent of all convicted offenders in many jurisdictions. In other words, theoretically the main offenders eligible for ICS are serious violators of the traffic laws and those convicted of nonviolent, nondrug 'hard-time' crimes. And they might be the least likely to recidivate in any event."

"'Hard-time' crimes means crimes that qualify under current sentencing guidelines for time in the state penitentiary?" Peter asked.

Hallam shook his head. "Again—*in theory*—yes. But *in practice*, lots of offenders who should go to a penitentiary spend their time in lower-security institutions. Our state high-security institutions are so crowded that more and more offenders of all kinds—even the very worst—are getting warehoused to county jails or work camps. 'Jails' aren't penitentiaries. Jails are only supposed to hold charged prisoners until they make bail or go to trial, and they're only supposed to hold convicted prisoners for a few days until they're taken off to prison. But because of penitentiary overcrowding, county jails are holding inmates who should be in medium- or even high-security state prisons."

According to Hallam, in any number of jurisdictions judges have found the overcrowded conditions in state penitentiaries—the "big houses" depicted in the movies—to constitute "cruel and unusual punishment," which is prohibited by the Constitution. State and local politicians—such as County Executive Eller—have to bring their correctional systems as a whole into compliance with court mandates by building new cell space or devising alternative means of controlling convicted offenders.

"It flows downhill," Hallam said. "The spillover from the state-level institutions becomes a problem for us. What the penitentiaries can't handle, the jails have to. Otherwise offenders go back onto the street in early release—or whatever it takes to meet the judge's decree. The result: *County* jails are overcrowded, meaning the counties have to build additional cell space, which is expensive. That's the real reason why Julio Eller's pushing for a cheaper alternative—in other words, for ICS. At least, Julio *hopes* it'll be cheaper."

Peter asked how early release worked.

"There's a rule of thumb: A typical inmate will serve half to two-thirds of his or her sentence. So if, as I estimate, the average sentence under today's sentencing guidelines is six years—that might apply to your garden-variety stickup artist or repeat check forger—the offender will be out on the street for the last two or three years under the supervision of the parole service."

"Which is you, right?"

"No, I'm *probation*. I'm responsible for convicted offenders who are released back to the community after trial because the judge thinks incarceration is inappropriate. My 13 officers and I are each carrying a caseload of about 210 right now. Jim Ayo, he's *parole*. He's responsible for convicts who still have time to do but are released under supervision. He and each of his 11 officers, for all of the county, have a caseload today of perhaps 175. What's more, the parole caseload is going up these days even more steeply than ours is."

Peter York was taking notes furiously.

"You mustn't forget," Hallam added, "that lots of probationers and parolees don't finish their stints without incident. Maybe 20 percent of probationers and an even higher percentage of parolees commit violations serious enough for revocation of their status. These are your typical recidivists, the ones who get recycled back into the system. They're detained again for technical violations, such as "breaking parole," or they're arrested for new crimes that they commit while on probation or parole. Here's a key point: Because its rules are so strict, and because the probationer is under close watch, ICS adds a whole set of new opportunities for offenders to commit technical violations, some of which will result in their reimprisonment. This kind of recycling back into the system, with a good chance that the repeater will end up in a cell instead of another stint on ICS, is called 'reprocessing.'"

Peter sensed from the emphasis Hallam gave the point that he'd have to think carefully through the implications of the reprocessing phenomenon before giving Hizzoner an assessment of Eller's ICS proposal.

"Of course," Hallam continued, "we don't get much reprocessing under conventional probation or parole. Our caseloads don't allow close enough supervision to catch 'em even in technical violations. But ICS would require more probation and parole officers to provide intensive supervision, with caseloads cut from upward of 200 to 25 or even 15 per probation officer."

Peter completed a quick mental calculation. Obviously, any move to intensive probationary or parole supervision would require a big increase in the numbers of officers on Hallam's and Ayo's forces. The increase in payroll would obviously depend on the number of offenders diverted into the intensive program and on the definition of *intensive*—in other words, the officer-to-client ratio.

Hallam gave Peter a worksheet showing the estimated basic cost per year per offender for each of four levels of correctional supervision. One of Hallam's assistants had worked up a report showing figures for two possible levels of ICS—intensive supervision from a DRC and parole to a residential CCC (see Table 6.2). The additional cost at each level for extra *rehabilitative* and *treatment* services (mostly substance-abuse counseling, plus job training for some offenders) appeared in Column 2, labeled *R&T*. Then in columns 3 through 5, Hallam had indicated the numbers of inmates or clients who might be expected in the county correctional system under three alternatives programs: Program 1, with no ICS option; Program 2, with the same number of convicted offenders under correctional supervision, but redistributed to take advantage of an ICS option; and Program 3, with an expanded throughput, made possible because the addition of ICS permitted judges to give a higher percentage of convicted offenders sentences other than suspended sentences or conventional probation.

Table 6.2 Estimated Population and Cost Statistics for Alternative Correctional Approaches

	(1)	(2)	(3)	(4)	(5)	(6)	(7)	(8)
	Cost in Thousands		Numbers Served			Cost in Millions		
	Basic	R&T	Program 1	Program 2	Program 3	Program 1	Program 2	Program 3
Incarceration	$18	$2	700	500	700	$14.0	$10.0	$14.0
ICS								
DRC*	$ 4	$3	—	100	300	—	.7	2.1
CCC†	$12	$3	—	100	100	—	1.5	1.5
Conventional								
Probation/Parole	$ 2	$0	1,400	1,400	1,200	2.8	2.8	2.4
			2,100	2,100	2,300	$16.8	$15.0	$20.0

*Daily Reporting Center.
†Community Corrections Center (residential).

Notes about Hallam's estimates: It costs $20 thousand/year to incarcerate a prisoner ($18,000 basic prison costs plus $2,000 R&T costs); it costs $7 thousand/year for an ICS client on the DRC schedule and $15 thousand/year on the residential arrangement; conventional probation or parole, which includes no R&T services, costs $2 thousand/year.

Hallam envisions three possible programs, distinguished by the ways in which incarceration, ICS, and conventional probation/parole are mixed.

Which program seems most efficient? Program 1, which assumes 700 behind bars and 1,400 in conventional probation/parole, for a total throughput of 2,100 at an annual cost of $16.8 million per year? Program 2, with 500 incarcerated, 200 in ICS, and 1,400 in conventional probation/parole at $15 million? Program 3, with 700 behind bars, 400 in ICS, 1,200 in conventional probation/parole, and a cost of $20 million?]

•　•　•　•　•

The Older Americans Act, passed by Congress in 1965, authorized the federal government to provide funds that state officials can use to buy meals for senior citizens. The meal-support program was never envisioned as a formal entitlement. That is, elderly Americans can't claim a *right* to a federally subsidized meal. Instead, Congress annually appropriates a lump sum of money, which is then distributed to states according to an allocative formula based on their populations of senior citizens. State officials, working with the county administrators who actually disburse the money, have considerable discretion under the law to decide how their allotments should be spread among local jurisdictions. The budgetary decisions of the state and local officials largely determine, for each locale, the number of meals to be prepared, the method of delivery, and even the kinds of food to be served.

Over the years, increasing food costs have effectively reduced the nutritional value of a dollar spent in the meals program. At the same time, the number of elderly Americans has increased. Local program administrators have therefore tried various expedients to stretch their federal dollars. By changing the mode of delivery (for example, switching from home-delivered meals to group service in senior citizen centers) or by relying more heavily on unpaid volunteers, officials in some locales have buffered their programs against the gradual shrinkage in the program's financial base. Even so, few program administrators have ever been able to meet the entire need. In most areas, there are substantial waiting lists of qualified elderly citizens for enrollment in the federally assisted meals program.

County Executive Eller had watched with interest, but with no deep level of involvement, as Bryn Geraci, who ran nutritional programs for the county's Department of Welfare Services, developed a highly popular approach to the senior citizens' meals program. Under Geraci's direction, the DWS program had gradually deemphasized congregate dining plans in favor of home-delivered hot lunches. Of course, the delivery approach cost more per plate than did the dining-center approach. But home-delivered hot meals apparently did a better job of meeting the needs of elderly citizens who had physical or psychological problems getting out for a daily lunch at a senior center. Furthermore, home delivery reduced pressures to institutionalize frail elderly citizens. In other words, Geraci's home-delivered meals program represented more than a nutritional supplement, for it supported eligible citizens' yearnings for independence and extended their ability to remain in their own homes.

Workers in the meal-delivery program had known for some time, however, that the effective shrinkage of available federal funds would sooner or later force the program into a crisis. Responding to inexorable financial pressures, and acting without County Executive Eller's knowledge, Bryn Geraci had negotiated a new understanding with Warden Tracy Grubb of the county jail. Geraci and Grubb hoped to launch a new voluntary work program at the jail, in which inmates would "donate their labor" by preparing hot meals and packing them for delivery to elderly citizens.

Warden Grubb had often expressed a desire to develop work programs, recreation programs—in fact, *any* kind of programs—that could be used to occupy some of the excess free time of her inmates. Grubb thought it critical to reduce the idleness that is a primary source of trouble in any prison. Geraci, who heard about Grubb's search for work-program ideas through the county workers' rumor mill, suggested that meals be prepared by inmates who wanted to earn "good-time" credits toward earlier parole. The prepared meals would then be delivered to eligible senior citizens by other volunteers, mostly from local churches and synagogues and a few neighborhood service organizations.

For years, the county had relied on Gus De Gustibus, Inc., to purchase and prepare the meals-program food. Obviously, DWS's contract with Gus De Gustibus couldn't be renewed if the jail program went into effect and the county correctional system became the official preparer of home-delivered meals. It made for a bit of a problem: Bryn Geraci had certainly been satisfied with the catering work of Gus De Gustibus. On the other hand, the new volunteer arrangement offered her a chance to expand and improve a program for some of the most deserving citizens in the county—this, moreover, in a period of cutback management throughout government. The use of virtually free labor by volunteering inmates of the county jail, with follow-up delivery service—also mainly by volunteers—would mean that labor costs could be all but eliminated from the meal-delivery program. Whereas hot lunches under the existing contract with Gus De Gustibus cost an average of $1.27 per meal, a program of alternating hot (Styrofoam-packaged) and cold (cardboard-boxed) lunches could be managed for $0.81 per meal. This was a nice way, indeed, not only to preserve a popular program but also probably to extend it by stretching federal dollars.

Bryn Geraci's staff, Tracy Grubb's county jail officials (and even the inmates), and of course the county's elderly citizens could be expected to see the new plan as a winner all around. The Gus De Gustibus relationship had been a satisfactory one while it lasted, but Geraci, after considering all the factors, found the case for change to be compelling. She expected just about everyone else—other than the proprietors and employees of Gus De Gustibus, Inc.—to react the same way.

●   ●   ●   ●   ●

Like Peter York, Emma Xavier worked on Hizzoner the mayor's immediate staff. She had heard about York's latest assignment—to research and report on County Executive Eller's ICS plan—and asked to see Peter briefly. Immediately upon entering Emma's office, Peter detected a certain awkwardness, almost an embarrassment, in her manner. Emma declared that she "didn't want to get out of line" but that there was "an angle to 'Eller's leniency plan'" that she thought worth calling to Peter's attention. Peter's assignment, of course, was to collect enough facts and opinions to support a rounded report to Hizzoner on the desirability of a move to ICS, taking both city and county concerns into consideration. He wasn't troubled at the thought of getting whatever input Emma wanted to give him.

"You know about my sister's boy, don't you?" Emma asked.

It had happened before Peter joined the mayor's staff, but word of a tragedy affecting anyone in an office finds its way even to newcomers. A drunk driver had hit and killed Danny Westa, the thirteen-year-old son of Emma's sister Sheila.

"Well, Sheila's been active . . . she's been *really* active in MADD, helping to sponsor the SADD chapter over at Bridger High and the like, ever since."

"Mothers Against Drunk Drivers," Peter interpolated.

Emma nodded, and added: "And 'Students Against Drunk Drivers' at the local high school. Anyway," she continued, "Sheila came to the house last night, very upset about this new sentencing plan . . . 'Eller's leniency plan.' The story about ICS in the *Tribune-Examiner* said it'll apply to drunk drivers."

By this point in his research, Peter knew that Emma was right: In most states, the majority of offenders selected for ICS are individuals with no prior pattern of career criminality who are convicted of "major traffic" offenses (a code word for drunk driving) or crimes against property.

"I can't begin to tell you what it does to a family, something like losing Danny," Emma said, speaking slowly. "Sheila's in counseling and under a doctor's care, and I don't know how long she can hold her job. She works in the city Housing Department. With Sheila's MADD work, and a depression she's fallen into, . . . well, her mind's not on her work, that's for sure." Emma described her sister's anger and outrage over the county executive's proposal for a new law that, she thought, would let drunk drivers off the hook. Emma ended with a low-key pitch for Peter "not to forget the Danny Westas who've been the victims of these guys that Eller means to give free rides from now on."

●   ●   ●   ●   ●

Marjorie Masters of County Executive Eller's staff—Peter York's next official interviewee after his meeting with Henry Hallam—said that some version of the standard two-dimensional sentencing-guideline framework is currently used by federal judges and in almost all state and lower courts. The first dimension in this framework ranks the seriousness/severity of a crime; the second ranks the offender's past criminal record and probability of rehabilitation. Currently, conviction of a crime high on the first dimension—especially a felony involving violence or a gun—earns the offender mandatory time behind bars. Mandatory hard time also results for a less serious crime if the offender ranks high on the second dimension.

In Masters's words: "A more favorable combination of seriousness/severity and record/rehabilitation potential probably gets the offender probation. The offender then stays on the streets as long as he or she remains 'clean,' which means in practice as long as the probation officer thinks the offender is clean. Since a typical probation officer has a caseload of from 175 to 225 clients, there's not much chance of close supervision, is there?"

Peter nodded agreement.

Marjorie Masters went on: "Yet there—in probation and parole—is where most convicted offenders are these days. Because of overcrowding in the prisons, 3 out of 4 convicted felons in the criminal justice system are under 'alternative sentencing.' That's a euphemism for probation or early release on parole."

County Executive Eller's proposal, Masters went on, was simply to add an intermediate level of sentencing between physical incarceration and conventional probation or early parole. "Under ICS, a convicted felon who has no record of violence or drug-related crime goes into an intensive supervision program. The individual has to keep a strict daily itinerary, hold a steady job, keep a curfew, and take extensive counseling and substance-abuse treatment if that's applicable. The individual must live in an approved residential location, and—this is why it's called 'intensive'—has to respond to random phone calls, as many as seven or eight a day to check on his or her whereabouts. In one version of ICS, the client also has to report every twenty-four hours to a designated DRC [the Daily Reporting Center mentioned in Hallam's display in Table 6.2]. In other versions, the offender has to wear an electronic beeper bracelet or live in a Community Corrections Center. A CCC or 'halfway house' gives an even tighter form of supervision."

"Pretty elaborate," York commented.

Masters nodded. "The caseloads would probably have to go down, when you average it all out, from maybe 200 per officer in conventional probation or parole to 20 or even fewer in ICS. *That* means more probation officers, more parole officers, and lots more social service workers to give counseling and treatment. Those extra workers and services all add to the costs. The bottom line is, ICS probably turns out to be cheaper than building new cells, but not by much. Also, the costs are spread differently: ICS increases labor costs and funnels money to nonprofit companies where most of the counselors work; new cell construction, of course, involves capital outlays and makes work for the building contractors."

• • • • •

Bryn Geraci and Tracy Grubb both had plenty to do during the few weeks that remained before the current contract with Gus De Gustibus lapsed. Together, the two of them had to arrange new supporting logistics for the senior citizens' meal service. Someone from the state's Department of Agriculture would have to plan and oversee the purchasing of food for the volunteer inmates to prepare, since Gus and Debra Springer—the proprietors of Gus De Gustibus—would have to relinquish these functions as well as food-preparation responsibility when their contract ended and the inmate program took effect. (Senior citizens and inmates, who averaged much younger ages, had different nutritional needs; Warden Grubb doubted that the current staff dietician could handle both the home-delivered meals and the in-house work-load.) Meal delivery schedules would also need revamping to accommodate the change to an all-volunteer force. But Geraci had already completed the hardest task—notifying the Springers in writing about the impending termination of their long-standing arrangement with the meals program.

•   •   •   •   •

Cindy Tatnall worked down the hall from County Executive Eller. Cindy was a special assistant responsible for "liaising" (the actual term in Cindy's job description) with the senior administrators of the county sheriff's force and county correctional staffs.

"What Margie Masters told you," Cindy said to Peter, "is correct as far as it goes. But there's more you should know.

"Here," Cindy said, directing Peter's glance to a diagram that she had roughed out on scratch paper. "You want to know about the cost picture—will ICS really save money, the way Julio Eller thinks it will? That depends partly on the inherent characteristics of ICS versus incarceration, at one extreme, and conventional probation or parole at the other. Almost as important, costs will also depend on the way we organize services in an ICS program—that is, on whether we provide rehabilitation and treatment, such as substance-abuse counseling, through public agencies or through privatization."

Peter looked at Cindy's diagram, a simple sketch of axes at right angles. Cindy labeled the axes as shown in Sketch 6.1.

"At one extreme, we have literal physical confinement—prison." Cindy pointed to the top range of her diagram along the vertical axis. "At the 'extreme of the extreme,' there's the incorrigible inmate who spends lots of time in solitary; then there's a lesser level of confinement—say time in an overcrowded cell in a high-security prison." As she spoke, Cindy drew her pencil tip in a downward direction. "Coming down still far-ther, there's the greater freedom an inmate has on 'easy time,' which might be time in a medium-security joint. And so forth."

Peter didn't get it.

"My point," Cindy said, "is that ICS is *also* a form of physical confinement, though we usually don't think of it that way. In fact, we usually think of it as just the opposite. But those telephone calls or electronic bracelets ensure that the offender's actions are limited to known, approved locations. ICS is still physical confinement, but just farther down on the continuum from low-security incarceration. At the least restrictive extreme, conventional probation or parole is also a method of confinement, but an extremely lax and uncertain one. The parolee can't leave the county; he or she has to check in from time to time. But given the caseloads that our probation and parole officers carry, who knows for sure from day to day what the clients are really doing or even where they really are?"

Cindy continued: "In theory, as the level of confinement decreases, you'd expect the cost of carrying out the sentence to decrease as well." Peter watched Cindy draw

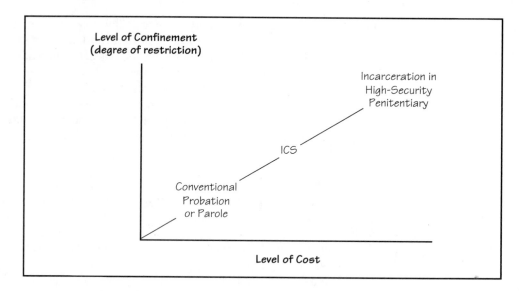

Sketch 6.1 Relationship between Level of Confinement and Level of Cost

the diagonal line, starting from the top right corner of her graph (high level of confinement and high cost—the maximum-security inmate) to the bottom left corner
(low level of confinement and relatively low cost—the conventional probationer or
parolee).

"Almost no one wants to privatize our high-security penitentiaries. But as we
move through the ICS programs toward conventional probation and parole, people
begin to make the case for privatization and contracting out." Cindy pulled her finger
down to the left, along the diagonal of her diagram. "Nonprofit firms from the private
sector already manage most community-based halfway houses for parolees. Private
nonprofit firms also do most of the substance-abuse counseling, working under contracts with the correctional department. That's true all around the country."

Peter nodded.

"What's more, private contractors already provide some of the services that are
needed at most institutions of incarceration: business services, such as food and laundry, and social services, such as alcohol and drug counseling.

"And so," Cindy concluded, "a new ICS program would add a whole new set of
questions. How should public and private implementation be mixed together at the
different points along the diagonal? What will be the impacts of different public-
private mixes on costs within the correctional system?"

•   •   •   •   •

Gus Springer, the founder of Gus De Gustibus, and his wife Debra, who managed the business end, had been political contributors of Julio Eller's since Eller had
first run for a seat on the Board of County Commissioners some twelve years earlier.
For most of that period, Gus De Gustibus had catered the county DWS's meals-
delivery program.

Debra Springer had once explained to Eller that the Gus De Gustibus contract with the DWS wasn't very profitable. For years, the Springers had been turning out 550 hot lunches every day at about a 5 percent markup over their costs. Why were Debra and Gus willing to accept so modest a profit margin? Partly, Debra claimed, because they thought the senior citizen service deserved support as a matter of plain civic responsibility. But she admitted that it was mainly because the arrangement served a worthwhile business interest for the firm. The meals contract guaranteed a steady cash flow from the DWS. The predictability of DWS payments let the Springers keep their employees at work through the ups and downs of the business cycle and the resulting fluctuations in demand for catering.

County Executive Eller looked at the letter he had just received from Debra Springer:

Dear Julio:

We have just been informed that the services of Gus De Gustibus, Inc., will soon be terminated as caterers for the county's meals program.

Gus and I hope very much that you will reconsider this decision. The idea that food preparation for the meals program will henceforth be conducted by prisoners of the county jail as a cost-saving measure flies in the face of the tradition that we have always honored, of not forcing area businesses and workers to compete with lower-paid public employees when services of equal value can be procured from private vendors. In this case, we are facing the possibility of layoffs in our workforce not only because of business going to a competing government agency but also because convicted criminals will now be doing the work on a supposedly "volunteer" basis.

After discussing the notification of the impending change in the meals program catering policy with John Spadely, Horace Epson, and Betsy Kwidzinsky [Eller recognized the names of these top officers of the local Business Council], Gus and I feel that a direct appeal to you for a reconsideration is in order. From the standpoint of Gus De Gustibus and its employees, serious economic implications are at stake here. But all of us who have discussed the new meals plan also agree that a matter of principle is involved.

Please give Gus or me a call so we can arrange to talk with you directly about the case for reconsidering the cancellation of our long-standing contract with the county.

Yours very truly,
/s/ Deb
Debra Springer
Vice President
Gus De Gustibus, Inc.

•   •   •   •   •

Hizzoner the mayor studied the letter from John Spadely, president of the Business Council. Spadely stressed that he had decided to contact the mayor directly only after discussing Claire Nagamura's recent *Tribune-Examiner* articles on "Eller's leniency plan" with other council members. Thanks to Nagamura's dogged pursuit and reporting of the ICS story, Eller's plan had become a matter of open discussion in the region, even though the proposal itself hadn't yet been formally introduced before the Board of County Commissioners.

Why, Spadely asked, had the mayor been silent regarding Eller's ICS plan? Why hadn't he assured his constituents that "this irresponsible, destructive plan to sprinkle convict halfway houses around the area" (Spadely's words) would be killed while still in the talking stage? Spadely's letter continued:

> The sentiment throughout the community is widespread that Eller's leniency plan would mean dozens of minijails scattered throughout our neighborhoods. To make matters worse, the criminals involved would not even be under direct control. They would be eating and sleeping, or at least regularly checking in, at centers in the middle of populated areas.
>
> This leniency plan for convicted criminals could become the loose canon of local politics. No one can tell where it would lead, and that is the reason why I and those for whom I speak think it necessary for you to assert leadership in opposition to any revision of the sentencing guidelines that are now in use.
>
> If you would like to discuss this important issue at greater length, I will be happy to set up a luncheon at Tenpins with some of the civic leaders whom I know to be deeply concerned.
>
> As ever,
> /s/ J.
> John Spadely
> Chairman and President
> First National Bank

• • • • •

The same day that County Executive Eller received Debra Springer's letter and the mayor heard from John Spadely, Peter York found a note from Cindy Tatnall on his desk:

> Peter:
>
> Did I mention that we were getting some labor economists from the university to do an input-output (I-O) study of the public-private issue? We want to find out the cost of different proportions of work in three categories of correctional functions by public and private teams and also how many jobs will be generated around the area.
>
> As you know, no one's seriously proposing that we throw our uniformed correctional officers out of work and hire private operators to take over guards' jobs in our prisons. (They're talking about that kind of privatization in some areas—but not here.) In other words, our studies assume that the *core correctional functions* will continue to be publicly provided. But different mixes of public and private are possible for the ancillary services needed to support the core functions.
>
> There are the so-called *essential business services,* such as laundry and plumbing and so forth; those functions could be done by civil servants, by inmates themselves, or by

contractors—or by some combination of the three kinds of workers. In a third category are *critical social services* such as job counseling and substance-abuse treatment; those functions could be done either by members of the corrections department or, as is common, by specialists from outside firms working under contract. You'll see that, because of union wage scales and civil service pay schedules, the costs of labor-intensive services differ, depending on whether they're provided by government employees or private contractors.

We asked the I-O people to consider how costs and total levels of employment might change if we move to different percentages of these functions carried out by public employees or under contract. So at a constant level of costs, how we mix public and private will influence how many jobs are supported.

Here's the preliminary table of the I-O people's findings. You should be able to interpret the figures with a little study. As you can see, the economists who did the research took two different cuts at the question: (1) an approach that relies mainly on public provision for all three categories of functions and services and (2) an approach in which services are privatized whenever it seems to make economic sense to do so.

Hope this helps you. Call me if you have questions.

Cindy

Input-output analysis, Peter York knew, is a technique that economists use to trace through the impact of a change in the demand for the products of a given industry. Those products (*outputs*) require certain raw materials (*inputs*). Labor is an important input in almost all production sequences. By how much will a change anywhere in the sequence change the demand for a particular input, such as labor? The answer will depend on the type of production process being used. In the ICS case, different ways of mixing public and private provision would correspond to different kinds of production processes (see Table 6.3).

Table 6.3 Costs to the Public and Jobs Created under Alternative Correctional Programs
Estimates assume equal numbers of inmates/clients served (from Column 5, Table 6.2) under both alternatives

| | (1) | (2) | (3) | (4) | (5) | (6) |
| | | Alternative 1 Mainly Public Provision | | | Alternative 2 Emphasize Contracting Out | |
Functions Performed or Provided	Total Costs (millions)	Distribution between Public/Private (percent)	Total Jobs	Total Costs (millions)	Distribution between Public/Private (percent)	Total Jobs
Confinement*	$ 7	100/0	160	$ 6	80/20	120
Business services	9	80/20	175	8	40/60	225
Social services	4	50/50	100	6	20/80	200
	$20		430	$20		545

*Confinement cost is estimated as a residual after the costs of directly charged and allocated business services and social services are deducted from the actual total cost of incarceration operations.

The salient finding in Cindy Tatnall's input-output study seemed to be that the higher the fraction of functions performed by private contractors, the more workers who would be employed. But—presumably because civil service pay scales were for some reason higher—private-sector employees working under contract would apparently carry significantly lower payroll costs per worker. Peter assumed that Cindy's I-O table would find its way, somehow, into the hands of local union leaders and others (including politicians) who were interested in the quality and level of economic activity in the area. All concerned would no doubt make it their business to think through the implications for their respective constituencies and then communicate their druthers regarding ICS to Hizzoner the mayor and County Executive Eller.

• • • • •

On his desk the next morning, Peter York found a note in the mayor's own hand:

Pete:

A delegation from Amnesty International will be in my office late tomorrow. The Amnesty people are making a national tour to survey American penal practices. I told the leader of the delegation that I'd brief his group regarding what I think we should do at the level of a local correctional system. The Amnesty people understand the pressures any mayor faces these days: "Get tough on crime," "Cut spending," etc. I know you haven't had time to do a thorough study of the ICS idea, but I need some thoughts now anyway.

Will you write up a one-page outline of initiatives you think I should get behind, briefly justifying why we should move in the directions you recommend?

• • • • •

Julio Eller wasn't altogether pleased that word of his ICS proposal had leaked to the press—although, to be fair, he had to admit that it was almost impossible to keep a major initiative secret for long from a diligent reporter with excellent sources, such as the indefatigable Claire Nagamura. Eller was even less happy about vague rumors to the effect that some individuals in his own county administration had doubts about the wisdom of the ICS plan and might drag their feet when preparing staff work to support the presentation of Eller's resolution before the Board of County Commissioners. Least encouraging of all were indications of significant opposition from some citizen groups. All the signs suggested that Eller should probably give his plan a second look. He arranged meetings with the following three individuals, whose inputs, he thought, might be helpful at this stage:

Sidney "Ham" Hambricht

Ham Hambricht had served as Julio Eller's campaign manager in the last two elections. Hambricht's particular achievement had been to position Eller as the candidate of suburban voters sometimes described as "enterprisers" or "upbeats." These voters tend to be relatively young (born after 1960), well educated, moderately affluent. They want efficient government, low taxes, clean and peaceful neighborhoods, and a favorable business climate. By reputation at least, these voters are also mildly anti-union and strongly "anti-bureaucrat" (whatever that means). Critics charge that Hambricht's campaigns, keyed on themes attractive to enterprisers and upbeats, alienated inner-city and minority voters. Eller now thinks he had better check out how ICS is likely to play with his base electoral constituency. Who better than Ham could advise him?

Cindy Tatnall

Cindy Tatnall's job put her in touch not only with the county correctional staff but also with the main law enforcement officials of the region—the city police, the county sheriff's department, the county courts, and the county attorney's office. Tatnall seemed the best person to help County Executive Eller brainstorm the pros and cons of ICS from the standpoint of administrative feasibility.

Mona Schwanke

Mona Schwanke of AFSCME[1] had already phoned County Executive Eller's office to request an appointment. Eller knew that Schwanke's call must have been motivated by rumors of impending changes in the division of work within the county correctional system. Eller had no doubt that Schwanke could represent the views not only of unionized civil servants in the county but also of those whom she liked to call "the good, hardworking people of the area."

Questions for Discussion
....

The following queries and exercises might help you frame your thoughts and organize a discussion of the case.

1. What's the story? What are the main conflicts, and how do they translate into specific choices to be made by the principal figures in the case?

2. Does the ICS plan sound, at first hearing, like a good idea? How about Bryn Geraci's cost-saving plan for the meals program—at first look, is it a good idea? Based on your assessment of John Donohue's analysis in our chapter reading, how do you feel about the proposed hybrid arrangements (part private, part public; part voluntary, part paid) in the ICS and senior citizens programs? In your opinion, are any aspects of a correctional system (or perhaps all aspects of such a system) inherently and unambiguously public in nature? What about the various functions in a program to support senior citizens (such as home-delivered meals)? Do any of the theories that are customarily used when assigning functions to private or to public institutions suggest how to proceed on the ICS proposal, which would probably result in increased contracting out? Do the paradigms of assign-

[1] *AFSCME:* The American Federation of State, County, and Municipal Employees.

ment suggest how to proceed on Bryn Geraci's proposal for the meals program, which would move work from the private sector into the county jail?

3. What do we know from the case write-up about the main players' relationships—personal and professional, private and public? Think especially about the relationships between (a) Julio Eller and Hizzoner the mayor; between (b) Eller and county officials Grubb and Geraci; between (c) Hizzoner and the Springers; and between (d) the mayor and John Spadley. Might any of their problems be less difficult if they had developed different kinds of working relationships than the ones depicted?

4. Obviously, neither the county executive nor Hizzoner the mayor controls the other. (There even seems to be some doubt about the degree of control that County Executive Eller has over subordinates in his own official family.) What efforts might Julio Eller have taken to create a situation in which he would now enjoy greater control—and hence have a better chance to implement initiatives that he favors? Which of the main ways of dealing with conditions of underdetermination (persuasion, restructuring, litigation, negotiation, strategic opposition) seems to you most applicable to the conflicts between Eller and the mayor? Most applicable to the rift between the mayor and the members of the Business Council?

5. What are the goals of County Executive Eller and Hizzoner the mayor? What criteria would you hope each would keep in mind as he deals with the other and with the proponents or opponents of policies that have real implications for each man's political future? To the extent that Eller and Hizzoner face overdetermined problems, would priority setting, parameter changing, or policy adjusting be useful techniques for them to employ?

6. "Sketch a model"; "Check the numbers." Can you outline the way offenders flow through the correctional system? How might a model of the process help one assess whether an ICS program would be more likely to decrease or to increase correctional costs? (Hint: Do you identify the reprocessing rate as a key variable in your model of the throughput? How do costs vary with the reprocessing rate? On what other variables in your model does the reprocessing rate in particular—and ICS program costs in general—depend?)

7. What implications do you draw from Cindy Tatnall's input-output estimates? Do her numbers make the ICS decision easier or harder? Why?

8. What points do you think Peter York should emphasize in the thought piece about the correctional system that he's to prepare for the mayor?

9. "Where you stand depends on where you sit." Put yourself successively in the positions of Ham Hambricht, Cindy Tatnall, and Mona Schwanke. How, in their shoes, would you recommend that County Executive Eller proceed in the ICS matter?

FOR FURTHER READING

For overview treatments of the New Theory, see

> Arrow, Kenneth, *The Logic of Organization* (New York: Norton, 1974).
> Garvey, Gerald, *Facing the Bureaucracy: Living and Dying in a Public Agency* (San Francisco: Jossey-Bass, 1993).
> Moe, Terry, "The New Economics of Organization," 28 *American Journal of Political Science* (November 1984), 733.

For additional discussions of the theory of the private-public distinction, see

> Bozeman, Barry, and Stuart Bretschneider, "The 'Publicness Puzzle' in Organizational Theory: A Test of Alternative Explanations of Differences between Public and Private Organizations," 4 *Journal of Public Administration Research and Theory* (April 1994), 197.
> Davis, Otto, and Andrew Whinston, "On the Distinction between Public and Private Goods," 57 *American Economic Review* (May 1967), 365; technical and difficult, but brilliant—a classic source on the subject.
> Musgrave, Richard, and P. B. Musgrave, *Public Finance in Theory and Practice* (New York: McGraw-Hill, 1980), chaps. 3–4; arguably still the most accessible presentation of the underlying economic theory of the private-public distinction.

Among the more influential recent works on privatization and contracting out (in addition to Donohue's *The Privatization Decision*) are

> Henke, Steven, ed., *Prospects for Privatization* (New York: Academy of Political Science Press, 1987).
> Kettl, Donald, *Sharing Power* (Washington: Brookings Institution, 1993).
> Savas, E. S., *Privatization: The Key to Better Government* (Chatham NJ: Chatham House, 1987).

The following books, taken together, provide a useful overview of the nonprofit sector:

> Herman, Robert D., et al., *The Jossey-Bass Handbook of Nonprofit Leadership and Management* (San Francisco: Jossey-Bass, 1994).
> O'Neill, Michael, *The Third America: The Emergence of the Nonprofit Sector in the United States* (San Francisco: Jossey-Bass, 1989).
> Salamon, Lester M., *America's Nonprofit Sector: A Primer* (New York: Foundation Center, 1992); probably the best overall survey.

On the strengths and weaknesses of voluntary help in public projects, see

> Brudney, Jeffrey, *Fostering Volunteer Programs in the Public Sector: Planning, Initiating, and Managing Voluntary Activities* (San Francisco: Jossey-Bass, 1990).
> Fisher, J. C., and K. M. Cole, *Leadership and Management of Volunteer Programs: A Guide for Volunteer Administrators* (San Francisco: Jossey-Bass, 1993).
> O'Connell, Brian, "What Voluntary Activists Can and Cannot Do for Agencies," 49 *Public Administration Review* (September–October 1989), 486.

Of special pertinence to the theories of the adversarial and cooperative images is

Kelman, Steven, "Adversary and Cooperationist Institutions for Conflict Solution in Policy Making," 11 *Journal of Policy Analysis and Management* (Spring 1992), 178.

On informal organizations in general, and iron triangles and issue networks in particular, see

Kirst, Michael W. "Policy Issue Networks: Their Influence on State Policy Making" 13 *Policy Studies Journal* (December 1984), 247.

Gormley, William T. "Regulatory Issue Networks in a Federal System" 18 *Polity* (Summer 1986), 595.

Meier, Peter, "An Evaluation of Community Development Block Grant Decision-making: Executive Dominance versus Issue Networks" 18 *Policy Studies Journal* (Spring 1990), 573.

Overman, E. Sam, "Iron Triangles and Issue Networks of Information Policy" 46 *Public Administration Review* (Special Issue: November 1986), 584.

Quirk, Peter, *Industry Influence in Federal Regulatory Agencies* (Princeton NJ: Princeton U. Press, 1981).

On intermediate criminal sanctions and community corrections, see

Byrne, James M., et al., *Smart Sentencing: The Emergence of Intermediate Sanctions* (Newbury CA: Sage, 1992).

Maynard-Moody, Steven, et al., "Community Corrections as an Organizational Innovation: What Works and Why," 46 *Public Administration Review* (July–August 1986), 301.

Petersilia, Joan, "Intensive Probation and Parole Supervision," in Michael Toney, ed., 17 *Crime and Justice* (Chicago: U. of Chicago Press, 1993).

▼◆●■▼◆●■▼◆●■▼◆●■▼◆●■▼◆

CHAPTER 7

Federalism and Intergovernmental Relations

If the most important distinction affecting the practice of public administration is, arguably, the one between the private and public sectors, the next most basic distinction may be the one between the national and the state or local levels of our government. This distinction was once captured with sufficient precision by the familiar term *federalism*. But that term is perhaps no longer adequate to describe our complex modern system of overlapping jurisdictions.

Most Americans can recollect stories heard in a civics class or read in a history text about the "Great Compromise," in which big-state emissaries to the 1787 Constitutional Convention made important concessions to the representatives of the small states. The bargain between the authors of the big-state Virginia Plan and the small-state New Jersey Plan made possible our federal union—a bilevel structure with a national government responsible for matters of general concern and a multitude of state governments, each responsible for issues of local interest. (Do you see how the distinction between "general concern" and "local interest" can be developed as a paradigm of assignment, a test for the apportionment of certain powers to the national government and the reservation of others to the separate states?)

Yet Americans today don't just have the two governments that the bilevel imagery, and the very word *federalism,* suggests. Collectively, Americans have multiple governments—some eighty-three *thousand* of them, by one estimate that's common in the literature. This figure includes the central government headquartered in Washington, the fifty state governments, thousands of county and municipal governments, and all manner of special districts (minigovernments set up to manage local school operations, consolidated planning for an area's sewer system, and the like). For the complexus of structures and processes in which the powers and responsibilities of the different levels of government have become enmeshed, public administrationists have coined the term **intergovernmental relations (IGR).**

Whereas, in contemporary parlance, *federal relations* refers to arrangements between Washington (that is, the national government) and the states, the broader term *intergovernmental relations* refers to national-state, state-local, national-local, and every other kind of relationship permitted within our system of decentralized, dispersed governmental powers. Officials are constantly adapting, modifying, and reinventing rela-tionships within our IGR system, giving rise to the variety of *isms* suggested by such terms as *cooperative federalism, regulatory federalism, picket-fence federalism,* and *executive federalism.* By the end of this chapter, you'll appreciate how these arrangements bear on the work of today's public administrators. You should also have some sense of the par-adigms of assignment that can be applied to our IGR system—that is, some sense of the principles by which different kinds of public functions are typically assigned to one or another level of government.

SECTION 1

The Design and Development of Our Federal System

Technically, a **federal system** is one in which at least two constitutionally independent levels of governmental power coexist. Ours is a federal system in this sense, as are the Australian, Canadian, and German systems, among others. In contrast, the British and the French governments are said to be **unitary systems** instead of federal. Although there exist local political districts, cities, and departments of government in Great Britain and in France, these subordinate jurisdictions possess no constitutionally inde-pendent powers of their own. Theoretically, if not practically, the counties in England and the *departements* in France can be abolished by legislative action in London or Paris. The states in our federal system aren't even theoretically subject to such an action by Congress.

As a government of **delegated powers**, the federal government possesses only those powers that "We the People" grant it in the U.S. Constitution. The so-called enu-merated powers include specific grants of authority to Congress, including the au-thority to raise armies, coin money, tax and spend for the general welfare, and regulate interstate commerce. The delegated powers also include powers which, though not spe-cifically enumerated, are "necessary and proper for carrying into execution" any of the specifically enumerated powers. In contrast, the governments of the fifty individual states possess **inherent powers**—authorities that inhere in the very existence of any state as an organized political entity. Thus a state government has all the powers that are implicit in the concept of a government, excepting insofar as some provision of the fed-eral or state constitution specifies otherwise. To underscore the Founders' intent in this area, the Tenth Amendment states that "powers not delegated to the United States by the Constitution, nor prohibited by it to the States, are reserved to the States respec-tively, or to the people."

A state's inherent powers include the power to issue regulations intended to pro-tect the health, safety, and welfare of its citizens. This comprehensive power, known as the **police power,** along with other inherent powers of the states such as the power to tax, aren't conferred by Congress. Hence they can't be abolished by Congress either.

As noted, a state's inherent powers don't give it unlimited authority even within its own borders. The people of each state arrange and limit the powers of their state gov-ernment; this they do through the provisions of the state constitution. Furthermore, a state must exercise even its inherent powers in ways that won't violate the federal Con-stitution or interfere with the implementation of national powers. The **supremacy clause,** in Article 6 of the Constitution, gives the national government a legal right-of-way over a state so long as the national government is itself exercising one of its delegated powers. Suppose, for example, that the legislators in a particular state passed a police law establishing certain standards of product safety, and then Congress, exercising its constitutional power to regulate interstate commerce, passed a federal law setting a uniform national product safety standard. If the state law interfered with the flow of commerce in a way that the courts found to be inconsistent with the requirements of the federal statute, the state law would be voided as a violation of the supremacy of the national government.

Under the doctrine of **federal preemption**, the states may also be prohibited from legislating in areas on which Congress has laid down a policy, lest state actions—even if they are broadly consistent with federal legislation—produce a crazy quilt of local laws concerning subjects that need uniform national regulation. Congress alone can give such uniformity—and then only if the states withdraw from the field once Congress has occupied it. In theory, the preemption doctrine doesn't expand federal authority beyond the limits of its constitutionally delegated powers. The mere assertion of a need for uniform treatment within a given policy area doesn't license Congress to usurp the states' police powers. In practice, however, the federal courts have interpreted Congress's delegated powers rather broadly, especially when the judges have been persuaded of a practical need for national uniformity. It results that the perceived need for uniformity has become an important paradigm of assignment: The federal courts will permit Congress to preempt—and hence "nationalize"—policy areas when uniformity seems necessary; meanwhile, policy areas that admit of diverse or experimental approaches remain fair subjects for legislation by the separate states.

Note that it wasn't, strictly speaking, the doctrine of federal preemption that moved the U.S. Supreme Court in the *Carbone* decision, excerpted in our case for Chapter 5, to void a local flow control law. In *Carbone,* Congress had not moved into the general field of waste disposal policy. Instead, the Court reasoned, the very fact that the Constitution itself gives Congress regulatory authority over interstate commerce implies a blanket prohibition against any state or local law—including the flow control ordinance reviewed in *Carbone*—which threatens to burden economic activity across state lines. The Court has taken to using the phrase *dormant power of Congress* to refer to such a blanket prohibition. On the other hand—and as we also saw in our casework for Chapter 5—because Congress's power over interstate commerce is plenary, members of Congress may indicate approval of an otherwise-questionable local action even when it appears to burden the stream of commerce. In such a case, the local law wouldn't conflict with Congress's dormant power because, by hypothesis, the power in question wouldn't any longer be in its dormant state. However, absent some positive indication of congressional approval, most state or local flow control ordinances turn out to be unconstitutional, whether or not Congress actively preempts them by passing a national waste control law of its own.

So far, we have been looking only at the constitutional dimensions of national and state power, not at the actual ability of legislators at either level of the system to translate their legal powers, whether delegated or inherent, into effective programs. To convert legal power into practical programs usually requires (among other things) money. The federal government has a great deal more of that than any state does, which is why state governments depend on grants of federal dollars for many of the functions that they perform. On the other hand, sometimes members of Congress impose requirements on the states without bothering to appropriate the needed money. Such federal legislation became a major source of conflict in the 1970s. We'll take this subject up soon in our discussion of "unfunded mandates."

What about the relations between a state and its constituent local jurisdictions: counties, cities, unincorporated areas within their borders, and special districts? The important point here is that local governments—which possess no constitutionally independent powers—are *not* to the states as our state governments are to the nation. In general, the powers of our county and city governments exist by delegation from the state legislatures. As creatures of the state legislatures, counties and municipalities are, in theory, subject to curtailment or even abolition at the whim of the higher lawmaking bodies.

Again, however, practice is more complicated than the legal theory might suggest. Many large city and major county governments are important players within our political system in their own rights. As such, they often act pretty much as independent operators and political entrepreneurs when dealing not only with their state governments but also with national leaders. The ascendancy of local governments as independent players has been one of the reasons why public administrators think today more in terms of an intergovernmental system than in terms of a traditional bilevel one.

Evolution of the Federal System

How did our complex pattern of intergovernmental relations evolve from a system based on what seems, in hindsight, to have been the much simpler model that the Framers of the Constitution envisioned?

In its extreme form, the bilevel model of our federal system involves two separate and independent sovereigns, national government and state government. The roots of this "separate and independent" concept are sometimes traced to the earliest days of the Republic—indeed, to the Father of the Constitution himself, James Madison. But it wasn't until the 1830s that the supporters of Andrew Jackson, a champion of local power, raised the bilevel theory to the status of an official constitutional doctrine. As president, Jackson packed the Supreme Court with justices bent on preventing the national government from encroaching on the prerogatives of the states. With some ups and downs, the Jacksonian concept, known as **dual federalism**, prevailed until well into the presidency of Franklin D. Roosevelt, when it yielded to the modern conception, known as **cooperative federalism.**

From Dual Federalism to Cooperative Federalism

The "dual" in the term *dual federalism* emphasized the separateness of national and state action—the expectation of President Jackson and his many followers that there was to be little intermixing of the two levels' authorities, programs, or purposes. Each government was "sovereign" within its sphere, and each supposedly proceeded with its own business pretty much independent of the other. The national government enforced tariffs, fought foreign wars, regulated interstate commerce, and the like; each state built its own roads, enforced contracts, chartered new cities, and generally exercised its most important inherent power—the police power—to ensure domestic tranquility and orderly commercial intercourse among citizens. The justices of the Supreme Court thought of themselves as the nation's constitutional referees, responsible for restoring the balance if either the national or any state government trespassed on the other's ground. The Court didn't hesitate to strike down acts of Congress that threatened the "reserved powers of the states"; in particular, this practice implied a rather narrow interpretation of Congress's interstate commerce power. Nor were the justices reluctant to declare state laws unconstitutional if they interfered with the power of Congress to legislate uniformly for the nation as a whole.

The Jacksonian emphasis on the states as separate, independent, and coequal political entities was consistent with the value of localism. We've seen that Americans have traditionally prized local interests, encouraged local loyalties, and, to the extent possible, demanded local self-government. But well before the end of the nineteenth century, the facts of national life had made it clear that dual federalism couldn't meet the needs of an industrial society. Between the presidency of Andrew Jackson (1829–1837) and that of Theodore Roosevelt (1901–1909), the U.S. economy had become national in scope. Corporations operated across state lines. It made no sense for dozens of state legislatures to regulate their own, limited portions of a single national flow of commerce. Thoughtful men and women recognized the need to coordinate local, state, and national policies. Prominent among the critics of dual federalism were America's Progressives, who—as we saw in Chapter 5—instinctively regarded localism as a threat to their agenda for centralization, synoptic decision making, and systemwide planning. The effort to transform dual federalism eventually gave rise to the system of cooperative federalism.

The decisive stimulus to change came in the 1930s. The crisis of the Great Depression showed the need for a more modern, more flexible division of national and state powers than the dual federalism paradigm implied. President Franklin D. Roosevelt and his advisers saw that responsibilities couldn't continue to be assigned exclusively to the federal government or to the states based on traditional, abstract notions of what was national and what was local. FDR recognized the need for a new paradigm to govern the allocation—and the sharing—of powers among the levels of government.

Roosevelt assembled a team of "braintrusters"—economists, lawyers, and professional public administrators who designed the sweeping programs known collectively as the New Deal. FDR and his advisers quickly learned that they would never be able to enact far-reaching new economic legislation without support from Congress, whose members' power bases remained in the states. FDR's braintrusters made common cause with the politicians on Capitol Hill. These coalitions between administrators and politicians anticipated a pattern that has since become familiar. In the modern issue-network context, relationships of mutual support routinely develop between those who participate in governance based on their intellectual expertise and those who participate because they've won election to public office. The emergence of this pattern over the years has given the lie to any lingering idea of a gap between policy makers and policy advisers. (We'll look closer at the relationship—not always easy—between politicians and policy professionals in our chapter reading.)

The initial emphasis of Roosevelt's advisers was on central planning, very much in line with the Progressive ideal of synoptic analysis. But the early New Dealers overreached themselves. Some major programs collapsed simply because they were unworkably ambitious and complicated. Most notably, midway through the 1930s, the colossal failure of the National Industrial Recovery Administration—the centerpiece of the legislative program known as the "first New Deal"—showed that teams of private businesspeople working with public administrators couldn't manage America's industrial sector from Washington. The job proved too big, the problems too complex. The wiser heads in Roosevelt's official family and in Congress finally abandoned the urge to central planning. Adopting the more traditional American course of agency-by-agency, problem-by-problem action, the lawmakers turned to passing federal statutes targeted on particular troubled industries (coal, commercial aviation, natural gas, securities) or intended to provide specific industrial protections (guaranteed collective bargaining rights for labor unions, minimum wage legislation). Historians have dubbed the aggregate of these narrowly targeted, piecemeal laws—most of them passed between 1935 and 1940—the "second New Deal."

To describe how the cooperative pattern works in practice, the political scientist Morton Grodzins suggested one of the most vivid, frequently invoked images in the literature, the so-called **marble cake metaphor.** Read on.

Morton Grodzins on the Marble Cake Metaphor

The American form of government is often, but erroneously, symbolized by a three-layer cake [corresponding to the national, state, and local levels]. A far more accurate image is the rainbow or marble cake, characterized by an inseparable mingling of differently colored ingredients, the colors appearing in vertical and diagonal strands and unexpected whirls. As colors are mixed in the marble cake, so functions are mixed in the American federal system. Consider the health officer, styled "sanitarian," of a rural county in a border state. He embodies the whole idea of marble cake government.

The sanitarian is appointed by the state under merit standards established by the federal government. His base salary comes jointly from state and federal funds, the county provides him with an office and office amenities and pays a portion of his expenses, and the largest city in the county also contributes to his salary and office by virtue of his appointment as a city plumbing inspector. It is impossible from moment to moment to tell under which governmental hat the sanitarian operates. His work of inspecting the purity of food is carried out under federal standards; but he is enforcing state laws when inspecting commodities that have not been in interstate commerce; and somewhat perversely he also acts under state authority when inspecting milk coming into the county from producing areas across the state border. He is a federal officer when impounding impure drugs shipped from a neighboring state; a federal officer when distributing typhoid immunization serum; a state officer when enforcing standards of industrial hygiene; a state-local officer when inspecting the city's water supply; and (to complete the circle) a local officer when insisting that the city butchers adopt more hygienic methods of handling their garbage. But he cannot and does not think of himself as acting in these separate capacities. All business in the county that concerns public health and sanitation he considers his business. Paid largely from federal funds, he does not find it strange to attend meetings of the city council to give expert advice on matters ranging from rotten apples to rabies control. He is even deputized as a member of both the city and county police forces.

The sanitarian is an extreme case, but he accurately represents an important aspect of the whole range of government activities in the United States. Functions are not neatly parceled out among the many governments. They are shared functions. It is difficult to find any governmental activity which does not involve all three of the so-called "levels" of the federal system. . . .

The federal grant programs are only the most obvious example of shared functions. They also most clearly exhibit how sharing serves to disperse governmental powers. The grants utilize the greater wealth-gathering abilities of the central government and establish nationwide standards, yet they are "in aid" of functions carried out under state law, with considerable state and local discretion. The national supervision of such programs is largely a process of mutual accommodation. . . .

From abattoirs and accounting to zoning and zoo administration, any government activity is almost certain to involve the influence, if not the formal administration, of all three planes of the federal system.

From Morton Grodzins, "The Federal System," in the President's Commission on National Goals, *Goals for Americans* (New York: American Assembly, 1960), pp. 265–267

SECTION ● ■ ▼ ◆ 2   The IGR System as It Works Today

Since the New Deal years, a complex, collaborative pattern has gradually emerged. The "feds" in Washington frame and finance all or major portions of many major new initiatives but leave it to state officials either to implement them or to come up with acceptable substitute policies. This pattern underlay the most popular of all New Deal programs, the Social Security Act of 1935, and it has been the model for much federal legislation in the years since.

Under the standard pattern, Congress passes a statute that either mandates or permits states to undertake certain efforts. Congress may send money to help, sometimes with a **pass-through**[1] or a **fenced-funds**[2] restriction. The city, state, or even regional implementation programs can be tailored, within limits, to meet local needs. The qualification "within limits" is critical: Typically the implementing officials must satisfy certain criteria or standards in order to remain in compliance with the federal statute. As was suggested in our study of the rule-making process in Chapter 4, Congress usually delegates at least a portion of the criteria- and standards-setting task to a federal administrative agency. Here are some examples of the standard pattern:

> *Education.* Under the Elementary and Secondary Education Act of 1965 (ESEA), the federal government provides grants to states and cities. The legislation contains a pass-through formula keyed on the numbers of low-income children in local school districts. This pass-through makes the local school boards the real administrators of ESEA funds. Board members must provide for special instruction to disadvantaged pupils, subject to periodic audits to ensure that the district is in compliance both with the general requirements of the statute and with detailed regulations issued by the U.S. Secretary of Education.

[1]*Pass-through:* A statutory requirement that a specified percentage of the funds must go directly to county or city governments, provided the latter meet certain criteria. To receive passed-through federal anti-poverty funds, for example, a city might have to show that a specified fraction of its current census roll consists of low-income citizens.

[2]*Fenced funds:* Federal money directed to designated kinds of private firms (for example, funding that is set aside to go to nonprofit service firms or to voluntary charitable organizations).

Environmental Protection. Under the Clean Air Act of 1970 and its amendments, state officials develop and implement plans to control smokestack releases from all except newly constructed electric plants, factories, and smelters. These state implementation plans are subject to requirements in elaborate rules issued by the administrator of the federal Environmental Protection Agency (EPA).

Natural Resources. Federal law requires state and local participation in land-use planning in locales that border on or contain federally owned lands. Under the Federal Land Policy and Management Act (usually shortened to FLPMA and pronounced "flip-ma"), plans are negotiated by public officials and private citizens. The completed plans are then administered locally, subject to federal review for compliance with minimum planning criteria set by the U.S. Secretary of the Interior.

Social Security. The Social Security Act of 1935, with its many amendments, was the pioneer event in the legislative history of cooperative federalism. The scope of programs now included under the Social Security umbrella is vast. This umbrella covers all elderly citizens, most disabled ex-workers, many survivors (widows), certain low-income aid recipients, and Medicaid beneficiaries. In an area such as Medicaid, benefit levels are set by the states subject to federal review for compliance with minimum standards published by the U.S. Secretary of Health and Human Services.

If, as noted, programs launched by state or local officials must satisfy criteria set forth in federal laws and administrative rules, they must also be broadly responsive to local political realities if they are to work. The resulting conflicts between the *demands of the rules* and the *imperatives of the place* define one of the toughest problems in day-to-day intergovernmental relations. Conflicts of this kind are among the main sources of overdetermination in our political system. (You won't be surprised to find that an example of the "rules versus place" conflict figures in our chapter case.)

The Rise of Regulatory Federalism

Sometime during the 1970s, critics began to argue that the word *cooperative* in the concept of cooperative federalism was a misnomer. The standard arrangement depended heavily on federal grants, and the programs implemented at the state and local levels were subject to close federal regulation. But the actual nature of the national-state relationship, the critics suggested, had become more coercive than cooperative. These commentators spoke of a system of **regulatory federalism**, claiming that a serious imbalance of power had emerged in the unfolding IGR pattern. Table 7.1 provides a background against which you can weigh the critics' claims.

On the top level of Table 7.1 (patterned on the breakout of private and public functions in Table 6.1) are programs that are initiated and funded by decision makers in Washington and then are actually implemented by federal administrators or by contractors working under the supervision of federal monitors. All three functions remain federal, either directly or "by proxy." Service in the U.S. military, in the foreign service, and in most slots within the federal justice system—for example, as a prosecutor or a paralegal aide in a U.S. Attorney's office—follows the federal provision pattern. The smoke jumpers of the U.S. Forest Service and the air safety inspection officers of the Federal Aviation Administration also embody the full federal provision approach.

Table 7.1 Ways of Distributing the Functions of Decision Making, Financing, and Implementation

	Decision Making	Financing	Implementation
Federal Provision			
Federal	x	x	x
State/Local			
Categorical and Block Grants			
Federal	x	x	
State/Local			•
Mandates*			
Federal	x		
State/Local		•	•
State Police Laws			
Federal			
State/Local	•	•	•

*Includes fully funded mandates, partially funded federal mandates that require matching state or local contributions, and unfunded mandates. Unfunded mandates in this sense include the ACIR categories discussed in the text—that is, most partial preemptions, crosscutting requirements, and crossover sanctions.

Funding Controls in Federal Grant Programs

On the second level of Table 7.1 are programs launched by Congress and funded in whole or in part by federal grants, but these are implemented either by state or by local civil servants or by contractors who are responsible to nonfederal officials.

A **categorical grant** contains severe restrictions with respect to the subject matter for which funds can be spent; the recipients of such funds must use them for rather narrowly specified purposes. A **block grant** involves sums of federal money given to a state or locality for programs of any description within a broad functional area. (A third category of federal grant, **revenue sharing**, refers to the provision of unrestricted funds; money is collected from taxpayers by the federal government and then is simply returned without strings to the states in accordance with some distribution formula. Revenue sharing occurred in the early 1970s but was gradually discontinued, leaving only categorical and block grants.)

A federal grant that is made specifically to fund physical upgrading of child care facilities would be categorical in nature. If the officials of an eligible city decided to accept such a grant, they would have to spend the money for the purpose specified, such as for the purchase of safety equipment. For such categorical grants, then, the feds are the decision makers and also provide financing, although state or local actors are the implementers. By contrast, a block grant in support of child care as a general function would imply a sharing of decision-making authority. Depending on the precise wording of the authorization, the local officials could decide whether to use the money to subsidize the upgrading of existing day care centers, to help working parents pay for child care, to experiment with innovative early education programs, or for similar purposes.

A General Accounting Office (GAO) study released shortly after the new Republican majority took power in Congress in 1995 revealed that only 11 percent of all federal grants were disbursed in the relatively unrestricted block form.[3] Even if the new Republican congressional majority were fully to fulfill its promise to devolve power from Washington to the states, it's unlikely that the categorical grant will come close to disappearing. For that matter, there's even little likelihood that the block grant will become the more common congressional grant instrument. There has always been a tendency for Congress to increase its own control over state and local spending, even when it has granted money in block form, by writing various special conditions (such as percentage pass-throughs) into the language of subsequent amendments.

Both categorical and block grants may require some contribution by the receiving jurisdiction. The term **matching funds** is often applied to such grants, although the actual share that a state or locale may have to contribute is frequently rather small. In many highway programs, for example, the state or locality only has to put up 10 percent of the total for a project that is otherwise within guidelines for a federal grant.

Public administrationists disagree regarding the effect that matching-funds programs have had on the health of our federal system. The lure of federal grants—in such fields as public works construction, health funding (joint federal-state financing pays for low-income Americans' Medicaid costs), and welfare—may distort budget decision making in the states and cities, producing spending patterns very different from what local decision makers would choose if the opportunity had never been offered to participate in conditional federal programs. Critics argue that the lure of federal funding often puts irresistible pressure on state and local officials to come up with the needed matching contributions. Ironically, the temptation may actually increase as the percentage share required to qualify for a federal grant decreases, since the smaller the ante required to play, the easier it may seem to get into the game. Even when waivers of federal requirements can be obtained—an increasingly common practice—it takes time and effort for local officials to complete the paperwork, and of course it's bothersome to have to "get permission" from the feds before undertaking an action in the way that seems best in local circumstances.

The Varieties of Unfunded Mandates

The third level in Table 7.1 contains the category of federal actions known as an **unfunded mandate,** under which the feds make the decisions. The states and locales are then left with the legal responsibility for implementation. The states and locales are also left with the bill—often for work that the local officials wouldn't have decided to do at all, had they been left with the choice. (Unfunded mandates can also be imposed by state lawmakers on county or city officials; by city council members on neighborhood organs of government such as precincts or wards; and so forth. The idea in every instance is the same: The higher authority gives the mandate; then the one who must execute the order must also find the resources.)

By the early 1990s, some state and local politicians were claiming that a quarter to a third of their budgets were going to fund programs mandated by Congress. Congress was generating unfunded mandates at the rate of about two hundred per decade, especially in regulations concerning the environment and workplace safety. In doing so,

[3]See U.S. General Accounting Office, *Block Grants: Characteristics, Experience, and Lessons Learned* (GAO-HEHS-7-95-74, February 1995), p. 4.

members of Congress not only were exercising the decision-making authority of the national government but also were preempting state and local officials' budgetary authority. Obviously, when Congress mandates that a state institute a program willy-nilly, it effectively sets itself up as the decision-making body for the allocation of the funds needed to comply. The money must then be raised through local tax increases or be diverted from other programs.

In the midterm elections of November 1994, Republican candidates for Congress offered voters a "Contract with America." In it they promised to impose no additional unfunded mandates on the states and to cut federal spending in absolute terms. They also promised to loosen some of the strings on any federal dollars Congress continued to send to the states by switching from categorical grants to block grants. In early 1995 the Republicans, having won their majority in Congress, tried to execute all the terms of their contract. In a flurry reminiscent of the "first New Deal" legislation of the initial hundred days of Franklin Roosevelt's presidency, the Republicans moved to decentralize political and administrative power. Success was mixed. The Senate didn't cooperate with House Republicans on some items; President Clinton vetoed others that managed to clear both houses of Congress. One bill that made it all the way into the statute books fulfilled the Republicans' promise to prohibit future unfunded mandates. Yet it should be remembered that Congress may repeal this restriction on its own power at any time. In any event, many state and local programs still exist—and will continue to exist—because federal laws already on the books require them, because grants of federal money make it possible for the states and localities to afford them, or because of a combination of federal mandates and federal funding.

The term *unfunded mandate* can be stretched to cover several other forms of federal action that impose financial or other burdens on state and local governments. A 1984 study of regulatory federalism by the Advisory Commission on Intergovernmental Relations (ACIR)[4] identified three techniques in addition to direct mandates by which the feds routinely force state and local governments to undertake programs framed in Washington:

Partial preemption. Specification of a minimum federal requirement (for example, a requirement that every state install a system to identify the fathers of children born out of wedlock and track "deadbeat dads") while leaving the state discretion to choose the exact mix of techniques for compliance.

Crosscutting requirement. A mandate that applies to a variety of programs, such as a ban against racial discrimination in educational programs, public works projects, and so forth.

Crossover sanction. A penalty imposed in one area to promote compliance with federal requirements in another; thus, federal funds to upgrade state roads may be withdrawn from states with lagging records of compliance with federal clean air regulations.

[4]*Advisory Commission on Intergovernmental Relations:* A study and advisory organization created by Congress in 1958 to identify and report on problems in IGR. The ACIR membership includes U.S. senators, governors, mayors of large cities, and other elected officials. In addition, senior federal executives and "public members" are appointed for their academic expertise in intergovernmental affairs. The ACIR staff, a permanent body, regularly publishes reports of high quality.

Like the direct unfunded mandate, all these practices impose a so-called **authority cost** on state or local governments; in addition to any spending that these techniques may force state or local governments to undertake, they reduce the affected officials' authority to set their own political and administrative agendas.

The bottom level in Table 7.1 shows a category which recognizes that many areas of legislation and administration—for example, those undertaken under the police power—remain within the province of state powers. It shouldn't be forgotten, however, that over the years, these areas of "reserved" powers have been reduced, both through Supreme Court interpretation and through federal legislation. The Court, for example, has interpreted the due process and equal protection clauses of the Fourteenth Amendment to the Constitution as severe limits on state lawmakers' powers in areas such as criminal justice policy, anti-obscenity legislation, and public schooling policy.

Picket Fence Federalism and Executive Federalism

Today's state air pollution control official may be recruited tomorrow for service in the air policy office of the federal Environmental Protection Agency—say to fill the post of an EPA official who left to work as an analyst in a private research firm that depends on contracts from the first worker's state conservation office. An identical in-and-out job pattern occurs in the areas of criminal justice, corrections, energy development, economic forecasting and development, educational policy, family services, health, social welfare, and transportation. These patterns lend validity to a concept known as **picket fence federalism.**[5]

Today, much of the American governance process is organized around a series of relatively separate policy areas such as environmental protection, criminal justice, and so forth. Each has its own set of applicable laws, its own flow of funds, its own population of circulating officials, and its own issue network. As Sketch 7.1 suggests, each program area can be thought of as a single slat in a fence. Participants within a given specialty interact freely with one another. But just as the individual slats never touch, the individual officials within a program area rarely interact with their counterparts from the neighboring slats. For example, federal, state-local, and private decision makers in the air quality area may constantly engage with one another, but they may have little interchange with their counterparts in criminal justice and other areas.

Picket fence federalism implies a pattern of interaction that is also called **executive federalism.** There exists a continuing need to adapt state and local demands to federally imposed requirements and, reciprocally, to adapt federal programs to state-local needs. In executive federalism, the elected lawmakers who frame the policies leave most of the activity of day-to-day cooperating to the appointive officials in federal, state, and local bureaucracies who are supposed to make the policies work. The system of executive federalism involves daily interactions among men and women in critical administrative positions: It is these relation*ships* among public officials that make intergovernmental rela*tions* work.

Picket fence federalism and executive federalism work largely through informal organizations—picket fence federalism, through relationships among officials within a

---

[5]The term was coined by U.S. senator (and former North Carolina governor) Terry Sanford in *Storm over the States* (New York: McGraw-Hill, 1967), p. 80.

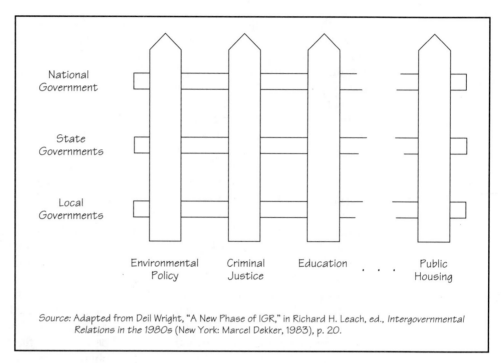

National
Government

State
Governments

Local
Governments

Environmental   Criminal   Education   . . .   Public
Policy   Justice   Housing

Source: Adapted from Deil Wright, "A New Phase of IGR," in Richard H. Leach, ed., Intergovernmental Relations in the 1980s (New York: Marcel Dekker, 1983), p. 20.

Sketch 7.1 Picket Fence Federalism

particular functional area; executive federalism, through regular contacts among administrators from the executive branches of the federal, state, and local governments. In executive federalism as in other manifestations of informal organizations, relationships tend to be continuing and friendly (or at least cordially adversarial). Personal familiarity is an important ingredient in the chemistry of federal-state-local cooperation. But—as in all informal relationships—there are dangers in these arrangements. Picket fence federalism intensifies the tendency of administrators to specialize. Policy professionals within a particular issue network or policy field may look to Washington—typically the main source of program funds—for their primary guidance. Common understandings and values among administrators within a "slat" in the system may put implementing officials at odds with local elected figures, who must be more concerned with overall balance among many programs that affect their areas than with the objectives of any particular one. (This issue is also explored in our chapter reading.)

Picket Fencing, Executive Federalism, and the "Determination Problem" Again

In Chapter 6, we emphasized the *inclusive* nature of informal organizations; that is, we emphasized the uses of issue networks as vehicles of information sharing and negotiation across the private-public boundary. By contrast, within the intergovernmental context, we should underscore the *exclusive* nature of picket fencing and policy making by executive officials.

The tendency under picket fence federalism for experts in one program area to exclude participants from neighboring issue networks is understandable. It is also regrettable. It's understandable because, by confining policy discussions and debates to the practitioners within a particular field such as environmental policy or criminal justice, the experts can facilitate deliberations and simplify analyses. Every participant with a position on a slat shares technical expertise with the others. Most of them may belong to the same profession or come from similar educational backgrounds, so they may think similarly about priorities. But the exclusive nature of these informal organizations is regrettable as well, because it may foster parochialism and close-mindedness. The participants in a problem-solving session within the field of environmental quality, criminal justice, or whatever, may tacitly agree to ignore issues or criteria that decision makers outside the network would regard as essential.

Picket fencing a field of policy may mitigate both underdetermination and overdetermination. It may mitigate underdetermination by reducing the fragmentation of the policy-making base and making it easier to control the direction of a line of decisions. But picket fencing may achieve this kind of policy integration by quietly arrogating control to a self-selected community of officials and interested private actors—the participants who have committed themselves to work within the relevant issue network. Similarly, picket fencing may mitigate overdetermination by effectively limiting decision making to individuals who are likely to share values and tacitly agree without further discussion about the criteria they think should be applied to the problems that interest them. Narrowing the basis of judgment by emphasizing the experts' criteria may promote consensus building. Nevertheless, critics of the picket fence pattern worry that priority setting and policy adjusting within relatively small circles of experts may end up excluding viewpoints that deserve representation.

By confining much of the policy dialogue not only to members of issue networks but also often to midlevel or even lower-level appointive officials of the executive branches of government, executive federalism carries the logic of exclusivity even further. In a system of fragmented authority, executive federalism may mitigate the problem of underdetermination by effectively reserving decision-making authority to a subset of actors from the executive branch (or, rather, from the executive branches, since they come from all levels of the system). And in a decision-making environment of multiple, contradictory criteria, executive federalism mitigates overdetermination by increasing the likelihood that a more limited set of criteria will be considered than if decisions were more broadly debated. Like picket fencing, the practice of executive federalism didn't just happen; it emerged in large part as a response to the pervasive problems of underdetermination and overdetermination in our system.

CHAPTER READING ▼ ▼ ▼

As Morton Grodzins pointed out in his discussion of the marble cake metaphor earlier in this chapter, few public programs of any significant scope today remain the responsibilities of any one level of government. In some combination or other, decision making, funding, and execution have become shared functions. In the following excerpt from a Brookings Institution study of federal grant programs, Paul Peterson, Barry Rabe, and Kenneth Wong outline a three-phase pattern of interaction between national and local officials. In their attempt to understand the conditions under which "federalism works," Peterson and his collaborators studied a variety of programs that involved federal financing and guidelines but required active state or local action for implementation. The study cases ranged across such diverse picket fence slats as hospital construction, the promotion of managed-care medical programs (health maintenance organizations), vocational education and education for disabled or disadvantaged children, federal rent subsidies, general community development, federal financial aid to "impacted" locales (locales with high concentrations of federal installations that enjoy exemptions from local taxes), and federal assistance to locales attempting to advance racial integration.

You should make a special effort to identify the paradigm of assignment that underlies our authors' reasoning: What basic principle, according to Peterson, Rabe, and Wong, should be used to apportion functions among different levels of government? How does the concept of a "collective action problem" (which we discussed in Chapter 6) figure in the authors' reasoning?

The expression the authors use early in the selection—"mutually accommodating intergovernmental relationships"—is a bit of a mouthful, but it identifies Peterson, Rabe, and Wong with those who see bargaining and mutual accommodation (rather than federal preemption or direct supervision) as the main techniques of coordination in our IGR system. The authors emphasize not only the *cooperative* but also the *evolutionary* aspects of the implementation process. That it may take a major new program a decade or more to mature is one of the more important findings of contemporary researchers. In fact, implementation scholars have concluded that it's usually unwise even to try for a systematic assessment of program success until a significant period has elapsed, during which unexpected effects are likely to occur and unexpected proponents or foes of the program are likely to lobby successfully for changes in the original terms. When dealing with our chapter case, it will be important to bear in mind these authors' depiction of implementation as a time-spanning, evolutionary process as well as one that involves officials from several levels of government and, often, from both the public and private sectors.

Peterson, Rabe, and Wong also stress that implementation typically involves at least two important kinds of actors—elective officials and their political advisers and, in addition, a special group of administrators whom our authors call **policy professionals.** The key players in the system of executive federalism often turn out to be these professionals. Administrators in the roles of advisers and analysts usually want to shape public policies in ways that are consistent with the standards of their specialized fields. But as we've noted, the "right way" when judged by technical or professional standards may not be the best way in terms of local political dynamics.

Conflict between local political leaders and policy professionals may be worsened by federal rules that have themselves been written by members of the professional group. Professional engineers, educators, or health experts may have shepherded the regulations through the rule-making process in the lead federal agency, mindful that engineers, educators, or health professionals at the local level may invoke the authority of those same rules in disputes with state or city political leaders. The technicians' way must sometimes be followed—even at the cost of political turmoil—because "the rules" require it or else federal funding will be lost. Does that sound like administrative black-mail, or what?

"Place-Bound" versus "Rule-Bound" in IGR

Paul Peterson, Barry Rabe, and Kenneth Wong

Suggestions by local elected leaders are often blocked by administrators who cite federal directives and expectations. Whenever administrative officials are relatively autonomous, local programs will be more responsive to federal expectations and will irritate local relations. The professional may be rule-bound, but the politician is place-bound.

[F]ederalism has become a buzzword. For some it conjures up images of a compassionate government that protects consumers and gives succor to the needy. For others it symbolizes an uncontrolled bureaucracy that grants special privileges to its chosen clientele and relentlessly writes regulations that stultify creativity and enterprise. If one is either uncritically for federalism or irrevocably against it, one hardly wants to understand how and when it works. . . .

Our findings concerning the federal role are more optimistic than has been typical in previous studies. Although we found examples of bureaucratic ineptitude, concessions to special interests, and inefficient use of federal resources, the dominant pattern was quite the opposite. Instead of conflict, we found cooperation. Instead of federal coercion, we found mutual accommodation on the part of national, state, and local officials. Instead of misappropriation of federal resources, we found ready acquiescence to federal guidelines at the state and local level. Above all, instead of a heavy federal presence, we found, for the most part, a cooperative system in which responsibility was shared among professional administrators at all levels of government.

Mutually accommodating intergovernmental relationships are founded on the reality that each participant needs the other. Federal agencies have crucial legal and fiscal resources; locals have the operational capacity without which nothing can be achieved. Cooperative relations are also facilitated by the fact that these programs belong to broad social movements with both national and local adherents. Professional administrators at all levels of government identify with the goals of these new programs, have been recruited to direct them, and as a result have a stake in making them work. . . .

There was considerable variety in the ways in which programs were designed and implemented. Instances of intergovernmental conflict and ineffectiveness occurred often enough to require us to consider the circumstances that affect program success. Our analysis of those circumstances is rooted in two basic distinctions: the extent to which a particular federal policy is focused on redistributive as distinct from developmental objectives, and the extent to which the agencies administering federal policy are exempt from local political pressures and are staffed by professionals who identify with policy goals. . . .

In general terms, the proper distribution of power between a central government and a large number of local governments can be readily stated. Policies and programs that affect the entire society more or less equally are appropriately assigned to the central government; national defense is the preeminent example. Policies and programs that affect only one subdivision of a society are appropriately assigned to local governments; the people in the community can then decide whether the benefits from a given program exceed the costs. People who value the program more than it costs for them to receive these benefits will, other things being equal, move to that community. Variations in policies will arise as each community offers a slightly different mix of public services and accompanying taxes to satisfy the demand of the relatively homogenous group of its residents. These local governments, with their different programs, all of whose effects are entirely local, will provide a higher level of satisfaction in a society than any uniform set of services provided by the central government. Playgrounds can be concentrated where young children are abundant; recreation halls for senior citizens can be clustered in adult communities; parks can be maintained at varying levels of care, depending on local aesthetic tastes.

It has been cogently argued, in fact, that to the extent all services can be decentralized a better fit can be achieved between what the public demands (that is, what services it is willing to pay for) and what is publicly provided. However, . . . local communities are much more subject to the influence of uncontrollable external economic forces than is the nation as a whole.

At the same time local governments are highly dependent on the local economic well-being of their communities. Their leaders are responsible for raising revenue from local sources to pay for many of the services they provide, and they must raise capital for longer-term projects in a bond market in which investors look at their financial capacity and prospects with cold, calculating eyes. . . .

Because of the constraints that open local economies place upon their governments, one can usefully distinguish between *developmental* and *redistributive* policies.

Developmental Policies

Developmental policies are intended to improve the economic position of a community in its competition with other areas. The kinds of policies properly considered developmental are much broader than those conventionally grouped under this term. Developmental policies do, of course, include plans to attract business and industry to a community through a combination of tax relief and special services. But many communities find that special concessions to particular firms and industries are not as efficient a way of promoting economic growth as providing effective public services that make a city a potentially

attractive home for productive employees and the firms that hire them. A high-quality infrastructure includes good roads, adequate utility and sanitation services, effective police and fire protection, quality schools, and pleasant parks and recreational activities.

Developmental policies to which the national government can contribute efficiently are those that aid a community's economic development but also have consequences for areas beyond that community. Transportation systems, for instance, not only facilitate commercial activities among a community's citizens but also increase trade and communication with other communities. The Constitution recognized the important role of the central government in such activities when it forbade states to erect tariffs or other barriers to commerce among themselves. . . .

Central government support of developmental goals is warranted because, if left to itself, a community would spend for such purposes only an amount equivalent to what it expected to gain from the resultant increase in its economic activity. It would not spend funds for any portion of a project that only benefited people living outside the community. Without central government support, localities would thus underspend for development.

Intergovernmental efforts on behalf of developmental objectives are marked by cooperative, mutually adaptive relations between central and local governments because the federal government, by aiding local economic development, is only assisting local governments in what they would otherwise want to do anyway. . . .

Because elected officials are well placed to gain politically from the success of developmental programs, they are disposed to promote them. Professional administrators and their staffs working in particular policy domains, however, have both fewer incentives and fewer chances to promote such programs. Professionals in one program area tend to be isolated from those in another and from other institutions and sources of political support. . . . School officials responsible for vocational education programs, for example, often find it difficult to mobilize business support for their training programs unless mayors or other prominent community leaders make this endeavor a priority.

Redistributive Policies

Redistributive policies are those that benefit low-income or otherwise especially needy groups in the community. One can roughly calculate whether a policy is redistributive by estimating whether those who pay for the service in local taxes are those who are receiving the services. If there is no overlap at all, such as in welfare assistance to those who pay no taxes, it is a case of pure redistribution.

"Redistribution" is a somewhat technical term not often used in common political parlance. Because it implies taking from one person or group and giving to another, the word emphasizes conflicts of interest among social groups. Participants in public debate, however, usually prefer to stress the mutuality of interests, so they define and defend redistributive programs in other terms. They speak of "social responsibilities," "social investments in the country's future," or more often, "serving populations with special needs." We do not object to this terminology . . . as long as these euphemisms do not gloss over the underlying tension between local redistribution and local economic development.

. . . If a community redistributes local resources to an especially needy segment of society, it will, other things being equal, attract members of that needy segment. Other communities will benefit because those in need will be cared for, and these communities will not have to bear the cost. If, however, a locality does not redistribute resources to help those in need, other localities suffer; either they must take up the burden or their residents must witness the resultant suffering. If, for example, only one city provides medical care for the indigent, housing for the homeless, welfare benefits for impoverished families and schooling for the handicapped, it would become a refuge for these needy groups but at cost it could not long sustain.

Locally designed redistributive policies thus pose what has come to be known as a collective action problem. This problem arises whenever a desired good or service available to one member of a group would be available to all. For example, one member of a community cannot enjoy clean air (outside an air-conditioned home) without other members also having the same opportunity. Even though all may value clean air, people will continue to pollute because they realize that even if they stop polluting, the air will remain dirty unless others also quit. Everyone waits for someone else to take the first step. In the absence of coordinated action or government intervention, what is commonly desired does not happen.

Redistribution from better-off members of a society to those in need is a good desired by most people. . . . For the good to be achieved effectively, all local communities must work toward it at the same time. Yet no local government will provide redistributive services on its own initiative for fear that it will be unduly burdened by a social problem while others escape the responsibility or, as is often said in this connection, free ride. Every community waits for another to provide the needed services, and, consequently, little happens.

Two solutions are possible. First, the central government may intervene and assume all responsibility for supplying a given service. When redistribution takes the form of a cash award based on some fairly well defined criteria, for instance, the central government alone can provide directly for those in need. The social security and medicare programs are well-known examples of federally funded and (largely) federally administered programs. When, however, commodities are to be distributed or services are to be performed—housing, education, medical care, food, legal assistance, or social services—the administrative complexity of the redistributive program may call for participation and cooperation by local governments. When this happens, central and local governments undertake joint responsibility for redistribution.

In such intergovernmental redistributive programs, local governments are asked to carry out responsibilities different from any they are likely to have initiated on their own. At first, they may react guardedly. How much actual—as distinct from symbolic—redistribution does the central government expect? How aggressively will the central government pursue its ostensible goals and enforce its stipulations? Will any overly zealous local government be saddled with obligations others have evaded? Is the central government going to sustain its program or is this just a passing episode?

Such questions often result in a three-phase evolution of intergovernmental relations during the early years of a redistributive program. In the first phase, because of the very newness of the program, the central government is likely to be vague in its objectives, imprecise in its stipulations, and inept in its administrative actions. As a result, local governments are likely to use program resources either for traditional local activities (usually developmental programs) or as substitutes for revenue that would otherwise have to be generated locally. Local administrators of preexisting programs will attempt to modify the new program so that it is consistent with established practice. The program's focus on those with special needs will be diffused.

As this diffusion becomes evident, groups supporting the new program's redistributive goals will ask the central government to monitor its implementation more closely. (They may even have anticipated such developments by writing strong language regulating program direction into the initial statute, thus bypassing the first stage.) In this second stage of a program's evolution, central government official prepare and disseminate more detailed regulations and guidelines, carry out more intensive audits, and conduct evaluations to see whether objectives are being realized. New professional administrators who are supportive and perhaps even enthusiastic proponents of the central government's policy take charge of local programs. Word from other communities gradually convinces local officials that they are not undertaking any commitment others are able to ignore. Compliance becomes so complete it is almost ritualistic. Local administrators become so attentive to the explicit and implicit guidelines of central government officials that even substantive policy objectives are at times subordinated to procedural regularity.

As responsiveness to federal requirements increases, however conflicts between local program administrators and local elected leaders may intensify. Elected leaders may resent the intrusion of federal rules into local decision making. The community's territorial autonomy, for which the elected

official is especially responsible, may seem violated by the plethora of federal regulations, audits, and evaluations. That local professionals identified with the program are responsible for its administration does little to assuage the politician's concern . . . for these professionals seem more committed to federal directives than to community concerns. Suggestions by local elected leaders are often blocked by administrators who cite federal directives and expectations. It is even possible—indeed likely—that federal regulations are used as an excuse for professional inaction that is actually motivated by quite other considerations. Many administrators have discovered that the most effective response to elected superiors is not that it *shouldn't* be done but that it *can't* be done. Federal regulations may be exactly the justification professional bureaucrats need to block changes they oppose in any case. Eventually, the elected official may feel that the array of seemingly mindless procedures imposed by federal regulations prevents the program from efficiently achieving its own objectives.

. . . [W]henever administrative officials are relatively autonomous vis-à-vis their elected officials, local programs will be more responsive to federal expectations and will inevitably irritate local relations. If administrators are not autonomous with respect to local elected officials, however—if they are political appointees rather than professionals—they will be less responsive to federal guidelines, and locally elected leaders will attempt to use federal resources for their own political and economic objectives. The professional may be rule-bound, but the politician is place-bound. . . .

While fiscal pressures, administrative practices, and constituency pressures produce results that vary from place to place, the combined effect of repeated conflicts over program regulations generates a third phase in the evolution of program administration. Facing complaints from local leaders and their legislative representatives, federal bureaucrats modify program guidelines and expectations once again. A new tolerance of local diversity, a new recognition that no single way of implementing a program is clearly preferable, and an appreciation of the limits as to what can be directed from the center steadily evolve. In the process, more experienced administrators emerge to guide program implementation. As Morton Grodzins pointed out years ago, cooperative intergovernmental relationships are primarily marked by a professionalized policymaking process. . . .

The third phase is not a return to phase one. There are no dramatic oscillations from complete permissiveness to detailed regulation and back again. Instead the third phase is more a synthesis, a discernment of the appropriate balance between what is desirable and what is possible.

From Paul Peterson, Barry Rabe, and Kenneth Wong, *When Federalism Works* (Washington: Brookings Institution, 1986), pp. 6–7, 10–20.

CHAPTER CASE

In the early 1990s, the United States remained one of a handful of major industrial nations without an explicit family policy. The United States belonged to an even-smaller circle of countries that had not implemented a comprehensive child care policy. That kind of political neglect of an issue so important to millions of Americans couldn't continue forever. Not surprisingly, the 1992 and 1996 presidential election campaigns included debates over the crisis of "family values." Powerful demographic, economic, and political factors—more women in the workforce than ever before, the emergence of women as a major electoral force—produced strong pressures for action.

The following scenario finds Kendra Quinn—whom we met in Case 3—drawn into an effort by local leaders (those place-bound politicians described by Peterson, Rabe, and Wong) to realize all the benefits they can from a series of federal family-policy initiatives. Several of these programs will require inputs of local private or public funds; they will also require local implementation—subject, of course, to those federal regulations that seem to have become as inevitable in our time as death and taxes. Kendra Quinn and the others must find a way to square proposed federal regulations with the needs of the local jurisdiction—a frequent problem in IGR and certainly a central concern in the following case.

CASE 6
··················

Dealing with "Disparate Impact" in Family Policy

Congress has passed three bills to serve as the framework of a new national family policy. The president quickly signed the first two bills into law but hasn't yet acted on the third (the so-called voucher program).

First, by means of a [hypothetical] amendment to the federal Tax Reform Act of 1984, Congress has increased the income tax credit that a "qualified working parent" can take to recoup some of the expenses he or she incurs for day care services. There's a debate under way regarding who may claim the credit as a qualified working parent, although a certain weight of opinion seems to have emerged behind an interpretation tying *qualified* to the word *registered* as it's used in the second bill.

Second, in the [hypothetical] Quality Day Care Act, Congress has imposed stricter regulatory standards on facilities (and on the persons who work in them) before they can be officially recognized as "registered child care centers." Subject to federal regulations, each state must promulgate new, stricter health and safety standards for day care centers and must define relatively stiff standards for the professional certification of caregivers.

Third, Congress has passed a [hypothetical] Supplemental Income Pre-School Assistance Act as a rider to another, broader bill in the field of primary education policy. This rider would set up a voucher system to support parental choice in child care arrangements. Parents would be able to draw on public funds (up to $200 per child per month, depending on the parents' income) when paying child care providers, who then can return any vouchers they collect to the government for reimbursement at the proper monthly rate.

These legislative actions were taken partly on the initiative of the congressional leadership and partly in response to demands from pressure groups. Prominent in various aspects of the lobbying effort were the African American civil rights leadership, the National Conference of Catholic Bishops, the National Council of *La Raza,* the National Organization for Women, and a loosely organized lobby of "child care professionals." The supporting coalition wasn't by any means monolithic, however. As is the common pattern in American politics, different groupings assembled to push for different elements in a single overall family-policy initiative. Prodding by the president also played a part in activating Congress to pass the tax credit and day care upgrading bills. Now, of course, the president wants to claim as much political credit as he possibly can for the family-policy initiative.

The wording of the third bill includes no explicit mention of the kinds of care providers who may accept vouchers and redeem them for reimbursement with public funds. Language in the congressional debates, however, suggested that care providers using the facilities of religious schools may qualify "if the programs that they offer are without religious content and if the facilities themselves qualify as 'registered child care centers' within the meaning of the Quality Day Care Act." Even boosters of the voucher program admitted that the initiative would be costly, since literally millions of parents who send children to certified day care centers would gain an entitlement to coupons that would eventually appear as claims on the Treasury. There were also constitutional questions. May taxpayers' money be used under any circumstances to support day care centers at religious schools and church halls, or would the acceptance of vouchers in such circumstances breach Thomas Jefferson's "wall of separation" between church and state?

All three bills easily sailed through Congress, though none of them commanded a majority large enough to override a presidential veto. A few days remain before the president must veto the voucher program, if he chooses to go that route, or else sign it into law.

•   •   •   •   •

Blair Songster, a recent addition to the White House staff, hadn't liked it very much the first time she heard her boss, Haney Brill, refer to the president as "The Man." The expression was just too slangy for Songster's taste. It made Brill sound flip and a bit vulgar, as if he were a play-by-play announcer given to snappy patter instead of a full Counsellor to the President of the United States. ("Who's Haney talking about," Blair wondered, "Stan Musial or the president?") To her ears, "The Man" also had a vaguely sexist ring. On the other hand, she had to admit that Haney—the demanding but very capable leader of the White House staff group to which Blair belonged—passed muster in almost every other way. And anyway, in Blair Songster's mind, Haney Brill's expression set a scenario for turnabout. The day was soon coming when some other senior White House aide—maybe Blair herself?—might refer to the president as "The Woman."

Songster hustled across the alleyway between the Old Executive Office Building and the West Wing of the White House. She was hurrying in response to a summons for a meeting in Brill's conference room, down the hall from the Oval Office itself. Two other junior staff aides from Haney's staff group converged, along with Blair, on the entrance to the West Wing. The presence of the three of them at the same time, all in apparent response to an identical E-mail instruction from Haney, probably meant that Brill had no specific assignment in mind for any one of his staff aides. Following his custom, Brill probably just wanted to mull over some issue or other with a few of his staff assistants.

"The Man is concerned about this family-policy initiative," Haney said when Blair and the others arrived. Brill himself had evidently come just a few minutes earlier from a meeting with the president. The problem of the voucher program—should the president veto it?—had been discussed, along with the implementation of the new tax credit and the mandate to upgrade child care centers. Haney continued: "The president doesn't want the several pieces of this family policy to be executed piecemeal. He wants enough coherence and impact in execution to ensure that expanded child care will be credited as a major accomplishment of his administration. But neither does he want to overreach and end up with a political white elephant because the courts reject the voucher program, because there's rampant cheating on the tax credit, or because too much 'pork'—favorite contractors' getting suspicious construction contracts—ends up in the effort to upgrade child care centers."

Eric Kanzler, one of Songster's colleagues in the staff group, asked if the president had indicated how he was leaning on the veto question.

"No," Haney answered, "The Man is still pondering his options."

Decision time on the veto was getting close. Brill knew that the president might call him back at any instant for a final word of advice. Should the president sign the voucher legislation, and thereby effectively incorporate it as a component of his own family-policy initiative? Or should he veto it on either constitutional or fiscal grounds? Haney said, "If the Man calls, as I expect he will, I'll want to bring one or two of you along to help me help the president decide what to do."

Kanzler, a lawyer, suggested that Songster and Jack Stone (the third member of the staff group in attendance) should review the Supreme Court's opinion in the *Lemon* case, which contained the Court's test for constitutionality when a governmental action raised doubts under the **establishment clause.**[1] Neither Blair nor Jack had heard of the *Lemon* case, so Eric said that he'd photocopy relevant portions of the opinion for the two of them to read (see Box 7.1).

"There's more I want you three to be thinking about," Haney Brill then said. He told Blair and the others that they should plan to attend a "strategy session" the following day. John Pospisil—like Brill, a full Counsellor to the President—would be present. So would several members of Congress: Irene Platt, Stuart Helfin, and Ellen Moe—all of whom served on the House Special Subcommittee on Primary and Secondary Education, the committee that had marked up[2] the new Quality Day Care Act as well as the rider to authorize a child care voucher program. The purpose of the strategy session, Brill said, would be to develop an implementation plan for the new family policy.

Platt, Helfin, Moe and the two presidential counselors held different opinions on various aspects of the family-policy initiative. But all were committed to a follow-through on the new legislation that would lay a basis for future growth. All knew of ambitious public programs that had come to ruin because of botched implementation. Congressional lore was rich in stories of the New Deal initiatives, such as the ponderous National Industrial Recovery program, that had fallen under their own bureaucratic weight. A few sitting members of the House still carried personal memories of President Lyndon Johnson's Great Society programs. For trying to do too much and failing, the Great Society programs ended up tarring a presidential administration with a reputation for ineptitude.[3] Pospisil, Brill, Congresswoman Platt, and the others were determined not to let happen to family policy what had happened to the early New Deal programs and the Great Society initiatives. The question for the next day's strategy session, then, would be: *How should the administrators who are responsible for interpreting and implementing the new tax provision, the Quality Day Care Act, and the voucher program (if the president signed it) approach their tasks, given the interrelated objectives of winning the best press and the broadest public support for an expanded federal child care initiative—all with an eye toward gradually extending the program in the future?*

Haney Brill told his assistants to do whatever research they had to so that they could participate intelligently in the next day's discussions. Brill turned to Songster:

"And Blair, I'm going to make you the coordinator of the whole megillah. I want you to stay in touch with the IRS people who'll have to interpret that 'qualified working parent' phrase of the new tax provision, and also with the team over in Health and

---

[1]Individual Supreme Court justices have expressed a desire to overrule the test set forth in the *Lemon* case, hoping to replace it with a test that—in terms of our analysis of the requirements of a good rule in Chapter 4—would strike a better balance among the requisites of transparency, congruence, and simplicity. Nevertheless, the Court has passed in numerous cases that presented the justices with opportunities to overrule, so *Lemon* remains the test under the establishment clause of the Constitution. See "The Supreme Court, 1994 Term," 109 *Harvard Law Review* (November 1995) 10: 170–180, 210–220.

[2]*Mark up:* The process during which members of a legislative committee hammer out the final wording of a bill before reporting it to the floor—that is, before sending it to the full house to be debated and voted up or down.

[3]In Chapter 11, we'll delve a bit more deeply into the history of some of the Great Society programs, and we will consider the diagnoses offered for these failures by implementation researchers.

BOX 7.1

Excerpt from Chief Justice Warren Burger's Supreme Court Opinion in *Lemon* v. *Kurtzman*, 403 U.S. 602 (1971)

Pennsylvania has adopted a statutory program that provides financial support to non-public schools by way of reimbursement for the cost of teachers' salaries, textbooks, and instructional materials in specified secular subjects. Rhode Island has adopted a statute under which the State pays directly to teachers in nonpublic elementary schools a supplement of 15% of their annual salary. Under each statute state aid has been given to church-related educational institutions. We hold that both statutes are unconstitutional. . . .

The language of the Religion Clauses of the First Amendment is at best opaque, particularly when compared with other portions of the Amendment. Its authors did not simply prohibit the establishment of a state church or a state religion. . . . Instead they commanded that there should be "no law *respecting* an establishment of religion." A law may be one "respecting" the forbidden objective while falling short of its total realization. . . . A given law might not *establish* a state religion but nevertheless be one "respecting" that end in the sense of being a step that could lead to such establishment and hence offend the First Amendment. . . .

Every analysis in this area must begin with consideration of the cumulative criteria developed by the Court over many years. Three such tests may be gleaned from our cases. First, the statute must have a secular legislative purpose; second, its principal or primary effect must be one that neither advances nor inhibits religion; finally, the statute must not foster "an excessive government entanglement with religion." . . .

Judicial caveats against entanglement must recognize that the line of separation, far from being a "wall," is a blurred, indistinct, and variable barrier depending on all the circumstances of a particular relationship. . . .

In order to determine whether the government entanglement with religion is excessive, we must examine the character and purposes of the institutions that are benefited, the nature of the aid that the State provides, and the resulting relationship between the government and the religious authority. . . . Here we find that both statutes foster an impermissible degree of entanglement.

Human Services, where the rules will have to be written to set federal health and safety standards under the Quality Day Care Act." Haney added that, since the HHS rule drafters would want to stay in touch with administrators at the state and local levels, Blair might have to make some trips beyond the Washington Beltway herself to gain a firsthand sense of the way the new family policy seemed to be playing out there in television land.

• • • • •

The tax credit amendment increased the amount that a qualified working parent could credit annually against income taxes—from a maximum allowed under the old law ($2,400 of expenses incurred for the day care of each child) up to a maximum under the new law of $3,000 per year. The amendment made no other changes in the wording of the pertinent statutes, so most commentators argued that the same interpretation of the phrase *qualified working parent* that had applied under the earlier version of the law should control the new arrangement as well. The earlier version, as interpreted by the Internal Revenue Service, required a parent (1) to have a job for which the employer paid Social Security taxes for the worker and (2) to send a child on a paying basis to a formal day care center of some kind—in most cases, to a center organized as a nonprofit business. This interpretation of the criteria for a working parent to be considered "qualified" in effect denied eligibility for the income tax credit to a working parent who relied on family-based day care or who sent a child to an informal facility and didn't pay a "market rate" (as judged by IRS auditors) to the care provider. It also excluded many workers whose wages were usually outside the Social Security system—daily home cleaners, many painters and odd-job workers, most proprietors of marginal service businesses.

Now, however, there was talk of a new lobbying effort to change the official interpretation of the new law's "qualified working parent" provision. The attempt to liberalize the eligibility for the tax credit would be spearheaded by some of the same coalition leaders who had pressured Congress to get the new family-law package passed in the first place.

Spokespersons for the African American leadership, the National Conference of Catholic Bishops, and the National Council of *La Raza* branded the existing interpretation of *qualified working parent* as discriminatory. They said that any requirement for professional out-of-home day care before a parent could receive benefits created a **disparate impact**—the legal term for a law or policy that helps or hurts members of particular groups, even though it may not be discriminatory on its face.[4] In many minority communities, it is common for care providers to be members of the extended family—grandparents, aunts, cousins, or sisters who look after children in their own homes. Specifically, family-based child care is probably the rule, not the exception, wherever Hispanic Americans have settled in sufficient numbers to preserve the core traditions of *la familia Latina*. In Latino communities, many informal providers enjoy the special relationship known as *comadre* with the mothers of the children for whom they provide in-home care. The pattern isn't much different among African Americans. Table 7.2 breaks out statistics about child care patterns among various demographic groups in the county where Kendra Quinn works.

---

[4]Another standard example of a disparate-impact rule is a regulation that imposes strength or other physical requirements for a particular class of jobs, requirements that may seem—and may even actually be—perfectly fair when tested against the peculiarities of the work (for example, lifting packages on a loading dock) but which have the inevitable effect of discriminating against women. Other kinds of physical job qualifications—such as those the airlines used to apply when selecting flight attendants—discriminated against men. (The courts have since struck these requirements down as illegally discriminatory under the federal Civil Rights Act of 1964, even though the airlines showed that the majority of both female and male passengers preferred an attendant force composed entirely of "stewardesses.") Much litigation may be needed in the years ahead before the courts can frame general standards that legislators and employers can use to tell when a disparate-impact law, rule, or policy is prohibited.

Table 7.2 Differing Patterns of Day Care Utilization, Estimated by Selected Racial or Ethnic Grouping (percent)

	Families Using Day Care	Accredited Centers	Home-Based Care or Baby-Sitting
African American	60	7	53
Latino	58	5	53
All Others	46	29	17

Few of the home-based care providers on whom Latinas and African Americans rely would be able to meet the rigorous training standards that the child care professionals—the main proponents of the Quality Day Care Act—were advocating. Observers have also expressed doubt that many of these home-based day care facilities could meet the stiffer safety standards that the states now had to promulgate. Finally, the pay that parents typically give to care providers under family-based or home-based arrangements are well below the legal minimum wage level—if, indeed, money changes hands at all.

Lined up against those who want the new tax credit to be applicable to home-based day care are most of the professionals in the care provider industry. The child care professionals claim that any interpretation which would allow the tax credit for family-based care would undermine efforts to upgrade the expertise of care providers. Besides, the nation's lawmakers had meant to emphasize professional care provision in high-quality facilities. Otherwise, why would Congress have passed the Quality Day Care Act? Under the approach advocated by the professionals, the expanded tax credit would apply only to parents who send their children to formal day care centers that have been officially accredited—"registered"—under the new Quality Day Care Act.

Joining those pressing for heightened professionalism (and hence a narrow interpretation of what makes a working parent "qualified") are quite a few politicians, lobbyists, and plain citizens who are seeking ways to cut the level of public spending, even if it means limiting the amount of money spent for programs such as child care by limiting the numbers eligible for benefits.

Government watchers know what to expect: If the IRS tries to confine the benefits of the tax credit to parents who pay market rates and send their children to formal day care centers, advocates for family-based child care will go to court arguing that the legislative history shows an intent by Congress to interpret the law broadly. If on the other hand officials revise the tax instructions to allow the tax credit for family-based or for informal child care arrangements, opponents from the other side of the issue will launch a legal challenge, arguing that the very existence of a companion Quality Day Care Act implies an intent by Congress to upgrade the industry, a goal allegedly inconsistent with tax breaks for "substandard" day care arrangements.

•   •   •   •   •

Excerpt from "Your Representative's Report," a monthly newsletter mailed to constituents on franked postage from Congressman Stuart Helfin's office.

HELFIN IN LEAD FOR CHILD CARE TAX BREAK. Congressman Helfin was one of twenty-four co-authors of the tax reform amendment that you have been hearing about. As a senior member of the Special House Committee on Primary and Secondary Education, Helfin was a leader in the legislative battle to increase the federal tax deduction for parents using qualified child care assistance by an additional $600 per year.

Opponents of this measure based their arguments in part on the claim that it would cost too much. In a major speech during the floor debate, which you might have seen on C-Span, Congressman Helfin pointed out that better child care would permit more working mothers to *become* wage earners, and hence taxpayers. (A Congressional Budget Office study found that the increase in taxes from additional earnings made possible by expanded child care nationally would offset the losses to the Treasury from the additional deduction.)

Further limits on the effective cost of the new deduction—and, Helfin pointed out in his C-Span speech, a further protection against abuse of the new tax provision—would come from the Internal Revenue Service. "To ensure that this new tax expenditure benefits only those who need it, and who use it in the way intended under the law, thirteen members of the Rural Caucus have signed a letter to the IRS suggesting that screeners of federal income tax returns during the early years of the program adopt a special by-mail audit program to ensure that taxpayers who claim the deduction can produce receipts or canceled checks for child care expenses that they actually incurred."

•   •   •   •   •

The new Quality Day Care Act requires the Secretary of Health and Human Services to set "minimum national day care standards." Administrators in each state must then write implementing rules and set up an inspection regime. In order to gain listing as a "registered" center, a day care facility must be certified by local inspectors as being in compliance with a "state compliance plan." The state compliance plan in turn must satisfy the national requirements set forth by the Secretary of HHS (assuming, of course, that the courts find the federal regulations, when finally issued, to be themselves reasonable interpretations of the congressional intent).

Of course, in actual practice, the personal involvement of the Secretary of Health and Human Services in these programs may end when someone within HHS is designated as the official responsible for implementing the Quality Day Care Act. Lower-level administrators will then begin the long and complicated process of drafting regulations. All the while, they will remain in touch with their key contacts on the relevant congressional staffs, within the relevant community of policy professionals (what do the experts think "minimum national day care standards" should require?), and especially in the states and localities, where all the above will finally have to be carried into implementation.

•   •   •   •   •

Excerpt from the "On the Lookout" section of The Network: A National Journal of Feminist Opinion:

Talk about Perverse Incentives!
Who's Helping Whom Here?

Nationally, women jobholders who work more than 40 hours per week pay about $100 per week per child for day care. Many middle-class parents can afford to send their infant children to higher-cost (up to $350 per week per child) fully regulated day care centers. Under the new regulatory legislation, these parents will gain both the benefits of improved child care service and also the benefit of the child care tax credit. If the voucher program gets signed into law, these middle-class and well-to-do parents—who already send their children to what are, in effect, "registered" facilities under any interpretation of the new law—will also qualify for a subsidy of up to $200 per month.

Observers of the day care industry have long known that many poor parents pass up job openings in order to care for their children at home. Their only realistic alternative is to leave their children with family members (who charge little or nothing for their services) or send them for semiformal home-based care with extremely low-cost providers. Such providers typically operate in facilities with little chance of qualifying for "registered" status; yet they are deterred

from upgrading because the costs of remodeling and wage increases are prohibitive. It's one of the clearest cases we've ever seen of disparate impact. To the extent that many low-cost providers will refuse to pursue registration and that eligibility for the tax credit is tied to children's attendance at registered centers, the registration requirement will make it impossible for many poor working parents to gain the tax benefit of the liberalized legislation. The new legislation turns out to be a cruel hoax!

Under the terms of the legislation as it now stands, the well-to-do will do well, but those who most need the benefits of a "national family policy"—the poor—will experience no change in their situations except a *loss* of the tax credit because of the new registration requirement! As one woman expressed it: "It's all an obvious case of indirect discrimination. The rules look neutral and impartial, but in their actual effect, they help some and hurt others. They hurt blacks and *Latinas,* and they hurt single working mothers. It's wrong that who cares for the kids should depend on whose kids they are, right?"

•   •   •   •   •

The president had used an Oval Office signing ceremony to underscore his support for the new $3,000 tax credit. In the speech he made when signing the credit amendment into law, he had stressed that a major goal of family policy should be to make child care more affordable and more widely available. Of course, affordability would contribute to availability, implying that nationally, thousands of additional centers would begin to appear after the tax credit and (perhaps) the voucher program began putting extra money into people's pockets. Where was suitable space going to come from? It was hard to imagine that key figures in the city's Bureau of Human Services wouldn't find themselves involved in the hunt for usable facilities. Among the local BHS figures who would doubtless play parts in the development of a more "parent-friendly" day care system were the director of the bureau, Aaron Haber; the head of the Housing Department within the bureau, Evelyn Alvarado; and one of Alvarado's staff assistants, Kendra Quinn.

Evelyn Alvarado informed Kendra Quinn that she wouldn't be surprised if Director Haber decided to set up a special department within the BHS. A new Department of Child Care would probably occupy a rung on the organizational ladder parallel to that of Alvarado's own Housing Department. But any restructuring would take time. Anyway, irrespective of Director Haber's plans for reorganization (or lack of them), Alvarado thought that "the responsible thing to do" would be to start thinking immediately about tasks that seemed likely to come her way under the impetus of the new legislation. She told Quinn: "We should begin right now tracking the progress of the federal rule makings. The IRS will be issuing a rule interpreting the tax-break provision. HHS will have to produce new regulations covering the health and safety requirements." Alvarado thought a second. "Actually," she continued, "we'll probably have to get into the rule-making business ourselves, at least indirectly."

Responding to a quizzical look on Kendra's face, Evelyn explained that the new Quality Day Care Act mandated the states to come up with compliance plans that would meet new *federal* standards for child care facilities. "Which means," Evelyn said, "that a team will be assembled in the *state* Department of Social Services to spell out procedures for *local* inspectors to follow when they check applicants for the status of 'registered' centers. It's like gears interlocking. Local officials—city building inspectors, child care experts on the county payroll, and so forth—will have to implement the state compliance plan. The state people wouldn't even think of acting without asking the implementers in city and county agencies what they think about it all."

"And that 'they' is 'us.'" said Kendra.

Evelyn nodded. The rule writers at the state level would have to stay in touch with the HHS team during the federal rule-drafting process; they would also be coordinating on a regular basis with the prospective implementers, administrators in the county's Department of Welfare Services and the city's Bureau of Human Services.

"Probably," Evelyn said, "the contacts between the local people (such as ourselves) and the state rule writers will be formalized somewhat through the creation of a committee with reps from various city, county, and state agencies. It'll be the panel members' job to help the state rule writers with their work." That gave Evelyn a thought. She considered it briefly and then said that Kendra should add an assignment to her current list of duties: to serve as Evelyn's all-purpose policy adviser, research assistant, and official delegate on the unfolding new family-policy initiatives. It meant, for example, that Kendra Quinn would serve as the Housing Department's rep on the interagency rule-drafting panel that Evelyn Alvarado expected would soon be set up.

• • • • •

As Alvarado had emphasized, any significant expansion in local day care offerings would involve prospective care providers in the search for usable space. As "City Housing Czar"—a title that local journalists had bestowed on her with good-humored overstatement—Evelyn Alvarado probably had better information about patterns of building utilization throughout the region than did anyone else, whether in government or in private real estate practice.

"The way these things work," Evelyn told Kendra, "is that all the private day care people who already have operations will start asking us about any new requirements under the amended laws. They'll ask about any changes in inspection standards and schedules and about how much time they'll have before they're expected to be in full compliance with the new rules." True, the drafting of new requirements would be the responsibility of the state-level administrators. Nevertheless, local citizens would expect Alvarado's people to be in regular touch with the state team. Interested parties would turn for the ungarbled word to officials with whom they had already developed a continuing rapport—namely, to Alvarado's staffers in the city Housing Department.

Evelyn continued: "Inspection standards will only be the beginning of it. We'll have folks deciding to go into the day care business. Those wanna-be providers will come to us wanting to know where they can get vacant space to set up shop."

Evelyn and Kendra considered the options. No doubt some care providers would build brand-new facilities that incorporated all the new standards (option 1). Others would want to expand and improve existing centers (option 2). Still other potential caregivers would search out existing buildings for conversion: the corner grocery store that had gone out of business but could become the corner child care center; the occasional old residence that could—with refurbishment and maybe a zoning variance—do service as a registered child care facility (option 3).

"I also suppose," Evelyn said, "it should be possible to get some of the space that will be needed simply by making better use of local public and private school facilities (option 4). Every grade school, whether public or parochial, has an assembly room; maybe some of those could be used for day care. Every church, temple, and synagogue has a hall." Lots of parishes were having serious financial difficulties. Alvarado had no reason to think that what she knew to be true within the area's Catholic community wasn't true in the Protestant and Jewish communities as well. Most pastors, she assumed, would be happy to offer day care services to their parishioners if they could collect some federal money for doing so—a real possibility if the president decided not to veto the voucher program on constitutional or fiscal grounds.

Alvarado and Quinn then added the final category of space to their inventory: space in the homes of relatives and close friends (option 5). Evelyn admitted in passing that she had virtually been "brought up by her 'Tia Paloma'" while her own mother worked long hours as a nurses' aide at Agnus Dei Hospital. If she were making the call, she wouldn't begrudge a liberal flow of federal funds so that the informal day care pattern which had worked for her could be expanded for others who desired that kind of arrangement.

Kendra Quinn also sympathized with those who hoped for a liberal interpretation of the new laws. She understood the feelings of parents who thought that child care vouchers should be negotiable as readily for day care in a parish-based facility as in a secular center. Quinn could also appreciate why most minority-group members thought they should qualify for the new tax break even if they opted for family-based arrangements rather than for day care in more expensive "registered child care centers." Of course, she knew, there was an additional wrinkle to be considered in connection with the tax credit. A tax credit provision only benefits individuals who earn enough in wages to pay income taxes in the first place. African Americans and Latinos in disproportionate numbers live close to the poverty line, where tax deductions—whether for mortgage interest payments, charitable giving, or child care expenses—are of little relevance. That fact too raised some hard questions, in Quinn's mind, of fairness and disparate-impact effects.

• • • • •

Congresswoman Ellen Moe was on the line to Haney Brill. The president owed Moe a favor or two, based on votes that she had recently cast for legislation that he supported. That little bit of history meant that a call from Ellen Moe to one of the president's counselors was worth taking, even if Brill had to interrupt a meeting with several of his staff assistants in order to do so.

Haney Brill expected that it must be payback time. Maybe Congresswoman Moe wanted White House help to get someone hired (or fired) in the executive branch. Maybe she wanted him to light a fire under some agency bureaucrat who was sitting on money or a development project ticketed for her economically troubled district up there in northeast Minnesota.

"No, Haney," Ellen said after a favorable comment about the recent strategy session and some banter about the political IOUs she held, "I'm calling to *do* you a favor, not ask for one."

"I'm not sure we want to get any deeper in your debt!" Haney joked.

"Let me tell you what's on my mind. Then you decide."

Moe, Brill knew, sat not only on the House Special Subcommittee on Primary and Secondary Education, a so-called **authorization committee**,[5] but also on two subcommittees of the Committee on Labor and Health and Human Services. The latter was the regular House **appropriations committee**[6] with funding authority in the family-policy area. Congresswoman Moe regularly engaged in the accepted legislative process known as bringing the bacon—"pork"—back to her congressional district. By longstanding tradition in the House of Representatives, members of appropriations committees enjoy something approaching moral entitlements to earmark modest sums for purposes they deem important in their home areas. (See Box 7.2.)

An appropriations committee member, after gaining behind-the-scenes support from his or her colleagues, earmarks funds by inserting a statement of committee intent—the reason for the earmark and its amount—into the report that accompanies the formal appropriations bill when it goes to the floor of the House. Naturally, there's some politicking and logrolling. Not every committee member usually gets approval for all that he or she might want. In general, however, members of appropriations

---

[5]*Authorization committee:* A committee or subcommittee in a legislative body with primary responsibility for producing bills that set legal permissions or requirements for agencies. A new program, such as a facilities-upgrading program, usually originates as an authorization bill.

[6]*Appropriations committee:* A legislative committee or subcommittee responsible for funding programs that have previously been authorized. For example, once a facilities-upgrading program has been enacted into law, an appropriations committee will usually recommend how much money should be allotted to support the authorization. The program may endure for years with an unchanged statutory mandate, while undergoing significant year-to-year variations in funding levels based on changing appropriations committee recommendations. Sometimes (but not frequently) the authorizing language will specify an appropriation. Conversely, sometimes appropriations committee members will report out bills that authorize new programs as well as fund existing ones. Nevertheless, in American practice the authorization and appropriations processes are distinct, and members of the two kinds of committees usually try to guard their turfs from trespass by each other.

BOX 7.2 ■ ■ ■

Earmarking Appropriations in the U.S. House of Representatives

... [I]f two hundred years of appropriations history is a guide, earmarked projects are here to stay.

Hardly anyone has a nice thing to say about the practice. The president and executive agencies do not want earmarks because they tie their hands and divert funds from their priorities. Authorizing committees do not want them in appropriations bills because the committees would rather do the earmarking in their own bills. Members of Congress who do not get what they regard as a fair share of funds complain that the practice is wasteful and demeaning. ... The news media and critics of Congress see corruption and vote buying behind just about every earmarked project.

Earmarks flourish because members of the Appropriations Committees would rather decide where funds are to be spent than let executive agencies make the determination. They flourish because the chief political value of serving on the Appropriations Committees is to bring home the bacon, not to guard the Treasury. They flourish because a spending bill with a lot of projects spread across the country is easier to pass than is one without them. They flourish in good times, when incremental resources are bountiful, and, it seems, even more in hard times when the budget is tight.

The truth is that most earmarks are relatively cheap; many can be crammed into tight budgets. And when funds are scarce, pork is prized because it may be the only kind of benefit that members can bring home. Programs, by contrast, are expensive because they typically provide nationwide rather than local benefits. Consider, for example, a proposal to improve U.S. education by upgrading teaching material. Even if this program were to start modestly, with only $100 allotted per student, the total cost would exceed $5 billion. Suppose, however, that instead of a national program a member of Congress earmarks $1 million to a local project. In the political arithmetic of budgeting, $100 may be too expensive but $1 million is affordable. Imagine that every member of Congress were to earmark $1 million. The total would be a bit more than $500 million, ... only one-thirtieth of 1 percent of total federal spending.

From Allen Schick, *The Federal Budget* (Washington: Brookings Institution, 1995), p. 141.

■ ■ ■

committees honor one another's most urgent earmarking priorities. As a general rule too, most members of Congress vote for the appropriations bills—earmarks and all—in pretty much the forms in which the regular appropriations committees report them.

Congresswoman Moe told Haney Brill that she was earmarking $2 million to support child care initiatives in her district. The plan—again, following a common practice in Congress—was to set aside that amount of federal money in the forthcoming budget year to support day care "demonstration projects." Other earmarks would also be taken by Moe's colleagues on the pertinent subcommittees and on the full Committee on Labor and Health and Human Services. A few noncommittee members had also wangled concessions from the committee leaders and would therefore have set-asides to dedicate to projects in their home areas. All these set-asides would add up to the not-untidy sum of a half-billion dollars—again, mostly for "demonstration projects," "special facilities," or "pilot programs." Collectively, the earmarks would funnel money—mostly in $1, $2, or $3 million increments—into some 250 of the nation's 436 congressional districts. (That's 435 "voting districts" plus the District of Columbia, which has a nonvoting "shadow representative" in Congress.) In turn, of the 250 members of Congress who would be bringing pork home from the Labor and Health and Human Services appropriation, some 75 had explicitly committed to earmark projects in support of the national child care initiative.

Congresswoman Moe told Brill that, irrespective of their party affiliations, the members of this "Caucus of 75" had pledged to work "on a bipartisan basis for a fiscally responsible family policy." They, like the president, wanted "a policy that would work." In line with the approach that the members of the recent strategy session in Brill's office had settled on, neither the members of the congressional "Caucus of 75" nor the president wanted another social program with nice symbolism but little staying power or provable beneficial results. Ellen Moe suggested that Haney swivel around and look at the document that should be coming through on his fax machine even as she spoke. He turned to watch the paper feed and, after a moment, retrieved the message.

"You got it? Good," Ellen said. "What you're holding are possible drafts of the earmaking language we in the 'Caucus of 75' are considering for the appropriations committee report. At an average of a $2-million earmark per representative, we're talking about $150 million that Congress will put selectively into districts to support child care. That's in addition," she emphasized, "to the tax expenditure [the amount of revenue that will be lost each year to the Treasury because of the credit that qualified working parents can deduct from their federal income taxes under the new legislation]. The $150 million will also be in addition to any money that flows into child care if the president signs the voucher bill."

The members of the "Caucus of 75," according to Ellen, couldn't commit in advance to support a position with which they or their constituents had severe reservations just because someone in the White House urged it. At the same time, Moe assured Brill, most of the 75 members who were bringing earmarks for child care back to their districts would value his advice on the best way to word the earmarking paragraphs in the committee report.

Haney thanked Ellen. Extra money from Congress—even the relatively modest sum of $150 million, and even if disbursed in the form of pork-barrel set-asides that were almost randomly distributed among 75 congressional districts—would surely help in the president's family-policy effort. Even more important, Haney thought, was the apparent willingness of the members of Congress from both parties to use their earmarking prerogatives in whatever way promised the best long-term family-policy payoff instead of individually calculating their potential political returns and directing their $2-million set-asides accordingly. ("How should I spend 'my' $2 million to maximize contributions to my next campaign?")

Haney told Ellen that he'd look over the alternative earmarking paragraphs as soon as his staff meeting was done and would call her back with his reactions. "And by the way," he added, "needless to say, Ellen: I owe you one."

"You owe me quite a few more than one," Congresswoman Moe replied with good humor; then she hung up.

Brill reconvened his meeting and quickly pushed through the remaining items on the agenda. After his assistants had left, he looked for the first time with care at the page that Ellen Moe had faxed to him:

ALTERNATIVE FORMULATIONS OF EARMARKING LANGUAGE

1. The [Labor and Health and Human Services] Committee is aware of efforts under way in the towns of [each member of the 'Caucus of 75' would insert the names of several towns or cities in the district] to upgrade child care facilities to bring them into compliance with the registration provisions of the Quality Day Care Act. The Committee earmarks $2 million for use in developing improved upgrading techniques at existing centers in these towns, which will also enable such centers to meet the standards issued pursuant to that Act.

2. The Committee is aware that many low-income parents may have trouble paying for high-quality child care services even with the help of the liberalized tax provisions of current law. The Committee earmarks $2 million to be administered by [insert here the title of the appropriate agency of local government in the pertinent congressional district], with the intent of supplementing the ability of parents whose family incomes, adjusted for the number of family members, fall below 125 percent of the official federal poverty line, and who fulfill the requirements of "qualified working parents," to defray the costs of child care.

3. The Committee is aware that many parents may have trouble paying for high-quality child care services even with the help of the liberalized tax provisions of current law. The Committee earmarks $2 million to be distributed by [insert here the title of the appropriate agency of local government in the pertinent congressional district], with the intent of supplementing the ability of "qualified working parents" to defray the costs of child care.

At the bottom of the page, Congresswoman Moe had penned:

Haney:

Which formulation—or any other phrasing you want to suggest—seems most likely to get $2 million spent in the most productive way in a congressional district?[7] Fax me your suggestions.

Ellen Moe

•　　•　　•　　•　　•

[7]In 1996, Congress passed a law providing for a presidential **line-item veto**. In limited cases, the president may veto a particular item in a federal spending bill instead of having to accept or reject the bill as a whole. The change applies mainly to *discretionary spending*—spending that is set in a current appropriations bill and not determined by legislation that establishes automatic entitlements to certain government benefits, such as Medicare and Social Security benefits. The actual effect of a new law often remains obscure for years,

Kendra Quinn and Gene Petitsaint got almost identical notes from their respective bosses, Evelyn Alvarado and Nora Smith. The notes contained time-and-place information about a meeting to be held with a visiting VIP from Washington. The visitor, a White House aide named Blair Songster, apparently had primary responsibility for coordinating interdepartmental actions (Health and Human Services, Labor Department, and so forth) at the federal level as well as state-local responses to the president's initiatives in the child care field. Songster was also supposed to expedite the writing of regulations for the Quality Day Care Act.

The notes from Alvarado and Smith described the forthcoming meeting as an opportunity for Songster to get input from locals around the country. Reportedly, Songster wanted to have an informal exchange of views with representatives from state, county, and municipal agencies who were likely to be involved in the implementation of the new child care laws. Songster was midway through a series of these get-togethers in Sunbelt cities. Kendra Quinn and Gene Petitsaint were told that the meeting with Songster would start sharply at 9 A.M., take the entire morning, and lap over a bit into the afternoon. It would be held in a large conference room of the BHS building. The agenda called for a working lunch of sandwiches and soda, to be served at noon, followed by a wrapup session ending no later than 2:30 P.M., so Songster could catch a cab to the airport for an afternoon plane to the next city she would visit.

Quinn and Petitsaint both expected to find a small group in attendance at the Songster meeting, the better to foster an open discussion of the many uncertainties that still remained in the new national family policy. Contrary to their anticipations, on the appointed day, Kendra and Gene observed that just about every unit of the city and county governments seemed to have sent a delegate. Also present at the meeting—showing the flag for Hizzoner the mayor, who wanted to cooperate with the feds on child care policy—was Peter York. In point of fact, the long invitation list had been Songster's idea. Plainly, the meeting wasn't to be a small working session. On the contrary, it became apparent that Blair Songster intended to "tell them, not ask them." Her mission wasn't so much to gather input as it was to give the folks in the provinces the Washington line. Obviously, certain implementation decisions had already been made at the White House level. Songster evidently thought it her job to explain "the president's position" (Read: the conclusions of Haney Brill and other Washington-based family-policy mavens) around the country in the hope that state and local officials could all agree to follow a common family-policy agenda.

According to Songster, the first, necessary requirement of a coherent and successful family policy was for regulations that could be uniformly implemented across the country and could withstand the court challenges that new federal regulations always prompt.

Blair Songster began by saying: "We think this family-values program is necessary, every bit of it—the tax break, the upgrading of child care centers. And if the pres-

until the courts have ruled on its constitutionality and meaning in concrete cases. But the new veto power, to take effect in early 1997, would probably apply to the "Caucus of 75" earmarks. No doubt, Congresswoman Moe's overture to the White House had a motive beyond the simple desire to get Haney Brill's opinion on the merits of the earmarks. A member of Congress who wants to add an item of expenditure to legislation may try to ensure that the president won't veto it when the bill comes to the Oval Office for signature by making a special effort (as Moe does here) to bring the wording of the spending provision into conformity with presidential preferences ident goes for the vouchers, well, we have to make sure that it's a 'clean' program, too—not overly complicated so it doesn't reach half the people it's intended to help (like food stamps), and absolutely free of corruption.

"We could design the programs in different ways," she continued. Then she set forth the polar cases that had been considered by a working group of members of Congress and White House staffers. The basic alternatives, Songster said, consisted of a strategy aimed at maximizing the number of children served and a strategy aimed at building administrative capacity by serving a much smaller number of children and troubleshooting potential problems before increasing the scale of the new child care services. Songster said that even though "maximizing the numbers" might seem the preferable strategy politically, the working group members had finally concluded that "minimizing mistakes and embarrassments" would best serve not only the president's political interests in the long run but also the interests of the nation's children.

"To sum it up," Songster said, "The aim in implementing the new legislation isn't—that's 'is *not*'—to get the number of additional kids in day care to go up fast. The aim is just the opposite: to build new child care capacity slowly and get the implementation of family policy right as we go."

Songster explained: "Our consensus in the working group is that too-rapid expansion of day care facilities would push the rule writers, both in HHS and in the states, to crank out a hastily drawn set of regs. It could also invite carelessness in program implementation as everyone tried to do to much too fast. Carelessness in rule drafting and implementation could lead to exploding costs and to questionable interpretations of eligibility and benefits. We'd get caught up in avoidable litigation." Songster then cited the problems in nursing homes back in the 1980s: fires in poorly regulated convalescent facilities, incompetent staffs in nursing homes—all the result, she contended, of expanding facilities too rapidly without ensuring the strict standards and close regulation.

Songster paused, apparently for reactions. When there were none, she went on: "I met with the Secretary [of HHS] herself to discuss this strategy—the 'Get it right' strategy, we call it—and before that, I met several times with the working group that included Haney Brill and John Pospisil. I also spoke with M.C.s Stu Helfin, Irene Platt, and Ellen Moe; Helfin chairs the House Special Subcommittee on Primary and Secondary Education. We think, given the mood in the country, that it's essential to prevent horror stories from coming out of the first year of these laws: We don't want cheating on the tax deduction, and we don't want people trading vouchers for money (assuming the president signs the bill), and we don't want the phrase *registered child care centers* to be interpreted loosely." Blair Songster paused briefly for effect: "We want the rules strict and clear, and we want the enforcement strict and uniform."

Now it was time for questions. For a half-minute or so, no one spoke. Then Kendra Quinn raised her hand and asked if Songster and the others in her working group had estimated the number of children who would, in the first year or so, be *excluded* from some or all benefits if the "Get it right" approach ended up—as it obviously would—denying registered status to home-based and informal day care arrangements. It was easy, Quinn noted, to think of a set of rules being drafted that would tie the "qualified working parent" provision to enrollment of the children in registered day care centers. Thus denial of registration could lead to further denials—of eligibility for the tax credit and even for voucher eligibility—if the Washington regulators wrote a strict set of rules and then held states to strict compliance.

Blair seemed to think it a fair question—not a very friendly one, but, yes, a fair one. She answered: "I have no firm estimate. One purpose of this trip is to get a sense . . . only impressionistic, I admit . . . of how the 'Get it right' approach we're suggesting will play around the country."

Kendra emphasized that she could give no more than a rough-and-ready, impressionistic response. She said that she and her boss, city housing director Evelyn Alvarado, had been doing some homework. They assumed it would be useful to project the increased demand for child care service—and hence for physical space dedicated to the family-policy mission—that seemed likely to materialize when the benefits in the new legislation become available. Blair was now implying that the rate of expansion would have to be a lot slower than Kendra and Evelyn had been expecting. The kind of program described by Blair would, to put it in plain terms, simply exclude most African Americans and Hispanics. Behind all the puffery and promises, was the vaunted national family policy just another middle-class program to give mostly white parents a tax break and upgrade the formal day care centers where well-off kids were already enrolled?

•   •   •   •   •

It was Kendra Quinn's first official meeting with Aaron Haber. She had, of course, seen the director around, and had met him several times at various kinds of social events and receptions for Bureau of Human Services staff members. This time, she saw, it was to be a meeting for serious business. Evelyn Alvarado was also in attendance.

Aaron Haber said that he'd been pleased with the initiative that Evelyn and her staffers—that meant Kendra—had taken to get BHS ready for the administrative phases of the new federal legislation. "But ad hoc responses won't cut it for long," he said.

As Evelyn Alvarado had expected, Haber was going to set up a new Department of Child Care within the BHS. The toughest immediate job would be one of "organizational design." Should the new office be within the Housing Department or a freestanding division within the BHS? Realizing that relations with the feds would, as these kinds of programs develop, be crucial, Haber wanted special thought to be given to "any IGR implications that we should keep in mind and, perhaps, build into our initial design and organization of the new child care office."

Aaron turned to Kendra and asked: "Why don't you take a few days to think through the issues raised by the new federal legislation in particular, and by the child care policy in general. What kinds of questions should we ask ourselves as we move to set up the new shop? What caveats and patterns of strain, if any, should be kept in mind when organizing and staffing the new outfit?"

•   •   •   •   •

"No," Evelyn agreed later that day to Kendra, "Aaron really didn't give you a very firm set of instructions. What he *did* give you is an opportunity to think this child care question through, putting some foresight and structure into it. After all, if the director had found the time to think the problem through for himself, he wouldn't need help now." The help Haber expected would come in the form of a brief memo from Kendra Quinn on the subject of child care organization.

Questions for Discussion
• • • • • • • • • • • • • • • • • •

The following queries might help you to frame your thoughts and organize a discussion of the case.

1. What's the story? What choices have to be made by whom? Where, if at all, do problems of underdetermination and overdetermination crop up in this scenario? How does a central tension discussed in the reading by Peterson, Rabe, and Wong—between "rule-bound" administrators and "place-bound" local politicians—show up in the situation?

2. In which of the Peterson, Rabe, and Wong categories—developmental programs and redistributive programs—would you place each of the components of the new federal family policy? Does the analysis by these authors of the relative difficulty of implementing federal developmental and redistributive programs suggest any points that the president and influential members of Congress should have borne in mind as they were working out the original outlines of the policy?

3. Do you think the voucher program passes the *Lemon* case's tests ("secular purpose," "neither advance nor inhibit," "no excessive entanglement")? When there is reasonable doubt about the constitutionality of a new law, do you think it's better to "go slow" lest an eventual adverse Supreme Court decision throw a field of public policy into disarray? Or is it better to move vigorously in the direction favored by elected leaders—perhaps in the hope that the momentum will actually help establish a climate of legitimacy? Taking constitutional uncertainties into consideration along with other factors, what would you advise the president to do about the voucher program?

4. How did the child care function—traditionally, a responsibility of the family—come to be a public responsibility? Which of the arguments in Chapter 6 for "taking functions public" seems to apply most directly to the child care issue?

5. "Check the numbers." What inferences do you draw from the estimates in Table 7.2? What implications, if any, do you draw from these figures for public policy, and how do they relate to the disparate-impact issue?

6. Blair Songster candidly states the options in child care policy as she and her White House cohorts see them: *Either* a narrowly defined new day care program that serves fewer children but is unlikely to self-destruct because of embarrassing incidents in implementation; *or* an expansive program serving larger numbers but at greater cost to the government and also more vulnerable to political and legal attack. Do you think that Songster and her White House colleagues have selected the correct course? Why or why not?

7. IGR is, among other things, about the division of authority among the national, state, and local levels of government. Do you think Congress should have been more specific in the wording of the new tax credit and the Quality Day Care Act, thereby delegating less discretion to the rule writers in the IRS and the Department of Health and Human Services? What case (if any) can be made for leaving

requirements so vague that the hammering out of concrete interpretations and implementation plans must be undertaken by administrators and ad hoc groups such as the team that met in Haney Brill's office and the congressional "Caucus of 75"?

8. What do you think of the approach that the members of the "Caucus of 75" have devised to give a modest financial boost to family policy? If you were in Haney Brill's position, which of the earmarking versions would you prefer to see in the report of the Labor and Health and Human Services appropriations committee? "Where you stand depends on where you sit." How might your viewpoint change if you were, say, a "poor-people's" advocate or a local elected official (say a mayor or county executive) instead of a presidential adviser?

9. Can you think of a better way to package a $150-million subsidy for the child care initiative than in seventy-five separate earmarks? What obstacles would you be likely to encounter if you tried to sell your better way to the "Caucus of 75"? Are the advantages of your way sufficiently greater than those of a pork-barrel approach to justify the effort?

10. Suppose you found yourself, as Kendra Quinn now does, tasked to think through the organization of an office in city government that will be created to implement the new family policy (whatever it turns out to be). Which paradigms of organization would you invoke when considering alternative ways of structuring a child care unit? How might the accumulated knowledge we have about the policy implementation process affect your thinking? In what ways might Quinn reflect her sensitivity to the "rule-bound versus place-bound" issue as she takes on the restructuring job that Director Haber has just given her? Remaining mindful of our discussions in this and earlier chapters about picket fence federalism, executive federalism, the workings of issue networks, and the role of policy professionals, what factors do you think Quinn should tell Haber to consider when he starts recruiting men and women to staff the new Department of Child Care?

FOR FURTHER READING

Among the standard works of the last few decades on American federalism are

Anton, Thomas J. *American Federalism and Public Policy* (New York: Random House, 1989); still, perhaps, the best single overview of the subject.

Derthick, Martha, "American Federalism: Madison's Middle Ground," 47 *Public Administration Review* (1987).

Elazar, Daniel, *American Federalism: A View from the States* (New York: Crowell, 1972).

Grodzins, Morton, *The American System* (Chicago: Rand McNally, 1966).

Walker, David, *Toward a Functioning Federalism* (Cambridge MA: Winthrop, 1981).

For accounts of more recent developments, see

Conlan, Timothy, *The New Federalism: Intergovernmental Reform from Nixon to Reagan* (Washington: Brookings Institution, 1988).

DiIulio, John, and Donald F. Kettl, *Fine Print: The Contract with America, Devolution, and the Administrative Realities of American Federalism* (Washington: Brookings Institution, 1995).

Hanus, Jerome J., "Intergovernmental Authority Costs," in Leach, Richard, ed., *Intergovernmental Relations in the 1980s* (New York: Marcel Dekker, 1983).

Nathan, Richard, "The Untold Story of Reagan's "New Federalism," 77 *Public Interest* (Fall 1984), 96.

Wise, Charles, and Rosemary O'Leary, "Is Federalism Dead or Alive in the Supreme Court? Implications for Public Administrators" 52 *Public Administration Review* (November–December 1992), 559.

Wright, Deil S., "Federalism, Intergovernmental Relations and Intergovernmental Management: Historical Reflections and Conceptual Comparisons," 50 *Public Administration Review* (March–April 1990), 168.

Useful case studies (the subject areas are indicated generally in the titles) include

Derthick, Martha, *The Influence of Federal Grants: Public Assistance in Massachusetts* (Cambridge MA: Harvard U. Press, 1970).

Gormley, William T., "Food Fights: Regulatory Enforcement in a Federal System," 52 *Public Administration Review* (May–June 1992), 271; on the workings of the regional offices of the USDA.

Keaney, Richard, and Robert B. Garey, "American Federalism and the Management of Radioactive Wastes" 42 *Public Administration Review* (January–February 1982), 14.

Kettl, Donald F., *The Regulation of American Federalism* (Baltimore: Johns Hopkins Press [1983], 1987); still a highly useful source on the workings of the U.S. Environmental Protection Agency.

May, Peter, and Walter Williams, *Disaster Policy Implementation: Managing Programs under Shared Governance* (New York: Plenum Press, 1986).

Morgan, David, and Robert England, "The Small Cities Block Grant Program: An Assessment of Programmatic Changes under State Control," 44 *Public Administration Review* (November–December 1984), 477.

On the problems of an American "family policy"—or lack of it—with particular reference to the child care issue, see

Berry, Mary Frances, *The Politics of Parenthood* (New York: Viking, 1993).

Besharov, Douglas, and Paul Tramontozzi, "Federal Child Care Assistance: A Growing Middle-Class Entitlement," 8 *Journal of Policy Analysis and Management* (1989), 313.

Gormley, William, *Everybody's Children: Child Care as a Public Problem* (Washington: Brookings Institution, 1995).

Note: "Into the Mouths of Babes: La Familia Latina and Federally Funded Child Care," 105 *Harvard Law Review* (April 1992), 1319.

CHAPTER 8

▽◆●■▽◆●■▽◆●■▽◆●■▽◆

Introduction to the Ethics of Public Roles

In the ideal institutional division of labor, public officials have just the powers they need to do what they're supposed to—no more, no less. The same is true for private individuals in their capacities as parents, entrepreneurs, contributors to charitable organizations, and so forth. A proper matching of functions to institutions lets private and public actors concentrate on where they have their comparative advantages. With the right private-public balance, everybody wins.

Many students of political theory think truly modern social thought began when Thomas Hobbes emphasized that private fulfillment depends on public order. Only if the government builds roads, establishes public schools, provides for the common defense, and satisfies the desires of all citizens for order in the neighborhood will citizens feel able to concentrate on inventing and manufacturing better mousetraps. On the other hand, it's important not to saddle government with too many responsibilities. The existence of a private sphere—a sphere of voluntary and free-market action—reduces the range of tasks that government officials must see to, making it possible to keep public power within manageable limits. (Think about the collapse of so many communist regimes. The old Soviet Union was almost all public sphere, a system that had to be managed entirely by government officials. In time the bureaucrats found that they just couldn't run every aspect of a complex economy. A lesson can be drawn: Everyone loses if the balance of private and public functions demands of public administrators more than they can—in Woodrow Wilson's words—"properly and successfully do.")

All of this suggests that the decision to declare a function as a public need, to move it out of private hands, shouldn't be taken lightly. Making a function a public responsibility alters the influence of the state in citizens' lives, usually enlarges the public budget, and often requires changes in the organization of government. The decision to take a function public also modifies the ethical and political obligations of the men and women who serve in public roles. *Roles* here refers to the patterns of action that are expected of the incumbents of public offices. Primary among these expectations are certain ought-tos and should-dos that derive from the general concept of a public role. We'll see that these obligations can be broadly divided into an official's duty to consider the consequences of his or her actions ("outcome-centered" considerations, in the language of moral philosophy) and a duty to employ acceptable means ("action-centered" restrictions). These two **general paradigms of obligation**—*general* because they apply to virtually all actions by anyone in any public role—are our subject in Section 1 of this chapter.

As noted, the general paradigms of obligation require an official not only to estimate the probable consequences (both positive and negative) of a public decision but also to control the actions that administrators take even in the pursuit of desirable outcomes. It's never enough that the outcomes are likely to be beneficial; *how* officials obtain those outcomes are critical factors as well. Official behavior must meet basic requirements of fairness, impartiality, and respect for the dignity of ordinary citizens. (How did you think you were treated the last time a traffic officer stopped you and issued a ticket? Whether you committed the violation or not was only part of it; *how* the officer dealt with you and followed though were just as important—as you no doubt concluded for yourself, especially if you thought you had grounds for grievance in any of these respects.)

In Section 2 of the chapter we'll take up certain **specific paradigms of obligation**—*specific* in that they involve special requirements based on particular kinds of roles. Perhaps the most obvious example is the special obligation of an official when in the role of a program implementer to obey orders. We have already (in Chapter 4) touched on the special duty of an official in an adjudicative role to act fairly when settling disputes. Later on (in Chapter 10), we'll deal with yet another specific paradigm, namely, the peculiar obligation of a service provider to put the needs of the client or patient first. Before we're done, we'll see how conflicting role-based duties can result in a demanding—and frequently an overdetermined—framework of moral demands.

SECTION ●■▼◆ 1   The Dilemma of Outcomes and Actions

We begin again, as we did in Chapter 6, by taking note of an important point of social and political philosophy: the value that we, as Americans, place on individual freedom and private choice. Ours is a system in which the freedom of a private individual to decide for himself or herself over a wide range of moral and economic affairs is highly prized. "To each his own" is the rule, not the exception. The primacy of the free market within the institutional division of labor is but one manifestation of the value that we place on a private citizen's freedom to pick and choose. The freedom of the marketplace enables an individual gradually to build up an inventory of possessions that reflects his or her private preferences.

Private Citizen, Public Official, and the Freedom to Choose

The freedom to pick and choose that's so central to the workings of a free-enterprise economy also extends in a general way to the social and moral realms. We are at liberty, for example, to select our personal friends and principal associates. The freedom of the private sector permits like-minded individuals to identify common concerns—that is, to identify themselves as members of particular subpublics in the sense discussed in Chapter 6—and to form associations. For this reason, the private sphere includes the realm of action that political philosophers call "civil society." In civil society, citizens freely engage one another in dialogue and debate; and if they so desire, they form groups—the voluntary associations, from churches to booster clubs such as Kiwanis and Rotary, that have traditionally played such an important role in American life. The freedom to make positive choices regarding one's associates also implies at least a limited right to exclude others from one's circle of intimate friends—although, to be sure, this right is far from an absolute. Legally as well as morally, exclusion on the basis of gender, race, or religion is prohibited in many kinds of undertakings.

Most of us take full advantage of the autonomy that we enjoy in the sphere of private activities—and for good reason. Freedom to choose permits us to economize on our personal energies and resources. We confine our strongest commitments to members of the family, close friends, and other favorites. We "save ourselves" for those whom we most deeply love, rejecting extreme obligations to persons we don't know.

Of course, freedom to choose isn't the same as freedom to harm. Simple decency (not to mention laws against negligence and malicious behavior) should prevent an individual from hurting others. But under most circumstances, the obligation not to do harm—which is what private tort law and the criminal justice system are all about—doesn't require individuals to undertake general obligations to do good. On the contrary, the imposition on private citizens of an affirmative duty of benevolence, if pushed too far, would destroy the area of personal autonomy that the private-public distinction preserves. We generally deem this area of autonomy a precious attribute of our tradition of freedom. For this reason, in the private sphere (though it seems harsh to say so), persons often may act without deep concern for the larger good of society—let alone of humanity—as a whole.

When we pass over from the private sphere to the public, however, the rules change. A person who accepts a public office isn't free to pursue private goals, to act arbitrarily, or to discriminate in behavior toward others. How is it that these dramatic changes in moral obligation come about almost automatically with the change from private to public action? That question has recently been the subject of several thoughtful essays by a leading American moral philosopher, Thomas Nagel.[1] An excerpt from an article in which Nagel discusses the obligations of public officials appears in Box 8.1. Nagel's analysis isn't always easy. But then neither is the problem that he's addressing, for it involves nothing less than the basis of the moral responsibilities of the men and women who accept public roles. Of all contemporary ethical and political theorists, Nagel perhaps provides the most solid philosophical grounding for a consideration of the ethics of public administration.

Nagel's Model: "The Problem of the Two Standpoints"

Nagel envisions an individual standing at the center of a series of concentric circles. Each circle represents a particular group of other persons. The innermost circle is symbolic of the individual's closest loved ones; the circles farther out represent groupings of persons who have more-distant connections to the individual at the center. Each

[1]See Nagel's *Equality and Partiality* (New York: Oxford University Press, 1991); and "Ruthlessness in Public Life," in Stuart Hampshire, ed., *Public and Private Morality* (Cambridge: Cambridge U. Press, 1978), p. 75.

BOX 8.1 ▬▬▬▬▬▬▬▬▬▬▬▬▬▬▬▬▬▬▬▬▬▬▬▬▬▬▬▬▬▬▬ ■ ■ ■

Thomas Nagel on the General Moral Obligations of Public Roles

When we try . . . to say what is morally special about public roles and public action, we must concentrate on how they alter the demands on the individual. . . .

Some of the moral peculiarity of official roles can be explained by the theory of obligation. Whoever takes on a public or official role assumes the obligation to serve a special function and often the interests of a special group. Like more personal obligations, this limits the claim that other sorts of reasons can make on him. . . . In a rigidly defined role like that of a soldier or judge or prison guard, only a very restricted set of considerations is supposed to bear on what one decides to do, and nearly all general considerations are excluded. With less definition, other public offices limit their occupants to certain considerations and free them from others, such as the good of mankind. Public figures sometimes even say and believe that they are obliged to consider only the national or state interest in arriving at their decisions as if it would be a breach of responsibility for them to consider anything else. . . .

But any view as absolute as this is mistaken: there are no such extreme obligations, or offices to which they attach. One cannot, by joining the army, undertake an obligation to obey any order whatever from one's commanding officer. It is not possible to acquire an obligation to kill indebted gamblers by signing a contract as a Mafia hit man. It is not even possible to undertake a commitment to serve the interests of one's children in complete disregard of the interests of everyone else. Obligations to the state also have limits, which derive from their moral content.

Every obligation or commitment reserves some portion of the general pool of motivated action for a special purpose. Life being what it is, each person's supply of time, power, and energy is limited. . . . In private life some exclusivity is necessary if we are to allow people to form special relations and attachments, and to make special arrangements with each other on which they can rely. For similar reasons larger groups should be able to cooperate for mutual benefit, or to form social units that may have a geographical definition. And it is natural that the organization of such cooperative units will include institutions, roles, and offices and that the individuals in them will undertake obligations to serve the interests of the group in special ways—by promoting its prosperity, defending it against enemies, etc. . . .

It may be that the added power conferred by an institutional role should be used primarily for the benefit of that institution and its constituents. The interests of mankind in general have a lesser claim on it. But this does not mean that prohibitions against harming others, directly or indirectly, are correspondingly relaxed. . . . [T]here is no reason to think that individuals in public roles are released from traditional moral requirements on the treatment of others, or that in public life, the end justifies the means. . . .

Two types of concern determine the content of morality: concern with what will happen and concern with what one is doing. Insofar as principles of conduct are determined by the first concern, they will be outcome-centered or consequentialist, requiring that we promote the best overall results. Insofar as they are determined by the second, the influence of consequences will be limited by certain restrictions on the means to be used.... The action-centered aspects of morality include bars against treating others in certain ways which violate their rights, as well as the space allotted to each person for a life of his own....

The interaction and conflict between these two aspects of morality are familiar in private life. They result in ... restrictions against harming or interfering with others, rather than requirements to benefit them, except in cases of serious distress. For the most part it leaves us free to pursue our lives and form particular attachments to some people, so long as we do not harm others....

There is no comparable right of self-indulgence or favoritism for public officials or institutions vis-à-vis individuals with whom they deal. Perhaps the most significant action-centered feature of public morality is a special requirement to treat people in the relevant population equally....

In respect to outcomes, public morality will differ from private in according them greater weight.... Within the appropriate limits, public decisions will be justifiably more consequentialist than private ones. They will also have larger consequences to take into account....

From Thomas Nagel, "Ruthlessness in Public Life," in Stuart Hampshire, ed., *Public and Private Morality* (Cambridge: Cambridge U. Press, 1978), pp. 77, 82–90.

---

of us can readily imagine this way of viewing the universe, with the self at the center and everyone else located a certain "emotional distance" away. Nagel calls the aspect of an individual taking this outlook the **personal standpoint.**

When we view the world from the personal standpoint, each of us experiences powerful egoistic urgings. ("If I am not for me," Hillel asked in the Talmud, "then who?") Self-interest and some degree of commitment to the interests of a relatively few "significant others" are compelling forces in human affairs. Each of us experiences a powerful sense of loyalty first to family (usually) and then to a small group of intimate friends. Within these innermost spheres of affection, personal likes and dislikes may be perfectly legitimate guides to behavior. It is natural—and for the most part, it's also appropriate—to favor family members, friends, and perhaps close professional associates when presenting gifts, distributing family resources, drafting wills, and so on. The emotional force of an individual's attachments diminishes as he or she moves to the circles of more-distant relatives, casual friends, neighborhood acquaintances, co-residents of the same city, and unfamiliar fellow countrymen. The human species, considered in the abstract, occupies the far outer ring. The individual's tie to mankind in general is highly attenuated and, for the most part, only intermittently expressed—as when a person is moved to contribute money after seeing a TV ad depicting a starving child somewhere across the sea.

When the universe is viewed from a position other than the egocentric vantage of the personal standpoint, however, the life of that suffering infant half a world away takes on a very different value relative to that of everyone else—including the value of one's closest friends and even one's own self. Nagel calls this alternative perspective the **impersonal standpoint.**

Intellectually if not emotionally, most human beings recognize a sense in which *all* human beings are of equal worth—those who are far off and unrelated as well as those who are in one's immediate circle of intimates. "We hold these truths to be self-evident, that all men are created equal, . . ." These are words we all recognize, and at some level in our consciousness we all probably accept them as true. Our ability (at least in our best moments) to appreciate the equality of all men and women derives from our capacity to think abstractly and, in doing so, to strip away the accidents of relationship, location, and degree of acquaintance. It's possible to "stand outside of one's self," even outside the entire system of concentric circles, and appreciate the common humanity of all. The nameless child who appears only as a fleeting face in the farthermost ring has every bit as much right to a fair chance in life as does one's own brother or sister, son or daughter. From the impersonal standpoint, the individual comes to see all men and women as equal to one another, at least in certain essential respects—in deserving a decent standard of living, for example, and in an entitlement to treatment with reasonable respect and dignity.

Now let's juxtapose the two standpoints. The individual who views the world egocentrically experiences powerful impulses of partiality, expressed as self-interest and a tendency to prefer family members, friends, and associates who have interests in common. In contrast, the impersonal standpoint requires benevolent, or at least impartial, behavior toward *all* others—those in the outermost ring as well as those within the individual's innermost circles of preferment. Nagel argues that most individuals, if they are honest with themselves, must admit that they can't satisfy both the urgings of partiality and the moral demands of impartiality in a completely reliable manner. Individuals, left to their own devices, vacillate irregularly between the pursuit of self-interest and its immediate extension, partiality toward intimates, and moments of altruism as expressed in a willingness to share impartially with the needy stranger as well as with the closest friend. Every individual experiences both impulses. Now the one force dominates, now the other. The uneasy juxtaposition of outlooks within every individual produces an inescapable problem, which Nagel calls the **problem of the two standpoints.**

Nagel suggests that there exists only one way to serve both the claims of partiality and the demands of impartiality. That is, there's only one way to create conditions under which individuals may continue to pursue their personal and group interests while, in society at large, the demands of the impartial standpoint are also being met. The answer lies largely in the institutional division of labor and, within the public sector, in the processes known as *role creation* and *role absorption*. Let's try to follow Nagel's argument.

Public Roles as Expressions of the Impersonal Standpoint

The private sphere gives individuals the opportunity to view the world from the personal standpoint. Within the institutions of the private sphere—especially the family and the market—individuals may act on behalf of their own interests and the interests of their close associates. But private action isn't enough. If social institutions consisted only of arrangements that supported individuals' freedom to choose, inadequate provision would have been made to express the impersonal standpoint. That standpoint represents a more fragile set of values—equality, impartiality—than the egocentric concerns of the personal standpoint do, but these nevertheless are values that just about all men and women recognize as important and, indeed, essential in a decent society. Unfortunately, if left to their own whims, most men and women will "favor their own." Self-interest and small-group prejudice make it risky to trust that individuals will act impartially even when they're dealing with friends, let alone in the interest of strangers. That's what's wrong with a society in which the institutional division of labor is tilted too far in favor of private action ("freedom to choose"), and hence is biased toward the personal standpoint in each individual. What about the interest of society as a whole? What about major subpublics whose members need more than mere hope that private decision makers will have the will and ability to help the disempowered, the needy, the vulnerable?

To promote actions that express the values of equal dignity and impartiality, men and women create public institutions—principally, the agencies of government—and set forth certain high expectations for the persons who fill positions in those institutions. The setting of expectations is an essential aspect of the process of **role creation,** since such expectations define roles in the most general sense of the word. Just as a role in a play requires an actor to utter preset lines, a social or organizational role requires the individual who fills it to behave in appropriate ways. **Role absorption** refers to the process in which the personality of an individual becomes, so to speak, partly fused with the requirements of the position. An individual whose personality has been absorbed in a role may be induced to meet the requirements of that role with a high degree of reliability, even though the demands may conflict with the role player's apparent self-interest. Soldiers *do* make sacrifices "above and beyond the call." Dutiful officials *do* adhere to the rules of their offices, even when it might be easier not to follow the established routines. (For their troubles, such officials are likely to be disparaged as "mindless bureaucrats.")

Naturally, role absorption is never complete. No human being acts as a soldier, a bureau chief, a police officer, or a welfare caseworker 100 percent of the time. An individual must divide his or her loyalties among the official role and various other roles, such as those of a parent, a community volunteer, an observant member of a religion, or a dutiful citizen. But while the individual is "on duty," the requirements of the role will concentrate the incumbent's attention and strongly direct his or her actions. The pay, psychological incentives (such as social prestige), and organizational context of a role can usually be arranged so that an individual filling it will conform far more closely to its demands than he or she would if simply left to act as a private person.

Many public roles originate in part to ensure that the impersonal standpoint will be expressed. Such roles are usually designed to meet the needs either of citizens in general or of large subpublics (the elderly, farmers, and so forth). It's customary to think of these groups as the "constituencies" or "clientele" of specific government agencies. Here we find the basis of our first general paradigm of obligation, namely, *the obligation of a public official to consider the likely consequences of his or her behavior for members of the pertinent constituency.* Furthermore, given the motivation behind much public role creation—to ensure the expression of the impersonal standpoint—there's a particularly strong expectation of impartiality in the way public officials treat the men and women with whom they come into contact. Here we find the basis of our second general paradigm of obligation, namely, *the obligation of a public official to act fairly, implying that "impartiality" may be the single most important action-centered restriction of all.*

Of course, role creation and role absorption can't guarantee a completely reliable or stable resolution of the tension between the values of partiality and impartiality. But public institutions may support a better balance of these values than if all individuals were simply left to reconcile the two standpoints as best they can through action in the private sphere, where there's virtually no affirmative duty to do good and where roles don't generally carry impartiality as a strong criterion of acceptable action. In the private sphere, "freedom to choose" would probably mean, in most cases, the freedom to behave partially not only when self-interested action is appropriate but also when self-interest or favoritism blinds the actor to the demands of impartiality.

An appropriate institutional division of labor, we've seen, requires a relatively large private sphere in which individuals enjoy rights to pursue their own interests (within limits) and give preferential treatment to others who are within their respective inner circles. Furthermore, the right to favor one's own interests extends to the group-forming process. Like-minded individuals may identify themselves as members of a subpublic and may organize to advance their purposes by any legal means, thereby exemplifying the pluralist behavior described in Chapter 6. Specifically, they may lobby government officials, encouraging policy makers to pass laws and implement programs that are favorable to their own interests. For these reasons, we expect self-interested behavior in the private sphere, both in free-market transactions and in group-based political action. Both forms of action are among the main expressions of the personal standpoint in a free society.

But we can't ask behavior in the private sphere to satisfy the human yearning for a society in which the needs of all are minimally satisfied and the demands of impartiality are met. To express the impersonal standpoint, the institutional division of labor also requires an active public sector. Institutionally, this sector consists mainly of government agencies staffed by officials filling public roles. Anyone who accepts a public role—whether election to office or appointment to an administrative post—accepts the general moral obligations that go with it. We've seen that, according to Nagel, the acceptance of a public office imposes two kinds of general ethical demands on an individual:

An **outcome-centered obligation** refers to a public officer's duty to consider the consequences that a decision or official action is likely to have for members of the subpublic which the official is supposed to serve.

An **action-centered restriction** encompasses all the legal principles and ethical values that impose limits on the means which an official may employ, even in the pursuit of desirable consequences.

From the juxtaposition of these two types of consideration derives the dilemma of outcomes and actions. Insofar as the outcome-centered criteria of administrative action prove inconsistent with the action-oriented restrictions that an official must observe, the dilemma of outcomes and actions represents a major cause of overdetermination in public administration.

The Making of a Moral Dilemma

Most of us accept that our status as human beings imposes moral duties on us. We demand honesty and compassion of ourselves when dealing with other persons, and we hope for the same in return. Most of us also acknowledge that the acceptance of a position in an organization, whether private or public, implies the acceptance of duties in addition to those which bind us simply because we're human. The duty to obey legal orders from superiors is perhaps the most explicit obligation of a member of an organization. This duty often proves to be of special and profound importance in public administration. (We'll take up the duty to obey in some detail in Section 2 of this chapter.) Professions such as accounting, engineering, law, and medicine are also kinds of organizations. The individual who accepts the mantle of professional accreditation accepts a further obligation to meet the ethical standards of the discipline, including the obligation to know and apply the **best practice** of the field when dealing with clients, patients, or other dependent individuals.

Work in a public organization implies the acceptance of a set of ought-tos beyond those obligations which result from the individual's status as a human being, as an occupant of a position in an organizational hierarchy, or as a professional. If private citizens have the *freedom* to do good for others—either because they foresee profit for themselves as well as their associates (this expectation is the basis of the market transaction) or because they're moved to offer services as volunteers, without compensation—public officials have an affirmative "*duty* to do good" in the sense that, at minimum, their roles oblige them to produce the particular services for the particular constituencies or subpublics that their agencies were set up to serve.

In the language of moral philosophy, public administrators must, to some extent at least, be practitioners of **consequentialist ethics.** The consequentialist, or outcome-centered, obligations of a public role require the official to consider the effects of a policy or a particular action not only on intimate friends but also on large numbers of citizens, many of whom are likely to be complete strangers to the administrator. As we'll see in the next chapter, the obligation to estimate outcomes or "count the consequences" complicates decision making in the public realm—especially when the admonition to "count" is taken literally, as it is in cost-benefit analysis, the standard method of formal policy analysis. Often it's virtually impossible—and sometimes it can seem downright immoral—to make numerical estimates of the effects of an official's actions.

Nagel notes that the attainment of a government position may permit the incumbent of a public role to take certain actions that would be illegal if performed by a private citizen. A public health officer may restrict citizens' freedom by declaring a general quarantine in the interest of a public health outcome; no private person may take such an action. In pursuit of a public safety outcome, a police officer may use force in circumstances that would result in a lawsuit against a private citizen who did the same. Some of the action-restricting demands of public office, then, may loosen the constraints that limit official behavior. But other action-centered restrictions narrow rather than broaden the range of means that an official may employ. In day-to-day American administrative practice, the main action-centered restrictions that work to narrow an official's freedom of action are of three sources. They originate, *first,* in our constitutional system (especially in the duty to observe due process of law in all official actions); *sec-*

ond, in the sheer needs of organizational discipline (the duty to obey a legal order from a superior); and *third,* in the special requirements of the impersonal standpoint for the incumbents of public roles (the duty of impartiality).

Because of the many and often severe limits in our system on the means that an official may employ—even in the pursuit of worthy ends—the paradigms of obligation frequently turn out to be in conflict within themselves. The outcome-centered considerations and action-centered restrictions often make for a dilemma:

The Dilemma of Outcomes and Actions

A public official is under a general obligation to achieve desirable outcomes for the citizens (members of the subpublic) whom he or she is pledged to serve, but the action-centered restrictions in our system may mean that the official must try to to do so through the use of means that severely narrow his or her freedom of action.

CHAPTER READING ▼ ▼ ▼

How do instances of the dilemma of outcomes and actions occur—and ultimately play out—in actual administrative practice? We can identify two levels at which this question commonly presents itself:

1. *General policy.* Suppose a policy carries both the promise of desirable consequences and the threat of unacceptable actions. What kind of test might be used to determine if the policy is a morally acceptable one after all the positives and negatives have been balanced out?
2. *Personal responsibility.* Suppose the general policy is known, but the specific application is ethically problematic. What factors should be considered by an administrator who feels called upon to execute a policy that raises the dilemma of outcomes and actions in a concrete case?

Again, there are no automatic moral formulas, no ethical catchphrases. At both levels, the morally correct answer will depend on circumstances and, of course, on the actor's values.

Our chapter reading deals with the so-called **three-pronged test** that judges use when they evaluate the constitutionality of a policy that seems, on its face, to be problematic in terms of outcomes and actions. You'll note when you read the opinions from *Michigan State Police* v. *Sitz,*[2] that different judges can draw opposite conclusions while employing the same test, depending on the values they bring to the case and the weights they assign to the circumstances. In Section 2 of the chapter, we'll go on to consider the action-centered restrictions that most frequently emerge to narrow an individual administrator's range of freedom, even when he or she is contemplating a move that's likely to lead to a desirable outcome. Again, the aim isn't to provide a simple formula, such as

---

[2]496 U.S. 444.

"Achieve the best consequence at all cost; let the end justify the means!" The point instead is to clarify the kinds of action-centered considerations that a public administrator is always obliged to take into account when faced with a morally ambiguous choice. Keeping these action-centered restrictions in mind won't guarantee the right choice. But failure to consider them is certain sooner or later to lead to a wrong one.

The following discussion of the three-pronged test occurred in the Supreme Court case that grew out of the Saginaw County, Michigan, highway checkpoint controversy. Under a roadway checkpoint policy instituted pursuant to a Michigan state law, Saginaw County troopers flagged all vehicles passing through a designated point and examined drivers for evidence of intoxication. Did the desirable consequences (reducing the drunk-driving rate) justify the actions taken (stopping motorists for breath checks)? A motorist named Rick Sitz argued that they did not. Sitz, who frequently traveled the span of roadway targeted for the roadblock procedure, sued to block implementation of the plan. Sitz claimed that an inspection by the sheriff's deputies would amount to an unreasonable seizure, a violation of his constitutional right to privacy. As such, Sitz claimed, the checkpoint policy transgressed one of the most compelling action-oriented restrictions that bind public officials.

The *Sitz* case reached the Supreme Court in 1990 as the culmination of a series of earlier cases about the proper interpretation of the Fourth Amendment, which reads in part: "The right of the people to be secure in their persons, houses, papers, and effects, against unreasonable searches and seizures, shall not be violated, and no Warrants shall issue, but upon probable cause, ..."

Background to the *Sitz* Case

In the 1976 case of *U.S. v. Martinez-Fuerte,*[3] the Court had approved the use by the U.S. Immigration and Naturalization Service of highway checkpoints to stop automobiles to detect illegal aliens. However, in *Delaware v. Prouse* (1979),[4] the Supreme Court invalidated a state plan which would have required motorists who approached random checkpoints on Delaware roads to produce their drivers' permits. The Court objected to the disproportion between the large number of drivers who would have to stop and the small fraction who would actually be found driving without valid permits. The value realized by society—identification of unlicensed drivers—didn't offset the costs of the checkpoint policy, reckoned in terms of inconvenience to motorists and the indignity of subjecting citizens even to momentary detainment. The majority opinion laid special stress on the fact that the operators of the roadblock stopped motorists even in the absence of any overt behavior that might give "probable cause" to suspect a particular driver of having broken the law.

(*Question:* How do you compare the social value of the consequence sought in the *Prouse* case—citation of unlicensed drivers—with the social value of the consequence sought in *Sitz*—arrest of drunk drivers? How do you react to the Supreme Court's use of a quantitative technique—the estimated ratio of drivers stopped to those who would

[3]428 U.S. 543.

[4]440 U.S. 648.

turn out to be without valid permits—in its attempt to evaluate the consequences of the Delaware checkpoint policy?)

In another 1979 lead-up case to *Sitz, Brown* v. *Texas,*[5] the Supreme Court had been asked to rule on the constitutionality of a demand by a police officer that a "suspicious" individual submit to a frisk. Did the officer's demand violate the individual's right to be secure from "unreasonable searches and seizures"? The Court, in finding against the officer's action, established the three-pronged test for Fourth Amendment cases:

> Consideration of the constitutionality of such seizures involves a weighing of the gravity of the public concerns served by the seizure, the degree to which the seizure advances the public interest, and the severity of the interference with individual liberty.

Does the three-pronged test seem to you a useful approach for reconciling the dilemma of outcomes and actions, assuming that the first two prongs (*gravity* and *degree*) relate to the outcomes side of the dilemma and that the third prong (*severity*) goes to the appropriateness of the action taken to achieve the desired outcome?

Bear in mind that in some cases there may be honest disagreement over the goodness or badness of the outcome that's being assessed. There are those who would argue that illegal aliens make a significant contribution to the American economy; hence the detection and expulsion of "illegals"—the end sought in *Martinez-Fuerte*—might not have unambiguously positive consequences. And there are certainly those who would argue that stopping and frisking a citizen, as in *Brown,* offends American conceptions of fair play unless there's evidence that the suspect presents a clear danger of some sort; "order maintenance" by police officers ceases to be an unambiguously desirable social outcome if it leads to the rousting of citizens for no better reason than that they appear shady or out of place to the local cop on the beat. However, *Michigan State Police* v. *Sitz* involved no such ambiguous judgments about social consequences. To this extent, *Sitz* differed from both *Martinez-Fuerte* and *Brown.* Few citizens would deny that the prevention of drunk driving is a "desirable outcome." The Michigan checkpoint policy clearly presented the issue of the balance between a positive public interest (sobriety on the highways) and the challenge to the privacy rights of those citizens who were stopped. The question: Notwithstanding the desirable outcome, did the Michigan policy involve an action prohibited under the Constitution?

The opinions in *Sitz* illustrate the kind of rhetorical argumentation that is typical when public officials must balance ends against means, consequences against constraints, outcomes against actions. Using techniques that exemplify paradigmatic analysis and the casuistic method, the justices reason by analogy from their holdings in prior cases. Chief Justice Rehnquist, for the majority, tries to present persuasive arguments for the sustainability of the checkpoint policy, based ultimately on the preponderant social value of the consequences sought. Associate Justice Stevens (joined by Justices Brennan and Marshall), in dissent, denies that the checkpoint policy can be squared with action-centered restrictions imposed by the U.S. Constitution itself.

[5]443 U.S. 47, citing *U.S.* v. *Prignoni-Poore,* 422 U.S. 873, 878–883 (1975).

Outcomes versus Actions in the Campaign against Drunk Driving: Two Views from the Supreme Court

No one can seriously dispute the magnitude of the drunk driving problem or the State's interest in eradicating it. . . . Conversely, the weight on the other scale—the measure of the intrusion on motorists stopped briefly at sobriety checkpoints—is slight. Justice William Rehnquist

CHIEF JUSTICE REHNQUIST delivered the opinion of the Court.

This case poses the question whether a State's use of highway sobriety checkpoints violates the Fourth and Fourteenth Amendments to the United States Constitution. We hold that it does not. . . .

Petitioners, the Michigan Department of State Police and its Director, established a sobriety checkpoint pilot program in early 1986. . . . Under the guidelines, checkpoints would be set up at selected sites along state roads. All vehicles passing through a checkpoint would be stopped and their drivers briefly examined for signs of intoxication. In cases where a checkpoint officer detected signs of intoxication, the motorist would be directed to a location out of the traffic flow where an officer would check the motorist's driver's licence and car registration and, if warranted, conduct further sobriety tests. Should the field tests and the officer's observations suggest that the driver was intoxicated, an arrest would be made. . . .

During the hour-and-fifteen minute duration of the checkpoint's operations, 126 vehicles passed through the checkpoint. The average delay for each vehicle was approximately 25 seconds. Two drivers were detained for field sobriety testing, and one of the two was arrested for driving under the influence of alcohol. A third driver who drove through without stopping was pulled over by an officer in an observation vehicle and arrested for driving under the influence. . . .

[At this point in his opinion, Chief Justice Rehnquist summarizes the history of the case before it reached the Supreme Court. A Michigan trial court and the Michigan Court of Appeals both held that the checkpoint operation violated the Fourth Amendment rights of those who were stopped.]

To decide this case the trial court performed a balancing test derived from our opinion in *Brown* v. *Texas,* 443 U.S. 47 (1979). As described by the Court of Appeals, the test involved "balancing the state's interest in preventing accidents caused by drunk drivers, the effectiveness of sobriety checkpoints in achieving that goal, and the level of intrusion on an individual's privacy caused by the checkpoints." . . .

As characterized by the Court of Appeals, the trial court's findings with respect to the balancing factors were that the State has "a grave and legitimate" interest in curbing drunken driving; that sobriety checkpoint programs are generally "ineffective" and, therefore, do not significantly further that interest; and that the checkpoints' "subjective intrusion" on individual liberties is substantial. . . .

No one can seriously dispute the magnitude of the drunken driving problem or the State's interest in eradicating it. Media reports of alcohol-related death and mutilation on the nation's roads are legion. The anecdotal is confirmed by the statistical. . . .

Conversely, the weight bearing on the other scale—the measure of the intrusion on motorists stopped briefly at sobriety checkpoints—is slight. We reached a similar conclusion as to the intrusion on motorists subjected to a brief stop at a highway checkpoint for detecting illegal aliens. . . . We see virtually no difference between the levels of intrusion on law-abiding motorists from the brief stops necessary to the effectuation of these two types of checkpoints, which to the average motorist would seem identical save for the nature of the questions the checkpoint officers might ask. The trial court and the Court of Appeals, thus, accurately gauged the "objective" intrusion, measured by the duration of the seizure and the intensity of the investigation, as minimal. . . .

With respect to what it perceived to be the "subjective" intrusion on motorists, however, the Court of Appeals found such intrusion substantial. . . . The court first affirmed the trial court's finding that the guidelines governing checkpoint operations minimize the discretion of the officers on the scene. But the court also agreed with the trial court's conclusion that the checkpoints have the potential to generate fear and surprise in motorists. This was so because the record failed to demonstrate that approaching motorists would be aware of their option to make U-turns or turnoffs to avoid the checkpoints. On that basis, the court deemed the subjective intrusion from the checkpoints unreasonable. . . .

We believe the Michigan courts misread our cases concerning the degree of "subjective intrusion" and the potential for generating fear and surprise. The "fear and surprise" to be considered are not the natural fear of one who has been drinking over the prospect of being stopped at a sobriety checkpoint but, rather, the fear and surprise engendered in law-abiding motorists by the nature of the stop. This was made clear in *Martinez-Fuerte*. Comparing checkpoint stops to roving patrol stops considered in prior cases, we said,

> [W]e view checkpoint stops in a different light because the subjective intrusion—the generating of concern or even fright on the part of lawful travelers—is appreciably less in the case of a checkpoint stop.

In [*U.S. v.*] *Ortiz,* we noted:

> [T]he circumstances surrounding a checkpoint stop and search are far less intrusive than those attending a roving-patrol stop. Roving patrols often operate at night on seldom-traveled roads, and their approach may frighten motorists. At traffic checkpoints the motorist can see that other vehicles are being stopped, he can see visible signs of the officers' authority, and he is much less likely to be frightened or annoyed by the intrusion. 422 U.S., at 894–895.

. . . Here, checkpoints are selected pursuant to the guidelines, and uniformed police officers stop every approaching vehicle. The intrusion resulting from the brief stop at the sobriety checkpoint is for constitutional purposes indistinguishable from the checkpoint stops upheld in *Martinez-Fuerte*.

The Court of Appeals went on to consider as part of the balancing analysis the "effectiveness" of the proposed checkpoint program. Based on extensive testimony in the trial record, the court concluded that the checkpoint program failed the "effectiveness" part of the test, and that this failure materially discounted petitioners' strong interest in implementing the program. We think the Court of Appeals was wrong on this point as well.

The actual language from *Brown* v. *Texas,* upon which the Michigan courts based their evaluation of "effectiveness," describes the balancing factor as "the degree to which the seizure advances the public interest." 443 U.S., at 51. This passage from *Brown* was not meant to transfer from politically accountable officials to the courts the decision as to which among reasonable alternative law enforcement techniques should be employed to deal with a serious public danger. Experts in police science might disagree over which of several methods of apprehending drunken drivers is preferable as an ideal. But for purposes of Fourth Amendment analysis, the choice among such reasonable alternatives remains with the government officials who have a unique understanding of, and a responsibility for, limited public resources, including a finite number of police officers. . . .

In *Delaware* v. *Prouse* . . . we disapproved random stops made by Delaware Highway Patrol officer in an effort to apprehend unlicensed drivers and unsafe vehicles. We observed that no empirical evidence indicated that such stops would be an effective means of promoting roadway safety and said that "[i]t seems common sense that the percentage of all drivers on the road who are driving without a licence is very small and that the number of licensed drives who will be stopped in order to find one unlicensed operator will be large indeed." 440 U.S., at 659–660. We observed that random stops involved the "kind of standardless and unconstrained discretion [which] is the evil the Court has discerned when in previous cases it has insisted that the discretion of the official in the field be circumscribed, at least to some extent." Id, at 661. . . .

Unlike *Prouse,* this case involves neither a complete absence of empirical data nor a challenge to random highway stops. During the operation of the Saginaw County checkpoint, the detention of each of the 126 vehicles that entered the checkpoint resulted in the arrest of two drunken drivers. Stated as a percentage, approximately 1.5 percent of the drivers passing through the checkpoint were arrested for alcohol impairment. . . . By way of comparison, the record from one of the consolidated cases in *Martinez-Fuerte,* showed that in the associated checkpoint, illegal aliens were found in only 0.12 percent of the vehicles passing through the checkpoint. . . .

In sum, the balance of the State's interest in preventing drunken driving, the extent to which this system can reasonably be said to advance that interest, and the degree of intrusion upon individual motorists who are briefly stopped, weighs in favor of the state program. We therefore hold that it is consistent with the Fourth Amendment. . . .

> *The Court appears to give no weight to the citizen's interest in freedom from suspicionless unannounced investigatory seizures. On the other hand, the Court places a heavy thumb on the law enforcement interest by looking only at gross receipts instead of net benefits.* Justice John Paul Stevens

JUSTICE STEVENS, with whom JUSTICE BRENNAN and JUSTICE MARSHALL join . . . , dissenting.

A sobriety checkpoint is usually operated at night at an unannounced location. Surprise is crucial to its method. The test operation conducted by the Michigan State Police and the Saginaw County Sheriff's Department began shortly after midnight and lasted until about 1 A.M. During that period, the 19 officers participating in the operation made two arrests and stopped and questioned 125 other unsuspecting and innocent drivers. It is, of course, not known how many arrests would have been made during that period if those officers had been engaged in normal patrol activities. However, the finding of the trial court, based on an extensive record and affirmed by the Michigan Court of Appeals, indicate that the net

effect of sobriety checkpoints on traffic safety is infinitesimal and possibly negative. . . .

In light of these considerations, it seems evident that the Court today misapplies the balancing test announced in *Brown v. Texas.* . . . The Court overvalues the law enforcement interest in using sobriety checkpoints, undervalues the citizen's interest in freedom from random, unannounced investigatory seizures, and mistakenly assumes that there is "virtually no difference" between a routine stop at a permanent, fixed checkpoint and a surprise stop at a sobriety checkpoint. . . .

There is a critical difference between a seizure that is preceded by fair notice and one that is effected by surprise. . . . This element of surprise is the most obvious distinction between the sobriety checkpoints permitted by today's majority and the interior border checkpoints approved by this court in *Martinez-Fuerte.* The distinction casts immediate doubt upon the majority's argument, but *Martinez-Fuerte* is the only case in which we have upheld suspicionless seizures of motorists. But the difference between notice and surprise is only one of the important reasons for distinguishing between permanent and mobile checkpoints. . . . In the latter case, . . . although the checkpoint is most frequently employed during the hours of darkness on weekends (because that is when drivers with alcohol in their blood are most apt to be found on the road), the police have extremely broad discretion in determining the exact timing and placement of the roadblock.

There is also a significant difference between the kind of discretion that the officer exercises after the stop is made. A check for a drivers' license, or of identification papers at an immigration checkpoint, is far more easily standardized than is a search for evidence of intoxication. A Michigan officer who questions a motorist at a sobriety checkpoint has virtually unlimited discretion to detain the driver on the basis of the slightest suspicion. A ruddy complexion, an unbuttoned shirt, bloodshot eyes or a speech impediment may suffice to prolong the detention. Any driver who had just consumed a glass or beer, or even a sip of wine, would almost certainly have the burden of demonstrating to the officer that her driving ability was not impaired. . . .

As I have already explained, I believe the Court is quite wrong in blithely asserting that a sobriety checkpoint is no more intrusive than a permanent checkpoint. In my opinion, unannounced investigatory seizures are, particularly when they take place at night, the hallmark of regimes far different from ours; the surprise intrusion upon individual liberty is not minimal. On that issue, my difference with the Court may amount to nothing less than a difference in our respective evaluations of the importance of individual liberty, a serious albeit inevitable source of constitutional disagreement. On the degree to which the sobriety checkpoint seizures advance the public interest, however, the Court's position is wholly indefensible.

The Court's analysis of this issue resembles a business decision that measures profits by counting gross receipts and ignoring expenses. The evidence in this case indicates that sobriety checkpoints result in the arrest of a fraction of one percent of the drivers who are stopped, but there is absolutely no evidence that this figure represented an increase over the number of arrests that would have been made by using the same law enforcement resources in conventional patrols. Thus, although the *gross* number of arrests are more than zero, there is a complete failure of proof on the question whether the wholesale seizures have produced any *net* advance in the public interest in arresting intoxicated drivers....

The most disturbing aspect of the Court's decision today is that it appears to give no weight to the citizen's interest in freedom from suspicionless unannounced investigatory seizures.... On the other hand, the Court places a heavy thumb on the law enforcement interest by looking only at gross receipts instead of net benefits.... This is a case that is driven by nothing more than symbolic state action—an insufficient justification for an otherwise unreasonable program of random seizures. Unfortunately, the Court is transfixed by the wrong symbol—the illusory prospect of punishing countless intoxicated motorists—when it should keep its eyes on the road plainly marked by the Constitution.

SECTION 2
Action-Centered Restrictions: Narrowing an Official's Range of Action

What does the individual administrator do when a careful consideration of the likely consequences of an act beckons in one direction, but the administrator's sense of duty—the requirements of the job description, say, or orders from a superior—seems to lie in the other? There are three main ways in which this kind of dilemma tends to emerge:

1. When general procedural requirements (for example, the constitutional obligation to observe due process) seem to require actions likely to produce consequences out of line with the outcome-centered demands of the official's role

2. When specific orders from a superior (the duty to obey) point toward an outcome that's inconsistent with the official's consequentialist obligations

3. When the duty of a public official to treat all persons in the relevant category equally (the duty of impartiality) seems likely to produce an unacceptable outcome.

These three categories overlap, but they can be taken as subheadings in a discussion of action-centered requirements that often collide with calculations of consequences.

Significantly, the concept of duty figures in a central way in each version of the dilemma mentioned in the forgoing list. You might want to pause here for a brief background discussion of the most influential approach in modern moral philosophy to the question of duty, that of Immanuel Kant. See Box 8.2.

Action-Centered Restriction 1: The Constitutional Requirement

No public action can be acceptable—even if a careful calculation of its consequences suggests it to be desirable—if it will deprive persons of procedural or substantive due process of law, both of which are guaranteed by the Fifth and Fourteenth Amendments to the U.S. Constitution:

> **Procedural due process** requires government officials to follow all the procedures that have been formally spelled out in the applicable laws, court decisions, or regulations of the agencies in which they work. The guarantee of procedural due process is probably the single most potent action-oriented restriction on public administrators in the American system of government.
>
> **Substantive due process**—which some would say qualifies more as an outcome-centered consideration than as an action-centered restriction—prohibits an official from using even a procedurally correct means if the result would offend most Americans' basic sense of right and wrong. Consider a "law" that denied blue-eyed people the vote or a regulation that taxed blonds at twice the rate of brunettes. Even if all legislative procedures were followed in passing such a statute, or if the prescribed routines were followed in writing the regulation, the outcomes would be deemed so fundamentally unfair that courts would declare them invalid.

Other important action-centered restrictions in the American constitutional scheme derive from the **right to privacy** (secured by the First, Third, Fourth, Fifth, Ninth, and Fourteenth Amendments when taken in combination) and the requirement of **equal treatment** under the law (secured by the Fourteenth Amendment). The guarantee of equal treatment—the exact words of the amendment are "equal protection of the laws"—can be considered as the constitutional provision that most directly expresses Nagel's impersonal standpoint and its associated values (fairness, impartiality) in the American political scheme.

Judicial interpretation of the due process clauses has been checkered, making it difficult to generalize much beyond the summary observation that judges have traditionally seen themselves as the special protectors of individual and minority rights. Perhaps an excerpt from one of the most famous Supreme Court decisions affecting the administrative process—the 1970 "New York welfare rights" case of *Goldberg* v. *Kelly*[6]— can best supplement the material we've already read to give the flavor of judicial reasoning in cases that involve administrators' actions that touch citizens' constitutional rights.

John Kelly, a disabled hit-and-run victim and recipient of "home relief" benefits in New York State and in the City of New York, was dropped from the welfare rolls when, without discussing his personal problems with his caseworker, he moved out of the

[6]397 U.S. 254 (1970).

BOX 8.2

Duty-Based versus Outcome-Centered Ethics in Immanuel Kant

No adequate discussion of the ethics of official action could ignore the analysis of duty offered by the most influential moral philosopher of modern times, the metaphysician and ethicist Immanuel Kant (1724–1804). Kant argued that the concept of a moral obligation can be formulated as a **categorical imperative**—that is, in such a way as to ensure that an individual will always ("categorically") choose duty over any calculation of consequences.

The categorical imperative is probably the most famous precept in the entire field of ethics. Certainly it is the most important maxim in the branch known as duty-based ethics, or **deontological ethics** (from the Greek word for *duty*), as distinguished from outcome-centered ethics, or **consequentialist ethics**.

The Categorical Imperative

Kant thought it possible to formulate a concept of duty that had universal validity. In Kant's thought, a *categorical* rule is one that binds an individual irrespective of circumstances and consequences. The antonym in Kant's system, *hypothetical*, applies to a rule that is valid only with reference to some ulterior objective. In other words, a hypothetical rule or imperative isn't universally binding; instead it depends for its force on the circumstances of the case and the effects likely to be achieved as a result of using it.

Kant gave two forms of the categorical imperative, one centered on the idea of a universal law and the other centered on the sacredness of human beings as persons who deserve respect as ends in themselves.

A Universal Law. In the first form, Kant urged all persons to "Act only on that maxim which will enable you at the same time to will that it be a universal law." Under this version, the ethical task facing an official in a morally problematic situation is to figure out the rule that, as rational beings, we would will all officials in all similar situations to follow. By definition, *that* is the rule a decision maker can wish to be a "universal law"; *that* therefore is the rule of action required in the specific case by the categorical imperative.

Consider a public health official who has gained some confidential information about certain persons who risk contracting a deadly disease such as AIDS. Suppose the official must decide whether to violate a professional confidence by divulging information about infected patients. Should the official, contrary to these patients' wishes, warn others?

Kantian reasoning might proceed in the following way: No one would will that any ground for the breaking of a professional confidence could ever be adopted as a universal maxim, for then every patient would know that privileged information isn't really privileged. There would literally be no such thing as a "professional confidence." But that outcome—"privileged information" that isn't privileged—is a contradiction in terms. Reason (not to mention common sense) suggests that a contradiction in terms can't be adopted as a universal rule of behavior. In other words, the rule under which the official might feel free to reveal the confidential information cannot possibly be adopted as a universal law. By this line of reasoning, the path of duty ("sublime duty," in Kant's words) is clear. It is also absolute: The administrator must not break the seal of privacy!

In contrast, a consequentialist bent on promoting "the greatest happiness of the greatest number" would proceed quite differently. The greatest-happiness principle comes to us from Kant's contemporary and arguably the most influential of all consequentialists, the utilitarian philosopher Jeremy Bentham (1748–1832), whose influence on public administration we'll take up in Chapter 9. As noted in the text, consequentialists argue that duty is a relative matter—relative to the situation. According to this view, the rightness or wrongness of an act depends on its effects. Hence one should do what's likely to produce the best consequences in the circumstances. "Best consequences" for whom? Depending on the decision maker's role, the consequences that count may be the effects of the act on humanity in general, on some subpopulation (such as a nation), or on a particular group of affected persons (say, disabled citizens or farmers) whose interests particular government officials are supposed to serve.

Using cost-benefit analysis, a follower of Bentham might try to estimate all the negative and positive effects of divulging or withholding the information. The analyst would then resolve the moral quandary based on the numbers rather than on an absolute Kantian rule.

Persons as Ends. Kant argued that the most important duty of all is the duty to recognize that every individual is an end in himself or herself. This duty forbids any person from ever treating another as a mere means. Here, Kant believed, was a universal law to which all human beings could subscribe, irrespective of the historical period in which they live or the official roles in which they earn their livings. In Kant's words: "Act so that in your own person as well as in the person of every other, you are treating mankind also as an end, never merely as a means." The "persons as ends" version is usually taken to mean that there's an absolute duty always to respect the autonomy and dignity of every other human being. Note, however, that Kant qualified his own maxim by prohibiting an individual from treating another human being *exclusively* as a means. Alas, that qualification leaves much room for judgment. To what degree may one person "use" another and still respect that person's autonomy and dignity? When does the taking of an "instrumental" view of another person begin to violate the spirit of what's supposed to be a morally absolute decree?

Kant's Enduring Influence

Some critics of duty-based ethics contend that Kant, in the end, gives us little more than words. These critics point out that it is as difficult for deontologists to apply the concepts of the "universal law" (first form) and "persons as ends" (second form) in practical situations as it usually is for consequentialists to count and weigh all the costs and benefits of a course of action. The public health official, say the anti-Kantians, might be no closer to a practical answer after a night worrying about abstract concepts of personal autonomy than he or she would be trying—however imperfectly—to predict the consequences of divulgence. ("If I don't tell on John and John ends up infecting Jane, and then Jane passes the virus on to . . ." and so forth.)

The critics of Kant are surely right when they insist that there exist no perfectly rational formulas for human conduct. We've noted that, in the ethical sphere, argumentation must be rhetorical rather than formally logical. On the other hand, the categorical imperative gives us a great deal more than mere words when it is considered within the rhetorical framework rather than as the kind of geometric ethical axiom that Kant apparently thought he had discovered. Kantian ethics demands that we consider what rule we'd like to have applied to ourselves before we apply it to others. One recalls the Golden Rule.

Perhaps we can't always precisely define what it means to act in accordance with a universal law or to treat other persons always as ends. But most of us think that we know concern for the general rather than the selfish interest when we see it, just as we recognize conduct that respects and empowers others rather than merely uses them. Because of the intuitive appeal of Kantian principles, and not because Kant's methodology finally settled any moral issues, the ethical thinking of the "philosopher of Königsberg" has exerted the powerful influence that it has over modern thought. Max Weber's disquietude over the dehumanizing overtones of scientific management and bureaucratic organization, discussed in Chapter 3, was rooted in the thinking of his German forebear, Immanuel Kant.

---

hotel where he had been living and into a friend's apartment. Frequent prior changes of address had made it extremely costly for welfare officials to keep track of him. The termination procedures did not guarantee Kelly an oral hearing at which he could offer evidence to support his claim of continued eligibility despite his frequent changes of address. Kelly's legal appeal eventually went to the Supreme Court.

At the time, some Court watchers considered *Goldberg* v. *Kelly* to be the most important procedural due process case of its era. As you read the following excerpt, pay particular attention to the effort that Justice William Brennan makes to identify the obligations of New York welfare officials, and the balance he tries to strike among competing criteria. The opinion begins with a description of the challenged procedures. These procedures should seem familiar even to a student who has never had an involvement with the welfare system, since they follow standard bureaucratic principles: hierarchy, reporting, routinization, and a preference for written records.

Justice William Brennan on Due Process Requirements

A caseworker who has doubts about the recipient's continued eligibility must first discuss them with the recipient. If the caseworker concludes that the recipient is no longer eligible, he recommends termination of aid to a unit supervisor. If the latter concurs, he sends the recipient a letter stating the reason for proposing to terminate aid and notifying him that within seven days he may request that a higher official review the record, and may support the request with a written statement prepared personally or with the aid of an attorney or other person. If the reviewing official affirms the determination of ineligibility, aid is stopped immediately and the recipient is informed by letter of the reasons for the action. Appellees' challenge to this procedure emphasizes the absence of any provisions for the personal appearance of the recipient before the reviewing official, for oral presentation of evidence, and for confrontation and cross-examination of adverse witnesses. However, the letter does inform the recipient that he may request a post-termination "fair hearing." . . .

The constitutional issue to be decided, therefore, is the narrow one whether the Due Process Clause requires that the recipient be afforded an evidentiary hearing *before* the termination of benefits. . . .

[W]hen welfare is discontinued, only a pre-termination evidentiary hearing provides the recipient with procedural due process.

For qualified recipients, welfare provides the means to obtain essential food, clothing, housing, and medical care. Thus the crucial factor in this case—a factor not present in the case of the blacklisted government contractor, the discharged government employee, the taxpayer denied a tax exemption, or virtually anyone else whose governmental entitlements are ended—is that termination of aid pending resolution of a controversy over eligibility may deprive an *eligible* recipient of the very means by which to live while he waits. Since he lacks independent resources, his situation becomes immediately desperate. His need to concentrate upon finding the means for daily subsistence, in turn, adversely affects his ability to seek redress from the welfare bureaucracy. . . .

The requirement of a prior hearing doubtless involves some greater expense, and the benefits paid to ineligible recipients pending decision at the hearing probably cannot be recouped, since these recipients are likely to be judgment-proof. But the State is not without weapons to minimize these increased costs. Much of the drain on fiscal and administrative resources can be reduced by developing procedures for prompt pre-termination hearings and by skillful use of personnel and facilities. . . .

We recognize . . . that both welfare authorities and recipients have an interest in relatively speedy resolution of questions of eligibility, that they are used to dealing with one another informally, and that some welfare departments have very burdensome caseloads. These considerations justify the limitation of the pre-termination hearing to minimum procedural safeguards, adapted to the particular characteristics of welfare recipients, and to the limited nature of the controversies involved. We . . . recognize the importance of not imposing upon the States or the Federal Government in this developing field of law any procedural requirements beyond those demanded by rudimentary due process. . . .

The city's procedures presently do not permit recipients to appear personally with or without counsel before the official who finally determines continued eligibility. Thus a recipient is not permitted to present evidence to that official orally, or to confront or cross-examine adverse witnesses. These omissions are fatal to the constitutional adequacy of the procedures.

The opportunity to be heard must be tailored to the capacities and circumstances of those who are to be heard. It is not enough that a welfare recipient may present his position to the decisionmaker in writing or secondhand through his caseworker. Written submissions are an unrealistic option for most recipients, who lack the educational attainment necessary to write effectively and who cannot obtain professional assistance. Moreover, written submissions do not afford the flexibility of oral presentations. . . . Particularly where credibility and veracity are at issue, as they must be in many termination proceedings, written submissions are a wholly unsatisfactory basis for decision. The secondhand presentation to the decisionmaker by the caseworker has its own deficiencies; since the caseworker usually gathers the facts upon which the charge of ineligibility rests, the presentation of the recipient's side of the controversy cannot safely be left to him. Therefore a recipient must be allowed to state his position orally. Informal proceedings will suffice; in this context due process does not require a particular order of proof or mode of offering evidence. . . .

Finally, the decisionmaker's conclusion as to a recipient's eligibility must rest solely on the legal rules and evidence adduced at the hearing. To demonstrate compliance with this elementary requirement, the decisonmaker should state the reasons for his determination and indicate the evidence he relied on, though his statement need not amount to a full opinion or even formal findings of fact and conclusions of law. And, of course, an impartial decisionmaker is essential.

Justice Brennan admits that a judge-made requirement for an oral pre-termination hearing will require new routines, increase costs, and add to the paperwork burden. The justice asserts, however, that welfare professionals should be able to use their administrative know-how to limit the costs of the expanded procedure. Do you agree? For that matter, do you think that such costs should even be an issue when due process is at stake?

Action-Centered Restriction 2: The Duty to Obey

We saw in Chapter 4 that administrators often enjoy substantial discretion when they function as administrative adjudicators or administrative rule makers. These are indeed important roles in our system of governance, but we shouldn't forget that, traditionally, there has always been an even more important administrative role: the so-called strictly ministerial role of an executor of higher orders, a *program implementer.* The Agriculture Department agent who's supposed to inspect fields for compliance with anti-erosion practices, the road builder in a state or municipal public works department, and the administrator who oversees mail-outs of Social Security checks are all program implementers. Their tasks are to execute policies enunciated by higher-ups in the political or administrative structure. The duty imposed by the Constitution itself on the president to "take care that the laws be faithfully executed" underscores the relevance of the program implementer's role at the very pinnacle of our government, in the "strictly ministerial" duties of the chief executive.

It stands to reason that the program implementer's role normally implies a narrowed range of discretion when compared with the adjudicator's and the rule maker's roles. If the task of the official is to execute some program or carry out some order issued by higher authority, the official's freedom is correspondingly reduced to actions that are consistent with the intent of the order giver. Given the importance of the program implementer's role, it's not surprising that the most important specific paradigm of obligation in American public administration has traditionally been the **executive paradigm,** centered on the administrator's duty to obey.

In the vocabulary of law, economics, and management science, the individuals who set the goals and issue the instructions are called *principals;* those who carry the orders out are the *agents.* An agent's primary obligation is to understand the intent of his or her principal and take those legal actions which will achieve the specified outcomes. The study of the relationships between individuals in these roles is called **principal-agent theory** (see Box 8.3).

The principals who are of main concern to many high-level appointive officials are the elected legislators who pass the laws that administrators then accept as the autho-

BOX 8.3 ■■■

Principal-Agent Theory

The rudiments of principal-agent theory emerged centuries ago to provide a legal and moral framework for relationships characterized by a division of labor. Each individual must, from time to time, rely on strangers who are more knowledgeable or more skilled than he or she is. In the words of the public administrationist Henry Kass:

> Agency developed out of the need to have free individuals represent one another's interests in an economically and socially specialized society like our own. In earliest times, those who acted for others were normally family dependents or bound servants who, in a real sense, were mere extensions of a *pater familias*. Agency originally arose out of the needs of unrelated, free individuals to serve and be served by others. . . . Viewed in another way, agency was one of the few institutions in such a world that sought to ameliorate the alienation and lack of trust that characterized a society of strangers with few organic bonds to one another. The ethics of agency allowed the isolated and specialized person in a pluralist society to trust, in Tennessee Williams's words, "the kindness of strangers." Specialized individuals, heavily dependent on one another, could give and receive basic services without experiencing exploitation as recipients or loss of freedom as providers.[7]

In modern agency theory, the employees of a private company serve the owners of a firm. They are obliged to "work the will" of their principals. Modern theorists extend this principle to the public bureaucracy: Administrators at any level are agents of their superiors. The obligation to obey runs from the street-level bureaucrat up to the top appointees in the hierarchy. The top appointees are responsible to elected officials. These officials are agents of the people, who put them into office. Thus workers at each intermediate tier are agents with respect to those above (from whom they take orders), and they are principals with respect to those below (to whom they give commands). In this way, agency theory becomes a way of conceptualizing the theory of democratic accountability and integrating it with the pyramidal model of classical organizational theory.

[7]Henry D. Kass, "Stewardship as a Fundamental Element in Images of Public Administration," in Henry Kass and Bayard Catron, *Images and Identities in Public Administration* (Newbury Park CA: Sage, 1990), pp. 115–116.

■■■

---

ritative statements of public intent. More narrowly considered, the higher-up of primary concern to the typical public administrator is the boss, commander, or manager who issues orders to lower-level officials. Let's refer to the broader of these two views as the **departmental version of the executive paradigm**, since it highlights the authority of the lawmakers over high-level officials of the executive branch. In this version, legislators pass a law that sets up a public program. It then becomes the responsibility of the top officials of some executive agency to implement the program. This they do, of course, by issuing further orders that administrators down the chain of command are expected to follow. We should then refer to the narrower view as the **organizational version of the executive paradigm,** since it emphasizes the duty of subordinates to carry out the legal orders of their superiors in an organizational hierarchy. *The central value in the executive paradigm is obedience to the principal,* whether that principal is a lawmaker (in the departmental version) or the worker's immediate boss (in the organizational version).

So important in so much of administrative practice is the obligation to obey that it would be useful here to consider one of the most provocative contributions ever made to this subject.

Intuitively, we all recognize that there are times when an administrator should *not* follow orders. The White House aides who did the bidding of superiors bent on obstructing justice disgraced the presidential administration of Richard Nixon. Eichmann at Auschwitz will stand for all time as a chilling example of obedience in the service not of duty but of demonic evil. Nevertheless, administrators typically work in environments where the *presumption* of the obligation to obey is powerful—so powerful that, in an extreme case, the administrative environment may promote a willingness on the part of officials to give up all sense of personal responsibility. The author of our next reading, the psychologist Stanley Milgram, refers to this kind of surrender of personal responsibility as **abrogation to authority.**

The ethics of the research methodology that Milgram used were hotly debated when his book *Obedience to Authority* appeared in 1974.[8] Many critics found Milgram's experimental findings even more disturbing than they found his laboratory techniques. Nor did all readers find convincing the theory Milgram offered to explain *why* individuals obey higher orders. Nevertheless, Milgram's concept of the **agentic state** is widely regarded as an important contribution to principal-agent theory. When in the agentic state, Milgram writes, "the individual no longer views himself as responsible for his own actions but defines himself as an instrument for carrying out the wishes of others."

You should find much to provoke your own thought as you read through the following excerpt, which can be taken as a contemporary statement of certain organizational requirements, psychological consequences, and moral dangers that are implicit in the executive paradigm.

[8]A few preliminary articles describing Milgram's experimental procedures and findings had appeared during the 1960s, mostly in scholarly journals. The full impact of the work wasn't felt, however, until Milgram published a highly readable account of his entire "obedience to authority" project in book form.

Stanley Milgram on the Agentic State

Obedience is as basic an element in the structure of social life as one can point to. Some system of authority is a requirement of all communal living, and it is only the man dwelling in isolation who is not forced to respond, through defiance or submission, to the commands of others. . . .

Obedience is the psychological mechanism that links individual action to political purpose. It is the dispositional cement that binds men to systems of authority. Facts of recent history and observation in daily life suggest that for many people obedience may be a deeply ingrained behavior tendency, indeed, a prepotent impulse overriding training in ethics, sympathy, and moral conduct. . . .

The moral question of whether one should obey when commands conflict with conscience was argued by Plato, dramatized in *Antigone,* and treated to philosophic analysis in every historical epoch. . . . The legal and philosophic aspects of obedience are of enormous import, but an empirically grounded scientist eventually comes to a point where he wishes to move from abstract discourse to the careful observation of concrete instances. In order to take a closer look at the act of obeying, I set up a simple experiment at Yale University.

[Milgram at this point describes the experiments that he conducted in the early 1960s. A subject, called the "teacher," would be brought into a laboratory and asked to help an experimenter test the effects of punishment on a learner. A second person, the learner, was strapped into a chair. The "teacher" read pairs of words which the subject later had to recall in proper sequence. The "teacher" was instructed to administer electric shocks for wrong answers. The subject was actually an actor, but few of the "teachers" whom Milgram tested gave evidence of suspecting that the shocks weren't real or that the learner's pain was feigned. In almost all cases, the "teacher" behaved as instructed, administering what he or she thought to be shocks of increasing intensity to a subject (who, for purposes of the experiment, proved a poor learner). "At 285 volts," Milgram comments, "his response can only be described as an agonized scream." Many "teachers" took the sequence to the highest level: 450 volts.]

A variation of the basic experiment depicts a dilemma more common than the one outlined above: the subject was not ordered to push the trigger that shocked the victim, but merely to perform a subsidiary act (administering the word-pair test) before another subject actually delivered the shock. In this situation, 37 of 40 adults from the New Haven area continued to the highest shock level on the generator. Predictably, subjects excused their behavior by saying that the responsibility belonged to the man

who actually pulled the switch. This may illustrate a dangerously typical situation in a complex society: it is psychologically easy to ignore responsibility when one is only an intermediate link in a chain of evil action but is far from the final consequences of the action. Even Eichmann was sickened when he toured the concentration camps, but to participate in mass murder he had only to sit at a desk and shuffle papers. At the same time the man in the camp who actually dropped Cyclon-B into the gas chambers was able to justify *his* behavior on the grounds that he was only following orders from above. Thus there is a fragmentation of the total human act; no one man decides to carry out the evil act and is confronted with its consequences. The person who assumes full responsibility for the act has evaporated. Perhaps this is the most common characteristic of socially organized evil in modern society.

The problem of obedience, therefore, is not wholly psychological. The form and shape of society and the way it is developing have much to do with it. There was a time, perhaps, when men were able to give a fully human response to any situation because they were fully absorbed in it as human beings. But as soon as there was a division of labor among men, things changed. Beyond a certain point, the breaking up of society into people carrying out narrow and very special jobs takes away from the human quality of work and life. A person does not get to see the whole situation but only a small part of it, and is thus unable to act without some kind of over-all direction. . . .

We must attempt to grasp the phenomenon [of obedience to authority] in its theoretical aspect and to inquire more deeply into the causes of obedience. Submission to authority is a powerful and prepotent condition in man. Why is this so?

The Survival Value of Hierarchy

Let us begin our analysis by noting that men are not solitary but function within hierarchical structures. In birds, amphibians, and mammals we find dominance structures, and in human beings, structures of authority mediated by symbols rather than direct contests of physical strength. The formation of hierarchically organized groupings lends enormous advantage to those so organized in coping with dangers of the physical environment, threats posed by competing species, and potential disruption from within. . . .

A clearer understanding will be found, I believe, by considering the problem from a slightly different point of view—namely, that of cybernetics. . . .

Consider a set of automata, *a, b, c,* and so on, each designed to function in isolation. Each automaton is characterized as an open system, requiring inputs from the environment to maintain its internal states. The need for environmental inputs (e.g., nourishment) requires apparatus for searching out, ingesting, and converting parts of the environment to usable nutritive forms. . . . To bring them [the automata] together, even in the most primitive and undifferentiated form of social organization, something must be added to the model we have designed. A curb must be placed on the unregulated expression of individual appetites, for unless this is done, mutual destruction of the automata will result. . . .

What will happen when we try to organize several automata so they function together? The joining of elements to act in a concerted fashion may best be achieved by creating an external source of coordination for two or more elements. . . .

Still more powerful social mechanisms can be achieved by having each subordinate element serve as a superordinate to elements in a level below. . . . The hierarchy is constructed of modules, each consisting of one boss with followers. . . . Each follower, in turn, may be superior to others below him . . . , the entire structure being built up of such interlocking units. The psychology of obedience does not depend on the placement of the module within the larger hierarchy: the psychological adjustments of an obedient Wehrmacht general to Adolf Hitler parallel those of the lowest infantrymen to this superior, and so forth, throughout the system. . . .

This analysis . . . alerts us to the changes that must occur when an independently functioning unit becomes part of a system. This transformation corresponds precisely to the central dilemma of our experiment: how is it that a person who is usually decent and courteous acts with severity against another person within the experiment? He does so because conscience, which regulates impulsive aggressive action, is perforce diminished at the point of entering a hierarchical structure. . . .

The critical shift in functioning is reflected in an alteration of attitude. Specifically, the person entering an authority system no longer views himself as acting out of his own purposes but rather comes to see himself as an agent for executing the wishes of another person. Once an individual conceives his action in this light, profound alterations occur in his behavior and his internal functioning. These are so pronounced that one may say that this altered attitude places the individual in a different *state* from the one he was in prior to integration into the hierarchy. I shall term this *the agentic state,* by which I mean the condition a person is in when he sees himself as an agent for carrying out another person's wishes. . . .

From a subjective standpoint, a person is in a state of agency when he defines himself in a social situation in a manner that renders him open to regulation by a person of higher status. In this condition the individual no longer views himself as a responsible for his own actions but defines himself as an instrument for carrying out the wishes of others. . . .

An authority system, then, consists of a minimum of two persons sharing the expectation that one of them has the right to prescribe behavior for the other. . . .

It is this ideological abrogation to the authority that constitutes the principal cognitive basis of obedience. If, after all, the world of the situation is as the authority defines it, a certain set of actions follows logically. . . .

The most far-reaching consequence of the agentic shift is that a man feels responsible *to* the authority directing him but feels no responsibility *for* the content of the actions that the authority prescribes. Morality does not disappear, but acquires a radically different focus: the subordinate person feels shame or pride depending on how adequately he has performed the actions called for by authority.

From Stanley Milgram, *Obedience to Authority* (New York: Harper & Row, 1974), pp. 1–11, 123–134, 142–146.

Action-Centered Restriction 3: The Duty of Impartiality

We've seen that the motivation behind much public role creation—to ensure the expression of the impersonal standpoint—establishes a strong expectation of impartiality in the way public officials treat the men and women with whom they come into contact. In Nagel's words: "There is no . . . right of self-indulgence or favoritism for public officials or institutions vis-à-vis individuals with whom they deal. Perhaps the most significant action-centered feature of public morality is a special requirement to treat people in the relevant population equally." To protect and advance the principle of impartiality in official conduct, public roles are commonly hedged about with elaborate codes of customs and rules designed to encourage their incumbents to treat their constituents or clients with the impartiality that the impersonal standpoint requires.

We can make the idea of impartiality and its context a bit more concrete with some examples: The off-duty police officer may be guided by the demands of his or her parental role, which implies a right to favor immediate family members. The government social worker when away from the office may devote the majority of his or her time to volunteer work for the Abortion Rights Coalition, Catholic Charities, the Lutheran Brotherhood, or the United Jewish Appeal. But when either the cop or the caseworker steps back into the public role, the pursuit of private agendas is supposed to end. Of course, favoritism and preferential treatment are permissible—in a sense, they are even mandatory—with respect to the particular constituency that the official's agency was created to serve *relative to other constituencies.* Social workers have a special responsibility to needy, vulnerable citizens; Social Security administrators, to the elderly; USDA officials, to farmers; and so forth. But *within the pertinent constituency,* there's an obligation of impartial treatment for all. Old men deserve the same consideration as old women do (and vice versa) when it comes time to process Social Security claims. Poor farmers should get the same level of attention and courtesy from the crop-subsidy administrators of the Department of Agriculture as the major agribusiness magnates do.

On the other hand, just as the duty to obey can be carried to an extreme, so might the duty of impartiality. The opposite side of the duty of impartiality is the problem of administrative compassion. This problem can arise out of the natural urge to draw distinctions among citizens and treat different persons differently. (You may recall from Chapter 4 that Jerry Mashaw's third model of justice—professional treatment—emphasized the need to treat clients and patients not as "cases" but as flesh-and-blood individuals who deserve individuated care.)

It's not always easy to frame a general rule that's reasonable, impartial, and compassionate all at the same time. That assumption underlies our next reading selection, an excerpt from another volume that (like Milgram's) provoked a heated reaction among public administrators when it first appeared. Victor Thompson's 1975 book *Without Sympathy or Enthusiasm: The Problem of Administrative Compassion* can be considered as an essay in priority setting. In this iconoclastic work, Thompson argued for the supremacy of impartiality among administrative values and urged administrators to reject compassion as a criterion of official action. Note how Thompson used the role concept, and the fact that he invoked the principle of impartiality in terms almost identical to those Thomas Nagel would use some years later in his essay on outcomes and actions—namely, the principle "that everyone in the same problem category is to be treated alike." (We'll find the same term, *problem category*, cropping up again in Chapter 10, in an excerpt from a revealing study of the way street-level bureaucrats often deal with clients such as welfare applicants.)

You might find Thompson's argument intuitively and emotionally offensive. The challenge, however, is to identify any missteps in his presentation (Are his premises correct? Are his logical inferences valid?) and then to frame a principled rebuttal expressed in a rhetorical argument for the inclusion of "compassion" and "enthusiasm" in the list of essential qualities for a public administrator.

Victor Thompson on the "Problem of Administrative Compassion"

A few years ago I read a short item in a Gary, Indiana, newspaper. . . . A state trooper had stopped a car that was driving down a country road at night without lights and weaving slowly back and forth across the road. The driver had no license. A woman was in the passenger side of the front seat. A man and a woman occupied the back seat. They were taken in and a ticket was issued and bond posted. Very simple. There was more information, however, that was irrelevant to the administrative problem and its disposition. A police reporter wrote up the whole case, including the additional, but administratively irrelevant, information. It seems the man driving the car had been blind from birth and had never experienced the feeling of driving a car. His wife and some friends decided to take him out on a quiet moonlit night on a quiet stretch of road and let him drive for a few minutes. The lights were not on because he did not need them. Of course, he had no driver's license. The car was weaving for obvious reasons. But all of these facts were irrelevant to the problem category that he represented to the police. Once this category had been established, the associated routines rolled out of the mill as inevitable as time. Could it have been different? Could the local organization have acted compassionately? That is the question I have set out to answer. . . .

Can modern organizations be compassionate? Can they "care"? Can organizations be depicted as good or bad, kind or cruel? From everything we know about modern organizations, the answer has to be "No!" . . .

In past times, with low mobility and very stable social relations, it was not always easy to separate the person from what he did day in and day out. The distinction between person and role was difficult to make. People became what they did and many modern names have come down to us from this period: Mason, Smith, Carpenter, Schumaker, etc.

An enormous increase in mobility, first geographic, then social, and finally psychological, has made the distinction between person and role easier for us to make. People can choose roles as they choose merchandise. As Max Weber said, one of the criteria of modern organization ("bureaucracy") is the separation of person and office, of personal rights and public rights, of person and role. With this modern discriminatory skill, it becomes possible to think of fashioning or designing organizations for achieving specific purposes just as we design physical tools or instruments for achieving certain purposes. Recognizing the organization as a designed tool or instrument adds several dimensions to our problem of administrative compassion.

There are at least two basic roles in tool construction. There is, of course, the "designer," an engineer with knowledge of the means to the accomplishment of various ends of other people. There is, too, the designer's client, the "person" who has a need for which a tool must be constructed. Let us call this role that of the "owner." . . .

An organization-tool uses people rather than inanimate things such as motors, cogs, and belts. People have values, goals, preference orderings, just as owners do. These values must be neutralized or else what is finally designed will be anything but a tool; whatever it might be would pull and haul in all directions, and its "accomplishments" would only be predictable, if at all, by systems analysis. It would have outcomes rather than outputs.

To avoid this result, to actually construct an organization-tool, an additional role is needed—that of "functionary." A functionary does his duty, applies his skills, performs his practiced routines, regardless of what goal or whose goal is involved. A screwdriver does not choose among goals or among owners. It does what it is "told." To induce individual persons to enter or perform the functionary role, designers and owners enter into an exchange contract with them, the employment contract. In return for sufficient values, such as salaries, prestige, power, and a chance at increasing one or more of these, the employee gives up his own values or uses for the organization in deference to those of the owner, thereby leaving a single, consistent ordering of values by virtue of which all behavior of functionaries can be coordinated and the relative success or failure of the organization-tool assessed. In public organizations we often use the term "servant" instead of or in addition to "functionary." The owner of the public organization in the modern period is, of course, "the people" (it used to be a feudal king).

As noted above, the test of the organizational tool, the criterion by which it is judged, kept, abolished, or modified, is external to the organization; it is the goal or preference ordering of the owner. There is no room for another test, such as the need of employees for "joy in work," or the need of clients for "compassion." We do not build tools to fight with themselves, to undo what they do. The goal of a public welfare organization, for example, is what the "public" wants for recipients of welfare, not what the welfare recipients want for themselves.

To recognize compassion in administration is to recognize another claim; it is to "steal" the owner's property. . . .

In the artificial system, all relationships are impersonal and abstract. There is not only no compassion; there is no way that compassion can be included.

Compassion cannot be prescribed. The idea of a designed role of "administrator of compassion" is ludicrous.

Theoretically, compassionate employees could be selected. However, competence to achieve the "owner's" goal will seem more important, and in the likely case of conflict between goal and compassion, only one choice is possible; compassion must go unless it indeed is the goal. Again, the design may meet public relations needs by special training in compassion for people in boundary roles such as counter clerk. But this is difficult to bring off. To sensitive clients, synthetic compassion can seem worse than none at all. In the final analysis, compassion is an individual gift, not an organizational one.

Whatever else a modern public (or private) organization is, therefore, it is a machinelike instrument or tool of an external power. It is an artificial system of prescribed roles and rules. It is not a person. It is not a parent or friend. It is an abstract system of interrelationships designed to achieve an externally defined goal. Roles are bundles of duties (and powers). They do not care; they have no feelings. Whereas a particular incumbent of a role may "care" for a particular client (or customer, etc.), the caring is not part of the organizational plan. In fact, such a caring relation between the incumbent of a role in a modern organization and a client is regarded as unethical, as giving the client "pull," perhaps in the form of nepotism or favoritism.

We are proud of the fact that modern administration, as compared with administration in the past, is relatively free of such "particularistic" behavior and is "universalistic" instead. We are proud of the fact that modern administration gives jobs to people who merit them rather than to people who need them. Departures from such impersonal (noncompassionate) performance are pounced upon by the media; the departures make good news stories precisely because they violate modern canons of good administration. Why should a modern role incumbent care about a client? Who cares for *him,* other than his family and close friends? He, too, is caught up in an abstract, impersonal network, the artificial system, the organization-tool. . . .

Most people in economically and politically underdeveloped countries cannot understand an abstract administrative order. Their relationships are personal, their obligations are personal, and they are unable to fashion organization-tools. That is why they are underdeveloped. For lack of organizations, their political actions, obligations, and interests are personal—"compassionate." There is no "public" interest. There is no "owner" of the public organizations, the accomplishment of whose goal is the test of said organization. Everyone simply gets all he can get. Compassion monopolizes administration.

Still the problem of administrative compassion remains. Most people are brought up in a small intimate group, the so-called nuclear family. Their earliest and most constant experiences involve emotional dependence and support—involve, that is, compassion. In a thousand ways, we come to need such treatment, to be treated as whole and unique individuals whose feelings are important. . . . We want administration to be universalistic (noncompassionate) in general,

but how could making a little exception in our case hurt anything, an exception that would have no perceptible effect on public administration but would do a tremendous amount of good for us? . . .

The continuing belief in favors—the belief that there is someone who can grant them and that it is all right to get them—is incompatible with the Kantian imperative, the golden rule, and the modern administrative norm, i.e., that everyone in the same problem category is to be treated alike. If I have the power to grant favors, I obviously believe in them and cannot truthfully say to a suppliant, "If I grant you an exception I will have to do the same for everyone else who is similarly situated."

Modern man needs to learn to be comfortable with impersonality. All this amounts to is giving a high value to . . . the achievement of established goals.

From Victor A. Thompson, *Without Sympathy or Enthusiasm: The Problem of Administrative Compassion* (University, AL: U. of Alabama Press, 1975), pp. 2–3, 8–10, 13, 17–18, 91.

 ## CHAPTER CASE

As the judicial debate in our chapter reading—the Supreme Court opinions in the *Sitz* case—suggests, one of the most important action-oriented restrictions is the constitutional protection of a citizen's right to privacy. This right also shapes up as one of the most problematical protections in a modern society. The patterns of interdependency in a nation such as ours raise hard questions every day about the extent to which actions taken in private may be permitted to impinge on the public welfare. How far should our freedom to pick and choose be protected when actions have a statistical chance of harming others—or worse, when likely ultimate consequences for others can't even be accurately assessed? This question is at the center of our chapter case, about HIV testing and AIDS intervention. The scenario raises the dilemma of outcomes and actions at two levels—at the level of broad social policy (What should a testing policy look like in general?) and at the level of individual impact (What should *this* public health professional, when dealing with *this* patient, do about *this* symptom of infection?).

An AIDS testing program might emphasize public health or, alternatively, could favor the protection of individual privacy rights by imposing strict action-oriented restrictions on public health officials. Why must we choose between the two values? For one reason, because, like most tests which rely on statistical methods, a test for the *human immunodeficiency virus (HIV),* the virus that causes AIDS, poses twin dangers. On one hand, a nonexistent condition may falsely show up as present. On the other, a condition that actually exists may not register in the test. These errors are known, respectively, as "false positives" and "false negatives." The false-reporting caveat applies not only to HIV testing but also to tests for drug use, for defective products on an assembly line, for carcinogens in the workplace, for infestations of vermin in a building, and so forth.

In HIV testing, the rates of false reporting have been estimated but aren't known exactly. In any event, these rates are probabilistic in the sense that they apply to entire batches of tests rather than to any one patient's specimen. (Note how probabilities figure critically at almost every point in our scenario; and as you do so, keep in mind the applicable rule of law, the Supreme Court's three-pronged test.)

An outcomes orientation would presumably favor tests that catch as many infected individuals as possible, even at the cost of overstating the number of false positives. But individuals who are known to have tested positively for HIV are likely to suffer from stigmatization and discrimination. These consequences result from what other people might hear about the patient's test results, whether those results are correct or not. In contrast, an action orientation keyed to the protection of individuals' privacy rights could lead to testing procedures that are likely to miss a higher percentage of persons who are, in fact, infected with the virus. This result could follow either because fewer individuals would be tested to begin with or because officials might adopt testing procedures biased toward producing false negatives rather than false positives.

HIV test results—again, whether correct or not—also seem to influence a patient's own decision to engage in or refrain from risky activities. In other words, no kind of testing regime has fully predictable consequences, either for society or for the individual. Multiple possibilities, all existing in a context of imperfect information, define exactly the kinds of indeterminacies that make public administration a realm of "proximate solutions to insoluble problems."

CASE 7

••••••••••••••••••

Public Health versus Privacy Rights: HIV Testing and AIDS Intervention

When, early in 1989, the encouraging word came out about the AIDS drug *zidovudine* (generally called *AZT),* Gene Petitsaint thought that for some of his college friends at the University of Washington, it must have been "the worst of good news." True, AIDS researchers had recorded no progress to speak of on either a preventive vaccine or a true cure. Infection with HIV therefore remained a 100-percent predictor of eventual deterioration to terminal AIDS. But clinical tests in the late 1980s suggested that treatment with AZT could significantly delay the onset of full-blown *acquired immuno deficiency syndrome (AIDS)* in infected individuals.

Health professionals at the University of Washington, as elsewhere around the country, put out the word: If you have any doubt of your HIV status, *get tested.* The chance apparently existed to postpone the onset of final-stage AIDS. But that chance required treatment while the infection remained in the asymptomatic state, based on knowledge of one's HIV status. The needed knowledge in turn could be gotten only by testing. At the time of the AZT announcement, the drug was costly—from $8,000 to $10,000 per year.[1] AZT also had side effects for some patients and, of course, could be taken only on prescription. In other words, an individual who merely suspected infection would find it almost impossible to get the drug legally without taking the further step of submitting to a test that would establish seropositivity—the term health professionals use when the test of a body serum, such as a blood sample, indicates the presence of a disease or infection (in this case, HIV infection).

"The earlier you know, the better"—that was the advice of Richard P. Keeling, president of the American College Health Association. Keeling, a frequent speaker on campuses, also strongly cautioned young people to undergo counseling before submitting to a test. Keeling further emphasized that individuals should undergo screening for the virus only under conditions that would permit them to know who might eventually gain access to test results. AIDS activists feared that information of the wrong kind in the wrong hands could block an infected individual's access to medical insurance. And laws against anti-AIDS discrimination notwithstanding, reports were common of social stigmatization, harassment on the job, and even discharges from employment under various pretexts.

No doubt, Petitsaint thought, individuals who feared they might have the virus now felt the pressures to find out for sure. But knowing for sure could itself, in a way, be dangerous, especially if the person had any doubt about his or her ability to control test information, should the result turn out to be positive. The AZT breakthrough—even if it had been all that it was initially reported to be—seemed a mixed blessing, a kind of bad news wrapping the good.

●   ●   ●   ●   ●

In late 1990 a Louisiana man was tried and convicted, under a new state law, for infecting a woman with the HIV virus. The offender, a dock worker named Salvadore Gambarella, admittedly knew of his own seropositive status when he entered into an affair with a female neighbor. Gambarella claimed to have informed his sexual partner that their liaison would put her at risk. However, the jury believed it when the woman, who later tested positive herself, denied that Gambarella had told her of the danger he posed.

On November 27, 1990, a *New York Times* reporter filed the following story with a New Orleans dateline.

In the last year, there has been a surge of prosecutions involving people with H.I.V., said Lawrence Gostin, executive director of the American Society of Law, Medicine, and Ethics, and head of the United States AIDS Litigation Project. Mr. Gostin said about 20 convictions had been logged around the country since the epidemic started.

---

[1] As we'll see, later developments cast something of a shadow over the initial optimism regarding AZT as a therapeutic agent. On the other hand, the cost of the drug also fell in the early 1990s. The estimated annual cost of recommended treatment today for an asymptomatic seropositive individual is in the range of $3,000–$4,000.

The man who prosecuted Mr. Gambarella, Steven Callahan, the Terrebonne Parish assistant district attorney, says the case tells people with H.I.V. "they have to be more responsible about their sexual behavior."

But others wonder. Many of these cases, particularly those resulting from criminal AIDS laws like the one here, trouble experts who say they reflect a new intolerance, demonize people with AIDS, and may even discourage people from seeking to learn whether they are infected with the virus. To know, these experts say, is to leave oneself open to prosecution. . . .

Half the states now have specific laws similar to Louisiana's, which makes the transmission of H.I.V. a crime. The law here, with its penalty of 10 years at hard labor and a fine of $5,000, is one of the toughest in the country. The law is "motivated by punitive or retributive motivations, not what's good for public health," said Mr. Gostin, who is also a professor of health law at Harvard University.[2]

• • • • •

For some time during his college years, Gene Petitsaint had expected to launch a career in government service. He had developed a special interest in health care. As the story of the apparent AZT breakthrough illustrated, there was always something new in medicine. Petitsaint took it for granted that the exploding costs of hospitalization and people's anxieties over access to quality treatment would ensure a continuing demand for government action. It made for a field in which a person could hope to find a well-paying job and maybe also even end up doing some good. Gene knew that not all of his college classmates could share that combination of expectations.

Gene hadn't known exactly what "policy planning" would entail in the public health department of a major city, but the recruiting letter he received from Dr. Nora Smith promised that he'd learn quickly. The position would involve a range of duties, embracing economic analysis and maybe some work with political overtones along with traditional public health work.

Soon after he left Seattle for the new job, Petitsaint began taking evening courses on subjects touching his field of work. In one of these courses, Dr. James Trussell, director of the Princeton University Office of Population Research, spoke about the statistics of AIDS testing. Highly technical lectures weren't to Gene's taste, but he had taken the maxim "Check the numbers" to heart. Jotting copiously as Trussell spoke, Gene tried to think through the underlying logic of the statistics of HIV testing and their implications for public health policy.

• • • • •

From the journal of Gene Petitsaint. Source: Notes and partial taping from a talk by James Trussell. Subject: "Dilemmas of testing policy."

I. Current procedure and its level of accuracy. According to Trussell, the U.S. Public Health Service recommends a two-step procedure for those who want to be screened or those (e.g., convicted prisoners) for whom HIV testing is mandatory.

Procedure. The individual first undergoes a screening test known as the *enzyme immunoassay (EIA)*. If a positive result occurs, the subject takes a *Western Blot (WB) test.*

[2]Adam Nossiter, "Man Is the First Convicted in Louisiana for Putting a Partner at Risk of H.I.V.," *New York Times*, Nov. 28, 1990, p. 7.

EIA costs about $6 per test; WB $50. Hence for cost reasons alone, there is an incentive to minimize use of the WB test. This is accomplished by breaking off the testing sequence if the EIA shows negative.

Error rates. EIA is thought to give a false positive result in 0.005 of cases, and a false negative in 0.01. The WB gives a false positive result at the 0.001 rate, and false negative at 0.01.

II. Statistical theory of testing. Trussell says that when tests are not perfectly accurate, as is the case with both the EIA and WB, a choice must be made between a testing procedure that minimizes false positives and one that minimizes false negatives. It's not possible simultaneously to minimize both kinds of error. In other words, a testing procedure that minimizes false positives will tend to return a higher number of false negatives out of a given population screened, and vice versa.

III. Philosophy of the Public Health Service procedure. Trussell emphasized that the two-stage testing approach is intended to minimize false positives, since one must test positive on both EIA and WB to be declared infected with HIV. Trussell referred to such a declaration as a "conviction." The procedure of branding an individual as infected only after a double indication of seropositivity is apparently intended to serve an individual's *privacy rights* by erring on the side of the judgment that is least likely to stigmatize even a person who tests positively in an initial screening.

Had the PHS mandated that everyone in the testing program receive both an EIA and a WB—with anyone testing positive on either being informed that he or she was infected—the strategy would be to minimize the risk of false negatives. Such a strategy—much more expensive than the one actually in use—would be aimed at the goal of containing the spread of HIV, since even an ambiguous indication of infection (resulting from a seropositivity showing on one, but not two, tests) would lead to a diagnosis that HIV is present. Such a diagnosis would trigger intervention of some kind (which could include a complete retesting of the "convicted" individual). This approach would be aimed at serving *public health* goals.

IV. Sensitivity to underlying HIV infection rate. Trussell went to the blackboard and outlined a tree diagram (see Sketch 8.1), speaking and adding numbers from memory as he drew:

> Suppose that the prevalence of HIV in a group is rare, only 0.2 percent (certainly an upper-bound estimate for low-risk persons in the United States as a whole) and that persons are tested at random. Then . . . if only the EIA test were used, 0.198 percent (= 0.002 × 0.99) of the population would be infected with the virus and would test positive, while 0.499 percent (= 0.998 × 0.005) would *not* be infected with HIV and yet would test positive. Thus, of those who test positive only 28.4 percent would be infected with HIV. The *predictive power* of a positive test result is poor.
>
> With the two-step procedure, we see that 0.19602 percent (= 0.002 × 0.99 × 0.99) would be infected with HIV and would test positive, whereas 0.0005 percent (= 0.998 × 0.005 × 0.001) would *not* be infected with HIV but would test positive. The predictive power of a positive result in the two-step procedure is 99.75 percent.

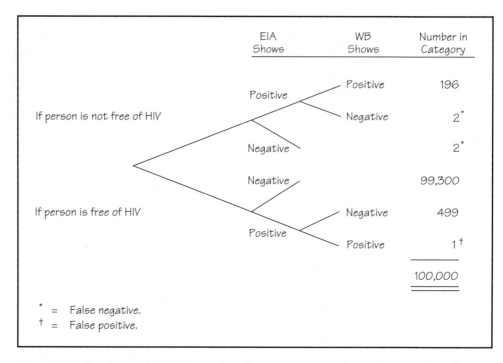

	EIA Shows	WB Shows	Number in Category
If person is not free of HIV	Positive	Positive	196
		Negative	2*
	Negative		2*
If person is free of HIV	Negative	Negative	99,300
		Negative	499
	Positive	Positive	1†
			100,000

* = False negative.
† = False positive.

Sketch 8.1 Breakout of HIV Testing Results in a Low-Prevalence (0.2% Infected) Population of 100,000 Tested Individuals

Trussell took a sip of water and then went on:

> The purpose of the two-step procedure is nicely illustrated by this example. It raises the predictive power of a positive test result from 28 percent to virtually 100 percent.
>
> Suppose, however, that the prevalence of HIV in another group is much higher, say 20 percent, which is probably less than the prevalence of HIV among homosexual men in some areas. . . . Using the same logic as before, we find that the predictive power of a positive result on the EIA test alone is 98.02 percent. With the confirmatory WB test, the predictive power rises to 99.998 percent. Therefore, the "rights" of those without HIV *seem* to be guaranteed, because virtually none will be falsely "convicted."
>
> But are the uninfected really protected? . . . Closer examination reveals that 33 percent of those "reprieved" by the WB actually would be infected with HIV. . . . If the behavior of the falsely "reprieved" is not modified, there is a high probability that this group will continue to spread HIV. The falsely "convicted" are protected at the expense of the larger pool of uninfected.

V. Sensitivity of procedure to purpose of testing. Later, in response to a query from the floor, Trussell answered:

In the high-prevalence case, what should be done? I would argue that the answer depends on the purpose of the test. If it is for screening for employment, immigration, or insurance, then one might wish to protect the rights of the falsely "convicted" by following the PHS guidelines. . . . However, when the purpose is for counseling the individual (especially when the testing is performed anonymously), then one cannot protect the rights of the falsely "convicted" and the uninfected simultaneously. Because the tests are not perfect, there is a trade-off between the two goals.[3]

After Trussell finished speaking, Petitsaint lingered to scribble some calculations, trying to fix the lecturer's points in his own mind. Gene multiplied a few numbers and then drew up a table containing comparative data for the two populations described by Trussell: a low-prevalence population, with a 0.2-percent HIV infection rate; and a high-prevalence one, with a 20-percent rate (see Table 8.1).

●   ●   ●   ●   ●

Shortly after Gene Petitsaint reported to his new job on Dr. Nora Smith's policy planning staff, the chairperson of a National Academy of Sciences panel announced a controversial new finding in AIDS research. Although the new information was more sociological in nature than it was medical, it had profound implications for the *epidemiology* of the HIV infection.

HIV positivity and AIDS, the National Academy study revealed, seemed to be confining itself to a relatively small number of at-risk subpopulations. These populations—sometimes called "recalcitrant communities"—included members of the homosexual community; intravenous drug abusers, who transmitted infection through the sharing of needles; the sexual partners of IV drug abusers; and prostitutes. On February 7, 1993, a panel member of the National Academy's study group, Allan Brandt of the Harvard Medical School, told a *New York Times* reporter: "Ten years ago, we were talking about quarantines, about isolating AIDS patients." Now "socially, AIDS patients have been quarantined, they have been isolated by their social inequality."

To be sure, cases of infection appeared outside these special populations. But the pattern of spread appeared much more sporadic and diffuse among individuals outside the identified groups than within the recalcitrant communities. Public health specialists recognized the epidemiological significance of this fact: While any case of HIV anywhere is tragic for the infected individual, the sporadic and diffuse nature of the pattern within the general population makes it difficult to sustain the chain reaction of additional infections. Some observers even concluded that the epidemic *as an epidemic* had been contained by making it a disease of a few "pariah" groups.

A spokesperson for the American Foundation for AIDS Research summarized the message that many drew from the National Academy's findings: "AIDS is a major problem but as it moves farther and farther from the 'mainstream of America,' it looks like we're going to ignore it. . . . The attitude has become, 'When I thought I was going to get infected, I was interested in AIDS, but now that I look around and see that my white, middle-class friends are not infected, I'm not interested.'"

[3]Based on James Trussell, "What Is the Purpose of HIV Antibody Testing?" 36 *Social Biology* (Spring–Summer 1989): 102–109.

Table 8.1 Gene Petitsaint's Calculation of False-Positive and False-Negative Test Results under the Public Health Service's Two-Stage Procedure

100,000 Individuals (underlying infection rate, percent)	False Positives	False Negatives
0.2	1	4
20.0	0 or 1	399

Queries: Which objective do you think should be primary: minimizing false positives? Or minimizing false negatives? Why? How, merely by changing the rules governing testing, could you bring about an outcome different from the one that the PHS procedure described by Trussell promotes? Based on your study of the Trussell presentation and Gene's computations ("Check the numbers"), which variable is more significant: the testing procedure itself? Or the way in which it is applied to different sub-populations?

The public health professionals in Gene Petitsaint's new circle of coworkers knew that Americans in general might forget the principal victims of the AIDS epidemic. But there was no way that AIDS victims could ever be far from the natural concern of a Haitian American immigrant such as Gene. Nor was there any way that city administrators, budget specialists, police officers, social caseworkers, or public health staffers—the kinds of officials with whom Gene, as a health professional, dealt every day—could ignore AIDS patients. The "socially disadvantaged segments" singled out by the National Academy panelists are more poor, on average, than most Americans. As a consequence, they are also far more likely than the average citizen to draw on public services, including homeless shelters, medical treatment in public hospitals, outreach functions of municipal social agencies, and welfare support. HIV victims—especially those in the category of IV drug abusers—are also among the most likely either to be unemployed before converting to full-blown AIDS or else to lose their jobs quickly when symptoms appear. When they lose their jobs, they also lose any private health insurance.

(Private insurance carriers, usually under cost-sharing arrangements with employers, provide most of the coverage that Americans have for major medical expenses. But as a result of technical limitations in some policies or the lapsing of insurance coverage when HIV-positive individuals lose their jobs, private insurance covers on average only about half the cost of full AIDS treatment for most victims of the syndrome. In the mid-1990s, Medicaid, the federal-state program to ensure medical care for poor Americans, became the primary funding source for 40 percent of all AIDS patients—and for a staggering *90 percent* of infected infants, many of them the children of drug-abusing mothers. Among health-care mavens, this trend is known as "the *Medicaid*ization of AIDS.")

Most estimates of total personal *and social* case costs for an infected individual lie in the range of $750,000 from the point of HIV diagnosis to the moment of death, although some estimates are well over $1 million. The social costs include the losses to society of the economic output that AIDS patients would have been able to contribute, had their disease not undermined their productivity. The social costs also include medical treatment and other costs displaced to taxpayers in general.

What about treatment during the final, full-blown stage of AIDS? It costs, on average, between $30,000 and $35,000 per year to treat an individual whose infection has progressed to the level of terminal illness. Such an individual faces the likelihood of repeated medical crises and multiple admissions to acute-care hospitals or special clinics. Total direct medical costs, from the onset of full-blown AIDS symptoms to the time of death, are probably about $75,000 per case. Again, most of this sum for the socially disadvantaged, who represent the majority of the cases, must come from public sources. Yet even with public support, the uncompensated costs to hospitals for treating AIDS patients may be as much as four times greater than those for patients with illnesses not related to HIV. Of course, these estimates don't even begin to reflect the anxiety, fear, pain, and suffering of the afflicted individuals and those close to them.

In sum, the exact pattern of the financial burden of AIDS treatment, though impossible to trace, is spread widely across society in the form of public funding out of tax revenues and insurance premiums paid by employees whose coworkers become ill. Cost shifting by private caregivers has also been an important factor. In the past, these caregivers have typically charged higher prices to paying patients, who have therefore ended up subsidizing low-income or indigent AIDS victims. However, the move in recent years to *managed medical care*—a code phrase for careful scrutiny of hospital costs and stiff competition among medical care providers—makes it unlikely that hospital administrators will be able to continue shifting costs to paying patients. Many public health experts expect the AIDS crisis to worsen in economic as well as medical terms. These experts cite the trend toward tightened financial discipline in the medical industry and the fact that this trend weighs with special force on the kinds of individuals who disproportionately wind up as AIDS patients.

●　　●　　●　　●　　●

In late 1992, officials at the federal Centers for Disease Control (CDC) in Atlanta expanded the list of diseases and symptoms used in defining the transition from asymptomatic seropositivity to full-blown AIDS. These officials recognized as symptoms of clinical AIDS a form of tuberculosis, cervical cancer, a previously excluded strain of HIV-related pneumonia, and a lower level of CD-4 cells. (CD-4 cells are critical in the proper functioning of the immune system, which HIV eventually destroys.) Federal health officials with a stroke thus increased the number of official cases of AIDS. Literally overnight, the caseload nationally jumped by about 60 percent, and the number of citizens qualifying for various categories of AIDS-related government benefits increased by almost as much. No doubt in medical and humanistic terms the action was justified—and perhaps even morally mandatory. But the change in levels of entitlement to public benefits made the AIDS epidemic even more difficult than it had previously been for public health policy makers. Nora Smith and her staffers had to worry about the rising costs of HIV testing and AIDS intervention.

As a professional health economist, Smith had made her views about HIV as a combined public health and public finance problem familiar to everyone in the policy shop:

> We're looking at an inevitable increase in the acute caseload as the numbers of HIV-positive cases—some of them in dormancy for years—convert to full-blown AIDS. We've got a time bomb. Every new infection today

threatens to bring a huge cost sometime in the future. Moreover, because HIV is infectious even before it becomes symptomatic, every new infection threatens the further spread of the disease to others with whom the individual engages in irresponsible behavior. Only a sensible HIV screening program will let us gauge the extent of the infection. And only if we can map the infection with reasonable accuracy will we be able to estimate the future demand for intensive care.

What should a sensible screening program look like?

• • • • •

From the journal of Gene Petitsaint. Source: Article by health policy experts Steven Nahmias and Charles D. Feinstein. Subject: "Screening strategies to inhibit the spread of AIDS."

A screening program for HIV is a method of identifying individuals who are infected. Screening should serve two purposes: (1) gather information on the spread of the virus; and (2) reduce the number of new infections. Little is known about the effect that screening has had in slowing down the spread of the virus. Does the knowledge that one is infected alter one's behavior? Perhaps. However, we do not feel that society can afford to rely on the personal ethics of the individual. A screening program should be coupled with a program of counseling and education and the progress of those found to be infected should be tracked. The behavior of those from high risk groups, in particular, should be monitored to curb the spread of the virus.

The cost of administering a screening program is an important part of the overall cost-benefit analysis. The Illinois program is one that has received a great deal of attention. Illinois began a mandatory pre-nuptial HIV screening program in January 1988. In the first year of the program, 155,458 newly betrothed people were tested at a cost of at least $5.4 million. The test results indicated that 26 individuals were infected with the virus (which includes those whose tests were falsely positive). Thus, the cost of detecting a single infection of HIV was at least $208,000.

Because the cost of detection per case was so high, this program has come under intense criticism. The high detection cost notwithstanding, we believe that a testing program for the general population could be designed to be cost effective. High detection costs can be justified if one or more future infections could be avoided for each detection. . . .

While identifying those who are infected is indeed the purpose of a screening program, the benefit of such an identification is determined by what happens after an HIV positive individual is identified. That is, unless there is a policy in place that exploits the identification of infected persons so as to reduce the spread of the virus, screening for HIV infection has little benefit beyond the value of the information.

Conditions under which screening should be preferred to not screening are therefore dependent upon public policy. The analysis required to determine such conditions is identical to that appropriate for any testing decision under uncertainty. . . . Indeed, one cannot possibly decide whether to screen unless one knows what the policy is and what effects that policy will have, as measured by the benefit. Further, one must have an understanding of the costs of errors in this situation. . . .

An approach to measuring the benefit of detecting a case of HIV infection begins with an estimate of the costs to society of AIDS. . . . Personal medical costs have been estimated to be between $27,000 and $70,000 per case (1989 dollars). Non-personal costs (including costs of tests) have been estimated to be between $16,000 and $21,000 per case (1989 dollars). Morbidity costs have been estimated to be approximately $17,000 per case (1989 dollars) while mortality costs have been estimated to be between $550,000 and $750,000 per case (1989 dollars).

Including morbidity and mortality costs in the total assumes that the individual otherwise would have been gainfully employed, and that the appropriate measurement of the benefit to society of that employment is the present value of lost future earnings. . . .

Based on these estimates, we may conclude that the cost of a case of AIDS is between $610,000 and $858,000 (in 1989 dollars). . . .

Assessing the benefit of detecting HIV is difficult since the benefit depends on what kind of individual is infected. Indeed, in all cases early detection of infection permits intervention and drug therapy that can delay, if not prevent, the onset of AIDS or other illnesses. If the individual is not in a high-risk group, these benefits might constitute the total benefit of detection. However, if the individual is a member of a high-risk group and therefore behaves in ways that tend to spread the infection, the major portion of the total benefit of detection is realized only if the infected individual does not infect others. Almost surely, such a realization entails alteration of the behavior of this infected individual. . . .

In particular, prostitutes and i.v. drug abusers seem to be characterized by precisely those behaviors that need to be altered. This is the essence of the difficulty: the benefit of screening such people is only realized if they cease being what or who they are, or society finds some other creative way of accommodating such behaviors. Hence, the relationship noted above between the value of a screening program and social policy. . . .

There should be follow-up to insure that infected individuals are not continuing to engage in activities that are likely to spread the virus. In principle, it is hard to imagine anyone opposing this point. The implementation, however, is somewhat problematical. Is it appropriate, for example, to enact legislation that makes knowingly spreading AIDS or the HIV infection a punishable offense? . . .

Suppose that screening has uncovered an infected adult. The goal of any post-screening activity is to effect a change in the behavior of the infected individual so that he or she is less likely to spread the virus to other uninfected adults. . . .

Suppose, for the sake of clarity, that the risk group in question is female prostitutes. Furthermore, suppose that, on average, infected prostitutes spread the disease to from 0 to 6 uninfected adults each year. Consider, then, the following hypothetical probability distribution:

$$g_0 = 0.34, g_1 = 0.24, g_2 = 0.18, g_3 = 0.12, g_4 = 0.08,$$
$$g_5 = 0.05, g_6 = 0.01$$

[I.e., 34% do not spread the virus; 24% infect 1 other person; etc.].... The mean of this distribution is 1.59, indicating that, on average, *each member* of this group is responsible for spreading the virus to 1.59 other uninfected adults each year.... Similar distributions would have to be estimated for other risk groups under study....

For each infected adult discovered from a particular risk group, there are several alternative actions available.... These actions might consist of the following in this case:

1. Take no action.
2. Education and counseling.
3. One-on-one intensive counseling.
4. Remuneration for not practicing.
5. Incarceration and isolation....

[O]ne could develop an expression for the expected cost associated with any policy. This objective function should also include costs of violating personal rights when implementing extreme actions (such as incarceration and isolation). Within this context, a policy is a function that chooses an action for each state of the system.... This analysis would ultimately lead to a set of policy decisions for each state and each risk group....

Policies can be modeled and characterized by the number of future infections caused by a single infected individual. That is, each alternative policy would yield, in general, a different probability distribution on the number of infections caused by a single infected individual. The expected cost of the number of new infections can be computed and thus serve as a measure of the benefit of the proposed policy.[4]

• • • • •

In the late 1980s and early 1990s, HIV test results for newborn infants ("neonates") were routinely collected in most of the nation's maternity wards and passed on to researchers at the Centers for Disease Control. The CDC researchers in turn used the information to track the spread of the epidemic. All testing mandated under the CDC program was anonymous; no direct association was drawn between test results, whether positive or negative, and specific babies.

The CDC discontinued neonate testing in 1995, in large part out of a desire to shift the focus from babies to their mothers, whom CDC doctors hoped would submit to voluntary testing early in their pregnancies. Nevertheless, the practice of anonymous screening is still followed in some states, counties, and cities as mandated by state or local public health ordinances. Nora Smith has had several conversations with

[4]From Steven Nahmias and Charles D. Feinstein, "Screening Strategies to Inhibit the Spread of AIDS," 24 *Socio-Economic Planning Sciences* (No. 4, 1990): 249–260.

Gene Petitsaint about the testing protocols that remained in force in their locale. These protocols are among those still based on the anonymous procedure: All newborns within legal reach of the Public Health Department are automatically screened using the two-step procedure. The resulting aggregate statistics are made known throughout the local public health community, but no baby is tested by name (except by special arrangement with a parent or legal guardian). Smith's concerns—she's said that it's time for Americans to rethink every aspect of HIV testing and AIDS intervention—have given Petitsaint reason to review his own views on AIDS policy. Should the current anonymous neonate testing practice be extended, discontinued, or modified?

Neonate testing in the area is carried out by medical technicians at local commercial laboratories under contracts with the city's Public Health Department. The technicians receive blood samples taken from newborns in area hospitals. Each laboratory services several local maternity wards. Under the guarantee of anonymity, the testing yields information only about the percentage of newborns at participating hospitals whose samples in a given batch test positive. As under the original CDC protocol, *which* individual babies have the infection remains unknown unless the mother asks for named testing.

Newborn seropositivity is known to be highly concentrated among the babies of women who are in the major at-risk categories, especially IV drug users and the sexual partners of addicts. These are also among the women who, out of financial necessity, tend to rely on public, inner-city hospitals for maternity services. Thus, although an epidemiologist looking at a given batch of anonymous blood tests wouldn't know which babies went with which results, he or she would inferentially expect any positives to be clustered within the population of newborns currently in those maternity wards which serve the highest concentrations of at-risk mothers.

One day Nora Smith called Gene Petitsaint in and asked him what he thought about mandatory *named* neonate testing—HIV testing of identified babies, whether the parent gave consent to do so or not. Apparently one of the doctors on the city's public health service field staff had been urging Smith to press for a change in the current policy. Before identified testing could occur anywhere in the state, laws currently on the books required informed consent by an individual (or, in the case of a child under age twelve, by a parent or guardian). As in many states, the only exceptions were for convicted offenders on their way to prison and for prostitutes already under criminal prosecution. If Smith, as head of the policy planning office, formally recommended that the state legislature pass a mandatory named neonate testing law (or a law which permitted counties and cities to pass mandatory named testing ordinances), the endorsement would surely push public health practice in that direction.[5]

Under a mandatory regimen, the blood specimen taken for HIV testing would carry its donor's name (Baby Jones, Baby Smith, and so on). Positivity could be linked to a specific individual. The baby could then be slated for special care and treatment, or at least—because seropositivity doesn't always indicate that the baby (as opposed

[5]In 1996 Congress amended the Ryan White Act, a federal statute that provides various kinds of financial support and legal protection to patients with AIDS. One provision of the amendments expresses Congress's intent to establish mandatory neonate testing as a national policy after the year 2000 unless the states, acting under their police powers, achieve significant progress by that time in the early identification of HIV cases.

to the mother) is infected[6]—for close observation. Most pediatricians reportedly favored such a practice. On the other hand, the views of obstetricians were more mixed. Many obstetricians feared that the "threat" of mandatory testing, whether applicable to the mother or to the baby, would deter some women from seeking professional obstetric services even for delivery, let alone early in pregnancy.

Although seropositive babies can't now be cured of their HIV infections, they can be given supportive therapies to strengthen them against the eventual onset of full-blown AIDS. Identified HIV testing could give early information vital to the care of babies facing severely foreshortened lives—lives with much pain and, often, abandonment through the early deaths of their mothers.

But Petitsaint knew that there were also arguments on the other side of the issue. Libertarians had long opposed proposals for mandatory named neonate testing. Barring freakish cases and the always-present danger of false positives, a baby's seropositivity could only be explained as a sequela (secondary result) of the mother's infection. Named testing of neonates would amount to named testing of new mothers, whether they had consented or not—contrary to law and in violation of the mothers' privacy rights. Some libertarians regarded named testing as doubly reprehensible because of its allegedly racist overtones, since everyone knew *which* populations of new mothers would be the primary targets of a mandatory program. Adversaries of the idea also argued that neonate testing would open the door for still more intrusive screening techniques, all justified as public health measures. The opponents of mandatory named neonate testing assumed that any weakening of the informed consent requirement would put society on the slippery slope to increasingly invasive forms of police and public health intervention in personal lives.

There were also opponents of mandatory testing who reasoned that for some new mothers it might be a perfectly rational choice to remain ignorant even if an HIV test were freely available and even if testing would be in the interest of their babies. Some individuals might reject testing lest confirmation of their suspected seropositive conditions increase their legal exposure or limit their sense of freedom to behave as they wished. Because the best way to remain ignorant was to withhold consent for any kind of testing, the best way to preserve the right to remain ignorant was to prohibit mandatory testing.

So bitter was the conflict between proponents of the contending positions on the testing issue that New York public health officials—the first in any state to react officially after the CDC discontinued its anonymous program—felt pressured to accept a weak compromise: All newborns would be tested for HIV on a named basis, but the testers would hold results confidential unless the mother explicitly consented to receive them.[7] Most parties conceded that this arrangement seemed the best that could be worked out, given the intense feelings on all sides. Still, commentators

---

[6]In as many as 70 percent of cases, a seropositive test result may reflect a response to the *mother's* antibodies, which have been passed on to the baby through the amniotic fluid. Of course, that still leaves 30 percent for whom seropositivity indicates that the antibodies are the *baby's* own, a diagnostic predictor of AIDS. Only with time, usually six months or so, can it be determined in which category a seropositive infant belongs. In short, neonate testing can establish a possibility of infection in the child and—false positives aside—its certainty in the mother.

[7]James Dao, "Mothers to Get AIDS Test Data under Accord," *New York Times*, Oct. 10, 1995, p. 1.

pointed out that the New York plan could leave seropositive newborns without follow-up observation unless mothers could be persuaded to receive the very information that they might not want to hear. On the other side, some women's advocates feared that reluctant new mothers would now be subjected to enormous pressure to give informed consent. The very process of pressuring them might, in effect, communicate information that the doctors had already acquired through the named testing program, whether the mothers in question gave formal permission to be told or not.

•   •   •   •   •

Early in 1993 European medical and sociological researchers reported significant reductions in the rates of HIV infection among members of "recalcitrant communities" who had been targeted for intensive programs of education, needle exchange, face-to-face counseling, and confidential contact tracing. Even IV drug abusers had responded to outreach, provided the investment of resources in the effort had been sufficiently intensive. Best of all, the European results seemed to confirm some encouraging American findings in this vein. The gay and lesbian communities of San Francisco and New York City, for example, had demonstrated that concerted educational efforts can pay off—at least temporarily—in communities with activist leaders and well-developed internal lines of communication.

As head of policy planning, Nora Smith had to take the targeted community approach seriously as a possible strategy for fighting the AIDS epidemic locally. Instinctively, she would have preferred a strategy less reliant on social action. Smith wasn't so sure about the effectiveness of public service announcements, counseling, and outreach efforts. She favored tactics tied more directly to known medical technologies (blood screening, contact tracing, direct condom distribution). But the whole field was confusing enough to justify consideration of any approach that seemed at all sensible on its face.

"Follow up on that information about the European experience," Nora instructed Gene. "Would intensive, targeted AIDS counseling work here in the United States, as it apparently has abroad?"

•   •   •   •   •

In the spring of 1993, word about AZT from the international AIDS conference in Paris was discouraging. Then came the European Concorde Study results. A major European effort to assess AZT using the most rigorous statistical techniques showed only marginal clinical effectiveness, if even that. In many cases, use of the drug did delay the onset of full-blown AIDS, just as the optimists had predicted at the time of the original talk about the AZT "breakthrough." But time and experience had now shown that, when the delayed symptoms of full-blown AIDS inevitably began to appear, the progression of the disease seemed swifter than among seropositive patients who hadn't used AZT. The sanguine expectations regarding AZT that Petit-saint so well remembered from the fuss raised by AIDS activists at the University of Washington seemed not to have been justified in the event.

A major exception to the discouraging news, however, seemingly applied to the special case when AZT was used in conjunction with other medicines as a prenatal HIV preventive. Statistically, untreated pregnant women who were HIV positive had a

25 to 30 percent probability of passing the infection on to their children before birth. With AZT plus supportive drug and nutritional therapies, researchers found the infection rate in utero dropped to slightly below 10 percent.

● ● ● ● ●

Gene Petitsaint wasn't quite sure how to dig into his new assignment—to give Dr. Smith an opinion on the workability of a European-type strategy of intensive targeting. Several of Gene's coworkers told him that a good person to contact was a fellow named Carlos Hersh. Hersh, who worked on a contract basis for the city's Bureau of Human Services, split his time among several of the city's emergency shelters. AIDS testing wasn't Hersh's specialty, but he knew as much as anyone could about the motives, behavior, and problems of the city's "recalcitrant communities."

Gene Petitsaint met Carlos Hersh in one of the tiny office cubicles of 1605 Front Street, a converted inner-city loft building that was used as a homeless shelter. Carlos listened as Gene described the studies of AIDS intervention strategies that had come out of Europe.

"I can speak about the homeless," Hersh commented. "They're my main professional concern. But, of course, the homeless include high fractions of unemployed people, impoverished individuals and families, homosexuals who have been rejected by their own families or communities and consider themselves outcasts, and substance abusers. I guess many of these groups qualify as 'recalcitrant communities.'"

Carlos continued: "Though we don't have exact figures, we strongly suspect, based on studies done in a half dozen or so cities, that the homeless population has an exceptionally high HIV rate. Different samples run from 10 percent to around 20 percent of the homeless population that's seropositive. In one study—in New York—a homeless shelter population was actually found to have a rate higher than 50 percent."

As Carlos spoke, Gene thought about James Trussell's illustrative prevalence rates—the "hypothetical" populations with 0.2 and 20 percent actual underlying HIV rates. Trussell's examples suddenly seemed pretty accurate representations of the underlying epidemiological pattern.

Hersh said that his experience counseling "down-and-outers," as he put it, lent support for intensive AIDS education. But, he emphasized, "anything less than a full-court press when working with people in these 'recalcitrant communities' is almost certain to be counterproductive."

Gene asked Carlos to explain what he had just said. What did he mean by a full-court press, and how could any level of HIV education ever be counterproductive?

Carlos replied: "Among members of at-risk populations—some gay populations, prostitutes, needle sharers—individuals who *think* they're clean, . . . that is, not infected, . . . respond reasonably well to education about safe sex, and all that. But among the same populations, when individuals find out through testing that they're HIV positive, they tend to take the news as a death sentence. They ask 'What the hell?' and they lose all discipline. That usually means more promiscuous, unprotected sex. It means ignoring needle-exchange programs even when they're available. It means that positive test results can lead to behavior that's likely to spread, not halt, the epidemic."

Carlos gestured at the peeling walls of the small office in which he and Gene were sitting. "I tried to start a counseling program about AIDS for the homeless here. There are other city shelters, but since this building is so easy for everyone to reach, I thought it would be the best place to set up a one-stop clinic: general education, needle exchange, HIV testing, close counseling for those who show positive." His expression telegraphed that the one-stop clinic had failed—perhaps hadn't ever even got off to much of a start.

"There was enough money to begin a modest operation," Carlos told Gene. "But there wasn't nearly enough to hire and train the people we need for intensive out-reach. Without street workers in constant touch, the people we'd most want to help would drop in at the clinic a few times, maybe submit to testing, then drop out. That was especially true for the ones who tested positive. Some visitors—especially the better-educated ones—refused testing to keep from getting information they didn't want to deal with. They had heard about legal liability. Anxiety about the law added to the natural fear of what a positive result would portend. It takes a lot of hands-on counseling to overcome that kind of averse attitude. The truth is, you can't even say that that attitude is completely irrational."

Gene interpolated: "Ignorance can actually be safer legally as well as more comfortable emotionally for the individual, and can also promote more responsible behavior. None of the factors in this HIV-AIDS area seems to work in the direction you'd expect."

Carlos nodded: "That's the paradox of information. If you want to fight AIDS with knowledge, you need more than cant about 'straight talk.' You need a big and intensive enough program on the streets—continuing one-on-one education, counseling, and support for the at risk and the already infected, so information doesn't lead to more of exactly the kind of behavior that spreads the infection."

•   •   •   •   •

The next time Nora Smith asked Gene into her office, Dr. Robert Tremblay was present. Gene had heard of Tremblay, the doctor who was pushing for Nora to give her official imprimatur to mandatory named neonate testing. Tremblay was speaking to Nora in the exasperated tones of someone who felt it necessary to repeat a simple truth for the third or fourth time. Whatever Tremblay was selling, Smith wasn't buying.

Apparently, the last round of anonymous testing of thirty-seven babies at four area hospitals had turned up a case of suspected neonatal HIV. One of the four maternity wards in the testing batch served the low-income Medicaid population from central-ward areas known to have a high HIV prevalence. Tremblay assumed that he could identify an extremely small group of infants in which the one infected baby would probably be found simply by focusing on the mothers and babies in the low-income ward. He proposed to survey the recently delivered mothers there for HIV-correlated traits. In the center-city area, skin color was one such trait. So was recent drug use or evidence of addiction. Tremblay could establish which of the mothers were women of color with a walk through the ward. Regular hospital admission workups—routinely available to Tremblay as a city public health officer—might suggest which of the new mothers, if any, were on drugs. Admission workups would also show whether any of the new mothers showed symptoms or sequelae of venereal diseases, another statistical correlate of HIV.

As nearly as Gene could make out, Tremblay was arguing that he had an unusual juxtaposition of factors in today's set of screening reports. He had a single positive result in the sample; he had a small population of mothers with well-known characteristics; hence he had an extraordinary opportunity by simple detective work to narrow the population containing the positive-test baby to an even smaller group than the population of thirty-seven newly delivered mothers. Only the babies in that tiny group from the inner city would have to be retested to identify by name the one with HIV antibodies. Facts he already had available, Tremblay said, contained all the information he needed to take two steps:

> *First*, by retesting—with or without the permission of the mothers involved—identify a baby who might need special care and probably wouldn't get it if Tremblay didn't move immediately to match the child with a named test result.
>
> *Second*, "intrude" on the privacy of the small group of mothers, one of whom might have passed HIV on to her child, and tell them that someone in their number was almost certainly seropositive and that she too would need extra medical advice and support.

"You can't do it, Bob. State law says 'informed consent' *before* you can test—or, in this case, before you can retest. In my opinion, the law even requires consent before you can act on the kind of information you now have from anonymous tests, that is, before you can go in and upset patients who might not want to hear what you have to say. It's one thing to give every pregnant woman or new mother generalized advice. It's a different matter to start scaring a small group, based on an invidious inference from test results that are theoretically anonymous."

"You're saying it's illegal?" Tremblay asked.

"It *might* be illegal," Nora answered. "It *surely* is unethical. And it's tinged with racism. Would you be able to do what you're proposing if the women out there were in suburban maternity wards, and white, and covered by Aetna or Prudential instead of Medicaid? And if you couldn't or wouldn't do it with them, what makes you think you've got the right to do it with this group?"

Tremblay's expression showed that Nora was making no more headway with him than his arguments for immediate intervention had made with her.

"Sure," Nora continued, "if you want, you can play missionary. 'Bob Tremblay, alias Dr. Schweitzer.' You can, if you insist, make the rounds of all the hospitals and barge in on all thirty-seven mothers, browbeating them about how *someone's* baby *might* be sick—but then again, might *not* be—and how they should all get tested and mend their loose ways. But you can't go out and actually identify the baby, and hence the mother, by comparing your supposedly anonymous result with racial data and privileged medical data and maybe those patients' financial data."

Tremblay reiterated that just those data formed a definite pattern of association with high-risk status for HIV. "At some point in any epidemic," he insisted, "public health *has* to take precedence. You do what you have to. You quarantine. If you don't know any better, you make people shave their heads or wear bells. You pass mandatory vaccination laws: Mommy doesn't want junior stuck with the needle? Tough! Little Tommy gets it anyway. You do *something*—you do whatever—to interrupt the progress of the disease. The earlier you do it, the less extreme the measures have to be."

But Tremblay saw that it wasn't washing, at least not with Nora Smith. "Forget the epidemic a minute, Nora, and just think about that kid the way I have to: as a *patient*. There's one baby over there in General Hospital whom we can help, and one woman we also might be able to help. We don't need mass screening, just a few tests on a small population of babies already identified as containing one known seropositive."

"I *can't* forget the epidemic, Bob," Nora shot back. "And I can't forget about the law, either."

"Ours not to reason why?" Tremblay asked, the sarcasm thick in his voice. "Well, Nora, you worry about the big picture. Maybe you're in the public policy business. But my main worry has to be that poor baby, whoever it is."

• • • • •

At the end of the workday, when most of the others in the office had left, Nora called Gene in again. She'd had word that Dr. Tremblay, as expected, had gone ahead and ordered named tests for seventeen babies in the maternity ward at General Hospital. Nora thought it was important for Gene to start "messing with the kind of hard case," as she put it, that mightn't have been written up in his public administration textbooks. Gene wasn't sure if Nora was referring to Bob Tremblay as a "hard case"; to the choice that Tremblay felt he'd had to make; or to the dilemma posed for Nora herself by the knowledge that a coworker was now probably a lawbreaker. Nora wanted Gene to help her think through what she should do—not only about the tests that Tremblay had just run but also about the larger issues. What position should the city's director of public health policy planning take on HIV testing and AIDS intervention?

Questions for Discussion

The following queries might help you frame your thoughts and organize a discussion of the case.

1. What's the story? What "circumstances of the action" and "conditions of the agents" should be kept especially in mind when thinking through the issues in this scenario?

2. Which aspects of the scenario should be taken as symptoms of underdetermination? What are the causes of underdetermination in the current situations of Nora Smith and Robert Tremblay and in the past experience of Carlos Hersh—all actors with jobs to do but incomplete control over important variables (including one another)? Which aspects of the scenario reflect incomplete or uncertain information? Which of the usual ways of dealing with conditions of underdetermination (persuasion, restructuring, and so forth) seems most likely to be helpful?

3. In what form or forms does the conflict between outcomes and actions present itself in this scenario?

4. Does mandatory named neonate testing sound, at first hearing, like a good idea? What about the proposal of some AIDS scholars for a testing program aimed at particular subpopulations based on statistical estimates of underlying infection rates or risky behavior patterns? At first look, does the Nahmias-Feinstein proposal for screening strategies seem like a good idea?

5. "Know the law." How (if at all) should the Supreme Court's three-pronged test be applied in the field of AIDS policy? Do you think a different balance between outcomes and actions should be struck in a testing policy for individuals in high-risk groups than for the population generally?

6. "Check the numbers." What implications for public health policy do you draw from the figures used in the presentation by James Trussell (Sketch 8.1)? What about the information presented by Carlos Hersh? How, if at all, do these data influence your thinking about HIV and AIDS policy?

7. In early 1996 AIDS researchers announced encouraging therapeutic results from a new drug, retonivir. When tested in conjunction with AZT on human subjects, retonivir significantly delayed the onset of complications in patients with AIDS. Such a "multidrug therapy," however, was projected to cost some $15,000 per patient, with related medications further boosting the annual cost above $70,000. Given the uncertainties (reminiscent of the initial expectations for AZT in "single-drug therapy") and given the costs, does this new breakthrough represent a "progression of circumstances" that leads you to modify any of your initial views about the desirable course for AIDS policy?

8. Which approach—the utilitarian (consequentialist) or the the Kantian (deontological)—seems to you more helpful in the kind of situation in which Dr. Tremblay finds himself?

9. What in your opinion should Nora Smith do about the information she's received to the effect that Dr. Tremblay has gone ahead and retested seventeen babies on a named basis without even trying to get their mothers' informed consent? Again: How, if at all, might the effects-based and the duty-based (consequentialist and deontological) approaches to ethics lead to different recommendations regarding the actions that the various figures in the case should take? "Discuss and defend": justify whatever action you think Smith should take.

10. How do the duties of procedural correctness, obedience to higher authority, and impartiality play out in the decisions that Nora Smith and Robert Tremblay have to make?

11. What criteria should policy makers try to realize when framing a policy for HIV testing? Are the items on your list consistent with one another, or might they lead to a problem of overdetermination? If the latter, what priorities would you assign to the different criteria that you have identified? (Remember: "HIV" isn't the same as "AIDS." How, if at all, should the priorities that are assigned to various criteria

differ in the cases of HIV testing and AIDS intervention?) How might parameter changing or policy adjusting be used to deal with any of the issues facing Nora Smith?

12. After digesting details of the scenario that might not have been obvious at first, and after thinking through the broader philosophical and political implications of the issues, do you feel the same way about mandatory named neonate testing as you did at first? About active testing and intervention programs targeted on particular segments of the population? What additional "progression of circumstances" can you imagine that might cause you to modify your opinions regarding the various decisions confronting Nora Smith?

FOR FURTHER READING

Some standard authors and works—all of them, thoughtful and rewarding—on the ethics of public administration are

Appleby, Paul, *Morality and Administration in Democratic Government* (Baton Rouge LA: Louisiana State U. Press, 1952).

Cooper, Terry, *The Responsible Administrator* (San Francisco: Jossey-Bass, 1990).

Denhardt, Katherine, *The Ethics of Public Service: Resolving Moral Dilemmas in Public Organizations* (New York: Greenwood, 1988).

Fleischman, Joel, et al., *Public Duties: The Moral Obligations of Government Office* (Cambridge MA: Harvard U. Press, 1981).

Frederickson, H. George, *Ethics and Public Administration* (Armonk NY: M.E. Sharpe, 1993).

Thompson, Dennis, "The Possibility of Administrative Ethics," 45 *Public Administration Review* (September–October 1985), 555.

Thompson, Dennis, *Political Ethics and Public Office* (Cambridge MA: Harvard U. Press, 1987); see especially chaps. 1–3, 5.

Works that link ethical issues to the principles of American constitutionalism are

Richardson, William, and Lloyd Nigro, "The Constitution and Administrative Ethics in America," 23 *Administration and Society* (November 1991), 275.

Rohr, John, *Ethics for Bureaucrats,* 2d ed., (New York: Marcel Dekker, 1988).

And see the following article, often (and correctly) referred to as a classic:

Bailey, Stephen, "Ethics and the Public Service," in Roscoe Martin, ed., *Public Administration and Democracy* (Syracuse NY: Syracuse U. Press, 1965), p. 382.

On the ethical implications of decision making in particular kinds of choice situations and in particular arenas of public policy, see

Bok, Sissela, *Lying: Moral Choice in Public and Private Life* (New York: Pantheon, 1978).

Glover, Jonathan, *Causing Death and Saving Lives* (New York: Viking Penguin, 1987).

Goodin, Robert E., *Protecting the Vulnerable* (Chicago: U. of Chicago Press, 1985).

Also see

Harmon, Michael, "The Responsible Actor as "Tortured Soul": The Case of Horatio Hornblower," 25 *Administration and Society* (November 1989), 283; also in Henry Kass and Bayard Catron, eds., *Images and Identities in Public Administration* (Newbury Park CA: Sage, 1990), p. 151.

Stewart, Debra, "Theoretical Foundations of Ethics in Public Administration: Approaches to Understanding Moral Action," 23 *Administration and Society* (November 1991), 357.

On principal-agent theory, see the Kass article referenced in Box 8.3 and

Moe, Terry, "The New Economics of Organization," 28 *American Journal of Political Science* (November 1984), 733.

Pratt, J. W., and R. Zeckhauser, *Principals and Agents: The Structure of Business* (Boston: Harvard Business School Press, 1985).

The literature on AIDS is voluminous and constantly changing. Useful recent sources include:

Keeling, Richard P., "HIV Disease: Current Concepts," 71 *Journal of Counseling and Development* (January–February 1993), 261.

Jonsen, Albert R., and Jeff Stryker, eds., *The Social Impact of AIDS in the United States* (Washington: National Academy Press, 1993).

National Commission on Acquired Immune Deficiency Syndrome, *America Living with AIDS: Transforming Anger, Fear and Indifference into Action* (Washington: 1991).

On the AIDS epidemic and public administration, see

Slack, James. D., "The Public Administration of AIDS" (Book Review), 52 *Public Administration Review* (January–February 1992), 77.

Levin, Martin, "The Day after an AIDS Vaccine Is Discovered: Management Matters," 12 *Journal of Policy Analysis and Management* (Summer 1993), 438.

▼◆ ● ■ ▼ ◆ ● ■ ▼ ◆ ● ■ ▼ ◆ ● ■ ▼ ◆

CHAPTER 9

Counting the Consequences: Formal Policy Analysis

In Chapter 8, we saw that one of the fundamental obligations of a public official is to consider the effects of a decision or action on the citizens whom the official is pledged to serve. Much brainpower has been invested in the development of ways to estimate the outcomes of official actions. The subfield of public administration known as **formal policy analysis** emphasizes the quantitative study of social benefits and costs. In this chapter we'll give special attention to the method most commonly used to estimate the outcomes of official decisions: *cost-benefit analysis,* or *CBA.* This is probably the single most widely used decision-making approach in modern public administration. Certainly it is the methodology most commonly relied on by administrators when they function as policy analysts and policy advisers. But CBA is also one of the more problematical and controversial intellectual frameworks in the field. We'll try to see why that, too, is the case.

Systems Analysis and Budgeting as Subfields of Public Administration

The role of the trusted counselor has existed as long as princes have recognized the need for sages at their sides. Traditionally, the members of "kitchen cabinets" have given advice based on political savvy, legal expertise, or simple common sense. In recent decades, however, something new has been added. As far as many policy makers are concerned, advice that is merely streetwise or commonsensical won't cut it anymore. Drawing on one of the most potent intellectual traditions in Western history—the geometrical tradition that we discussed in Chapter 1—these practitioners demand analytical backup that is formal, quantitative, rationalistic, and systematic.

In the 1600s, influential thinkers tried to apply the algebraic methods of the great physicists and mathematicians—Galileo and Newton, Descartes and Pascal—to the social realm. René Descartes and his contemporary Thomas Hobbes believed that the human condition could be improved through the application of the right analytical methods. For most of the intellectual heroes of the seventeenth century, these methods had to be quantitative. Descartes and Hobbes explicitly championed geometrical reasoning as the method of *all* sound thinking. (It was Descartes's excesses on this score that led Pascal to muse about the "ridiculous" posture of geometers who try to use mathematics on problems that call for applications of the discerning intellect.)

The eighteenth-century Scottish moral philosopher Hutcheson derived algebraic formulas to compute the amount of "benevolence" that a person displayed when dealing with others. Another major figure of the "century of enlightenment," the French encyclopedist Diderot, included an entry entitled "political arithmetic" in his compendium of all knowledge. And in Italy the first modern criminologist and penal reformer, Beccaria, developed a mathematical calculus to be used when computing sentences, so as to ensure that a convicted criminal's punishment would fit the crime and achieve the maximum deterrent effect on other would-be miscreants.

A bit later came the British penal reformer and philosopher Jeremy Bentham (1748–1832). The modern aspiration not merely to list but also to measure the effects—literally to *count the consequences*—of a proposed course of action probably owes more to the influence of Bentham's version of consequentialist philosophy than to any other single source. (Our chapter reading includes a thumbnail description of Bentham's philosophy, known as **utilitarianism**.) Bentham popularized the greatest-happiness principle mentioned in Chapter 8, the notion that public policies should promote "the greatest happiness of the greatest number." From him we get the idea of a "felicific calculus"—Bentham's coined term for a computational procedure that he regarded literally as an algebra of happiness. In the same spirit, that exemplar of our own American Enlightenment, Ben Franklin, codified a systematic "prudential algebra" to be followed when dealing with complicated issues in which multiple considerations must be juggled and balanced (see Box 9.1).

More than two centuries after Bentham outlined the felicific calculus and Franklin described his prudential algebra—and more than a hundred years after Woodrow Wilson called for a "science of administration"—we find an influential cadre of administrative theorists and practitioners still working to advance the formal methodology of policy analysis. Their aim is the same as Bentham's and Franklin's was, to help decision makers "judge better." They have tried to advance this effort by moving beyond mere careful, comprehensive analysis of the kind that the Progressives of a century ago espoused and developing a rigorous new quantitative methodology.

The Emergence of Formal Policy Analysis as a Subfield of Public Administration

If the spirit of modern formal policy analysis traces ultimately to the intellectual heroes of seventeenth-century science, most of its standard methodologies and techniques derive more proximately from the operations researchers, systems analysts, mathematical economists, and public-sector budget analysts who, beginning during World War II, developed this subfield of contemporary public administration.

The discipline known as **operations research** originated as a response to the troubles that American and British air crews were having in bomb runs over Germany. The Allied air commanders commissioned teams of mathematicians and scientists to figure

BOX 9.1 ■■■

Formal Policy Analysis, Ben Franklin Style

To Joseph Priestley

London, September 19, 1772

Dear Sir,

In the affair of so much Importance to you, wherein you ask my Advice, I cannot for want of sufficient Premises, advise you *what* to determine, but if you please, I will tell you *how*. When those difficult cases occur, they are difficult, chiefly because while we have them under Consideration, all the reasons *pro* and *con* are not present to the Mind at the same time; but sometimes one Set present themselves, and at other times another, the first being out of Sight. Hence the various Purposes or Inclinations that alternatively prevail, and the Uncertainty that perplexes us.

To get over this, my Way is to divide half a sheet of paper by a Line into two Columns; writing over the one *Pro*, and over the other *Con*. Then, during three of four Days Consideration, I put down under the different Heads short Hints of the different motives, that at different times occur to me, *for* or *against* the Measure. When I have thus got them all together in one View, I endeavor to estimate their respective Weights; and when I find two, one on each side, that seem equal, I strike them both out. If I find a Reason pro equal to some two reasons con, I strike out the three. If I judge some two Reasons *con*, equal to some three Reasons *pro*, I strike out the five; and thus proceeding I find at length where the Ballance [sic] lies; and if, after a Day or two of further Consideration, nothing new that is of importance occurs on either side, I come to a Determination accordingly. And, tho' the Weight of Reasons cannot be taken with the Precision of Algebraic Quantities, yet when each is thus considered, separately and comparatively, and the whole lies before me, I think I can judge better, and am less liable to make a rash Step, and in fact I have found great advantage from this kind of Equation, in what may be called *Moral* or *Prudential Algebra*. . . .

Excerpted from Adrienne Koch, ed., *The American Englightenment* (New York: George Braziller, 1965), p. 89.

■■■

out what flight formations of B-17 and Lancaster bombers would minimize their exposure to Luftwaffe fighters and German antiaircraft batteries. World War II operations research was, in effect, a hugely successful instance of formal systemwide analysis and planning. The analysts figured out how the American and British fliers could modify their formations so their gunners could bring maximum concentrated firepower against the German interceptors. These operations researchers went on to recommend the altitudes at which the Allied attackers should make their bomb runs. By varying their flight plans in calculated ways—or sometimes, in ways that were totally random, so no one could predict an attack pattern—Allied crews were eventually able to confuse the German antiaircraft gunners, who had to resort to sheer guesswork when they set the altitudes for their flak shells to explode.

After World War II, U.S. Air Force Chief of Staff Henry "Hap" Arnold asked friends in private industry to keep the operations researchers together as a source of continuing advice on air tactics and strategy. The result was the granddaddy of American think tanks, the California-based RAND Corporation (note the acronym for *R&D,* or *research and d*evelopment). In due course, the RAND researchers recruited logicians and mathematical economists into their ranks, thereby laying the basis for a new interdisciplinary field called **systems analysis** (see Box 9.2).

Formal Policy Analysis in Government Decision Making

The two key figures in the development and spread of formal policy analysis within government were both brought into public service in the early 1960s by Robert McNamara. McNamara, appointed as Secretary of Defense by President John F. Kennedy, called Charles Hitch and Alain Enthoven to the Pentagon from the RAND Corporation, where they had made names for themselves as budget theorists. Both were experts in the whole bag of techniques that eventually became the discipline of systems analysis. Under McNamara, Hitch and Enthoven took charge of budgeting for the Pentagon, where in 1961 they instituted the reform known as *program budgeting.* To support the new budgeting approach, Hitch and Enthoven established the first high-level systems analysis team in the federal government. The members of the Hitch-Enthoven team eventually carried the gospel of systems analysis to other federal agencies, where their skills were in great demand. These "whiz kids" eventually spread formal policy analysis to the budget offices and programming divisions of many state and municipal governments. The Hitch-Enthoven staffers popularized the technique—with which you have already become familiar—of summarizing complex issues in simple numerical tables.

Cost-Effectiveness Analysis

Enthoven sometimes described the core ideas of systems analysis as little more than "sophomore economics." Enthoven was referring to a basic principle that underlies the technique known as **cost-effectiveness analysis.** Cost-effectiveness analysis was central to the effort by McNamara, Hitch, and Enthoven to remodel defense planning around the budget process, while at the same time recasting that process to incorporate certain new techniques, called *performance budgeting* and *program budgeting* (discussed in the next section).

The lesson Enthoven wanted to teach was that it's generally best to spend no more dollars on any program, such as the purchase of bombers, than will bring you to what economists call the *point of marginal returns.* Beyond this point (see Sketch 9.1), extra dollars will yield less and less in the way of improved performance and hence will be better spent for some other purpose—for example, to buy fighter planes or tanks or warships. Ultimately, the same principle applies to government as a whole. Thus, beyond the point of marginal returns in the defense field taken as a whole, extra dollars spent on military preparedness will yield less and less in the way of improvements in national security and hence would be better spent on education, health care, or some other kind of program.

BOX 9.2 ■■■

The Vocabulary of Systems Analysis

Systems analysts draw their techniques from a variety of disciplines but rely especially on economics, computer science, linear algebra, and statistics. The following terms give no more than a sense of what formal analysts are up to these days.

Chi-Square Analysis

A statistical technique used to tell whether a distribution of effects could reasonably have occurred by chance. For example, were those successful Allied bombing runs in World War II simply luck? Or was the improved survival rate so improbable that some deeper causal factor had to be at work—namely, the benefits of formal analysis as applied to the bombing tactics?

Decision Tree

A technique in which an analyst carefully diagrams the possible options open to a decision maker at every stage in the unfolding of a project. Each "branch" in the tree leads to a later decision, at which point additional options are noted. Variations of the decision-tree technique include:

Probability Tree Analysis, in which the cumulative effects of a series of chance events or probabilities are computed; Sketch 8.1 gives an example of this technique.

Game Tree Analysis, in which successive generations in the branching process denote the responses of different "players"—usually adversaries—to the decisions or "moves" made by others at prior stages in the exfoliation of the branches.

Program Evaluation and Review Technique (PERT), used to plan complex projects that involve interdependent sequences of decisions and production efforts. We'll have an example of PERT charting in our case for Chapter 11.

Critical Path Method (CPM), used to identify the specific sequence of branches or production efforts that determines the minimum time needed to complete a project with many interdependent parts.

Game Theory

A formal method of deciding the best course of action for an individual to adopt when that person is in a situation of *strategic interdependence;* that is, when his or her best course of action will depend on the course followed by one or more adversaries, and vice versa. (Do you recall the decisions that Roman Drnda and Walt March had to make as they faced off against each other in the RIFfing situation in Case 2? Drnda and March could have used game-theory techniques to decide which course of action might be the safest for each to pursue.)

Internal Rate of Return (IRR)

The interest rate at which the net present value of an investment will equal zero. You will see a few pages farther on, when we consider cash-flow analysis and cost-benefit analysis, that the value of a stream of future expenditures and revenues depends critically on the interest rate. In business decision making, it's often required that the IRR of a project exceed the expected discount rate, that is, the interest rate at which money can be borrowed. Otherwise, the decision maker would probably be better off putting any extra cash in the bank and collecting interest instead of spending it to finance the project. We'll see an example of this application of the IRR in our chapter case.

Linear Programming

A mathematical optimizing technique used to compute which way productive facilities—such as a school or a factory—should be employed when different output mixes are possible (Teach more English or more biology? Produce computer chips or test tubes?); when the outputs are linearly proportional to the amounts of resources used as inputs; and when multiple constraints (such as budgetary limits) "bind" the effort. Another example of a problem suitable for proximate solution using linear programming methods is the one in Chapter 1 about the mix of workers in an organization. Most economists and systems analysts would think first of linear programming as the technique of choice in the priority-setting, parameter-changing, and policy-adjusting problem of Box 1.2. Instead of modifying the givens of the problem in one or more of the ways described in Chapter 1, a linear programmer would accept the constraints and would seek for the least-wasteful combination of x- and y-type workers.

Prisoners' Dilemma

A situation of strategic interdependence in which adversaries can improve their outcomes if they cooperate with one another but in which noncooperation or even treachery *appears to* promise an even higher reward to the one who "defects." In fact, if either adversary refuses to cooperate, everyone ends up worse off. The prisoners' dilemma—so-called for criminals whom a district attorney tempts to "rat on each other"—is probably the game-theory problem that has had the greatest impact in social science. (Drnda and March in Case 1 were in such a dilemma. Game theorists have worked out ways of dealing with such situations.)

Regression Analysis

A statistical technique used to tell whether and how strongly two or more variables correlate with one another. A high correlation doesn't necessarily mean that either variable causes the other. But it does imply that forces are at work such that when one variable appears, a predictable level of the other is likely to be found as well.

Risk-Benefit Analysis and Expected Value (EV)

A variation on cost-benefit analysis in which explicit treatment is given to probability and uncertainty. Risk-benefit analysis hinges on the concept of an *expected value*, which is akin to that of discounting. The value of an uncertain promise of $50 is obviously less than that of a sure thing, an immediate $50 payment. An analyst may take the risk of nonpayment into account by adjusting the *absolute value* ($50) for the probability of actual delivery. The expected value of a $50 payment that the receiver thinks has only a 50-50 chance of being made is given by

$$EV = (\$50) \times (0.5) = \$25$$

Spreadsheet Analysis (*What-if* Analysis)

Analysis, usually done on a computer with commercial spreadsheet software, in which a problem is solved using one set of assumptions, and then results are recomputed when the analyst changes the givens. In the cost-benefit tables presented in this chapter (see Table 9.2, page 369), estimates of net present value are computed based on an 8-percent interest rate. Using spreadsheet software, results can be recomputed automatically and almost instantaneously to show the effects of changes in the interest rate, changes in the assumed streams of costs and revenues, and so forth.

Survey Research

A set of social science techniques, mostly developed since the 1930s, used to sample public opinion. The *tracking polls* that campaigners use to monitor a candidate's popularity are probably the most familiar example. *Contingent value analysis,* a polling method employed to measure the value that citizens impute to nonmarket goods such as environmental quality, is an increasingly popular application of survey research in public administration. We'll see an example of contingent value analysis later in the chapter.

Note that in cost-effectiveness analysis, the inputs and outputs are measured differently: in billions of dollars along the vertical axis in Panel A; in numbers of bombers along the horizontal axes in both panels; and in a separate "effectiveness measure" of some kind (say, destructive power) along the vertical dimension of Panel B. The linear relationship between dollars and bombers in Panel A shows that after an initial production run, each new bomber costs about the same as the last one did, whether it does or doesn't yield the same amount of combat value that the previous "copy" of the plane added. But in Panel B, the inflection of the curve at the so-called marginal-returns point suggests that a major drop-off occurs there in the rate at which effectiveness continues to increase with additional inputs of dollars. The early systems analysts tried to emphasize that financial planning (How many dollars?) had to go along with production planning (How many bombers?) and tactical planning (How much potential combat value?—which turns out not to depend in a simple, linear way on either of the first two numbers). To the whiz kids, financing and planning were obverse sides of the same coin: an improved budgeting process.

Performance Budgeting and Program Budgeting

The performance budget represented another step in the campaign of the rationalists to supplant the line-item budget. You may recall from Chapter 5 (Box 5.1) that a line-item budget shows dollars and the items of personnel or equipment that the dollars will buy—the *inputs* to the governance process. In line-item budgeting, an increase in an appropriation corresponds to an increase in the number of people employed, in

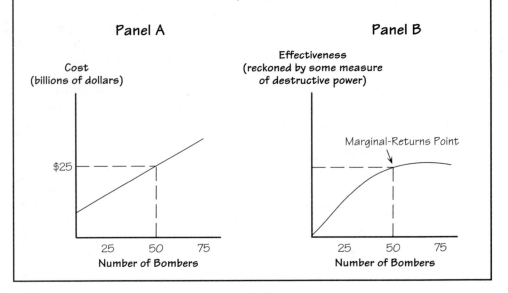

The aim is to identify the dollar outlay (in this example, $25 billion) that will purchase that number of vehicles (50 bombers) yielding the highest ratio of effectiveness to cost. The assumption is that the effectiveness can be quantified, but not necessarily by using the same measure—dollars—that is used to quantify the cost.

Panel A

Cost
(billions of dollars)

$25

25   50   75
Number of Bombers

Panel B

Effectiveness
(reckoned by some measure
of destructive power)

Marginal-Returns Point

25   50   75
Number of Bombers

Sketch 9.1 Cost-Effectiveness Analysis

the equipment they will have available, in the extra contract-service workers (cleanup crews, office-machine maintenance specialists) they may hire, and so forth. But will the increased spending of taxpayers' dollars produce a proportionate increase in the effectiveness of government programs? There's no way to tell by looking at a line-item breakout of dollars and inputs.

One way to begin evaluating effectiveness is to see how spending relates to *outputs* and (if possible) *outcomes*—the essence of **performance budgeting.** The performance budgeter focuses not on the personnel or equipment per se but on the benefits they can generate—in other words, on their effectiveness. It is this shift in focus that establishes the close conceptual relationship between performance budgeting and cost-effectiveness analysis.

Obviously, the choice of performance measures is critical to the design of a performance budget. McNamara's Pentagon analysts in the 1960s had to devise performance measures for the bombers, ships, tanks, and other units of military equipment that they would ask Congress to buy. How much destructive potential (along the vertical axis in Sketch 9.1, Panel B) could be delivered by so many bombers (along the horizontal axes in both panels)? With the spread of performance budgeting to agencies other than the Department of Defense, similar performance-measure questions had to be asked for social programs. Budgeters in the educational field had to decide what quantitative index they would use to measure the effectiveness of teaching programs;

police administrators had to find measures for their programs (reduction in violent crime rates? in citizens' perceptions of the safety of their streets as measured by public opinion polls?). As James Q. Wilson emphasized in his discussion of police administration (Chapter 3), the choice of performance measures often influenced analysts' estimates of effectiveness. Critics of formal policy analysis saw the possibilities for analysts to "tweak" the numbers and hence rig the results.

In theory, **program budgeting**—the innovation for which McNamara, Hitch, and Enthoven became most famous—carried both cost-effectiveness analysis and performance budgeting to higher levels of sophistication. Program budgeters try to quantify not only input measures but also (in James Q. Wilson's terminology) output measures and outcome measures in a way that will permit direct comparisons.

In performance budgeting, an increase in outlays will be explicitly tied to an expected increase not only in inputs like personnel or equipment but also in some output: more bombing (or better bombing), more or better teaching, better policing, and so forth. But when is "more bombing" preferable to spending money on "more teaching" or "better policing"? When resources are scarce, as they always are, what justifies a change in one activity at the expense of another (more bomber pilots, say, and fewer teachers? or more teachers and fewer cops)? The formal policy analysts wanted to make such value assessments across broad lines of competing programs. In a program budget, information is supposed to be displayed in a way that will permit a decision maker to achieve not only the efficient level of spending for each individual program but also the right proportion of programs to one another. When the correct amounts of defense, education, public safety, and so forth have been identified, the budget has achieved *program balance*—the objective of program budgeting. Table 9.1, based on the writings of the Brookings Institution budget expert Allen Schick, and Schick's own commentary in Box 9.3, suggest the progression of concepts from the line-item format through the performance budget to the program budget.

We can perhaps refine our understanding of the term *program balance* in Table 9.1 by returning briefly to the story of the whiz kids. Hitch, Enthoven, and their crew came to the Pentagon fired with enthusiasm to "rationalize" the U.S. defense budget. They found, however, each service trying to maximize its own budget and build its pet weapons systems. Navy planners had blueprints for submarine-launchable nuclear missiles; Air Force staff officers had their pat justifications for new intercontinental missiles and land-based bombers. Organizing the defense budget by separate armed services not only invited constant battling for spending shares but also prevented program optimization. Sound familiar? It should. The whiz kids were fighting the perennial American political battle—systemwide planning versus local interest—in a new arena.

Table 9.1 Basic Concepts in Public Budgeting

Type of Budget	Primary Purpose	Items Displayed	Primary Value
Line-item	Control	Inputs	Legality
Performance	Management	Agency outputs	Efficiency
Program	Planning	Agency missions	Program balance

BOX 9.3 ——————————————————————————————— ▪▪▪

Allen Schick on Control, Management, and Planning in Budgeting

Although every budget process includes aspects of control, management, and planning, one function tends to predominate. As a practical matter, these three functions are competitive; emphasis on one diminishes use of the others. Central authorities must be selective in their use of the crowded days and months of the fiscal year. If they use the central budget apparatus to maintain close surveillance over the spending actions of agencies, it is unlikely that they will have the opportunity or the capability to plan or manage through the budget process. . . .

   Control in budgeting is the process of enforcing the limitations and conditions set in the budget and in appropriations, and of securing compliance with the spending restrictions imposed by central authorities. If the budget details the allowances for items of expense, the central budgeters will be required, or at least tempted, to monitor agency actions in order to enforce the limits. If restrictions are imposed on the spending discretion of agencies, the budget power will be used to uphold these restrictions. *Management* involves the use of budgetary authority, at both agency and central levels, to ensure the efficient use of staff and other resources in the conduct of authorized activities. In management-oriented budgeting, the focus is on agency outputs—what is being done or produced and at what cost, and how that performance compares with budgeted goals. *Planning* refers to the process of determining public objectives and the evaluation of alternative programs. To use the budget for planning, central authorities must have information concerning the purposes and effectiveness of programs. They must also be informed of multiyear spending plans and of the linkage between spending and public benefits.

   Thus, if the budget process is dominated by a control orientation, its range of concerns is limited: How can the agencies by held to the expenditure restrictions—both in detail and in the aggregate—that have been established by the legislature and the central executives? What reporting procedures should be used to enforce propriety in expenditure and accuracy in the accounts? What limitations should be placed on agency authority to spend for personnel, equipment, travel, and other items? A management-oriented budget process, on the other hand, is concerned with operation rather than with control, that is, with the efficiency rather than the legality of expenditure. What is the best way to organize for the performance of an authorized activity? What is and what should be the cost of performing a unit of work? What is the maximum productivity derived from a unit of input? And finally, a planning orientation encompasses a broad range of policy concerns. What are the objectives of the government and the missions of its agencies, and how are these expressed in the budget? What criteria should be used for evaluating programs and for computing their costs and benefits? What is the effectiveness of program A compared to program B?

   The crucial issue is the balance among these vital functions at the central levels. . . . Each function has its distinctive budget classification: items of expense in the case of control, activity accounts for management budgeting, and the program categories for planning. A different budget skill is associated with each perspective: accounting is the traditional skill of budget controllers; public administration is the usual background of budget managers; economics and systems analysis is the specialized discipline of budget planners. . . .

[M]ost governments begin with control and its line-item form. . . . [G]overnments face the problems of preventing financial improprieties; and of limiting agency spending to authorized levels. For this reason, government budgeting inevitably "begins with indispensable efforts to promote 'accountability' by preventing public funds from being stolen, used for unauthorized purposes, or spent at uncontrolled rates. . . ."*

The management orientation, which marks the second stage of budgeting, is reflected in the movement for performance budgeting and the concomitant redesign of expenditure accounts, the development of work and cost measures, and adjustments in the roles of central budgeters and in their relationships with agencies. . . .

[Program budgeting] represents the third stage of U.S. budgeting, the planning orientation. In this stage, the determination of public objectives and programs becomes the key budget function.

*Citing Bertram Gross, "The New Systems Budgeting," 29 *Public Administration Review* (March–April 1969): 117.

From Allen Schick, *Budget Innovation in the States* (Washington: Brookings Institution, 1971), pp. 4–9.

As civilians, the whiz kids had no stake in the interservice competition. They chose to view the Navy's sub-launched missiles, the Air Force's land-based missiles, and strategic bombers as substitutable elements in a single "package" of strategic programs. (Among Pentagon insiders, "program packaging" became the slang term for the program budgeting procedure.) In other words, the reformers simply decided to treat the armed services *for budgetary purposes* as if they didn't exist. Across the entire defense budget, the whiz kids applied the same procedure. They lumped programs of the Army, Navy, and Air Force together based strictly on the military objective: strategic deterrence of a massive attack, fighting limited wars (such as in Korea and Vietnam), and so forth.

So taken was he with the packaging concept that President Lyndon Johnson ordered budgeters in all federal offices to adopt the whiz kids' approach. For example, the anti-poverty programs of the Office of Economic Opportunity were to be lumped in with those of the Bureau of Indian Affairs and the Department of Housing and Urban Development, and systems analysts were to seek for the best balance among expenditures on defense programs, anti-poverty programs, antitrust enforcement, and so forth. But program budgeting at this grandiose level proved much too complicated. President Johnson's successors acquiesced when their senior administrators urged quiet abandonment of the effort.[1] Nevertheless, the aspiration of the program budgeters to display the links between dollars spent and values gained—"how much bang for the buck," in

[1]Again, it was Allen Schick who provided the best account of the dismantling of program budgeting in its more lavish forms. See "A Death in the Bureaucracy: The Demise of Federal PPB," 33 *Public Administration Review* (March–April 1973): 146.

Defense Department lingo—retains a hold on the imaginations of many public administrators. One finds the techniques of performance budgeting and program budgeting widely used today, if not in overarching systems, then in specific programs in which the need for performance measures and agreement on policy objectives don't overtax officials' analytical capabilities.

SECTION 2

Cash-Flow Analysis and Cost-Benefit Analysis

An important move beyond cost-effectiveness analysis occurred when the whiz kids asked themselves why they should settle for the merely intuitive conviction that the best solution, in problems like the one in Sketch 9.1, Panel B, occurs where a curve measuring different quantities (combat effectiveness versus number of airplanes, say) begins to flatten out. Why not make a direct comparison of the value of financial outlays with the values of the outcomes that are being sought? The trick is to measure the costs of a given course of action on the same scale that the analyst uses to measure the benefits. Different versions of this precept—simple enough to state, but often very hard to achieve in practice—lie at the core of the two key analytical techniques that we want to focus on for the next few pages: **cash-flow analysis (CFA)**, the basis of most investment decision making in the private sector, and **cost-benefit analysis (CBA)**, the primary technique of policy advice in the public sector.

Private-Sector Financial Analysis: CFA

The purpose of a cash-flow analysis is to tell a business decision maker whether the stream of net revenues that customers are expected to generate when they purchase units of a good or service will, over a period of years, cover the outlays that a producer must make in order to produce the items in question.

Table 9.2 shows a simplified CFA for the EMS—emergency medical service—operation in a region that we have already visited, the four-county St. Croix area in northern Minnesota and Wisconsin. Let's assume that the service has ten ambulances and a total staff of thirty basic emergency medical-service professionals. The director of the EMS operation now wishes to purchase four additional ambulances; lease a light aircraft to provide both scheduled and emergency air-evacuation runs to major hospital centers south of the St. Croix area (including the Mayo Clinic in Rochester, Minnesota); and upgrade ten staff members to full paramedic status.

The total initial capital outlay required for the proposed upgrading is $550 thousand, shown in Row 0 of Table 9.2 under Column 2 (Capital Investment). The $550-thousand entry is a negative amount because, as a capital outlay, it is a debit—money to be spent rather than received, albeit spent with some hope of recovering a stream of positive payments over time. Note also the final entry in Column 2. A $100-thousand credit reflects the director's estimate that, at the end of year 10 of expanded operations, the new ambulances will be salvageable at the indicated figure; that is, it should be possible to sell them as used equipment for a sum projected as $100 thousand. (Obviously, the projection of *any* salvage value for used ambulances ten years into the future represents a highly iffy estimate. The $100-thousand figure is used only for illustrative pur-

Table 9.2 Cash-Flow Analysis of Proposed St. Croix–Area EMS Expansion (dollars in thousands)

(1)	(2)	(3)	(4)	(5)	(6)	(7)
	Net Outlays		Annual Net Cash Receipts	Columns 2 + 3 − Column 4	@ 8-Percent Discount	
Year	Capital Investment	Annual Expenses			Discount Factor	Present Value
0	− $550*			− $550	1.000	− $550.0
1		− $200†	$150	− $50	.926	− $46.3
2		− $200	$150	− $50	.857	− $42.9
3		− $200	$150	− $50	.794	− $39.7
4		− $200	$150	− $50	.735	− $36.8
5		− $200	$150	− $50	.681	− $34.1
6		− $200	$150	− $50	.630	− $31.5
7		− $200	$150	− $50	.583	− $29.2
8		− $200	$150	− $50	.540	− $27.0
9		− $200	$150	− $50	.500	− $25.0
10	$100†	− $200	$150	$50	.463	$23.2
NPV						− $839.2

*Covers three equipped new ambulances ($500,000) plus one-time special paramedic training to upgrade the basic medical-service force ($50,000).

†Covers annual lease of air evacuation plane ($100,000) and increments to salaries of upgraded and additional EMS workers ($100,000).

‡Projected salvage value of used ambulances, end of year 10.

poses. Besides, it's important to get in the habit of reading tables carefully. Recall our maxim, "Check the numbers," and challenge figures that seem out of line.)

Column 3 shows estimated net annual expenses—additional salaries, fuel and other supplies, and so forth. It would cost an extra $200 thousand each year (over and above current annual expenses for the basic-level service) to run the upgraded operation.

Column 4 of Table 9.2 shows the director's assumptions regarding revenues. Where will the expected stream of positive payments come from, and to what extent are such payments likely to defray in whole or in part the initial capital investment? Some users of the medical service, the director projects, should be billed in exactly the same way that a private businessperson would bill a client for professional services. (A typical response by an ambulance service may cost a paying client from $50 to $300, depending on the nature, distance, and difficulty of the call.) But not all clients pay for ambulance service, nor do the service providers themselves always bill all customers who have the ability to pay. Many emergency services don't even come close to breaking even. For the sake of our example, let's assume that user fees from direct payments by clients and reimbursements by insurance companies should yield a stream of revenues in the amount of $150 thousand for each of the ten years that the service will operate in the expanded mode.

Now look for a moment at the figures for any one of the outyears—say year 4. Expenses and expected receipts net to a figure of *minus* $50 thousand (Row 4, Column 5). But just as a dollar promised four years hence isn't worth a dollar in hand today, a net cash outflow in a future year (such as − $50 thousand) doesn't have the immediate negative effect of dollars spent today. The analyst must take the "time value of money" into consideration. **Discounting** is the standard method used to estimate the so-called present value of a future benefit or cost. (**Compounding** is discounting in reverse—working from a present sum to an expected future value if the sum is saved in an account paying a given rate of compound interest.) Because various benefits and costs expected at different points in the future can all be discounted and then added up, a complete present value analysis yields a single number: the **net present value (NPV)**. The NPV is the equivalent worth today of an entire stream of future expenditures and revenues, such as the stream of expected outlays (Column 2 and Column 3) and projected receipts (Column 4) in Table 9.2.

One can use commercial software programs, hand held calculators, or interest tables with pencil and paper to discount future sums and compound present ones. Table 9.3 is a standard table of discount factors; it assumes that sums are compounded annually (an unrealistic assumption, but again, useful for illustrative purposes) and that the future amounts to which compounded savings will grow are realized at the end of a payout year. An assumed net payout of $50 thousand at the end of year 4 of extended EMS operations in our example, discounted back to the present at 8 percent, will have a present value of only

$$− \$50 \text{ thousand} \times .735 = − \$36.8 \text{ thousand}$$

In this equation, the coefficient .735 comes from the cell given by the intersection of Row 4 and Column 4 in Table 9.3.

Applying these principles to the figures in Table 9.2 and working backward from Row 10, we find that the present value of a $100-thousand salvage recoupment ten years hence, after deducting the projected $50-thousand net payout, is only $23.2 thousand (discounted at 8 percent). Similarly, the present value of the expected $50-thousand net loss expected in year 9 of the expanded operation is *minus* $25 thousand. And so forth, up through all the remaining rows until we reach "year 0"—that is, the present day. The present value of the proposed initial $550-thousand capital investment, of course, is

$$− \$550 \text{ thousand}$$

since the outlay is negative and occurs at the (undiscounted) starting point of the entire process.

(Incidentally, when net outlays and receipts are expected to remain constant over the entire period of the analysis, it isn't necessary to multiply each year's net figure by its own appropriate discount rate. Instead, the constant annual figure can be multiplied by a single coefficient known as the **annuity factor.** The annuity factor is found in Table 9.4. As we will presently see, the annuity factor plays an important role in decisions about the relationship of public to private provision. The annuity factor comes into play when computing the level of public subsidy that might be appropriate for a program with a negative cash flow.)

It should be clear that the critical figures in Table 9.2 are in Column 7, for these show the present values that movement into the new line of operation—in this case, into advanced-level EMS operations—should generate. Taking care to subtract costs

Table 9.3 Discount Factors (present value of $1)

Periods until Payment	(1) 2%	(2) 4%	(3) 6%	(4) 8%	(5) 10%	(6) 12%	(7) 14%	(8) 16%	(9) 18%
1	.980	.962	.943	.926	.909	.893	.877	.862	.847
2	.961	.925	.890	.857	.826	.797	.769	.743	.718
3	.942	.889	.840	.794	.751	.712	.675	.641	.609
4	.924	.855	.792	.735	.683	.636	.592	.552	.515
5	.906	.822	.747	.681	.621	.567	.519	.476	.437
6	.888	.790	.705	.630	.564	.507	.456	.410	.370
7	.871	.760	.665	.583	.513	.452	.400	.354	.314
8	.853	.731	.627	.540	.467	.404	.351	.305	.266
9	.837	.703	.592	.500	.424	.361	.308	.263	.225
10	.820	.676	.558	.463	.386	.322	.270	.227	.191
11	.804	.650	.527	.429	.350	.287	.237	.195	.162
12	.788	.625	.497	.397	.319	.257	.208	.168	.137
13	.773	.601	.469	.368	.290	.229	.182	.145	.116
14	.758	.577	.442	.340	.263	.205	.160	.125	.099
15	.743	.555	.417	.315	.239	.183	.140	.108	.084
16	.728	.534	.394	.292	.218	.163	.123	.093	.071
17	.714	.513	.371	.270	.198	.146	.108	.080	.060
18	.700	.494	.350	.250	.180	.130	.095	.069	.051
19	.686	.475	.331	.232	.164	.116	.083	.060	.043
20	.673	.456	.312	.215	.149	.104	.073	.051	.037
21	.660	.439	.294	.199	.135	.093	.064	.044	.031
22	.647	.422	.278	.184	.123	.083	.056	.038	.026
23	.634	.406	.262	.170	.112	.074	.049	.033	.022
24	.622	.390	.247	.158	.102	.066	.043	.028	.019
25	.610	.375	.233	.146	.092	.059	.038	.024	.016
30	.552	.308	.174	.099	.057	.033	.020	.012	.007
40	.453	.208	.097	.046	.022	.011	.005	.003	.001
50	.372	.141	.054	.021	.009	.003	.001	.001	.000

From Erich A. Helfert, *Techniques of Financial Analysis,* 4th ed. (Homewood IL: Richard Irwin, 1977), tab.4-10. Complete discount tables can be found in almost any textbook on accounting or financial analysis.

(the figures in Column 2 and Column 3) and to add net receipts (in Column 4) so as to get net outlays for each year, we sum up the present-value figures in Column 7 to get a *negative* NVP of

$$- \$839.2 \text{ thousand}$$

Evidently, the proposed expansion and upgrading of the St. Croix regional EMS would be a losing proposition, at least in "profit and loss" terms. The cash flows likely to be generated from payments for services over the assumed ten-year economic life of the project won't even come close to recouping the outlays that the director of the opera-

Table 9.4 Annuity Factors (present value of $1 received annually for *n* years)

Years (n)	(1) 2%	(2) 4%	(3) 6%	(4) 8%	(5) 10%	(6) 12%	(7) 14%	(8) 16%
1	.980	.962	.943	.926	.909	.893	.877	.862
2	1.942	1.886	1.883	1.783	1.736	1.690	1.647	1.605
3	2.884	2.775	2.673	2.577	2.487	2.402	2.322	2.246
4	3.808	3.630	3.465	3.312	3.170	3.037	2.914	2.798
5	4.713	4.452	4.212	3.993	3.791	3.605	3.433	3.274
6	5.601	5.242	4.917	4.623	4.355	4.111	3.889	3.685
7	6.472	6.002	5.582	5.206	4.868	4.564	4.288	4.039
8	7.325	6.733	6.210	5.767	5.315	4.968	4.639	4.344
9	8.162	7.635	6.802	6.247	5.799	5.328	4.946	4.607
10	8.983	8.111	7.360	6.710	6.345	5.650	5.216	4.833
11	9.787	8.760	7.887	7.139	6.495	5.937	5.453	5.029
12	10.575	9.385	8.384	7.536	6.814	6.194	5.660	5.197
13	11.343	9.986	8.853	7.904	7.103	6.424	5.842	5.342
14	12.106	10.563	9.295	8.244	7.367	6.628	6.002	5.468
15	12.849	11.118	9.712	8.559	7.606	6.811	6.142	5.575
16	13.578	11.652	10.106	8.851	7.824	6.974	6.265	5.669
17	14.292	12.166	10.477	9.122	8.022	7.120	6.373	5.749
18	14.992	12.659	10.828	9.372	8.201	7.250	6.467	5.818
19	15.678	13.134	11.158	9.604	8.365	7.366	6.550	5.877
20	16.351	13.590	11.470	9.818	8.514	7.469	6.623	5.929
21	17.011	14.029	11.764	10.017	8.649	7.562	6.687	5.973
22	17.658	14.451	12.042	10.201	8.772	7.645	6.743	6.011
23	18.292	14.857	12.303	10.371	8.883	7.718	6.792	6.044
24	18.914	15.247	12.550	10.529	8.985	7.784	6.835	6.073
25	19.523	15.622	12.783	10.675	9.077	7.843	6.873	6.097
30	22.396	17.292	13.765	11.258	9.427	8.055	7.003	6.177
40	27.355	19.793	15.046	11.925	9.779	8.244	7.105	6.234
50	31.424	21.482	15.762	12.234	9.915	8.304	7.133	6.246

From Erich A. Helfert, *Techniques of Financial Analysis*, 4th ed.(Homewood IL: Richard Irwin, 1977), tab. 4-11. Complete annuity tables can be found in almost any textbook on accounting or financial analysis.

tion wants to make. Because *from a business standpoint* the initial $550-thousand investment shouldn't be made, the EMS director who is pushing for expansion would have a hard time convincing a local banker to loan the service the money it needs for expansion.

But does a negative NPV mean that the proposed expansion can't be justified under any circumstances? Not necessarily. The expanded and upgraded EMS might be justifiable politically on the grounds that it would contribute to the social welfare of the citizens of the St. Croix area. Even if user fees wouldn't cover more than a fraction of the costs, a subsidy from tax receipts might be justified to make up the difference and ensure that the population gets the higher level of emergency service that the director wants to provide. Whether or not such a subsidy should be offered will depend, at least in part, on the results of a cost-benefit analysis.

An actual CFA can, of course, become extremely complicated. In the real world of business decision making, analysts can make few of the kinds of simplifying assumptions that we used in the forgoing illustration (only a ten-year time horizon; annual rather than quarterly or daily discounting). We also assumed that we were working, in Column 2 through Column 4, with reliable projections of outlays and income. In a real CFA, large envelopes of uncertainty may surround such estimates. Yet private-sector decision making invariably benefits from the analyst's ability to make two simplifications that aren't usually available to public-sector decision makers:

1. The only *costs* the analyst need consider are those associated with dollar purchases of equipment, financial services, labor, and the like. *External effects on others needn't be considered*—unless, of course, the producer is *forced* to pay for any public bads that he or she produces, say in the form of a "pollution tax" or capital outlays to meet a regulatory requirement.

2. The only *benefits* a private-sector analyst need consider are those returned to the organization in the form of revenues from sales. Whether or not the required stream of revenues will be forthcoming will depend on the willingness and ability of customers to buy the goods; in other words, it won't depend on the *social* value (or harm) of the items sold, or on whether the items might be needed by persons who can't afford to pay market prices for them.

As noted, neither of these conditions holds true in the case of public-sector decision making, which is why a different methodology is needed to "count the consequences" of public actions. In a capitalist economy like ours, *private* value ("profit") dominates a decision maker's business calculations, whereas *social* value should be the key consideration for a public analyst, adviser, or policy maker.

Public-Sector Financial Analysis: CBA

Cost-benefit analysis, with its many variations and elaborations, is probably the premier contribution of economists to contemporary public administration. Economists usually think of a policy or a course of action as a series of "transformations." A *transformation* is any process in which inputs (such as land, labor, and equipment) are combined to produce one or more outputs. Different inputs in different amounts can be combined to produce different kinds of outputs or different levels of the same output. Some of these combinations of inputs will prove to be more efficient than others, and some will be less efficient. Rationality requires the manager to choose the policy that gives "the most for the least," the economist's definition of efficiency. This policy is sometimes said to be the one with the best **cost-benefit ratio** (a shorthand expression, we'll shortly see, that must be used with some care).

The ability to measure both costs and benefits using a common **numeraire**, dollars, was one of the principal improvements claimed by the proponents of CBA over cost-effectiveness analysis. Costs include any net direct charges that will have to be borne by the developers of the project, such as the salaries that will have to be paid to workers, the outlays that must be made for land and equipment, and so forth. For purposes of cost-benefit analysis (although *not* usually for purposes of cash-flow analysis), costs also include negative external effects. Similarly, the benefits of a public project include dollar estimates of any positive external effects that are likely to result from the undertaking, since such effects represent gains from the standpoint of any citizens who end up better off because of them.

Market Prices versus Willingness to Pay

Strictly speaking the value of positive outcomes in a CBA should be computed not on the basis of market prices (as in cash-flow analysis) but rather on the basis of what economists call **willingness to pay (WTP).** Conversely, the negative worth, or "disutility," of adverse outcomes and public bads should be computed as the number of dollars that all affected individuals would be willing to pay, if a mechanism were available for doing so, to eliminate the harm. The WTP figure, if obtainable, is usually a truer gauge of the social worth of a project than is the market price, which is the same for everyone. In a competitive market, those who are indifferent as well as for those who assign a high value to a good or service must pay the same price to buy it. In contrast, the WTP measure takes into account variations in preferences, and so it gives a better gauge of the item's true value.

Yet the WTP figure is usually an exceedingly difficult one to assess with any precision or reliability, and so analysts often resort to rough "guesstimates." In some cases, they simply take actual or simulated market prices as reasonable proxies for citizens' WTP, while realizing that this practice usually understates the true values. Indeed, because WTP information is almost never available in direct form, much of the art of CBA lies in the devising of indirect ways to assign dollar amounts to outputs (or, in some cases, in simply having the *chutzpah* to use market prices as indicators of WTP).

The difference between a consumer's WTP and the market price that he or she actually must pay for a good or service brings us to the technical term **consumer surplus,** a concept developed by one of the pioneers of neoclassical economics, the Englishman Alfred Marshall (mentioned in Chapter 5). Economists use this term to refer to a kind of windfall benefit that consumers achieve when free-market forces drive down prices and promote *allocative efficiency* (the condition that obtains when every resource is used in its most efficient way). Sketch 9.2 shows a typical supply-and-demand graph—in this case, for the standard fictional product that most economics teachers use to illustrate market dynamics: the widget. The downward-sloping demand curve indicates that consumers will purchase fewer and fewer widgets as the price per widget increases. The market-clearing price (where supply and demand meet) is shown to be $25 per unit, at which price 100 widgets are purchased. If widget makers sold their items at, say, $50 apiece, the demand curve shows that a certain number of consumers would still buy some. In other words, some customers would be willing to pay $50, indicating that they value a widget at more than the actual $25 market-clearing price.

The hachured triangle in Sketch 9.2 is known as the area of consumer surplus—a measure of some consumers' aggregate willingness to pay an above-market price for a given good or service. The trapezoidal area enclosed by the heavy black boundary is the total WTP area.

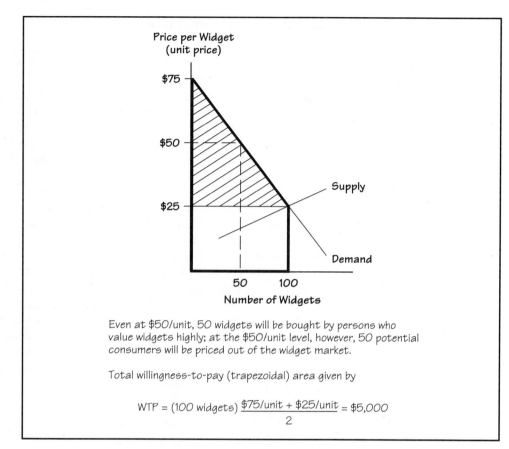

Price per Widget
(unit price)

$75

$50

Supply

$25

Demand

50   100

Number of Widgets

Even at $50/unit, 50 widgets will be bought by persons who
value widgets highly; at the $50/unit level, however, 50 potential
consumers will be priced out of the widget market.

Total willingness-to-pay (trapezoidal) area given by

$$\text{WTP} = (100 \text{ widgets}) \frac{\$75/\text{unit} + \$25/\text{unit}}{2} = \$5,000$$

Sketch 9.2 Supply, Demand, and Willingness to Pay

Compare, now, the total WTP area with the rectangular area beneath the hachured triangle. The area of this rectangle is given by the *total revenue formula (TR):*

Price × number of widgets sold = TR

Substituting numbers from Sketch 9.2 into the formula gives:

$25/unit × 100 widgets = $2,500

From the total revenues that a private producer expects to gain over the projected life of the widget factory must be subtracted the operating costs of production, which yields the net cash inflows in a CFA. These net cash inflows are easier to estimate than total social benefits are, since they are based on relatively "hard" economic data, say about production costs and expected market prices. On the other hand, a glance at Sketch 9.2 shows that the annual undiscounted cash inflow numbers in a CFA (in our example, the total revenues—TR = $2,500—earned each year from widget sales at $25/unit) are virtually certain to be much smaller than the numbers used as estimates of the WTP area in a CBA.

CFA, CBA, and the Institutional Division of Labor

We've seen that the conception of an institutional division of labor implies a distinction between functions that can best be performed by private businesspersons operating in free markets and functions that belong to Woodrow Wilson's category of "what government can properly and successfully do." Private-sector undertakings are paid for by fees—the money that buyers shell out, item for item, to purchase goods or services in markets. In CFA, the stream of fees paid by buyers must produce revenues that more than cover the producer's stream of costs. You'll recall that those costs include the producer's initial investment and all subsequent expenditures (including wages paid to workers and the cost of raw materials).

In contrast, public-sector undertakings are usually paid for out of taxes. Such undertakings are socially beneficial but may prove impossible to finance through fees, often—as we saw in Chapter 6—because market failures of some kind prevent private sellers from recovering enough revenues to produce a profit over the useful life of the facility that's needed to make the product in question. A proposal to "take a private function public" complicates the decision-making process because it calls for an inherently more difficult evaluation technique: cost-benefit, rather than cash-flow, analysis. A CFA is likely to have indicated the financial infeasibility of such a project, at least as assessed from a private business standpoint. A CBA, however—which takes both positive and negative externalities into account and which (ideally, if not often practically) uses WTP rather than competitive market prices—will often indicate the desirability of moving forward even though the enterprise fails the CFA test. The *social* value of such an enterprise may justify public provision or a public subsidy, even though it would be a losing proposition for a private entrepreneur.

Two important questions occur:

1. When can a policy analyst say that a particular project should be launched? In other words, what are the cost-benefit criteria for saying "Go!" to a proposed public project?

2. How does the possibility of mixed signals from a CFA and a CBA for the same project relate to the current trend toward privatization and contracting out?

Box 9.4 discusses the first question: when to say "Go!" to a project. The focus of the following text is on the second question.

Project Analysis in an Era of Privatization

No development in public administration, we have seen, has been more important than the move toward privatization, reflecting as it does a widespread belief that our institutional division of labor has somehow gotten out of kilter. What the trend toward privatization means, in concrete terms, is that government agencies are producing some goods and services that might better be produced privately. Furthermore, fees instead of tax funds could be used to pay for some of these goods, thereby permitting citizens to regain some of the efficiencies and freedom associated with free-market decision making.

But the move to privatize public functions greatly complicates the methodology of formal policy analysis. In many cases, both cost-benefit analysis and cash-flow analy-

BOX 9.4

When to Say "Go!" to a Project:
Cost-Benefit Ratio versus Greatest Net Benefit

We have referred to the cost-benefit ratio as if it, by itself, can be used as a decision-making criterion. The idea would be to choose the course of action with the highest ratio of gains to costs. In many cases, the ratio test will indeed indicate when a project should be undertaken (always assuming, of course, that all costs and benefits have been included and properly measured, which are frequently heroic tasks in themselves). But two authorities, Edith Stokey and Richard Zeckhauser, have pointed out that the ratio test is itself but a special instance of a more fundamental rule: "In any choice situation, select the alternative that produces the **greatest net benefit.**"*
When the decision maker is bound by a resource constraint, or when a selection must be made from among mutually exclusive projects, the choice that maximizes benefits by the greatest-net-benefit test may not be the same choice that the cost-benefit ratio would indicate.

You should therefore use the term *cost-benefit ratio* guardedly, as a shorthand expression for a selection to be made from a list of tests tailored to the circumstances of the case. The following list comes from Stokey and Zeckhauser:

1. When choosing one project from a number of candidates, select the one which promises the greatest net benefit.

2. When deciding whether to accept or reject when only a single project is being considered, and where there are no constraints on costs, adopt the proposal if the net-benefit number (that is, NPV) exceeds $0.

3. When deciding on the best scale for a project (assuming it has a positive NPV), expand the size until the marginal benefit—the value added by the next increment of increase—equals that increment's marginal cost.

4. When deciding which of a number of projects to launch *subject to a cost constraint* (usually a total number of dollars to invest), calculate the net benefit of each project per initial cost, rank projects in decreasing order, and select projects for implementation by working down the list until the available dollars are used up.

*A Primer for Policy Analysis (New York: Norton, 1978), p. 137.

sis are relevant. Additionally, officials have to deal with important follow-up questions: When should the private users of a project be required to help defray its costs by paying fees for the services that they use (the way visitors pay to enter a national park)? Conversely, when is it justifiable for public officials to subsidize enterprises out of tax funds? At what level, in justified cases, should a public subsidy be set?

In the era of privatization, one sometimes encounters cases in which cost-benefit and cash-flow calculations both show positive net present values. Society will be better off if such a project is undertaken (net social benefits exceed net social costs), but commercialization is feasible, since the discounted cash flow of the project is also positive. On the other hand, when the cost-benefit ratio is negative and the cash flow is positive, private providers will be able to make a profit even though the net social benefits are (by hypothesis) negative. Finally, there is the case in which the results of a CBA are positive but the CFA for the project is negative, meaning that the project can only be produced with public funding. Even in this case, however, administrators or elected officials may want to "hit up" users for a fee to defray some of the costs.

When, then, should private payments or user fees be charged for the use of public facilities? And when should public subsidies be offered to help private-sector providers of goods and services? These are two of the most important questions regularly faced by public administrators. In an era of privatization and commercialization, much controversy is inevitable over the "split" that should be set, in a given project or service (such as emergency medical assistance), between financing out of user fees and financing by public subsidy out of tax revenues. Again, we encounter one of our pervasive and persistent problems: the problem of underdetermination. The fact that user fees *can* be used to defray part of the cost of a socially beneficial operation doesn't necessarily mean that such fees *should* be set at the highest level that the traffic will bear. The balance that should be struck is, ultimately, a policy decision calling for value judgments.

Public Subsidies for Private Undertakings

Kirk Harlow and Duane Windsor, two Texas-based experts in public financing, have devised an approach to the subsidy issue.

Assume that a CFA has been conducted for some service that private actors are thinking of providing, and that it shows a negative NPV. (Note that the level of user fees assumed in such a CFA—exemplified by Column 4 in Table 9.2—is a key variable in the estimate of the NPV figure.) Further assume that a CBA shows the project or service in question to be socially desirable. Therefore the policy makers decide to provide a public subsidy adequate to bring the present value of the project up to zero. When policy makers decide to "make up the difference" through a subsidy, they are in effect promising to pay a fixed amount over the life of the project. ("The difference" to be made up in our EMS example would be the negative $839.2 thousand at the bottom of Table 9.2.) A stream of fixed payments over a specified number of years is called an **annuity.** Consequently, the correct way to evaluate a subsidy is by assessing the NPV of the policy makers' promise (the annuity). The present value of an annuity is computable from the factors in Table 9.4, according to the formula:

$$\frac{\text{NPV}}{\text{annuity factor}} = \text{annual subsidy}$$

Using the **Harlow-Windsor method,** the value of a subsidy is therefore computed by taking the negative NPV figure derived from a CFA, dividing it by the appropriate annuity factor, and changing the sign of the result from negative to positive. We will find this method useful in our chapter case.

SECTION 3

Modern Criticisms of Formal Policy Analysis

The techniques of formal policy analysis, with cost-benefit analysis at their center, have today become standard intellectual equipment, particularly for public administrators serving in the roles of policy analysts and advisers. A basic familiarity with the methods and vocabulary of analysis is a virtual requisite of effective work in many government assignments. This is not to say, however, that the impulse to "count the consequences" has gone unchallenged. Three difficulties in formal policy analysis seem to have preoccupied the critics:

1. An alleged *operational* weakness (Can the key variables in public policy problems be measured to the required degrees of accuracy and precision?)
2. An *ethical* weakness (Do we demean precious values, such as human life, when we try to put dollar signs on them?)
3. A *cognitive* weakness (Even if all needed calculations are theoretically possible and ethically acceptable, do we as finite humans have the mental prowess to make them?)

We will consider the cognitive critique—which has given rise to an entire school in modern decision theory, known as incrementalism—in Chapter 11.

The Operational Criticism: Measuring the Unmeasurable, "Monetizing" the Nonmonetary

The main operational criticism of formal policy analysis is centered on the assumption, basic to cost-benefit analysis, that expenditures can be directly compared with outcomes by measuring both costs and benefits in dollars. The measurement of values in dollar terms is known as **monetizing** them. Some values are easy to monetize (for example, "the price of sugar" when sugar is traded in a competitive market); some values are of intermediate difficulty (the value of water service provided by a regulated utility company); some values are formidably hard to measure in pecuniary terms (the value of a sunset unobstructed by smog; the value of a human life). More often than not, unfortunately, public administrators in policy analyst–adviser roles are called on to assess problems involving values at the difficult extreme of the spectrum.

We've noted that the free market automatically prices costs, revenues, and profits (the factors under study in cash-flow analysis) in common, dollar terms. But this fact may be irrelevant in social decision making. It is usually far harder in cost-benefit analysis than in cash-flow analysis to draw up two columns of positive and negative dollar figures that can be totaled and directly compared. The operational objection to formal policy analysis, if correct, is especially powerful, for it suggests that public administrators can't legitimately transfer the well-established private-sector technique of CFA to the arena of government decision making. The operational criticism, if true, supports the ironic words generally attributed to Wallace Sayre, an eminent mid-twentieth-century scholar of public administration: "Public and private management are fundamentally alike in all unimportant respects."

BOX 9.5 ━━━━━━━━━━━━━━━━━━━━━━━━━━━━━━━━━━━━ ■ ■ ■

A Contingent Value Analysis of Prince William Sound

To see what Americans would pay to avoid a repeat of the 1989 Exxon Valdez oil spill, the State of Alaska surveyed 1,043 people in the 50 states.

First, interviewers described the consequences of the Exxon spill and offered a description of a program for preventing future oil spills.

> ... Although the cost would be high, the escort ship program makes it virtually certain there would be no damage to Prince William Sound's environment from another large oil spill during the 10 years it would take all the old tankers to be replaced by double-hulled tankers. ...

Then the interviewers explained who would pay.

> All the oil companies that take oil out of Alaska would pay a special one-time tax which would reduce their profits. Households like yours would also pay a special one-time charge ... in the first year of the program.

Next they estimated the program cost. The dollar figure was randomly set at four different levels.

> At present, Government officials estimate the program will cost your household a total of ($10, $30, $60, $120). ... This money would only be used for the program to prevent damage from another large oil spill in Prince William Sound.

Those who said they would vote for the program were asked if they would pay a larger amount ($30, $60, $120, $250). Those who said they would not vote for the program were asked if they would pay a smaller amount ($5, $10, $30, $60).

The median response—the answer that represented the 50th percentile of all answers—was $31. The average dollar figure was a considerably higher, $94. Interpreted as the answer to a popular referendum, the median represents the majority view that households would collectively be willing to pay about $2.8 billion to prevent another spill. Interpreted as a kind of marketing survey, the average suggests that households would collectively pay $8.6 billion to buy a spill-free environment for Prince William Sound.

From Peter Passel, "Disputed New Role for Polls: Putting a Price Tag on Nature," *New York Times*, Sept. 6, 1993, p. 36.

━━ ■ ■ ■

As we have seen, the consequences that must be counted in a CBA theoretically include all immediate *and* ultimate, direct *and* indirect, internal *and* external effects of the proposed action. Yet it may be impossible to price many social effects in competitive markets, or even to quantify them in meaningful ways. How, for instance, should a land-use planner evaluate the dollar benefits of a particular kind of development (building a recreational complex in a little-visited area of a state, for example, as opposed to flooding the same property by constructing a dam for hydroelectric power)? Even if the planner can put dollar amounts on the benefits of a resort versus the benefits of power generation, how does he or she go about balancing these benefits against the value of leaving the area as an undeveloped wilderness?

Have modern formal policy analysts devised satisfactory ways of handling such issues? Judge for yourself. Box 9.5 contains a description of a recent application of the technique known as **contingent value analysis,** perhaps the most sophisticated systematic methodology for monetizing values—in this case, environmental values—that are held by large numbers of people but are not readily expressible in market behavior.

CHAPTER READING

The most difficult cost-benefit analyses of all are those which involve value-of-life determinations. The ethical critique of cost-benefit analysis, which is also the subject of our chapter reading, expresses the revulsion many persons feel when they see values that somehow seem sacred become profaned by an effort to count or weigh them. How can a public health or public safety official put a dollar value on the lives that might be saved by a new immunization program, a changed traffic pattern, or an investment in upgraded emergency medical services? The following selection by the Harvard political scientist Steven Kelman suggests that the value-of-life questions raised in these kinds of programatic decisions are problematic morally as well as analytically.

Take special note of Kelman's explicit treatment of cost-benefit analysis as an expression of Bentham's philosophy of utilitarianism. Kelman seems to suggest that the derivation of CBA from utilitarianism is enough in itself to make this methodology somewhat suspect on moral grounds. Do you agree? Additionally, Kelman makes use of the distinction between the private sphere and the public one to argue against the methodology in which a decision maker uses data gleaned from private exchanges in markets to assess benefits. We have already seen that this kind of methodology is, technically speaking, of doubtful accuracy. Do you accept Professor Kelman's claim that this methodology is morally as well as analytically flawed?

Is Cost-Benefit Analysis Ethically Suspect?
Steven Kelman

Depending on the moral importance we attach to the right or duty involved, cost-benefit questions may become irrelevant to the outcome of a moral judgment.

At the broadest and vaguest level, cost-benefit analysis may be regarded simply as systematic thinking about decision-making. Who can oppose, econo-

mists sometimes ask, efforts to think in a systematic way about the consequences of different courses of action? The alternative, it would appear, is unexamined decision-making. But defining cost-benefit analysis so simply leaves it with few implications for actual regulatory decision-making. Presumably, therefore, those who urge regulators to make greater use of the technique have a more extensive prescription in mind. I assume here that their prescription includes the following views:

(1) There exists a strong presumption that an act should not be undertaken unless its benefits outweigh its costs.

(2) In order to determine whether benefits outweigh costs, it is desirable to attempt to express all benefits and costs in a common scale or denominator, so they can be compared with each other, even when some benefits and costs are not traded on markets and hence have no established dollar values.

(3) Getting decision-makers to make more use of cost-benefit techniques is important enough to warrant both the expense required to gather the data for improved cost-benefit estimation and the political efforts needed to give the activity higher priority compared to other activities, also valuable in and of themselves.

My focus is on cost-benefit analysis as applied to environmental, safety, and health regulation. In that context, I examine each of the above propositions from the perspective of formal ethical theory, that is, the study of what actions it is morally right to undertake. My conclusions are:

(1) In areas of environmental, safety, and health regulation, there may be many instances where a certain decision might be right even though its benefits do not outweigh its costs.

(2) There are good reasons to oppose efforts to put dollar values on non-marketed benefits and costs.

(3) Given the relative frequency of occasions in the areas of environmental, safety, and health regulation where one would not wish to use a benefits-outweigh-costs test as a decision rule, and given the reasons to oppose the monetizing of non-marketed benefits or costs that is a prerequisite for cost-benefit analysis, it is not justifiable to devote major resources to the generation of data for cost-benefit calculations or to undertake efforts to "spread the gospel" of cost-benefit analysis further. . . .

Like the Molière character who spoke prose without knowing it, economists who advocate use of cost-benefit analysis for public decisions are philosophers without knowing it: the answer given by cost-benefit analysis, that actions should be undertaken so as to maximize net benefits, represents one of the classic answers given by moral philosophers—that given by utilitarians. To determine whether an action is right or wrong, utilitarians tote up all the positive consequences of the action in terms of human satisfaction. The act that maximizes attainment of satisfaction under the circumstances is the right act. . . .

[F]or a broad range of individual and social decisions, whether an act's benefits outweigh its costs is a sufficient question to ask. But not for all such decisions. These may involve situations where certain duties—duties not to lie, break promises, or kill, for example—make an act wrong, even if it would result in an excess of benefits over costs. Or they may involve instances where people's rights are at stake. We would not permit rape even if it could be demonstrated that the rapist derived enormous happiness from his act, while the victim experienced only minor displeasure. We do not do cost-benefit analysis of freedom of speech or trial by jury. . . .

In the most convincing versions of non-utilitarian ethics, various duties or rights are not absolute. But each has a *prima facie* moral validity so that, if duties or rights do not conflict, the morally right act is the act that reflects a duty or respects a right. If duties or rights do conflict, a moral judgment, based on conscious deliberation, must be made. Since one of the duties non-utilitarian philosophers enumerate is the duty of beneficence (the duty to maximize happiness), which in effect incorporates all of utilitarianism by reference, a non-utilitarian who is faced with conflicts between the results of cost-benefit analysis and non-utility-based considerations will need to undertake such deliberation. . . . Indeed, depending on the moral importance we attach to the right or duty involved, cost-benefit questions may, within wide ranges, become irrelevant to the outcome of the moral judgment. . . .

In order for cost-benefit calculations to be performed the way they are supposed to be, all costs and benefits must be expressed in a common measure, typically dollars, including things not normally bought and sold on markets, and to which dollar prices are therefore not attached. The most dramatic example of such things is human life itself; but many of the other benefits achieved or preserved by environmental policy—such as peace and quiet, fresh-smelling air, swimmable rivers, spectacular vistas—are not traded on markets either.

Economists who do cost-benefit analysis regard the quest after dollar values for non-market things as a difficult challenge—but one to be met with relish. They have tried to develop methods for imputing a person's "willingness to pay" for such things, their approach generally involving a search for bundled goods that *are* traded on markets and that vary as to whether they include a feature that is, *by itself,* not marketed. Thus, fresh air is not marketed, but houses in different parts of Los Angeles that are similar except for the degree of smog are. Peace and quiet is not marketed, but similar houses inside and outside airport flight paths are. The risk of death is not marketed, but similar jobs that have different levels of risk are. Economists have produced many often ingenious efforts to impute dollar prices to non-marketed things by observing the premiums accorded homes in clean air areas over similar homes in dirty areas or the premiums paid for risky jobs over similar non-risky jobs.

These ingenious efforts are subject to criticism on a number of technical grounds. It may be difficult to control for all the dimensions of quality other than the presence or absence of the non-marketed thing. More important, in a world where people have different preferences and are subject to different constraints as they make their choices, the dollar value imputed to the non-market things that most people would wish to avoid will be lower than otherwise, because people with unusually weak aversion to those things or unusually strong constraints on their choices will be willing to take the bundled good in question at less of a discount than the average person. . . . To use the wage premiums accorded hazardous work as a measure of the value of life means to accept as proxies for the rest of us the choices of people who do not have many choices or who are exceptional risk-seekers. . . .

A second problem is that the attempts of economists to measure people's willingness to pay for non-marketed things assume that there is no difference between the price a person would require for *giving up* something to which he has a preexisting right and the price he would pay to *gain* something to which he enjoys no right. Thus, the analysis assumes no difference between how much a homeowner would need to be paid in order to give up an unobstructed mountain view that he already enjoys and how much he would be willing to pay to get an obstruction moved once it is already in place. Available evidence suggests that most people would insist on being paid far more to assent to a worsening of their situation then they would be willing to pay to improve their situation. The difference arises from such factors as being accustomed to and psychologically attached to that which one believes one enjoys by right. But this creates a circularity problem for any attempt to use cost-benefit analysis to determine *whether* to assign to, say, the homeowner the right to an unobstructed mountain view. For willingness to pay will be different depending on whether the right is assigned initially or not. The value judgment about whether to assign the right must thus be made first. (In order to set an upper bound on the value of the benefit, one might hypothetically assign the right to the person and determine how much he would need to be paid to give it up.)

Third, the efforts of economists to impute willingness to pay invariably involve bundled goods exchanged in *private* transactions. Those who use figures garnered from such analysis to provide guidance for *public* decisions assume no difference between how people value certain things in private individual transactions and how they would wish those same things to be valued in public collective decisions. In making such assumptions, economists insidiously slip into their analysis an important and controversial value judgment, growing naturally out of the highly individualistic microeconomic tradition—namely, the view that there should be no difference between private behavior and the behavior we display in public social life. An alternative view—one that enjoys, I would suggest, wide resonance among citizens—would be that public, social decisions provide an opportunity to give certain things a higher valuation than we choose, for one reason or another, to give them in our private activities.

Thus, opponents of stricter regulation of health risks often argue that we do not value life infinitely, and therefore our public decisions should not reflect the high value of life that proponents of strict regulation propose. However, an alternative view is equally plausible. Precisely because we fail, for whatever reasons, to give life-saving the value in everyday personal decisions that we in some general terms believe we should give it, we may wish our social decisions to provide us the occasion to display the reverence for life that we espouse but do not always show. By this view, people who not have fixed unambiguous "preferences" to which they give expression through private activities and which therefore should be given expression in public decisons. Rather, they may have what they themselves regard as "higher" and "lower" preferences. The latter may come to the fore in private decisions, but people may want the former to come to the fore in public decisons. They may sometimes display racial prejudice, but support antidiscrimination laws. They may buy a certain product after seeing a seductive ad, but be skeptical enough of advertising to want the government to keep a close eye on it. In such cases, the use of private behavior to impute the values that should be entered for public decisions, as is done by using willingness to pay in private transactions, commits

grievous offense against a view of the behavior of the citizen that is deeply engrained in our democratic traditions. It is a view that denudes politics of any independent role in society, reducing it to a mechanistic, mimicking recalculation based on private behavior.

Finally, one may oppose the effort to place prices on a non-market thing and hence in effect incorporate it into the market system out of a fear that the very act of doing so will reduce the thing's perceived value. To place a price on the benefit may, in other words, reduce the value of that benefit. Cost-benefit analysis thus may be like the thermometer that, when place in a liquid to be measured, itself changes the liquid's temperature.

Examples of the perceived cheapening of a thing's value by the very act of buying and selling it abound in everyday life and language. The disgust that accompanies the idea of buying and selling human beings is based on the sense that this would dramatically diminish human worth. Epithets such as "he prostituted himself," applied as linguistic analogies to people who have sold something, reflect the view that certain things should not be sold because doing so diminishes their value. . . . "[P]riceless" . . . [is] reserved for a subset of things not for sale, such as life or health.

From Steven Kelman, "Cost-Benefit Analysis: An Ethical Critique," 5 *Regulation* (No. 1, January–February 1981): 33–40.

▲ ▲ ▲

 ## CHAPTER CASE ● ● ●

Few kinds of change are more wrenching in a community than the closing of a business. The anxiety of workers who fear layoffs begins with the first rumor of a plant shutdown. If closure actually occurs, the damage to the economy and social stability of the region may persist for years. Talk of such a closing provides the background for the following scenario. Anton Kurvaszy fears that the rumored plans of a local corporation, Polaris Paper Company, to end operations at its old paper-stock plant at Half Day Rill in Apostle County could give the region just the kind of "negative push" it doesn't need. Closure of Polaris's mill could worsen the spiral of economic contraction that's been underway since "Carter killed the cows."

    Tied to the future of the old mill out at Half Day Rill, it turns out, are a series of additional questions, all seemingly unrelated to one another. These questions have to do with the appropriateness of federal subsidies for regional economic development, a proposed expansion of the federal prison industries program, the flood-control benefits of an upgraded dam on the Upper St. Croix River (also at Polaris's Half Day Rill site), the market for recycled paper in the four-county area, and a proposal to upgrade the St. Croix region's emergency medical service. . . . But wait! All this is getting ahead of ourselves. It's *your* job to figure out "What's the story?"

Before you start sorting through the complexities of the case, it might be helpful to ask yourself a few questions. Have you fixed in your own mind the way that our institutional division of labor generates not only an *allocation of functions* (functions reserved to private institutions versus functions assigned to government) but also a *distinction of methodologies* for estimating outcomes (CFA versus CBA)? Can you explicate the justifications for cash-flow analysis in private-sector decision making and cost-benefit analysis in the public sphere? Following up the same line of thought, can you see why the assumptions and requirements of CBA tend to make public decision making far more difficult, contentious, and value-laden than decision making in private businesses?

Try not only to identify the key technical questions raised in the following scenario—whether CBA or CFA applies, how the amounts of any public subsidies to St. Croix-area private businesses might be decided—but also to confront deeper philosophical and moral issues such as the ones broached in our chapter reading by Steven Kelman. How should the worth of a human life saved by a paramedic be reflected in the balance sheet of social choice? Is the governance process somehow dehumanized, as Kelman contends, by the very attempt to perform a CBA for Len Palchaterian's proposal to upgrade the St. Croix EMS? What's the value of a *private*-sector job that is saved by a *public* subsidy? In the circumstances of the following case, who would be the most appropriate providers of any subsidies that you think might be warranted: local taxpayers? the federal government? (You might find a starting point for an answer to this question in our paradigms of assignment—especially the ones discussed in the Peterson, Rabe, and Wong reading in Chapter 7 relative to the allocation of functions among the different levels of government.)

A final tip: The scenario contains exactly the kinds of interlocking issues that so often make for problems of underdetermination in public administration. A team approach may be especially useful, in which different individuals keep track of different themes and then try to view the picture as a whole—once it begins to take shape—from their particular vantage points. ("Where you stand depends on where you sit.") The weight of detail may overburden the analyst who works alone, but a dialogic approach can often help members of a study team untangle the knots and isolate the connections that give pattern to seemingly unrelated subplots of the story.

CASE 8

....

Regional Economic Development: The Dam, Dump, and Mill Out at Half Day Rill

At her desk in the Old Executive Office Building just across from the White House, Blair Songster looked at the bundled packet of papers in her in-basket. It was a proposal to install a new stationery plant at a federal prison somewhere in the upper

Midwest. The package had been forwarded by Songster's boss, Haney Brill, who was just back from a trip and behind in his work. Formally, the proposal came from Warden John Smarck of the Federal Correctional Institution in the small Minnesota town of Vikingsholm. But Songster, scanning Smarck's cover letter, noticed that more was involved than simple permission to spend already-available money for new paper-making machines and printing presses. Warden Smarck wanted approval for federal agencies with regional offices in the midwestern states to make special purchases of customized stationery. That stationery—to be manufactured out of 100-percent-recycled paper stock—would be produced in the Vikingsholm prison factory.

Multiple departments and bureaus of the federal government would have to modify their procurement procedures if Smarck's plan were accepted. Smarck's proposal would also require purchases of paper at subsidized prices. These unusual requirements had brought the package for action to Haney Brill's desk in the White House Domestic Council. Warden Smarck's request couldn't be handled as a simple internal Bureau of Prisons issue; high-level approval was needed. Brill had bucked the problem to Blair Songster for study and a recommendation.

Someone had clipped to Smarck's package a *Washington Post* news item from a few months earlier. The article reported the president's pledge to support recycling by requiring federal agencies to purchase paper made with recycled stock, even at higher cost, as a way of "priming the pump" for the recycling industry. Also in the stack was a letter from Minnesota Congresswoman Ellen Moe of the district in which the prison was located. Moe endorsed the proposal. She had added a paragraph underscoring the depressed condition of the region. The proposed new stationery plant at Vikingsholm, Moe insisted, would provide needed stimulation for regional businesses.

Blair Songster leafed through some of the other memos and attachments in the stack, trying to determine exactly what questions she was going to be required to answer before she settled in to study the contents in detail. Blair rechecked the buck slip from Haney Brill. Brill had wide-ranging responsibilities for issues of domestic policy, especially when they had political overtones. In a time of continuing concern over budget deficits, presidential aides had to ferret out programs that couldn't be justified economically and then offer them up for sacrifice. "Unless an initiative is going to pay its way by producing more benefits on some demonstrable scale than it will cost, it shouldn't be funded"—that, Brill had stressed to his assistants, was the default rule these days for White House decision making. The default rule was to be overridden only on a showing of very, very good reasons indeed for doing so. Brill's note of transmittal follows.

Blair—

Ellen Moe wants the president to order federal agencies to support a new printing plant at a federal prison in her district by buying its goods even at above-market prices. She seems to have bought the old "for want of a nail" argument: If we give them that nail—the subsidy for paper produced at the prison—there's a better chance to win the battle of economic stimulation in her area. Let me know pretty quick what you think we should do.

Haney

• • • • •

The story had started a month or so earlier in Larch City, Minnesota. (Blair Songster had never heard of Larch City, but in the course of her research, she saw on an area map that it wasn't far from the town of Vikingsholm in southern Larch County.) In their separate suites of the Jackson Building in Larch City, two influential figures in the St. Croix region—Anton Kurvaszy and Andy Byce—had been spending some considerable amounts of time pondering certain problems in the four-county area.

A circled date on Anton Kurvaszy's calendar indicated that it was again near time to make a presentation at the next development-plan meeting of the St. Croix Development Commission. Kurvaszy had five items to think through. This is how they appeared on the pad before him:

1. Polaris Company—mill closing

2. Vikingsholm-UNICOR connection

3. Subsidy for "Winter Wonderland"?

4. AWA-Polaris connection

5. Proposal for EMS upgrading

In the ten days or so that remained before Kurvaszy had to make his presentation, he with his staffers would be expected to prepare answers for questions that the county commissioners would eventually ask. Which of the projects made sense as area development initiatives? What public funding would be required? Could user fees be charged to help defray expenses? Would any of the projects create local nuisances or threaten environmental controversies? If so, the politicians better know it before constituents started complaining.

By any measure, item 1 on Kurvaszy's list presented the most serious issue. Closure of Polaris Paper Company's old wood-pulp mill at Half Day Rill, long rumored, seemed more and more likely. Only the "enviros"—some avid environmentalists who had long wanted all improvements removed from the Upper St. Croix watershed—might, on balance, welcome a shutdown. And even the enviros would regret the impact of a plant closing on locals who'd end up out of work.

Any problem touching one of the St. Croix area's major firms, such as Polaris, affected prospects for economic growth in the region. For this reason, the possibility of a plant closing also became the official concern of the planning director of the four-county development commission. But fortunately, Kurvaszy had learned, there seemed a chance to save the Half Day plant and the jobs that would stay with it. The day before, Stansford Byrne, a senior executive of Polaris, had taken Kurvaszy to lunch in the nearby town of Vikingsholm. Also in attendance were Warden John Smarck and Lieutenant Sandy Zysman of the Vikingsholm Federal Correctional Institution, a medium-security prison that housed some 825 inmates. At lunch, the four had discussed a possible alternative to a phase-out of the old mill.

Zysman headed the prison industries program (officially known by the acronym *UNICOR*) at Vikingsholm. Zysman and her superior, Warden Smarck, were always on the lookout for ways to expand the prison's UNICOR program. Byrne, Smarck, and Zysman all hoped they could agree on a single project that would justify both a reversal of Polaris's plant-closure plans and an expansion of Vikingsholm's jobs-for-inmates program. Sandy Zysman thought she had come up with an idea for just such a project.

Currently, Stan Byrne said, the workforce of forty full-time employees out at the old mill converted wood into pulp and then processed the pulp into raw paper stock. From Half Day the stock was transferred by truck to other plants within the Polaris network for finishing, or it was sold to "external" papermakers who processed it into stationery, artists' construction paper, specialty wrap, and other finished goods. Byrne was willing to explore any economically sensible way of extending the Half Day operation. Absent an economically viable plan, however, the best Byrne could promise Polaris's workers was an orderly phase-out at Half Day Rill and, for some, transfers to jobs at plants elsewhere in the company's network. (Polaris had operations in Minnesota, Wisconsin, the Upper Peninsula of Michigan, and Ontario, Canada. But all these plants were too far away for workers displaced from Half Day to take transfer jobs unless they moved their families out of the four-county region.)

"To keep the old mill in service," Byrne said, "we obviously have to turn a profit. *How much* profit? Well, that's a different question. Different people within the company probably have different ideas about the answer. Anyway, we can't operate profitably at any level, high or low, now. Our product's too expensive; the equipment is ancient and inefficient—it can't use recycled paper, so it has to run entirely on fresh pulp. Pulp is okay with us, but it leads to constant friction with the nature lovers. What's more, at Half Day, with our old equipment, we can't produce some of the newer kinds of paper that today's stationers prefer." Byrne passed around some samples of the specialty papers Polaris was producing at its state-of-the-art plants.

Byrne continued: "If we're to keep operating out at Half Day Rill, we have to raise the efficiency of that operation, which means:

"*One,* heighten the head at the old mill dam. Among other things, that'll let us generate hydroelectric power to drive the plant in the most efficient and environmentally responsible way.

"*Two,* expand the onsite landfill at Half Day Rill.

"*Three,* get a reliable supply of affordable feedstock (either virgin wood pulp or recyclable paper). And

"*Four*—probably the most difficult—lay on a long-term contract with a purchaser who'll guarantee the cash flow we'd need to justify refurbishing the plant."

Byrne spoke briefly about his main worries. The area's environmentalists could be counted on to resist both the head heightening of the dam and the landfill expansion. There were also "inside problems" at Polaris. Byrne didn't go into details, but the others picked up on his allusion to the chairman and chief executive officer of Polaris, a crusty, lifelong resident of the St. Croix named Francis X. Doherty. Doherty, a subscriber to "old-line American economic values" (as he described them), believed that corporate money should be invested where it will earn the highest return for the company's stockholders. If he held true to form, Doherty's inclination would be to close the antiquated mill if there existed another way to invest Polaris capital with a prospect of higher return.

Byrne then briefly touched on some of the other items that he'd have to address if a way were to be found to keep the mill in operation. First were the requirements to raise the head of the old dam and equip it for hydroelectric generation. That would cost some money—about $3.5 million, Polaris's engineers had estimated. The good news, Byrne added, was that Polaris might not have to bear the head-heightening costs in their entirety. Byrne was apparently already in negotiations with a woman named Marilyn Taverner from a large midwestern land-development firm, Karelia Corporation. Karelia might be persuaded to help pay for any dam work that Polaris undertook out at the Half Day site.

Anton Kurvaszy nodded. Kurvaszy too had been approached by Taverner. It seemed that Karelia's planners were eyeing the Half Day Rill area for development as a major resort site. Head heightening of the dam there would make the spot more attractive for recreational development. Because Karelia stood to benefit from an improvement in the Half Day Rill dam, Byrne hoped to wheedle a one-time cash contribution from the corporation to defray some of the cost of head heightening. Byrne said he had in mind a figure in the range of a half-million dollars. Karelia would then develop its "Winter Wonderland" project on vacant land adjacent to Polaris's Half Day Rill property.

And then, Byrne said, there was the issue of the old landfill on the Half Day Rill site. The existing dump would have to be enlarged if the mill were to be kept operating. The word *landfill* provoked Kurvaszy's interest. Even before the lunch meeting with Bryne, Smarck, and Zysman, Anton Kurvaszy had been toying with the idea of a formal linkup between his current pet project, the Area Waste Authority, and Polaris's landfill operation. Why not bring the Polaris dump into the regional waste disposal system? The Vikingsholm lunch, however, wasn't the right occasion to talk about the landfill. Kurvaszy wanted to keep the focus on the main subject—Smarck and Zysman's plan for a connection between the Polaris paper operation and the Vikingsholm prison factory. Kurvaszy therefore merely mentioned that he wanted to talk at some future time about the Half Day Rill landfill.

•   •   •   •   •

As federal officials, John Smarck and Sandy Zysman justified their budgets as much on political as on economic grounds. They weren't familiar with the kinds of calculations that Francis X. Doherty, a businessman to his marrow, would demand of Byrne. Byrne explained that Doherty mightn't be satisfied unless Byrne developed a plan for the mill with an internal rate of return (whatever that meant) well above the interest rate at which Polaris would have to borrow money to finance the project. For his own part, Byrne said he'd be willing simply to settle for a positive net present value—a much easier test than the more sophistocated (and more demanding) internal rate-of-return comparison that Fran Doherty liked to use when making corporate decisions. After all, Byrne said, Polaris over all was doing pretty well these days, financially speaking. On a relatively small and isolated operation such as the one out at Half Day Rill, the corporate conscience might be better served if Polaris kept employees at work and maintained the company's presence in the St. Croix region, even if it carried a modest opportunity cost. The "rational" decision on the Half Day Rill plant based on a standard business analysis might not be the best decision in human—or, frankly, in political—terms.

Stan Byrne also had to be concerned lest Polaris refurbish the mill and introduce a new product line but then not be able to generate enough customer demand to pay for the operation. Byrne didn't disguise his hope that Smarck and Zysman had found the way to write the kind of long-term contract that he had in mind. Under the plan that Zysman had developed for UNICOR expansion, the Half Day mill would be refitted with some of the new technology that was revolutionizing paper production around the country. Such a conversion would enable the Half Day workers to produce a high-quality semigloss paper stock entirely out of postconsumption paper.[1] Vikingsholm-UNICOR would then buy all the stock produced at the Half Day mill. Inmates in the new plant that Sandy Zysman hoped to set up in the prison complex would, in turn, produce a distinctive stationery for use in federal agencies.

The director of the Bureau of Prisons had already given Smarck and Zysman permission to expand their UNICOR program. Zysman figured that it would cost $3.5 million to buy the papermaking and printing equipment needed to get the new jobs-for-inmates operation under way. The needed funding had already been appropriated by Congress and budgeted for Vikingsholm. Thus, figuratively speaking, Smarck and Zysman had the money for an expansion of the prison factory in their pockets, leaving it only to be determined what specific kind of jobs-for-inmates program would be funded. For various reasons, Zysman favored the stationery operation over other possibilities—assuming, of course, that federal offices would buy all the stationery that Vikingsholm-UNICOR could produce. Table 9.5 shows Sandy Zysman's workup of the expected cash flow for the proposed new plant.

Unfortunately, even with the new papermaking and printing technology that Zysman wanted to install at Vikingsholm, stationery made from recycled paper would be more expensive than if made from virgin wood pulp. For this reason, federal agency buyers would have to pay more for Vikingsholm paper than they would for stationery of roughly comparable quality if they continued to purchase it from non-UNICOR vendors (although non-UNICOR paper might not have distinctive watermarks, and much of it would probably not be produced from 100-percent recycled paper). The "surcharge" that government purchasers would have to pay, Zysman estimated, would amount over all to an annual federal subsidy of a bit more than $737,000 (based on the Windsor-Harlow method, using a 6.710 annuity factor).

●　　●　　●　　●　　●

Down the hall in the Jackson Building from the suite occupied by the St. Croix Development Commission Planning Division, Andy Byce was also working through some issues that he thought could be of consequence to citizens of the four-county region.

---

[1]*Post-consumption paper:* What most of us mean when, in ordinary conversation, we speak of "recycled paper." Paper that has been used in newspapers, packaging, stationery, and so forth, and then taken through the recycling operation is known as postconsumption paper. Waste from a papermaking operation that never goes into a commercially usable product, but is immediately recycled, is known as *preconsumption feedstock.*

Table 9.5 Cash-Flow Analysis of Proposed Stationery Production Project at Vikingsholm-UNICOR (dollars in thousands)

(1)	(2)	(3)	(4)	(5)	(6)	(7)
		Outlays		Estimated Annual Receipts (if sold at market prices)	@ 8 Percent Discount	
		Annual Expenses				
Year	Capital Investment	Stock @ $75/Ton	Other		Discount Factor	Present Value
0	− $3,500				1.000	− $3,500.0
1		− $1,800	− $250	$1,800	.926	− $231.5
2		− $1,800	− $250	$1,800	.857	− $214.3
3		− $1,800	− $250	$1,800	.794	− $198.5
4		− $1,800	− $250	$1,800	.735	− $183.8
5		− $1,800	− $250	$1,800	.681	− $170.3
6		− $1,800	− $250	$1,800	.630	− $157.5
7		− $1,800	− $250	$1,800	.583	− $145.8
8		− $1,800	− $250	$1,800	.540	− $135.0
9		− $1,800	− $250	$1,800	.500	− $125.0
10	$500	− $1,800	− $250	$1,800	.463	$115.6
NPV						− $4,945.8
Required Annual Subsidy						$737.1 *

*Computed using the Harlow-Windsor method, based on a 6.710 annuity factor (8-percent discount over ten years; see Table 9.4).

For years, Andy Byce and his partner Boyce Winkwiak had been surveying properties all over the St. Croix. They had compiled file drawers full of information touching all manner of concerns across the St. Croix. One such concern was flood-proneness. Under the federal Flood Disaster Protection Act of 1973, owners of homes and businesses in the floodplains of flowing rivers must purchase special insurance in order to qualify for mortgages from federally insured banks or thrift institutions. The slightest movement of a line on a survey map could determine whether a citizen who lived in the watershed of a flood-prone river had to buy the extra coverage. In the flat boglands and brushy forests of northwest Wisconsin, the Upper St. Croix in both of its branches was such a river. As the flood zones appeared on the current maps, approximately 6,500 area residents fell under the flood-insurance mandate. Andy Byce and Boyce Winkwiak had helped draw those maps.

Byce and Winkwiak worked out of their offices in Larch City on the Minnesota side of the St. Croix gorge, but they had almost as many jobs in Wisconsin as in their own state. Byce and Winkwiak had been retained on and off during the late 1970s and early 1980s to survey the Upper St. Croix flood zones over in Wisconsin. This work, completed under the auspices of the Apostle County commissioners, had finally produced a complete set of maps. The floodplain determinations of Byce, Winkwiak, and the other area civil engineers had won quick approval by reviewers in the Federal Emergency Management Agency. FEMA approval meant that banks and thrifts could make loans to flood-prone property owners as long as the latter paid the additional premiums for flood insurance. Different levels of premium applied, depending on a building's location within the St. Croix's 25-year, 50-year, or 100-year flood zone. On average, mandated insurees paid about $300 annually.

One or both branches of the Upper St. Croix had overflowed a few times within recent memory, but never by enough to flood the properties of more than 10 percent or so of the Apostle County residents whose locations required them to pay into the program. Those few area residents who did suffer damage later seemed happy with the services they received. They reported that claims adjusters from both FEMA and participating private insurance companies had been quick to settle and were fair in their levels of award. But that still left almost 6,000 citizens in Apostle County laying out $300 a year for federally mandated insurance that most of them thought they didn't need.

Andy Byce sat at his drafting table, thinking. He rechecked some calculations he had made about the old dam near Polaris Paper Company's mill out at Half Day Rill. It should be possible, at not too much cost, to institute a water-storage regime on the southern branch of the Upper St. Croix. That would lead to a redrawing of the flood maps. If the head of the existing low dam at Half Day Rill were raised by just a few feet, water in the occasional wet season that might otherwise end up in basements of homes and businesses could be held in the large lake that would form behind a raised Half Day Rill dam.

Byce had to admit that not every location would survey to a location uphill of a newly drawn floodplain. As many as a few hundred would have to continue taking out insurance even under the kind of flood-prevention regime that Byce had in mind. Furthermore, it would cost something to complete the engineering work, resurvey parts of Apostle County, and draft new maps so FEMA inspectors could approve the new flood zones. Still in all, it seemed reasonable to estimate the collective value of the project at about $1.8 million annually. Byce based that estimate on the insurance costs some 6,000 property owners would be able to avoid following the raising of the dam and redrawing of the floodplain:

$$6,000 \times \$300/\text{year average insurance charge} = \$1.8 \text{ million/year.}$$

As a civil engineer with some experience in such matters, Byce knew that it would probably take a one-time outlay of twice the $1.8 million figure, give or take, to raise the Half Day Rill dam head. Byce would have to think a bit more about the cost side of the kind of project he had in mind. He also had to acknowledge that the benefits from dam-head heightening would be diffuse. A $1.8-million benefit to a single individual can induce action that isn't likely to be forthcoming if, instead, the same sum is divided among thousands of small-sum beneficiaries. Byce knew that the diffuseness of the $300-per-year benefits might make it hard to mobilize all who stood collectively to benefit. Practical difficulties aside, however, Byce thought it pleasant to consider the possible gains for some 6,000 St. Croix–area residents if money to raise the dam head could somehow be made to appear.

Still working with the $1.8-million figure (the annuity, or *annual* collective payment), Andy Byce noted that the ten-year *undiscounted* *total* benefit of head heightening would equal $18 million. He reached for his calculator, keyed in an 8-percent rate, and noted the discounted present value of such a ten-year collective saving. Byce rechecked the figure and smiled. He thought his good pal and hunting partner, Apostle County Manager Guy Ambrose, would be interested to learn that—at least in theory—it might be possible to launch a project with a collective present value of a tad more than $12 million[2] to flood-prone residents of the county if they could find a way to pay a modest lump sum toward head heightening today.

• • • • •

All in all, Anton Kurvaszy had reflected to himself when he returned to his Larch City office following the lunch with Byrne, Smarck, and Zysman, the proposed Polaris-Vikingsholm arrangement didn't seem to be quite the kind of deal envisioned in the legislation that authorized jobs-for-inmates programs in federal prisons. Anton flipped to this description in a Bureau of Prisons brochure:

The Mission of UNICOR

Federal Prison Industries, Inc., also known by the title UNICOR, is a public corporation wholly owned by the federal government. UNICOR provides opportunities for inmates of correctional institutions to engage in useful, paying work. Today UNICOR products range from auto parts to X-ray components. Federal Acquisition Regulations require federal agencies with requirements for products that are available from UNICOR to buy them if they are competitive in price and quality with comparable items offered on the open market.

• • • • •

Should agencies of the federal government ever be asked to buy UNICOR goods at higher-than-market prices? Would it even be legal to do so? Private suppliers regularly complain of "unfair competition," citing prison-industries use of "cheap convict labor." Furthermore, no government procurement officer ever likes to be *ordered* to buy certain products willy-nilly, as would have to occur if Vikingsholm stationery were to find a mandated market in federal agencies. The budget officers in the agencies selected to become captive customers wouldn't relish having to find extra money for a high-cost supplier like Vikingsholm-UNICOR.

On the other hand, what if the Vikingsholm stationery would really be unique? Some commercial papermakers were using recycled stock too. But maybe enough additional features could be added to the Vikingsholm product to distinguish it from competitors' paper. The selling point, Kurvaszy supposed, would be "special-watermark, special-weight, custom-printed stationery" for federal agencies' use. Uniqueness would appear to exempt the product from the statutory requirement of market competitiveness based on lowest price. Additionally, there was the current government policy to promote recycling, even if it had to be done at some cost in the forms of jacked-up waste disposal fees and higher prices for products made with recycled feedstocks. The "Made with 100% recycled paper" mark on Vikingsholm-UNICOR paper just might provide the margin of justification for some high muckety-muck in Washington to order federal agencies to buy UNICOR stationery.

According to Mary Martengrove, who had excellent contacts among the local enviros, many thoughtful conservationists and environmentalists now thought that

[2]$1.8 million × 6.71 (@ 8 percent over ten years) = $12.078 million.

recycling would need government support for years to come. Currently, the market for postconsumption paper, plastics, and so forth was strong enough for private recyclers to make a go of the business without subsidies. But that situation might not last. The bottom in the recycling market had been known to drop precipitously in the past. That awareness scared many potential entrepreneurs away. With the promise of long-term public subsidies, however, investors could enter the business being confident of a cushion in the event the market for this or that recycled product went south.

This line of thought led to another idea in Anton Kurvaszy's mind. Kurvaszy was looking for ways to increase the recycling percentage in the four-county area's waste stream. Suppose the new Area Waste Authority contracted to supply some of the recycled paper that Polaris would need as feedstock if operations at the mill were extended. It surely was an idea worth discussing with Stan Byrne—along with that other idea in Kurvaszy's mind, the one about disposing some unrecyclable wastes from the four-county area in an expanded landfill on Polaris's Half Day Rill site.

Kurvaszy phoned Byrne: "At our lunch yesterday, Stan, you said something about the need for Polaris to expand the landfill at the Half Day Rill site. Let me hear more."

Byrne seemed a bit puzzled at Kurvaszy's choice of topic, but he responded to Anton's request. Safe, convenient, low-cost disposal waste facilities, Byrne stressed, are a must in the paper industry: "Paper milling produces gobs of waste. The closer the wastes can be dumped to the mill, the better. It saves on transportation costs." Byrne had assumed that he would simply order the landfill sealed if and when Polaris closed the old mill. "But if we *don't* close the mill," he said, "we'll have to expand the pit—it's almost full."

Byrne paused, apparently thinking for the first time about the implications. He realized that keeping the dump in service might not be quite as simple a process as it would be to order it sealed. "I suppose we'll need a team of engineers, and maybe lawyers, to make sure that a new landfill's environmentally engineered. We're operating under different laws today, and in a different climate of opinion, from when the landfill at Half Day Rill went into service."

Anton asked how much all that—the engineering, the lawyering, and of course the physical work to expand the dump—would cost. Whatever the estimate, might it be possible, for a few dollars more, to extend the dump's capacity beyond the foreseeable extent of Polaris's needs?

"Cost a lot? No," Stan Byrne answered. "Getting the environmental approvals—that's an engineering problem and an administrative one, not an economic hurdle. We already have all the land we'd need for a huge new landfill, and then some."

Anton then said that he had it in mind for the AWA not only to sell Polaris recycled paper from the four-county waste stream but also to pay tipping fees to Polaris for AWA's use of the Half Day landfill as a disposal site for nontoxic household wastes. He referred to some figures that he had scribbled on the back of an envelope: "Suppose AWA guarantees you 18,000 tons per year of recyclable paper, say at $20 per ton, for a yearly total of $360,000. At the same time, say that AWA pays you $20 per ton to take 10-, 11-, maybe 12,000 tons of nonrecyclable trash, averaging $210,000 per year total. That would be trash you'd add to mill wastes for the dump. The tipping fee might help you generate the cash flow you need to go ahead on the Vikingsholm-UNICOR deal."

Table 9.6 Estimated Outlays and Receipts by Polaris to Extend Working Life of the Mill at Half Day Rill (dollars in thousands)

Outlays					
One-Time Capital Investments			Annual Cash Expenses		
Heighten Dam Head	New Equipment	Expand Landfill	Pulp @ $20/Ton	Labor, O&M, and Other	Total
3,000*	1,500[†]	1,500[‡]	$360	$620	$980

Receipts					
For general waste disposal services: Tipping fees to be paid by AWA at Half Day Rill @ $20/ton	For use by Karelia of improved land at Half Day		For sales of 24,000 tons/year of special stock to Vikingsholm-UNICOR		
	If One-Time Fee	If Annual Lease	@ $60/ton	@ $75/ton	@ $90/ton
$210[§]	$500	$50	$1,440	$1,800	$2,160

*Covers Polaris's share of $3.5 million one-time construction costs to raise the head of the Half Day Rill dam.

[†]Covers purchase of a new de-inking machine and continuous-process pulping equipment which runs on co-generated hydroelectricity and uses 100-percent recycled paper as feedstock.

[‡]Covers excavation and environmental-sealing charges incurred in connection with the expansion of the landfill at the mill site. Assumes that Polaris can obtain all necessary variances to expand the landfill and put it in general service (instead of using it exclusively as a receptacle for Polaris waste).

[§]Assumes that half of all dumped waste under the four-county operation—a total of 10,500 tons/year (see Table 5.2)—goes to the expanded landfill at the Polaris site near Half Day Rill, at the negotiated tipping fee of $20/ton.

Byrne promised Kurvaszy that he'd give serious thought to the landfill idea. Byrne hung up and turned to his computer. He pulled his cash-flow spreadsheets onto the screen and added changes to reflect a possible additional income stream in the form of AWA tipping fees (see Table 9.6 and Table 9.7). Byrne looked at the bottom-line figures, taking particular note of the NPV and IRR calculations. Byrne wondered if the possibility of a linkup with AWA would influence Francis X. Doherty's reaction to a proposal for an extension of operations out at Half Day Rill.

•   •   •   •   •

At Anton Kurvaszy's request, Mary Martengrove had remained in touch for some weeks now with Len Palchaterian, director of the St. Croix regional emergency medical service (EMS). It didn't surprise Mary when Anton assigned her the action on Len's latest request for help. Palchaterian hoped to expand and upgrade his operation, and Mary assumed that the assistance he needed would have to come, if at all, in the form of a subsidy from the four counties.

"Something new has been added," Mary said as she stared at the table of figures before her. It contained Palchaterian's latest CFA of his upgrading project (see Table 9.8). Currently, Palchaterian's medical teams provided *basic medical service (BMS)* and occasional routine medical transportation throughout the St. Croix area. The BMS level included the splinting of broken limbs, the administration of oxygen to patients taken with sudden shortness of breath or chest pains, and, of course, rush runs as

Table 9.7 Cash-Flow Analysis of Proposed Refurbishment of Polaris Mill at Half Day Rill (dollars in thousands)

Assumes head heightening of the Half Day Rill dam, guaranteed revenue stream to Polaris under long-term contract with Vikingsholm-UNICOR, and use of recycled paper from AWA.

(1)	(2)	(3)	(4)	(5)	(6)	(7)
		Outlays		Annual Cash Receipts*	@ 8-Percent Discount	
	Capital Investment	Expenses			Discount Factor	Present Value
Year		$20/Ton Pulp	Other			
0	− $3,000[†]				1.000	− $3,000.0
1	− $3,000[‡]	− $360[§]	− $620	$2,010	.926	− $1,824.2
2		− $360	− $620	$2,010	.857	$882.7
3		− $360	− $620	$2,010	.794	$817.8
4		− $360	− $620	$2,010	.735	$757.1
5		− $360	− $620	$2,010	.681	$701.4
6		− $360	− $620	$2,010	.630	$648.9
7		− $360	− $620	$2,010	.583	$600.5
8		− $360	− $620	$2,010	.540	$556.2
9		− $360	− $620	$2,010	.500	$515.0
10	$500	− $360	− $620	$2,010	.463	$708.4
NPV						$1,363.8
IRR						5 percent

*$1,800 thousand/year from Vikingsholm-UNICOR plus an estimated $210 thousand annually in AWA tipping fees at the expanded landfill on Polaris's Half Day Rill site.

†Covers new mill equipment plus cost of landfill expansion.

‡Estimated total cost (to Polaris) of dam upgrading—that is, $3.5 million net of Karelia's contribution of $500,000.

§18,000 tons/year of postconsumption paper from AWA for use as feedstocks at a negotiated fee of $20/ton.

needed to local clinics and emergency rooms. Palchaterian now wanted to raise his operation from basic to the higher level, known as *advanced medical service (AMS)*. The AMS level would require Palchaterian's squads to develop a capability for more-rapid response to emergency calls. The AMS rating would also require a staff trained to provide true paramedic treatment in emergency cases: defibrillation, tracheotomies, and so forth.

Martengrove, looking at Palchaterian's latest workup, frowned. She compared the current proposal with his earlier cash-flow estimates. Len's initial capital investment proposal had been upped from $550 thousand to $1.1 million (compare Table 9.8 with Table 9.2). The increase reflected Palchaterian's belief, now, that it would be preferable to buy rather than to lease an air-evacuation plane. Since the SCDC would actually own the aircraft, it also could be sold for salvage at the end of the planning period instead of being turned back to a leasing company as a total write-off.

As indicated in Column 4 of Table 9.8, Palchaterian still counted on $150 thousand in annual user fees, both directly from clients and from insurance companies, to defray part of the cost of the expanded EMS operation. But Palchaterian had added a

Table 9.8 Len Palchaterian's Revised Cash-Flow Analysis for a Proposed St. Croix–Area EMS Expansion (dollars in thousands)

(1)	(2)	(3)	(4)	(5)	(6)	(7)
	Outlays*		Estimated Annual Cash Receipts		NPV Calculation	
					@ 8-Percent Discount	
Year	Planned Capital Investment	Estimated Net Expenses	User Fees	Recreational Charges[†]	Discount Factor	Present Value
0	− $1,100				1.000	− $1,100.0
1		− $275	$150	$100	.926	− $23.2
2		− $275	$150	$100	.857	− $21.4
3		− $275	$150	$100	.794	− $19.9
4		− $275	$150	$100	.735	− $18.4
5		− $275	$150	$100	.681	− $17.0
6		− $275	$150	$100	.630	− $15.8
7		− $275	$150	$100	.583	− $14.6
8		− $275	$150	$100	.540	− $13.5
9		− $275	$150	$100	.500	− $12.5
10	$200[‡]	− $275	$150	$100	.463	$81.0
NPV						− $1,175.1
Required Annual Subsidy						$175.1

*Covers new ambulances and one-time paramedic training courses, as in the original plan, plus purchase of an air-evacuation craft. Figures in Column 3 also reflect the higher salaries of a generally upgraded EMS force.

[†]A $200,000/year recreation charge would increase the NPV to − $504.2, which would still require a subsidy, at the level of $75.1/year. Elimination of the recreational charge would yield an NPV of − $1,846, implying a $275.1 annual subsidy.

[‡]Projected salvage value of used ambulances and air-evacuation craft after ten years of service.

new column (Column 5) to reflect projected income—$100,000 every year—that hadn't come up in his earlier conversations about the EMS upgrade. What, Martengrove asked Kurvaszy, are "Recreational Charges"?

"I'm sorry, Mary," Anton said in mild embarrassment. "I should have filled you in." Kurvaszy cleared his throat, the signal that he wanted to talk. "You might have heard about the Winter Wonderland proposal. Palchaterian wants to draw off some of the Winter Wonderland revenues to help pay for his EMS upgrading. That's what he means by 'Recreational Charges.'"

Everyone in the St. Croix who read the newspapers or listened to the radio knew that developers from Chicago (or St. Louis, or somewhere) had been talking up a grand new development project for the area. A big outfit named the Karelia Corporation wanted to build a world-class resort complex in the four-county area. Karelia hoped over a three-decade period to develop:

A "Winter Wonderland" based on a network of cross-country ski trails and snowmobile trails plus an Olympic-grade ski jump, bobsled, and luge complex

A rock-climbing school and course—one of the most complete and most scenic in the world

A rustic-cabin development followed by a complete "Christmas Village" of luxury rental units, expected eventually to take on the cachet of Aspen or Vail

A world-class luxury resort hotel with a PGA Tour–quality thirty-six-hole golf course

A new casino-gambling complex, to be developed by members of the Thunder Bay band on a small plot of Chippewa land on the Minnesota side of the St. Croix gorge

A small airport, designed primarily for executive craft but capable of landing 727-class commercial jets.

Mary said she was impressed.

Anton agreed: "When these promoters start pushing the buttons, big-think gets catchy. Even in small-town U.S.A." The governor of the State of Minnesota was said to be lobbying bankers in New York and Singapore; Karelia still needed investors. Minnesota legislators were reportedly prepared to support the Karelia development with tax breaks and expedited regulatory procedures. Lawmakers in Madison, Wisconsin, were also thought to be favorably inclined, although they apparently hadn't yet committed themselves. Anton suspected that the Wisconsinites wanted to see exactly how the development modules were to be divided with Minnesota.

But Mary still didn't understand Len Palchaterian's logic. How did Karelia's Winter Wonderland project get tied in with Palchaterian's CFA for EMS upgrading?

"When Palchaterian got wind of Karelia," Anton explained, "he figured it'd help his case if he added a special charge on users of any new outdoor facilities. I gather that federal agencies already use charges of this kind. The Park Service nicks mountain climbers for 'insurance premiums'; the service builds up a fund to spend when rescuers have to go hunt for the inevitable few who get lost or injured in national parks. It'll be the same with Winter Wonderland. Some folks will end up lost on the ski trails, and some will get hurt scaling the gorge. Len's medics will be called out. According to him, Winter Wonderland will increase the demand for EMS. Why shouldn't Karelia users help pay for it?"

Was Karelia's development scenario plausible? Mary pointed out that if Winter Wonderland never materialized, Palchaterian's projected "Recreational Charges" wouldn't exist either. Anton then showed Mary a table of figures that a Karelia Corporation executive, Marilyn Taverner, had given him (see Table 9.9).

"This Marilyn Taverner," Anton continued, "has talked to everyone from the governors of the two states on down. She's assured anyone who'd listen that Karelia wants to use the Winter Wonderland module to kick-start the overall project. Support Winter Wonderland, and everything else in the scenario should follow in due course." Thus, Anton said, "Karelia wants 'development support' now in exchange for the promise to generate jobs and business over time as the post–Winter Wonderland phases unfold." Mary understood that when Karelia said "development support," it meant "public subsidy."

Anton continued: "Winter Wonderland should require relatively little initial capital investment and should be the least controversial part of the Karelia plan, environmentally speaking. The Winter Wonderland development will consist of low-impact facilities: cross-country ski runs and a network of fully engineered snowmobile

Table 9.9 Marilyn Taverner's Cash-Flow Analysis of Proposed Winter Wonderland Development (dollars in thousands)

Assumes $100,000/year recreation charge to EMS and the existence of the high-head dam at Half Day Rill, built with a $500 contribution to Polaris from Karelia in Year 1.

(1)	(2)	(3)	(4)	(5)	(6)	(7)
	Planned	Expenses		Estimated	@ 8-Percent Discount	
	Capital	Recreational	O&M,	Cash	Discount	Present
Year	Investment	Charges*	Other	Receipts	Factor	Value
0	−$3,500†				1.000	− $3,500.0
1	− $500	− $100	− $100	$550	.926	− $138.9
2		− $100	− $100	$575	.857	$321.4
3		− $100	− $100	$600	.794	$317.6
4		− $100	− $100	$625	.735	$312.4
5		− $100	− $100	$650	.681	$306.5
6		− $100	− $100	$675	.630	$299.3
7		− $100	− $100	$700	.583	$291.5
8		− $100	− $100	$725	.540	$283.5
9		− $100	− $100	$750	.500	$275.0
10		− $100	− $100	$775	.463	$266.2
NPV						− $965.6
Required Annual Subsidy						$143.9

*Eliminating the recreational charge to EMS, with all other factors held constant, yields a NPV to Karelia of − $294.7, implying a subsidy of $43 thousand/year. A $200,000/year recreation charge, instead of $100,000/year, would decrease Karelia's NPV estimate to − $1,636.5, requiring a subsidy of $243.9 thousand/year.

†Covers grading of area around the new lake to be formed by the high-head dam at Half Day Rill and construction of low-maintenance trails and supporting structures (warming houses, sauna facilities, concessions).

routes. There'll be simple structures along routes running from the St. Croix gorge to Half Day Rill: new warming houses, concessions, saunas, and stuff. Even without the ski jump and other Olympic paraphernalia—that's to come later—Winter Wonderland should attract people for winter sports from as far as the Twin Cities, maybe from Milwaukee and even Chicago. Once tourists get the image of the St. Croix as a wintertime vacationland, the stage will be set for the other Karelia projects."

Mary noted the stream of receipts projected in the Taverner CFA (Column 5 in Table 9.9). She supposed that commercial success might build on itself over time. Taverner's CFA showed a return of more than a half-million dollars in receipts the first full year, building annually thereafter to an estimate of a bit more than three-quarters of a million dollars in year 10.

Anton gestured toward the regional map on his wall. "If Karelia gets what it hopes to from Polaris—Marilyn Taverner has been negotiating with Stan Byrne—the Winter Wonderland trails will all converge on the planned site of a rustic-cabin village near Half Day Rill. The Karelia people hope to talk Polaris into raising its dam head. Head heightening would turn what's now a pond into a fair-sized lake." Anton explained that the new lake would make the area perfect for four-season recreation:

nordic skiing in the winter; fishing and, eventually, tour-quality golf in the summer. Of course, he admitted, if the dam head remained low, there'd not only be no extension of the mill but also would be no big, beautiful lake to develop *around*. And Karelia would invest less initially in the whole project, based on a smaller stream of expected receipts, since the attractiveness of the area for tourist development would be correspondingly diminished. On the other hand, Anton told Mary, the Karelia developers hadn't left it entirely up to Polaris to decide for or against head heightening. Marilyn Taverner had apparently made at least a tentative offer to pay some of the cost of upgrading the dam.

The stage was getting crowded! Mary Martengrove wondered whether anyone else might be in the act. The *dramatis personae* included, besides Palchaterian, the decision makers from Polaris and now this Marilyn Taverner from Karelia. Was anyone else in the wings waiting to make an appearance? For example, what about the idea that Andy Byce had described to Mary a few days earlier over coffee at the Gopher Grill? Andy, born promoter that he was, had talked about organizing an Upper St. Croix Watershed Association. The association would consist of property owners who would chip in toward a study of re-damming the southern branch of the Upper St. Croix River at Half Day Rill with an eye to cutting their current flood-insurance burdens.

•   •   •   •   •

Mary studied the Karelia figures (Table 9.9). She could think of no plausible conditions under which the Karelia planners could expect Winter Wonderland to generate a cash flow high enough for a positive net return. Karelia hoped to make up the deficit, however large, through a subsidy from four-county taxpayers' funds, to be funneled to Karelia through the SCDC. Marilyn Taverner claimed that a "modest" subsidy for Winter Wonderland would be a down payment on economic development for the entire region. The subsidy would enable Karelia to get started on Winter Wonderland. In turn, Winter Wonderland, the project that would establish the St. Croix as a multisport recreational mecca, would lay the basis for Karelia's longer-term development plan to materialize.

Speaking of subsidies, Mary pointed out to Anton that a sizable contribution from tax funds would apparently also be needed to support Len Pachaterian's proposal for EMS upgrading—even if Len got the recreational charges from Karelia.

Anton chuckled briefly. "You picked that up too, did you? If you look at the figures, the level of an EMS subsidy would depend on the level of any recreational charge. Since any charge paid to the EMS would have to come out of Karelia's Winter Wonderland cash flow, if Karelia were required to pay a hefty recreation charge, it would need an even larger subsidy than otherwise." The four counties would collectively have to come up with almost $320,000 annually. "How the figure gets divided between the medics and the developers," Anton said, "seems little more than a bookkeeping decision."

Mary asked if the county commissioners understood all the items on their agenda—Len Palchaterian's EMS proposal, Marilyn Taverner's Winter Wonderland plan, the need for as much as a $320,000 annual subsidy, and, maybe most important, how all these issues connected to the Polaris-Vikingsholm deal?

"The commissioners certainly appreciate the need for regional development," Anton replied. "And so do the county managers. Within reason, they also seem willing to come up with subsidy money—*if* the benefits to the area will justify the amount they'll be asked to spend." At that, Anton saw that Mary understood what he needed from her.

•　•　•　•　•

Most of us today take for granted the availability of emergency ambulance service: Just dial 911. Yet local governments have routinely undertaken to provide basic emergency medical service only since World War II. Not until Congress passed the Emergency Medical Services Systems Act of 1973 did significant efforts start to help all communities reach a high uniform national standard of service. Today the push is on almost everywhere to raise emergency service levels, even though some critics doubt that the benefits of upgrading are worth the costs. An advanced-level EMS—the kind Len Palchaterian wanted for the St. Croix—should be able to meet the so-called "eight-minute standard." In cardiac-arrest cases, lifesaving chances sharply increase if a highly trained medical team reaches the patient within eight minutes of the attack. However, in areas of low population density and long response distances, such as the St. Croix, it's sometimes difficult at any economically feasible level of service to ensure that the eight-minute standard can regularly be met.

Mary Martengrove knew from her discussions with Len Palchaterian that it would be hard to predict how many lives might be saved if the EMS got upgraded equipment and a more highly trained paramedic force. Even with a rapid-response capability, the distances within the four-county area would make it impossible even to approach a perfect lifesaving record. Palchaterian admitted, reluctantly, that professional opinion in the emergency-medicine community favored a pattern of expenditures different from the one he was advocating. Most emergency medical planners thought that, in areas of low population density, extra money shouldn't usually be spent to upgrade; rather, it was generally best to buy additional personnel and equipment at the *same* (BMS) level of skill and sophistication. Additional medics spread throughout an area, each with a shorter mean driving time to a caller, usually meant better service than did a smaller EMS force of more highly trained paramedics. Fewer responders translated into increased average distances and hence more time to reach patients. On balance, faster equipment and higher skills rarely offset the time penalty of sparser area coverage.

Why, then, did Palchaterian want to upgrade rather than simply expand and disperse his operation? Mary put it to Len: "Suppose you could count on the extra money. Why would you spend it upgrading to AMS instead of using it to extend existing service at the BMS level?"

Len explained that emergency medicine, a tough calling under any circumstances, is particularly demanding in the long, harsh winters of the St. Croix. Morale in the force is a critical factor. Len thought his people would value the professional prestige implicit in paramedic status and possession of an air-evacuation capability. Palchaterian added a few stories of a personal nature. He described two separate cases of accident victims who were hurt while out on traplines and whose lives almost certainly could have been saved if his EMSers had been able to fly them down to the Mayo Clinic.

General statistics, Len argued, didn't necessarily apply to the St. Croix, where the peculiarities of weather and the nature of citizens' activities made trauma relatively more common as a source of severe emergencies than were heart attacks and strokes. It was Palchaterian's best guess, based on a dozen years' experience, that the gains from an AMS capability when dealing with trauma and freezing cases would end up saving about the same number of additional lives as would a faster-response BMS force, with its improved capability in cardiac cases. Palchaterian estimated that the savings in additional lives attributable to an upgrading might range from 1 every other year to 3 lives each year. However, Len preferred to leave it to Mary to put any dollar values on the lives that might be saved—assuming that such estimates were necessary for the kind of analysis that Anton Kurvaszy had asked her to conduct.

It didn't take Mary Martengrove much of a literature search to identify the most frequently cited experts on value-of-life assessments. The journals with the latest findings were too specialized for the local library collections, but an interlibrary loan request and a two-day wait brought her the references she needed on microfilm.

● ● ● ● ●

From the journal of Mary Martengrove. Subject: Value-of-life estimates for use in cost-benefit analyses.

How Much Will Individuals Pay to Reduce Life-Threatening Levels of Risk?

The government faces a variety of opportunities to reduce risk. Airplane cabin fire protection costs $200,000 per life saved; automobile door protection standards save lives at $1,3 million each; Occupational Safety and Health Administration (OSHA) asbestos regulations save lives at $89.3 million each; Environmental Protection Agency (EPA) asbestos regulations save lives at $104.2 million each; and a proposed OSHA formaldehyde standard costs $72 billion per life saved. . . . Which of these policies should be pursued, and which provide benefits that are not commensurate with their costs?

In a democratic society, the appropriate starting point for analyzing these tradeoffs is the value individuals bearing the risk place on the improved safety. Over the past two decades, there has developed a substantial literature on the value of these risk-money tradeoffs. The greatest emphasis has been on the tradeoff involving mortality risks and wages. . . . In situations in which no market data are available, such as some environmental risks, one can use surveys to derive a market value as if a market for the good existed. This paper explores these different approaches to establishing appropriate economic values for risks to life and health. . . .

[The author here describes various measurement techniques, beginning with economic studies of the increases in wages that workers typically demand in exchange for accepting riskier kinds of jobs. The author moves on to describe survey research techniques, all of which] involve eliciting responses to a simulated market context using variants of a procedure known as "contingent valuation," which ascertains individual preferences contingent upon some hypothetical market scenario. . . .

A survey might ask respondents directly how much of a wage increase they would require to accept a given risk increase. A variant of this approach is to process in iterative fashion. Rather than seeking a response to an open-ended question, the willingness-to-pay value may be adjusted until the respondent indicates indifference. . . .

A principal benefit of survey methodologies is that they provide insight into classes of outcomes that cannot be addressed with available market data. One such benefit category is altruistic benefits, which by their very nature will not be reflected in market risk-taking decisions. . . .

A major concern with survey valuations of health risks is that the responses will be reliable only to the extent that individuals understand the tasks to which they are responding. A matter of particular concern is the processing of risk information presented in survey context.

Consider two different valuation studies of the same health outcome using surveys involving different risk levels. The first of these studies . . . focuses on individuals' valuations of the risks from bleach and drain opener, chloriamine gassings, child poisonings, and hand burns, among others. These morbidity effects are by no means catastrophic, but the estimated values the respondents attach to them are in excess of $1 million in three cases. . . .

Individuals who are willing to pay one dollar to reduce the risk of bleach gassing by 1/1,000,000, will exhibit an implicit value for the injury of $1 million, but this response may not reflect the underlying risk-dollar tradeoff so much as it does the inability of individuals to deal with extremely low probability events. . . . [T]he usual range of experience with risk is with hazards of much greater frequency. The evidence in the psychology and economics literature . . . indicates there is a tendency to overestimate the magnitude of very low probability events, particularly those called to one's attention. Survey methodologies may elicit individual valuations as perceived by the respondent, but one must ensure that what is being perceived is accurate. Errors in risk perceptions may be a particularly salient difficulty.

A final concern with respect to survey valuations is whether the respondents are giving honest and thoughtful answers to the survey questions. In practice, truthful revelation of preferences has proven to be less of a problem than has the elicitation of meaningful responses because of a failure to understand the survey task. Strategic misrepresentation can also be addressed by using a survey mechanism that is designed to elicit a truthful expression of preferences, such as hypothetical voting on a political referendum. . . .

Policy Implications

Although the value-of-life literature is now roughly two decades old, the essential approach became well established in the 1970s. The appropriate measure of the value of life from the standpoint of government policy is society's willingness to pay for the risk reduction, which is the same benefit formulation in all policy evaluation contexts.

Economists have had the greatest success in assessing the risk-money tradeoff using labor market data. Although the tradeoff estimates vary considerably depending on the population exposed to the risk, the nature of the risk, individual income level, and similar factors, most of the reasonable estimates of the value of life are clustered in the $3 million–$7 million range. Moreover, these estimates are for the population of exposed workers, who generally have lower incomes than the individuals being protected by broadly based risk regulations. Recognition of the positive elasticity of the value of life with respect to worker earnings will lead to the use of different values of life depending on the population being protected. Taste differences may also enter, as smokers and workers in very hazardous jobs, for example, place lower values on health risks.

The 1980s marked the first decade in which use of estimates of the value of life based on risk tradeoffs became widespread throughout the Federal government. Previously, agencies assessed only the lost present value of the earnings of the deceased, leading to dramatic underestimation of the benefit value. In large part though the efforts of the U.S. Office of Management and Budget, agencies such as OSHA and EPA began incorporating value-of-life estimates in their benefit evaluations. Policy makers' recognition of the nonpecuniary aspects of life is an important advance.

Given the range of uncertainty of the value-of-life estimates, perhaps the most reasonable use of these values in policy contexts is to provide a broad index of the overall desirability of a policy. In practice, value-of-life debates seldom focus on whether the appropriate value of life should be $3 million or $4 million—narrow differences that cannot be distinguished based on the accuracy of current estimates and the potential limitations of individual behavior underlying these estimates. However, the estimates do provide guidance as to whether risk reduction efforts that cost $50,000 per life saved or $50 million per life saved are warranted. . . .[3]

•   •   •   •   •

Table 9.10 shows Mary Martengrove's rough cut at a cost-benefit workup for the EMS upgrading. Her estimates, she later explained to Anton Kurvaszy, reflected two different assumptions about the lifesaving results of upgrading. Assuming that the higher level of service resulted in the saving of 1 life every other year at a half-million dollars valuation per life saved—Mary's low estimate—the present value of Palchaterian's proposal, discounted over a ten-year period, netted out to a negative figure (Column 5). Alternatively, assuming that the upgrade would result in the saving of 3 lives per year at $1 million per life—the high estimate—the benefits turned dramatically positive (Column 6).

[3]From W. Kip Viscusi, "The Value of Risks of Life and Health," 31 Journal of Economic Literature (December 1993): 1912–1913, 1939–1943.

Table 9.10 Cost-Benefit Analysis of Proposed St. Croix–Area EMS Expansion (dollars in thousands)

(1)	(2)	(3)	(4)	(5)	(6)
	Net Direct	Benefits		PV @ 8-Percent Discount	
Year	Costs*	Low Estimate†	High Estimate†	Low Estimate	High Estimate
0	− $1,100	$500	$3,000	− $600	$1,900
1	− $275	$0	$3,000	− $254	$2,523
2	− $275	$500	$3,000	$193	$2,335
3	− $275	$0	$3,000	− $218	$2,164
4	− $275	$500	$3,000	$165	$1,948
5	− $275	$0	$3,000	− $187	$1,856
6	− $275	$500	$3,000	$142	$1,717
7	− $275	$0	$3,000	− $160	$1,589
8	− $275	$500	$3,000	$122	$1,472
9	− $275	$0	$3,000	− $138	$1,363
10	− $75	$500	$3,000	$197	$1,354
NPVs				− $740	$20,220

*Net direct costs in each year equals the algebraic sum of Column 2 and Column 3 in Table 9.8.

†Low estimate based on $500,000 value of 1 life saved every other year.

‡High estimate based on $1 million valuation per life of 3 lives saved every year.

What if, at the forthcoming development-plan meeting of the SCDC, Kurvaszy were asked to make a *comparative* evaluation: Which project—EMS upgrading or Winter Wonderland—showed the more favorable cost-benefit figures?

Martengrove's thinking had proceeded along some such lines as the following: On the negative side of the ledger, Winter Wonderland would impose a *loss* of aesthetic, environmental, and recreational values for those St. Croix–area residents who were repulsed at the thought of hordes invading the region every weekend for cross-country skiing and snowmobiling. Mary knew that the redoubtable Finn Ebertsen of Brownlea, Wisconsin, was organizing a citizens' group bent on blocking the Winter Wonderland development. She had spoken with Ebertsen and had tried to gauge the number of area residents who felt strongly against further development. "Theoretically," Mary told Anton, "these opponents should be willing to pay something to prevent further development."

Mary showed Anton her cost-benefit table for Winter Wonderland, in which Column 3 gave her estimate of that "something," based on conversations with some of Finn's environmentalists over in Apostle County (see Table 9.11).

Mary said that her Column-3 numbers were no more than guesstimates. Short of a careful, systematic study—say a formal contingent value analysis—who could say what the real values of recreational and aesthetic losses might be, especially since exactly the same effects might be judged differently by different evaluators? Many in the area wanted to keep the Upper St. Croix basin as wild as they could. But others wouldn't consider development as a cost at all—indeed, quite the opposite. The "pros" and the "antis" seemed pretty evenly balanced, as far as Mary could see. Suppose, she

Table 9.11 Cost-Benefit Analysis of Proposed Winter Wonderland Development (dollars in thousands)

Assumes optimistic estimates of area residents' valuation of Winter Wonderland's recreational potential, a high level of business surge, and the flood bonus.

(1)	(2)	(3)	(4)	(5)	(6)	(7)	(8)
	Costs		Benefits			@ 8-Percent Discount	
Year	Direct	External Lost Recreation	Direct WTP	Business Surge	Flood Bonus	Discount Factor	Present Value
0	− $3,500					1.000	− $3,500
1	− $700	− $1,200	$500	$150	$1,200	.926	− $46
2	− $200	− $1,200	$500	$200	$1,200	.857	$428
3	− $200	− $1,200	$500	$250	$1,200	.794	$436
4	− $200	− $1,200	$500	$300	$1,200	.735	$441
5	− $200	− $1,200	$500	$350	$1,200	.681	$443
6	− $200	− $1,200	$500	$400	$1,200	.630	$441
7	− $200	− $1,200	$500	$450	$1,200	.583	$437
8	− $200	− $1,200	$500	$500	$1,200	.540	$432
9	− $200	− $1,200	$500	$550	$1,200	.500	$425
10	− $200	− $1,200	$500	$600	$1,200	.463	$416
NPV							$354*

Column 2: Sum of columns 2–4—Taverner's estimate of net direct benefits, from Table 9.9.

Column 3: Martengrove's guesstimate of the WTP of St. Croix residents who, fearing threats to the environment, put a negative value on Winter Wonderland and would, theoretically, pay some amount to block the development.

Column 4: Martengrove's guesstimates of all positive WTP values not captured in user fees or reflected in her estimate of the dollar value of the business surge.

*NPV would equal − $3,308 if the flood-bonus credit were one-third (instead of two-thirds) of Andy Byce's estimate.

had asked herself, that half the 120,000 residents of the four counties opposed development and put an equivalent value of only $20 per person on rejection of Winter Wonderland. That would generate, in Column 3, a negative externality of $1.2 million annually.

The numbers in Column 4 and Column 5 represented Mary's rough figures for direct and external benefits to citizens of the four counties, should the Karelia plan unfold as the corporate planners hoped it would. "Suppose Winter Wonderland becomes a reality," Mary later explained to Anton, "and it pulls visitors into the area. Users of the ski trails, and snowmobile runs, and the rest, pay direct fees (Column 4). Their presence should also generate general business for restaurants, souvenir shops, and so forth, in the area. That kind of business surge wouldn't occur in the absence of the development, so it's an added net benefit (Column 5)."

Anton Kurvaszy understood the technique: Mary was merely proposing a "straw man," a table of estimates based on her general understanding of the region's economic dynamics. The idea was to use rough, back-of-the-envelope figures as a basis for dialogue. Anton might want to dispute one or more of Mary's quantitative hunches: "I think *this* set of numbers is too low"; "But you forgot to include *that* bundle of effects in your estimate of external effects." Through successive modifications, even a rough workup such as Mary's can, over time, be transformed into a useful display of pertinent data.

Mary derived the flood-bonus estimates in Column 6 of Table 9.11 after talking with Andy Byce. Byce had recognized the tie-in between the talk of dam-head heightening out at Half Day Rill and the possibility of a dispersed benefit in the form of reduced insurance premiums for some 6,000 building owners in Apostle County. Andy had claimed a $1.8-million annual bonus, but Mary knew of his irrepressible boosterism. Andy's enthusiasm often expressed itself in inflated numbers when he was talking up development projects for the St. Croix region. "Cut Andy's numbers by a third," Mary had counseled herself when entering the figures in Column 6.

●　　●　　●　　●　　●

Francis X. Doherty completed the morning's dictation and dismissed his secretary. He glanced at his desk calendar and reached for a sheet of stationery, the kind with just his name at the top instead of the formal Polaris letterhead. Doherty unscrewed an ancient Sheaffer fountain pen. He used it only for signing and for writing the occasional note that he wanted in his own hand. Doherty thought for a moment and then wrote:

> Ellen:
>
> I am miserable to have to write this. I don't think I've ever missed one of your fundraisers. But an unavoidable conflict has come up. My grandson Brian just made the varsity gymnastics squad at Northwestern. Their first meet is in Omaha. There's no way I can think of missing it—even, my dear, if it means I'm not there for your campaign kickoff dinner.
>
> Enclosed anyway is my check for four plates.
>
> Surely there will be other times and other ways that I can show support for your outstanding work as our congresswoman. It's clear that your campaign this time will be a tough one. But be of cheer! The opposition made a grievous political error when they picked an Ivy League glamor boy to run against you. If a record of achievement counts for anything, your reelection is assured; but even if good looks and elegance are to be decisive in this election, remember—to most of your constituents, there's never been a politician more glamorous than you.
>
> Faithfully,
> Fran

Francis X. Doherty reread the note. He folded it and placed it along with a personal check in an envelope. On the front he wrote *E.M.* and marked the envelope "Personal and Confidential." He buzzed, and when the secretary entered his office, he instructed her to send the letter by delivery service to Congresswoman Moe at her Cannon Building office on Capitol Hill.

For five terms, Ellen Moe had represented the district with diligence and integrity. She was one of Minnesota's most successful bread-and-butter politicians.

Her attentiveness to constituents and her success bringing money into the area had earned the congresswoman a large, loyal following. It was also true that many who knew her—especially those who remembered her from high school days—did indeed regard Ellen Moe as a kind of glamorous figure. But the puffery in his note notwithstanding, Doherty knew that Moe's political chic wouldn't be enough to pull *this* election out against the articulate, well-financed candidate who opposed her. Fran Doherty wondered if he could do anything to help Ellen besides offering a few encouraging words and making a modest contribution to her campaign chest.

•   •   •   •   •

The day after he spoke with Stan Byrne about the expanded landfill possibility, Anton Kurvaszy asked Mary Martengrove if she had ever heard of "an SNT": a **single negotiating text.** Mary's expression made it immediately clear that she hadn't. Anton cleared his throat, and Mary sat down to listen.

The SNT was a device used in the 1978 Camp David meeting that Jimmy Carter arranged between the president of Egypt, Anwar Sadat, and the prime minister of Israel, Menachem Begin. "Egypt and Israel were formally at war. There were so many issues outstanding," Anton said, "and the peace negotiations were going to be so complicated, that Carter's people had to find a way to bring some order into the talks. President Carter's advisers came up with the so-called SNT."

All this was interesting, Martengrove thought, but she didn't see how it related to any of the projects Kurvaszy had her working on for the forthcoming development-plan meeting of the SCDC. Kurvaszy went on: "The Polaris-Vikingsholm project is pretty complicated—maybe not as complex as Camp David was, but complicated nonetheless. There are quite a few players. Each has obligations; each has to act on behalf of interests that others don't share. I don't think any one of us has tried to see the big picture, or for that matter, to locate all the different ways we could collectively foul up our chances to put a deal together."

In the SNT procedure, Kurvaszy explained, someone tries to identify the main concerns of all parties. The analyst produces a single text outlining, in the simplest possible terms, a "package" of agreements. The principals review the text and react. The author of the first-draft SNT asks clarifying questions, seeking out potential points of convergence, and then drafts a new version. So it goes. Ideally, all parties move closer with each round toward a center that gradually reveals itself through the dialogic process. The peace agreement between Egypt and Israel emerged after President Carter's aides had gone through more than twenty SNTs, each of which incorporated adjustments based on the parties' reactions to earlier versions.

Now Mary saw it coming.

Anton told Mary to think through the interests of the different parties who would have to be involved in an AWA-Polaris-Vikingsholm deal. She should also, he said, consider whether there might be any point in bringing Andy Byce into the talks. Anton ran through the kinds of questions he wanted Mary to ask: "Who *wants* what out of a deal to keep the old mill up and running? Who *needs* what in exchange for his or her contribution to the arrangement?" Mary was to see if she could produce a single document in which would be identified the necessary participants to a deal, the various parties' interests, and (if possible) an outline of the kinds of agreements that might make everyone, on the whole, better off than they would be in the absence of an integrated understanding.

• • • • •

County Manager Guy Ambrose of Apostle County, Wisconsin, and Arne Temple, his counterpart in Burnt County, usually got together before each development-plan session of the SCDC. Fellow "cheeseheads" (as they referred to themselves in the good-humored way of Wisconsinites), the two county managers found it helpful to talk through forthcoming agenda items. It made sense for Ambrose and Temple to pick each other's brains and consider whether they should bring coordinated positions representing Wisconsin's interests into the commission's meetings.

Ambrose and Temple had both heard that the commission would probably be considering a request from Len Palchaterian for a subsidy to the regional EMS. Arne Temple had also picked up word that Anton Kurvaszy might propose a subsidy for Karelia Corporation's development project, the Winter Wonderland idea that everyone was getting so excited about. Guy Ambrose said that he liked what he had heard about Winter Wonderland. Still, if public money had to be spent, he wasn't sure that it should come from the local tax base—or, if it did, that any extra funds should go to the medics or the Winter Wonderland developers. Ambrose had no trouble listing other Apostle County projects—potential competitors for tax monies—that deserved support. Arne Temple saw parallels to several items on his own wish list for Burnt County:

> Widening the shoulders along more than a hundred miles of county roads that needed work
>
> Expanding the county's free library system, including funding for new storefront branch offices in towns not currently served (The "inequity" in the existing system bothered folks.)
>
> Completely refurbishing the interior of the Apostle County Courthouse, including replumbing of the jail, where officials feared that the courts would force prisoner releases on grounds of ill treatment
>
> Hiring additional caseworkers in the county welfare office, where backlogs were hurting people whose problems certainly qualified them as among the neediest citizens of Apostle County
>
> Approving grants to the towns of Gull, Martinsville, and Zane so that each could initiate an official festival day (parade, bratwurst roasts, and the like) patterned after the popular "Muskie Festival" in the town of Borton

Public money spent on these projects wouldn't be available to funnel through the SCDC into EMS upgrading or Winter Wonderland support. Of course, the converse was also true.

• • • • •

Under the auspices of the Federal Executive Institute at the University of Virginia, high-level government officials gather from time to time for seminars in Charlottesville, a short drive from Washington. At the most recent FEI gathering, Haney Brill had been one of three speakers on the subject of White House administrative procedures. Brill, knowing he needed a break from the West Wing pressure, had arranged to stay an additional day and a half as a full participant in the seminar. On returning to Washington, he had used every waking hour to work through the accumulated papers on his own desk. As soon as he finished with the problems that absolutely required his personal action, he would be buzzing for Blair Songster and his other assistants. He'd want reports on problems—such as the Vikingsholm-UNICOR subsidy—that had been farmed out to subordinates before and during his trip to Charlottesville.

Blair Songster knew that she had better have something ready when the call came from Haney Brill. She reviewed her materials, which now included memos of telephone conversations with contacts that Blair had developed in the Bureau of Prisons, Polaris Company, the St. Croix Development Commission, and Karelia Corporation. Blair swiveled her chair to look out the window, across toward Haney's West Wing office. Haney would soon reach the bottom of the pile in his in-basket. If Blair was any judge, Haney would be just about ready to pick up his phone and ask her what she thought about the package of papers from Minnesota.

Questions for Discussion
. . . .

Anton Kurvaszy, Stan Byrne, Blair Songster, and the other actors in this scenario have to make certain decisions based on their estimates of gains and costs to their own institutions. At the same time, they have to think about potential impacts on organizations other than their own. It's a textbook case (literally!) of underdetermination. As they sort out their situations, the characters in the case might find it useful to ask themselves questions like the following ones.

1. What's the story? What are the critical conflicts in the case, and in what ways might they be resolved? Do you see any ways that potential conflicts might be converted to opportunities through joint action?

2. "Sketch a model." Can you pull together the various "subplots" into a simple model that brings the major relationships among the principal figures into view and reveals how they depend on one another?

3. Potential flood-bonus benefits are widely diffused over many citizens of Apostle County, creating a collective action problem (Remember? From Chapter 6?). Would the transaction costs of organizing a St. Croix Watershed Association be so high that it hardly seems worth trying to involve flood-prone citizens in formal discussions of area development plans? How, for their parts, should Stan Byrne and Marilyn Taverner deal with Andy Byce and the flood-prone residents whom he would like to organize? That is, how should Byrne and Taverner respond to the possibility that the flood-zone residents of Apostle County might "free ride" if Polaris and Karelia invest money to raise the head of the dam at Half Day Rill?

4. Which criteria of public assignment (again, from Chapter 6) apply most directly to the provision of emergency medical service? Based on your theory of the proper institutional division of labor, how *in general* would you like to see the EMS function be structured in the United States: Through fully tax-supported public pro-

vision? Complete privatization? Some kind of public-private hybrid? "Discuss and defend"; justify your preference.

5. "Circumstances make the case." Do any special circumstances in the four-county region make you think that your general preference for a particular form of emergency medical organization should be modified for the St. Croix region *in particular?*

6. Suppose you had the time and research support to conduct thorough analyses not only of the projects on Anton Kurvaszy's list but also of the initiatives that Guy Ambrose sees as potential competitors for public funding. How would you decide which efforts from the two lists should be undertaken, assuming that limited funds would require the setting up of priorities among them?

7. How convincing do you find the approach used in contingent value analysis? Would this approach prove useful to Mary Martengrove as the staffer from whom Anton Kurvaszy wants cost-benefit recommendations regarding possible subsidies for EMS upgrading and the Winter Wonderland development? Can you, for each of the projects discussed in the case write-up, explain the possible relevance of a CFA and a CBA? If you were an official responsible for a recommendation or a decision on project financing, under what circumstances would it be most important to see both kinds of analysis?

8. What do you think of Mary Martengrove's estimates of costs and benefits for the EMS proposal (Table 9.10) and for the Winter Wonderland development (Table 9.11)? What numbers would you use when assessing the benefits of lives saved? Does your reading of the Kelman article persuade you that maybe *formal* policy analysis may be inappropriate, even misleading? If so, what other modes of policy evaluation might you consider employing in the EMS and Winter Wonderland evaluations?

9. What level of subsidy or subsidies (if any) would you suggest be funded by the SCDC, and how should any public money be divided in support of EMS upgrading and Winter Wonderland? "Discuss and defend"; justify the approach you favor.

10. Do you regard Congresswoman Ellen Moe and Polaris Company CEO Francis X. Doherty as significant players in this scenario? Are there ways in which their long-standing friendship could be brought into play? Would it, in your opinion, be appropriate to trade on their relationship?

11. What do you think Mary Martengrove's first draft of an SNT should look like? If Blair Songster were asked by Haney Brill to prepare an SNT to structure a meeting of federal officials and interested parties from the St. Croix region, how might Blair's outline differ from Mary's? ("Where you stand depends on where you sit"— and sitting next door to the White House is a lot different from sitting in Larch City's Jackson Building.)

12. What would you, if you were in Blair Songster's position, tell Counsellor to the President Brill when he asks Blair for (*a*) "a summary briefing of the situation up

there in Ellen Moe's district"; *(b)* an explanation of the federal interest—and especially the president's stake, if any—in the situation; and *(c)* a recommendation for approval, rejection, or modification of Warden Smarck's request.

FOR FURTHER READING

An important stock-taking article—a piece that, among other things, suggest why it's important to appreciate the fundamentals of formal policy analysis—is

> Guzzle, Celona, "Essential Skills for Financial Management: Are MPA Students Acquiring the Necessary Competencies?" 45 *Public Administration Review* (November–December 1985), 840.

Among the readily available introductory works on formal policy analysis—excellent introductory sources, all—are

> Quade, E. S., *Analysis for Public Decision Making* (New York: North Holland, 1975); long the basic introductory work, still useful and highly readable.
>
> Stokey, Edith, and Richard Zeckhauser, *A Primer of Policy Analysis* (New York: Norton, 1978).
>
> Weimer, David L., and Aidan R. Vining, *Policy Analysis: Concepts and Practice* (Englewood Cliffs NJ: Prentice-Hall, 1989).

A lucid introduction to cost-benefit analysis is

> Gramlich, Edward, *A Guide to Benefit-Cost Analysis* (Englewood Cliffs NJ: Prentice-Hall, 1990).

For a more advanced—though still accessible—treatment of cost-benefit analysis, with many instructive examples, see

> Keeney, Ralph, and Howard Raiffa, *Decisions with Multiple Objectives: Preferences and Value Tradeoffs* (New York: Wiley, 1976).

The Harlow-Windsor method of subsidy computation, with examples, is developed in easily understood terms in

> Harlow, Kirk C., and Duane Windsor, "Integration of Cost-Benefit and Financial Analysis in Project Evaluation," 48 *Public Administration Review* (September–October 1988), 918.

Excellent references on the specific ethical obligations of an administrator when serving in the analyst-adviser's role are

> Gutmann, Amy, and Dennis Thompson, *Ethics and Politics: Cases and Comments* (Chicago: Nelson-Hall, 1990); see especially chap. 3 ("using citizens as means") and chap. 5 ("the ethics of policy analysis").

McRae, Duncan, and James Wilde, *Policy Analysis for Public Decisions* (Belmont CA: Wadsworth, 1979); especially chaps. 3 and 8.

Wolfe, Charles, "Ethics and Policy Analysis," in Joel Fleischman et al., eds., *Public Duties: The Moral Obligations of Government Office* (Cambridge MA: Harvard U. Press, 1981).

On the evaluation of human life, see—in addition to the article excerpted in the text from the writings of Kip Viscusi (the acknowledged authority on the subject)—

Rhoads, Steven E., "Do Economists Overemphasize Monetary Benefits?" 45 *Public Administration Review* (November–December 1985), 815.

The techniques of formal policy analysis can also, of course, be used to confuse, delay, and obfuscate as well as to clarify issues; see

Jenkins-Smith, Hank, and David Weimer, "Analysis as Retrograde Action: The Case of Strategic Petroleum Reserve," 45 *Public Administration Review* (July–August 1985), 485.

◆ ● ■ ▼ ◆ ● ■ ▼ ◆ ● ■ ▼ ◆ ● ■ ▼ ◆

CHAPTER 10

Making the Human Connection: Motivating the Worker, Serving the Citizen

"Making bureaucracy work" means making it work *accountably*—in compliance with the policies set forth by elected representatives of the people. But it also means that the day-to-day activities in our bureaucracies should be made meaningful to the individuals who actually staff the organizations of industry and government. Is it possible to reconcile workers' yearnings for personal fulfillment with the imperatives of the institution? The question has emerged wherever the large organization has made its appearance, whether in the form of the modern corporation, the mass-production factory, or the sprawling public bureaucracy. Such masters of nineteenth-century social thought as Alexis de Tocqueville, Charles Dickens, and Karl Marx pondered the problems of workplace dehumanization. To this list must be added the name of the great theorist of bureaucracy, Max Weber. Even Frederick Winslow Taylor recognized that an intolerable work environment couldn't be efficient in the long run.

There are those who doubt that hierarchical structures can ever adequately meet human needs. As we saw in our study of classical organizational theory (Chapter 3), the structures envisioned by Max Weber, with their clearly drawn lines of authority and supervision, are meant to ensure workers' compliance with higher orders. Yet—as Weber admitted—impersonal design and the routinization of many bureaucratic procedures tend to undermine humane relationships. Can bureaucracy be given a human face as it appears both to its own members (the bureaucrats themselves) and to the outsiders with whom the bureaucrats come into contact (ordinary citizens, clients, customers)?

SECTION 1 ● ■ ▼ ◆

Motivation in the Modern Organization: The Human Relations Approach

The classical theorists, we've seen, were preoccupied with the problems of direct supervision. They expected to manage employees by commands and standardized rules; they envisioned workplaces in which managers would exercise close surveillance over subordinates. More recent thinkers, in contrast, have focused on the problem of motivating workers—on *worker motivation*. The concern is to foster attitudes that will incline workers toward behavior that's helpful to the organization even in the absence of detailed commands and without close surveillance by superiors. The loosening of external controls—a corollary of the move to more marketlike organizational forms—requires greater attention to the "internal" influences on workers' behavior: What values do employees bring to the workplace? What motivations drive their actions? An organization that is diminished at its core—in terms of its members' morale and commitment—won't even be a very effective tool.

Perhaps the most important twentieth-century stimulus to a style of thinking that's today known as the **human relations approach** came out of a series of experiments in the late 1930s called the *Hawthorne studies*. One purpose of these studies was to subject certain doctrines of Taylor's scientific managers to controlled empirical tests.

The Hawthorne Studies

The Western Electric factory at Hawthorne, Illinois, in suburban Chicago was an equipment-manufacturing division within the AT&T corporate structure. The workers in each of many specialized divisions produced precision parts for assembly into finished telephone sets. An observer might have thought the work tedious and inherently error-prone. Yet the manufacture of reliable equipment—long a premier value in the AT&T scheme—required extreme care by Western Electric employees at every stage in the process. The Hawthorne plant seemed an excellent site at which to study the relationship between working conditions and workers' performance.

A team of visiting researchers found that the Western Electric employees had developed elaborate informal relationships which supplemented, and in some cases virtually replaced, the authority relationships formally prescribed in the AT&T organization charts. In all departments of the plant, the assembly-line workers—not the supervisors—effectively set performance standards for everyone in each of hundreds of small-scale informal organizations. The workers decided among themselves what seemed a fair sharing of the load, how strenuously each member of the group had to labor, and even when a given individual could take time off from work. These standards both set limits to what the bosses could demand and established criteria for the employees. Prudent supervisors rarely interfered with the group's norms, threatened its solidarity, or reversed a decision that had been ratified by its members. The discovery of this dynamic seems to have contributed to the conceptualization of the **zone of acceptance** as an important aspect of employer-employee relationships (see Box 10.1).

The Hawthorne researchers concluded that the scientific managers had seriously overstated the motivational value of physical conditions and economic incentives. It seemed a surprising finding. Logically, the need of owners and subordinates to divide the product of their joint labors implied an unreconcilable opposition of interests: How much of the company's economic surplus should go to profit? How much to wages? The same logic suggested that Frederick Winslow Taylor had been correct when he suggested the piece-rate pay schedule as a way to prevent "soldiering," since piece rates

BOX 10.1 ■■■

The Zone of Acceptance

Workers normally accept positions in organizations expecting to receive orders from superiors. But obedience is conditional. While some conditions may be explicit, written into the employment macrocontract (for example, employers may agree not to prescribe a dress code), others are likely to be informal. Employees gradually develop a sort of common law among themselves which specifies the kinds of commands that their superiors may give them. Workers will obey commands to the extent that they see them as lying within a *zone of indifference*. Chester Barnard—himself a retired senior AT&T executive—coined this term because he observed that most employees are indifferent about choices between any two instructions that lie *within* the zone.* If the boss says "Try it this way," the workers will accept the command and obey; if the boss says "No, do it that way instead," the workers will be just as willing to respond. An order *outside* the zone of indifference, however, will either be disobeyed outright or—if followed at all—followed grudgingly and with possible intent to sabotage.

Because the zone of indifference encompasses all orders that workers accept as legitimate, students of organizations, following Herbert Simon's usage, also refer to it as the **zone of acceptance.**[†] Simon's term probably gives the better description of the phenomenon: the willingness of subordinates to obey the orders they receive from higher authorities.

The zone of acceptance is subject to change over time. The words of the original macrocontract may take on new meanings. Evolving practices among workers may rise to the status of expectations, even "entitlements." Effective managers engage workers in continuous dialogue to ensure that expectations are understood all around and that commands from above will lie within the bounds of the acceptable. In a sense, then, *the effectiveness of direct supervision depends on a successful ongoing process of mutual adjustment.* This fact is consistent with the conception of an organization as a negotiated order, which we discussed in Chapter 3 (Box 3.2).

*The Functions of the Executive (Cambridge MA: Harvard U. Press, 1938), pp. 168–169.

[†]Administrative Behavior (New York: Free Press, 1947), pp. 12, 116.

■■■

would tie workers' wages directly to their individual outputs.[1] But neither the belief in an inherent antagonism between "capital" and "labor" nor Taylor's belief in the efficacy of a more rational incentive scheme proved out at Western Electric.

[1]*Piece-rate pay schedule:* A pay arrangement in which a worker isn't "on salary" but instead is compensated a certain amount per unit of output, the way a seamstress may be paid a fixed sum for every shirtwaist or dress she turns out.

In one set of Hawthorne experiments, researchers modified factors in the workers' environment. The experimenters divided telephone-relay assemblers into two work groups. In one room the physical conditions of work were varied, and workers' responses to the changes were observed. Observations were also taken of the workers in the other room, where conditions remained constant. The researchers found that productivity rose almost irrespective of the direction of change in a particular workplace factor. Higher-intensity lighting increased output; a switch to a lower intensity produced an additional increment of improvement; and, amazingly, a reversion back to higher intensity further improved—rather than degraded—worker performance. Even more remarkably, productivity gradually rose even among the workers in the control group, for whom conditions hadn't changed.

The Hawthorne researchers concluded that it wasn't, after all, physical and economic conditions (the "organization of technics") that determined productivity. Rather, the "organization of human relations" best explained the spurts in productivity that occurred under these carefully controlled conditions. Workers responded to managerial displays of *human* concern. Within broad limits, what mattered to workers was the belief that their bosses were interested in them, as symbolized by the variations that were being made in the environmental factors of work. Members of both the experimental group and the control group knew that they were "special." What made them so wasn't changes or constancy in illumination levels but their membership in a cohort of workers whose every act was being studied and whose every response was being evaluated. Hence **Hawthorne effect** refers to the response of workers to an expression of supervisory interest in their welfare.

The Hawthorne researchers' discovery was an important contribution to management studies. Still, it should be pointed out that subsequent experiments have shown that Hawthorne effects may produce only temporary responses. Permanent productivity improvements usually need more than merely symbolic displays of human interest. Often, productivity improvements require managers to back their expressions of concern with tangible incentives (higher pay) or to vary workers' physical circumstances in basic ways, such as through technological improvements.

The Rise of the Human Relations Approach

It would be difficult to overstate the impact of the Hawthorne studies on management theory and practice. The Western Electric findings were probably the most powerful stimuli to the search that ensued for ways to humanize the workplace. This search gave rise from the 1940s through the 1960s to a burgeoning literature. No single contribution to the literature of the human relations approach has been more influential than the one from which our next reading selection comes. We turn now to Douglas McGregor's explication of his famed *Theory Y,* with its roots in the doctrines of the clinical psychologist Abraham Maslow and its broader grounding in a philosophy of history.

McGregor insisted that organizational relationships must reflect the physical and psychological realities of a given stage in the the development of industrial civilization. Just as the industrial workers decribed by nineteenth-century writers such as Tocqueville, Dickens, and Marx experienced conditions fundamentally different from those of their forebears (the feudal serfs who had worked the land in medieval times), McGregor argued that the average clerical or manufacturing worker of today labors under conditions fundamentally different from those experienced by the assembly-line hand of an earlier generation. Changed historical conditions change workers' needs, and hence their motivations. McGregor's thesis contradicted the classical theorists' belief that it should be possible to develop a generic theory of organization, true for all humans in all circumstances and all eras.

Douglas McGregor on Theory X and Theory Y

The conventional conception of management's task in harnessing human energy to organizational requirements can be stated broadly in terms of three propositions. In order to avoid the complications introduced by a label, I shall call this set of propositions "Theory X":

1. Management is responsible for organizing the elements of productive enterprise—money, materials, equipment, people—in the interest of economic ends.

2. With respect to people this is a process of directing their efforts, motivating them, controlling their actions, modifying their behavior to fit the needs of the organization.

3. Without this active intervention by management, people would be passive—even resistant—to organizational needs. They must therefore be persuaded, rewarded, punished, controlled—their activities must be directed. . . .

Behind this conventional theory there are several additional beliefs—less explicit, but widespread:

4. The average man is by nature indolent—he works as little as possible.

5. He lacks ambition, dislikes responsibility, prefers to be led.

6. He is inherently self-centered, indifferent to organizational needs.

7. He is by nature resistant to change.

8. He is gullible, not very bright, the ready dupe of the charlatan and the demagogue.

The human side of economic enterprise today is fashioned from propositions and beliefs such as these. . . .

The findings which are beginning to emerge from the social sciences challenge this whole set of beliefs about man and human nature and about the task of management. The evidence is far from conclusive, certainly, but it is suggestive. . . .

Perhaps the best way to indicate that the conventional approach of management is inadequate is to consider the subject of motivation. In discussing this subject I will draw heavily on the work of my colleague, Abraham Maslow of Brandeis University. His is the most fruitful approach I know. . . .

Physiological and Safety Needs

Man is a wanting animal—as soon as one of his needs is satisfied, another appears in its place. This process is unending. It continues from birth to death.

Man's needs are organized in a series of levels—a hierarchy of importance. At the lowest level, but preeminent in importance when they are thwarted, are his physiological needs. Man lives by bread alone, when there is no bread. Unless the circumstances are unusual, his needs for love, for status, for recognition are inoperative when his stomach has been empty for a while. But when he eats regularly and adequately, hunger ceases to be an important need. The sated man has hunger only in the sense that a full bottle has emptiness. The same is true of the other physiological needs of man—for rest, exercise, shelter, protection from the elements.

A satisfied need is not a motivator of behavior! This is a fact of profound significance. It is a fact which is regularly ignored in the conventional approach to the management of people. I shall return to it later. . . .

When the physiological needs are reasonably satisfied, needs at the next higher level begin to dominate man's behavior—to motivate him. These are called safety needs. They are needs for protection against danger, threat, deprivation....

Social Needs

When man's physiological needs are satisfied and he is no longer fearful about his physical welfare, his social needs become important motivators of his behavior—for belonging, for association, for acceptance by his fellows, for giving and receiving friendship and love.

Management knows today of the existence of these needs, but it often assumes quite wrongly that they represent a threat to the organization. Many studies have demonstrated that the tightly knit, cohesive work group may, under proper conditions, be far more effective than an equal number of separate individuals in achieving organizational goals.

Yet management, fearing group hostility to its own objectives, often goes to considerable lengths to control and direct human efforts in ways that are inimical to the natural "groupiness" of human beings. When man's social needs—and perhaps his safety needs, too—are thus thwarted, he behaves in ways which tend to defeat organizational objectives. He becomes resistant, antagonistic, uncooperative. But this behavior is a consequence, not a cause.

Ego Needs

Above the social needs—in the sense that they do not become motivators until lower needs are reasonably satisfied—are the needs of greatest significance to management and to man himself. They are the egoistic needs, and they are of two kinds:

1. Those needs that relate to one's self-esteem—needs for self-confidence, for independence, for achievement, for competence, for knowledge.
2. Those needs that relate to one's reputation—needs for status, for recognition, for appreciation, for the deserved respect of one's fellows....

The typical industrial organization offers few opportunities for the satisfaction of these egoistic needs to people at lower levels in the hierarchy. The con-

ventional methods of organizing work, particularly in mass production industries, give little heed to these aspects of human motivation. If the practices of scientific management were deliberately calculated to thwart these needs—which, of course, they are not—they could hardly accomplish this purpose better than they do.

Self-Fulfillment Needs

Finally—a capstone, as it were, on the hierarchy of man's needs—there are what we may call the needs for self-fulfillment. These are the needs for realizing one's own potentialities, for continued self-development, for being creative in the broadest sense of that term....

[M]anagement finds itself in an odd position. The high standard of living created by our modern technological knowhow provides quite adequately for the satisfaction of physiological and safety needs. The only significant exception is where management practices have not created confidence in a "fair break"—and thus where safety needs are thwarted. But by making possible the satisfaction of low-level needs, management has deprived itself of the ability to use as motivators the devices on which conventional theory has taught it to rely—rewards, promises, incentives, or threats and other coercive devices.

Neither Hard nor Soft

The philosophy of management by direction and control—*regardless of whether it is hard of soft*—is inadequate to motivate because the human needs on which this approach relies are today unimportant motivators of behavior. Direction and control are essentially useless in motivating people whose important needs are social and egoistic. Both the hard and the soft approach fail today because they are simply irrelevant to the situation.

People, deprived of opportunities to satisfy at work the needs which are now important to them, behave exactly as we might predict—with indolence, passivity, resistance to change, lack of responsibility, willingness to follow the demagogue, unreasonable demands for economic benefits. It would seem that we are caught in a web of our own weaving.

In summary, then, of these comments about motivation:

Management by direction and control—whether implemented with the hard, the soft, or the firm but fair approach—fails under today's conditions to provide effective motivation of human efforts toward organizational objectives. It fails because direction and control are useless methods of motivating people whose physiological and safety needs are reasonably satisfied and whose social, egoistic, and self-fulfillment needs are predominant.

For these and many other reasons, we require a different theory of the task of managing people based on more adequate assumptions about human nature and human motivation. I am going to be so bold as to suggest the broad dimensions of such a theory. Call it "Theory Y," if you will.

1. Management is responsible for organizing the elements of productive enterprise—money, materials, equipment, people—in the interest of economic ends.

2. People are *not* by nature passive or resistant to organizational needs. They have become so as a result of experience in organizations.

3. The motivation, the potential for development, the capacity for assuming responsibility, the readiness to direct behavior toward organizational goals are all present in people. Management does not put them there. It is a responsibility of management of make it possible for people to recognize and develop these human characteristics for themselves.

4. The essential task of management is to arrange organizational conditions and methods of operation so that people can achieve their own goals *best* by directing *their own* efforts toward organizational objectives.

From Douglas McGregor, "The Human Side of Enterprise," in Bennis and Schein, eds. *Leadership and Motivation: Essays of Douglas McGregor* (Cambridge MA: MIT Press, 1966), pp. 5–16.

The Organizational Culture Approach

Douglas McGregor's closing admonition bears repeating:

> The essential task of management is to arrange organizational conditions and methods of operation so that people can achieve their own goals *best* by directing *their own* efforts toward organizational objectives.

The most obvious way to attain congruency between individual and organizational objectives is by fostering a sense of identification between the person and the agency in which he or she works. The aim in this kind of effort is to achieve coordination of all employees' activities by standardizing the values that animate workers as they make their everyday decisions. *Coordination by standardization* in this special, psychological sense is a major theme in contemporary organizational thought. When this form of coordination succeeds, it can release workers' energies, galvanize commitment, and achieve direction without coercion. When overdone, however, it can amount to brainwashing—a kind of programming of human behavior that critics liken to robotization.

Even the administrative managers recognized the potentialities of coordination by standardization in this special sense. Luther Gulick admitted that coordination could be achieved both psychologically, by "the dominance of an idea," and organizationally, through "a structure of authority."[2] But Gulick and his colleagues never stressed the *human factor,* as it's generally called, thinking as they did that the major frontier in administrative theory still lay in the development of rational structures and operational procedures (the "canons of efficiency"). It remained for writers such as Chester Barnard and Herbert Simon, both of whom faulted the classical thinkers for their narrowness of outlook, to bring coordination through psychological standardization into a central position in administrative study. The ideas of Barnard and Simon matured in work of the sociologist Philip Selznick, usually credited as the seminal contributor to the modern theory of **organizational culture.**

Selznick's *Leadership in Administration,* published in 1957, contained an explicit attack on the administrative managers' teaching that universal canons of efficiency could be applied to any organization. Selznick stressed the importance of emotional and symbolic factors in all human experience; he also argued that the emotional and symbolic value of an organizational experience is essentially unique rather than universal.

What we observe in the actual functioning of a typical business firm or government agency, Selznick claimed, are two quite-different but related systems, the *organization,* properly so-called, and the *institution.* (For now, we'll add quotation marks around these terms to emphasize the special sense in which Selznick uses them.) The "organization" is instrumental, a formal structure of offices and roles, rationally engineered to *achieve efficiency.* The "institution" is that aspect of the system in which participants *find meaning.* The "institution" consists of the framework of symbols and values to which members commit themselves emotionally, not just rationally. Selznick contended that what is truly institutional—the basis of employees' loyalty and purpose—is also specific to the time, place, and membership of the group. Hence, although a given organizational paradigm may be used as the underlying template for many different kinds of structures (there are thousands of structures we recognize as bureaucracies; and thousands more in which we discern the basic pattern of the market), every "institution" is unique.

The institutional leader is the person who can cultivate a shared view among workers of the nature, rightness, and importance of the organization's principal tasks. These tasks, together with the values they embody, define what's special about the organization—what sets it apart from all other organizations. As such, these tasks define the **distinctive competence** of the organization. The faithful performance of these tasks can serve as the basis for collective pride. Selznick called the cultivation of meaning **value infusion.** Workers in a value-infused environment accept and act on common premises for their everyday actions. (Selznick acknowledged the sources of this "common premises" concept in the writings of Barnard and Simon.) Employees in a value-infused work context will try to advance the agenda of the organization and will perform its critical tasks up to standard even if their self-interest, narrowly defined, urges them to shirk or subvert, and even if their day-to-day activities can't be measured or easily monitored.

Underlying the theory of value infusion is the conviction that most men and women aspire to more than mere personal gain. The wellsprings of human motivation are spiritual and emotional as well as material and rational. (As that genius of the dis-

[2]In fairness, it should be noted that Gulick and his collaborator, Lyndahl Urwick, also recognized the importance of the Hawthorne experiments, to the extent of including a summary of the Western Electric studies in their famous symposium volume *Papers on the Science of Administration* (see the bibliographical reference at the end of the chapter).

cerning intelligence, Blaise Pascal, once observed, "The heart has reasons that the reason doesn't know."[3]) The organization in the sense of a rationalized structure can't answer the yearning of the human heart for meaningful work, but a value-infused environment—an "institution" in Selznick's sense—can.

Selznick's doctrine of value infusion has become a staple of modern administrative study. It underlies the recognition that, in order to flourish, a firm or public agency needs more than a cunningly devised scheme of incentives (such as a pay scale that rewards productivity rather than mere seniority). An organization, whether a private firm or a public agency, also needs a sense of common dedication among its employees. Goal diversity and moral hazard are less likely to emerge in an organization with a well-developed corporate culture.

On the other hand, too strong an organizational culture may have disadvantages, especially when external contingencies require members to abandon an existing conception of the institutional mission. Workers who have internalized one set of values may resist ideas that don't fit into the established patterns of thought. Programmed to think one way, employees may ignore signals of institutional trouble and may fight change even when the need for adaptation would be evident to individuals whose outlooks are less strongly shaped by a mature organizational culture. This kind of recalcitrance can be considered as an example of the *trained incapacity* that Robert Merton analyzed more than four decades ago in his study of the bureaucratic personality (the first reading excerpt in Chapter 4).

SECTION 2
● ■ ▼ ◆

Service Professionals: Making the Human Connection

Many cases in public administration touch broad issues of public policy. Others deal with relatively impersonal questions of organizational structure or procedure. But perhaps the most important cases are the ones that involve the seemingly narrow and personal concerns of specific people—people with names (not just Social Security numbers), people with faces (not just manila folders in some bureaucrat's cabinet) . . . above all, people with worries about the way they're going to be treated by the representatives of a distant government bureaucracy.

Ironically, the hardest contacts to humanize may involve the very officials whose roles bring them into constant touch with some of the most vulnerable of our citizens. There's always the danger that police officers, social caseworkers, on-site inspectors and other regulatory agents, clerks in state motor vehicle departments and federal passport offices, and others who work in face-to-face instead of "paper-to-paper" environments will become inured to the troubles of the citizens with whom they deal. The literature is filled with stories of worker burnout, inhuman caseloads, excessive rule-boundedness, impossible demands for impartial treatment, and the depressing conditions in which "faceless bureaucrats" so often must interact with citizens (symbolized by the sparse and grungy physical appearance of many motor vehicle departments and welfare offices).

Yet the call to service—one of the traditional appeals of government work—has become increasingly powerful in recent decades. It's not hard to understand why the

[3]*Pensées* (Thoughts), No. 229.

role of a service provider should have a peculiar capacity to inspire a sense of fulfillment in public administrators. Set against the forces of depersonalization in the modern organization are countervailing impulses not merely to serve but also to *care*. The urge to help is one of the most basic of responses. Literally millions of public jobs today give officials the opportunities to satisfy that most decent of human drives. The question isn't whether the negative or positive forces will prevail but how the process of value infusion can be used in public agencies—especially in human-service agencies—to ensure that the forces of humanization will win.

The Coming of the Service Professional

The Progressives seem to have envisioned a corps of public administrators consisting mostly of clerks in the bottom and middle ranks of government agencies and experts in such technical fields as accountancy, engineering, forestry, and so forth at the top. Absent from this clerks-and-experts picture is the **service professional** who works in immediate contact with citizens—often with some of the most needy and dependent citizens in our society. The typical service professional is neither a program implementer in the normal sense nor an adjudicator; rather, today's service professional is a caregiver, a comforter, a counselor—a "helper." The citizen who receives the service is a patient or client, not an anonymous citizen standing in line or an impersonal entry on some government mailing list.

Service professionals have been represented in the ranks of public administrators since colonial days. Public schoolteachers probably head the list. But only in relatively recent decades have service professionals in many other specialties become civil servants in large numbers. The 1930s saw a vast expansion in welfare-oriented programs, the prototypes of today's efforts in "family building," job training and counseling, and a variety of programs in support of families with dependent children (*welfare* as the term is commonly used). The Great Society programs of the 1960s added a whole new set of service-oriented roles to the public service. The specially trained public schoolteacher who has charge of learning-disabled students, the young lawyer who serves indigent clients in a federally funded legal aid office, the state unemployment counselor on whom laid-off citizens depend for job-placement services are all guided primarily by a **service paradigm.** As the term suggests, the central value in this paradigm is service *as measured by the needs of the client or patient,* rather than by orders from above or an abstract judgment of "deservingness."

Of course, a service professional who works as a government official (in contrast with a therapist or lawyer in private practice) can have a public obligation to serve clients only after legislators have launched a program, established an organization to administer it, and provided for the salaries of the agency's employees. Nevertheless, the emphasis in the service professional's role is on the client (or patient, or applicant for help) rather than on the program.

A fundamental tenet in most counseling, therapeutic, and other "helping" practices is the nonjudgmental posture of the professional: The deservingness or moral culpability of the client—often key considerations, as we saw in Chapter 4, for administrators when acting in adjudicative roles—are irrelevant when the obligation is client service. The helper must take whatever action, within reason, will best meet the needs of the client, patient, or claimant for service. The client-centered orientation also distinguishes the work of the service professional from that of the traditional program implementer. Many government lawyers, chaplains, counselors, doctors, and therapists feel more compellingly bound by their client obligations and the **best practice**[+] of their professions than by the duty to obey higher orders. The same goes for many government employees in the fields of public education and in the criminal justice system. In large numbers, workers in these fields regard themselves as service professionals first, and program implementers only secondarily.

[+]*Best practice:* In most professions, certain preferred problem-solving approaches and "treatment protocols" have been developed to guide practitioners. These methods include "generally accepted accounting principles," "best engineering practice," "medical practice guidelines," and so forth, depending on the field. In general, a professional is obliged to know and follow the best practice of the field. In our reading selection in Box 4.1, Jerry Mashaw refers to this obligation when he notes that the proper defense of a service provider's actions, when challenged, typically hinges not on adherence to an abstract code of values or obedience to higher orders, as in the judgmental and executive paradigms (discussed in Chapters 4 and 8, respectively), but on his or her use of "sound professional judgment."

CHAPTER READING   ▼ ▼ ▼

In the early 1970s Jeffrey Prottas, a graduate student in a joint Harvard-MIT public policy program, conducted a now-famous study of street-level bureaucrats in four Boston-area social work agencies. Prottas's account of his findings takes us into a world that most Americans never experience firsthand, the world of "tenuously controlled chaos" where frontline public officials deal daily with individuals in deeply troubled circumstances.

One might have thought that the employees of local welfare departments, public housing offices, veterans' hospitals, and inner-city emergency medical facilities would be guided unambiguously by the value of client service. But Prottas's study demonstrated that the demands of routine program implementation, administrative adjudication, and nonjudgmental assistance to clients quickly become confounded. Try to identify some of the ways in which the program implementer's, adjudicator's, and service provider's roles—although distinguishable in theory—jumbled one into another. How did the circumstances of the action and conditions of the agents create problems of extreme difficulty (if not downright impossible problems) by bringing multiple roles and conflicting paradigms of obligation into play?

The Day-to-Day Work of Street-Level Bureaucrats: The Massachusetts Welfare Department

Jeffrey Prottas

The limiting feature is boredom and the fear of being bureaucratized. Workers do not think of themselves as clerks or bureaucrats but as as social workers. They look for opportunities to do something other than the routine processing of simple cases, but the preferred cases are difficult to generalize about because workers are hesitant to admit that they prefer certain clients to others; this would be judgmental, the gravest sin in the social worker's cosmology.

This is a story about magicians. But is it not a story about old crones in secluded hovels turning princes into frogs. It is about modern, mundane magicians, with powers more relevant to urban crises than to sleeping princesses. Times have changed for magicians as for everyone else. The outputs of vast pharmaceutical laboratories can change princes into frogs (or anything else) far more easily and quickly than can even the most skilled old crone. What is called for in modern magic is mass marketing—the capacity to change a great number of citizens into a limited number of creatures economically and efficiently. For such magic 9 A.M. to 5 P.M. is a more propitious time than the full of the moon, and printed forms conjure better than bat-wings—and are more readily available. These modern magicians are organization men and women. They work for welfare departments, police departments, hospitals, housing authorities, courts, and so forth, and if they can't change a citizen into a frog they can certainly do a goat and will generally try for a sheep. These practitioners of modern magic are frequently called bureaucrats—street-level bureaucrats (but who knows what Merlin was called behind his back). Their occult task is to turn ordinary citizens into "clients" (or "suspects," "patients," or any other trade name for client). . . .

The Welfare Department as a Research Site

The welfare department is a huge bureaucracy with a great effect on the lives of its clients. Moreover it is in many ways an archetypical bureaucracy. It is rule-bounded and hierarchical in structure. The discretion granted its street-level bureaucrat is, at least formally, quite minimal—yet even a short period of observation indicates that considerable discretion is in fact exercised by its street-level bureaucrats. In this sense it was chosen as a "best case," a highly bureaucratic organization with little formal street-level discretion but substantial actual discretion.

Another consideration that made the welfare department an attractive research site was the quasi-professional status of its street-level bureaucrats. Welfare workers are called, and think of themselves as, social workers. Indeed, the very first paragraph of

their contract with the department states "all employees in the representation unit have professional status and all work assignments are of a professional nature." In reality, a Master of Social Work is very rarely encountered in the department. . . .

The work units of a local office are primarily of two kinds: intake units and district units. The responsibility of the intake unit is to accept and process applications from new clients. When the duties of the intake worker have been completed the case is passed on to a district unit where it becomes the responsibility of another welfare worker, who becomes the client's social worker and so responsible for all aspects of the client's case. . . .

In one office an intake worker would handle perhaps 6 or 8 new cases a week, in another 12 would be typical. The larger offices were the busier.

The clientele of the offices also differed. Of the six, two were in white ethnic areas, one in a transitional area, one in a predominantly black area, one in a black and Spanish-speaking area, and one had an unusual percentage of General Relief cases (who tend to be single white males). Everywhere the workers were overwhelmingly white, college-educated, young, and female.

Generally differences among clients had little impact on worker behavior. The only pattern that did emerge was related to social class. Workers tended to be more sympathetic to applicants whom they characterized as "working class" than to "poor" applicants. The operational distinction was obscure but revolved around work history and previous experience on welfare. Such clients also tended to be deferential to workers and ignorant of the welfare system. As these characteristics are highly regarded by workers for work-related reasons, it is difficult to be certain of the balance between work-related and social preferences. . . .

Work in the Welfare Department. . . .

It is the primary duty of the intake unit to receive applicants and determine eligibility. This involves receiving, verifying, and processing new applicants for welfare grants. Under the present system there are two general categories of aid administered through the Massachusetts Welfare Department: General Relief and Aid for Families with Dependent Children (AFDC). AFDC is the largest program and is federally subsidized. It is largely limited to female-headed households with children under the age of eighteen. Compared to General Relief its benefits are generous and its rules complex. The complexity of its rules is largely a function of the great number of subsidiary benefits built into the system through which eligible clients can receive special additional aid. For an intake worker it differs from General Relief primarily because it takes considerably longer to receive and process the application. General Relief is a state-funded program designed primarily to serve unemployed single men, or unemployed men and women without children. . . .

Gaining Access.   From the client's point of view, gaining access is what the intake unit is all about. . . . For the client the decision can always be understood in terms of making a request or desisting from doing so. In some cases that decision is spontaneous (based on information or needs beyond the worker's ability to affect) but in many cases the client's decisions are not made without regard for the behavior of the intake worker. The worker provides (or fails to provide) information on which to base decisions and also provides clues to the way requests will be received, and the likelihood and value of any benefits that might flow from those requests. . . .

Intake Worker.   It is the job of the intake worker to properly categorize the new applicant. The formal categorization of an applicant has several components. The first and the simplest is the initial determination of eligibility for the core category of the department (either AFDC or General Relief). The remaining components involve determinations of eligibility for the numerous special categories that further subdivide the primary one. Thus some AFDC clients receive food stamps and some do not, some receive special diet grants and some do not, some receive new furniture and some do not. It is the task of the intake worker to make these decisions. . . .

The intake unit operates under a great number of rules defining procedures and has numerous invari-

able and routine responsibilities. Yet the content of the workday is highly uncertain since it depends on the number and circumstances of the applicants who apply. Applicants may be compliant and cooperative or aggressive and demanding; the quality of the day depends on such variations and the variations cannot be anticipated. . . .

It is impossible to say how long a typical interview will take. As a rule AFDC interviews are substantially longer than General Relief applications, but the complexity of individual cases and the attitudes of individual applicants introduce large variations. Moreover, there are constant interruptions from other clients on the telephone and from other workers in person. Some interviews are interrupted as many as ten times. Even at that, the initial interview is often the longest single piece of time a worker will donate to a case. After the initial interview a worker will rarely spend more than twenty minutes at a stretch on any one case. The actual processing of a case is done in bits and pieces and strung out over a period of four to five weeks. The overall impression is one of tenuously controlled chaos. Workers are always behind in their paperwork and always struggling to catch up on their backlog of cases. . . .

The Initial Interview: Basic Eligibility Determination.   The standard application form is the bureaucracy's primary tool for the routinization of the intake worker's job. In theory the form is self-explanatory and unambiguous; it can be filled out by the applicant alone. In practice it cannot. It is too long and the intent of the questions too unclear. Of course the intent of the questions is perfectly clear to the intake worker because he knows the use to be made of the answers. For this reason the form is highly routine for the worker and standardizes much of basic eligibility determination. It is also characteristic of this form that the applicant's answers to certain critical questions must be supported by certain documents. This has the dual effect of minimizing the worker's ability to interpret applicant responses and of putting the primary burden of completing the application on the applicant, as applicants must obtain the documents on their own. In this way the exchange of information between worker and applicant is highly stylized with regard to basic eligibility determination. The worker poses the question required by the form and the applicant must respond with a specific piece of information.

The Application Form: Ritual as a Limit on Discretion.

The catechism of the application form allows little variation in the players' parts and this is its intent. Yet even here a certain element of variation can be introduced.

The first section of the AFDC application is related to children, specifically, their number and ages. The AFDC grant is a function of these facts, or rather it is a function of those that can be documented by birth certificates. . . . The second proof an applicant must provide is an up-to-date rent receipt. This, like birth certificates, is documentation and so has an unambiguous bureaucratic meaning. . . . The worker does have certain responsibilities and alternatives with regard to rent receipts and these serve to emphasize the largely ritualistic nature of the rules. What constitutes a valid rent receipt is largely up to the intake workers. . . . The last sections of the application form deal with applicant's economic situation. . . .

Applicants rarely compartmentalize their circumstances in quite the same way as the welfare department. They often wish to respond to questions in ways that frequently do not answer and almost invariably go beyond the question asked. To some degree workers are inclined to let them tell their story. Intake workers think of themselves as social workers and generally wish to know something about their clients and their clients' problems. It is during the exchange of this sort of information that workers form a judgment about the applicant and that judgment determines how much information they will give to the applicant and how much extra effort they will be willing to expend on that applicant's case. . . .

[T]he worker does not want to have to respond to demands or questions from the applicant that will substantially complicate the processing of the case or lead to conflict. The most common and easiest way for an intake worker to control the interview with the applicant is to fall back on his official responsibilities. The worker emphasizes that the application form must be completed and that it will eventually cover all the areas the applicant wished to discuss. In

this way the applicant can be cut off or directed without the worker taking personal sponsibility. . . .

In any interaction it is possible to raise the cost of continuing the interaction by making the other person uncomfortable or by showing a negative attitude toward him. The intake worker is in a particularly good position to do this (or its reverse, inducing gratitude and cooperation by considerate behavior) because the worker represents a public body with the "color of law" and society's blessing. Moreover, the applicant has come to the worker for a benefit and so comes as a supplicant. This gives the intake workers a tremendous advantage in the personal elements of control in interactions. (All this is aside from the advantages, to be discussed shortly, that result from superior knowledge.) . . .

The practice of informally rejecting applications is common in all the offices. While taking an application the worker may discover that the applicant is ineligible for aid, perhaps having too many assets or being eligible for veterans benefits or disability. Rather than accept the application and then process it as rejected after the documentation proves ineligibility, the worker simply informs the applicant that he or she will be found ineligible and that there is no reason to submit an application. Generally the applicant will acquiesce, either having understood the worker's argument or because he or she has simply understood the conclusion, that no money will be forthcoming. This is, of course, illegal. No investigation was made, no documents gathered, and no formal rejection, with the opportunity to appeal, will be made. Workers know this. They know that the citizen has a right to apply but they feel that it is reasonable for them to try to dissuade him from doing so if the only result will be pointless filling out of forms and setting up of files.

By this procedure intake workers have set up an informal pre-screening routine. . . .

Distribution of Special Services.

The system of welfare grants is very complicated, especially in the area of special programs to which some, but not all, applications are entitled. These programs can represent a considerable amount of money for a recipient and, in many cases, workers have de facto discretion in the distribution of these services.

The amount of discretion varies with the amount of information the applicant has about the welfare system, and with the number of recipients receiving the special grant. For example, some grants are not part of the basic AFDC aid package, but are being received by so many clients that their absence will cause a supervisor to question the workers. The food stamp program is of this type.

The eligibility requirements of the food stamp program are submitted with those of the AFCD program. Therefore all AFDC recipients are eligible for food stamps. The value of food stamps is so clear that few recipients decline to apply. . . . The program is so widely used that the worker has very little discretion over its distribution.

This is in marked contrast to the worker's role in many other special programs. Many of the grant categories of the welfare department apply to only a small percentage of clients. In those cases few clients are knowledgeable enough to request the grant and their absence (absence in any given case) is not cause for supervisor concern.

In many ways the supplemental medical diet program is the most important special program distributed by the intake worker. In practice, if not in theory, it is highly discretionary. This program is designed to supplement the basic grant of those clients who have a medical problem requiring a special diet. It is a very generous program by welfare standards and can increase a client's grant by as much as 15 percent. The primary eligibility requirement is the possession of a form, signed by a doctor, attesting to the client's (or her children's) medical need. Intake workers can easily steer an applicant to a clinic or a doctor whose sympathy for welfare clients is well known. Such an attitude is not at all uncommon, especially in free clinics. In these clinics the doctors will sign the diet form if the flimsiest medical basis can be invented.

. . . The only check on the worker is from the client, and, to a lesser degree, from the doctor. The worker's influence is attenuated just to the degree that the applicant's knowledge matches his own. If the applicant knows the rules and the tendencies of local clinics as well as the worker she can proceed regardless of the worker's attitude—but this amount of knowledge is rare. . . .

Another area where the intake workers exercise considerable discretion is the computation of income of AFDC applicants. A certain amount of that income is deductible from the applicant's grant and so what is considered income can be very important. Income from a regular job is, more or less, inevitably included, but occasional income from irregular or part-time work may not be if the worker does not press the applicant to report it all.

On many occasions workers will clearly signal clients they wish to help that they do not wish to be told about minor occasional income. Aside from any other considerations, such income greatly complicates grant computation. . . .

The Priorities of the Intake Worker. The formal expectations of the welfare department on the intake worker have a schizophrenic character. The rigidity of many of the eligibility rules is designed to assure a high degree of uniformity in the treatment of applicants. In the apparent interests of equity all clients are expected to respond to a standard series of tests in standardized ways. If this policy were carried to its logical conclusion, the discretion of the intake worker would be limited to acting or failing to act as a facilitator in the process of obtaining documents and proofs. However there is another force at work which represents the desire to not only treat all applicants alike, but to treat each applicant according to the applicant's individual merits and needs. This is manifested in the tremendous complexity of the rules and the multitude of special programs and exceptions. These complexities have two results: the worker, who has access to information about the rules, is able to dispense that information differentially and so, on his own discretion, affect the distribution of the department's programs. At the same time this complexity reduces the intake worker's accountability to superiors. The requirement that benefits be tailored to the unique needs of the client makes it impossible to judge the appropriateness of variations among applications without knowledge of their unique characteristics. The intake worker's superiors do not interact directly with applicants and so are dependent on the intake worker for information about clients. . . .

"All Things Not Being Equal." All things being equal intake workers express a preference for simple cases over complicated ones, but sometimes all things are not equal. In fact the limiting feature to this preference is boredom and the fear of being bureaucratized. As mentioned earlier, intake workers do not think of themselves as clerks or bureaucrats but as as social workers. They look for opportunities to behave as social workers, which means an opportunity to do something other than the routine processing of simple cases. For this reason all workers will spend more time and effort on some cases than the minimum they could get away with.

These preferred cases are difficult to generalize about, partly because workers are hesitant to admit that they prefer certain clients to others; this would be judgmental, the gravest sin in the social worker's cosmology. In accordance with social worker jargon the only differences that workers will admit to as an explanation for the undeniable differences in the treatment of different cases is "need."

But in the context of the intake worker's daily activities "need" has at least two meanings. The simplest refers to real differences in the situation of applicants; some children are sick and must have special diets, some families have no beds to sleep on, no pots to cook in. These are real needs and although they may be responded to to greater or lesser degrees, intake workers are, on the whole, serious about their responsibilities and these needs are reflected in the worker's efforts. But when these needs are broadly similar, there remains another sort of need which influences how much personalized attention an applicant will receive. In these roughly comparable cases differences in need reflect the applicant's apparent inability to look out for her own interests and her predilection to accept the worker's help as a gift and not merely her due. Ignorance of departmental processes is a precondition for demonstrating helplessness. Applicants who have these characteristics can generally expect a sympathetic hearing, good quality information, and even a little extra effort from an intake worker.

An excellent example . . . was the treatment of an AFDC applicant from Virginia. This applicant was very pleasant and soft-spoken, answered all questions with apparent candor, allowed the worker to direct the interview, and accepted without question the worker's judgments. Her situation was complicated: she had been on welfare in Virginia and so the department needed documentation from them that the case was closed without incident. (The fact that the applicant ingenuously admitted to having still been on welfare in Virginia just prior to leaving was proof to the worker that she was honest, ignorant of the system, and so not trying to play on the worker's trust.) The normal procedure in these cases is for the applicant to write to her worker in Virginia asking that the proper notification be sent to the worker in Massachusetts. This can be expected to take some time.

In common with many AFDC applicants awaiting final approval this client was having trouble obtaining housing. In this case an opportunity existed to obtain low-cost housing if the application could be quickly finalized. The case worker went to extraordinary lengths to facilitate the process. She repeatedly called Virginia to get them to send the necessary form, she provided the landlord with assurance that the client would be eligible, and so forth.

Finally, when it proved impossible to get a response from Virginia in time to obtain the low-cost housing, the worker simply went ahead without it! She told her supervisor that she had had verbal assurance from Virginia that the forms were in transit. She processed the application in one day (four to six weeks being typical) and attained the supervisor's signature the same day (two weeks being typical). Of course this is an extreme case but lesser examples are common. For "good" applicants explanations are longer, information clearer, and the benefit of the doubt available.

Applicants with contrasting attributes receive contrasting treatment. Aggressive applicants who seem to know the ropes are mistrusted by intake workers. Aggressiveness takes some of the initiative from the worker and implies that benefits received will be accepted as earned and not as conferred. Moreover, workers do not feel that these applicants are as needy because they appear quite capable of protecting their own interests and so the worker need not be as concerned with doing so.

Worse than a merely aggressive attitude is aggression combined with knowledgeability. It allows the applicant to make requests that cannot easily be ignored and it can make it harder to keep the case simple. Moreover, knowledge implies the possibility of using the worker in a manipulative fashion. If the "correct" answers are known it is possible that the applicant is conning the worker. Being conned is an indication of inexperience and an inability to judge clients and so is very threatening to workers. . . .

The Number of Rules

Because public service bureaucracies are concerned with numerous or complex characteristics of their clientele, tremendous situational variation exists in the process of categorizing clients. As such organizations have a very strong commitment to "distributive justice," they naturally are constrained to issue rules designed to regularize the categorization in as many cases as possible. This means that they must produce rules saying that if X situation pertains then the street-level bureaucrat must take Y action. Because the relevant client characteristics are numerous and complicated, and generally presented in idiosyncratic ways, many such rules are needed. This represent nothing more (or less) than the agency's attempt to insure that its definition of "equality" prevails, and further, to see that such equals receive equal treatment. For example, in the case of a welfare department, two applicants, one with a five-year-old child and the other with a six-year-old child are entitled to the same grant payment. Yet an applicant with a seventeen-year-old is not "equal" to the other two but falls into a different category and hence is entitled to different treatment. In pursuit of justice, therefore, many public service bureaucracies produce very large numbers of rules. . . .

. . . In extreme cases the core rules of an agency may become so demanding that the street-level bureaucrat's chronic inability to respond will cause an official change in procedures. . . .

In the more common case street-level bureaucrats begin to develop time-consuming techniques in less central and less monitored aspects of the agency's work. This represent the first deviation from the formal equality of the rules. Public service bureaucracies, aware that, *in toto,* the demands of their rules exceed the resources of their street-level bureaucrats, accept and even come to depend on areas of routine noncompliance. So institutionalized is this that a new bargaining tool has entered the repertoire of public service unions, the "work-in," where all administrative rules are rigidly enforced—at the cost of a complete breakdown in the substantive goals of the agency. The single-minded enforcement of parking rules by policemen is an obvious case in point.

Discretion. The excess of rules also has the effect of introducing discretion into this formally prescriptive system. Most administrative rules are not part of the organization's core technology (that is, they are not indispensable for the processing of every client) although they may play a role in the proper processing of any given client. The great number of such rules and the fact that their applicability must be decided on a case-by-case basis makes the effective monitoring of their use inherently difficult. In effect, therefore, their use becomes discretionary.

From Jeffrey Manditch Prottas, *People Processing: The Street-Level Bureaucrat in Public Service Agencies* (Lexington MA: Lexington Books, 1979), pp. 1, 18–20, 23–27, 29–32, 34, 36, 38–40, 92–93.

▲ ▲ ▲

 CHAPTER CASE ● ● ●

Most observers of street-level bureaucrats have uncovered patterns similar to those reported by Prottas. The problems of multiple and ambiguous roles appear to be fairly common in agencies concerned with direct human services. So do departures from prescribed procedures under the pressures of rule ambiguity and, sometimes, punishing workloads. We might expect to find the picture drawn by Prottas duplicated in many motor vehicle departments, probation and parole offices, large public hospitals, publicly run counseling operations of all kinds (domestic battering, substance-abuse, and so forth), and agencies set up to assist homeless citizens. Which brings us to our chapter case.

Every day, public administrators who deal with America's homeless citizens must make Solomonlike choices. How is an official to allocate 100 beds in a public shelter when 1,000 homeless individuals may need places for the night? How should the manager deal with needy persons when there's room in the inn, but the applicants don't satisfy some official qualification for shelter? As an officeholder, the administrator is a role player with rules to observe and routines to follow. A distinguished American social theorist, James March, writing in collaboration with a Norwegian student of public administration, Johan Olson, has described institutions as "collections of interrelated rules and routines that define appropriate actions." What's appropriate varies with the role:

> The accountant asks: What does an accountant do in a situation such as this? The bureaucrat asks: What does a bureau chief do in a situation such as this? . . . The process involves determining what the situation is, what role is being fulfilled, and what the obligations of that role in that situation are.[1]

Yet few situations provide unequivocal cues or evoke clear-cut rules. Often, administrators find themselves simultaneously playing multiple roles and required, therefore, to deal with conflicting interpretations of appropriate action. When should an official obey an explicit command that conflicts with the individual's duties as a service professional? What if the command conflicts with the apparent demands of fairness in the circumstances of the case? How should a professional react when the best practice of the field raises a conflict with feelings of humaneness, with the rules of the organization, even with the formal laws of the jurisdiction? Suppose that you (like Linda Vega in our scenario) were approaching a new job that you knew would require hard decisions about the treatment of homeless persons. What insights and resolutions related to the role-based obligations of public administrators would you try to fix in your own mind preparatory to assuming your duties?

CASE 9

....

Helping the Homeless: The Shelterers' Dilemmas

It would be going too far to say that Linda Vega decided on a career in public administration the night she heard Roger Detweiler speak on homelessness. But Linda always recalled the occasion as an event of significance in her life. One of Linda's professors at City College in New York City had encouraged his students to learn "how administration works in the real world." Detweiler, who had quite a reputation as a social advocate, liked to bear down on the nitty-gritty issues—especially issues of basic physical accommodations for the city's growing population of homeless persons.

The portion of the talk that made the lasting impression on Linda concerned what Detweiler simply referred to as "the toilet problem."

[1]James March and Johan Olson, *Rediscovering Institutions* (New York: Free Press, 1989), pp. 160–161.

"If you don't have a home, you don't have regular access to a sink, a mirror, a bathroom," Detweiler asserted. "Imagine: You're a mother with two children, both girls, but no home. Suppose you and the kids survived the night in one of the city's emergency shelters. No one stole your shoes. From what you can tell, neither kid caught anything infectious during the night—the open dormitory was filled with strangers coughing and wheezing and worse. Anyway, you apparently survived. But the three of you have to leave the shelter at 8:30—that's the rule. You've no place to go: no job for you, no day care for the girls. And you can't go back to your EAU [Emergency Assistance Unit, where shelter beds are assigned] until nightfall. What's your biggest problem now?"

Detweiler paused. "Getting to a bathroom—so you won't disgrace yourself, won't dirty clothes that you haven't enough money to launder anyway. *Getting to a bathroom*, that's your biggest problem! The 'comfort stations' in the parks? They're dirty, dangerous, and likely to show your girls a side of life that you'd rather they not have to learn right now. The department stores? The restaurants? Unless you're a customer, don't even think about it."

Detweiler next told how a lawyers' advocacy group had petitioned the state supreme court to order the installation of additional public toilets throughout the City of New York; how the court rejected the request, suggesting that accessible public toileting facilities are not required under the state constitution; how a foreign company had offered to install some low-cost (25 cents per entry) facilities in exchange for advertising space on the sides of the kiosks that would contain the toilets. Detweiler spoke with low-key outrage, arguing that public toilets *were* a requirement of a decent and orderly society, particularly one in which thousands of citizens lived destitute and homeless.

Linda didn't forget the picture drawn by Roger Detweiler of that desperate mother trying to solve a problem that most Americans never have to give so much as a thought. When her courses at City College permitted, she wrote term papers about homelessness. One time she did a project on shelter planning: "You have x number of cubic feet in a municipal shelter," the problem write-up specified. "Fire regulations and public health considerations require y cubic feet per bed; the mayor has allocated no more than z dollars to equip and run the shelter—beds, blankets, food for soup lines, and employees' salaries. You can increase the number of beds by keeping an open dormitory layout, or you can reduce crowding and provide some privacy for occupants by enclosing bedding areas with partitions. Fewer beds mean fewer breakfasts to provide—but also fewer people served, in a city with literally hundreds of thousands on the streets. How many beds should be procured, and how should they be arranged within the facility? How far should the 'amenity level' be compromised to increase the numbers accommodated and cut unit costs?"

Linda would never have called herself an expert on homelessness, but she read and occasionally clipped news items on the subject. A few years after the Detweiler talk, when she landed her new job in a part of the country where she, as a Latina, had always wanted to spend time, Linda was glad that she had finished City College with an engineering degree ("the math comes in handy"), and gladder still that she had learned something about one of the critical human problems of the day.

• • • • •

From the journal of Linda Vega. Source: Article by Gordon Berlin and William McAllister, "Homelessness," Brookings Review (Fall 1992).

Each story [of a homeless individual or family] begins with a set of predisposing conditions, usually severe poverty. Then something happens—a worker loses a job, a mentally ill person decompensates [that is, goes off medication], drug users turn homes into crack houses, or a building is emptied because of abandonment, arson, or conversion.

Still, the next step is not usually the street. Evicted or otherwise pushed out of a home, the newly homeless travel a circuit of friends, relatives, and others willing and able to provide temporary shelter or to lend money. After a while, most people can contribute enough to the household to remain there, or they find a place of their own. But for others, having exhausted the good will and resources of kin as well as friends, the final stop is a shelter or the street. . . .

Ending homelessness means providing housing at a price homeless people can afford. But the homeless have very little money, and fairness suggests they should not be favored at the expense of similar poor people who have managed not to become homeless. The housing, then, would have to be very minimal, at a time when standards for housing quality are higher than ever. This conflict between income, equity, and standards is the central dilemma for homeless policymaking.

• • • • •

What apparently drove the flow of homeless individuals in New York City was the pressure of more than half a million persons living doubled up with relatives and friends or in severely substandard quarters. Evictions and other calamities—including, in many cases, rejection by relatives—meant that perhaps a hundred thousand persons at any point in time were searching for some kind of shelter. Bed space in the city's shelters and single-room-occupancy hotels (SROs) was limited. Turnover in public housing and low-cost private housing spaces rarely exceeded twenty thousand per month. The overflow had no place to go but the streets.

As homelessness worsened through the 1980s and into the 1990s, no doubt some New Yorkers tried to put the growing army of "street people" out of their minds. But there was no way to put them out of sight. All about the city, disheveled persons lugged their lives' accumulations in shopping bags or wheeled them from corner to corner in shopping carts. Panhandlers, most claiming to be homeless as well as broke, accosted commuters at subway stations.

As city politicians and administrators perforce directed increasing attention to the problem, the courts imposed stricter and stricter shelter habitability standards. Some New York political leaders and administrators interpreted the court ruling in the leading case, *McCain* v. *Koch*, as establishing an unconditional legal right to shelter for any citizen of New York who appeared at an EAU claiming homelessness. Whether it had been formally mandated or not, that was the policy that city officials eventually adopted (see Box 10.2). Unfortunately, though, the tightening of habitability requirements may actually have made it more difficult for city officials to solve the problem.

BOX 10.2

McCain v. Koch

A Ms. Yvonne McCain and others, homeless heads of families who were dissatisfied with conditions in city shelters, sued the mayor of New York, Edward Koch, and the New York City Departments of Social Services (DSS) and Housing, Preservation, and Development (HPD).

From McCain v. Koch, *511 North Eastern Reporter, 2d Series, Argued in the Court of Appeals of New York April 22, 1987; decided June 4, 1987.*

The appeal involves . . . various aspects of the immensely difficult human, social and governmental problems presented in New York City and other large urban areas by the plight of homeless destitute families with children. Plaintiffs . . . are destitute families who have been granted and are receiving emergency housing aid. In their complaint seeking an order compelling defendants [Mayor Koch, DSS, and HPD] to provide them with "safe, suitable and adequate emergency housing," [the plaintiffs] describe specific conditions encountered by families lodged in hotels and motels, including instances of rooms without furniture, bedding or appliances, apartments without adequate heat, hot water, plumbing or electricity, and unguarded buildings infested with rodents and vermin and plagued with crime. Defendants reject any suggestion that they are indifferent to the plight of the homeless and cite, among other documents, the 1987 Report of the Mayor's Advisory Task Force on the Homeless as evidence that the City is doing "a 'creditable job' in what the Advisory Task Force described as the 'monumental task' of housing and feeding a homeless population. . . ." Plaintiffs reject these conclusions and assert that defendants still do not provide "emergency housing that meets the most basic standards of civilized society." . . .

[A prior court ruling cited by the defendants] *does not* direct defendants to provide housing where none is being provided. It applies only *"[w]hen a family is not denied* emergency housing, assistance and services" (emphasis added). Its provisions, insofar as they prescribe minimal standards, are:

"DSS and HPD shall, arrange so far as is practicable in the placement in emergency housing, that such housing:

"a. contains a bed for each family member, or a crib in the case of an infant, with a clean mattress and pillow and with clean and sufficient sheets and blankets;

"b. contains a sufficient number of clean towels;

"c. contains sufficient space for the family based on City laws governing residential units [citation omitted];

"d. has accessible to it a sanitary bathroom with hot water;

"e. is sufficiently heated pursuant to City law;

"[f]. contains basic furniture essential for daily living;

"[g]. has window guards as required by the laws governing residential multiple dwellings;

"[h]. has locks on the . . . housing unit's outside doors." . . .

These minimum standards provisions were first imposed by [the New York State] Supreme Court on June 20, 1983. . . .

Defendants contend next that they have no legal obligation to provide plaintiffs "with any emergency housing" under State or Federal constitutional or statutory law. Without such underlying obligation, the argument goes, there can be no substantive basis for . . . compelling compliance with minimum standards. The argument misconstrues the scope and effect of the [earlier Supreme Court] order . . . [I]t benefits only those families who have qualified for and are receiving emergency housing aid and the direction that the housing must meet prescribed minimum standards applied only when DSS and HPD have undertaken to provide the housing. . . .

Supreme Court decided that defendants, having undertaken to provide the homeless with emergency shelter, were obliged to furnish shelter meeting minimum standards. It reasoned that "[i]n a civilized society, a 'shelter' which does not meet minimal standards of cleanliness, warmth, space and rudimentary conveniences *is no shelter at all*" (127 Misc. 2d, at 24, 484 N.Y.S. 2d 985; emphasis added) and that in providing sub-minimum shelter the defendants were, in effect, denying *any relief* to the homeless. . . .

With the adoption of the departmental regulations (18 NYCRR 352.3[g],[h]), there can be no question about the minimum level of habitability which defendants now must meet when they undertake to provide emergency housing.

Most New Yorkers who were homeless or in fear of becoming so hoped, before all else, to qualify for an apartment in public housing. Since vacancies were scarce and competition for units stiff, candidates for low-rent public housing tried to find ways to improve their priorities for selection. Heads of families had an edge over single individuals; homeless heads of families received even higher priorities. The highest priorities of all went to those who could show that they had gone through the horrendous experiences of losing their homes and staying for extended periods first in emergency shelters and then in one of the infamous SRO "welfare hotels." Thus, although the city's shelter program is technically separate from public housing, the two systems are indirectly connected by most applicants' awareness that admission to a homeless shelter usually served as the first step to SRO assignment; from an SRO, the lucky ones could go on to permanent public housing.

Some analysts contended that the amenity level of the emergency shelters was the crucial variable in New York City's homelessness problem, inasmuch as it helped to determine the rates of flow within the system. Linda Vega recalled the fuss by local television news anchor people and talk-radio hosts when the *New York Times* reported on an interview with Nancy Wackstein, an advocate for the homeless and, for a time in the early 1990s, director of the New York City Office on Homelessness and Single Room Occupancy Housing. So ran the *Times* article of July 12, 1992:

The education of Nancy Wackstein, crusader for the poor, is a subject that Ms. Wackstein herself talks about with a lacerating irony. The advocate who made her reputation vilifying the city for dumping homeless children into welfare hotels says she now understands why it is so hard to empty the hellholes. . . .

Ms. Wackstein took office convinced that the city could move homeless families out of drug-infested welfare hotels in no time at all. In a frenzy of activity, she goaded city bureaucracies to fix up city-owned apartment buildings faster and move homeless families into them more quickly, "That was our big mission," Ms. Wackstein said. "It was the Mayor's campaign issue. Boy, I believed it. I approached it with energy and passion. When we started in the spring there were 1,200 families in welfare hotels. By August [1990], we were down to 150."

But the welfare hotels filled up, faster, it seemed, than they had been emptied. Again, more than 1,000 of the 5,200 homeless families in the city live in welfare hotels.

"I thought that if you just provided 8,000 units of permanent housing for a couple of years, you'd address the problem. I failed to understand that the universe of potential homeless families is very large. There are probably 200,000 ill-housed welfare families in the city.

"The municipal government will never be able to solve this alone."

That simple insight made Ms. Wackstein understand that the city had to regulate the number of people coming into homeless shelters. The unspoken reason that the city made people stay in shelters a long time before they got housing was in fact, she said, "to discourage more ill-housed people from checking into the system. The awfulness of shelters also deterred mothers living doubled up with relatives from bringing their children to shelters."[2]

Something about the Wackstein interview kept nagging at Linda Vega. Wackstein's description of the New York shelter system implied a relationship between the reputed amenity level of the city's emergency shelters and the number of street people who, by asking for shelter, took the first step to high-priority eligibility for affordable public housing. The better the reputation of the shelters, the more individuals who would choose to become homeless—primarily by leaving crowded conditions with relatives—and apply for shelter space. Linda suspected that a simultaneous reverse relationship existed between the number of individuals in shelters and the *actual* (as opposed to the *reputed*) amenity level. Legal limits on occupancy were sometimes observed in the breach. An increase in the number of applicants for emergency shelter meant that additional bodies would end up being crammed into a fixed volume of space. Thus an increase in the numbers petitioning for shelter would cause a decline in the amenity level. That effect would eventually be reflected in a lowered reputation—and hence in the reduced attractiveness—of the shelters as an intermediate stage on the way to a public housing assignment.

"Suppose the city throws more money into the shelter system," Linda thought, "making them more attractive. More families try to use them, spurred by their aware-

[2]Celia Dugger, "Memo to Democrats: Housing Won't Solve Homelessness," *New York Times*, Jul. 12, 1992, "Week in Review" Section, p. 22.

ness that the shelters are the gateway to affordable permanent housing. Eventually, though, word gets out about the crowding. Some people who would otherwise deliberately put themselves on the street to qualify for shelter—the first step toward a public housing apartment of their own—stay doubled up with relatives. Sooner or later, the opposite forces balance out.

Linda shook her head, mentally sketching a model of the opposite forces: "With all other things held equal, the lower the number of beds, the higher the amenity level. Hence the worse the backlog of people applying for shelter space. If the system isn't 'tuned' just right, a perpetual mismatch between the number of beds and the number of applicants is inevitable—an impossible situation, politically and administratively!"

•   •   •   •   •

Some time after Linda Vega read the account of the Wackstein interview, she received the letter from Evelyn Alvarado about the junior-level job in the Housing Department of the Bureau of Human Services. Would Linda be willing to leave New York for parts west? (She would.) Could she start in the new position immediately? (She could.) There were all sorts of problems waiting for Linda to work on if she took the BHS job, Ms. Alvarado had stressed, problems that needed the kind of energy, diligence, and New York gutsiness that a person like Linda could bring to a new life in a new location.

Linda adapted quickly to the sunniness and warmth of the Southwest, and to a local Latino culture with which she could easily identify. Her first assignment was to read through what seemed like a mountain of reports. The document that most interested her was a hundred-page booklet referred to around the office as "the CHAS." Congress had passed the Cranston-Gonzalez Affordable Housing Act of 1990, which consolidated some of the twenty or more programs authorized by Congress for homeless assistance. Cranston-Gonzalez required each municipality that benefitted from federal housing grants to develop a *Comprehensive Housing Affordability Study—CHAS.*

Linda focused on the sections of the CHAS that dealt with homelessness and affordable housing. According to the CHAS, there was a long waiting list for admission to vacancies in local public housing units. As in New York, federal law required city housing authorities to give certain preferences in these waiting lists. Homelessness, as evidenced by quartering in an emergency shelter, was a prime qualification to go to the head of the line. But in her new city as in her old one, the problems of scarcity were easier to handle on nights when potential users stayed doubled up with relatives—or even camped outside on the streets—instead of applying for emergency shelter space.

•   •   •   •   •

It had become the tradition in the BHS to initiate new employees by detailing them to the scutwork jobs in the agency. Linda Vega's breaking-in stint was to "sit the night shift" in the Agua Blanca Housing Project, a small public apartment complex with an attached emergency shelter for homeless individuals and families. The shelter received joint funding from federal, state, and city sources. The Housing Department officials who managed Agua Blanca had their work cut out to comply with federal requirements, state social welfare policies, and pressures from city-based politicians.

"It won't be as hard as it may sound," Linda's new boss, Evelyn Alvarado, said of the night-shift duty. "Just hang out in the Agua Blanca office from eleven to three o'clock to take any phone calls from residents—you know, complaints about fights in the building, or druggies around the place, or whatever. Our occupants aren't shy. They let us know, *pronto,* about noise, about neighbors who keep live-in lovers or visitors too long, and . . . yes . . . about homeless people congregating near the place. 'Congregating' is shorthand for 'giving Aqua Blanca a skid-row reputation.'

"When you get a complaint," Evelyn told Linda, "you just ring the local cops or, if the problem sounds serious, [Sheriff] Al Rilleau's office over in county—the way the folks who called you should have done in the first place. For the rest, just sit there, watch TV if you want, and maybe use the quiet time to catch up on any paperwork."

It sounded easy enough.

"The only real work comes in connection with the Agua Blanca emergency shelter. The night-shift person for the apartment complex runs the shelter too. Most of the takers for bedding show up earlier in the evening, but there's the occasional straggler who shows up after eleven o'clock asking for space."

"And what do I do then?"

"You give it to them," Evelyn replied. She added that there was talk of a possible "new city policy on admissions to shelters," but she stressed that Housing Department practice had always in the past been to give shelter to anyone asking. *Anyone.*

"And if there's no room?"

Evelyn replied: "We've got twenty-seven beds at Agua Blanca. The shelter's a Quonset hut hooked to the apartments by a corridor. We used to put overflow people in blankets on the floor, even using the connecting passage for sleeping room on rare nights. The apartment residents complained, but we did it anyway if anyone needed room for the night."

"You put extras on the floor?"

"I said, 'we *used to,*'" Evelyn answered. "No more. You weren't here yet when we had a rash of fires around town. Arson. Some deaths. Fire regulations, now they're *strictly* enforced. So if there's no room—when the limit of twenty-seven is reached—no one else can be admitted."

Evelyn frowned briefly and switched to another topic. She started to say something about "'covering' for Sheila Westa" when the phone rang. Distracted, Evelyn broke off. She gave Linda a good-luck signal and waved her off, assuring her that Grant McLaren—whom Linda would relieve at the Agua Blanca front desk—would tell her everything she needed to know about "the Westa situation."

•   •   •   •   •

Despite Evelyn's assurances, Linda found Grant McLaren to be a bit unsure himself about the procedures that acting managers of the Agua Blanca should follow. McLaren wasn't one of the regulars in the job; he freely admitted to knowing little about the "hands-on side of the housing business." Though he was an experienced member of Evelyn Alvarado's Housing Department staff, until relatively recently, McLaren had never actually run either a public housing building or an emergency shelter. He had spent most of his career as a paper-pusher of some sort in head-quarters. His primary emotion seemed one of relief that Linda Vega would be taking the night shift for a while. With one more person sitting rotation as an acting man-ager, McLaren would have to pull fewer details himself. The job, he told Linda, had more than its share of hassles but few professional or personal satisfactions.

McLaren was obviously uncomfortable as he explained the unusual situation involving Sheila Westa. It came out that Sheila, a popular and able worker in the Housing Department, had suffered the worst kind of personal tragedy. Her son had died in a traffic accident. Sheila, who had worked herself up into management in the Housing Department, didn't seem able to pull her official life back into shape, even after an extended period of bereavement. Somehow, she managed her family affairs. She even found the emotional resources to participate in community activities: She was a United Way collector, an active member of the local MADD chapter, and a helper in various ways at the high school where her boy would have graduated. But Sheila just wasn't cutting it any more on the job.

About six months after Danny Westa had died, Sheila began experiencing bouts of severe clinical depression. Ironically, she had just been promoted to the rank of a full building manager and had been assigned to Agua Blanca. Quickly, a pattern of absenteeism emerged. On several occasions when she had actually made it in to work, minor crises broke out among Agua Blanca residents or in the shelter area. Sheila, working at about half speed, proved incapable of handling incidents that most of the other permanent managers in the system would have finessed easily.

Until Sheila's doctor found a drug that would combat her depression, Grant explained to Linda, Sheila's friends in the department were all pitching in to "cover" for her.

"Cover for her?"

Sheila was supposed to rotate with two other permanent Agua Blanca managers so the manager's chair would be filled around the clock. In fact, however, for the last two or three months, Sheila had called in unable to take 1 shift out of 5. Other mem-bers of Evelyn Alvarado's staff took Sheila's shifts as favors to her, and also as ges-tures of the esprit within the Housing Department.

"You see," McLaren said, "when one of us subs for Sheila, what we do is, well, we phone her periodically at home. She usually answers, even on night shifts. I know it's hokey, but the idea is to have a basis for tapping her judgment. If there are prob-lems, maybe you talk to her. We get her to give 'instructions' over the phone about handling whatever's the problem. So, see, it's effectively having her do the manage-ment. Then we just sign Sheila's log and worksheet to keep her current."

Linda finally got what Grant was telling her. McLaren and the others were ensur-ing that Sheila Westa—who had presumably already used up all her sick days—would continue to draw her check. The books always showed her present for duty as assigned.

Linda couldn't disguise her doubts about the Westa arrangement. "Is this 'cov-ering' all right? I mean, signing for someone else? I'm not objecting to Mrs. Westa's getting paid"—although Grant's account made it clear that Sheila was drawing checks for hours not worked. But Linda said that she thought she would "feel queazy falsify-ing a logbook showing this Sheila Westa to be present when she's really not on the job, and even 'phoneying it up' with the telephone stunt."

Whether Grant agreed with Linda or not on the merits of her position (Linda couldn't tell what he thought), he made it clear that everyone on the team expected everyone else to support one of their own: "We all love Sheila, and she's been through hell, and she's going through more hell right now with this depression thing. We're all sure her doctor will find the right medicine combination soon, and she'll be back at 100 percent. We're just tiding her over."

●　　●　　●　　●　　●

Linda Vega was a week into her night-shift work when word of the rumored policy change—the one that Evelyn Alvarado had mentioned when she described the tradition of taking *anyone* in who needed a bed for the night—became official. Homelessness was becoming a problem of such visibility and unpopularity that the politicians apparently found it necessary to take dramatic action.

"I assume you've been following the brouhaha in City Council," Evelyn said one day to Linda.

Indeed she had, Linda replied. In fact, the battle over shelter policy would have been hard to miss. It was all over the local news. Just the night before, Linda had seen clips of City Councilman Warren Slaby's latest speech on the subject. Slaby had made a career of the "family values" issue. For several weeks, he had been the protagonist of a bitter debate. Slaby claimed that it was long past time to stop supporting "immoral lifestyles" and sheltering "hippies too unhinged to get permanent legal addresses for themselves." In his speech the previous day, Slaby had introduced a resolution amending the statement of intent governing city funding for emergency shelters. The Slaby amendment passed with a comfortable margin. Under its terms, a single large converted loft building near the old skid-row section of town—1605 Front Street— would be used as an open-dormitory-type shelter for single individuals. All other emergency facilities that were supported in whole or in part by city funds were to become "family shelters." According to the Slaby amendment, the "exclusive purpose" of these shelters would be "to provide centers for short-term housing and other social services to 'at-risk' families."

The new rule took effect immediately. "Needless to say," Evelyn commented, "after all the political posturing, Slaby and his crowd didn't in the end provide any extra dollars for all those 'other social services' that their amendment refers to. So we'll just continue to run Agua Blanca as we have, as an ordinary homeless shelter. Except, I don't see any way to get around the 'families only' restriction." Evelyn knew that strict enforcement of the Slaby amendment would leave dozens of needy single men and women without shelter beds; the 1605 building by itself wasn't nearly big enough to handle all the demand. At the same time, the space dedicated for family service—Agua Blanca, Pavillion, and every other shelter (except 1605) in the city's system—would probably exceed the demand.

●　　●　　●　　●　　●

Milo Andrews, an old-timer in the Housing Department, recognized the troubled look on his good friend Evelyn Alvarado's face. Milo also held down one of the hardest jobs on Evelyn's staff: general manager at 1605 Front Street.

Evelyn motioned Milo into her office and gestured toward a memo lying on her desk. The paper bore the state senate letterhead. The top typed line identified the document as a "Declaration of Legislative Intent."

The legislators over in the state house were rethinking their policy on homelessness, just as Slaby and other city-level politicians had done. "You know Tom Opperman. [Opperman was an *L.A.*—a legislative assistant—to State Senator Manuel O'Haire.] Opperman sent this memo over to [BHS Director] Aaron Haber."

Evelyn explained that the housing appropriations bill had just completed markup in the state senate. The bill would be passed and signed into law within a few days. The appropriation would contain all state matching-fund money, to be combined with funds from Washington under Cranston-Gonzalez and other federal housing laws, in support of shelter funding, housing subsidies, and public housing construction throughout the state. "It's an omnibus budget bill, said Evelyn. The way Manny O'Haire has structured it, the point is to put a new twist on the way all money in the housing area will be spent from now on."

Milo knew that Senator O'Haire had been making speeches about the need to get at the "root causes" of homelessness. Milo had been a close observer of the political scene long enough to know that, although Manny O'Haire did his own thinking, he counted heavily on Tom Opperman for criticism and advice.

Evelyn continued: "Manny says he wants to stop throwing money at symptoms and get at the causes of homelessness. Either on his own initiative or because the senator told him to, Opperman's tried to explain what that means in the area of shelter policy. I gather that O'Haire's planning to read portions of Opperman's memo into the legislative record. . . ." Senator O'Haire had an impeccable record on issues of human and minority rights. In the entire state legislature, he alone might get away untarnished if he proposed a change in shelter policy that the area's service professionals would have called heartless and mean-spirited coming from anyone else.

Tom Opperman had bootlegged a draft of his memo to Evelyn Alvarado's boss, Aaron Haber, with a note informing Haber that if he wanted to continue getting state funds, he should prepare for a change in the way his people implemented emergency shelter programs within the city. Similar notes had no doubt gone to other shelter officials all over the state.

Milo listened while Evelyn unburdened herself: Opperman wanted to make the shelters less comfortable, maybe even less safe. Opperman talked of budget tightening, but the real motive was to make it even more miserable for the homeless. To hear Evelyn tell it, the cutbacks that Opperman was proposing in shelter funding and in the level of "nonessential amenities" would require her to cut security services at all city shelters (fewer night guards), reduce services and facilities (probably including a removal of the free laundry machines, and certainly discontinuance of free breakfasts at most of the city's shelters), and cancel work orders to install partitions in the city's dormitory-type shelters with the aim of making them more "family friendly."

Evelyn frowned. "I certainly haven't thought through the implications. Except. . . ."

"Except?" Milo prompted.

"Except, well . . . except: How can we possibly obey the kind of policy Opperman's pushing? The answer is, we can't. Or at least, *I* can't."

Milo suggested that Evelyn cool off. True, the new policy would be unpleasant to implement. But, Milo said, "unpleasant comes with our territory." In the course of his career, he had had to do lots worse than what Opperman wanted.

Evelyn had thought that Milo Andrews would be the first person to understand how destructive Opperman's "slash and burn" policy (as she characterized it) would be to the "human philosophy" she had tried to cultivate in the city's shelter administration. Evelyn declared that she simply wasn't ready to "just hold her nose and obey whatever comes out of the legislature."

"Then what *do* you plan to do?" Milo, still unruffled, asked Evelyn.

"I don't know. That's why I'm talking to you."

Evelyn asked Milo to read Opperman's memo and give her his ideas: How should she, as the city's housing official with responsibility for shelter administration, advise her managers to act under the new policy? How, for that matter, should Milo Andrews react. He, as an actual shelter manager, would probably soon be on the receiving end of an order (again, in Evelyn's words) "to trash his own facility as a way of deterring people from asking for help there."

Later at his desk in the office at 1605 Front Street, Milo scanned the Opperman document:

Senate Committee on Finance
Subcommittee on Social Program Oversight

DECLARATION OF LEGISLATIVE INTENT

Supplement to the preambular statement of the sense of the Senate, Title I, S. 396

Our homeless population is disproportionately Anglo. In large part, this imbalance exists because Latinos who are at risk of homelessness are far more likely than Anglos to have extended family members nearby willing to take them in. A higher percentage of our Anglos are transients, relatively recent arrivals, or from dysfunctional families and hence without immediate sources of assistance.

The combined Anglo and Latino populations of *potential* shelter clients far exceed the numbers that we are now accommodating, and also exceed the numbers than we ever could shelter in any reasonably efficient way.

For years, we have been spending in the range of $250,000 annually of federal (McKinney Act, Cranston-Gonzalez Act) funds for shelter expansion and support. This is in line with national tendencies. These have long emphasized a response to homelessness through the provision of emergency sheltering with federal subsidies. But the evidence suggests that it is time to change our policy. This can be done without jeopardizing our federal dollars. Both Congress and HUD [federal Department of Housing and Urban Development] are moving toward increased reliance on an affordable housing strategy and toward efforts to provide the homeless with job skills and substance-abuse treatment which will help them make the transition from homelessness.

In the shelter business, supply creates its own demand. Individuals who have alternative prospects for decent housing consume emergency shelter funds that could be better expended on other housing-related programs. We do not want to keep overloading our system and end up undermining the political legitimacy of programs needed by the truly destitute. The worst way to help the most needy is to help the only-partly needy.

The best way to deter the partly needy is by emphasizing in every possible way the barebones, emergency nature of our temporary shelters. Funds currently programmed, or actually being spent, on nonessential amenities, such as free meals and personal services, should be diverted to more useful purposes. Federal dollars currently slated for shelter augmentation should be reprogrammed into drug treatment and similar social programs. Such programs not only are meritorious in their own right but also cut to the root causes of homelessness in a way that providing emergency shelter does not. Such reprogramming might result in some reduction of services and lowering of amenity levels in our shelters, but that seems an unavoidable cost of an overdue change in policy.

Milo reread the memo and then kicked back in his seat and reflected. For a while during the late 1980s and early 1990s, Milo knew, officials in many cities were feeling sorely pressed to reduce overcrowding in their homeless shelters. Some intentionally kept their facilities dirty and noisome so that no one who wasn't utterly desperate would apply to sleep in them. It was a politically supportable and relatively efficient strategy. By keeping demand for shelter artificially low relative to the true level of potential demand, the so-called deterrent approach eliminated pressures to provide costly additional facilities. It also choked off one of the spigots that controlled flows of people into permanent public housing.

"Circumstances make the case." Milo was familiar with the maxim. Evelyn might have overreacted to the Opperman plan; there were worse sins than purposefully making certain public services inconvenient and inaccessible. On the other hand, can it *ever*, under *any* circumstances, be acceptable for a public administrator—even when acting under a legislative mandate—to implement a policy of purposeful degradation of needed human services? On reflection, Milo concluded that Evelyn was right to ask questions before simply committing to follow the legislative lead. But Milo was no more sure about the right answers than she seemed to be.

•   •   •   •   •

Linda Vega was happy in her new job, her new city, and her new digs, but she tried to keep up with the major news from her once- and always-beloved New York. A filler story in the second section of the morning *Trib'-Examiner* one day caught Linda's attention. Housing officials in New York, it said, had decided that the city could no longer guarantee both shelter to all citizens who claimed homeless status *and* acceptable safety, privacy, and comfort for all sheltered individuals. Under a new program, admission to New York City shelters would be denied to persons found to have reasonable alternative housing accommodations. Curious, Linda dropped into the public library that evening. She leafed through the back issues of the *New York Times* there and finally located the news item that she sought:

New York's new policy on homelessness sounds straightforward: the city will shelter only families who have no adequate place to live, screening out those with apartments of their own or friends or families they can stay with. . . .

In about a month, the caseworkers who counsel the homeless will be plunged into a new role of weighing which families are in sufficiently dire straits to be deemed homeless, and thus entitled to shelters.

Specifically, they will have to decide when families should be required to stay doubled up. And they will be faced with complex questions: When is an apartment too crowded to be safe? When does a building have enough drug dealing in the hallways to be considered hazardous? . . .

"Overworked, undertrained social services workers will be playing God," said Steve Banks, coordinating lawyer for the Legal Aid Society's Homeless Family Rights Project.[3]

The *Times* reporter noted that a staff of seventeen city administrators had been assigned to make the critical determinations—with the understanding, however, that the investigators were to "stay away from subjective judgments" when they issued their crucial decisions on homelessness claims.

● ● ● ● ●

Carlos Hersh had the note from Evelyn Alvarado in his pocket. He was to appear as soon as he could get downtown to the BHS headquarters offices following his shift at Pavillion. Hersh provided psychological and substance-abuse counseling at the city's homeless shelters. Currently, he was spending more and more of his time at the Pavillion shelter—and understandably so, for he seemed to be having more success out there than with the programs he had instituted at several inner-city facilities.

The Pavillion shelter, a converted mansion that the city had acquired on tax delinquency, was far out on River Road in a comfortable, almost-suburban residential neighborhood. Pavillion took its nickname from the large porch, a formal veranda, which surrounded the grand old building on three sides. The facility also had a sizable front lawn dotted with picnic tables and other outdoor furniture. A few small businesses (toney restaurants, boutiques) and several dozen well-kept, landscaped homes stood within sight of the shelter.

For some time, Carlos Hersh's counseling efforts at Pavillion had been attracting unexpectedly large numbers of homeless individuals seeking help for substance-abuse problems. Hersh suspected that his clientele wouldn't change appreciably even if, under the Slaby amendment, only families were permitted to remain overnight at Pavillion. Nothing in the Slaby restriction prevented anyone who desired—whether single or attached to an intact family—from taking advantage of the Pavillion's so-called nonresident services. These consisted mostly of formal counseling and (just as important) simple informal socializing on the Pavillion lawns. The Pavillion offerings also included preliminary psychiatric diagnostic services—in some cases, preparatory to the handing over of a troubled individual's file to administrators in city or county mental health agencies.

Hersh had learned that the people who most need counseling are also often the ones most suspicious of any arrangement that bespeaks authority, institutionaliza-

[3]Celia Dugger, "New York Confronts It's Own Shelter Rule," *New York Times*, Aug. 12, 1993, p. B1.

tion, or regimentation. Emotionally or medically troubled individuals, many of whom had experienced physical restraint or even ill treatment in prior hospitalizations, often feared what they thought they would find inside a shelter. But Carlos knew that a smile and a few coins for bus fare would often bring clients out on day trips to the Pavillion's picnic tables. There visitors to the shelter could enjoy soft drinks, escape the harassment to which street people are subject in the business districts, and begin the process of "just talking," which is how Carlos liked to start the counseling experience. "Come and just hang out; you don't have to stay overnight at the shelter," Carlos told street people who showed signs of need. Carlos had found these invitations to be the least threatening, and hence the most effective, way to reach the city's vulnerable.

But Carlos also knew that the often-unkempt picnic tablers were straining relations with members of the nearby community. Episodes of disorderly conduct by residents (loitering off Pavillion grounds, urinating in public) had caused the local residents to mobilize. The neighbors didn't distinguish among sheltering, counseling, simple provision of human contact on the lawn, or, for that matter, any of the other services that they (incorrectly) suspected to be going on at Pavillion, such as HIV testing and out-patient AIDS treatment. The neighbors had hired a lawyer to petition for a re-zoning of the area, which would force Pavillion to close.

Hersh's very success with the day-trippers, who were visiting in increasing numbers, was actually making it easier for the neighbors to brand the shelter a public nuisance. Carlos wondered if he should give his professional assent when Evelyn Alvarado, who controlled the contract under which he worked for the BHS, asked the expected question that afternoon: whether, for political reasons, the one successful outreach strategy that Carlos had found for the people he was professionally committed to serve should be scrapped.

• • • • •

One day early in her second week at Agua Blanca, Linda Vega found a note from Evelyn Alvarado: "L., Please see me ASAP."

"Why don't you take 'the duty' this week?" Evelyn asked, although her tone made it clear that Linda was getting an order, not receiving a request. "Think of it as another example of the hazing we give to newcomers," Evelyn added, without unkindness.

Linda hadn't heard of "the duty."

"Oh," Evelyn said, "I guess I assumed that you would have picked up on it in random talk around the office."

Evelyn continued: "You know, if you've waded through the small print in the CHAS, that public housing rules let visitors in city-owned apartment buildings stay for two weeks—no longer." Evelyn explained that a family on an extended visit in public housing with relatives or friends effectively evades paying rent, since rents in public housing depend on the number of people in the apartment, not counting visitors. "There's lots of pressure on our renters to take in cousins and sisters and aunts. It overloads the buildings, adding noise and maintenance problems. Then too, all those strangers in the building make the regular tenants nervous. We get calls pretty quick from other tenants when a visiting family overstays the two-week limit."

"Here," Evelyn waved two salmon-colored slips; "this week's quota of petitions for further exceptions. You can add them to any paperwork you've saved up to do tonight at the shelter." Both petitions, it happened, involved visitors who wanted to extend stays at the Agua Blanca.

Evelyn continued: "These extension requests need decisions by early tomorrow. If the decisions are to evict, word goes to [County Sheriff Albert] Rilleau first thing in the morning. If for some reason you decide to extend either petitioner beyond the two-weeks' visitation they've already had, . . . well, then *you*'ll have to handle the complaints from neighbors. And *you*'ll have to write something up explaining why there should be a waiver of rules that are pretty clear." Evelyn passed the salmon-colored slips over to Linda.

On one:

Request for Extension. Family Diano, mother/3 chldrn with cousin Diano family, Apt. 5D, Agua Blanca. Rating, 6. Persons in excess of rated capacity of unit, visitors included: 3. Visitor Diano long-time city resident. Evicted from rental house, Census 6.02 [a central ward census tract with upward of 66 percent low-income population], for nonpayment of rent. Full-time-employed as waitress. Resident Diano baby-sits the cousin's kids while visitor Diano working. (Will continue taking kids during day even if Visitor Diano moves elsewhere.) Visitor Diano will be homeless, family-shelter-eligible if required to leave.

On the other:

Request for Extension. Couple (female) Johnson & Strawski. With female resident Eberle, Apt. 1E, Agua Blanca. Rating, 4. Persons in excess of rated capacity of unit, visitors included: − 1. Both visitors apparent transents [sic] in area. In local area job hunting about 1 month. Neighbor complains homosexual association, seeking strict enforcement of 2-wk limit. Visitor Strawski employed as part-time taxi driver. Visitor Johnson artist. Petitioners will be homeless, single-shelter-eligible if required to leave.

"Jobs like this aren't so easy, I admit," Evelyn said as she brushed past Linda on her way out. "As you know—or maybe you don't—under municipal ordinance, formally the [BHS] director himself has to make these visitor-eviction decisions, which means that we take our turns doing the dirty deed for the boss. It's not pleasant, turning those people onto the street, which is what we have to do in most cases. But you might as well see right away what the territory looks like, and what comes with it."

Linda took note of the deadline that Evelyn set before she left the office: "I'll be back first thing tomorrow. Tell me then what you decide to do about the two extensions."

●　　●　　●　　●　　●

1605 Front Street—the singles-only emergency shelter that Milo Andrews ran—had become increasingly crowded in the aftermath of the Slaby policy change, as more homeless singles who were turned away from the "family service" shelters sought bed space at the converted loft structure on Front Street.

Andrews strolled the floors of his facility, thinking about the Opperman memo. He wondered if it would even be possible to render the place less accommodating— or, to tell the truth, more dehumanizing—than the open rows of bunks already made it. But he knew that "cutback management" throughout the city would probably force him to find a way to reduce service even further than he already had, irrespective of any instructions issued pursuant to the O'Haire bill.

The fact was that budget cuts had been having their effects for some time on essential city services across the board. Most critical, they had forced the city to close several firehouses despite the recent increase in the arson rate. The mayor himself had recently appeared on television to stress that the fire hazard in the inner city had risen to the level of a public emergency. Hizzoner exhorted administrators of public agencies and facilities to set an example of "scrupulous attention to fire safety."

The building at 1605 was full, its occupancy limit of seventy-nine having been reached more than a half-hour earlier. Assuming that no fights would break out and that he'd have no emergency medical or substance-related incidents to handle, Milo supposed that he could count on a few quiet hours until he turned his office over to the night manager at eleven.

Suddenly, there appeared at the entrance a woman alone, and then an instant later, a mother with two children. Both women urgently requested shelter. Milo discerned in the first woman all the signs of a battered spouse seeking refuge but too embarrassed or too scared to admit the real reason for her homelessness. The mother, nervously chain-smoking, also seemed close to the end of her emotional tether. Since the fire limit at the shelter was in the form of a total-occupancy restriction, not a bed number, Milo knew that he couldn't legally even permit the women and children to doze the night away on couches around the building. Unless, of course, he bent the rules.

But if he did that tonight, why not tomorrow . . . and thereafter? And if he did it for scared, exhausted women (either with or without kids), why not for the single men whom he regularly turned away? And if he could talk himself so easily into disobeying the rules even for these obviously needy and miserable applicants, what was the point of the rules to begin with—or of his obligation to follow them?

●　　●　　●　　●　　●

Linda Vega sat at her desk in the Aqua Blanca office. Before her were the salmon-colored slips with the extension requests from "Family Diano" and "Couple Johnson & Strawski." Not much was occurring to distract her from the decision she had to make about the visitation petitions. Traffic was for some reason light, and all evening Linda had received only a single phone call—not from an apartment resident but from Milo Andrews about a problem that Linda might be able to help him handle "if they could find money for a cab somewhere in the loose change of the BHS budget," as he Milo it.

Almost midnight and quiet—the Quonset was only half full. Under the "families only" rule, the population of residents for the night consisted mostly of children whose mothers had long since coaxed them to sleep.

Linda started at the unexpected sound. Two figures turned through her office door and moved to her desk. The man seemed about thirty years old and, Linda immediately saw, of rough cut. With him was a woman (girl?), not more than fifteen in Linda's judgment. Twice, the man—Steve Mc-something—referred to the two of them as "a couple." At several points during his little speech requesting space in the shelter, Steve nodded with a certain tenderness toward the girl, whom he called "my Zoe." He asked for "a few days' space" and said he could pay "if it was within reason."

Linda studied the couple. Both were disheveled. Steve and Zoe had identical tattoos of cobras on their upper right arms. Indeed, they came across as a steady twosome, but Linda doubted that they constituted "a family" in the sense intended by the City Council members who had overwhelmingly passed the Slaby amendment. Linda discerned no evidence of abuse, duress, or fear in the young woman's eyes or demeanor. Yet something about their manner—not just Zoe's vague silence and apparent exhaustion but also Steve's nervously supplicating manner—suggested that the two needed help. Linda certainly believed that they were homeless. But she feared that the unkempt appearance of the two, compounded by Steve's gravely tone of voice, might upset—or even frighten—the children of families in the shelter. At any rate, Linda was satisfied in her own conscience that Steve and Zoe represented unlikely candidates for the "family building" mission that Councilman Slaby and his cohorts had made the legal purpose of the Aqua Blanca facility.

A strange thought occurred to Linda. For some time, she had carried an image in her mind of a dispirited mother with two frightened, unkempt girls in tow looking for beds by night and safe, clean toilet facilities by day. Linda shifted uncomfortably as she realized that she had always somehow filled the face of the older youngster in that mental picture with features strikingly like the those of the wan girl named Zoe who now stood before her.

Questions for Discussion

The following queries might help you to frame your thoughts and organize a discussion of the case.

1. What's the story? Or, rather, what are the interwoven stories in the case? State, as simply as you can, the main issue or issues that Evelyn Alvarado, Linda Vega, and Milo Andrews have to resolve.

2. The case write-up alludes to several different sheltering strategies that have been tried in New York City. Can you describe the main approaches? What were the strengths and weaknesses of each?

3. "Know the law." Did the court in *McCain* v. *Koch* establish a universal right to shelter? If the "universal right" interpretation was, in your opinion, an incorrect reading, what motive might have been behind it? How did the "universal right to shelter" reading, when combined with tough new habitability standards, change the nature of the shelterers' problem?

4. "Sketch a model." Linda Vega, referring to the New York shelter system as it worked at the time of the Wackstein interview, concludes: "If the system isn't

'tuned' just right, a perpetual mismatch is inevitable." What will be mismatched with what? What kind of model do you suppose Linda had in mind? How might such a model, if explicitly sketched out, be used when framing a sheltering strategy?

5. Based on your reading of the selection from Jeffrey Prottas, what steps would you take, if your were responsible for a group of public administrators with direct people-to-people responsibilities—such as shelter managers—to improve the chances of efficient, caring discharge of their duties?

6. For that matter, how "caring" should shelter managers try to be? What's your sense of how Victor Thompson's thesis regarding "the problem of administration compassion" (from Chapter 8) bears on the issues in this case? In the same vein, how does the requirement of impartiality relate to the way Linda Vega should handle the two visitation applications? To the way she should deal with the request of Zoe and Steve for shelter? Would any "progression of circumstances" have led you to modify your view of the decisions that Linda should make regarding "Family Diano," "Couple Johnson & Strawski," or Zoe and Steve?

7. We also saw in Chapter 8 that public officials must take consequences into account because they work in agencies created to serve the interests of particular subpublics or of the public generally. The "confused homeless" surely constitute a subpublic of proper concern to Carlos Hersh, given his obligations as a service professional. The residents of the neighborhood around the Pavillion shelter also constitute a distinct subpublic. What criteria should Evelyn Alvarado use when weighing the claims of these two subpublics as they relate to the practices that Carlos Hersh has developed at the Pavillion?

8. How, in your opinion, should Linda Vega react to Grant McLaren's instructions about "covering" for Sheila Westa? Consider the "progression of circumstances" and the "conditions of the agents": Does the fact that McLaren is evidently passing on instructions with the approval of higher-ups (specifically, Evelyn Alvarado) make a difference in your answer?

FOR FURTHER READING

Probably the best starting point for a deeper study of the motivational issues raised in this chapter is the seminal (if somewhat difficult and abstract) book cited in Box 10.1:

Barnard, Chester, *The Functions of the Executive* (Cambridge, MA: Harvard U. Press, 1938).

Two standard accounts of the Hawthorne experiments, by leaders of the Hawthorne research team, are

Henderson, L. J., et al., "The Effects of Social Environment," in Gulick and Urwick, eds., *Papers on the Science of Administration* (Clifton NJ: Kelly [1937], 1973), 143.

Roethlisberger, F., and Dickson, W. J., *Management and the Worker* (Cambridge MA: Harvard U. Press, 1939).

For a superior summary and critique of the Hawthorne experiments, and of the human relations approach in general, see also

Perroux, Charles, *Complex Organizations: A Critical Essay* (Glenview IL: Scott, Foresman, 1973), chap. 3.

From the Hawthorne experiments and Barnard's *Functions of the Executive* onward, the human relations approach can be traced through the following authors and titles:

Maslow, Abraham, "A Theory of Human Motivation," 50 *Psychological Review* (July 1950), 370.

Argyris, C., *Integrating the Individual and the Organization.* (New York: Wiley, 1964).

Ouchi, William, *Theory Z* (New York: Avon, 1981).

Organizational culture theories in public administration (and in the literature of business administration) are traceable through:

Selznick, Philip, *Leadership and Administration* (Berkeley CA: U. of California Press, 1957); the seminal theoretical treatment.

Kaufman, Herbert, *The Forest Ranger* (Baltimore: Johns Hopkins Press, 1960); a kind of counterpart to Selznick and the classic empirical treatment of the subject.

Peters, Thomas, and Robert Waterman, *In Search of Excellence* (New York: Warner Books, 1983); the highly readable blockbuster work on corporate culture.

Wilson, James Q. *Bureaucracy: What Government Agencies Do and Why They Do It* (New York: Basic Books, 1989); especially chap. 6.

DiIulio, John, "Principled Agents: The Cultural Bases of Behavior in a Federal Government Bureaucracy," 4 *Journal of Public Administration Research and Theory* (July 1994), 277; a superb summary article.

On "ethical climate" in modern organizations—one of the most important aspects of organizational culture—see

Victor, Bart, and John Cullen, "The Organizational Bases of Ethical Work Climates," 33 *Administrative Science Quarterly* (March 1988), 101.

Street-level bureaucrats have been extensively studied; fine follow-up sources to the Prottas reading are

Blau, Peter, *The Dynamics of Bureaucracy* (Chicago: U. of Chicago Press, 1955).

Lipsky, Michael, *Street-Level Bureaucracy: Dilemmas of the Individual in Public Services* (New York: Russell Sage Foundation, 1980); the standard work on the subject.

Kelly, Marisa, "Theories of Justice and Street-Level Discretion," 4 *Journal of Public Administration Research and Theory* (April 1994), 119.

Two classic accounts of "abrogation to authority" carried to demonic extremes—in the one case, through deference to higher orders; in the other, through submission to group opinion—are

Arendt, Hannah, *Eichmann in Jerusalem: A Report on the Banality of Evil* (New York: Viking, 1963).

Janis, Irving, *Groupthink: Psychological Studies of Policy Decisions and Fiascos* (Boston: Houghton-Mifflin, 1982).

On the organization, management, funding—and "humanization"—of service-provision agencies, see

Agranoff, Robert, *Intergovernmental Management: Human Service Problem-Solving in Six Metropolitan Areas* (Albany NY: State U. of New York Press, 1986).

Handler, Joel F., *Law and the Search for Community* (Philadelphia: U. of Pennsylvania Press, 1990).

Hasenfeld, Yeheskel, ed., *Human Services and Complex Organizations* (Newbury Park CA: Sage Publications, 1992).

On the ethics of service to the weaker members of society, see

Goodin, Robert, *Protecting the Vulnerable* (Chicago: U. of Chicago Press, 1985).

See also, for a different perspective on the specific ethical orientations of different administrative roles,

Jos, Philip, and Sam Hines, "Care, Justice, and Public Administration," 25 *Administration and Society* (November 1993), 373.

CHAPTER 11

Modern Decision Theory and Implementation Research

After the end of World War II, there appeared two thinkers whose rejection of classical organizational theory and synoptic analysis decisively influenced modern decision-making theory. Herbert A. Simon, who was trained in management studies and considered himself an administrative theorist, eventually won the Nobel prize in economics—impressive testimony indeed to the interdisciplinary impact of his work. Charles E. Lindblom, an economist by education, emerged in the 1950s as one of the most prominent members of the Yale school of political science. The Yale researchers insisted on studying how people actually behave, rather than how the philosophers say they *should* behave. This realistic approach quickly became the orthodoxy of a generation of social scientists, and it made the Yalies the most influential political analysts of the early postwar decades. Simon and Lindblom eminently illustrated the claim of public administration to be considered a truly architectonic discipline.

For our own part, we study Simon and Lindblom not because all public administrationists—let alone all social scientists—accept their teachings. Thoughtful scholars have taken issue with Simon's campaign to put "deciding" (decision theory, in today's vernacular) at the center of administrative analysis.[1] And Lindblom has put off some readers with his rather puckish dismissal of the entire rationalistic tradition in public administration. Critics wonder how seriously they should take an approach to decision making that Lindblom has whimsically called "muddling through."

But despite the controversy their writings engendered (or perhaps because of it), Simon and Lindblom helped to structure the core debates in the subfields of public administration known as *modern decision theory* and *implementation research*. That's why students of the subject continue to read—and respect—their works even today. That's also why we'll turn, in Section 1 of this chapter, to the debate over synoptic planning and incremental adjustment. Then, in Section 2, we'll take up two contrasting implementation approaches: top-down planning (or forward mapping) and bottom-up planning (or backward mapping).

[1]See, for example, the exchange between two leading contemporary public administrationists, Michael Harmon and Jay White: "'Decision' and 'Action' as Contrasting Perspectives in Organization Theory," 49 *Public Administration Review* (March–April 1989): 144–150; and White's response, ibid.: 150.

Synoptic Analysis versus Incremental Adjustment

Simon, Lindblom, and their many followers went beyond the *political* objections to systemwide planning that we considered in Chapter 5. Simon and the others argued that the fundamental limit in the decision-making process isn't so much interference by politicians on behalf of local interests as it is the *cognitive* bounds which limit the analyst's own information-processing capacities.

Under the synoptic decision-making model, a rational decision maker is supposed to

1. Make explicit the goals or ends to be pursued.
2. Take a comprehensive survey of the factors relevant to the problem at hand, identifying all possible means toward the given ends.
3. Carefully calculate the cost of each possible means and choose the one that will lead to the goal or goals at minimum cost, thereby satisfying the definition of efficiency used by most economists.

Incrementalists such as Simon and Lindblom, however, argued that two kinds of difficulties frequently emerge when one tries to undertake the herculean task envisioned by systemwide planners.

First, there's a **values problem.** The administrator often finds it impossible to specify a clear-cut set of goals, all of which are to be achieved simultaneously. And the notion of identifying a single, unambiguous goal to pursue is, in the realm of public policy, often simply out of the question. We have uncovered repeated examples of how the multiple but inconsistent values that administrators feel obliged to advance lead to problems of *overdetermination.*

Second, there's a **complexity problem.** By this term, incrementalists actually refer to two subproblems: (1) the inherently complex nature of many administrative situations and (2) the inherent limits of the administrator's own intellectual capacities. We've seen that it's in the nature of administrative situations to involve many variables in complex and often-weak relationships with one another. The analyst can't ignore some factors and concentrate on a limited set of others. The result is the kind of *underdetermination* with which we've become familiar. The decision maker is also likely to suffer from a shortage of information—another factor contributing to underdetermination—and a lack of time to study the limited information that may be available.

Concern with the problem of insufficient raw data, compounded by the problem of the decision maker's own information-processing deficiencies, led Simon to reject the concept of synoptic analysis and the optimizing model of decision making in favor of the alternative approach called **incremental adjustment.**

As expounded by the neoclassical economist Pareto, the optimizing model of consumer behavior posits that a rational person—for instance, a careful shopper in a store—will constantly reassess the gains and costs of different possible bundles of goods. New items come onto the market; price levels fluctuate; consumers' preferences change over time. The shopper supposedly takes all this information in and adjusts his or her purchasing plans accordingly. As we have also seen, the method of formal policy analysis that's known as *cost-benefit analysis* transfers this imagery from its original setting, in the market for consumer goods, to the realm of political and administrative choice. Ideally, the policy analyst totes up *all* the negatives of a proposed course of action (the costs), *all* the positives (the benefits), and then repeats the procedure for *all* courses of action that might be taken in the circumstances.

Is there somehing wrong with this picture? According to Simon, there surely is.

Simon argued that the synoptic requirements of the optimizing model—prohibitively difficult for the lone consumer in a supermarket or shopping mall—are unrealistic to the point of fantasy for a decision maker acting on the public's behalf in the context of a modern administrative organization. Complete calculations may be feasible for exceedingly simple problems, problems in which the term *all* in the forgoing account of the cost-benefit procedure is a small number and in which both the costs and the benefits of an action are readily quantifiable. But when these requisites can't be satisfied (which is usually), cost-benefit analysis may be as difficult to put into practice as was the Progressives' ideal of systemwide planning—and for many of the same reasons. Simon gave a new name, **bounded rationality**, to the limits of human information-processing capabilities. In doing so, he changed the basic vocabulary of administrative science.

Bounded Rationality and "Satisficing": Enter "Administrative Man"

Simon argued that human rationality quickly runs up against three kinds of boundaries:

> On one side, the individual is limited by those skills, habits, and reflexes which are no longer in the realm of the conscious. His performance, for example, may be limited by his manual dexterity or his reaction time or his strength. His decision-making processes may be limited by the speed of his mental processes, his skill in elementary arithmetic, and so forth. . . . This is the field that has been most successfully cultivated by the followers of Taylor and which has been developed in time-and-motion study. . . .
>
> On a second side, the individual is limited by his values and those conceptions of purpose which influence him in making his decision. If his loyalty to the organization is high, his decisions may evidence sincere acceptance of the objectives set for the organization; if that loyalty is lacking, personal motives may interfere with his administrative efficiency. . . .
>
> On a third side, the individual is limited by the extent of his knowledge of things relevant to his job. . . . In this area, administrative theory is concerned with such fundamental questions as these: What are the limits of the mass of knowledge that human minds can accumulate and apply? How rapidly can knowledge be assimilated? . . . How effective is the system of communication to channel knowledge and information to the appropriate decision-points? What types of knowledge can, and what types cannot, be easily transmitted?[2]

[2]Herbert Simon, "The Proverbs of Administration," 6 *Public Administration Review* (Winter 1947) 53: 64–65.

Bounded rationality helps explain why so many problems in public administration are underdetermined. Sheer inadequacy of information or understanding (or both) often prevents even the most insightful decision maker from daring to act as if all variables and their interrelationships were known and—at least in the sense of being mastered intellectually—under control. According to Simon, bounded rationality forces decision makers in circumstances of any complexity to forgo optimizing and content themselves instead with **satisficing**.

The satisficing model of decision making applies to a figure who made his first appearance in the writings of Simon: the figure of **administrative man,** who deals day in, day out with the complexities and uncertainties that are standard fare for public managers. Unlike the **economic man** of the optimizing model, administrative man (and woman) can't—except in trivial cases—tote up all the negatives and compare them with all the positives. Instead, the practicing administrator must try to cope as tolerably well as he or she is permitted by bounded rationality—by inadequate knowledge and limited information-processing capabilities. Satisficing presupposes a willingness just to get along by settling for proximate solutions.

The various theorists of incrementalism have put their distinctive twists on the concept, and some have been more explicit than others in spelling out the links between their own work and the seminal ideas of Simon. But all incrementalists acknowledge the difficulty of the values problem and the complexity problem; all emphasize the limiting effects of inadequate information; and all argue that change should be undertaken gradually and experimentally—through stepwise moves from positions that themselves will have been been reached through a series of prior experimental moves. Bounded rationality explains why prudent decision makers often shrink from projects of comprehensive reform or systemwide planning in any literal sense. Overly ambitious moves by a decision maker, or moves that are taken too quickly, may carry excessive risks. Such moves tend either to introduce errors in policy that will offset any expected gains or else may simply overburden the ability of affected workers to absorb new rules and work effectively within new structures. The failure of comprehensive industrial planning in the "first New Deal" (we covered the too-ambitious initial designs of FDR's braintrusters in Chapter 7) exemplified some of the dangers that Simon and his followers sought to avoid in future public policy making.

Working Out the Details: How Incremental Adjustment Gets Carried Out in Practice

In 1959, Simon's disciple Charles Lindblom published his famous article introducing the incrementalist technique that he called "muddling through." Eschewing any attempt at synoptic analysis—also called the **rational-comprehensive method**—Lindblom's decision maker makes a series of "successive limited comparisons" among "relatively few values and relatively few alternative policies."

According to Lindblom, synoptic (or rational-comprehensive) analysis may be the decision-making method preferred in theory, but it is incremental adjustment that most policy advisers and decision makers use in practice to deal with the values problem and the complexity problem. What's more, Lindblom contended that the piecemeal methods he recommended generally produce "rational" policy choices: that incremental adjustment usually works. In the following reading selection, note that Lindblom explicitly regards muddling through as a form of coordination by mutual adjustment. As you read, ask yourself if you are persuaded that Simon, Lindblom, and others of their school have found in incrementalism a solution for the most common source of underdetermination in public administration, namely, the kind of fragmentation of authority among diverse agencies and program offices that produces incentives for multiple decision makers to operate at cross-purposes.

Charles Lindblom on "Muddling Through"

Ideally, rational-comprehensive analysis leaves out nothing important. But it is impossible to take everything important into consideration unless "important" is so narrowly defined that analysis is in fact quite limited. Limits on human intellectual capacities and on available information set definite limits to man's capacity to be comprehensive. In actual fact, therefore, no one can practice the rational-comprehensive method for really complex problems, and every administrator faced with a sufficiently complex problem must find ways dramatically to simplify.

An administrator assisting in the formulation of agricultural economic policy cannot in the first place be competent on all possible policies. He cannot even comprehend one policy entirely. In planning a soil bank program, he cannot successfully anticipate the impact of higher or lower farm income on, say, urbanization—the possible consequent loosening of family ties, possible consequent eventual need for revisions in social security and further implications for tax problems arising out of new federal responsibilities for social security and municipal responsibilities for urban services. Nor, to follow another line of repercussions, can he work through the soil bank program's effects on prices for agricultural products in foreign markets and consequent implications for foreign relations. . . .

In the method of successive limited comparisons, simplification is systematically achieved in two principal ways. First, it is achieved through limitation of policy comparisons to those policies that differ in relatively small degree from policies presently in effect. Such a limitation immediately reduces the number of alternatives to be investigated and also drastically simplifies the character of the investigation of each.

For it is not necessary to undertake fundamental inquiry into an alternative and its consequences; it is necessary only to study those respects in which the proposed alternative and its consequences differ from the status quo. The empirical comparison of marginal differences among alternative policies that differ only marginally is, of course, a counterpart to the incremental or marginal comparisons of values . . .

It is a matter of common observation that in Western democracies public administrators and policy analysts in general do largely limit their analyses to incremental or marginal differences in policies that are chosen to differ only incrementally. They do not do so, however, solely because they desperately need some way to simplify their problems; they also do so in order to be relevant. Democracies change their policies almost entirely through incremental adjustments. Policy does not move in leaps and bounds.

The incremental character of political change in the United States has often been remarked. The two major political parties agree on fundamentals; they offer alternative policies to the voters only on relatively small points of difference. Both parties favor full employment, but they define it somewhat differently; both favor the development of water power resources, but in slightly different ways; and both favor unemployment compensation, but not the same level of benefits. Similarly, shifts of policy within a party take place largely through a series of relatively small changes, as can be seen in their only gradual acceptance of the idea of governmental responsibility for support of the unemployed, a change in party positions beginning in the early '30s and culminating in acceptance of the Employment Act of 1946.

Party behavior is in turn rooted in public attitudes, and political theorists cannot conceive of democracy's surviving in the United States in the absence of fundamental agreement on potentially disruptive issues, with consequent limitation of policy debates to relatively small differences in policy.

Since the policies ignored by the administrator are politically impossible and so irrelevant, the simplification of analysis achieved by concentrating on policies that differ only incrementally is not a capricious kind of simplification. In addition, it can be argued that, given the limits on knowledge within which policy-makers are confined, simplifying by limiting the focus to small variations from present policy makes the most of available knowledge. Because policies being considered are like present and past policies, the administrator can obtain information and claim some insight. Non-incremental policy proposals are therefore typically not only politically irrelevant but also unpredictable in their consequences.

The second method of simplification of analysis is the practice of ignoring important possible consequences of possible policies, as well as the values attached to the neglected consequences. If this appears to disclose a shocking shortcoming of successive limited comparisons, it can be replied that, even if the exclusions are random, policies may nevertheless be more intelligently formulated than through futile attempts to achieve a comprehensiveness beyond human capacity. Actually, however, the exclusions, seeming arbitrary or random from one point of view, may be neither.

Suppose that each value neglected by one policy-making agency were a major concern of at least one other agency. In that case, a helpful division of labor would be achieved, and no agency need find its task beyond its capacities. The shortcomings of such a system would be that one agency might destroy a value either before another agency could be activated to safeguard it or in spite of another agency's efforts. But the possibility that important values could be lost is present in any form of organization, even where agencies attempt to comprehend in planning more than is humanly possible.

The virtue of such a hypothetical division of labor is that every important interest or value has its watch-

dog. And these watchdogs can protect the interests in their jurisdiction in two quite different ways: first, by redressing damages done by other agencies; and, second, by anticipating and heading off injury before it occurs.

In a society like that of the United States in which individuals are free to combine to pursue almost any possible common interest they might have and in which government agencies are sensitive to the pressures of these groups, the system described is approximated. Almost every interest has its watchdog. Without claiming that every interest has a sufficiently powerful watchdog, it can be argued that our system often can assure a more comprehensive regard for the values of the whole society than any attempt at intellectual comprehensiveness.

In the United States, for example, no part of government attempts a comprehensive overview of policy on income distribution. A policy nevertheless evolves, and one responding to a wide variety of interests. A process of mutual adjustment among farm groups, labor unions, municipalities and school boards, tax authorities, and government agencies with responsibilities in the field of housing, health, highways, national parks, fire, and police accomplishes a distribution of income in which particular income problems neglected at one point in the decision process become central at another point.

Mutual adjustment is more pervasive than the explicit forms it takes in negotiation between groups; it persists through the mutual impacts of groups upon each other even where they are not in communication. For all the imperfections and latent dangers in this ubiquitous process of mutual adjustment, it will often accomplish an adaptation of policies to a wider range of interests than could be done by one group centrally.

Note, too, how the incremental pattern of policy-making fits with the multiple pressure pattern. For when decisions are incremental—closely related to known policies—it is easier for one group to anticipate the kind of moves another might make and easier too for it to make correction for injury already accomplished.

Even partisanship and narrowness, to use pejorative terms, will sometimes be assets to rational decision-making, for they can doubly insure that what one agency neglects, another will not; they specialize personnel to distinct points of view. The claim is valid that effective rational coordination of the federal administration, if possible to achieve at all, would require an agreed set of values. . . . But a high degree of administrative coordination occurs as each agency

adjusts its policies to the concerns of the other agencies in the process of fragmented decision-making I have just described.

From Charles E. Lindblom, "The Science of 'Muddling Through,'" 18 *Public Administration Review* (Winter 1959): 1.

SECTION **2**
● ■ ▼ ◆

Planning and Implementation: Forward Mapping versus Backward Mapping

Simon and Lindblom published their most influential works between 1945 and 1965. Their arguments on behalf of incremental adjustment might have warned practitioners off from some of the more ambitious public ventures that were launched under President Lyndon Johnson's Great Society agenda. The 1960s was a decade of governmental activism reminiscent of the "first New Deal" years, and federal staff workers devised a host of ambitious new social programs, most of them to be carried out by program implementers in the states and cities. Congress appropriated, and bureaucrats spent billions. Yet for all the hoopla and initial optimism, major outlays of public funds had disappointingly few positive effects. Congress's much-heralded "Model Cities" legislation yielded embarrassingly few examples of successful urban renewal. Later, employment-training initiatives under the Comprehensive Employment and Training Act of 1973 (the CETA program) took on the taint of gross inefficiency and, in some cases, downright corruption. The term **implementation gap** entered the vocabulary of public administration, referring to the discrepancy between lofty intentions and actual results.

What went wrong?

Incrementalists, of course, blamed massive programs that allegedly required levels of planning and management far in excess of the available capabilities. The most eminent incrementalist in the intellectual succession from Simon and Lindblom was the University of California political scientist Aaron Wildavsky. With one of his students, Jeffrey Pressman, Wildavsky tried to explain the implementation gap based on a study of one of the most notorious Great Society failures. Pressman and Wildavsky's 1973 volume *Implementation* did as much as any single work to establish implementation research as a recognized subfield of public administration.[3]

Pressman and Wildavsky told of the ill-fated effort by Washington-based planners in the Economic Development Administration (EDA) to create jobs for the hard-core unemployed of Oakland, California (see Box 11.1). The headquarters staffers acted as if they had only to enunciate a goal and its realization should follow pretty much as a matter of course. But a continent separated the policy makers in Washington from the intended beneficiaries "out there" in one of the nation's westernmost cities. To administer the Oakland project required a large new organization that stretched from EDA head-

---

[3]Wildavsky, a scholar and teacher of rare magnanimity, published prolifically and often with co-authors. He insisted that multiple names on the jackets of his books be listed alphabetically. Everyone who knew Wildavsky also recognized that practice as the way of one scholar—whose name, after all, started with W—to nudge his students and less-well-known colleagues into the academic spotlight.

BOX 11.1

What Went Wrong with the Oakland Project?

In 1965, administrators in the Washington headquarters offices of the U.S. Economic Development Administration (EDA), a division of the Commerce Department, hatched a plan for the construction of a new docking, loading, and transportation complex on the Oakland side of San Francisco Bay. The plan won support from virtually all federal, state, and Bay Area municipal officials who reviewed it. Labor leaders were equally supportive, as were the private-sector industrialists who stood to gain from an inpouring of federal funds. The EDA idea bore all the textbook signs of sure success.

At the end of the day, however, Oakland officials found themselves without the expected new transportation hub and without the promised new employment base. Pressman and Wildavsky telegraphed their finding in this tongue-in-cheek subtitle:

> How great expectations in Washington are dashed in Oakland; or, why it's amazing that federal programs work at all, this being a saga of the Economic Development Administration as told by two sympathetic observers who seek to build morals on a foundation of ruined hopes.

A Defective Causal Theory

The concept dreamed up by planners in Washington—to stimulate jobs by promoting a fancy new seaport complex in Oakland—seemed attractive enough at first look. But a critical examination of the causal theory underlying the enterprise would probably have suggested that the planners had settled on an inappropriate way to achieve the objective in view. The EDA planners hoped to create permanent jobs for Oakland's hard-core unemployed. Yes, the capital outlays required for major dockside projects would create construction jobs, but *not* jobs for the area's hard-core unemployed. Oakland in fact already had plenty of unfilled jobs. The EDA project would indeed create additional ones, but of the wrong kind. The existing vacant jobs in the area, as well as the ones which would come into being as a result of the marine-terminal construction, by and large required skilled workers. In short, the population targeted by the EDA planners—the long-term unemployed—couldn't compete for the positions that the project would create.

A policy maker needs a model or causal theory which correctly predicts how the goal is to be achieved. Given their goal, the EDA planners should have provided the hard-core unemployed with the training they'd need for the jobs that were already available instead of creating new jobs that couldn't be filled by the intended beneficiaries of the plan.

The Perils of Administrative Complexity

Pressman and Wildavsky used the Oakland project as a prime example of the perils of administrative complexity.

The authors studied the timetable and decision-making structure of the Oakland project. Pressman and Wildavsky found dozens of "decision points," most of which required approvals by multiple players. Decision makers from the private sector as well as from all levels of government had to be represented in every discussion. The fact that all participants had a say in the conduct of the work meant also that everyone held a kind of veto power over at least a portion of the effort.

The vulnerability of a project to delay, Pressman and Wildavsky concluded, depends on the number of decision points, the number of participants whose clearance is required for each decision, and the intensities of the conflicts that divide the participants. In all, seventy separate agreements had to be arranged in order for the Oakland project to succeed. The number of players and their patterns of preference are largely aspects of the political context in which a policy is to be carried out. The number of participants (political, business, labor, local community) and their inherent diversity of interests built potential conflicts into the organization of the project. The players in the Oakland game demanded repeated justifications of one another's concerns and interests. Failure at any one decision point interrupted forward movement in the overall enterprise. The lapse of time permitted problems to develop that might not have materialized if the project had proceeded apace.

Vulnerability to Political Conflicts

Rapid turnover among the participating federal, state, and even local officials contributed to the impression of a stop-and-go project. Meanwhile, unforeseen external forces were undermining community support for the project. The early coalition of politicians, administrators, industrialists, labor spokespersons, and community leaders fragmented in squabbles among the groups. Throughout the period of the project, racial tensions were worsening in the Bay Area. The EDA planners found themselves in negotiations with battling factions, trying to deal with posturing and hidden agendas among representatives of the very communities that the original architects saw the project as helping. Internal conflict eventually helped defeat the best-laid plans of the EDA administrators.

---

quarters near the Potomac River to a work site in coastal California. The members of that implementing organization never successfully cleared the Oakland construction project of the bugs that turned up, in part because much of their time had to be spent wringing the bugs out of an administrative organization that had to be set up from scratch.

Pressman and Wildavsky struck a theme taken up by all subsequent implementation researchers: Projects above some threshold of complexity, such as big public works projects, are vulnerable to the same kinds of problems in administration that complex intellectual tasks are in policy analysis. There's the danger that planners will forget how unpredictable (and how cussedly refractory) the world can be—and how limited are human beings' capacities to control events. When the EDA planners set up an unnecessarily complex organization to manage a project that was inherently complex in its own right, they worsened what would have been, even in the best of cases, a problem with too many variables for easy control. It was a classic example of underdetermination.

Incremental Adjustment Considered as Backward Mapping

Wildavsky's successors extended the critique of synoptic planning, and hence the incrementalist decision making model, to the approach called *backward mapping,* which was first outlined in the early 1980s by the implementation researcher Richard Elmore.

Motivated by a desire to understand the phenomenon known as the *implementation gap*—an important theme in public administration since the 1960s—Elmore wanted an analytical framework for implementation study that could serve both as a diagnostic device (that is, an analysis of what has gone wrong with failed public programs, like the Oakland project) and a prescriptive theory (that is, a statement of conditions under which different implementation approaches seem advisable). In the following selection Elmore contrasts backward mapping with the contrary implementation approach—called, naturally, forward mapping.

Richard Elmore on Mapping as an Implementation Paradigm

[T]here are at least two clearly distinguishable approaches to implementation analysis: *forward mapping* and *backward mapping.* Forward mapping is the strategy that comes most readily to mind when one thinks about how a policymaker might try to affect the implementation process. . . .

Forward mapping of a federal policy might being with a statement of congressional intent. It would then outline federal agency regulations and administrative actions consistent with that intent. It would elaborate a division of responsibilities between central and regional offices of the federal government (or among federal, state, and local administrators) such that each implementing unit had a clearly defined mission. It would then state an outcome, usually in terms of an observable effect on a target population, consistent with the initial purpose of the policymaker. . . .

The details of forward mapping are less important for our purposes than the underlying logic. Forward mapping begins with an objective, elaborates an increasingly specific set of steps for achieving that objective, and states an outcome against which success or failure can be measured. It is consistent with the standard framework of policy analysis and with conventional techniques of management science and decision analysis (**program evaluation and review technique [PERT] and critical path method [CPM]**). Insofar as implementation analysis is treated at all in textbooks on policy analysis, it is treated as forward mapping.

What the textbooks do not discuss are the weaknesses of forward mapping and its severe limitations as an analytic technique. The most serious problem with forward mapping is its implicit and unquestioned assumption that *policy makers control the organizational, political, and technological processes that affect implementation.* The notion that policymakers exercise, or ought to exercise, some kind of direct and determinant control over policy implementation might be called the "noble lie" of conventional public administration and policy analysis. Administrators legitimate their discretionary decisions by saying that their authority is delegated and controlled by elected and appointed policymakers. . . .

The logic of backward mapping is, in all important respects, the opposite of forward mapping. It begins not at the top of the implementation process but at the last possible stage, the point at which administrative actions intersect private choices. It begins, not with a statement of intent, but with a statement of the specific behavior at the lowest level of the implementation process that generates the need for a policy. Only after that behavior is described does the analysis presume to state an objective; the objective is first stated as a set of organizational operations and then as a set of effects, or outcomes, that will result from these operations. Having established a relatively precise target at the lowest level of the system, the analysis backs up through the structure of implementing agencies, asking at each level two questions: What is the ability of this unit to affect the behavior that is the target of the policy? And what resources does this unit require in order to have that effect? In the final stage of analysis the analyst or policymaker describes a policy that directs resources at the organizational units likely to have the greatest effect. . . .

Forward mapping assumes that organizational units in the implementation process are linked in essentially hierarchical relationships. . . . Backward mapping assumes essentially the opposite: The closer one is to the source of the problem, the greater is one's ability to influence it; and the problem-solving ability of complex systems depends not on hierarchical control but on maximizing discretion at the point where the problem is most immediate.

Applying forward and backward mapping to the same problem gives much different results. The analytic solution offered by forward mapping stresses factors that tend to centralize control and are easily manipulated by policymakers: funding formulas, formal organizational structures, authority relationships among administrative units, regulations, and administrative controls (budget, planning, and evaluation requirements). The analytic solution offered by backward mapping stresses the dispersal of control and concentrates on factors that can be influenced only indirectly by policymakers: knowledge and problem-solving ability of lower-level administrators, incentive structures that operate on the subjects of policy, bargaining relationships among political actors at various levels of the implementation process, and the strategic use of funds to affect discretionary choices.

From Richard F. Elmore, "Backward Mapping," in Walter Williams et al., *Studying Implementation* (Chatham, NJ: Chatham House, 1982), pp. 19–22.

Forward Mapping as a Paradigm of Implementation

Forward mapping is the implementation approach associated with synoptic analysis and top-down planning. As Elmore describes it, forward mapping begins with as precise a statement as possible of the policy maker's intent and proceeds through a sequence of increasingly more specific steps to define what is expected of implementers at each lower level in the organization. This mapping-out process, when complete, yields a comprehensive plan. As such, it gives a position of special importance to staff officials. The staffers who surround the leader work out the details (often in some such form as a PERT diagram) and also perform the follow-up functions emphasized by the classical organizational theorists: They ensure that the milestones are met and that the pathways in the PERT diagram are observed. After the frontline operators execute the plan, the staff officials complete the cycle by comparing the actual outcome with the commander's original objective. The test of success thus becomes the achievement of a kind of congruency between the initial vision and the postimplementation results.

When to Use Forward Mapping

Under what circumstances, if any, will the kind of organization and planning procedure exemplified in the Oakland case succeed? The logic of forward mapping suggests that top-down planning may be most appropriate when:

1. *The project in question is a relatively simple one, making it possible to anticipate needs and forestall problems through advanced planning.*

This condition is also, we have seen, a requisite for the adoption of a synoptic approach. To tell when the level of complexity in a proposed new program exceeds some critical threshold must always remain a matter of judgment and must be strongly affected by the circumstances, the quality of the workers available to complete the project, and the resources of the project leadership (including their determination, ingenuity, and rapport with the hands-on workforce).

2. *There exist good reasons to base policy on a broad statement of intent issued by a high-level decision maker.*

An office holder may have campaigned on a promise to achieve some definite outcome for constituents. A president, a governor, or a city manager may have an overall strategy that requires the completion of a specific subprogram without substantial change because it represents an essential component in the larger design. For these or similar reasons, the nature of our political system may induce a decision maker at the pinnacle to issue a top-down order in the hope that subordinates will find a way to execute the superior's will without modifying it in the implementation process.

3. *The nature of the policy area in question makes it unwise to delegate broad discretionary authority to the frontline workers.*

Where deviations from approved procedures may trespass on individuals' rights (as in police work) or may have catastrophic consequences (as in medical experimentation or health and safety inspections), close surveillance and pervasive controls may be justified. Such situations may imply a preference for

A classically *bureaucratic* approach to organization, with none of the freedom to innovate that market-mimicking structures are supposed to encourage
A strongly directive approach to coordination (vesting in superiors a high degree of *direct supervision* over subordinates—as in combat units, crime control squads in crackdown policing, emergency rescue teams, and the like)
A strict *compliance* approach to implementation (establishing an absolute understanding in subordinates of their obligation to follow the rules, with minimum room allowed for exercises of discretion)

4. *The implementation effort fits unambiguously within the mission responsibilities of a highly regarded existing agency, and so the appropriate organization and procedures to be used for the job never become subjects of discussion.*

Forward mappers tend to accept the *existing* organizational structure as a given. This approach seems most appropriate when the qualifications of the organization are not debatable and when the pertinence of the mission to that organization is beyond question. When faced with the need to get certain kinds of military jobs done, for example, the president doesn't solicit potential implementing organizations for bids; he or she simply reaches for the red phone to "call in the Marines."

5. *The frontline officials must take detailed instructions from above because the policy area has few knowledgeable experts, who must therefore "program" the implementers.*

Sometimes there *does* exist One Best Way. In such cases, superiors usually want that way to be used, meaning that subordinates should adhere strictly to whatever procedures are set forth by the experts who are most likely to know the way to go. Often this requirement involves a statement of *best practice*. Where there's a best way to do a job—especially one that touches on health or safety—we don't want workers experimenting. Airline passengers want to know that the best engineers in the business have written the rules governing safety inspections and that the frontline Federal Aviation Agency workers are following those rules instead of personal hunches or whims.

6. *There is a high level of confidence in the causal theory underlying the policy, and so planners can predict the effects of executing programmed actions even in the absence of additional learning.*

Just as knowledge of what works may be either concentrated within a small population of experts or diffused among many workers, it may also be relatively more or relatively less certain. The more certain the body of causal theory, the greater will be the justification for forward mapping. Planners who prescribe in any degree of detail the work that operators are to undertake and the ways they're to carry it out had better be pretty sure that the assigned tasks will lead to the outcomes they expect!

7. *The undertaking is a short-term or one-time activity, with little need or opportunity for learning and adaptation over time.*

Forward mapping leaves little flexibility, but then flexibility may be unnecessary or even undesirable. The nature of the effort may leave no time for learning and no tolerance for experimentation. Space launchings and disaster-relief efforts present interesting mixed cases. The National Aeronautics and Space Administration and the Federal Emergency Management Agency both need to engage in "organizational learning" over time, incorporating new knowledge and adapting to new technologies. But each individual instance of NASA and FEMA activity requires quick, reliable execution of whatever procedures exist at the moment.

Backward Mapping as a Paradigm of Implementation

Backward mapping assumes that the administrators who will best understand the possibilities and problems in a project are those who, in the course of actual implementation, will gain hands-on experience: the street-level bureaucrats, not the paper-pushers back at headquarters.

Forward mappers, who see it as the implementers' job to execute the detailed plans of staffers, expect strict *compliance* by the frontline workers with higher orders. This expectation allows little room for *discretion* among workers at the implementing end of the project. Therein, according to Elmore, lies a severe shortcoming of the forward-mapping approach. In most organizations, Elmore argued, formal authority descends by degrees from central decision makers at the top of the pyramid through the intervening tiers to the ultimate implementers at the bottom of the structure. It's a paradigm of organizational structure with which we have become thoroughly familiar.

Elmore goes on to describe a reverse, *upward* flow of "the informal authority that derives from expertise, skill, and proximity to the essential tasks that an organization performs." Forward mappers recognize the first part of this formulation, but Elmore contends that they tend to ignore the second: the actual authority that frontline workers have to advance or frustrate action based on their own goals, their special skills, and their knowledge of the locale in which the staffers' plans must actually be implemented. (It seems likely that Elmore's concept of informal authority owes something to the Barnard-Simon *zone of acceptance,* discussed in Box 10.1.) Backward mappers conclude that the frontline implementers should be permitted—indeed, should be encouraged— to exercise their special knowledge of local conditions and their unique feel for the breaking event.

Local conditions and concerns enter into the backward mapper's thinking in yet another way: Backward mappers deem it as big a mistake to forget how local leaders can damage a project if their views are ignored as it is to forget how local implementers can help if their expertise is fully used. Almost any implementation scheme eventually exposes those who are responsible for its execution to resistance, unless those who are likely to be affected see reasons to support it or, at least, not to sabotage it. Planners who neglect to consider the desires and special problems of interested individuals in the locale of intended effect are apt also to forget that affected individuals can organize coalitions to resist programs that they judge to be harmful or intrusive. Activists can lobby for legislative changes, can litigate in the courts, can appeal to public opinion, and can manipulate formal procedures in the administrative process. In short, they often can tie up a program that they don't like—almost indefinitely. That, in fact, is exactly what they did in Oakland.

Backward mappers enter the implementation game expecting those who will be affected by a new program to form coalitions that may oppose, modify, or advance the effort (another example of local interests' organizing against ideas forced on them from above; another example, too, of our pluralistic political process at work). Continuing negotiations are likely to be necessary to adjust plans and accommodate changing interests. The backward mapper therefore tries to create what Elmore calls a "bargaining arena," which is open to the representatives of all affected local interests. The parties will use this arena and the bargaining that will go on continuously within it to shape—and reshape . . . and *re*-reshape—the implementers' original plan for change. The relationship between backward mapping and bargaining is the subject of our chapter reading, which follows our next topic.

When to Use Backward Mapping

We have already listed some circumstances under which the forward-mapping approach has its comparative advantage. In contrast, an implementation researcher should think first of backward mapping when:

1. *Complexity exceeds the threshold beneath which forward mapping is a realistic strategy.*

When, for whatever reason, it proves impossible to accept the overriding lesson of the Pressman-Wildavsky study—Simplify!—it may make sense to try to cope with complexity by backward mapping, thereby shifting authority to frontline workers who may discern practical difficulties and emerging opportunities that never even occur to a top-down planner.

2. *The aim is to change deeply rooted or ill-understood patterns of behavior in some target population.*

Backward mapping is most likely to apply when the objective is to modify behavior, especially when merely commanding change seems unlikely to bring it about (for example, moving poorly motivated individuals "from welfare to workfare" merely by threatening to cut off their benefits; or achieving change in the behavior of domestic abusers merely by ordering batterers to get control of themselves). Implicitly, the individuals in the target population will need to have their incentives modified or their habitual patterns of response altered—processes that usually take time, during which it may be possible to devise improved methods.

3. *The street-level bureaucrats either really do know the problem best or are presumed to be best able to learn.*

Frontline workers often are very able as well as very knowledgeable. Notwithstanding the desire of top leaders to keep agents under control, it is sometimes best to give them freer rein.

4. *The policy area or administrative role is one in which the frontline workers should be allowed some discretionary latitude.*

We saw in Chapter 8, Section 2, that strict compliance with a precise set of higher orders may be required of program implementers as a corollary of their duty to obey. In contrast, the adjudicative and especially the service provider's roles often require room for the exercise of discretion.

5. *Uncertainties exist at the top about the appropriate causal theory for the problem, implying a need for a "plan" that is flexible and open to adjustment as the implementers learn about the mechanisms that they are working with.*

Bottom-up planning will sometimes succeed where top-down planning would fail, simply because workers on the scene may best be able to discern the critical variables in the situation; in other words, they may be best able gradually to develop a correct causal theory of the problem. Furthermore, the ultimate implementers should be able to respond to any changes in these variables more quickly and more knowledgeably than planners far away in headquarters might be able to do.

6. *Adaptation over time is likely to be a requirement of successful program execution, especially over the long haul.*

We saw in Chapter 7 that implementation researchers emphasize the need to take an evolutionary view of most public programs and projects. Too rigid a plan or too minutely specified a set of rules can become a straightjacket. The ultimate outcome of an implementation effort will be as much a product of the chemistry between the day-to-day implementers and the members of the targeted population as it will be of the original conception of the enterprise.

7. *Questions exist regarding the most appropriate organization for the task.*

The existing outfit may not be the most suitable one. When it's not obviously a mission "for the Marines" or a job for the smoke jumpers—in other words, when the optimal choice of the organization for the assignment is unclear—the experimental attitude of the backward mapper may be the appropriate one. "Restructuring" is a frequent result when one goes the backward-mapping route. In some instances, a special new organization may evolve as the leader tries to piece together needed units from various parts of an existing structure.

To sum up: The backward mapper adopts the following two rules:

Enlist the administrative officials who are closest to the problem in a creative effort to solve it, instead of imposing detailed plans on them from above.

Involve all interested parties in the problem-solving process, thereby inviting a continuous striving for adjustments as individuals grope toward better appreciations of their own and others' concerns.

Backward mapping thus calls to mind the *negotiated order* of the bargaining theorists. At any instant, the backward mapper's "plan" is little more than a tissue of bargains, fragile in nature and subject to continuing negotiation and revision. This conception often proves a nice match for the kinds of systems that we encounter in public administration: underdetermined systems with fragmented structures of authority, dispersed information, and incomplete control. In such systems, decision making tends to be piecemeal; solutions emerge through incremental adjustment.

CHAPTER READING

In *The Manager as Negotiator,* two experts in modern bargaining theory, David Lax and James Sebenius of the Harvard Negotiating Project, point up the relationship between backward mapping and situations that call for coordination by mutual adjustment rather than direct supervision. Lax and Sebenius refer to the decision-making technique that's appropriate to such situations as **indirect management**—really, another term for the special requirements of the kinds of underdetermined problems that we've seen to be characteristic of public administration. You should find in the following selection not only an interesting case study—an account of President Gerald Ford's effort in 1976 to forestall a feared national public health hazard, the influenza "epidemic that wasn't"—but also a synthesis of certain ideas that we've so far treated separately: mutual adjustment, shared (in the sense of "fragmented") authority, and negotiation as an essential management skill.

Backward Mapping and Indirect Management: A Case Study—The Swine Flu Scare

David Lax and James Sebenius

What does a situation of shared authority and resources but concentrated accountability mean for managers? At a minimum, it calls for tools beyond those of traditional administration. To give up the illusion of control is not to give up the game.

Negotiating is a way of life for managers, whether renting office space, coaxing a spare part from another division, building support for a new marketing plan, or working out next year's budget. In these situations and thousand like them some interests conflict. People disagree. And they negotiate to find a form of joint action that seems better to each than the alternatives.

Virtually everyone accepts the importance of bargaining to sell a building, resolve a toxic waste dispute, acquire a small exploration company, or handle like situations. Yet negotiation goes well beyond such encounters and their most familiar images: smoke-filled rooms, firm proposals, urgent calls to headquarters, midnight deadlines, and binding contracts. Though far less recognized, much the same process is involved when managers deal with their superiors, boards of directors, even legislators. Managers negotiate with those whom they cannot command but whose cooperation is vital, including peers and others outside the chain of command or beyond the organization itself. Managers even negotiate with subordinates, who often have their own interests, understandings, sources of support, and areas of discretion.

In a static world, agreements once made generally endure. Yet change calls on organizers to adapt. And rapid changes call for new arrangements to be envisioned, negotiated, and renegotiated among those who know the situation best and will have to work with the results. . . .

Managers often find that their formal authority falls far short of their responsibilities and their success is dependent on the actions of others outside the chain of command. Though people in this predicament may yearn for more control, there is often no practical way to follow the textbook advice to match authority with responsibility. "Indirect management" is the name we give to this increasingly important phenomenon of concentrated responsibility but shared authority and resources. It calls for a very different approach from traditional line management. . . .

Textbooks urge that authority be carefully matched to responsibility, that control and accountability dovetail. [But often] this match does not hold and often cannot hold. . . . [M]anagers bear responsibility for production that is carried out through organizations or units that they do not directly "control." In such cases of "indirect management," the importance of the manager-as-negotiator dramatically increases.

. . . With the rise of complexity and interdependence, with increasing professionalization, with heavier emphasis on the role of information, with new organizational forms, and with the continuing decline in the automatic acceptance of formal authority, indirect managerial skills promise to be ever more necessary. . . .

As organizations have taken novel forms, become "flatter," involving matrix concepts, and the like, the ease of applying traditional notions of accountability has declined. . . .

Implications for Indirect Managers

What does a situation of shared authority and resources but concentrated accountability mean for managers? At a minimum, it calls for tools beyond those of traditional administration. Formal authority will be insufficient, commands will go unheeded, management systems will be inaccessible, and organizational culture will not flow across boundaries. Instead, the manager must create and modify networks of linked decisions and agreements. But this carries several implications.

Managers depend on "outsiders" for results. Consequently, managerial jobs are thus defined more by the required network of agreements than by organizational boundaries. In fact, this observation renders less interesting the old conundrum of just where the organization "stops." An indirect manager who stops where her organization does cannot do her job.

Sometimes, the required networks of linked agreements and decisions are not fully "inside" any set of organizations. In these cases, the networks' porosity and visibility will open them to many of the pressures that are often associated with legislatures. Interest groups, regional organizations, legislators, as well as other local, state, and private entities may seek to intrude on indirect managerial processes that would have been invisible had they been carried out "inside" organizations. Moreover, the obvious discretion associated with indirect managerial activities invites review by courts and administrative law judges. . . .

Apart from yearning for the old hierarchy, we see two broad approaches to the challenge of indirect management.

Seeking a Better Match of Authority and Accountability

The first response is to change the situation itself, to seek a better match of authority and responsibility. This may be done by renegotiating purposes, realigning expectations and accountability, and/or increasing authority and resources. This is an appealing course, but it is often impossible for individual managers who increasingly find themselves in such situations. . . .

Making the Most of an Indirect Management Situation

Beyond trying to wriggle out of the situation, managers may simply seek to be more effective. Instead of wishing for more control and ineffectually applying traditional tools, they must acknowledge that they face networks of linked agreements and that effective action requires extensive negotiation. To give up the illusion of control is not to give up the game.

We now present a basic approach to indirect management. Like direct production, the place to start is with a careful specification of desired results, followed by a delineation of the "production function" or required network of linked agreements. Then it is possible to determine the most promising bases for influencing needed decisions and agreements.

Desired Results—The Central Interest in Indirect Management Negotiations. A first question to ask is about the nature of the "product," or desired results. . . .

The capacity to specify the product will drive many subsequent management problems. Where characteristics can be well specified, management by means of formal agreement or contract is a possibil-

ity; where characteristics of the desired product elude such description, other approaches are needed. . . .

The Required Networks of Linked Agreements. After a careful attempt to specify the "product," a second step involves specifying the network of linked agreements most likely to yield it. Two related sets of questions facilitate this analysis. First, who is needed to carry out each part of the specified "production" process? To what must each agree, and what sort of decisions must be made? Second, to whose action or inaction is the desired result likely to be vulnerable? In effect, the desired product will come about through a network of linked agreements and decisions among the critical parties. Often, it is most efficient to begin with the desired result and carefully "map backward" through the necessary chain of actors and events. . . .

Obtaining Desired Agreements and Influencing Decisions. . . . Having looked at the product, the network, the parties whose involvement is needed at each stage, and to whom the results may be vulnerable, it is time to analyze the bases for potential agreement and decision. . . .

An Example of Indirect Management: Swine Flu Immunizations

Early in 1976, ominous signs began to appear of a possible major epidemic or "pandemic" of what looked like "swine influenza." This was particularly fearsome, since in 1918 an apparent swine flu pandemic had struck down some half a million Americans including a disproportionately large number of young parents and soldiers. Much uncertainty about the proper interpretation of the scientific evidence and many conflicting opinions about the appropriate government response to this health threat followed the early signs of a possible pandemic.

In any case, though, in a dazzling display of bureaucratic entrepreneurship, the Assistant Secretary of Health, Theodore Cooper, and Dr. David Sencer, the Director of the Centers for Disease Control (CDC), convinced then-President Gerald Ford to endorse a program to immunize "every man, woman, and child in the United States," as Ford put it publicly, against swine flu. The program was scheduled to start in the summer of 1976, before flu season began. In short, Cooper and Sencer obtained a mandate—the authority and resources to carry out the program they had advanced.

. . . Ultimately, the swine flu program foundered. Insurers refused to provide insurance for vaccinations; Congress not only had to pay for the vaccine, but also had to pass special liability-assuming legislation; timetables slipped; and distribution of the vaccine fell far short of the president's goal, a situation fortunately relieved by the persistent *failure* of the disease to make an appearance. Vaccinations, however, caused occasional bad side effects and some three hundred deaths which were intensively publicized. In shambles, the program was suspended. It is now widely recalled as as public health fiasco. . . .

Despite the possible ill-conceived nature of the original decision and the ultimate fate of the program, this situation provides a useful vehicle to analyze a particular indirect managerial problem in some detail. In retrospect, it is fairly obvious that this situation was not amenable to the techniques of direct management. Neither managers' orders nor their equivalent here, "doctors' orders," proved very potent.

Consider the situation as of March 1976, when with mandate in hand, Cooper and Sencer faced the problem of accomplishing universal swine flu immunizations by early the next fall. Had Cooper and his associates carefully brainstormed, or "mapped backward" from what ultimately needed to be done, their list would have included the following: people had to be convinced to go to health centers; injections had to be provided; plans and explanations for private physicians as well as state and local health bodies had to be in place; air guns and syringes had to be distributed along with the vaccine. Consent forms had to be printed and distributed. Monitoring and statistical reporting systems had to be installed. The vaccine itself had to be ordered, then produced in bulk, bottled, and insured. It also had to be paid for with funds appropriated for the purpose. These had to be legislated by Congress after being requested by Ford.

This "backward" recitation of requisite actions carries an immediate implication of the people and organizations who needed to agree to perform these tasks. The public had to be convinced to go and connect with syringes and air guns; the media had to convey much of the necessary information. Private and public physicians had to be convinced of the crisis and instructed about what to do. State and local health bodies had to formulate plans and coordinate them with the national Department of Heath, Education and Welfare. Pharmaceutical companies needed to make the vaccine; in turn, they had to be insured by private insurers or, as it turned out, by the federal government. HEW was responsible for procuring the vaccine, for completing field trials and other tests, and for coordinating the entire effort. Congress needed to appropriate the money and to deal with liability questions when the insurers balked. All of these early steps needed to be cleared through channels in the Ford Administration. . . .

Cooper, of course, "directly controlled" only a small fraction of this long chain of actors needed to implement his policies. Yet many held him and CDC head Sencer accountable for the program's ultimate perceived failure; Cooper, for example, was not reappointed by the next administration. . . .

Of course, this example—of shared authority and resources, combined with tight political accountability—defines the situation as one of indirect management. Though Cooper and Sencer did not have access to the traditional tools of public administration (personnel systems, budget systems, information systems, ability to alter organizational structure, and so forth), many techniques nevertheless existed that could have enhanced the chances for success.

Though the above discussion focuses on Cooper's problem of managing the swine flu program itself, Cooper had a variety of larger interests at stake. "Failure" would mean not only that his personal career was likely to suffer, but the Centers for Disease Control and other units formally subordinate to him would almost certainly lose substantial credibility. Future immunization programs would take place under a shadow and innovative preventive health initiatives would face much higher hurdles than before. Cooper and Sencer, understandably, focused on the immediate substantive issues and managed for the short-term, worst case—a major epidemic—which, it turned out, was regarded by many as unlikely. The more likely outcomes seemed outside their field of vision, as did some of the other interests that rode on the performance of the swine flu program.

A look at the organization of that small part of the network under Cooper's direct control shows a traditional organization on strict programmatic lines. After all, the Department of Health, Education and Welfare and the Centers for Diseases Control had always carried our immunization programs along such lines. No matter that this program envisioned vaccinating twice as many people as had ever before been run through such a program and in half the time. Information requests and orders were transmitted through a structured many-leveled hierarchy. In other words, nominal program channels were the conduits for information. It frequently took a long time for a crucial piece of information (e.g., that insurers were reluctant to insure the vaccine at all) to reach those who desperately needed it for managerial purposes. Yet program managers needed, on a timely and continuing basis, a vast amount of legal, public relations, scientific, production, logistical, and coordination related information. Timely information is crucial for direct managers; for indirect ones in a crisis, it is still more so.

The need for such information argues strongly for establishing a structure for this project rather than relying on the existing program management structure. . . .

Having diagnosed the situation as one of indirect management, having noted the central roles of uncertainty and information, and having tentatively prescribed a project-management system for the direct managerial aspects, it is now time to turn to the indirect managerial task. The problem at the time could be easily stated: How could Cooper get those outside HEW to do what he wanted? What means existed to get them to agree to act in accord with his program, especially since he would be accountable for what they did or did not do?

The relevant chain of actors and tasks can be identified by asking two questions: One, who needs

to do what for the program to work? And two, to what and whom are the desired program results vulnerable? As noted above, the chain of actors stretches back from the public, to the media, to state and local health bodies and private physicians, through pharmaceutical and insurance companies, to the Congress, to the Centers for Disease Control, to HEW, and to the rest of the administration. The discussion that follows considers how a manager can get these required actors to go along with program idea. . . .

The General Public. To go along, members of the general public had to be convinced that the shots would be safe, available, and effective. Further, they had to perceive their alternatives to a decision to go along with the program as painful and dangerous. . . .

Advocates of immunization had to base their appeal on scientific credibility and the legacy of previous successful immunization programs, such as that for polio. Through a televised image of Gerald Ford receiving a swine flu shot, presidential authority would be invoked. In other times this may have been potent, but as a campaigner that year in tight presidential primary and election races, Gerald Ford needed to "borrow" authority. In fact, to persuade the public, it may have been necessary to have a more vivid image: swine flu actually sighted in the southern hemisphere (where the flu seasons alternate with those in the northern hemisphere), bodies, a genuine crisis atmosphere. All of these elements, however, point to the key role of the media in the "production" of public immunization.

The Media. . . . The swine flu program clearly had any number of easily foreseeable public relations vulnerabilities. First, in advance of an actual epidemic, members of the media could simply ignore the program or attack it on any number of grounds. If the vaunted "consensus" of top scientists in favor of the program were to unravel, it would look contrived (in fact, there were prominent defectors from the consensus). Ford's announcement of the swine flu decision the day after his North Carolina primary loss to Ronald Reagan did not help the program's image.

Moreover, in any sustained national immunization drive, one could readily predict that "temporally coincident deaths" would occur. . . .

Rather than appoint an inexperienced doctor as the informal press liaison, the program managers might have tapped a great deal of in-house media expertise at HEW. When three deaths occurred in a Pennsylvania clinic, local officials there conveyed a great deal of confusion and intimated that it must have been a batch of "bad vaccine." Some early planning by HEW officials could have alerted local public health people everywhere to this statistically foreseeable possibility and helped the Centers for Disease Control to change the "bad vaccine" image that ultimately and unnecessarily resulted. Recognizing the crucial role of the media as part of the entire immunization program—for which Cooper and Sencer were held accountable—it is hardly too much to suggest that some media-wise input should have been sought early on and emphasized thereafter by indirect program managers.

State and Local Health Bodies and Private Physicians. These groups represented the implementation capability of the program. Though Cooper had little "direct authority" over them, a number of factors might have enhanced the chances of their agreement with his vision. If they had shared Cooper and Sencer's perception of the problem and concurred in the scientific judgment, strong professional norms and shared purposes of protecting public health should have guaranteed their participation.

Conversely, if upon revealing all evidence and analysis that the Centers for Disease Control had, these groups remained unenthusiastic, then who else would have been likely to go along? Yet in some early dealing with key state and local public health bodies, there was a great deal of dissent about the nature of the threat and the possible response. Physicians and public health professionals in these meetings pointed to any number of difficulties in mounting a universal program. They pointed to the opportunity cost of swine flu in terms of other programs. They seriously questioned the scientific merit of the program. These questioning voices should at least have given some pause to Sencer and Cooper. Information should have flowed in *two* directions here. An

unjustifiable certainty and arrogance with respect to "the proper response"—which they "knew"—ended up costing the two dearly.

The Congress. If the job had been done well with state and local physicians and the media, keeping the program separate from "politics" should have gone a long way toward maintaining congressional support. It then would have become a fairly simple matter to keep the appropriate congressional committees informed and designate someone or some unit to be the official source of ongoing information. Many congressional complaints had their origins in the apparent lack of someone at HEW that was "in charge."

The Pharmaceutical Companies. It should have been fairly straightforward to manage this relationship contractually. HEW had a long-term relationship with these companies and could expect relatively easy bargaining with them over this program given the many immunization programs with which they would deal jointly.

The Insurance Companies. The insurance companies were an essential ingredient in the production of the vaccine. Moreover, a "will not insure" decision would have appeared to convey to the public fatal misgivings about the safety of the program. A simple prescription was appropriate to this twofold vulnerability. Given the program's central reliance on insurance companies, HEW officials should have probed their motives and procedures and sought to understand them better. Instead, they did not deal or negotiate with them directly, but only through the vaccine manufacturers. In dealing only with the manufacturers, HEW program managers incurred substantial unnecessary risks. . . .

In review, . . . backward mapping would have revealed the long chain of actors that encompassed the "production function." This chain displayed the classic symptoms of an indirect management situation: shared authority and resources but concentrated accountability for program results. The many scientific and managerial uncertainties suggested the key role of information and communication, and implied that the direct organizational effort should have been organized more along project lines than by existing programs. These direct managerial decisions would have complemented the larger, indirect task of getting people to agree or decide to go along with their plan.

The answers to two questions would have offered indispensable insight: What was needed for success, and to whom and what was the program vulnerable? A minimum prescription would have been to focus attention on and try to understand entities that turned up in answer to these questions. The harder managerial task was influencing them to go along with the program. Standard tools of administration did not appear to offer much help. Instead, the methods of bargaining and persuasion should have been used. . . .

An acute consciousness of the indirect managerial aspects of the program might have prevented considerable grief. And that is the case in almost all indirect management situations.

From David A. Lax and James K. Sebenius, *The Manager as Negotiator* (New York: Free Press, 1986), pp. 1–2, 314–319, 320–323, 329–338.

CHAPTER CASE

Domestic violence is a serious—and apparently an increasing—problem in our society. Long before the murder trial of O. J. Simpson dramatized the domestic violence problem, police officials and social workers had suspected the extent of intrafamilial abuse and were trying to do something about it. But what?

If ever a problem begged for a comprehensive response, this would seem to be it. Lack of dramatic action to deal with abusers may condemn literally hundreds of thousands of victims to living in continuous fear of beatings, injury, and even death. For this reason, Congress and virtually all states have tightened the domestic violence laws. Additional legislation seems likely in many locales. Typical are laws which would require that police officers arrest batterers and that judges put them in jail. Unfortunately, however, data on the causes and possible cures of abusive behavior are patchy and even contradictory. If we have no valid causal theory of the domestic violence problem, if we haven't solid evidence about the kinds of programs that will actually reduce the number and severity of incidents, should we act cautiously instead of boldly and dramatically?

As you consider the issues that concern the key figures in this case (State Senator O'Haire, legislative aide Tom Opperman, Sheriff Al Rilleau, and Linda Vega, among others), you might want to bear in mind the following questions:

1. Does our level of knowledge about the domestic violence problem, applied in a framework based on the Supreme Court's three-pronged test (discussed in Chapter 8), justify a sweeping new law? Or does incremental adjustment provide a more suitable legislative philosophy?

2. Which approach should the implementers of a policy for dealing with domestic violence adopt: forward mapping or backward mapping? How will this choice be influenced by the nature of the problem, the ability of responsible officials to gather information about the frequency of violent incidents, and the relationship between policy makers (Senator O'Haire and his colleagues) and the officials who will have to deal with abusers and their victims?

CASE 10

·················

Dealing with Domestic Violence:
A "Night in Jail" Law for Spouse Abusers?

Sheriff Al Rilleau glanced over at the Tuesday morning *Tribune-Examiner,* squinting to focus on the headline under his wife Rachel's tapping fingertip:

Bill Moves toward Vote in Capitol:
Jail for Wife Beaters!

"Just what we need," Rilleau muttered.

"It *is* just what we need!" Rachel replied.

"No, I didn't mean it in a negative way," Rilleau protested. "It's probably a good bill, and I hope they pass it into law. But a new law always raises questions for the cops who've got to put it in effect"—as though Rachel didn't know.

Rilleau, leaving the breakfast table, sighed. "I better ask some of our local 'bright eyes' what new responsibilities and procedures they're dreaming up for us." The *they* were the legislators who, according to the *Trib'-Examiner* piece, would soon approve a stiff new domestic violence law.

"Well, I don't care what your new responsibilities and procedures are, just so they help those poor women!" That was Rachel's parting shot as her husband squared his cap and left for his office in the county building.

•   •   •   •   •

Usually, Al Rilleau took no special interest in the FBI reports on violent crime. Certainly Rilleau never went out of his way to track the national statistics on murders, rapes, and other so-called Index Crimes. But he kept the relevant local-area data always in the front of his mind and could hardly help noting whether the norms for his bailiwick were above, below, or on a par with the national crime rates. Almost 40 percent of the trouble calls to which his sheriff's deputies responded during any given week involved domestic violence, a figure that closely paralleled the national statistic. In fact, all other crimes of physical violence *combined* demanded less of Rilleau's and his officers' time than did battering cases within families.

In his office, Sheriff Rilleau settled at his desk to read the news article with some care.

Jail for Wife Beaters!

by Claire Nagamura

In recent years, some feminist leaders, police administrators, and social workers have urged not only more intensive counseling but also tougher treatment of spouse beaters. (Domestic abuse takes many forms, *all of them serious, but the representative offender is a male who has a continuing married or unmarried relationship with a woman and who develops a pattern of battering his partner.) Many proponents of the tougher stance recommend "night in jail" laws. Under such a law, a police officer responding to a domestic violence call may not simply tell the abuser to cool off, as was traditional in many jurisdictions, but must arrest and hold him for a specified period behind bars.*

Wife battering is the most frequent cause of physical injury to women. In the majority of cases, the behavior leading up to an incident is just what the stereotype suggests: A habitually abusive husband or live-in boyfriend loses control and pounds on the nearest "object." If that object happens to be his wife or girlfriend, the result is abuse—often escalating to aggravated assault or even homicide. Almost one-third of women murdered in the United States are victims of their male partners.

Laws have been passed in fifteen states requiring arrests in domestic abuse cases. In nineteen states, laws mandate arrest for the violator of a court order issued to protect the victim of a previous battering incident. We now bid to join the list with a mandatory "night in jail" rule for spouse batterers. The proposed bill is expected to pass handily in both houses, and the governor has assured feminist advocates that he will promptly sign it into law.

What Works Best?

In 1984 a pioneering study in Minneapolis compared the deterrent effects of three kinds of police responses: mediation of the quarrel by the responding officers (the traditional law enforcement approach to domestic violence); requiring the batterer to cool off by leaving the house for eight hours or more; and arrest of the abuser, followed by a night in jail. The researchers found the night in jail was most effective in changing behavior. But Dr. John Stoppa, a sociologist specializing in criminology at the University of New Mexico, said that follow-up studies to the Minneapolis survey show mixed results. Analyses of battering cases in Colorado Springs (Colorado) and Miami (Florida) confirmed that prompt arrest of a domestic offender deters repeat episodes. However, three other studies—in Charlotte (North Carolina), Milwaukee (Wisconsin), and Omaha (Nebraska)—showed arrests correlating with *increases* in subsequent violence. "Arresting a batterer may end up boomeranging against the victim," Stoppa said, "by adding to the buildup of rage and resentment in the abuser."

Economic Conditions Count

Searching beneath the inconsistencies in the research, analysts found that arrest was associated with an increased subsequent propensity to violence for batterers who were unemployed but that it correlated with a decrease for batterers who held jobs throughout the period of the offense, arrest, and follow-up observation period. Relative to the results expected in the absence of a jail-time requirement, for both employed and unemployed abusers, offenders who were subjected to criminal prosecution proved less likely to recidivate than did those who were merely arrested, jailed, and released the next morning without prosecution. The recidivism rate further declined as a direct function of the stiffness of the sentence.

Rilleau refolded the newspaper and pitched it. He swiveled, reaching for a dog-eared telephone directory to double-check his recollection of Ernie Guerrero's number. It was after 9 o'clock in the morning; Guerrero would probably be starting his third hour of work at the county attorney's office. Guerrero answered after one ring, and Rilleau skipped the pleasantries. "Ernie, this 'night in jail' bill that's coming up for a vote in the legislature: I take it it's going to pass."

Ernest Guerrero hadn't been out of law school for more than a year or two, and his post as deputy assistant county attorney was his first professional appointment. Guerrero confessed that he hadn't been following the progress of the bill, but he knew enough to assure Rilleau that "almost everyone in the DA business" liked what they had heard about it.

"Can you check the wording of the bill and tell me what I think about it?" Rilleau asked.

Guerrero laughed. "Sure, if a quick opinion will do."

The next day, Rilleau's fax machine contained the promised memo from Guerrero:

MEMORANDUM OF LAW

TO: Sheriff Albert Rilleau
FROM: E. Guerrero, Deputy Assistant County Attorney
SUBJECT: Pending Domestic Violence Act

This memorandum is in response to your phone request for an opinion regarding the subject bill (will be codified as 23 *Stat.*—), apparently a sure bet for quick passage, which will provide, in pertinent part:

(Subpart 2 (A)) Each county, or at the discretion of the relevant boards of county commissioners or their equivalents, several counties acting in concert, and incorporated municipalities within such county or congregate of counties, will not later than 45 days after this law becomes effective,

(a)   develop a plan to deal with domestic abuse, provided that the plan will include a minimum requirement of mandatory incarceration or prosecution in any instance in which a responding local law enforcement officer finds an adult person physically abusing a family member, or on the basis of substantial evidence, finds an adult person to have perpetrated such an act of abuse within a brief period before the police arrived on the scene; and

(b)   develop a full-service approach to domestic violence prevention and suppression, which may include but not be limited to pre-event intervention upon reasonable cause, shelters for victims, and counseling and therapy for the batterer.

Each such county or multicounty plan is to be recorded in the office of the state attorney general and is to have the force of law.

Commentary

On the face of it, the new statute, if passed, will create an entitlement for physically abused individuals in a domestic violence situation to receive police assistance and some combination of police action against the abuser and therapy for the victims upon any officer's finding of a physically abusive situation. Within 45 days of signing by the governor, your department, our office, and city and county social service workers have to provide personnel and facilities so that all entitled individuals will be able to gain the benefits created by this law. You and the others (the county's Department of Welfare Services crowd, the shelter staffers from the city's Bureau of Human Services, etc.), along with someone from our office and probably representatives from probations and parole, will have to negotiate the exact plan.

Let me clarify the words *entitlements* and *benefits* in this context.

In 1983 the Supreme Court said that a person has a legal entitlement to a benefit if an official must provide such benefit whenever certain substantive predicates are met (*Hewitt* v. *Helms,* 459 U.S. 460, 472). The wording of the proposed domestic violence law will establish such a "substantive predicate," namely, a finding by a police officer of recent physical abuse against a family member. However, we won't know exactly what benefit(s) the abused person would then be entitled to until the plan for our area has been drawn up. All we know now, from the wording of the law, is that the follow-up actions called for in the plan will be mandatory. A responding officer will have to use judgment in each case to tell whether the predicates have been satisfied, but—depending on the plan—may have no discretion in the way he or she reacts if abuse (the factual predicate) is found to exist. Also, depending on the plan, we in County Attorney may have no discretion in deciding whether or not to prosecute.

I interpret *benefits* here as including the battered woman's entitlement to have her abuser arrested. But note that, although the press refers to the statute as a "night in jail" law, the wording permits several options: (1) arrest followed by incarceration and release, (2) arrest followed by release *without incarceration* but with subsequent prosecution, (3) arrest followed by incarceration and prosecution, or (4) some combination of all the above. The full-service requirement also gets the public health types, social workers, and maybe some others into the act. The final plan will be mandatory, not permissive; but county officials have the discretion within the 45-day limit to decide which procedure to use.

Additional Considerations

I gather that there have been problems in other states with "night in jail" laws when the statute or the implementing regulations require that *both* parties be arrested (and/or jailed, and/or prosecuted) when both seem to have inflicted injury, even if one party inflicted the injury in self-defense. These simultaneous busts are known as *dual-arrest incidents.* The words of the pending bill go to the injurers' actions, not their motives. Police officers operating under mandates such as the ones indicated in the proposed statute often refuse to take chances on not enforcing the letter of the law, so they arrest both parties in a dispute even when a little discretion might be called for.

You should also be aware that mandatory arrest laws sometimes deter victims or neighbors from reporting violence, since a report amounts to a guarantee that one (or both) parties will spend some time behind bars.

Litigation is likely before anyone will be sure how the courts will read the new law, and then experience in actual implementation will be needed before we'll know if it's part of the solution or part of the problem—if it positively affects the batterer or further enrages him; if it deters the abuser or merely intimidates the victim in a way that prevents the police from even being called.

Across the bottom of his memo, Guerrero had scribbled in a broad hand: *"Now if we can only get the judges to cooperate when they sentence these guys!"*

● ● ● ● ●

Sheriff Rilleau had been impressed on several occasions when he had dealt with Linda Vega during minor disturbance calls at the Agua Blanca public housing units. The two had also served together on a United Way subcommittee for a while after Vega had discontinued her breaking-in duty at Agua Blanca and moved to full-time work on Evelyn Alvarado's staff in the BHS headquarters building. Like Ernie Guerrero, Linda Vega had about her the confident way of a comer; like Ernie too, Linda had the kind of energy and imagination that qualified her as one of those whom Al Rilleau dubbed "bright eyes."

Rilleau phoned Evelyn Alvarado to ask if she could "lend Linda Vega" to help him on a special project for a few days. Linda, Al had said, could "give him a social service slant on the pending night-in-jail bill." Evelyn was happy, as ever, to win some goodwill by lending the services of a BHS staff member to a requesting local official. Evelyn Alvarado knew that Al Rilleau knew that she would feel free someday to call in a return favor from the sheriff's shop.

It was Rilleau's thought that Vega could help him prepare for the county officials' negotiations—the interagency planning process for implementation of the proposed new law. Rilleau also assumed that Vega might turn out to be the Housing Department administrator assigned to coordinate the shelter component of the plan. For the period of time she was assigned to the sheriff's office, Vega would help Rilleau think through any changes that might be desirable in his department.

● ● ● ● ●

The conclusions reached in the pioneering 1984 Minneapolis study regarding the deterrent effect of night-in-jail laws convinced U.S. Attorney General William French Smith to issue a formal statement officially recommending arrest as the standard police response in domestic assault cases. In 1984, however, police in most states could not legally make warrantless arrests for misdemeanors unless the offense occurred in the officer's presence. Battery, unless aggravated, was (and remains) a misdemeanor in most jurisdictions. Therefore, in response to Attorney General Smith's mandatory-arrest recommendation, legislators across the nation (except only in Alabama and in West Virginia) passed laws waiving the ancient common-law rule prohibiting warrantless arrests for out-of-sight misdemeanors.

Under the new laws, police officers could make warrantless arrests on the scene of a domestic incident if they had probable cause to believe that a misdemeanor has been committed or that a restraining order has been violated. That change in the law opened the way for stern responses by police officers who thought they found evidence of domestic violence. Nevertheless, domestic violence laws continued to be underenforced through the 1980s. Until states actually began passing night-in-jail laws in the early 1990s, an average of only 3 to 5 percent of battering incidents across the nation resulted in arrests.

Most experts attributed the reluctance of law enforcement officials to make arrests to cultural factors—to patterns of habit and value among police officers that led to leniency toward batterers. Sheriff Rilleau thought that, on this subject at least, the experts were probably right. When Rilleau had broken into police work, the professional law enforcement officer's book on domestic violence read very differently from the way it does now. In the old days, rookie cops everywhere were taught to treat domestic disputes as private matters, subject only to civil action by the victim. ("She can leave him; she can divorce him.") Many cops still saw the domestic violence call as an occasion for mediation: Stop the violence; cool the situation; find a compromise. Get back to *real* police work.

As a young patrolman, Al Rilleau hadn't heard of a single case of nonlethal domestic violence in which an officer actually cuffed a batterer and took him to lockup, let alone completed the paperwork needed for a follow-up criminal prosecution. Nor would change come quickly. Across the country (and certainly in Rilleau's department), respected officers trained in the old negotiative tradition remained alive and well and probably handled domestic violence calls pretty much as they had been taught in earlier days. Rilleau had no doubt that the practitioners of the old ways were passing the same techniques—which they regarded as compassionate, humane ways of resolving battering episodes—on to the young officers coming up. Rilleau never met a cop who liked a wife beater. Still, it was common in the squad cars and locker rooms to hear guardedly empathetic comments about the "terrific pressure" that the typical batterer presumably experienced: "Too much beer, too little work, absolutely no hope—and besides, who really knew what 'drove him to it' behind closed doors?"

Whether he agreed with the goals of the new law or not (and from what he knew, based on Claire Nagamura's news article and Ernie Guererro's memo, he did agree), Rilleau doubted that it would be as easy as the politicians apparently thought to turn attitudes, practices, or priorities on their heads within the sheriff's department. He recalled an analysis in an old police administration text by a British criminologist named Chatterton:

Perhaps the greatest fault in the traditional police response to domestic violence is not best described as an unwillingness to act, but overwillingness to assume the "judgment of Solomon." There is evidence that police do have judgmental attitudes to the behavior of women victims which they may consider contributory to the man's violence, e.g., if they think the woman is "nagging," "hysterical," or "a sluttish housewife."

Chatterton . . . recognizes the prevalence of this tendency not to enforce the law in practical policing. . . . As Chatterton explains further, the legal victim did not always prove to be a moral victim. He develops a model in which he identifies the four combinations of these tendencies in which the legal evidence and constructs of moral blameworthiness are in accord or at variance, and shows the impact this has on arrest decisions. . . . [See Sketch 11.1.]

Chatterton discusses in some detail one case he attended where the moral blamelessness of the husband and the moral blameworthiness of the wife governed the officer's decision not to arrest from a moral perspective, though from a legal perspective evidence for arrest was more than sufficient. . . . The entry [in the officer's day book] read "Domestic

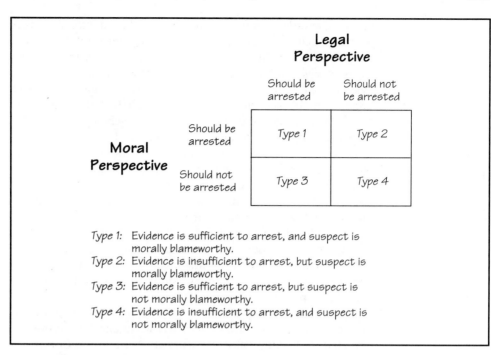

Sketch 11.1 Combining Legal with Moral Judgments in a Police Officer's Decision to Arrest

dispute. Parties advised." The officer in conversation with Chatterton explained his decision not to arrest by referring to the moral characteristics of the father, whom he considered a good worker and provider, counterposed against the mother who kept a slovenly home and was difficult and "mouthy." . . .[1]

•   •   •   •   •

From the journal of Linda Vega. Subject: Successful programs dealing with domestic violence.

Given the impetus to night-in-jail laws that the 1984 Minneapolis study had provided, it wasn't surprising that the nearby city of Duluth developed one of the first and most noteworthy mandatory-arrest organizations. Court officials, the police, and various social-agency policy makers worked their approach out with women's rights advocates.

In Duluth, the members of a central council, the Domestic Abuse Intervention Project (DAIP), coordinate responses in all battering cases. Police, probation officers, shelter managers, and domestic counselors participate. On the criminal justice side, swift arrest followed by vigorous criminal prosecution are key elements. Follow-up involves monitoring of the assailant's whereabouts and conduct, especially when a

[1]From Susan S. M. Edwards, *Policing "Domestic" Violence* (London: Sage Publications, 1989), pp. 94–96.

protective order has been issued to prohibit additional contact between him and the victim. Such protection orders are strictly enforced. Batterers are closely monitored, sometimes through "saturation surveillance." Pretrial probation programs for assailants involve weapons forfeiture and, often, no-contact orders. Thereafter, domestic violence cases receive "fast-track court scheduling" and expedited trials. The Duluth approach also sets aside resources for rehabilitation for the assailant.

DAIP workers mobilize shelter and psychological as well as medical support services for the victim. Because many victims of domestic abuse know little of their legal rights, DAIP professionals or volunteer workers brief the women, who may seek restraining orders or decide to press charges against their assailants. The latter course effectively commits the victim to testify against her abuser—often, a forbidding prospect. Trained participants in support groups that are organized by county attorney's representatives accompany the women into court.

Under these procedures, Duluth officials increased the misdemeanor assault conviction rate in domestic abuse cases from 20 percent to more than 80 percent. On the rehabilitative side, DAIP administrators over the life of the program to date have arranged for special counseling and other supportive social services for 200 to 250 assailants per year.

Linda Vega had extracted this information from a long article on domestic violence law in a 1993 *Harvard Law Review*. To check for more recent developments, she phoned the Duluth Police Department. One Ellwood Dormsjo, who had been with the DAIP from its inception, confirmed the information that Linda had assembled from published material. He added: "By the way, a prof over at the 'U' here"—Dormsjo was referring to the Duluth campus of the University of Minnesota—"has done some further studying.[2] You can give her a call: Dr. Melanie Shepard in the School of Social Work. Dr. Shepard is one of the authorities on the 'battered wife syndrome.' What she found will surprise you."

Dormsjo continued: "This Dr. Shepard spent five years measuring everything you can imagine in DAIP. Then she ran her statistics on the computer. Her numbers show that a batterer is less likely to repeat if he's arrested, prosecuted, and sentenced to time in jail. But the correlation is far from certain. And—here's the surprise—the longer the guy's been abusing the woman before he gets arrested and caught up in the criminal justice system, the more likely he is to mend his ways."

Dormsjo was right; that finding *did* surprise Linda.

"A batterer does it once, and if he's caught and arrested, he's more likely—quite a bit more likely, according to the numbers—to repeat. But if a batterer has a pattern of abuse going on for some time, and *he's* finally put through the treatment—same DAIP treatment as the first offender—he's more likely to *not* recidivate. Damned if I can figure it!"

•   •   •   •   •

Linda Vega took a fresh sheet of paper and tried her hand at a PERT diagram of a domestic violence response plan for the local area, assuming that the new bill

[2]Melanie Shepard, "Predicting Batterer Recidivism Five Years after Community Intervention," 7 *Journal of Family Violence* (No. 3, September 1992): 167–177.

became law and, hence, that administrators from the relevant agencies would have to work out procedures for implementing the get-tough policy. Working slowly, fitting pieces together as in a puzzle, Vega sketched a pattern of boxes connected by arrows. Each box contained an "event," and each arrow showed which events led to which other ones.

First comes the precipitating *incident*, which someone has to *report* (events 1 and 2). The police dispatcher orders a response. *Arrival* is the next event: Cops reach the scene and check it out. If they find that violence has been perpetrated, they make the required *arrest*—or, if appropriate, they arrest both parties involved. From this fourth event box (arrest), Vega split off two arrows to indicate the start of multiple paths, one to be followed by the abuser, and the other by the victim.

On path 1, the offender goes to *jail*. The next morning, there's an *arraignment* (usually after a public defender is assigned to the case); this is an important event because it takes the batterer out of police hands and puts him into the jurisdiction of the courts. Usually the judge orders a *release*, probably letting the abuser return home with a warning, but sometimes freeing him under an order to stay away from the victim (another two-arrow split). In cases of serious injury, the judge may decide to hold the offender without bail, in which case he goes back to jail (that now makes three arrows). If the county plan calls for mandatory prosecution, the offender must wait for the *trial*. Then there's *sentencing* and whatever *follow-up* the county negotiators come up with to implement the new law.

Meanwhile, on path 2, the responding officers have contacted someone from social welfare services, who comes to the home and arranges medical *treatment* for the victim and, probably, a night (at least) in a *shelter*. Now the BHS, the nearest hospital or clinic, and the Housing Department are in the network, along with the cops and the courts. The next morning, while the batterer is being arraigned, the victim is with a social worker undergoing an intensive personal *evaluation*, mainly to determine whether she should return home or stay a while longer in the shelter (yet another two-arrow split). If there are kids, an additional set of caseworkers—the folks from "juv'y" (Juvenile Services)—may become involved. None of this takes into account the possible participation of private nonprofit organizations and volunteers (churches, women's support groups, and so forth). Some weeks down the road, there'll probably be a quick trial in which the victim is a prosecution witness, assuming that she gets the moral and legal support that such a role requires. New law or not, most such trials end with a suspended sentence.

Vega looked over her diagram, noting the pattern of organizational involvement, timing, and coordination: police, corrections, the courts, her own Housing Department in the BHS, other social agencies, and probably an oddment of private firms working for any of the above under contract. "Jail for Wife Beaters!" the headline over Claire Nagamura's article had read. But to administer a night-in-jail law would take a lot more than some willing police officers and a few extra cubic feet of cell space. For that matter, it wasn't even clear to Vega that the police should have the primary organizational responsibility for implementation of such a law. (Should social workers instead of the police take the lead?) And it certainly wasn't obvious how the complex of cooperating agencies—cops, county attorney, courts, public health, several units of city BHS and county DWS—should be brought together in pursuance of the "full-service" provisions of the proposed new law.

• • • • •

Tom Opperman hung up the phone, his brow furrowing slightly. "That stuff of Dr. Shepard up in Duluth," he thought, "seems thin, like a lot of research in sociology. But it also seems to say that the 'battered wife syndrome'... well, it's *lots* more complicated than appears on the surface."

It had been Opperman's job to check out the night-in-jail bill before State Senator O'Haire irrevocably committed himself to a positive vote. Was the proposal based on a sound understanding of the problem that the lawmakers hoped to fix? Opperman's assignment had taken him into several bodies of literature. He had reviewed current writings on behavior modification and deterrence and had reviewed the work of the so-called implementation researchers. (Should domestic legislation be centered on a firm statement of a policy objective? Or on a definition of certain behavior that lawmakers hoped to change?) Naturally, Opperman had read up on the subject of spouse abuse. Pursuing leads uncovered in the library, he eventually found himself on the phone with the same Melanie Shepard whom Ellwood Dormsjo had mentioned to Linda Vega.

Professor Shepard's work established one behavioral profile for nonhabitual abusers and a different pattern for long-time batterers. Was that surprising? What implications did the evidence—sketchy as it seemed—have for public policy? Ultimately, Opperman thought, the aim should be prevention rather than just punishment after the fact. In this connection, the Shepard work seemed suggestive. It stood to reason that first-time or nonhabitual abusers wouldn't have records. Neither the police nor social workers could be expected to prevent violence when there was no basis to expect it. Longtime batterers, on the other hand, were precisely the ones for whom there should be a trail of incidents inviting special attention—perhaps surveillance; surely intervention to prevent the next episode, especially when the next episode might be fatal and when, surprisingly, intervention actually seemed to work best in the cases of habitual abusers.

Opperman had also come across some of the same information that Ernie Guerrero cited in his memo to Al Rilleau: suggestions to the effect that the denial of any discretion to responding police officers might lead to overly rigid applications of the law, especially in dual-arrest situations; hints to the effect that the *mandatory* in mandatory arrest laws might deter reporting and hence might worsen the very problem they were intended to solve.

Maybe, Opperman concluded, he should think a bit more about this domestic violence bill. By political instinct as well as by conviction, his boss, Senator O'Haire, leaned strongly toward voting for the night-in-jail law. But maybe the senator should pause and consider before adding his voice to the expected overwhelming majority when the bill came up for a vote.

Opperman frowned. Delay for further study mightn't be the politically opportune play. Any wavering about the night-in-jail bill by Senator O'Haire now, Opperman realized, would raise the ire of some loyal members of his constituency. Spokeswomen for most feminist groups wanted this legislation; they wanted it badly, and they wanted it *now!* These voters constituted an important bloc. In the past, voters who leaned to the liberal side on social and gender issues had always been able to count on the senator for support when crucial bills came up, and they had repeatedly repaid him with financial and electoral support.

• • • • •

From the Journal of Linda Vega. Source: Albert J. Reiss. Subject: Contrasting approaches to the control of harmful behavior.

Many, if not most, social control systems are organized as a mixture of compliance and deterrence models of law enforcement. Still, when faced with a potential or actual violation, the two systems behave differently. When faced with a potential violation, the deterrence-based system will mobilize its detection system to await the actual violation so that it may catch and punish violators; the compliance-based system correlatively will attempt to prevent its occurrence. To prevent violations, compliance systems may use *threats* of punishments, but to actually carry out a punishment is a signal of its failure to prevent the noncompliance. . . .

[T]he levying of a penalty in compliance systems is a mark of its failure to secure compliance, whereas the levying of a penalty is a mark of success in deterrence-based systems. In deterrence systems, penalties serve notice that all violators will suffer a similar fate; in compliance-based systems, they serve notice that the law enforcement system has been unable to secure compliance.

Compliance and deterrence law enforcement systems differ also in their organization for the mobilization of law. Compliance systems are organized to induce conformity either by providing incentives towards that end or by using means that prevent unwanted conditions. They are primarily proactive in their mobilization. . . . Deterrence law enforcement systems are organized to detect and process violations once they have occurred. They vary in their mix of proactive and reactive mobilization forms, but on balance depend on reactive mobilization. . . .

The core violation in a compliance system is often dubbed a "technical" violation, behavior that violates a condition or standard that is designed to *prevent* harm or unwanted conditions. In contrast, the core violation in a deterrence system is *immediately harmful* behavior. . . .

Typically, compliance and deterrence systems differ as well in their presumptions of sociocultural causality. Deterrence systems rest on presumptions about the causal effect of sanctions, especially the power of sanctioning violators to deter future violations. . . . Compliance systems presume knowledge of what causes violations and of how to prevent them if causal conditions are manipulated.[3]

• • • • •

[3]From Albert J. Reiss, Jr., "Selecting Strategies of Social Control over Organizational Life," in Hawkins and Thomas, eds., *Enforcing Regulation* (Boston: Kluwer-Nijhoff), pp. 24–26.

Linda Vega sat in the vestibule, out of Al Rilleau's direct line of sight, waiting for Richardson—Deputy Todd Richardson. After some cajoling, Sheriff Rilleau had agreed to let Vega ride with a patrol team to see how officers responded to domestic violence calls. "You can turn on the TV any night and see camera teams reporting on cops' live-action jobs," Linda had argued. "You mean I can't see firsthand what I'm supposed to help you reorganize?"

Al had grunted reluctant agreement with Linda's logic. "Okay. Start with Richardson. I guess I can't object if he won't." What Rilleau didn't say (and didn't have to) was that cops don't much like outsiders on their cases. But then, who does?

"Remember, if there's a d.v.—which is likely, they come in all the time—you stay out of it." Rilleau winked: "And we just won't tell Guerrero, who handles county liability, that you were along for one of our rides."

A few minutes before 7 o'clock, Richardson appeared and introduced himself. "Bob Peña—he's my partner this week." Richardson pointed to the fortyish-looking deputy approaching the two of them. "Peña, he don't like Watch 2—family man, and I guess the wife complains when he's on nights."

"Miss Vega here. She's riding tonight," Richardson told Peña.

The local Latino community was close-knit, and Peña knew about Linda Vega. A New Yorker . . . college . . . that pretty much said it. Talk was, she was working on the sheriff's plan for the new d.v. procedure. Peña, along with everyone else in the department, expected quick passage of the proposed law, but he certainly didn't understand why Rilleau had to go outside the department for help.

"Riding? No way," Peña snapped.

"It's from Al," Todd countered, knowing that nothing else had to be said.

It was shaping up to be quite a patrol. Peña didn't like nights; Richardson didn't seem to like partnering with Peña; and it didn't do much for either of them, this business of getting looked over by "the girl" (as both thought of Linda) from the BHS. Besides, Richardson knew that if the rumors were right, Peña himself didn't fare very high on the home front.

Peña, at the wheel, cruised the blue-and-white out Candelaria to the near part of West Patrol Section. Calls came sporadically through the radio crackle: "Accident, 19th and Broad: 6, please respond." "Complaints from Herman at the Forum. Some rowdiness. Who takes it?" "Carolyn, Jake: Raise hq."

Then: "16. Fighting again, 1586 Hebrides basement. Neighbor call."

"Away we go," Richardson said, without excitement. "*Again.* Second call, and it's just Wednesday."

"Take 'B-Vista' here, right through to Hebrides," Richardson ordered. Both officers seemed to have forgotten Vega's presence in the back seat.

"Rodriguez, . . ." Peña said, "he has too much pressure. Berkman's [meaning Berkman Trucking Company] laying off. Rodriguez's afraid he's next to go. What'll he do then?"

Todd broke in. "I don't want to hear about it. You can't hit the wife and kids. No matter why. It's the second call this week on Rodriguez."

Peña—who seemed tense but in no hurry—slowed off Buena Vista, took a dog-leg turn down the street with the missing sign, and drew up before 1586. Hebrides was familiar to both Richardson and Peña, a street where people had their work cut out to keep from slipping backward. Still, it was the kind of overbuilt block on which, at another time, there might be a sense of neighborhood—not now, though, with the noise from the Rodriguez place and all.

Richardson, first out of the car and quick to the door, gave a perfunctory holler. There was no direct answer—only a shouted expletive, apparently not directed at him. He tried the door and, finding it locked, smashed the knob with a swing of his knee. Peña, lagging behind, shook his head, whether in sadness or anger, Vega couldn't tell.

After an interval, Vega followed Richardson and Peña into the basement. The place was much too small for—how many? Linda counted six, including the baby. A rotating fan hadn't done much with the heat or the fetid air. A women in her early thirties, her dress ripped at both sleeves, was crawling, with a knife in her hand. Rodriguez stood away from her; blood was flowing down his right arm. The older children were obviously in terror.

"Call General," Richardson ordered, meaning the hospital. "It might be an artery." When Peña failed to move, Linda tried the phone. Getting no dial tone, she turned to the oldest child, a girl of about twelve years with swollen, tearful eyes, and asked: "¿Hay teléfono arriba?"

The girl crept backward, to a pile of pillows on the floor, without reply. Then the boy, perhaps six years old, but with brighter eyes, answered for her: "Nadie está arriba. Pero vamanos a Tía Elenora; ella tiene teléfono."

Linda followed the boy from the basement, across a patch of yard to a small apartment behind 1582.

"Necessita teléfono," the boy explained, pointing to Linda. "¡Sangre, sangre! Ésta vez, el sangre está en la silla nueva y mi camion."

Linda completed the ambulance call and pondered the boy's statement. He was used to violence. His major concern seemed to be the blood on the new chair and on his toy truck.

Linda returned with the boy to Rodriguez's place. Richardson had pressed a handkerchief as a makeshift compress to the man's arm. The paring knife, still bloody, remained in the woman's hand. A girl age two or three, dirty and wailing, clung to her knee.

"Sonovabitch!" Richardson exclaimed, glancing quickly at the man's wound and his own now-bloody hands. Peña assumed that his partner was upset for having forgotten to don the latex gloves that patrol officers carry in the age of AIDS.

"This . . ."—Richardson, skipping a word, pointing at Rodriguez—"goes to General, then to jail. I'd take him right to lockup, but Al would suspend me."

"*She* has the knife, and you're sending *him* to jail?" Peña asked, incredulously. "If either goes, both do!"

Richardson looked at the woman, on her feet now, trying to pull a sleeve over an exposed bra strap. Neither officer assumed that she had ripped her own clothes or that Rodriguez hadn't been responsible for the swelling at her lip.

So, Linda could see, *that* was the deal: If Richardson insisted on taking the man, Peña'd make sure the wife—who'd face the more serious, "aggravated" charge—went too. Linda wondered about the kids. What happened to them? It wasn't a nice choice to think about, whether the cops took both their parents or left both of them, maybe to start at it again as soon as the three visitors were out the now-broken door.

"Just leave him, and he'll make it," Peña continued. "I know this family. She leaves him to visit her parents. Sometimes for weeks at a time. He stays here with the kids—and works a full-time job too. He's an okay *muchacho*. He just needs a break in the pressure."

Richardson's expression showed his displeasure at Peña's letting it all out this way—in front of Rodriguez . . . in front of Vega, too!

Then Peña got to what (Linda later figured) was really on his mind: "You know, Richards', Rodriguez here, he came over only a few years back—probably wet. You jail him, and he's history, He'll be deported. So," Peña concluded, with more belligerence in his tone than would have been common in most of the disputes that occasionally flare up between partners: "So, what do we do?"

•　•　•　•　•

Linda Vega looked at the photocopy of the letter from Senator O'Haire. Evelyn Alvarado had asked Linda to "think a bit about it." Under the seal of the State Senate, it read in part:

Ms. Evelyn Alvarado
Director, Department of Housing
Bureau of Human Services
207 BHS Building

Dear Ms. Alvarado:

As I am sure you know, the legislature is considering favorable action on a bill that would require certain police actions in domestic violence cases. This bill, strongly supported by many public-interest groups, is generally known as the "night in jail" bill. It would, among other things, require your office (along with others) to participate in various aspects of a full-service program by providing shelter and counseling services to the victims of domestic abuse. I am sure that you, under Director Haber's guidance, have been developing plans to carry out the BHS portions of an implementation program.

Since support for the domestic violence bill is overwhelmingly strong, both among legislators and in the public generally, we have not held formal hearings. While I am not convinced that this decision was necessarily a mistake, I nevertheless am of the opinion that I and other senators could only profit from a fuller discussion of the issues raised by the bill.

Although this is short notice, I wonder if you and Director Haber could meet with me, other members of the senate and our staffs, and representatives of other agencies slated to participate in the full-service approach. I have taken the liberty of scheduling a breakfast meeting (with continental buffet), at which time we would all appreciate your advice concerning the best kind of policy to adopt. Please feel free to bring any other specialists from your office and also to designate one of your own staff to make the BHS presentation about this most important question.

Sincerely,
/s/ Manuel O'Haire
Manuel O'Haire
Senator
4th District

Evelyn Alvarado told Linda Vega that Senator O'Haire held these little breakfast get-togethers with some regularity. The format provided a relatively informal way for interested parties to air their thoughts. And attendees at Manny O'Haire's breakfast sessions didn't have to worry about the procedural niceties of formal hearings. Anything said stayed off the record; even that relentless ferret of information, *Trib'-Examiner* reporter Claire Nagamura—a frequent invitee to O'Haire breakfasts "on background"— scrupulously observed the "no attribution" understanding. And Senator O'Haire himself was good at stimulating give-and-take among those around his tables. Everyone usually left with a better sense of the issues under discussion.

Linda, whom Evelyn elected to make the Housing Department's informal presentation (surprise!), thought yet again of the Rodriguez experience. She tried to think less about what Richardson and Peña had actually done that night than about the options they would have had if the new law had already been passed and the county plan had been put into place. She was still musing: What options *should* they have had?

• • • • •

At the same moment that Evelyn was assigning Linda to prepare a brief presentation for the forthcoming breakfast get-together, Sheriff Al Rilleau was at his desk across town, unfolding a letter from State Senator Manuel O'Haire. It began:

Sheriff Albert Rilleau
Headquarters, Sheriff's Department
P.O. Box 1829
County Building

Dear Sheriff Rilleau:

As I am sure you know, the legislature is considering favorable action on a bill that would require certain police actions in domestic violence cases. . . .

Questions for Discussion

The following queries might help you frame your thoughts and organize a discussion of the case.

1. What's the story? Who must make what choices? What "circumstances of the action" and "conditions of the agents" are relevant to the decisions that different actors in the scenario must make? How does the conflict between synoptic decision making aimed at once-and-for-all solutions and incremental decision making based on piecemeal, stepwise adjustments present itself to the figures in the case?

2. How do you feel, in general, about the proposed new domestic violence policy? Does a night-in-jail law sound, at first hearing, like a good idea? Why? Or why not?

3. What relevance does the dilemma of outcomes and actions (Chapter 8)—and the related three-pronged constitutional test—have to the problem of policy formulation and implementation in the area of domestic violence?

4. Does a "deterrence" or a "compliance" approach seem better-suited to problems of domestic violence? Why? Which kind of organization should be assigned primary responsibility for implementation of the kind of domestic violence law (if any) you would favor? For example, would you put police in the deterrent role? One of the city or county social work agencies in a preventive role? If, in your opinion, the evidence about what works in domestic abuse cases doesn't support a clear recommendation, what does *that* fact suggest about the kind of approach that might be appropriate for implementation?

5. Consider the first four events in Linda Vega's notes for a PERT diagram: the battering *incident,* the *report* to police, the patrol team's *arrival,* and the *arrest.* How many different possibilities can you foresee for breakdowns or unexpected consequences to occur, even in these initial events? Does it seem likely that careful analysis of domestic violence can minimize the danger of unwanted unexpected consequences and, thus, justify the forward-mapping implementation approach? How would you proceed with the outline of an implementation plan if the current version of the night-in-jail bill is enacted?

6. Charles Lindblom's essay on "muddling through" is one of the best-known articles in the literature of public administration, and there's every reason to suppose that State Senator O'Haire would have come across it at some point. Suppose the senator decides that the currently proposed night-in-jail bill should be shelved and a less-sweeping domestic violence statute offered in its place. Suppose Senator O'Haire asked you to help him frame the new bill. Using the method of successive limited comparisons, which criteria would you emphasize, and which alternatives would you consider when drafting the substitute legislation?

7. Which police or social worker actions in cases of domestic abuse should, in your opinion, be made mandatory? Which actions should be left to the discretion of frontline officials? "Discuss and defend"; justify your answer.

8. Given the circumstances found at the Rodriguez home, what should officers Richardson and Peña have done? (Remember: At the time of the incident, no night-in-jail law was on the books; the officers therefore had considerable freedom to do what they thought the situation required.) What generalizations, if any, do you draw from your reactions to the Rodriguez incident regarding an overall policy for dealing with domestic violence?

9. After digesting details in the case that might not have been obvious initially, do you feel the same way about the proposed night-in-jail law as you did at first? How, if at all, have your feelings changed as you considered this case?

FOR FURTHER READING

The standard sources on the debate between the synopticists and the incrementalists are

Braybrook, David, and Charles Lindblom, *A Strategy of Decision* (New York: Free Press, 1963), pp. 105–106.

Simon, Herbert, "Introduction to the Second Edition," *Administrative Behavior* (New York: Free Press, 1947).

See also

Behn, Richard, "Management by Groping Along," 7 *Journal of Policy Analysis and Management* (Fall 1988), 643.

Etzioni, Amatai, *The Active Society* (New York: Free Press, 1968), p. 285; on the approach—intermediate between synopticism and incrementalism—called *mixed scanning.*

Etzioni, Amatai, "Mixed Scanning Revisited," 46 *Public Administration Review* (January–February 1986), 8.

On implementation research see (in addition, of course, to the classic Pressman-Wildavsky study discussed in the text)

Alexander, Ernest R., "From Idea to Action: Notes for a Contingency Theory of the Policy Implementation Process" 4 *Administration and Society* (February 1985), 403.

Edwards, George C., ed., *Public Policy Implementaion* (Greenwich CT: JAI Press, 1984); a fine symposium volume by experts in the field whose insights haven't been rendered obsolete by the passage of more than a dozen years.

Goggin, M. A., et al., *Implementation Theory and Practice: Third-Generation Research* (Glenview IL: Scott, Foresman, 1990); an innovative study with a strong theoretical orientation by a team of prominent implementation researchers.

Mazmanian, Daniel, and Paul Sabatier, *Implementation and Public Policy* (Glenview IL: Scott, Foresman, 1983).

Williams, Walter, ed., *Studying Implementation* (Chatham NJ: Chatham House, 1982); like Williams's other book (cited next), especially useful for the light it sheds on implementation research in the 1970s, when scholars and practitioners were still trying to establish the subfield and coin its core concepts.

Williams, Walter, *The Implementation Perspective* (Berkeley CA: U. of California Press, 1980).

A classic book that develops the conception of implementation as a series of "games" is

Bardach, Eugene, *The Implementation Game: What Happens after a Bill Becomes a Law* (Cambridge MA: MIT Press, 1977).

And, for an excellent article that is complementary to Elmore's seminal essay on backward mapping, see

Sabatier, Paul, "Top-Down and Bottom-Up Approaches to Implementation Research," 6 *Journal of Public Policy* (January 1986), 21.

Interesting case studies in implementation are

Derthick, Martha, *New Towns In-Town* (Washington: Urban Institute, 1972); one of the earliest studies and still regarded as among the best.

Levin, Martin, and Barbara Ferman, *The Political Hand: Policy Implementation and Youth Employment Programs* (New York: Pergamon, 1985).

May, Peter, and Walter Williams, *Disaster Policy Implementation: Managing Programs under Shared Governance* (New York: Plenum Press, 1986).

Nathan, Richard, *Turning Promises into Performance: The Management Challenge of Implementing Workfare* (New York: Columbia U. Press, 1993).

◆ ● ■ ▼ ◆ ● ■ ▼ ◆ ● ■ ▼ ◆ ● ■ ▼ ◆

CHAPTER 12

Postscript: What Government Can Properly and Successfully Do

We study public administration because some of us will actually become government officials. But public administration is as important for the general citizen as it is for the student bound on a career in public service. In a democracy, we all need to know what we may sensibly ask government to do. Because power flows from the people and accountability returns to them—in other words, because the people are supposed to be "the boss"—we also should know what level of performance we have a right to expect from government. For these reasons, Woodrow Wilson, more than a century ago, wrote that the primary object of administrative study should be to discern "what government can properly and successfully do."

It's as pertinent to ask this question today as it was in Wilson's time. But we are no more likely to find final answers than our predecessors were. We've seen that Americans in every generation have felt the need to reopen one or more of the defining issues of governance. What's private? What's public? The responses have varied over time. Along with them, the institutional division of labor has shifted as well. Equally mutable have been notions of the proper division of responsibilities in our system of intergovernmental relations. Much the same story can be told about the relative powers of the legislative, executive, and judicial branches. Ours has been a political system not only in *being* but also in *becoming*—evolving, ever adapting to changed circumstances.

The New American State as it began to emerge a bit more than a hundred years ago represented one of the most distinctive and important of our nation's institutional adaptations. The decades since the great bureaucracy-building binge began have seen the rise of a vast bureaucratic apparatus: the complex of administrative and executive capabilities that political scientists call **state capacity.** The pace of public-sector growth has slowed, but in absolute terms the size of government continues to increase. There's no end to this trend in sight. Understandably, therefore, the search is on for ways to improve state capacity, to create "a government that works better and costs less."[1]

---

[1]Subtitle of the *Report of the National Performance Review*—The Clinton Administration "Reinventing Government" Initiative, conducted under the direction of Vice-President Al Gore (Washington: U.S. Government Printing Office, Sept. 7, 1993).

Organizational and procedural arrangements figure in important ways in administrative study, which is why we've spent as many pages as we have on issues of structure and process. It goes almost without saying that more-efficient organizations and improved procedures can add to state capacity. Nor should advances in techniques of analysis be slighted; Woodrow Wilson's "better methods of executive action" remain important today, as they were a hundred years ago. But in the quest for administrative excellence, all the improved organizational structures, procedures, and analytical methods taken together can't substitute for the right kinds of people—people equipped with the knowledge and sensibilities needed for the unusually complex problems that define the work of today's public administrators.

The theologian Reinhold Niebuhr once referred to democracy as a search for "proximate solutions to insoluble problems."[2] Niebuhr might have been writing about problem solving in the public sector. The "proximate solutions" characterization becomes more pertinent all the time. Our cases should have demonstrated, if nothing else, that Niebuhr's formulation gives a far more apt description of today's problem-solving challenges than does the Progressives' original conception of the public administrator's task. The Progressives, we've seen, thought that administrators were in the business of applying universal truths to solve determinate problems. Remember Luther Gulick's "canons of efficiency"? The scientific managers' notion of a One Best Way, like the scientific conservationists' "maximum sustainable yield" and the administrative managers' belief in "organization as a technical question," all assumed that expert administrators would be dealing with problems for which technical expertise could yield optimal solutions.

But that was then. This is now. The history of public administration records a process of growth not only in the scope of the subject but also in its difficulty—and in the complexity of the kinds of problems that our officials confront daily. Public administration has become a realm of problems that are mostly without determinate solutions. As the philosophers Jonsen and Toulmin wrote of the practice of casuistry (see Box 1.1), so may it be said of problem solving in public administration: It is "the analysis of complex cases in the light of a thousand difficulties."

All our cases have been intended to sharpen your problem-solving skills—not simply by pointing up the importance of the substantive knowledge of the field (civil service rules, organizational theories, and the like), or by providing practice in table reading and formal analysis, but also by giving you a feel for the *texture* of problem solving in the public sector today. We've seen that the kind of judgment required by an administrator who must act from a position of inadequate control (underdetermination) and usually under multiple, inconsistent constraints (overdetermination) requires a special way of thinking and a special kind of preparation.

The virtues of the practicing administrator today are the traditional virtues of the casuists: circumspection, discernment, moral acuity, prudence. All of which means that it is just these kinds of intellectual and moral qualities that are the real stuff of "state capacity." In the end, what government can properly do depends largely on what it can successfully do, and that depends in turn on the capabilities of the people who staff it— a relatively small population of persons who hold elective offices or serve as judges in our higher courts plus the much larger number of individuals who work by appoint-

[2]*The Children of Light and the Children of Darkness* (New York: Scribner's, 1944), p. 118.

ment as administrative adjudicators, analysts, policy advisers, executive decision makers, program implementers, and so forth. What we may reasonably ask government to do mostly boils down to what we can and should feel entitled to ask our public officials to do.

Woodrow Wilson may have erred in that famous essay with which we opened our study when he called for a "science of administration." Today one is more likely to hear public administration called a "craft"[3] or likened to a professional "practice"[4] than described as a science. There are theories—we've covered dozens of them in the forgoing pages—but no single, universally applicable theory, no mature "science of administration." Yet if Wilson was wrong in some ways, he was right on in others—and never more so than when he described the work of public administrators as "great and important enough to attract the best minds." It remains so to this day.

[3] See, for example, the symposium on "the craft of public management" in 8 *Journal of Policy Analysis and Management* (Spring 1989): 284.

[4] Terry L. Cooper, "Hierarchy, Virtue, and the Practice of Public Administration: A Perspective for Normative Ethics," 47 *Public Administration Review* (July–August 1987): 320.

GLOSSARY

Following each entry, the number in parentheses indicates the chapter in which the defined term was introduced or, when it seems more likely to help the reader, the chapter in which the term is principally discussed. The index should also be checked for page references to additional treatments of the term.

Abrogation to authority. The surrender of personal responsibility by a member of an organization who has entered the **agentic state.** (8)

Action-centered restrictions. Legal principles and ethical values that limit the means a public official may employ even in the pursuit of desirable consequences. (8)

Administered decision making. As distinct from **negotiated decision making,** decision making by a superior in a hierarchical structure who has the legal authority to direct and supervise the actions of one or more subordinates. (6)

Administrative adjudication. The quasi-judicial process in which an administrative decision maker resolves a dispute or allocates benefits. (4)

Administrative law. The branch of law that defines the structural framework of administrative agencies, specifies the procedures that officials of these agencies are to follow when carrying out their duties, and outlines the rights and legal obligations of citizens in their dealings with administrative agencies. (4)

Administrative law judge (ALJ). An official in an administrative agency who conducts courtlike hearings and renders formal opinions in cases before they go to the top administrator or commissioners in the agency. (4)

Administrative man. An administrator who, recognizing the limits of **bounded rationality,** adopts a **satisficing** approach to decision making and settles for proximate rather than exact or optimal solutions to problems. (11)

Administrative management school. A school of organizational theorists in the classical tradition who, in the 1930s, formulated certain **canons of efficiency** and tried to apply them to improve the structure and workings of the federal government. (3)

Administrative managers. A shorthand term for the members of the **administrative management school.** (3)

Administrative Procedures Act of 1946. The statute that established the procedural framework of modern federal **administrative adjudication** and **administrative rule making** and also provided the model for many similar state and municipal statutes. (4)

Administrative rule making. The process by which an administrative regulation is conceived, drafted, debated, and finally issued as a formal order with the force of law. (4)

Adversarial imagery. An imagery of the private and public spheres as being separate arenas of activity, and of spokespersons for private business and public regulatory officials as being essentially hostile to one another. **(6)**

Adverse selection. The tendency for less-able, less-energetic individuals to apply for work in an organization because **incentive impairments** cause the better candidates to seek employment elsewhere. **(2)**

Agentic state. The psychological state in which an individual regards himself or herself as a mere instrument for carrying out the will of organizational higher-ups. **(8)**

Algorithm. A problem-solving routine consisting of steps to be followed in exact order. **(1)**

Annuity. A stream of payments to be made periodically (usually annually) and in fixed amounts for a specified period. **(9)**

Annuity factor. A coefficient used to **discount** or **compound** an annuity payment, as in the **Harlow-Windsor method** of evaluating the amount needed in a public subsidy. **(9)**

Appointment by merit. The personnel principle under which a candidate for the civil service must demonstrate qualifications for the position based on some objective, politically neutral factor. **(2)**

Appropriations committee. A legislative committee or subcommittee with the primary responsibility for recommending funding for agencies and programs that have previously been authorized. **(7)**

APT (Administrative, professional, or technical worker). An official in a midlevel career grade (generally "white collar" but not yet a senior position) who fills a civil service job that requires a professional credential, B.S.-level technical training or higher, or the ability to apply administrative skills in significant degree. **(2)**

Asymmetric information. A situation in which two or more individuals have different degrees of access to important information, as when subordinates know more than their superiors do about the day-to-day work and hence can change routines or even disobey orders without being caught. **(2)**

Asymmetric preferences. In **integrative bargaining**, a situation in which negotiators attach different levels of importance to the values that define the various dimensions in the negotiation, sometimes permitting each bargainer to get a better deal on his or her higher values by making sacrifices along dimensions of lesser value. **(5)**

Authority cost. The loss of authority that effectively occurs when officials at a higher level of government impose a requirement, such as a federal **unfunded mandate,** which impairs the ability of lower-level (usually state or city) officials to set their own political and administrative agendas. **(7)**

Authorization committee. A legislative committee or subcommittee which has the primary responsibility for proposing the legislation that defines the legal authority of a government agency or the purposes and limits of a government program. **(7)**

Backward mapping. An implementation approach in which planners identify a condition or pattern of behavior that policy makers think should be changed and then consider the structure of potential implementing agencies, working upward from the lowest-level units—assessing each unit's ability to affect the behavior and estimating the resources needed for the unit to have that effect. **(11)**

BATNA. In bargaining theory, the best alternative to a negotiated agreement; also known as a reservation price or a walking-away price. **(5)**

Best practice. Problem-solving approaches or treatment guidelines that practitioners are expected to know and follow, especially in fields that involve the provision of human services, such as counseling and medicine. **(10)**

Block grant. Federal funds that the receiving state or local government officials may spend on any programs within a broadly specified functional area. **(7)**

Bounded rationality. Limits on human information-processing capabilities that prevent a decision maker from engaging in true **synoptic analysis** except in analyzing the simplest of problems. **(11)**

Bureaucracy. An organizational structure displaying the following characteristics in significant degree: appointment by merit, tenure for employees, assignment of workers to specialized units, a hierarchical authority structure, rationalized authority, and organization of work under explicit rules (preferably in written form). **(3)**

Bureaucratic rationality model. The model of administration (closely related to the **executive paradigm**) in which the main value is efficient realization of goals that have been set by higher authorities. **(4)**

Canons of efficiency. According to the members of the **administrative management school,** a body of administrative knowledge expressible as a set of universal principles of efficient organization (a **generic theory of organization**). **(3)**

Cash-flow analysis (CFA). A technique used to tell a business decision maker whether and by how much the revenues that the buyers of a good or service are expected to generate will, over a period of years, cover the outlays a producer would have to make to produce the items in question. **(9)**

Casuistry. A problem-solving approach with a long history in ethics and statecraft in which an analyst carefully considers circumstances and motives when trying to decide what action to take when faced with a moral, legal, or administrative quandary. **(1)**

Categorical grant. A federal grant that, unlike a **block grant,** narrowly restricts the purposes for which recipients (usually state and local governments) can spend the funds. **(7)**

Categorical imperative. A moral requirement that is universally binding, exemplified in Immanuel Kant's ethical system by the duty never to treat another human being merely as a means. **(8)**

Charismatic organization. An organization in which the leader's authority derives from his or her ability to inspire followers (his or her grace, or *charisma*). **(3)**

Civil service tenure. A legal right, attained after a period of satisfactory performance in a civil service job, not to be fired except under a few unusual circumstances, such as demonstrated incompetence or a general cutback in government staffing. **(2)**

Coalition formation. In bargaining theory, the process in which several negotiators form an alliance based on an agreement (and often on a series of **side-payments**) that should yield each coalition member a better outcome than he or she thinks can be gained through continued independent bargaining. **(5)**

Collective-action problem. The problem that results when **free riders** can take advantage of some *privately* produced **nonexcludable good**, which will therefore be underproduced unless the members of the community figure out how it can be provided *collectively,* with everyone paying his or her fair share. **(6)**

Commercialization. As distinct from **privatization**, the transfer of a function from government to private industry even though it could be performed efficiently either by a government agency or by a private firm. **(6)**

Community power structure. An **informal organization** of influential citizens who, working mostly behind the scenes, dominate public decision making in a given locale. **(6)**

Comparable worth. A personnel concept under which pay reflects the economic value of the skills that the worker must bring to the position, as judged by labor or personnel experts rather than as fixed by market forces. **(2)**

Complexity problem. In modern decision theory, the thesis that it's rarely possible to engage in **synoptic analysis** because of the inherent complexity of most real-world problems and the inherent limits of human intellectual capacities. **(11)**

Compliance model. An approach to enforcement aimed at bringing behavior into conformity with a law or rule by providing incentives toward that end or by preventing conditions that tend to induce disobedience, based on a theory of what causes violations and what changes in causal conditions should prevent them. **(11)**

Compounding. The method used to project the probable value at some future time of a present benefit or cost, the future value being the amount to which the present figure should grow if saved in a bank account paying an assumed rate of interest. **(9)**

Congruence. The quality of a rule whose wording describes exactly what actions the rule writers intended to require and exactly what actions they wanted to prohibit, so that reading the rule brings the mind of the reader into "congruence" with the intent of the rule writers. **(4)**

Consequentialist ethics. The approach to ethics in which the overall consequences (effects, outcomes) of an act are taken as the proper basis of moral choice. **(8)**

Constitutional law. The provisions of the U.S. Constitution and judicial interpretations of those provisions which, in establishing the basic powers of government and setting forth the procedural and substantive rights of persons, create the framework for all subordinate bodies of public law, such as **administrative law. (4)**

Consumer surplus. The value (generally given in dollars) that buyers in a free market derive from the competitive process which drives the price of an item down to where the producers of the item can just cover their costs; for most buyers, that level—the market-clearing price level—is beneath the **willingness-to-pay** level. **(9)**

Contextual goal. A criterion or objective other than the main goal of the organization which a worker must nevertheless try to achieve even while pursuing the official goal. **(1)**

Contingent claims contract. An agreement in which the parties list a series of future actions to be taken if specified conditions occur. **(5)**

Contingent value analysis. A procedure for **monetizing** a value (such as environmental quality) based on interviews in which respondents estimate how much they'd be willing to pay either to bring the value into existence or to prevent harm to it. **(9)**

Contracting out. The process by which private individuals or companies, working under government contracts, undertake functions (such as garbage pickup or prison management) that are generally recognized as public responsibilities. **(6)**

Cooperative federalism. The theory of the federal system that emphasizes cooperative action and an intermixing of the functions and powers of the different levels of government. **(7)**

Cooperative imagery. An imagery of the spheres of private and public action as being populated by private citizens and public officials who work in continuous, close, and generally cordial contact with one another. **(6)**

Coping organization. An agency or business firm in which neither outputs nor outcomes can be effectively observed. **(3)**

Cost-benefit analysis (CBA). A technique of **formal policy analysis** used to tell a public-sector decision maker whether and by how much the stream of social benefits expected over the life of a public project will offset the social costs that will have to be incurred in order to produce the benefits. **(9)**

Cost-benefit ratio. A summary number that's usually expressed in reverse order from the terms in the expression—that is, as the present value of a stream of expected future benefits divided by the present value of the corresponding stream of projected costs; a positive ratio may indicate that a project should be launched, but because this procedure is sometimes misleading, the ratio should be checked for agreement with the **greatest net benefit** calculation. **(9)**

Cost-effectiveness analysis. A type of formal policy analysis in which the aim is to display the relationship between the dollar cost of producing different levels of a good or service and its estimated worth or effectiveness at each level, using a measure of "effectiveness" other than dollars. **(9)**

Counterpart organization. The process by which an administrative agency is created with a jurisdiction that narrowly corresponds to a particular industry—a pattern which may be extended to a counterpart **oversight committee** that has legislative jurisdiction over both the agency and the industry. **(6)**

CPM (Critical Path Method). An extension of the **PERT (Program Evaluation and Review Technique)** in which a planner uses the PERT breakout of the separate steps needed to complete a program for the explicit purpose of estimating the minimum time (the time required to traverse the "critical path" through the PERT sequence) required to complete the work. **(11)**

Craft organization. An agency or business firm in which outcomes but not outputs can be observed. **(3)**

Crosscutting requirement. A form of **unfunded mandate** in which federal decision makers prescribe a condition or requirement and make it applicable to a variety of programs (as in "All programs that get federal funds, from agriculture to welfare, must satisfy nondiscrimination requirements"). **(7)**

Crossover sanction. A form of **unfunded mandate** in which federal decision makers impose a penalty in one area of policy unless state and local officials comply with federal requirements in another (as in "States not in compliance with federal clean air regulations lose federal highway funds"). **(7)**

Cybernetic theory. The formal study of control mechanisms and processes—the mechanisms and processes by which an organization of any kind adapts to external influences (**organizational contingencies**) and internal forces (such as **goal diversity**) that threaten its stability. **(3)**

Defective information. Any deficiency in the knowledge needed to deal with a given situation that results in a lack of control over the situation, thus making it an **underdetermined problem. (1)**

Delegated powers. The enumerated and implied powers granted to Congress in Article 1 of the U.S. Constitution. **(7)**

Deontological ethics. The approach to ethics in which duty or motivation is regarded as the proper basis of moral choice (as in "Human beings should do what duty demands"; or "The intent of the actor, not the consequence of the act, is the primary determinant of guilt or innocence"). **(8)**

Departmental version of the executive paradigm. The **specific paradigm of obligation** that emphasizes the duty of executive-branch officials to carry out the intent of the lawmakers who authorized the program that they are implementing. **(8)**

Deregulation. The easing of publicly-imposed rules on a regulated industry. **(6)**

Deterrence model. An approach to enforcement aimed at preventing disobedience to a law or rule through threats of punishment for violators, based on a system to detect and process infractions after the fact. **(11)**

Developmental policies. Policies that are intended to improve the economic position of a community in its competition with other communities. **(7)**

Dialogic process. Reasoning or argumentation that occurs in the form of a dialogue, discussion, or debate rather than in solitary, silent contemplation. **(1)**

Dilemma of outcomes and actions. The situation in which a public official has trouble satisfying the **outcome-centered obligations** applicable to the situation because of **action-centered restrictions** that limit his or her freedom of action. **(8)**

Direct supervision. A **paradigm of coordination** under which the efforts of different individuals or units are harmonized by assigning one individual the authority to issue instructions to them and monitor their actions. **(3)**

Discerning intelligence. The style of thinking that draws on common sense and intuition and that emphasizes attention to the details and peculiarities of the problem at hand. **(1)**

Discounting. The method used to estimate the present value of a future benefit or cost, defined as the amount that would grow into the future figure if it were allowed to compound at the interest rate assumed applicable over the period. **(9)**

Disparate impact. The differential impact of any law or policy that has the effect of helping or hurting members of one group relative to another, although no discriminatory intent may be evident in the terms of the policy or even have been present in the minds of those who adopted it. **(7)**

Distinctive competence. The tasks, together with the values they embody, that define what's special about an institution and so can serve as the basis for collective pride. **(10)**

Distributive bargaining. Negotiation between two adversaries with directly opposed interests who bargain along a single continuum, implying that a favorable move for one bargainer involves a loss for the other. **(5)**

Dual federalism. The now-discarded theory of the federal system under which the national and state governments were seen as separate and "sovereign" within their respective spheres. **(7)**

Earmark. A sum of money that legislators direct to be spent on a specific project or purpose; the earmarking language may be in the appropriations bill itself but is more likely to appear in the **appropriations committee** report that accompanies a money bill to the floor and explains the legislative intent. **(5)**

Economic man. The fictional decision maker of economic theory who is all-knowing and completely rational and, hence, capable of adopting a **maximizing** posture in all choice situations. **(11)**

Employment macrocontract. A hypothetical contract in which employees collectively agree to work within a hierarchical structure and accept **administered decision making** instead of insisting on individual item-by-item contracting (**negotiated decision making**). **(3)**

Equal treatment. The **action-centered restriction** that requires a public official when dealing with citizens to act impartially toward all members of the same category. **(8)**

Establishment clause. "Congress shall make no law respecting an establishment of religion" (Amendment 1, U.S. Constitution). **(7)**

Executive budget. A budgeting format that emphasizes coherence in financial planning, to be achieved by a chief executive (or staffers acting in his or her name) who develops a comprehensive budget based on balanced estimates of program requirements and departmental needs. **(5)**

Executive federalism. The practice in which congressional lawmakers frame general policies but then largely leave it to executive-branch officials from all levels of government to work with one another in formulating and carrying out implementation plans. **(7)**

Executive paradigm. The governing **specific paradigm of obligation** for an administrator when filling the role of **program implementer**, centered on the duty to obey the official's principal, who may be either a lawmaker (in the **departmental version of the executive paradigm**) or the official's immediate boss within the organizational hierarchy (in the **organizational version of the executive paradigm**). **(8)**

External diseconomy. A harmful **external effect**; also called a **public bad**. **(6)**

External economy. A beneficial **external effect**; also called a **public good**. **(6)**

External effect. An effect of some private action or transaction that benefits or harms individuals other than those immediately involved in the transaction. **(6)**

Federal preemption. The constitutional doctrine under which federal courts may void legislation by a state that touches an area for which Congress has already laid down a single national policy. **(7)**

Federal system. A system of government with at least two constitutionally independent levels of power; in the U.S. system, the national (federal) level and the state level. **(7)**

Fenced funds. Money in a federal grant that's reserved for specified localities or designated kinds of private firms, such as nonprofit service firms. **(7)**

Formal policy analysis. The subfield of public administration that embraces the development and application of quantitative problem-solving techniques. **(1)**

Forward mapping. An implementation approach which begins with a high-level statement of an ultimate objective, after which planners detail the steps that specified units—descending through the organizational levels—are to follow in pursuit of the stated goal. **(11)**

Fragmentation of authority. A characteristic of the American political system in which the parceling out of legal jurisdictions over the various aspects of a problem often leaves no one decision maker with the authority to take full control, thus necessitating multiple authorities somehow to work out a joint solution. **(1)**

Free rider. An individual who derives a benefit from a **public good** (or from the prevention of a **public bad**) without contributing to the cost of producing it. **(6)**

Functional management. The organizational scheme of Frederick Winslow Taylor, who wanted every worker in a factory to report as needed to several different bosses, each of whom would specialize in a different function. **(3)**

Game theory. The formal study of **strategic interaction.** **(1)**

General paradigm of obligation. A framework of expectations applicable in some degree to all actions of a public official, involving—at minimum—the obligation to work for desirable consequences and the duty to respect all citizens' rights while doing so. **(8)**

Generic theory of organizations. A theory of organizational structure that members of the **administrative management school** thought they could apply to any kind of organization because it was putatively derived from universal truths of human motivation and behavior. **(3)**

Geometrical intelligence. The style of thinking that emphasizes abstract reasoning, deduction, and—where possible—quantitative methods, as in **formal policy analysis.** **(1)**

Goal displacement. The process whereby a worker loses sight of the real objective that an organization exists to achieve and pursues some other goal, such as perfect adherence to the customary routines whether they make sense or not. **(4)**

Goal diversity. Divergences among the values or objectives of different individuals in an organization, including the divergence of members' goals from the official goals of the organization itself. **(1)**

Greatest net benefit. In **cost-benefit analysis,** the appropriate principle to use when deciding whether to launch a project: "In any choice situation, select the alternative that produces the **greatest net benefit.**" **(9)**

Harlow-Windsor method. A method, based on the **annuity** concept, of evaluating the amount needed in a public subsidy. **(9)**

Hawthorne effect. The tendency of workers to respond with higher morale and productivity when their supervisors show special interest in their welfare. **(10)**

Human relations approach. The movement to "humanize the workplace" through the design of job procedures that are consistent with workers' emotional needs and responsive to their yearnings for self-fulfillment. **(10)**

Human resources approach. The movement within public personnel administration to deemphasize concern with the intricacies of civil service **position classification** and enhance public employees' professionalism while developing more flexible public-sector career patterns than have been traditional. **(2)**

Impersonal standpoint. The outlook in which all human beings are seen as equal in worth irrespective of their relationships (or lack of relationships) with the viewer. **(8)**

Implementation gap. The discrepancy between the intended achievements of a new public program and the more modest results (or, sometimes, the completely unwanted consequences) that often emerge when the plan is implemented. **(11)**

Incentive impairments. Flaws in organizational structures or procedures that weaken workers' motives to perform diligently and in the service of the larger goals of the organization. **(2)**

Incremental adjustment. The decision-making approach that emphasizes the need to undertake changes gradually, experimentally, and in small steps. (11)

Independent regulatory commissions (IRCs). Administrative agencies set up outside the legislative and executive branches, often to regulate economic activity in particular industries. (4)

Indirect management. A management approach which emphasizes negotiation because an official responsible for implementing a program or policy finds that the resources needed to carry out the mission are shared among other actors, with whom the official must therefore bargain for cooperation. (11)

Informal coordination. The practice in most large organizations in which line officers constantly consult staff officials, and, reciprocally, staff officials constantly advise the line officers, over whom they have no formal command authority. (3)

Informal organizations. Patterns of continuing but unofficial relations that facilitate communication and negotiation outside of formal channels and often across the boundaries that divide formal organizations from one another (including the boundaries between private firms and public agencies). (6)

Information absorption. Losses or distortions of information going either up or down the chain of command. (3)

Informational bargaining. Bargaining that emphasizes knowledge sharing, even among putative adversaries, leading to a view of negotiation as a continuous process of constructive communication rather than as a dispute-settling procedure. (5)

Inherent powers. Powers—such as the **police powers** of the fifty states—whose existence is inherent in the very existence of an organized political entity. (7)

Input-output analysis. A statistical technique used by economists to predict how a change in demand for a raw material, an intermediate product, or a finished good anywhere in the stream of commerce will affect the demand for the factors of production (land, labor, and materials) elsewhere throughout the economy. (6)

Institutional division of labor. The balance between activities that remain in the private sector and those undertaken by government; the concept can be extended to include the division of public activities among the national, state, and various local levels of government. (6)

Instrumental theory of institutions. The view that institutions are merely tools, to be modified freely in whatever way will make them more useful. (6)

Instrumentalist. One who subscribes to the **instrumental theory of institutions.** (6)

Integrative bargaining. Bargaining in situations that involve multiple dimensions and often several bargainers who seek opportunities to negotiate package deals that would be impossible in **distributive bargaining.** (5)

Intergovernmental relations (IGR). The entire set of arrangements and relationships among officials at two or more levels of government—national-state, state-local, national-local, county-city–special district, and so forth. (7)

Internal rate of return (IRR). The interest rate at which the **net present value** of an investment will equal zero. (9)

Internal service unit (ISU). A unit in a larger organization that produces billable goods or services, such as cars in a motor pool, which members of the organization may "rent" by paying a fee. (3)

Iron triangle. An **informal organization** of individuals from one or more administrative agencies, legislative committees or subcommittees, and an industry under the agencies' regulatory authority who (in theory) cooperate to advance the interests of the industry. **(6)**

Issue network. An **informal organization,** fluid and somewhat diverse in membership, that facilitates flows of information among parties from the private and public sectors, providing a forum for bargaining and cooperative problem solving. **(6)**

Judgmental paradigm. The governing paradigm of **administrative adjudication,** the central value of which is fairness in the determination of "who deserves what." **(4)**

Kaldor-Hicks principle. The notion that a decision which threatens to create winners and losers may be acceptable even though it's not **Pareto optimal** if its beneficiaries will have their situations sufficiently improved so that some of their gains could (at least theoretically) be used to offset the losses of those who would otherwise be made worse off. **(5)**

Legislative micromanagement. The practice of legislators' imposing detailed rules and requirements on appointed officials, thus severely limiting the latters' freedom to exercise their own judgment. **(4)**

Line-item budgeting. A budgeting procedure in which appropriations are broken out into "inputs"—such as personnel, operations and maintenance, and so forth—with no systematic effort to relate these items to the programs they support (let alone to the effectiveness of those programs). **(5)**

Line-item veto. The power of a chief executive, such as a president or governor, to strike out particular items of expenditure within an appropriations bill instead of having to accept or veto the bill as a whole. **(7)**

Line-staff distinction. In classical organizational theory, the distinction between the *doers* who carry out the primary purposes of the organization (line work) and the *thinkers* who collect information, conduct analyses, present options, and recommend actions (staff work). **(3)**

Marble cake metaphor. A figure of speech used to describe **cooperative federalism** and its characteristic intermixing of national, state, and local powers, the way chocolate and vanilla swirls intermix in a marble cake. **(7)**

Matching funds. Funds that one jurisdiction or level of government (usually a state or local government) must contribute toward the financing of a public program as a condition of receiving major funding for the program from some other level (usually the federal government). **(7)**

Matrix organization. An organizational structure in which individuals are assigned from skill-based "home units" (such as engineering or marketing departments) to a team assembled for a particular project, after which they return to their home units for new project-team assignments in response to the changing needs of the overall organization. **(3)**

Maximizing. In economics, the effort to find the solution to a problem that yields the highest value ("maximizes utility"), taking all costs into account; in general, synonymous with **optimizing.** **(5)**

M-form (multidivisional) organization. A structure in which (unlike the **U-form organization**) semi-independent divisions function, for *operating* purposes, as separate companies, leaving the chief executive and top staff officers free to concentrate on long-range planning and financing for the organization as a whole. **(3)**

Method of successive limited comparisons.   An incremental decision-making approach, also called "muddling through," in which the decision maker considers only a few policies that differ slightly from those presently in effect and ignores some possible consequences even of the policies that are considered, trusting that someone in another organization will object if the simplification causes problems for anyone else. **(11)**

Miles's Law. A maxim of administrative analysis that says, "Where you stand depends on where you sit." **(1)**

Mission-driven organization. An organization in which, within limits, a flexible attitude is taken toward rules so that workers can do what's needed to carry out the mission rather than being straightjacketed by habitual routines. **(2)**

Mixed-mode entity. An organization in which members' values are partly aligned but also partly divergent, producing both opportunities for cooperation and the potential for internal conflict. **(3)**

Model. A simplified representation of the main variables in a problem and their relationships with one another; when the model emphasizes causal links—that is, when certain variables are identified as causes of specified effects—it's called a *causal theory.* **(1)**

Monetizing. To measure a value in dollar terms. **(9)**

Moral hazard. The tendency of workers not to perform with due care or diligence because **incentive impairments** make it unlikely that shirkers will suffer any adverse consequences even if they fail to perform up to standard. **(2)**

Moral judgment model. A model of administration, closely related to the **judgmental paradigm,** under which the primary obligation is to see that every individual receives the proper benefits (or pays the right penalty), often based on some law or formal regulation which sets forth a schedule of entitlements that the official is administering. **(4)**

Mutual adjustment. A **paradigm of coordination** under which individuals within units or members of different units in an organization harmonize their efforts by informally communicating (including negotiating) with one another. **(3)**

Negotiated decision making. As distinct from **administered decision making,** decision making that results from a freely made agreement or contract, often entered into after explicit bargaining. **(6)**

Negotiated order. A way of conceiving an organization in which relationships of authority, allocations of duties, and so forth are seen as being constantly renegotiated and incrementally revised at all organizational levels. **(3)**

Net present value (NPV). The equivalent worth today of a entire stream of expected future expenditures and revenues (or costs and benefits), netted against each other and properly discounted. **(9)**

Network organization. A loose market-mimicking organizational structure under which individuals or teams are free to arrange joint ventures with other individuals and teams, both inside and outside the organization. **(3)**

New American State. A term in the scholarly literature used to describe the administrative institutions set up by the **Progressives.** **(6)**

New Theorists. A school of scholars who, drawing most of their premises from economic theory, emphasize the quest for efficiency as a driving force in social life and the power of self-interest as the main motivator of human behavior. **(2)**

Nonexcludable good. A product or process with spillover effects (also called **external effects**) that make it impossible to confine its benefit or harm to the individuals responsible for bringing the product or process into existence. (**6**)

Numeraire. Any system of units, such as dollars, used to express in numbers the measure or quantity of some item. (**9**)

One Best Way. The **scientific management** doctrine that there always exists a single, most efficient way to deal with a problem and that this way can be discovered through careful observation and scientific analysis. (**1**)

Operations research. A field of technical analysis, pioneered in military planning but now in more widespread application, aimed at **optimizing** a tactic, strategy, or public program through the use of quantitative techniques. (**9**)

Opportunism. The tendency of workers whose personal objectives conflict with the goals of the organization to take advantage of loopholes in the rules or weaknesses in organizational procedures. (**3**)

Optimizing. In **operations research** and **systems analysis**, the effort to find the solution to a problem that yields the highest value after deducting all costs; in general, synonymous with **maximizing**. (**5**)

Organizational contingency. Any change in the external environment that calls for organizational adaptation in order to keep the organization functioning effectively. (**1**)

Organizational culture. The framework of emotional associations, symbols, and values that endow membership in an institution with coherence and meaning. (**10**)

Organizational layering. The addition of intermediate tiers in a pyramidal structure, consisting in the main of midlevel managers appointed to prevent the **span of control** from increasing excessively as an expanding organization adds to the number of its frontline workers; also called **organizational thickening**. (**3**)

Organizational version of the executive paradigm. The **specific paradigm of obligation** that emphasizes the duty of a subordinate official to obey the legal orders of his or her superiors in the organizational chain or command. (**8**)

Outcome-centered obligation. The obligation of a public official to consider the consequences of a decision or action both for members of the subpublic which the official is supposed to serve and for the public generally. (**8**)

Overdetermined problem. A problem, typical of those encountered in public administration, in which so many criteria have to be realized that the range of solutions is severely narrowed or—more often—in which the criteria are inconsistent with one another, so that the decision maker must weight them or even sacrifice some criteria outright. (**1**)

Overinclusiveness. A defect in the phrasing of a rule as a result of which more actions appear to be permitted or prohibited by the rule than its authors actually intended. (**4**)

Oversight committee. A legislative committee or subcommittee (often identical to the pertinent **authorization committee**) responsible for supervising an administrative agency or monitoring the execution of a public program. (**4**)

Paradigm of assignment. A set of principles used to assign different functions to different kinds of institutions. This term may apply to the assignment of functions to private or public institutions, to different levels of government (national, state, and local), or to different branches of government (legislative, executive, and judicial). (**1**)

Paradigm of the case. A framework of ideas used to order the data in a case, develop a **model** of the problem, and propose a line of response; often the paradigm comes from a store of fairly standard frameworks that public administrationists use when thinking about the assignment of functions to private or public institutions, ways of structuring organizations and coordinating workers' actions, and issues of moral obligation. **(1)**

Paradigm of coordination. A pattern of authority relationships and communication links, such as the **direct supervision** or **mutual adjustment** patterns, used to ensure that the efforts of different workers in an organization contribute to a common goal. **(1)**

Paradigm of obligation. A set of principles that define the duties or moral obligations of the incumbent of a role. **(1)**

Paradigm of organization. A coherent framework of concepts commonly used as a pattern for structuring organizational relationships, as for example on a hierarchical pattern or on a free-market pattern. **(1)**

Parameter changing. A way of dealing with an **overdetermined problem** in which the actor redefines one or more factors (parameters) in order to eliminate, or at least to reduce, the element of inconsistency that is the usual cause of the overdetermination. **(1)**

Pareto optimality. A situation in which no individual can be made better off without making at least one other person worse off. **(5)**

Partial preemption. A form of **unfunded mandate** in which federal decision makers specify a minimum requirement to be fulfilled by state or local officials but leave the latter to choose the exact mix of techniques that they will use to achieve compliance. **(7)**

Pass-through. A statutory requirement for funds in a federal grant program to bypass the state agency that normally would receive the money and, instead, go directly to local governments or to other specified recipient organizations. **(7)**

Pendleton Act of 1883. The federal law that set up the framework of the modern merit-based civil service. **(2)**

Performance budgeting. A management-oriented budgeting approach in which spending categories are explicitly related to program outputs, the aim being to help a decision maker decide how efficiency might be improved either by varying the amount of money spent or by changing the outputs that the money is used to purchase. **(9)**

Performance measurement. The process by which analysts and managers try to produce quantitative evaluations of an organization's *outputs* (day-to-day activities and work products) and *outcomes* (social consequences of the outputs). **(3)**

Personal standpoint. The outlook of an individual who, putting himself or herself at the center of a series of concentric circles, feels a declining sense of concern moving farther out through the spheres of family members, close friends, mere acquaintances, and so forth. **(8)**

PERT (Program Evaluation and Review Technique). A planning technique in which an analyst diagrams the steps that must be carried out to complete a complex project, taking special care to identify procedures that must be completed in sequence and those which may be completed in parallel. **(11)**

Phronesis. The Greek term, usually translated as "practical wisdom," for the kind of knowledge that Aristotle argued was needed in ethics and politics and what we today call *public administration.* **(1)**

Picket fence federalism. A figure of speech used to describe the practice in which intergovernmental policies are worked out in **issue networks** operating more or less independently of one another (the "slats" in the fence). **(7)**

Pluralists. Members of a school of political analysts who see public policy making as a process driven by groups that individuals organize to pressure government for remedies when market failures harm them or when the production of a particular **public good** by government can benefit them. **(6)**

Police powers. The power of a state government to legislate on behalf of the health, safety, and welfare of its citizens. **(7)**

Policy adjusting. A way of dealing with an **overdetermined problem** in which goals (which are implicit in the policies being pursued) are changed in such a way as to eliminate, or at least reduce, the element of inconsistency that is the usual cause of the overdetermination. **(1)**

Policy-administration gap. The idea espoused by the **Progressives** that a clear separation was possible and appropriate between policy makers, who formulated goals, and administrators, who were merely to execute orders from above. **(1)**

Policy professionals. Participants in the policy process whose influence is based on academic credentials, technical expertise in particular policy areas, the access their active participation in **issue networks** gives them to useful information, and the support they receive from one another based on shared professional values and policy objectives. **(7)**

Politics-administration gap. The doctrine, often used interchangeably with the doctrine of the **policy-administration gap,** that politicians and public administrators work in essentially separate spheres of action, the former mainly as policy makers and the latter in "strictly ministerial" capacities as policy implementers. **(1)**

Position classification. The process in which personnel experts grade and categorize the work of an agency, giving rise to a hierarchy of jobs that are graduated by civil service grade, covered by detailed position descriptions, and filled by employees paid according to their grades, adjusted for years in the rank (seniority). **(2)**

Positional bargaining. The technique, most often employed in **distributive bargaining,** in which adversaries posture by announcing "positions" that may or may not truthfully represent their demands or intentions. **(5)**

Primary basis of aggregation. In classical organizational theory, the main principle used to group line functions together. **(3)**

Principal-agent theory. The theory of the relationship between a *principal* (who gives instructions) and an *agent* (who agrees to carry them out), focusing on the reciprocal duties and rights of the individuals in these roles and on ways to ensure that obligations on both ends will be met. **(8)**

Principled bargaining. The underlying approach of **integrative bargaining,** in which negotiators avoid posturing, make honest exchanges of information, and try to accommodate one another's reasonable interests. **(5)**

Priority setting. A way of dealing with an **overdetermined problem** in which a decision maker reduces inconsistency by concentrating on the conditions or criteria that seem most important while deemphasizing or even ignoring the less-weighty ones. **(1)**

Privatization. As distinct from **commercialization,** the transfer of a function from government to private industry because the government is performing inefficiently or, at least, because it's thought that private suppliers can provide the service substantially more efficiently. **(6)**

Problem of the two standpoints. The dilemma that results when a person tries to reconcile the **personal standpoint** with the **impersonal standpoint** and finds that it's impossible to satisfy both the urgings of partiality and the moral demands of impartiality in a completely reliable manner. **(8)**

Procedural due process. The constitutional requirement for officials to follow all applicable legal procedures when acting in their official capacities. **(8)**

Procedural organization. An agency or business firm in which outputs but not outcomes can be observed. **(3)**

Production organization. An agency or business firm in which both outputs and outcomes can be observed. **(3)**

Professional treatment model. A model of administration (closely related to the **service paradigm**) under which the supreme obligation is to treat each client or patient compassionately and nonjudgmentally while providing individuated service based on the person's needs. **(4)**

Program budgeting. A planning-oriented budgeting approach in which analysts evaluate competing programs, trying to achieve not only the efficient level of spending for each program (as in **performance budgeting**) but also the right balance of spending among different programs. **(9)**

Program implementer. The role of an administrator whose responsibilities are, in theory, "strictly ministerial" because they call for relatively few exercises of discretionary judgment, but rather the obedient (and often "routine") execution of programs already in place or policies enunciated by political or administrative higher-ups. **(8)**

Progression of circumstances. Conditions in a specific situation that represent departures from the **paradigm of the case**; in **casuistry,** a case analyst takes the progression of circumstances into account before judging culpability or recommending a course of action. **(1)**

Progressives. "Good-government" activists who, starting roughly in the 1880s, pushed for the adoption of merit-based public personnel administration, scientific management techniques, and systemwide planning. **(2)**

Public bads. Negative **external effects** or **external diseconomies.** **(6)**

Public goods. Positive **external effects** or **external economies.** **(6)**

Public provision. The form of public action in which government officials *decide* to provide a service, *finance* the program out of public funds, and *implement* it by having civil servants actually do the work. **(6)**

Pure bargaining. Bargaining in which each party is guided mainly by his or her expectations of what the other will accept. **(5)**

Radial expansion. Growth in which an organization expands along all dimensions at the same time—horizontally in a process driven by the addition of frontline workers, and vertically through the addition of midlevel managers in an attempt to maintain a workable **span of control** at every tier in the pyramid. **(3)**

Rational-comprehensive method. Another term for synoptic analysis. **(11)**

Rational-legal organization. An organization, the purest expression of which is **bureaucracy,** whose members accept authority because it is rationally justified, systematically organized, and explicitly controlled. **(3)**

Redistributive policies. Policies that benefit low-income or otherwise needy groups by means of public programs paid for, in the main, by citizens other than the ones who receive the services. **(7)**

Reduction in force (RIF). A cutback in the workforce, usually because of budgetary belt tightening, vanishing demand for the services that the workers provide, or withdrawal of the statutory authorization for the programs they administer. **(2)**

Regulation. The form of public action in which legislators and administrators impose legal requirements on private businesses but leave the private actors to finance and actually implement the actions needed for compliance. **(6)**

Regulatory federalism. A term with negative connotations which is used to suggest that the federal government often abuses its superior constitutional authority and financial power by burdening state and local governments with inappropriate **unfunded mandates** and other regulatory requirements that carry excessive **authority costs. (7)**

Resting place. In bargaining theory, a "natural" or intuitively "fair" distribution within a bargaining range. **(5)**

Revenue sharing. A category of aid, rather popular in the 1970s but now discontinued, by which federal funds would be allotted to states and localities based on some distribution formula but otherwise without strings, meaning that the receiving officials could spend the money for whatever public purpose they wished. **(7)**

Revolving door. A figure of speech for the practice in which government employees move to private-sector jobs within industries that come under the policies of the agencies in which they serve; meanwhile private-industry workers are moving the other way—to positions in public agencies with regulatory responsibilities for the industries to which they will someday return. **(6)**

Rhetorical argumentation. A style of reasoning, argument, or justification that commonly involves a **dialogic process** and that emphasizes intuitive, estimative judgments—"guesstimation," probable rather than rigorous reasoning, and assessments of concrete circumstances which call for exercises of the **discerning intelligence** and *phronesis.* **(1)**

Right to privacy. The **action-centered restriction** under which a public administrator must refrain from undue intrusions into the personal activities or histories of citizens. **(8)**

Role absorption. The process in which an individual comes to identify personally with the requirements of a position, making it likely that he or she will fulfill the obligations of the role even if they go against the role player's apparent self-interest. **(8)**

Role creation. The process by which people seek to promote actions that they consider desirable by setting up institutions, both public and private, which consist of roles that imply expectations of appropriate behavior for the individuals who fill them. **(8)**

Rule-boundedness. The organization of work under rules that are both explicit and detailed, usually with the intent of ensuring that regular, routinized procedures are followed and arbitrary action is minimized, but often with the additional effect of inhibiting workers from exercising judgment when the circumstances call for a response that hasn't been anticipated in the rules. **(4)**

Rule-driven organization. An organization in which fulfillment of the mission may be sacrificed because employees must follow the routines or obey the rules even when those make it harder to get the job done. **(2)**

Rules-versus-standards debate. The continuing debate regarding the relative benefits of carefully drawn rules that limit administrative discretion and more loosely formulated standards that allow administrators to use their judgment when circumstances seem to call for "tailored" action. **(4)**

Satisficing. A decision-making approach in contrast with **maximizing** or **optimizing**, characterized by a willingness just to get along and settle for proximate solutions. **(11)**

Scientific management. The Progressive Era movement led by Frederick Winslow Taylor, who envisioned a "science of work" based on experimentally validated principles that could be used to design production processes for maximum efficiency. **(2)**

Secondary (tertiary, etc.) bases of aggregation. In classical organizational theory, principles that supplement the **primary basis of aggregation;** used when making further breakouts in the line structure or when grouping supporting functions together that don't conveniently lend themselves to aggregation under the primary principle. **(3)**

Senior Executive Service (SES). A cadre of senior federal civil servants who are supposed to function as a career elite, taking general instructions from the political appointees above them and seeing to the implementation of policies through skillful management of the civil servants in the sub-SES ranks. **(2)**

Service paradigm. The governing **specific paradigm of obligation** for an administrator in the role of a **service professional,** centered on the duty to give assistance, service, or treatment while taking special account of the client's or patient's circumstances and needs. **(10)**

Service professional. A worker accredited in one of the "caring professions," such as nursing or social work. **(10)**

Side payment. In bargaining theory, a bribe paid by one negotiator that helps to induce one or more other negotiators to engage in **coalition formation** with the first. **(5)**

Simplicity. The quality of a rule—for example, "Speed limit: 55 miles per hour"—that is easily remembered, needs little interpretation, and requires few data inputs to apply (just look at the speedometer). **(4)**

Single negotiating text (SNT). A document prepared to facilitate **integrative bargaining** by offering participants a summary of their current positions (as understood by the drafter of the SNT) and proposals for possible "package deals"; as the participants react to each draft SNT, clarifying their thinking and responding with counterproposals, the negotiation moves incrementally along within a coherent framework. **(9)**

Span of control. The ratio of superiors (generally normalized to 1) to the number of subordinates who report to them on a given tier in an organization. **(3)**

Specialized-line approach. An organizational approach in which line workers, organized into specialized units, are expected to develop so much expertise within their areas of responsibility that they needn't depend on staff experts but can do their own "brain work." **(3)**

Specific paradigm of obligation. A framework of expectations that adds a kind of twist or special emphasis to the **general paradigms of obligation** (which apply to *all* public roles) by requiring an official to stress a particular value based on the specific kind of role the official is filling, such as the duty of the **program implementer** to stress obedience or the duty of the **service professional** to stress individualized treatment of a client or patient. **(8)**

Spoils system. The nineteenth-century public personnel system in which politicians doled out patronage jobs to their political supporters, sometimes without reference to the appointees' qualifications (or lack of them). **(2)**

Staff approach. An organizational approach featuring a staff that is large, high in quality, and powerful—a cadre of intelligence gatherers, analysts, and planners who do most of the organization's critical thinking. **(3)**

Standardization. A **paradigm of coordination** under which each worker is "programmed" to produce outputs that have been predesigned to fit with others, as in a factory-system based on the principle of interchangeable parts. **(3)**

State capacity. The entire apparatus of governmental institutions that's in place to anticipate and analyze problems of public concern and then to devise and implement solutions; the term has come to refer especially to *administrative* institutions and processes. **(12)**

Strategic interaction. An approach to a situation (such as a **pure-bargaining** situation) in which several decision makers have goals of their own to pursue but none can control the others, so each actor tries to calculate which course of action will best advance his or her own interests, mindful of the strategies that the adversaries might pursue—and also of the adversaries' efforts to do the exactly the same. **(1)**

Strategic misrepresentation. Taking an untruthful position in a bargaining process; also called *insincere reporting*. **(5)**

Street-level bureaucrat. Officials such as police officers and welfare caseworkers who come regularly into direct contact with citizens and whose work enables them to exercise considerable discretion because they are not under constant surveillance (as are "paper shufflers" who sit at desks in open offices). **(3)**

Subpublic. A group of citizens who are affected by any **external effects** of supposedly private actions, meaning that a new subpublic comes into being whenever a new external effect appears. **(6)**

Substantive due process. The constitutional obligation of an official to avoid an act that will offend common decency or fundamental fairness, even if the official follows the prescribed formal procedures (the obligations of **procedural due process**) when performing the act. **(8)**

Supremacy clause. "This Constitution, and the Laws of the United States which shall be made in Pursuance thereof; . . . shall be the supreme Law of the land; . . . any Thing in the Constitution or Laws of any State to the Contrary notwithstanding" (Article 6, U.S. Constitution). **(7)**

Synoptic analysis. The approach to planning and decision making that emphasizes comprehensive study of all relevant factors and options. **(5)**

Systems analysis. An interdisciplinary field whose practitioners aim at **optimizing** the use of resources over entire systems of linked efforts, taking into account not only different possible combinations of means but also alternative sets of objectives. **(9)**

Theory of market failures. The theory that the benefits of free exchange (freedom to choose, promotion of efficiency) make government action an appropriate substitute for market transactions only when market failures, such as monopolies or **external effects,** crop up. **(6)**

Three-pronged test. A Supreme Court test to determine when an intrusion into a citizen's privacy (as in a police search) is constitutional, based on a weighing of the value the authorities are trying to advance (such as crime prevention), the degree to which the intrusion will help officials realize the value, and the severity of the interference with the individual's privacy. **(8)**

Traditional organization. An organization in which the leader's orders are acknowledged as legitimate because (and only if) they are in accordance with custom. **(3)**

Trained incapacity. The difficulty a worker may have performing a task because training for some other aspect of the job has produced habits or deficiencies that inhibit the carrying out of the first task. **(4)**

Transaction costs. The costs in time, energy, and emotional drain lost in the process of bargaining, plus any further costs incurred in acquiring information. **(6)**

Transparency. The quality that a rule possesses when its wording is so clear that everyone who must follow it interprets its requirements not only correctly but also uniquely, that is, in exactly the same way. **(4)**

U-form (unitary) organization. A structure in which (unlike the **M-form organization**) the day-to-day operations of all units as well as long-range planning and financing functions remain under the full command of a single leader and his or her immediate staff. **(3)**

Underdetermined problem. A problem in which a lack of information or lack of control—usually signaled by the ability of some decision makers to arbitrarily change the conditions under which others must act—makes it impossible for any decision maker to come up with a unique or exact solution. **(1)**

Underinclusiveness. A defect in the phrasing of a rule as a result of which fewer actions appear to be permitted or prohibited by the rule than its authors actually intended. **(4)**

Unfunded mandate. A provision of federal law that imposes requirements on state or local governments without providing funds for implementation. **(7)**

Unitary approach. An organizational model in which, ideally, a single chief executive masters the entire work of the organization and issues orders for subordinates at successively lower tiers to transmit down the line in increasing detail to the front-line workers. **(3)**

Unitary principle. The doctrine that each subordinate in an organization should report to only one superior and that the entire hierarchy should build to a single commander from whom all orders ultimately emanate. **(3)**

Unitary system. In contrast with a **federal system,** a system of government with a single center of constitutional power; although subordinate jurisdictions may exist, they derive all their authorities from the supreme power. **(7)**

Utilitarianism. A version of **consequentialist ethics** aimed at achieving "the greatest happiness of the greatest number," theoretically requiring that the outcomes of an act be evaluated as a balance of gains and costs across society as a whole (rather than with reference to a particular **subpublic**). **(9)**

Value infusion. The process by which an institutional leader inculcates common values in the members of an organization, which the members then use as starting points for their everyday actions. **(10)**

Values problem. In modern decision theory, the thesis that it is rarely possible for a problem solver to specify a clear-cut set of goals, all of which can be achieved simultaneously. **(11)**

Voluntarism. A mode of production in which workers act without compulsion and without compensation or, at least, for less than they would be able to command if their labor were priced in a free market. **(6)**

Willingness to pay (WTP). The amount in dollars that all persons in a given population (usually, members of a community) would be willing to pay in order to achieve some benefit or to eliminate some harm. **(9)**

Zone of acceptance. The set of instructions that employees will accept as legitimate and willingly obey. **(10)**

Acknowledgments (continued)

INDEX

ABOUT THE AUTHOR

▼ ◆ ● ■ ▼ ◆ ● ■ ▼ ◆ ● ■ ▼ ◆ ● ■ ▼ ◆ ●

GERALD GARVEY has a doctorate from Princeton University, where he has been a professor of politics since 1971. He has also served on the faculties of the U.S. Air Force Academy and Georgetown University. At Princeton, he currently teaches public administration, public management, and the introductory course on American democracy.

Garvey brings practical experience as well as academic preparation to the field of public administration. Both before and since his appointment at Princeton, he has served in various capacities as a public official and as a private consultant to government agencies. His assignments have included service as a Pentagon planner, as executive secretary of President Johnson's task force on Native American programs, on the general counsel's staff in the Office of the Secretary of the Air Force, as head of the New Jersey State Energy Crisis Study Commission, and as project director of the effort to modernize Federal Energy Regulatory Commission procedures through computerization.

Garvey has published books and scholarly articles on a wide range of topics in American government, public administration, and political economy.